ENDORSEMENTS

"If you've ever struggled with how to apply God's Word to real-life problems, this book is for you. June Hunt and the Hope for the Heart team have created a truly life-giving resource that points people to the hope found in Christ."

—Sheila Walsh, author and cohost of *Praise and Better Together* on TBN

"This book is a powerful tool for anyone seeking biblically grounded wisdom on life's toughest challenges. Whether you're a pastor, counselor, or simply someone looking for guidance, *The Care and Counsel Handbook* provides clear, compassionate, and scripturally sound answers."

—Dr. Mark Batterson, *New York Times* bestselling author of *The Circle Maker*

"June Hunt and Hope for the Heart have created an invaluable resource for anyone offering hope and help to others. *The Care and Counsel Handbook* delivers biblical wisdom and practical guidance—quickly, clearly, and compassionately. Every pastor, counselor, and caring Christian will want this book."

—Drs. Les and Leslie Parrott, founders of The Parrott Institute for Healthy Relationships at Olivet Nazarene University

"I cannot overstate the significance and importance of this new resource, *The Care and Counsel Handbook*, from June Hunt and the excellent Hope for the Heart team. I recommend this comprehensive resource for every church and ministry organization entrusted with the care of God's people in their most trying circumstances."

—Dr. Mark M. Yarbrough, president of Dallas Theological Seminary

"Life is full of challenges, but God's Word offers solutions. *The Care and Counsel Handbook* is a powerful guide to help you navigate struggles with clarity, wisdom, and biblical truth."

—Taya Kyle, author, executive director of TACKF - Service Marriage Strong, and widow of *American Sniper* Chris Kyle

"For decades, counselors, coaches, and, in particular, those struggling with life's toughest questions have sought out words that bring hope. This book from Hope for the Heart represents 100 biblical, understandable, life-impacting responses to so many of those questions. You need a good Bible dictionary nearby when you study Scripture. You need this book if you are a people helper or just someone who needs to know God's Word on the most important questions you're facing today. Highly recommended."

—Dr. John Trent, president of Strong Families

"This book is an incredible resource for individuals, pastors, churches, and ministries who love God's Word and are seeking to offer biblically grounded care and counsel. The wisdom contained in its pages will help you minister effectively and compassionately in bringing hope to those who need it."

—Jack Hibbs, senior pastor at Calvary Chapel Chino Hills

"My respect and admiration for June Hunt is boundless. This easy-to-use reference guide reveals her love of God and deep compassion for helping people. With practical and biblical advice, she continues to be a counselor extraordinaire, and her unique story illustrates how to rise above the noise of any situation. Designed with essentials in mind, *The Care and Counsel Handbook* includes an integrated whole-person approach across 100 difficult issues, and the team at Hope for the Heart reaches beyond counseling to transform us to become more like Jesus."

—Nick Vujicic, founder and president of Nick V Ministries

"Every pastor, counselor, and ministry leader needs this handbook. It provides biblically sound, easy-to-use guidance on life's toughest challenges that people face today. I highly recommend it!"

—Dr. Robert Jeffress, senior pastor at First Baptist Church Dallas

"At a time when so many are desperate for direction, *The Care and Counsel Handbook* offers practical, biblically rooted solutions for real-life struggles. Hope flows for those who need it personally and for those who want to be equipped to help others. This is an essential resource for all longing for God's truth. I strongly encourage you to read it—and to share it with a friend."

—Geof Morin, president and CEO of Biblica

"A great resource for when life's challenges threaten our peace and hope. Biblical encouragement with clear insight into the 'how to' for victory in life's hardest places!"

—Becky Brown, president and LPCC of New Life Ministries

"*The Care and Counsel Handbook* is a very helpful, clearly written, concise, biblical and practical guide to dealing with 100 key issues from abortion to worry. Highly recommended for all people helpers including professional counselors and therapists, pastors, chaplains, lay counselors, and anyone involved in caring for others."

—Rev. Dr. Siang-Yang Tan, senior professor of clinical psychology at Fuller Theological Seminary

"The power of God's Word is undeniable. The Bible holds answers for all of life. This resource does a wonderful job of making it easy to find these answers in a simple, systematic way. Hope for the Heart has provided another fantastic resource, one filled with treasure that has earthly and eternal impact. This book is a great gift for those struggling with life issues."

—Gary Blackard, president and CEO of Adult & Teen Challenge U.S.A.

"For any leader, caretaker, mentor, or friend who is walking with someone in need of guidance for navigating life's struggles, *The Care and Counsel Handbook* offers biblically grounded, practical wisdom. This is a much-needed resource that provides something more than just advice—it offers hope."

—Aubrey Sampson, pastor, author, and podcaster

"I love June Hunt! For more than forty years, she and Hope for the Heart have helped people understand how to apply biblical principles to life's biggest questions. This handbook distills the insight of decades into an easy reference, scripturally backed tool. If you want to know where in the Bible to look for godly counsel on any of the 100 topics covered, this book is for you."

—Greg Stier, founder of Dare2Share

"King David asked God to deliver him from all his fears. If such a mighty man of God needed help with his fears, anxieties, and worries . . . how much more do we? I have never come across a resource that addresses the many concerns we all have, and in such a deep and biblical way. This is a must-have resource."

—Gary Wilkerson, president of World Challenge

"One does not write a book like this without decades of research, real life expertise, and a devotion to seeing people who are struggling find hope. Whether you are looking for the core passages of Scripture that speak to a common source of pain or looking for clear instruction on how to guide someone to greater freedom, this book is a treasure trove of helpful nuggets."

—Dr. Marcus Warner, president of Deeper Walk International

"Once again, June Hunt and the Hope for the Heart team have hit a home run! *The Care and Counsel Handbook* is an invaluable resource to help caregivers focus and give those we serve our undivided attention, without having to search through volumes of supplemental materials. I highly recommend this resource for leaders who desire to effectively and efficiently achieve maximum results in ministry.

—Pastor James Ward, senior pastor at INSIGHT Church

"I'm honored to endorse June Hunt's upcoming resource, *The Care and Counsel Handbook*. This comprehensive resource is a culmination of forty years of ministry and her vision to offer biblical hope and practical help for life's toughest challenges. As someone who has witnessed the powerful impact of her counsel and coaching *Keys* in my clinical practice, I believe this new tool will empower and equip pastors, counselors, and ministry leaders seeking wisdom for the toughest topics. I'm confident this handbook will equip a new generation to tackle emotional, mental, and spiritual struggles with grace and wisdom."

—Dwight Bain, founder of The LifeWorks Group

"We know many people today, especially young people, are struggling with anxiety and are searching for meaning and purpose. *The Care and Counsel Handbook* offers practical, biblically rooted solutions for real-life challenges. June Hunt and the Hope for the Heart team have created an essential resource for anyone seeking to care for others with God's truth."

—Dr. Len Munsil, president of Arizona Christian University

"June Hunt encompasses the definition of *unique*: being the only one of its kind, unlike anyone else. Her passion for the Word of God, the hearts of people, and the integrity of ministering through the power of the Holy Spirit is one of a kind. This resource is the culmination of her life work in many ways, as she has taken the wisdom entrusted to her for over forty years and shared it with all of us. Digest this material and share it with others that God entrusts to you."

—Dr. Gary and Barb Rosberg, cofounders of The Rosberg Group and America's Family Coaches

"*The Care and Counsel Handbook* is a unique and definitive resource for people of faith, whether it's those who are seeking help or those who provide the needed guidance. And if solid biblical truth and integration are important, you can have confidence that June Hunt and the leadership team at Hope for the Heart have honored Scripture throughout this comprehensive reference. It's a library of wisdom rooted in Christ, providing real answers to real problems."

—Dr. Robert Sloan, president of Houston Christian University

"In an era where individuals of all generations are accustomed to rapid searches and expect clear, concise, and applicable responses to their concerns, this well-organized resource provides biblically sound wisdom to meet people where they are in their search for truth."

—Dr. Rita M. Murray, founder and principal of Performance Consulting, LLC

"A perfect blend of quick-reference practicality and theological depth. This handbook provides concrete, biblical wisdom for immediate support situations while offering substance for deeper study, exactly what every care ministry needs."

—Rolfe Carawan Jr., president of Transformed Living

"*The Care and Counsel Handbook* ensures our 2,100 chaplains, serving over 6,000 worksites every week, and caring for over 425,000 employees and 1 million family members, are now the best equipped 'Messengers of Hope' in the workplace! The topics are in alignment with what we track as employees open up to chaplains about their life issues, problems, addictions, grief, and questions. These simple to use resources are a go-to for chaplains on the frontlines encountering thousands of issues every day, of which they need some quick context, help, and direction to bring immediate help to someone in need!"

—Jason Brown, president and CEO of Marketplace Chaplains

"The *Care and Counsel Handbook* is a treasure house of wisdom for an impressive waterfront of life issues. While relevant to every demographic of life, I know it will be a powerful, biblically based tool of great value for our nation's military and veteran populations. This expertly crafted handbook is a must-have resource for any counselor, life coach, ministry leader, or lay person interested in bringing excellent care to those who desperately need it."

—Bob Dees, major general in the U.S. Army (Ret.) and president of the National Center for Healthy Veterans

THE CARE AND COUNSEL HANDBOOK

A Quick Reference Guide
of Biblical Answers *for*
100 REAL-LIFE ISSUES

HOPE *for the* HEART

The Care and Counsel Handbook: A Quick Reference Guide of Biblical Answers for 100 Real-Life Issues

Published by Forefront Books, Nashville, Tennessee.
Distributed by Simon & Schuster.

Library of Congress Control Number: 2025911157

Print ISBN: 978-1-63763-473-8
E-book ISBN: 978-1-63763-474-5

Cover Design by Jonathan Lewis, Jonlin Creative
Interior Design by PerfecType, Nashville, TN

Printed in the United States of America

DISCLAIMER

Information, resources, and products provided by Hope for the Heart (HFTH), whether in print or electronic forms, and/or as part of any direct or affiliated website, Learning Management System, or social media platform, are general in nature and are not intended to provide or be a substitute for advice, consultation, or treatment with a duly licensed mental health practitioner or other medical professional, and do not qualify participants to identify or practice as a professional mental health therapist or counselor. **Alert**: Given the sensitive nature regarding many of the topics and issues that HFTH addresses, individuals should be aware of potential emotional and/or psychological reactions that may arise due to current or past traumatic experiences, and therefore take any appropriate precautions to safeguard one's overall well-being. This information and these resources and products are intended to provide practical faith-based guidelines and biblical principles for balanced living and are not a replacement for medical advice. Professional services should be pursued whenever necessary and/or appropriate. By utilizing any HFTH information, resources or products, individuals acknowledge that HFTH is not providing direct clinically oriented mental health treatment or therapy, and that such usage does not create or constitute a therapeutic relationship between any individual and HFTH. As a condition to such use, every person who uses HFTH's information, resources, or products agrees to defend, indemnify, and hold harmless HFTH and its licensees, affiliates, and assigns, as well as the officers, agents, and employees of HFTH and its licensees, affiliates, and assigns, from and against any and all claims, liabilities, losses, damages, costs, charges, causes of action, suits, fees, recoveries, judgments, penalties, and expenses (including reasonable attorneys' fees and expenses), which may be made against, imposed upon, or suffered by HFTH as a result of, related to, or in connection with such use. Additionally, certain views and opinions that might be expressed in such information, resources or products may be those from sources other than HFTH and do not necessarily represent the views of HFTH nor imply an endorsement by HFTH.

HOPE *for the* HEART

Because hope means everything.

At Hope for the Heart, hope gets real.

We know life is a series of challenges. But finding help shouldn't be.

That's why we create simple, easy-to-use resources. Professionally informed, all rooted in God's Word. We provide clear answers and practical guidance on over 100 real-life issues, helping you understand and apply the Bible to your life and those you serve.

It's all life-giving counsel that's key to living whole and free. For God's heart is to see you live abundantly and share the hope you have in Christ.

So that whatever you're facing—or whoever comes to you—you have every reason for hope, for every challenge in life.

Because hope means everything.

For everything that was written
in the past was written to teach us,
so that through the endurance
taught in the Scriptures and
the encouragement they provide
we might have hope.
(ROMANS 15:4)

www.hopefortheheart.org

The Complete System of Care

Giving you every reason for hope, for every challenge in life.
Because hope means everything.

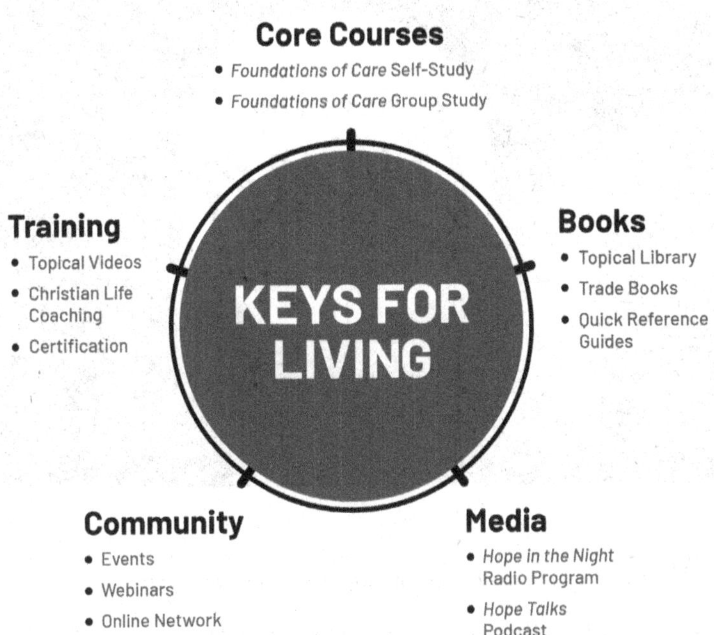

Designed with the whole person in mind, Hope for the Heart's Complete System of Care provides a comprehensive library of resources and training tools that are all professionally informed, rooted in God's Word. Centered around our 100+ topic *Keys for Living Library,* these practical, biblical resources ensure you have everything you need when getting to the heart of common life issues.

Whether for personal help or training purposes, it's all key to being completely equipped for effective care and counsel. From practical guidance in our books to deeper insights through courses, events, and media, these tools work together to help you experience freedom and transformation in Christ—and equip you to share that hope with others.

Explore our resources today and get the tools you need to take better care of yourself and others.

www.hopefortheheart.org

Keys for Living Library

This book contains excerpts from our *Keys for Living Library.*

Developed by June Hunt and the Hope for the Heart team, the *Keys for Living* are short, helpful books with clear answers from God's Word and concise, practical guidance on life's challenges. Our library consists of *Keys for Living* books on more than 100 topics.

Visit our website to learn more and order any of our *Keys for Living* books.

www.hopefortheheart.org

CONTENTS

Foreword . . . 1
Preface . . . 5
Three Helpful Concepts for Effective Biblical Care & Counsel . . . 15
Three Inner Needs . . . 16
Four Points of God's Plan . . . 18
How to Have a Transformed Life . . . 21
The Abortion Dilemma . . . 23
Abuse Recovery . . . 31
Adoption . . . 39
Adultery . . . 47
Aging Well . . . 55
Alcohol & Drug Abuse . . . 61
Alzheimer's & Dementia . . . 69
Anger . . . 75
Anorexia & Bulimia . . . 83
Anxiety . . . 91
Assurance of Salvation . . . 99
Atheism & Agnosticism . . . 107
The Bible: Is It Reliable? . . . 113
The Blended Family . . . 121
Boundaries . . . 127
Bullying . . . 135
Caregiving . . . 141
Child Evangelism . . . 149
Childhood Sexual Abuse . . . 157
Chronic Illness & Disabilities . . . 163
Codependency . . . 171
Communication . . . 177
Conflict Resolution . . . 185
Confrontation . . . 193
Considering Marriage . . . 201
Crisis & Trauma . . . 209
Critical Spirit . . . 221
Cults . . . 227
Dating . . . 235
Death & Heaven . . . 241
Decision-Making . . . 249
Depression . . . 257
Divorce . . . 267
Domestic Abuse . . . 275
The Dysfunctional Family . . . 283
Employment . . . 291
Envy & Jealousy . . . 297

Ethics & Integrity 303
Evil & Suffering . . . Why? 311
Fear 319
Financial Freedom 325
Forgiveness. 333
Friendship 341
Gambling 347
God: Who Is He? 353
Grief. 363
Guilt & Shame 373
Habits & Addictions. 381
The Holy Spirit 387
Homosexuality & SSA. 395
Hope 401
Identity & Self-Image 409
Infertility 417
Intimacy 425
Jesus: Is He God? 431
Leadership 439
Loneliness 447
Lying vs. Truthfulness 455
Manipulation. 463
Marriage 471
Mentoring, Coaching, and Discipling .479
Midlife Crisis 487
New Age Spirituality 495
The Occult 501
Overeating 509
Parenting 515
Perfectionism 523
Pregnancy . . . Unplanned 531
Prejudice 539
Pride & Humility 545
Procrastination 551
Prosperity Theology. 559
Purpose in Life 567
Reconciliation 573
Rejection & Abandonment 579
Salvation 587
Satan, Demons, and Satanism 595
Self-Worth 603
Sex and Human Trafficking 609
Sexual Addiction 615
Sexual Assault & Rape Recovery. 623
Sexual Integrity 631
Single Parenting 641

Singleness 649
Spiritual Abuse 655
Spiritual Warfare 663
Stealing 671
Stress 677
Success Through Failure 685
Suicide Prevention. 691
Teenagers. 699
Temptation 705
Terminal Illness 713
Time Management. 721
Trials 727
The Unbelieving Mate. 737
Verbal & Emotional Abuse 743
Violence 749
Widowhood 755
Worry. 763
Notes 771
A Legacy of Hope 783

FOREWORD

By June Hunt

I've always noticed gaps. Empty spaces. *Holes*. Perhaps you have too. It's a curious thing to notice—because a gap, by definition, is what's missing.

How well I remember speaking at a leadership conference when I suddenly learned that I needed to prepare a final 5-minute talk. The focus was this: "What have you done that could help those in this audience—right now?"

What immediately came into my mind were the frequent comments said to me: "I've never heard anyone else speak on the many topics you address on radio, such as manipulation and procrastination . . . spiritual abuse, childhood sexual abuse, and verbal and emotional abuse."

At the time, there were hardly any Christian resources on these important topics. Yet as a former Youth Director at a mega church and later the College & Career Director, I had come alongside many young victims of abuse. Sadly, I saw a huge hole that needed to be filled.

So, I began my talk with these words: "I look for holes—holes that need to be filled." A hole often refers to a problem that needs to be fixed. I thought about three kinds of holes: *potholes, plot holes,* and *holes in our hearts*.

1. A *pothole* is a hole in a road that makes driving uncomfortable and bumpy. Drivers try to avoid potholes. (In reality, we need to learn how to navigate around different kinds of *abusers* and bumpy people with a *critical spirit.)*

2. A *plot hole* is a hole in a story indicating something significant is missing in the narrative. (Likewise, if we are seeking to help someone whose story is stuck, silenced, or they've lost the words to tell their story—we can learn how to provide *counseling* to give them help and *hope.)*

3. A *hole in the heart* refers to someone who has suffered a significant loss in life, whether the loss of a person, the loss of employment, or even the loss of a precious pet. (We need to learn how to help people in the throes of *grief, divorce, death,* and even in the loss of *employment*.)

What about you? Maybe there's a hole in your life. Or perhaps the Lord has revealed to you a topic, demographic, or area of potential ministry that needs attention—*your attention*. I pray and trust this book will help you find the answers you need . . . and equip you to offer hope in the very places others feel lost or broken. That's been my story, and it's why we created this resource.

Looking back, when I began speaking at conferences, teaching inductive Bible studies, and leading a Sunday morning class, I simply had a hunger to learn the Word of God. Yet early on, I noticed that people had fewer questions about the Bible and more questions about their problems like anger and abuse, depression and divorce, forgiveness and fear, and so much more.

Clearly, they had holes. Some strugglers needed to know that the Word of God spoke directly to their needs, but for most others, the hole was one of application—they knew God's Word, but didn't know how to apply His truth to their trials. So, I searched the Scriptures for answers, hoping to fill those empty holes with answers.

In 1986, I was asked to broadcast a national radio program which we called *Hope for the Heart*, presenting God's truth for today's problems. For three years I taught a course called *Counseling Through the Bible.* Working with a small team, we created simple outlines with clear, biblical truths on 96 topics—concise, bullet-pointed reference tools. We called them *Keys—Biblical Counseling Keys*—because I wanted to help people unlock what God's Word said about their challenges. Over time, these *Keys* grew into what is now our 100+ volume *Keys for Living Library*—the foundation of Hope for the Heart and the resource you are now holding.

Today, a similar hole still exists. Now, we have access to all the world's knowledge online, yet people are still struggling. The problem is the gap between *information* and *wisdom*—between knowing about something versus applying what you know. The Bible speaks to the value of wisdom: "*Get wisdom. Though it costs all you have, get understanding*" (Proverbs 4:7).

This book is the culmination of 40 years of seeking God's wisdom . . . of prayerfully filling the holes. For some, it will provide new knowledge—biblical answers to personal struggles. For others, I believe it will help connect what you know in your head with what you long to experience in your heart.

Whether it's for your own life—or for someone you love—my prayer is that this resource will bridge the gap between helplessness and lasting hope . . . between giving up versus moving forward . . . between feeling unprepared versus being equipped to confidently help others.

Candidly, this is a big book! That's because there are big needs. The questions are many, but God's Word truly addresses all the issues we face in life. That's why I want to encourage you with a lesson I've learned over the years.

When I started those Bible studies, I didn't know where the Lord would lead. I simply did what He put in front of me. When I saw a missing piece, I tried to fill the hole and meet the need. And as I took one step after another, the Lord opened more doors and expanded our ministry in a way I never could have imagined.

So, remember . . . you don't need to have all the answers. Just take the next step. Whether you're looking for help for yourself or someone else, begin where you are. Jesus said, *"Ask and it will be given to you; seek and you will find; knock and the door will be opened to you"* (Matthew 7:7).

In this book, we've organized 100 real-life topics so you can find God's answers quickly and easily. Pray. Seek His wisdom. Do what's in front of you. And trust Him to be faithful to work in and through you . . . *"The one who calls you is faithful, and he will do it"* (1 Thessalonians 5:24).

As I look back over a lifetime of ministry—thousands of callers on *Hope in the Night,* countless conversations at conferences and ministry events—I see how God used those simple steps of faith. Through speaking, radio, writing, and counseling, God continues to use Hope for the Heart to fill the holes and lead people to the hope of Christ.

Now, four decades later, with over 100 topics in our *Keys for Living Library,* translated into 35+ languages and used in over 60 countries—I am deeply grateful to God for all He has done. Truly, *"He is able to do immeasurably more than all we ask or imagine"* (Ephesians 3:20). And I believe the Lord will do even more wonderful things your life as you take steps of faith and fill your mind with His Word and seek to meet the needs of those in front of you.

How thankful I am for *you.* For your desire to seek God's wisdom—for yourself and for those under your care. Be encouraged, friend, you are not alone. The Bible says, *"The LORD himself goes before you and will be with you; he will never leave you nor forsake you. Do not be afraid; do not be discouraged"* (Deuteronomy 31:8). This is my favorite Scripture. You could personalize this passage: *"The LORD himself goes before me and will be with me; he will never leave me nor forsake me. I will not be afraid; I will not be discouraged."*

Whatever issue you or someone you love is facing, never forget, *there is hope*—guaranteed hope, an assured hope that will never fail. That's why we created this resource. Not only to help you find biblical answers—but so you can live and lead with the matchless hope of Christ. Try to comprehend how extraordinary these words are, spoken by the Lord Himself, to fill the holes in your life and give you hope for your heart . . .

"'I know the plans I have for you,' declares the LORD, 'plans to prosper you and not to harm you, plans to give you hope and a future'" (Jeremiah 29:11).

Yours in the Lord's hope,

June

June Hunt
Founder and Chief Servant Officer
Hope for the Heart

PREFACE

Life is both beautiful and complicated. We all experience times of great joy and great struggle. Each day brings opportunities to manage confusion, turmoil, and decisions, while also working to maintain our relationships and responsibilities. There are seasons we may feel like we can't make it through the day without some measure of stress and worry. As finite people, trying to do it all on our own burns us out, saps our strength, and may ultimately leave us depleted and defeated.

As we strive to care well for people we serve—in ministry, our families, loved ones, and even ourselves—we often discover we need much more than sheer willpower, grit, or caffeine to keep every plate spinning. We need a source of strength that doesn't fade when times get tough. We need *hope* to pull us through. Because in these moments of doubt, confusion, and weariness . . . we discover that *hope means everything.*

At Hope for the Heart, our mission is to help people find the hope that never fails and never ends—the hope of Jesus Christ. Only He can give you a lasting hope that weathers every storm of life and empowers you to keep going each day. This unshakable hope is found in God's perfect written Word—the Bible.

God's Word: The Foundation of Effective Care & Counsel

Where do you go for information? Answers and direction? Comfort and support? Wise counsel and truth? God's heartbeat on a matter? For the Christ follower, it's God's Word—the Bible. There is no greater treasure in all the universe. Indeed, His Word is for all people, for *"he is not far from any one of us"* (Acts 17:27). He gave us the Scriptures so that we would have clear guidance, constant encouragement, and enduring hope: *"Everything that was written in the past was written to teach us, so that through the endurance taught in the Scriptures and the encouragement they provide we might have hope"* (Romans 15:4).

A foundational Bible verse to reflect on and lean into is found in 1 Kings 22:5, *"First seek the counsel of the Lord."* For those who have given their lives to Christ, it's a firm foundation. For those seeking to understand how God's truth can change their lives, it's an open invitation. May God give us eyes to see, ears to hear, and His Spirit to know and understand His will.

This passage in 1 Kings describes how Jehoshaphat, king of Judah, responds to king Ahab's invitation to wage war. Jehoshaphat had a history of seeking God when faced with matters of great consequence. His counterpart, however, was often more motivated by ambition and other priorities. The Hebrew phrase used in verse 25 is *devar Yahweh*. It means "the word of the Lord," and the root is *dabar* or "speech." The literal translation would go something like this: "Before we consider a matter or make a decision, let us first see what God would *say* to us. What would be His words?"

In the beginning, at the dawn of our created world, God's Word was there. It was with Him and in fact, it was Him (John 1:1). Like a master artist poised before a canvas of unlimited and unimaginable potential, God spoke all things into being. His very breath brought mankind to life.

Over and over, throughout the pages of Scripture, we see the Creator making an effort to communicate who He is and how He loves. He spoke with Adam and Eve in the garden. He called Abraham out of his home, giving him everlasting promises. He spoke to Moses through a burning bush, and then to His people by inscribing His commandments on stone. He spoke through priests and prophets. And then, God sent His one and only Son to speak directly to us through the power of relationship and the message of the cross.

Jesus . . . Immanuel . . . God with us, was the *Logos* according to John in his gospel. This means that Jesus was the spoken Word of God—His speech, as it were—and His counsel. During the Last Supper, the disciple Philip implored, *"Lord, show us the Father and that will be enough for us"* (John 14:8). Jesus answered, *"The words I say to you I do not speak on my own authority. Rather, it is the Father, living in me, who is doing his work"* (v. 10). To strengthen and seal this thought, Jesus told us, *"Heaven and earth will pass away, but my words will never pass away"* (Matthew 24:35). This should give us peace of mind and assurance that we can stand confidently on all that Scripture teaches us.

In James 3:13–18 (NASB), after describing wisdom from "below," James then compares it to the wisdom "from above." This identifies the source of wisdom as God Himself, the voice of our heavenly Father:

- That is ***First Pure***
  - — God's voice is not tainted by worldliness or selfish gain.
  - — God's voice is holy and true to His Word.
- That is ***Peaceable***
  - — God's voice is something that soothes the spirit and calms the soul.
  - — God's voice is not contentious.
- That is ***Gentle***
  - — God's voice is approachable, and He is easily entreated.
  - — God's voice is spoken with kindness.

- That is ***Reasonable***
  - God's voice is practical and does not create confusion.
  - God's voice is applicable to whatever is going on in our lives.
- That is ***Full of Mercy***
  - God's voice is not critical or judgmental.
  - God's voice is compassionate and loving.
- That is ***Full of Good Fruits***
  - God's voice is a commitment to action.
  - God's voice is something that leads to measurable results.
- That is ***Unwavering***
  - God's voice is impartial, showing no favoritism.
  - God's voice is firm and enduring for all generations.
- That is ***Without Hypocrisy***
  - God's voice is genuine and transparent.
  - God's voice is a reflection of Christ.

Only through the grace and truth found in the Word of God are we able to effectively care for the whole person. Consider the following quote from psychiatrist Dr. James Fisher, made after nearly fifty years of mental health practice. It's an important reminder of the power of God's Word.

> If you were to take the sum total of all authoritative articles ever written by the most qualified of psychologists and psychiatrists on the subject of mental hygiene; and if you were to combine them and refine them and cleave out the excess verbiage; and if you were to have these unadulterated bits of pure scientific knowledge concisely expressed by the most capable of living poets; you would have an awkward and incomplete summation of the teachings of Christ, particularly the Sermon On the Mount; and it would suffer immeasurably in comparison.[1]

The Care and Counsel Handbook represents the cornerstone of the very hope upon which our ministry was founded—the hope of God's Word. It is truly a one-of-a-kind biblical resource that not only offers hope, but also celebrates the beautiful wisdom, guidance, and counsel of God based on the principles in His timeless Word. This book is part of our Complete System of Care—our vast library of biblical resources—which we believe provides a trustworthy road map for anyone seeking godly guidance and direction. All of our resources serve as a compass, pointing to the "true north" of God's Word, covering more than 100 topics on what the Bible says about the everyday issues of life.

This book is also the culmination of a 40-year vision given to Hope for the Heart's founder, June Hunt, to bring biblical hope and practical help to those looking for answers and support . . . and to those who feel called to care for others in their time of need. The pages that follow give each of us the opportunity to hear and understand what God has to say to us about the real issues of life.

The Story of the *Keys*

Since her early days as a church youth director, young adults director, conference speaker, and longtime teacher and radio host of *Hope in the Night*, June Hunt's dedication to Scripture and the transformational power of the Holy Spirit has been a hallmark of Hope for the Heart and every aspect of our ministry. Spanning four decades in radio, print, and face-to-face teaching and counseling, her model of providing God's truth for today's problems—to see minds, hearts, and lives changed—has impacted people around the world in 60+ countries and 35+ languages. This resource is the embodiment of June's God-given vision and life's work.

But June did not always have hope. She discovered the truth of who God is gradually as an inquisitive child who desperately needed hope amid a chaotic and painful childhood. Growing up in a home that did not always feel safe, June eventually encountered the gospel as a young teen. Although her relationship with her father was difficult and hurtful, she saw her mother's tender heart and learned over time that they needed to lean on Christ and God's Word when life became complicated. June saw how the Lord transformed her mother as she studied His Word. In time, June chose to place her faith in Christ and surrendered her life to Him. That decision changed everything.

As June began to study God's Word for herself, she learned how to explore the Bible and understand how God provides answers for the challenges of life. She applied her innate logical approach and problem-solving skills to decipher what the Bible had to say about topic after topic. In doing so, she learned not only how to lovingly counsel others directly from God's Word, but also how to develop a unique way of sharing God's truth about real-life challenges. This became the foundation of a lifelong biblical counseling, coaching, and caregiving ministry.

There are many different theories, models, and approaches to counseling. Colleges and seminaries, mental health centers, and ministries are filled with books and ideas on how best to help those who are lost, brokenhearted, in need of direction, or simply have unanswered questions. Birthed out of a three-year *Counseling Through the Bible* training course and live training events called Biblical Counseling Intensives, the Lord gave June a dynamic, versatile, and practical framework that incorporates both God's Word and biblical counseling theory into a proven model that has touched millions of lives.

Now consolidated in our *Keys for Living Library*, these resources bring in-depth biblical integration and practical guidance on a myriad of topics that give truth and hope so a life can be transformed. Unlike secular theories that place man at the center of a counseling paradigm, at Hope for the Heart, we believe God is the center and ultimate source of healing and well-being. That's why our *Keys for Living* books explain in common language how to use God's Word to address our everyday struggles, challenges, and questions. These resources are practical, relevant, consistent, and translatable guides for navigating life.

The Care and Counsel Library addresses 100 real-life topics and speaks to many of today's most prevalent issues. The chapters herein offer practical, biblical guidance on everyday challenges, and are based on the content in our *Keys for Living Library* on the same topics. Each of the full *Keys for Living* books provide additional in-depth content and serve as a broader and more complete reference for each topic. You can find our *Keys for Living* books and other biblical resources at www.hopefortheheart.org.

The Format of the *Keys*

Building a structurally sound home without well-designed plans and blueprints is impossible. With the same mindset for our mission of building structurally sound, biblical counseling resources that speak to everyday life struggles, each *Keys for Living* topic is organized into four distinct sections: Definitions, Characteristics, Causes, and Steps to Solution. This simple, uniform structure provides a firm foundation and a consistent framework from topic to topic.

Building on this foundation, each of the *Keys* facilitates personal growth, and proves to be a valuable tool to care for and counsel others. The *Keys* not only unlock and open doors, providing a safe pathway for growth and change, but they also help close off avenues of unhealthy, unbalanced, and ungodly values and false beliefs. The *Keys* truly serve as a guiding light through Scripture toward the hope we all long for and need.

Here is a closer look at the structure:

Definitions develop your understanding of the problem from God's perspective.

- Identify word origins and meanings

- Explain, clarify, and distinguish terms and concepts
- Use biblical illustrations and real-life situations
- Present myths and truth, as well as common questions and answers
- Include applicable scriptures for quick reference

Characteristics seek to be a spotlight of truth, convicting and exposing the need for change.

- Describe both physical and emotional symptoms
- List obvious and not-so-obvious characteristics
- Reveal appropriate and inappropriate behavior
- Include checklists and self-assessments
- Serve as a tool to identify the associated problem

Causes bring to light legitimate inner needs that we sometimes try to meet in illegitimate ways.

- Reveal the underlying reasons for the symptoms
- Distinguish between surface and root causes
- Identify the basic God-given need(s) we seek to fulfill
- Expose a wrong belief system and how we seek to meet our own needs
- Pinpoint a scriptural principle that applies to the right belief

Steps to Solution give concrete action plans for breaking bondages and building Christlike character.

- Feature a key memory verse
- Present a key biblical passage that applies to the associated issue
- Identify biblical principles to act upon to bring about change
- Outline practical steps to victory and ultimate healing
- Include illustrations and scriptures to memorize for the renewing of your mind

Additionally, three core concepts are embedded into every *Keys for Living* book, providing a tightly woven, common thread that reinforces our dependency on the Lord, His Word, and His work on the cross. Summarized here, you can read more about these concepts in the following pages.

- **Three Inner Needs**—We are all created with three basic inner needs: the need to be loved, the need for significance, and the need for security. Each of these needs can be legitimately met in a relationship with Jesus.

- **Four Points of God's Plan**—Christ is our ultimate hope, and His purpose for us is salvation. The problem is sin, the provision is the Savior, and our part is surrender.

- **How to Have a Transformed Life**—God's purpose is for us to be conformed to the character of Christ, His priority is to change our thinking, and His plan is for us to rely on His strength to be all He created us to be.

The Complete System of Care

We are all called to care. That doesn't just mean caring for others. It also means taking care of ourselves. That's why we created the Complete System of Care. It offers a holistic approach to addressing mental, emotional, relational, and spiritual life issues. Centered around our 100+ topic *Keys for Living Library,* the practical, biblical resources in our Complete System of Care ensure you have everything you need when getting to the heart of common life issues. Each resource is professionally informed and rooted in God's Word. From practical guidance in our books to deeper insights through video training courses, inspiring events, and media platforms, these tools work together to help you experience freedom and transformation in Christ—and to share that hope with others.

One distinctive feature of this system is the continuum it represents—from finding appropriate resources for self-care to caring for a loved one or friend. Our Complete System of Care provides guidance and tools for the various roles where individuals need to be equipped to help others . . . whether you're a pastor, ministry leader, professional counselor, life coach, or an everyday Christian who feels called to care.

At Hope for the Heart, we have learned over the years that effective care and counsel requires both an authentic, caring relationship and a solid understanding of human behavior. Whatever your role in the kingdom, God gives us opportunities to be His ears, His voice, and His compassionate heart . . . to counsel and comfort others. *"Let the message about Christ, in all its richness, fill your lives. Teach and counsel each other with all the wisdom he gives"* (Colossians 3:16 NLT).

The truth is, Christian counseling isn't undertaken exclusively by highly trained mental health clinicians. It also takes place over coffee cups; on the basketball court; in hospital rooms and countless homes, schools, and offices; across cities, states, and countries; wherever two or more people share honest thoughts, concerns, and burdens with one another. All it takes is a decision to share and a willingness to listen. Then, we have the opportunity to invite God and His Word to penetrate hearts and provide the counsel and hope we need to face life's challenges.

Hope for the Heart resources can be used by professionals and lay counselors; pastors and chaplains; Christian life coaches, educators, and ministry leaders; roommates and neighbors; strangers and friends. We believe that by

God's grace, His Word can be understood by the hurting heart, be shared in discipleship, and be modeled within the home and community.

So whether you are a Christian looking for answers or you want to better serve those under your care as a leader, parent, or friend—you have every reason for hope, for every challenge in life. *Because hope means everything.*

Making Disciples

We must remember that we cannot fix, transform, change, heal, or save anyone. However, we can introduce people to the One who is able to do all these things and more. Just before He ascended to heaven, Jesus told His followers, *"Go and make disciples of all nations, baptizing them in the name of the Father and of the Son and of the Holy Spirit, and teaching them to obey everything I have commanded you"* (Matthew 28:19-20). This is our mission statement as those who serve Christ, the Great Commission given by the One who came as the Living Word. He promised to send the Holy Spirit, the Comforter, who would remind us of His truth (John 14:24-26). Now, even today, we have the joy of speaking His words over our own lives as well as to those who need grace, truth, support, encouragement, and, most of all, *hope*!

The call to action is to make disciples—to see those the Lord has entrusted into our care grow closer to Him, mature in their faith, and ultimately become ambassadors of reconciliation as the apostle Paul described in 2 Corinthians 5:18-21. Remember that the gospel came to us only on its way to the next person.

Hearing the Voice of the Good Shepherd

In a beautiful metaphor found in John 10:4-5, we see (and hear) the voice of the Good Shepherd. Jesus says, *"His sheep follow him because they know his voice. But they will never follow a stranger; in fact, they will run away from him because they do not recognize a stranger's voice."* By learning to recognize the voice of the Lord, we will always be able to discern that of the imposter.

In fact, when learning to identify counterfeit money, U.S. Treasury agents are trained by studying only real currency, not fake bills. If what they are inspecting fails to match what they have been taught to recognize as authentic, they automatically know the bill is counterfeit. *The truth alone reveals the imposter.* What an important principle for every believer.

Our prayer is that this resource will become a trusted tool whenever you need to hear what God has to say about a matter, or when you have a concern of the heart, are burdened for a loved one, have an unanswered question, or need godly wisdom and direction for a pressing issue. We pray that by studying God's truth, you will learn to recognize the authentic voice of the Shepherd.

May you be like Philip, who joined the Ethiopian eunuch to guide him in what he was reading from the scroll of Isaiah (Acts 8:25–39). Or Peter, who spoke truth and good news to Cornelius, opening the door for countless Gentiles to find faith and salvation (Acts 10:34–43). Or Priscilla and Aquila, who *"explained the way of God even more accurately"* to Apollos (Acts 18:26 NLT). Or Barnabas and Saul, who spent a year making disciples in Antioch where they were first called Christians (Acts 11:26).

For countless people across the globe, *hope means everything*. Yet for many, hope remains a distant thought, an elusive dream of a better tomorrow, or simply an honest and heartfelt prayer to the One who they hope can make a difference. And what should our response be as those who follow Christ, believe in His promises, and rest in His provision?

June Hunt likes to put it this way: "There are no hopeless situations, only people who have grown hopeless. There really are biblical solutions for all of life's struggles."

As you answer the call to care for those God places in your path—even amid your own trials and struggles—may you recognize His voice, be strengthened by His love, and may the Lord work in and through you to do more than you can ask or imagine as you seek His counsel and reflect His care.

> I pray that from his glorious, unlimited resources he will empower you with inner strength through his Spirit. Then Christ will make his home in your hearts as you trust in him. Your roots will grow down into God's love and keep you strong. And may you have the power to understand, as all God's people should, how wide, how long, how high, and how deep his love is. May you experience the love of Christ, though it is too great to understand fully. Then you will be made complete with all the fullness of life and power that comes from God. Now all glory to God, who is able, through his mighty power at work within us, to accomplish infinitely more than we might ask or think. Glory to him in the church and in Christ Jesus through all generations forever and ever! Amen. (Ephesians 3:16–21 NLT)

THREE HELPFUL CONCEPTS FOR EFFECTIVE BIBLICAL CARE & COUNSEL

The chapters in this resource provide detailed, practical guidance from God's Word on 100 topics. While it is helpful to know what the Bible says specifically about individual topics, it can also be beneficial to understand a few concepts that apply to all people, for any topic or issue.

That's why we want to encourage you to familiarize yourself with three foundational concepts found in all of our *Keys for Living* books. In the following pages, you'll find information about the Three Inner Needs, Four Points of God's Plan, and How to Have a Transformed Life.

The Three Inner Needs provides a helpful framework for understanding what often lies beneath many of the issues we face. Many times, we seek to meet our needs for love, significance, and security in illegitimate ways instead of seeking to meet those needs through Christ.

The Four Points of God's Plan provides a simple framework for sharing the gospel with someone, regardless of what challenge they are facing. We believe that true, lasting change first begins with a relationship with Jesus Christ, so it is important to point people to the Lord and remember the ultimate need people have—salvation.

How to Have a Transformed Life provides biblical insight on God's purpose, priority, and plan for each person. This gives people a target to aim for as they seek to grow and change.

These three concepts work together to provide you with a biblical, overarching framework that can be applied to any topic or issue when helping others. We pray these three concepts will be useful to you as you seek His guidance and serve those under your care.

Let the wise listen and add to their learning,
and let the discerning get guidance.
(PROVERBS 1:5)

THREE INNER NEEDS

We all have three inner needs: the needs for love, significance, and security.[2]

Love—to know that someone is unconditionally committed to our best interest

"My command is this: Love each other as I have loved you" (JOHN 15:12).

Significance—to know that our lives have meaning and purpose
"I cry out to God Most High, to God who fulfills his purpose for me"
(PSALM 57:2 ESV).

Security—to feel accepted and a sense of belonging
"Whoever fears the LORD has a secure fortress, and for their children it will be a refuge" (PROVERBS 14:26).

The Ultimate Need-Meeter

What do our inner needs reveal about us and our relationship with God?

God did not create any person or position or any amount of power or possessions to meet our deepest needs. People fail us, and self-effort also fails to meet our deepest needs. If a person or thing could meet all our needs, we wouldn't need God! Our inner needs draw us into a deeper dependence on Christ and remind us that only God can satisfy the longings of our hearts. The Lord brings people and circumstances into our lives as an extension of His care, but ultimately only He can satisfy all the needs of our hearts. The Bible says,

"The LORD will guide you always;
he will satisfy your needs in a sun-scorched land
and will strengthen your frame.
You will be like a well-watered garden,
like a spring whose waters never fail."
(ISAIAH 58:11)

All along, the Lord planned to meet our deepest needs for . . .

Love—*"I* [the Lord] *have loved you with an everlasting love; I have drawn you with unfailing kindness"* (JEREMIAH 31:3).

Significance—*"'I know the plans I have for you,' declares the* LORD, *'plans to prosper you and not to harm you, plans to give you hope and a future'"* (JEREMIAH 29:11).

Security—*"The* LORD *himself goes before you and will be with you; he will never leave you nor forsake you. Do not be afraid; do not be discouraged"* (DEUTERONOMY 31:8).

Our needs for love, significance, and security can be legitimately met in Christ Jesus. Philippians 4:19 makes it plain: *"My God will meet all your needs according to the riches of his glory in Christ Jesus."*

FOUR POINTS OF GOD'S PLAN

Whether you're trying to make sense of your past, trying to overcome something in the present, or trying to make changes for a better future, the Lord cares about you. He loves you. No matter what challenges you or your loved ones are facing, no matter the pain or difficult feelings you may be experiencing, no matter what you've done or what's been done to you, there is hope. And that hope is found in Jesus Christ.

God has a plan for your life, and it begins with a personal relationship with Jesus. The most important decision you can ever make is whether you will receive His invitation. If you have never made that decision, these four simple truths can help you start your journey together with Him.

"I know the plans I have for you," declares the LORD,
"plans to prosper you and not to harm you,
plans to give you hope and a future."
(JEREMIAH 29:11)

1. God's Purpose for You: Salvation

— What was God's motivation in sending Jesus Christ to earth? To express His love for you by saving you! The Bible says, *"God so loved the world that he gave his one and only Son, that whoever believes in him shall not perish but have eternal life. For God did not send his Son into the world to condemn the world, but to save the world through him"* (John 3:16–17).

— What was Jesus' purpose in coming to earth? To forgive your sins, to empower you to have victory over sin, and to enable you to live a fulfilled life! Jesus said, *"I have come that they may have life, and have it to the full"* (John 10:10).

2. The Problem: Sin

— What exactly is sin? Sin is living independently of God's standard—knowing what is wrong and doing it anyway; also knowing what is right and choosing not to do it. The apostle Paul said, *"I know that nothing good lives in me, that is, in my sinful nature. I want to do what is right, but I can't. I want to do what is good, but I don't. I don't want to do what is wrong, but I do it anyway"* (Romans 7:18–19 NLT).

— What is the major consequence of sin? Spiritual death, eternal separation from God. The Bible says, *"Your iniquities* [sins] *have separated you from your God"* (Isaiah 59:2). Scripture also says, *"The wages of sin is death, but the gift of God is eternal life in Christ Jesus our Lord"* (Romans 6:23).

3. God's Provision for You: The Savior

- Can anything remove the penalty for sin? Yes! Jesus died on the cross to personally pay the penalty for your sins. The Bible says, *"God demonstrates his own love for us in this: While we were still sinners, Christ died for us"* (Romans 5:8).
- What is the solution to being separated from God? Belief in (entrusting your life to) Jesus Christ as the only way to God the Father. Jesus said, *"I am the way and the truth and the life. No one comes to the Father except through me"* (John 14:6). The Bible says, *"Believe in the Lord Jesus, and you will be saved"* (Acts 16:31).

4. Your Part: Surrender

- Give Christ control of your life, entrusting yourself to Him. Jesus said, *"Whoever wants to be my disciple must deny themselves and take up their cross and follow me. For whoever wants to save their life will lose it, but whoever loses their life for me will find it. What good will it be for someone to gain the whole world, yet forfeit their soul?"* (Matthew 16:24–26).
- Place your faith in (rely on) Jesus Christ as your personal Lord and Savior and reject your "good works" as a means of earning God's approval. The Bible says, *"It is by grace you have been saved, through faith—and this is not from yourselves, it is the gift of God—not by works, so that no one can boast"* (Ephesians 2:8–9).

Has there been a time in your life when you know you've humbled your heart and received Jesus Christ as your personal Lord and Savior—giving Him control of your life? If not, you can tell God that you want to surrender your life to Christ in a simple, heartfelt prayer like this:

"God, I want a real relationship with You.
I admit that many times I've chosen to go my own way
instead of Your way.
Please forgive me for my sins.
Jesus, thank You for dying on the cross
to pay the penalty for my sins.
Come into my life to be my Lord and my Savior.
Change me from the inside out and make me the person
You created me to be.
In Your holy name I pray. Amen."

What Can You Now Expect?

When you surrender your life to Christ, you receive the Holy Spirit, who empowers you to live a life pleasing to God. The Bible says, *"His divine power has given us everything we need for a godly life"* (2 Peter 1:3). Jesus assures those who believe with these words:

"Truly I tell you, whoever hears my word
and believes him who sent me
has eternal life and will not be judged
but has crossed over from death to life."
(JOHN 5:24)

HOW TO HAVE A TRANSFORMED LIFE

Reaching the Target: Transformation!

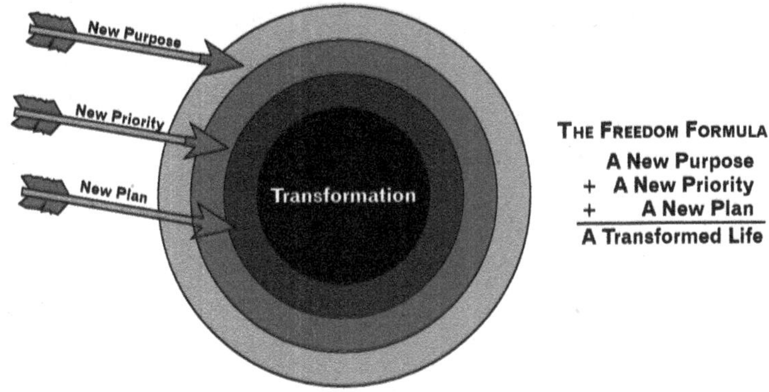

Target #1—A New Purpose

God's purpose for me is to be conformed to the character of Christ.

"Those God foreknew he also predestined to be conformed to the image of his Son" (ROMANS 8:29).

"I'll do whatever it takes to be conformed to the character of Christ."

Target #2—A New Priority

God's priority for me is to change my thinking.

"Do not conform to the pattern of this world, but be transformed by the renewing of your mind" (ROMANS 12:2).

"I'll do whatever it takes to line up my thinking with God's thinking."

Target #3—A New Plan

God's plan for me is to rely on Christ's strength, not my strength, to be all He created me to be.

"I can do all things through Christ who strengthens me" (PHILIPPIANS 4:13 NKJV).

"I'll do whatever it takes to fulfill His plan in His strength."

THE ABORTION DILEMMA

Answering the Tough Questions

God's Heart on Life

God meets the needs of those He creates by providing for them both before birth and after birth.

"The Almighty, who blesses you with . . . blessings of the breast and womb" (GENESIS 49:25).

God is the sovereign Creator/Maker of everyone—the One who uniquely forms and knits together each person in the womb according to His plan and purposes.

"Did not he who made me in the womb make them? Did not the same one form us both within our mothers?" (JOB 31:15).

God has personal, precise interaction with His creations while they are in the womb, even teaching them as they are developing into the unique persons of His design.

"You desired faithfulness even in the womb; you taught me wisdom in that secret place" (PSALM 51:6).

God is intimately acquainted with each individual child. Even before He forms a child in the womb, He has a plan and purpose for each and every one.

"From birth I have relied on you [God]*; you brought me forth from my mother's womb. I will ever praise you"* (PSALM 71:6).

God sets each life apart and calls each one to a specific purpose while they are still in their mother's womb and, when the time is right, He fulfills His purpose in their lives.

"God, who set me apart from my mother's womb and called me by his grace, was pleased to reveal his Son in me so that I might preach him among the Gentiles" (GALATIANS 1:15–16).

God oversees the entire life of every child.

"From birth I was cast on you; from my mother's womb you have been my God" (PSALM 22:10).

God makes known the value He places on an unborn child by the penalty He sets forth for anyone who would injure that child while still in the mother's womb.

"If people are fighting and hit a pregnant woman and . . . there is serious injury, you are to take life for life" (EXODUS 21:22–23).

God is personally present and involved in the conception, formation, and birth of all life; He personally witnesses the death of every person He creates; and at the appointed time He will satisfy His demand that an accounting take place for the cost of every life.

"I will demand an accounting for the life of another human being" (GENESIS 9:5).

Because of the LORD's great love we are not consumed,
for his compassions never fail.
(LAMENTATIONS 3:22)

The Two Main Positions in the Abortion Argument

Pro-life

The pro-life position is that life begins at the moment of conception and that all human life is precious and made in the image of God. Therefore, an unborn baby should receive constitutional protection of life.

This position is in agreement with the biblical position, which values the life of the unborn baby the same as the life of the mother.

"If people are fighting and hit a pregnant woman and she gives birth prematurely but there is no serious injury, the offender must be fined whatever the woman's husband demands and the court allows. But if there is serious injury, you are to take life for life, eye for eye, tooth for tooth, hand for hand, foot for foot, burn for burn, wound for wound, bruise for bruise" (Exodus 21:22–25).

Pro-choice

The pro-choice position is that a female has the right to choose whether or not to have an abortion because an unborn child is considered to be part of the mother. Some believe that a fetus is only a "potential person" (*Roe v. Wade*, 1973) and, therefore, should not be entitled to constitutional protection. Those who prioritize "reproduction rights" believe the decision about the life or death of the unborn baby should be solely the choice of the pregnant mother. However, this "choice" often disregards the "rights" of the father of the child and results in the absolute absence of choice for the unborn.

This position invites God's great disfavor because it provides no protection for the innocent, unborn life.

"There are six things the LORD hates, seven that are detestable to him: haughty eyes, a lying tongue, hands that shed innocent blood" (PROVERBS 6:16–17).

The Bible gives us this instruction for sharing truth with others:

Opponents must be gently instructed,
in the hope that God will grant them repentance
leading them to a knowledge of the truth.
(2 Timothy 2:25)

Primary Influences that Cause a Woman to Choose Abortion[3]

1. **Fearing parental response**—"Since I'm not married, I will let my parents down and they'll be angry at the baby's father."

2. **Fearing rejection and ridicule**—"I don't want my pregnancy to be exposed. I'll be rejected by those I want to respect me."

3. **Fearing financial responsibility**—"I can't afford a child."

4. **Fearing the inability to care for the child**—"I'm unprepared for single parenting."

5. **Fearing a non-supportive partner**—"I'm involved in an abusive relationship. I was abandoned."

6. **Fearing a pregnancy resulting from rape or incest**—"I don't want a reminder of this."

7. **Feeling the timing is inconvenient**—"This will interfere with my education, job, lifestyle, etc."

8. **Feeling rushed to make a decision**—"I feel pressured by parents, the baby's father, an abortion counselor, etc."

9. **Feeling it is wrong to bring an unwanted child into the world**—"I just don't want this child or any child now."

10. **Feeling it is just another means of birth control**—"I have a right to eliminate any child I may have."

11. **Feeling that a fetus is not a person**—"This is not a person, but just a blob of cells."

12. **Feeling no moral conviction**—"I don't feel an abortion is morally wrong."

God is Sovereign over LIFE

L—Length of Life

"All the days ordained for me were written in your book before one of them came to be" (Psalm 139:16).

I—Inmost Being

"For you created my inmost being" (Psalm 139:13).

F—Frame

"My frame was not hidden from you when I was made in the secret place" (Psalm 139:15).

E—Embryo

"You knit me together in my mother's womb" (Psalm 139:13).

I have set before you life and death, blessings and curses.
Now choose life, so that you and your children may live.
(Deuteronomy 30:19)

My Personalized Plan

Seek wise advice and listen to the truth concerning the life I am carrying in my womb.

— Though this baby may be unplanned, that does not mean the baby is a mistake.

"Now the one who has fashioned us for this very purpose is God" (2 Corinthians 5:5).

Sacrifice my desires in favor of what is best for my unborn child's future.

— I will not let my potential problems dictate whether or not I carry my baby to term.

"My sacrifice, O God, is a broken spirit; a broken and contrite heart you, God, will not despise" (Psalm 51:17).

Strive to prioritize the life of my unborn child above the perceived losses and fears I currently have.

— I will remember that God still has a plan for my life and for the life of my unborn child.

"Peace I leave with you; my peace I give you. I do not give to you as the world gives. Do not let your hearts be troubled and do not be afraid" (John 14:27).

Submit to God's will, recognizing that not everyone will support my decision to have my child.

— I will share with my baby's father and my family that I've made my decision to have the baby.

"Let this be written for a future generation, that a people not yet created may praise the LORD" (PSALM 102:18).

Serve my unborn child, encouraging him/her to grow and thrive.

— I will do whatever I can to secure the best future for my baby.

"Whoever wants to become great among you must be your servant" (MATTHEW 20:26).

Surround myself with supportive people.

— I will seek out positive role models to offer encouragement throughout the pregnancy, birth, and raising or adoption of my child.

"God has put the body together, giving greater honor to the parts that lacked it, so that there should be no division in the body, but that its parts should have equal concern for each other. If one part suffers, every part suffers with it; if one part is honored, every part rejoices with it. Now you are the body of Christ, and each one of you is a part of it" (1 CORINTHIANS 12:24–27).

Key Verse to Memorize

"Before I formed you in the womb I knew you, before you were born I set you apart."
(JEREMIAH 1:5)

Shelter myself in God's will, asking Him to guide my next steps.

— I will seek God's wisdom, asking Him to guide me and lead me in future decisions.

"Praise be to the name of God for ever and ever; wisdom and power are his. He changes times and seasons; he deposes kings and raises up others. He gives wisdom to the wise and knowledge to the discerning" (DANIEL 2:20–21).

Questions & Answers

Question: "What does the Bible say about the sanctity of life?"

Answer: The Bible is not silent about the value, worth, and sanctity of life, especially in terms of the unborn child in the womb.

God created humankind in His image. God uniquely formed human beings to be His image-bearers and gave them a special dignity, personal freedom, and individual accountability above all the works of creation. The right to life of every unborn human being is inherent by virtue of being created in the image of God.

"God said, 'Let us make mankind in our image, in our likeness, so that they may rule over the fish in the sea and the birds in the sky, over the livestock and all the wild animals, and over all the creatures that move along the ground.' So God created mankind in his own image, in the image of God he created them; male and female he created them" (GENESIS 1:26–27).

Human life begins at conception and human beings have been made to be in relationship with God, who created each person's inmost being, knit together in their mother's womb.

"For you created my inmost being; you knit me together in my mother's womb. I praise you because I am fearfully and wonderfully made; your works are wonderful, I know that full well. . . . Your eyes saw my unformed body; all the days ordained for me were written in your book before one of them came to be" (PSALM 139:13–14, 16).

From conception until natural death, every human life is sacred because every human life has been created by God.

"This is what the Lord says—your Redeemer, who formed you in the womb: I am the Lord, the Maker of all things, who stretches out the heavens, who spreads out the earth by myself" (ISAIAH 44:24).

Human life, even before conception, is designed by God for a specific purpose. Every human life must be recognized, respected, and protected as having the rights of a person and the irrevocable right to life.

"Before I formed you in the womb I knew you, before you were born I set you apart; I appointed you as a prophet to the nations" (JEREMIAH 1:5).

Human life is precious and deserves to be saved. All life is precious. Therefore, deliberately terminating human life after conception is a sin against God for which individuals are held accountable. Extremely rare situations exist where saving the life of the mother can result in losing the life of the baby. However, this is a matter of trying to save one life or two lives, as opposed to causing the death of one or both.

"The fruit of the righteous is a tree of life, and the one who is wise saves lives" (PROVERBS 11:30).

Human life must be protected and defended from conception to natural death. We are ethically bound to defend all human life from destruction, whether by surgical abortion or use of drugs, devices, or procedures with the intent of terminating human life.

"Rescue those being led away to death; hold back those staggering toward slaughter. If you say, 'But we knew nothing about this,' does not he who weighs the heart perceive it? Does not he who guards your life know it? Will he not repay everyone according to what they have done?" (PROVERBS 24:11–12).

Human life must be publicly and peacefully proclaimed as sacred. Those who make up the Christian church, including and led by Christian ministers and ministries, should be public witnesses regarding the intrinsic and irrevocable dignity of all human life, from conception to natural death.

"This day I call the heavens and the earth as witnesses against you that I have set before you life and death, blessings and curses. Now choose life, so that you and your children may live" (DEUTERONOMY 30:19).

Human life at conception defies that a fetus is just a "mass of tissue."

According to the Bible, a fetus is not merely a mass of tissue. God's Word does not distinguish between a "potential baby" and a "newborn baby." In the Bible, the same Greek word *brephos,* which means "babe," is used to describe both a fetus and a newborn baby.

Fetus: *"When Elizabeth heard Mary's greeting, the baby leaped in her womb"* (Luke 1:41).

Babies: *"People were also bringing babies to Jesus for him to place his hands on them"* (Luke 18:15).

Human life at conception negates that females have the right to choose abortion by asserting, "It's her body!" A woman should have rights over her own body, but in pregnancy there are at least two different bodies, two different heartbeats, two different brain wave patterns, two different genetic codes (DNA), and often two different genders and blood types. Every woman has choices within her own life, but not the freedom to destroy the life of a developing human being within her.

"I have cared for you since you were born. Yes, I carried you before you were born" (ISAIAH 46:3 NLT).

Key Passage to Read

Psalm 139:13–16

Human life is unique from all other forms of life. A human being is defined as a member of the species Homo sapiens. All human beings have their own genetic codes (DNA), singularly unique and established at conception. The DNA of a human fetus is distinct not only from animals, fowls, and fish, but also from the mother's DNA.

"Not all flesh is the same: People have one kind of flesh, animals have another, birds another and fish another" (1 CORINTHIANS 15:39).

Question: "How can someone who's had an abortion experience true healing?"

Answer: True healing begins when we take full responsibility for the past, receive God's love and forgiveness, extend forgiveness to others, rebuild trust, embrace our God-given worth, and live with renewed purpose in Christ.

"He heals the brokenhearted and binds up their wounds."
(PSALM 147:3)

ABUSE RECOVERY

From Surviving to Thriving

God's Heart on Abuse

God hears the cry of the abused.

"You, LORD, hear the desire of the afflicted; you encourage them, and you listen to their cry" (PSALM 10:17).

God understands the pain of abuse.

"He [Jesus] *was despised and rejected by mankind, a man of suffering, and familiar with pain"* (ISAIAH 53:3).

God strengthens and upholds the victim of abuse.

"Do not fear, for I am with you; do not be dismayed, for I am your God. I will strengthen you and help you; I will uphold you with my righteous right hand" (ISAIAH 41:10).

God confirms the abuse victim's value and worth.

"Are not five sparrows sold for two pennies? Yet not one of them is forgotten by God. Indeed, the very hairs of your head are all numbered. Don't be afraid; you are worth more than many sparrows" (LUKE 12:6–7).

God gives hope to victims of abuse.

"'I know the plans I have for you,' declares the LORD, 'plans to prosper you and not to harm you, plans to give you hope and a future'" (JEREMIAH 29:11).

God offers healing from the pain of abuse.

"He heals the brokenhearted and binds up their wounds" (PSALM 147:3).

God wants to be a refuge to the abused and help them process their emotions and experiences with Him.

"Trust in him at all times, you people; pour out your hearts to him, for God is our refuge" (PSALM 62:8).

God wants to transform victims' hearts and minds with His Word.

"Let God transform you into a new person by changing the way you think. Then you will learn to know God's will for you, which is good and pleasing and perfect" (ROMANS 12:2 NLT).

God wants those who've been abused to establish boundaries in their life and relationships.

"Guard your heart above all else, for it determines the course of your life" (PROVERBS 4:23 NLT).

God wants abuse victims to help others who have experienced abusive treatment.

"The Father of compassion and the God of all comfort . . . comforts us in all our troubles, so that we can comfort those in any trouble with the comfort we ourselves receive from God" (2 CORINTHIANS 1:3–4).

God calls for abusive people to change.

"Give up your violence and oppression and do what is just and right" (EZEKIEL 45:9).

God will one day end all abuse and pain.

"He will wipe every tear from their eyes, and there will be no more death or sorrow or crying or pain. All these things are gone forever" (REVELATION 21:4 NLT).

"You intended to harm me,
but God intended it for good
to accomplish what is now being done,
the saving of many lives."
(GENESIS 50:20)

Replacing Lies with Truth

Lie: "I am worthless and insignificant."

Truth: You matter to God. You have God-given worth because God created you, and that worth can never be taken from you.

"For you created my inmost being; you knit me together in my mother's womb. I praise you because I am fearfully and wonderfully made" (PSALM 139:13–14).

Lie: "No one will ever accept me."

Truth: The Lord chose you, accepts you, and will never reject you.

"I have chosen you and have not rejected you. So do not fear, for I am with you; do not be dismayed, for I am your God. I will strengthen you and help you; I will uphold you with my righteous right hand" (ISAIAH 41:9–10).

Lie: "I am unlovable."

Truth: God loves you, and nothing can separate you from His love.

"I am convinced that nothing can ever separate us from God's love. Neither death nor life, neither angels nor demons, neither our fears for today nor our worries about tomorrow—not even the powers of hell can separate us from God's love. No power in the sky above or in the earth below—indeed, nothing in all creation will ever be able to separate us from the love of God that is revealed in Christ Jesus our Lord" (ROMANS 8:38–39 NLT).

Lie: "I deserve to be abused."

Truth: No one deserves to be abused—no one. Each person should be treated with respect as God's image-bearer.

"Show proper respect to everyone" (1 PETER 2:17).

Lie: "There is no hope for me."

Truth: No matter how deep the pain, with God, there is always hope.

"There is surely a future hope for you, and your hope will not be cut off" (PROVERBS 23:18).

Key Verse to Memorize

You, God, see the trouble of the afflicted;
you consider their grief and take it in hand.
The victims commit themselves to you;
you are the helper of the fatherless.
(PSALM 10:14)

Lie: "I have no control over what happens to me."

Truth: God has given you free will, and you do have control over the choices you make and the actions you take.

"For we are each responsible for our own conduct" (GALATIANS 6:5 NLT).

Lie: "God doesn't care about me."

Truth: God cares deeply about you and wants you to come to Him with your burdens.

"Give all your worries and cares to God, for he cares about you" (1 PETER 5:7 NLT).

Lie: "God is disappointed in me and wants nothing to do with me."

Truth: God has compassion for you—He is with you and desires a close relationship with you.

"The LORD is gracious and compassionate, slow to anger and rich in love. The LORD is good to all; he has compassion on all he has made. . . . The LORD is near to all who call on him" (PSALM 145:8–9, 18).

My soul is in deep anguish.
(PSALM 6:3)

Emotional Side Effects of Abuse

1. **Low self-worth**[4]

   "Consider the ravens: They do not sow or reap, they have no storeroom or barn; yet God feeds them. And how much more valuable you are than birds!" (LUKE 12:24).

2. **Dependency**[5]

   "You open your hand and satisfy the desires of every living thing. The Lord is righteous in all his ways and faithful in all he does. The Lord is near to all who call on him, to all who call on him in truth. He fulfills the desires of those who fear him; he hears their cry and saves them" (Psalm 145:16–19).

3. **Fearfulness**[6]

   "God has not given us a spirit of fear, but of power and of love and of a sound mind" (2 Timothy 1:7 NKJV).

4. **Excessiveness**

   "Offer your bodies as a living sacrifice, holy and pleasing to God—this is your true and proper worship. Do not conform to the pattern of this world, but be transformed by the renewing of your mind. Then you will be able to test and approve what God's will is—his good, pleasing and perfect will" (Romans 12:1–2).

5. **Compulsiveness**

   "By grace you have been saved through faith. And this is not your own doing; it is the gift of God, not a result of works, so that no one may boast" (Ephesians 2:8–9 ESV).

The Lord is close to the brokenhearted.
(Psalm 34:18)

Common Beliefs of Abuse Victims: A Personal Checklist

- ☐ I am worthless and unlovable.
- ☐ I need the approval of others to feel good about myself.
- ☐ I must do everything I can to bring about change when I see it is needed.
- ☐ I am responsible for the behavior and feelings of those around me.
- ☐ I am better off with bad love than with no love at all.
- ☐ I am bad if I feel angry.
- ☐ I am terrible because I hate my abuser.
- ☐ I am weak for having needs.
- ☐ I must give in to others because they are wiser and stronger than I am.
- ☐ I must be unlovable if the people I care about reject me.
- ☐ I must keep peace at any price.
- ☐ I will be loved if I am good.
- ☐ My feelings are less important than the feelings of others.
- ☐ My mistakes only confirm my worthlessness.

The Difference Between Guilt and Shame

Shame is a painful emotion of disgrace caused by a strong sense of real or imagined guilt.

Shame can be a response to what was done to you, but guilt is a response to something you have done.

Shame focuses on who you *are*, whereas guilt focuses on what you've *done.*

Shame creates an inner desire to maintain rigid control over emotions and behavior, while guilt creates a desire to change or justify emotions and behavior.

Shame produces inner loneliness that fosters unhealthy dependencies, whereas guilt produces inner longings that foster healthy repentance in relationships.

Shame steals the joy of your salvation, while guilt confessed restores joy in salvation.

Restore to me the joy of your salvation
and grant me a willing spirit, to sustain me.
(Psalm 51:12)

My Personalized Plan

Look to the Lord: God will listen to me, strengthen me, and help me rise above abuse. Being abused can distort my view of God, but I will remember that God loves me. He is for me, and He is with me. He desires to heal and restore me and set me free. I can trust Him.

"Look to the Lord and his strength; seek his face always" (1 Chronicles 16:11).

Talk to someone: Because I have been abused (or am currently being abused), I need to tell someone. If they don't believe me, I will tell someone else. Talking to someone can be the first step toward healing and recovery for me. I know that God can use my friends, family, and counselors to comfort me and to help me heal and grow.

"Two people are better off than one, for they can help each other succeed. If one person falls, the other can reach out and help" (Ecclesiastes 4:9–10 NLT).

Key Passage to Read

Lamentations 3:19–26

Address physical issues: Whether or not the abuse I endured was physical—I may have physical issues that need to be addressed. There may be literal wounds or lingering pain in my body that needs healing.

"I am suffering and in pain. Rescue me, O God, by your saving power" (PSALM 69:29 NLT).

Process my emotions: Painful, hidden emotions like anger and hurt still affect my well-being and relationships. I will give myself time to grieve and process this pain.

"In my distress I called to the LORD; I cried to my God for help" (PSALM 18:6).

Replace lies with truth: As I read His Word, I will begin to see myself through God's eyes.

"You will know the truth, and the truth will set you free" (JOHN 8:32).

Set boundaries: In abusive relationships, boundaries that are designed to keep me safe are often crossed. To prevent further abuse, it's important for me to establish and maintain firm boundaries.

"Above all else, guard your heart, for everything you do flows from it" (PROVERBS 4:23).

Help others: I can take the bad things that have happened to me and use them for good. God can use my painful experience to help others.

"The Father of compassion and the God of all comfort . . . comforts us in all our troubles, so that we can comfort those in any trouble with the comfort we ourselves receive from God" (2 CORINTHIANS 1:3–4).

Questions & Answers

Question: "Why didn't God stop my abuse from happening?"

Answer: Knowing that God permitted your abuse but in no way caused your abuse or condoned it is critical. God hates evil and violence and will one day totally obliterate all evil and evil practices. He will pronounce eternal judgment on all who persist in their evil ways.

"I will punish the world for its evil,
the wicked for their sins.
I will put an end to the arrogance of the haughty
and will humble the pride of the ruthless."
(ISAIAH 13:11)

Question: "I've discovered that my daughter is a 'cutter.' Why would she intentionally hurt herself?"

Answer: Those who deliberately inflict repeated pain on themselves—such as cutting, burning, or biting their bodies or reopening barely healed wounds—are seeking relief from overwhelming emotional pain. Self-inflicted harm becomes a temporary coping mechanism to release tension or the shame of abuse.

Any form of self-injury is a cry for help. These strugglers need to know on a very deep level that they don't have to shed their blood to relieve their emotional pain because Jesus has already given His life for them.[7]

You were redeemed . . . with the precious blood
of Christ, a lamb without blemish or defect.
(1 PETER 1:18–19)

ADOPTION

A Child Born in the Heart

God's Heart on Adoption

Adoption is a picture of God's love—showing how God joyfully welcomes us into His family.

"Even before he made the world, God loved us and chose us in Christ to be holy and without fault in his eyes. God decided in advance to adopt us into his own family by bringing us to himself through Jesus Christ. This is what he wanted to do, and it gave him great pleasure" (EPHESIANS 1:4–5 NLT).

Adoption is a picture of salvation—showing how God sets us free and becomes our Father.

"When the right time came, God sent his Son, born of a woman, subject to the law. God sent him to buy freedom for us who were slaves to the law, so that he could adopt us as his very own children. And because we are his children, God has sent the Spirit of his Son into our hearts, prompting us to call out, 'Abba, Father.' Now you are no longer a slave but God's own child. And since you are his child, God has made you his heir" (GALATIANS 4:4–7 NLT).

Adoption is a picture of security—showing how we belong to God as His children and heirs.

"You have not received a spirit that makes you fearful slaves. Instead, you received God's Spirit when he adopted you as his own children. Now we call him, 'Abba, Father.' For his Spirit joins with our spirit to affirm that we are God's children. And since we are his children, we are his heirs. In fact, together with Christ we are heirs of God's glory" (ROMANS 8:15–17 NLT).

Adoption is a picture of hope—showing the glorious future that awaits God's children.

"We believers also groan, even though we have the Holy Spirit within us as a foretaste of future glory, for we long for our bodies to be released from sin and suffering. We, too, wait with eager hope for the day when God will give us our full rights as his adopted children, including the new bodies he has promised us. We were given this hope when we were saved" (ROMANS 8:23–24 NLT).

Adoption is a picture of holy royalty—showing how God views His chosen people.

"You are a chosen people, a royal priesthood, a holy nation, God's special possession, that you may declare the praises of him who called you out of darkness into his wonderful light" (1 PETER 2:9).

Adoption is a picture of being treasured—showing the depths of God's love for His children.

"You are a people holy to the LORD your God. Out of all the peoples on the face of the earth, the LORD has chosen you to be his treasured possession" (DEUTERONOMY 14:2).

Adoption is a picture of rejoicing—showing God's joy in His children.

"He brought out his people with rejoicing, his chosen ones with shouts of joy" (PSALM 105:43).

Adoption is a picture of planning and purpose—showing God's will for His children.

"In him we were also chosen, having been predestined according to the plan of him who works out everything in conformity with the purpose of his will" (EPHESIANS 1:11).

Adoption is a picture of promise—showing character qualities God intends for His children.

"As God's chosen people, holy and dearly loved, clothe yourselves with compassion, kindness, humility, gentleness and patience" (COLOSSIANS 3:12).

Adoption is a picture of loving assurance—showing the proof of God's love for His children.

"We know, brothers and sisters loved by God, that he has chosen you" (1 THESSALONIANS 1:4).

In their hearts humans plan their course,
but the LORD establishes their steps.
(PROVERBS 16:9)

Should You Consider Adopting a Child?

Don't Adopt . . .

If you secretly feel that an adopted child is second best to having a biological child.

If you are looking for a child to fill your emotional needs.

If you are seeking your identity through parenting.

If you fear dealing with inherited weaknesses.

If you and your spouse are not in complete agreement about the adoption.

If you are attempting to save your marriage.

If you are uneasy about biological origins being revealed or discovered.

A person may think their own ways are right,
but the LORD weighs the heart.
(PROVERBS 21:2)

Do Adopt . . .

If you have a happy, stable marriage that is flexible enough to include another person.

If you can truly love and accept a child who is not born to you.

If you and your spouse are ready for a lifelong commitment to love a child sacrificially.

If you are realistically prepared to accept the bad times along with the good times.

If you and your spouse believe adoption is God's will for you.

If you can accept possible rejection and can wait patiently for love and acceptance.

If you have an understanding of godly discipline for children.

Key Verses to Memorize

"Forget the former things;
do not dwell on the past.
See, I am doing a new thing!
Now it springs up; do you not perceive it?
I am making a way in the wilderness
and streams in the wasteland."
(ISAIAH 43:18–19)

By wisdom a house is built,
and through understanding it is established.
(PROVERBS 24:3)

Telling a Child About Adoption

Why should we tell our adopted child?[8]

Adoption is good; therefore, positive attitudes about adoption should be developed early.

The older a child is, the harder adoption is to accept.

Being truthful reinforces the values of honesty and trust.

When a child is told early in life, adoption becomes an accepted part of family life.

What should we tell our adopted child?[9]

Develop positive attitudes involving warmth, comfort, pleasure, security, and love in association with the word *adoption*.

Begin setting the stage with adoption stories, as well as with the child's own personal story.

Explain age-appropriate details of the story and answer all questions honestly.

Be prepared to talk about emotions and feelings when your child initiates conversations or when you sense special opportunities.

When should we tell our adopted child?

0–3 Years: During your child's infancy and toddler years, begin using the word *adoption* in a loving way.

3–5 Years: During your child's early years, begin talking about the child's personal adoption.

5–8 Years: Continue the dialogue during early school years and be prepared to answer all your child's questions honestly.

8–12 Years: Draw out feelings and emotions during the preteen years and help your child understand the past. Be accepting of the child's differences.

Understand God's Concept of Adoptive Love

Adoptive Love is . . .

Selective: It makes a conscious decision to love.
"In love he predestined us for adoption to sonship through Jesus Christ, in accordance with his pleasure and will" (EPHESIANS 1:4–5).

Extensive: It extends beyond family bloodlines.
"For God so loved the world that he gave his one and only Son, that whoever believes in him shall not perish but have eternal life" (JOHN 3:16).

Creative: It provides a new identity.
"If anyone is in Christ, the new creation has come: The old has gone, the new is here!" (2 CORINTHIANS 5:17).

Legal: It includes the guarantee of a child's inheritance.

"Now if we are children, then we are heirs—heirs of God and co-heirs with Christ" (ROMANS 8:17).

Redemptive: It gives freedom to the one in fear or bondage.

"The Spirit you received does not make you slaves, so that you live in fear again; rather the Spirit you received brought about your adoption to sonship" (ROMANS 8:15).

My Personalized Plan

I will . . .

Remember my own spiritual adoption.

— I will remember that God adopted me into his family through Christ.

— I will reflect on how God is my Father, and I'm called to reflect His love.

"God decided in advance to adopt us into his own family by bringing us to himself through Jesus Christ. This is what he wanted to do, and it gave him great pleasure" (EPHESIANS 1:5 NLT).

Key Passage to Read

Romans 8:15–18

Pray regularly.

— I will pray through the entire adoption process, every step of the way.

— I will tell God about my hopes, fears, worries, and struggles.

"Do not be anxious about anything, but in every situation, by prayer and petition, with thanksgiving, present your requests to God. And the peace of God, which transcends all understanding, will guard your hearts and your minds in Christ Jesus" (PHILIPPIANS 4:6–7).

Talk with my spouse.

— I will regularly talk with my spouse, ensuring we are in agreement about adopting a child.

— I will share my concerns and be receptive to what my spouse thinks and feels.

"Let us therefore make every effort to do what leads to peace and to mutual edification" (ROMANS 14:19).

Seek wise counsel.

— I will talk with trusted friends and family about the decision to adopt.

— I will talk with others who have adopted to educate myself on the process.

"In an abundance of counselors there is safety" (PROVERBS 11:14 ESV).

Settle practical matters.

— I will address issues related to finances, housing, and other parental matters.

— I will address the impact the adoption will have on other family members.

"Do your planning and prepare your fields before building your house" (PROVERBS 24:27 NLT).

Trust God's plan.

— I will trust God's timing for the adoption, understanding there might be setbacks.

— I will celebrate what God is doing through this process as I lean on Him each day.

"Trust in him at all times, you people; pour out your hearts to him, for God is our refuge" (PSALM 62:8).

Questions & Answers

Question: "How can I connect with my grown daughter whom I gave up for adoption and have only recently met? She now has little children of her own."

Answer: There are many ways you can show that you care about her. For example, to begin reconnecting with her:

— Send her cards and letters on a regular basis.

— Invest spiritually in her by praying for her and her family daily.

— Send meaningful items that can minister to her and to her family.

Regardless of your daughter's response to you, remain consistent in your efforts to maintain contact. Focus on giving rather than on receiving.

"It is more blessed to give than to receive."
(ACTS 20:35)

Question: "My husband and I went through the process of in vitro fertilization. We just had precious twins. Although we have three more frozen embryos, my husband now says he doesn't want any more children. Morally, what should we do?"

Answer: You are involved in an ethical decision that still affords you several positive options. Instead of terminating the three little lives of your making, you have better choices.

— Wait! After a period of time, he may want more children.

— Investigate the option of putting your embryos up for adoption.

I have set before you life and death. . . . Now choose life,
so that you and your children may live.
(Deuteronomy 30:19)

ADULTERY

The Snare of an Affair

God's Heart on Adultery

Adultery breaks God's heart because . . .

Adultery violates God's command:
"You shall not commit adultery" (Exodus 20:14).

Adultery separates people God has joined together.
"They are no longer two, but one flesh. Therefore what God has joined together, let no one separate" (Matthew 19:6).

Adultery can result from wrongful divorce and remarriage.
"He answered, 'Anyone who divorces his wife and marries another woman commits adultery against her. And if she divorces her husband and marries another man, she commits adultery'" (Mark 10:11–12).

Adultery is sexual immorality.
"The body . . . is not meant for sexual immorality but for the Lord, and the Lord for the body" (1 Corinthians 6:13).

Adultery involves engaging the body of Christ in a sinful sexual act.
"Do you not know that your bodies are members of Christ himself? Shall I then take the members of Christ and unite them with a prostitute? Never!"
(1 Corinthians 6:15).

Adultery is a sin against the adulterer's own body.
"All other sins a person commits are outside the body, but whoever sins sexually, sins against their own body" (1 Corinthians 6:18).

Adultery denies God's ownership of our physical bodies.
"Do you not know that your bodies are temples of the Holy Spirit, who is in you, whom you have received from God? You are not your own; you were bought at a price. Therefore honor God with your bodies" (1 Corinthians 6:19–20).

Adultery violates God's sexual instructions to husbands and wives.
"Each man should have sexual relations with his own wife, and each woman with her own husband. The husband should fulfill his marital duty to his wife, and likewise the wife to her husband" (1 Corinthians 7:2–3).

Key Verses to Memorize

For the Unfaithful Spouse

Flee from sexual immorality. All other sins
a person commits are outside the body,
but whoever sins sexually,
sins against their own body.
(1 CORINTHIANS 6:18)

For the Faithful Spouse

Because of the LORD's great love
we are not consumed,
for his compassions never fail.
They are new every morning;
great is your faithfulness.
I say to myself, "The LORD is my portion;
therefore I will wait for him."
(LAMENTATIONS 3:22–24)

Adultery creates a barrier between husbands and wives that separates them from the love they previously had for one another, whereas:

"Neither death nor life, neither angels nor demons, neither the present nor the future, nor any powers, neither height nor depth, nor anything else in all creation, will be able to separate us from the love of God that is in Christ Jesus our Lord" (ROMANS 8:38–39).

Adultery breaks up marriages and results in children not being raised by parents in an intact family unit as God intended.

"The Creator 'made them male and female,' and said, 'For this reason a man will leave his father and mother and be united to his wife, and the two will become one flesh.' . . . Therefore what God has joined together, let no one separate" (MATTHEW 19:4–6).

"God blessed them and said to them, 'Be fruitful and increase in number; fill the earth and subdue it'" (GENESIS 1:28).

But a man who commits adultery has no sense;
whoever does so destroys himself.
(PROVERBS 6:32)

Possible Outer Signs of Adultery

- — Change in behavior
- — Less spontaneity
- — Less sexual intimacy
- — Change in spending patterns
- — Change in schedule
- — More unaccounted time away from home
- — More faultfinding
- — Less personal conversation
- — More emotional distance
- — Less vulnerability in sharing

— More unexpected gifts ("guilt gifts")
— Less discussion of future plans
— More anger at being questioned

Whoever walks in integrity walks securely,
but whoever takes crooked paths will be found out.
(Proverbs 10:9)

Characteristics of Adulterous Temptation

T—Tasting forbidden fruit—Feeling lured by lust

E—Emotional enticements—Focusing on feelings

M—Minimizing the marriage—Devaluing the marriage commitment

P—Physically withdrawing—Avoiding home and family

T—Temporal over the eternal—Prioritizing pleasure over principle

A—Anger over accountability—Blaming over resolving problems

T—Twisting the truth—Lying about the attraction

I—Imagining the illicit—Fixating on fantasy thinking

O—Objecting to accusations—Defending the "third party"

N—Neglecting the Lord—Hardening the heart toward the Lord

Adultery's Insidious Deception

Adultery is so deceptive because it . . .

— **Skews** objectivity.
— **Feels** good physically.
— **Numbs** emotional pain.
— **Gives** an illusion of being loved.
— **Makes** both parties feel desirable.
— **Gives** a false sense of significance.
— **Provides** a temporary sense of security.
— **Gives** a false feeling of belonging/connection.
— **Diverts** attention away from family/marital problems.
— **Can be wielded** as a weapon to punish the resented spouse.

"You may be sure that your sin will find you out."
(NUMBERS 32:23)

Adultery's Deceptive Draw

When asked, "Why were you drawn into adultery?" the response is almost always among these answers:

"**I blamed** my marriage partner for my problems."

"**I rationalized**: God understands my situation."

"**I failed** to look at the lifelong consequences."

"**I assumed** my mate would never change."

"**I believed** it would make me happy."

"**I opened** the door of compromise."

"**I thought** I wouldn't be caught."

"**I hardened** my heart."

"**I was lured** by lust."

Changes for Good the Adulterer Must Make[10]

Confess the adultery.

"Confess your sins to each other and pray for each other so that you may be healed" (JAMES 5:16).

Commit yourself to your covenant partner completely.

"The LORD is the witness between you and the wife of your youth. You have been unfaithful to her, though she is your partner, the wife of your marriage covenant. Has not the one God made you? You belong to him in body and spirit. And what does the one God seek? Godly offspring. So be on your guard, and do not be unfaithful to the wife of your youth" (MALACHI 2:14–15).

Cut all ties with the third party.

"For there is nothing hidden that will not be disclosed, and nothing concealed that will not be known or brought out into the open" (LUKE 8:17).

Choose where to place your thoughts when tempted.

"Finally, brothers and sisters, whatever is true, whatever is noble, whatever is right, whatever is pure, whatever is lovely, whatever is admirable—if anything is excellent or praiseworthy—think about such things" (PHILIPPIANS 4:8).

Consider the difference between love and lust.

"Husbands, love your wives, just as Christ loved the church and gave himself up for her" (EPHESIANS 5:25).

Count the cost.

"The trouble they cause recoils on them" (PSALM 7:16).

Communicate godly sorrow.

"Godly sorrow brings repentance that leads to salvation and leaves no regret, but worldly sorrow brings death" (2 CORINTHIANS 7:10).

My Personalized Plan

For the Unfaithful Spouse

I will . . .

1. **Confess my adultery to God and to my spouse.**

   "Confess your sins to each other and pray for each other so that you may be healed" (JAMES 5:16).

2. **Recommit myself to my covenant partner in word and action—**completely.

   "First seek the counsel of the LORD" (1 KINGS 22:5).

   "The wisdom that comes from heaven is first of all pure; then peace-loving, considerate, submissive, full of mercy and good fruit, impartial and sincere" (JAMES 3:17).

3. **Call on the phone (not meet) and cut all ties with the person with whom I have been involved.**

   "Can a man scoop fire into his lap without his clothes being burned? Can a man walk on hot coals without his feet being scorched?" (PROVERBS 6:27–28).

4. **Avoid anything that may jeopardize my commitment to my spouse.**

   "Above all else, guard your heart, for everything you do flows from it. . . . Let your eyes look straight ahead; fix your gaze directly before you. Give careful thought to the paths for your feet and be steadfast in all your ways. Do not turn to the right or the left; keep your foot from evil" (PROVERBS 4:23, 25–27).

5. **Consider the feelings of my mate.**

   "When anyone becomes aware that they are guilty in any of these matters, they must confess in what way they have sinned" (LEVITICUS 5:5).

For the Faithful Spouse

1. **Have a forgiving heart toward my spouse.**

   "If you forgive other people when they sin against you, your heavenly Father will also forgive you. But if you do not forgive others their sins, your Father will not forgive your sins" (MATTHEW 6:14–15).

2. **Don't try to change my mate but leave room for God and His Word.**

   "The word of God is alive and active. Sharper than any double-edged sword, it penetrates even to dividing soul and spirit, joints and marrow; it judges the thoughts and attitudes of the heart. Nothing in all creation is hidden from God's sight. Everything is uncovered and laid bare before the eyes of him to whom we must give account" (HEBREWS 4:12–13).

3. **Don't blame myself for the adultery.**

   "Each of us will give an account of ourselves to God" (ROMANS 14:12).

4. **Don't minimize the seriousness of my spouse's infidelity.**

   "Do not offer any part of yourself to sin as an instrument of wickedness, but rather offer yourselves to God as those who have been brought from death to life; and offer every part of yourself to him as an instrument of righteousness" (ROMANS 6:13).

5. **Trust God with every uncertainty I now face.**

   "You have searched me, LORD, and you know me. You know when I sit and when I rise; you perceive my thoughts from afar. You discern my going out and my lying down; you are familiar with all my ways" (PSALM 139:1–3).

Create in me a pure heart, O God,
and renew a steadfast spirit within me. . . .
Restore to me the joy of your salvation
and grant me a willing spirit, to sustain me.
(PSALM 51:10, 12)

Questions & Answers

Question: "What commonly characterizes those who get involved in adultery?"

Answer: The lying lure of adultery is subtle. It begins slowly by laying a foundation in the heart and mind based on dissatisfaction and selfishness, then quickly deepens in danger. Typically, people who become involved in adulterous relationships . . .

— Find fault in their marriage partner
— Disregard their marriage covenant
— Rationalize their wrong actions as being "right"

Ultimately, they indulge in selfish pleasures to the extent that they develop a heart that is hardened toward the desires of God.

A person may think their own ways are right,
but the LORD weighs the heart.
(PROVERBS 21:2)

Question: "My husband has been unfaithful to me. Is it possible for me to ever trust him again? Is it possible for him to change?"

Answer: It is possible for your husband to change, and it is possible for you to trust him again. But . . .

— First he must develop a godly sorrow over his lack of commitment to you and the marriage covenant.
— Then he needs to identify the key that opened the door to adultery.
— Through marriage counseling, he must admit and understand his weaknesses and then devise a plan to keep from walking through that door again.
— Pray that he will see his sin as God sees it and hate his sin as God hates it. Pray, too, that you will be open to trusting him once he has proven himself to be trustworthy.

Key Passages to Read

For the Unfaithful Spouse
Colossians 3:1–15

For the Faithful Spouse
Romans 12:9–21

It is possible for God to change anyone who is willing to have a changed heart.

"For nothing will be impossible with God."
(LUKE 1:37 ESV)

AGING WELL

Living Long & Finishing Strong

God's Heart on Aging

God will carry you and sustain you each day.

"Even to your old age and gray hairs I am he, I am he who will sustain you. I have made you and I will carry you; I will sustain you and I will rescue you" (ISAIAH 46:4).

God wants you to trust Him, knowing that your time is in His hands.

"I trust in you, LORD; I say, 'You are my God.' My times are in your hands" (PSALM 31:14-15).

God wants you to rest in Him—in His promises, His character, and His salvation.

"Truly my soul finds rest in God; my salvation comes from him. Truly he is my rock and my salvation; he is my fortress, I will never be shaken" (PSALM 62:1-2).

God wants you to live without fear and to be both comforted and strengthened by His presence.

"So do not fear, for I am with you; do not be dismayed, for I am your God. I will strengthen you and help you; I will uphold you with my righteous right hand" (ISAIAH 41:10).

God wants you to reflect on what He's done for you and others in the past.

"I will remember the deeds of the LORD" (PSALM 77:11).

God wants you to become fully mature in Christ.

"He is the one we proclaim, admonishing and teaching everyone with all wisdom, so that we may present everyone fully mature in Christ" (COLOSSIANS 1:28).

God wants you to tell the next generation about Him—about His character and His works.

"We will not hide these truths from our children; we will tell the next generation about the glorious deeds of the LORD, about his power and his mighty wonders" (PSALM 78:4 NLT).

God wants you to mentor and influence others with His truth.

"The things you have heard me say in the presence of many witnesses entrust to reliable people who will also be qualified to teach others" (2 TIMOTHY 2:2).

God wants you to take care of yourself physically and spiritually.

"Physical training is of some value, but godliness has value for all things, holding promise for both the present life and the life to come" (1 Timothy 4:8).

God wants you to live in the present and not worry about the future.

"Do not worry about tomorrow, for tomorrow will worry about itself. Each day has enough trouble of its own" (Matthew 6:34).

God wants you to finish the race, looking forward to your reward from Him.

"I have fought the good fight, I have finished the race, I have kept the faith. Now there is in store for me the crown of righteousness, which the Lord, the righteous Judge, will award to me on that day—and not only to me, but also to all who have longed for his appearing" (2 Timothy 4:7–8).

Key Verse to Memorize

"Even to your old age and gray hairs
I am he, I am he who will sustain you.
I have made you and I will carry you;
I will sustain you and I will rescue you."
(Isaiah 46:4)

God wants you to live with an eternal perspective.

"Therefore we do not lose heart. Though outwardly we are wasting away, yet inwardly we are being renewed day by day. For our light and momentary troubles are achieving for us an eternal glory that far outweighs them all. So we fix our eyes not on what is seen, but on what is unseen, since what is seen is temporary, but what is unseen is eternal" (2 Corinthians 4:16–18).

"Is not wisdom found among the aged?
Does not long life bring understanding?"
(Job 12:12)

Negative Effects of Aging

Illness: As our bodies age, we become more vulnerable to physical illness and injuries. Consequently, we need to prioritize keeping both our physical and spiritual lives healthy.

"The human spirit can endure in sickness, but a crushed spirit who can bear?" (Proverbs 18:14).

Isolation: As family and friends begin to pass away and mobility restricts movement, we can become isolated. The loss of loved ones or severe health issues can cause more restrictive isolation.

"The Lord your God is living among you. He is a mighty savior. He will take delight in you with gladness. With his love, he will calm all your fears. He will rejoice over you with joyful songs" (Zephaniah 3:17 nlt).

Denial: If you deny the truth about changes in your life, you cannot adapt to each change and embrace the growth that comes through maturity.

"Be honest in your evaluation of yourselves" (ROMANS 12:3 NLT).

Fear: If you hide "the real you" from others, it often becomes harder to develop safe and mature relationships based on honesty and trust. When you place your trust in God, He will drive away the fear and empower you to be "real" in all situations.

"There is no fear in love. But perfect love drives out fear, because fear has to do with punishment. The one who fears is not made perfect in love" (1 JOHN 4:18).

Bitterness: Always wanting and expecting things to go *your way* leads to resentment against God and others when your expectations are not met. This leads to bitterness that hardens your heart, making it difficult to accept the unpredictably of life.

"See to it that no one falls short of the grace of God and that no bitter root grows up to cause trouble and defile many" (HEBREWS 12:15).

Pride: Placing your trust solely in your own efforts and believing that you can be successful and content living apart from God leads to an exaggerated sense of self-importance.

"In his pride the wicked man does not seek him; in all his thoughts there is no room for God" (PSALM 10:4).

Rebellion: For the Christian, disobeying God by seeking fulfillment through greed, power, or immoral choices can derail your testimony and your influence on others.

"'Only acknowledge your guilt—you have rebelled against the LORD your God, you have scattered your favors to foreign gods under every spreading tree, and have not obeyed me,' declares the LORD" (JEREMIAH 3:13).

Losses Leading to Discontentment

Loss of **control**	Loss of **health**
Loss of **hope**	Loss of **income**
Loss of **independence**	Loss of **home**
Loss of **loved ones**	Loss of **dreams**
Loss of **reputation**	Loss of **purpose**

Transitions[11]

T—Thoughts of one's own mortality

R—Reassessment of lifelong goals and values

A—Achievement of goals, yet failing to find fulfillment

N—Normal changes biologically and physiologically

S—Sexual drive diminishing in the male, increasing in the female

I—Insufficient financial resources

T—Traumatic illness or death of parents, family, or close friends

I—Identity misplaced in a person, a job, or social status

O—Offspring at difficult age and/or leaving home

N—Narrowing of job opportunities

S—Social emphasis on youth

There is a time for everything,
and a season for every activity under the heavens.
(ECCLESIASTES 3:1)

How to Overcome Loneliness

Loneliness can be overcome by . . .

- — Filling an empty table with dinner guests
- — Making holidays festive by starting new traditions
- — Calling others on the phone
- — Inviting friends to attend a movie or event
- — Joining a book club
- — Sending cards, letters, or emails to family members and acquaintances
- — Letting go of grudges and extending forgiveness
- — Taking time to visit those in need of company

"Then the righteous will answer him, 'Lord, when did we see you hungry and feed you, or thirsty and give you something to drink? When did we see you a stranger and invite you in, or needing clothes and clothe you? When did we see you sick or in prison and go to visit you?' The King will reply, 'Truly I tell you, whatever you did for one of the least of these brothers and sisters of mine, you did for me'" (MATTHEW 25:37–40).

My Personalized Plan

A—Accentuate the positive.

— Realize your feelings are usually determined by your thinking.

— Guard the thoughts that come into your mind.

— Look for the good in people and circumstances, asking God to reveal His good purposes for you.

"Whatever is true, whatever is noble, whatever is right, whatever is pure, whatever is lovely, whatever is admirable—if anything is excellent or praiseworthy—think about such things" (PHILIPPIANS 4:8).

G—Get on the highway to health.

— Sleep at least seven to eight consecutive hours every day.

— Get regular medical checkups.

— Engage in exercises that stimulate your brain.

"Dear friend, I pray that you may enjoy good health and that all may go well with you, even as your soul is getting along well" (3 JOHN V. 2).

I—Initiate involvement.

— Volunteer your time and assistance with an organization or cause you believe in.

— Encourage others by talking with them.

— Form a neighborhood Bible study group.

Key Passage to Read

2 Corinthians 4:17-5:10

"Whoever sows generously will also reap generously" (2 CORINTHIANS 9:6).

N—Notice the roses.

— Take time to identify and renew previous interests.

— Learn to relax and play.

— Gain new appreciation for the beauty in nature.

"Jesus said, 'Let's go off by ourselves to a quiet place and rest awhile'" (MARK 6:31 NLT).

G—Grow in grace.

— Reflect on how God has orchestrated your life.

— Appreciate how God has shown you His love throughout your life.

— Meditate on the goodness and greatness of God.

"Grow in the grace and knowledge of our Lord and Savior Jesus Christ. To him be glory both now and forever!" (2 PETER 3:18).

Search me, God, and know my heart.
(PSALM 139:23)

Questions & Answers

Question: "Is affection important to an elderly person?"

Answer: Our need to feel loved, valued, and accepted by others does not diminish with age. Hugs, kisses, and loving touches communicate affection, concern, and encouragement in a way that words alone cannot. That said, we must respect the personal comfort level of all people, regardless of their age. If someone you care about is not comfortable with physical affection, then communicate your love in a nonphysical manner—with smiles, a gentle tone of voice, and caring words.

Greet one another with a kiss of love.
(1 PETER 5:14)

Question: "How can I handle the time demands of an elderly loved one?"

Answer: Develop a reasonable schedule, providing quality and quantity of time. Send notes, cards, or make phone calls to the loved one. Include in your schedule short, frequent pop-in visits along with regular appointments. If your loved one needs more supervision and care than you can reasonably provide yourself, ask other family members to help or arrange for a licensed caregiver. If you are providing care on a regular, long-term basis, remember to take care of yourself as well. Getting proper rest and emotional support from others will help you approach your caregiving tasks with more energy, patience, and enthusiasm.

There is a proper time and procedure for every matter.
(ECCLESIASTES 8:6)

ALCOHOL & DRUG ABUSE

Breaking Free & Staying Free

What Is God's Heart on Substance Abuse?

God's heart is that we surrender our bodies to Christ, not to an addiction.

"I urge you, brothers and sisters, in view of God's mercy, to offer your bodies as a living sacrifice, holy and pleasing to God—this is your true and proper worship" (ROMANS 12:1).

God's heart is that we allow Him to transform us through the renewing of our minds.

"Do not conform to the pattern of this world, but be transformed by the renewing of your mind. Then you will be able to test and approve what God's will is—his good, pleasing and perfect will" (ROMANS 12:2).

God's heart is that we not allow anything to replace Him in our lives and rule over us as gods.

"You shall have no other gods before me" (EXODUS 20:3).

God's heart is that we cultivate an intimate, personal relationship with Him as our provider.

"His divine power has given us everything we need for a godly life" (2 PETER 1:3).

"God will meet all your needs according to the riches of his glory in Christ Jesus" (PHILIPPIANS 4:19).

God's heart is that we develop God-empowered control in every area of our lives.

"The grace of God has appeared that offers salvation to all people. It teaches us to say 'No' to ungodliness and worldly passions, and to live self-controlled, upright and godly lives in this present age" (TITUS 2:11–12).

God's heart is that we glorify Him in all that we think, say, and do.

"Whether you eat or drink or whatever you do, do it all for the glory of God" (1 CORINTHIANS 10:31).

God's heart is that we not lose hope when we relapse, but that we confess our sin of misplaced dependence, thank Him for His forgiveness, and seek His help to continue the fight.

"If we confess our sins, he is faithful and just and will forgive us our sins and purify us from all unrighteousness" (1 JOHN 1:9).

God's heart is that we choose our friends and associates wisely because of the influence they have on us.

"Blessed is the one who does not walk in step with the wicked or stand in the way that sinners take or sit in the company of mockers, but whose delight is in the law of the LORD, and who meditates on his law day and night" (PSALM 1:1–2).

God's heart is that we not dwell on our faults and failures, but rather that we focus on the work God is doing in us now and the wonderful plans He has for us in the future.

"'I know the plans I have for you,' declares the LORD, 'plans to prosper you and not to harm you, plans to give you hope and a future'" (JEREMIAH 29:11).

"See, I am doing a new thing! Now it springs up; do you not perceive it? I am making a way in the wilderness and streams in the wasteland" (ISAIAH 43:19).

God's heart is that we overcome anything that keeps us in bondage, and that we live in the victory accomplished when Jesus overcame the world for us.

"Everyone born of God overcomes the world. This is the victory that has overcome the world, even our faith. Who is it that overcomes the world? Only the one who believes that Jesus is the Son of God" (1 JOHN 5:4–5).

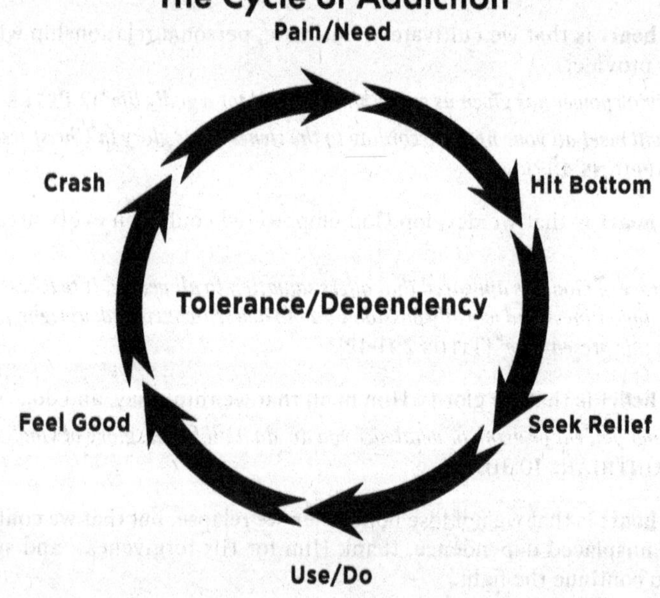

Feeling Pain/Experiencing a Need: A significant source of pain or an unmet need (either of which might be physical, emotional, psychological, relational, and/or spiritual) leads to a person who is hurting.

"Even in laughter the heart may ache, and rejoicing may end in grief" (PROVERBS 14:13).

Hitting Bottom: The pain or need sends a person spiraling into a state of hopelessness and despair.

"How long must I wrestle with my thoughts and day after day have sorrow in my heart?" (PSALM 13:2).

Seeking Relief: At the bottom of this cycle, a person naturally seeks relief by using or doing something to alleviate the pain.

"Listen to my cry, for I am in desperate need; rescue me from those who pursue me, for they are too strong for me" (PSALM 142:6).

Using/Doing: In an attempt to eliminate the pain or need, a person uses a substance or acts out a behavior.

"For you have spent enough time in the past doing what pagans choose to do—living in debauchery, lust, drunkenness, orgies, carousing and detestable idolatry" (1 PETER 4:3).

Feeling Good: The initial result is experiencing some relief from the pain/need at any cost.

"At one time we too were foolish, disobedient, deceived and enslaved by all kinds of passions and pleasures. We lived in malice and envy, being hated and hating one another" (TITUS 3:3).

Crashing: Relief is short-lived, and the effects of feeling good wear off, leaving the user with crushing disappointment. This leads back to the pain/need, exacerbated by added guilt, shame, and despair.

"When you were slaves to sin, you were free from the control of righteousness. What benefit did you reap at that time from the things you are now ashamed of? Those things result in death!" (ROMANS 6:20–21).

The Serenity Prayer

God, grant me the serenity to accept
the things I cannot change,
courage to change the things I can,
and wisdom to know the difference.
Living one day at a time,
enjoying one moment at a time,
accepting hardships as the
pathway to peace,
taking, as Jesus did, this sinful world
as it is, not as I would have it.
Trusting that God will make
all things right
if I surrender to his will,
so that I may be reasonably happy
in this life
and supremely happy with him
forever in the next.
Amen.
—*Reinhold Niebuhr* (1892–1971)

Self-Inflicted Damage from Addiction[12]

Lack of self-control

Social problems

Financial difficulties

Risky behavior

Health risks

Toxic withdrawal

You were taught, with regard to your former way of life,
to put off your old self, which is being corrupted
by its deceitful desires;
to be made new in the attitude of your minds;
and to put on the new self, created to be like God
in true righteousness and holiness.
(EPHESIANS 4:22–24)

Addiction's Impact on Others[13]

Relationship wreckage

Codependency

Wounded emotions

Betrayed trust

Chaotic conflicts

Violence and injury

People are slaves to whatever has mastered them.
(2 PETER 2:19)

12 Steps to Freedom

1. **Admit you are powerless over your dependency.**
   "Indeed, we felt we had received the sentence of death. But this happened that we might not rely on ourselves but on God, who raises the dead" (2 CORINTHIANS 1:9).

2. **Realize that the God who made you and saved you has the power to restore you.**

   "Though you have made me see troubles, many and bitter, you will restore my life again; from the depths of the earth you will again bring me up. You will increase my honor and comfort me once more" (PSALM 71:20–21).

3. **Yield your will to the will of God.**

   "Trust in the LORD with all your heart and lean not on your own understanding; in all your ways submit to him, and he will make your paths straight" (PROVERBS 3:5–6).

4. **Face reality—face your true self.**

   "Search me, God, and know my heart; test me and know my anxious thoughts. See if there is any offensive way in me, and lead me in the way everlasting" (PSALM 139:23–24).

5. **Admit your struggle with sin, both to God and to someone else.**

   "Confess your sins to each other and pray for each other so that you may be healed. The earnest prayer of a righteous person has great power and produces wonderful results" (JAMES 5:16 NLT).

Key Verse to Memorize

My eyes are ever on the LORD,
for only he will release my feet from the snare.
(PSALM 25:15)

6. **Accept God's help to change past patterns.**

   "Humble yourselves, therefore, under God's mighty hand, that he may lift you up in due time. Cast all your anxiety on him because he cares for you" (1 PETER 5:6–7).

7. **Confess your defects and daily failings.**

   "Create in me a pure heart, O God, and renew a steadfast spirit within me. Do not cast me from your presence or take your Holy Spirit from me. Restore to me the joy of your salvation and grant me a willing spirit, to sustain me" (PSALM 51:10–12).

8. **Ask forgiveness of those you have offended.**

   "If you are offering your gift at the altar and there remember that your brother or sister has something against you, leave your gift there in front of the altar. First go and be reconciled to them; then come and offer your gift" (MATTHEW 5:23–24).

9. **Make restitution where you have wronged others.**

   "If they give back what they took in pledge for a loan, return what they have stolen, follow the decrees that give life, and do no evil—that person will surely live; they will not die. None of the sins that person has committed will be remembered against them. They have done what is just and right; they will surely live" (EZEKIEL 33:15–16).

10. **Keep a clean slate when you realize you have been wrong.**

    "The grace of God has appeared that offers salvation to all people. It teaches us to say 'No' to ungodliness and worldly passions, and to live self-controlled, upright and godly lives" (TITUS 2:11–12).

11. **Pray to know God's path for your life.**

    "Show me your ways, LORD, teach me your paths. Guide me in your truth and teach me, for you are God my Savior, and my hope is in you all day long" (PSALM 25:4–5).

12. **Reach out to others with your hands and your heart.**

    "Carry each other's burdens, and in this way you will fulfill the law of Christ" (GALATIANS 6:2).

My Personalized Plan

I will . . .

Admit that I need help to stop my addiction, letting go of pride and stubbornness.

"Whoever conceals their sins does not prosper, but the one who confesses and renounces them finds mercy" (PROVERBS 28:13).

Abandon the shame of my addiction and face it head-on with God's help, thereby loosening its grip on me.

"Let us then approach God's throne of grace with confidence, so that we may receive mercy and find grace to help us in our time of need" (HEBREWS 4:16).

Key Passage to Read

Matthew 6:9-13

Adjust my life to reflect the changes I am making by replacing old thoughts and habits with new, healthy ones.

"Throw off your old sinful nature and your former way of life, which is corrupted by lust and deception. Instead, let the Spirit renew your thoughts and attitudes. Put on your new nature, created to be like God—truly righteous and holy" (EPHESIANS 4:22–24 NLT).

Acquire new habits, friends, and ways of coping.

"If anyone is in Christ, he is a new creation. The old has passed away; behold, the new has come" (2 Corinthians 5:17 ESV).

Accept that my addiction has caused me to hurt others and myself. I will make amends, forgiving when it is needed and accepting forgiveness when it is given.

"Who can discern their own errors? Forgive my hidden faults. Keep your servant also from willful sins; may they not rule over me" (Psalm 19:12–13).

Questions & Answers

Question: "If I am a habitual, compulsive drinker and drug user, can I really change and permanently stop?"

Answer: Yes. Although habits, compulsions, and addictions are highly resistant, they are not impossible to change.

Repeating actions actually alter the brain, making it more difficult to change. However, new patterns of behavior can be learned, which, in turn, can also alter the brain. Replace bad habits and addictions with good, healthy habits and activities with supportive people.

If you are a Christian, you have *His Word* to help change your way of thinking, *His church*—often with specialized community groups to support your life change—and *His Spirit* to empower you from within to follow through to stop abusing alcohol and drugs.

It is God who works in you to will
and to act in order to fulfill his good purpose.
(Philippians 2:13)

Question: "Is it possible to use drugs and alcohol without becoming addicted?"

Answer: Yes, just as every drug is different, everyone's physical reaction is different.

Because of the destructive risk of addiction, using unnecessary drugs is dangerous. We need to remember that our bodies are not our own—they belong to God.

Do you not know that your bodies
are temples of the Holy Spirit,
who is in you, whom you have received from God?
You are not your own; you were bought at a price.
Therefore honor God with your bodies.
(1 Corinthians 6:19–20)

ALZHEIMER'S & DEMENTIA

Doing What's Best for Your Brain

God's Heart on Memory

Six things God wants us to remember . . .

To trust in His forgiveness

"I, even I, am he who blots out your transgressions, for my own sake, and remembers your sins no more" (ISAIAH 43:25).

To remember His promises

"He remembers his covenant forever, the promise he made, for a thousand generations" (PSALM 105:8).

To recall God's work in our lives

"Do not forget the things your eyes have seen or let them fade from your heart as long as you live" (DEUTERONOMY 4:9).

To remember His miracles

"Remember the wonders he has done, his miracles, and the judgments he pronounced" (1 CHRONICLES 16:12).

To obey His commands

"Remember all the commands of the LORD, that you may obey them . . . I am the LORD your God" (NUMBERS 15:39, 41).

To hold fast to what we have received

"Remember . . . what you have received and heard; hold it fast" (REVELATION 3:3).

Six things God wants us not to do . . .

Fear or be afraid

"Do not be afraid; you will not be put to shame. Do not fear disgrace; you will not be humiliated" (ISAIAH 54:4).

Dwell on the past

"Forget the former things; do not dwell on the past" (ISAIAH 43:18).

Fail to recall His benefits

"Praise the LORD, my soul, and forget not all his benefits" (PSALM 103:2).

Forget His teaching

"My son, do not forget my teaching, but keep my commands in your heart" (Proverbs 3:1).

Neglect what pleases Him

"And do not forget to do good and to share with others, for with such sacrifices God is pleased" (Hebrews 13:16).

Be discouraged

"The Lord himself goes before you and will be with you; he will never leave you nor forsake you. Do not be afraid; do not be discouraged" (Deuteronomy 31:8).

Common Characteristics of Early-Stage Dementia

Dementia symptoms in its early stages can include:[14]

- Forgetting recently learned information
- Increasing difficulty with planning or organizing
- Asking the same questions over and over
- Losing track of dates, seasons, and time
- Getting lost
- Not remembering names
- Having trouble coming up with the right word
- Misplacing or losing items
- Exercising poor judgment when dealing with money
- Experiencing mood and personality changes

Common Characteristics as Dementia Progresses

Dementia symptoms as the disease progresses may include:[15]

- Forgetting events or personal history
- Being unable to recall personal information
- Struggling with basic tasks
- Using the wrong word, mispronouncing words, speaking in confusing sentences
- Withdrawing from social situations
- Showing an increasing tendency to wander and become lost
- Experiencing trouble controlling bodily functions
- Showing poor judgment

— Being argumentative
— Requiring around-the-clock assistance

Signs and Symptoms of Alzheimer's Disease[16]

Cognitive symptoms:

— Difficulty with memory
— Difficulty with language
— Difficulty with recognition of objects
— Difficulty with time/place/event orientation

Noncognitive symptoms:

— Apathy
— Adversarial-like actions
— Anxiety
— Aggression

Key Verses to Memorize

The Father of compassion and
the God of all comfort . . .
comforts us in all our troubles,
so that we can comfort
those in any trouble with the comfort
we ourselves receive from God.
(2 CORINTHIANS 1:3–4)

Physical symptoms:

— Tremors/rigidity/slowness of movement
— Restlessness or agitation
— Impaired motor ability
— Compromised immunity

Keep Your Brain Healthy for Life

Protect your brain . . . practically.

— Take up sports that are less aggressive, such as table tennis or golf.
— Wear a seat belt when in a vehicle, and a helmet if riding a bicycle or motorcycle.
— Get at least seven hours of quality sleep every night. Go to bed and wake up at the same time every day, even on weekends.[17]

"[The Lord] *grants sleep to those he loves*" (PSALM 127:2).

Nourish your brain . . . nutritionally.

— Stay hydrated with water and avoid drinks with added sugar.[18]
— Maintain a healthy weight. Limit portion size to control calorie intake, and be as physically active as you can be.[19]

- — Eat more good fats and avoid eating bad fats. Balance protein, good fats, and carbohydrates. Get lots of dietary antioxidants.[20]

"Then God said, 'I give you every seed-bearing plant on the face of the whole earth and every tree that has fruit with seed in it. They will be yours for food'" (GENESIS 1:29).

Strengthen your brain . . . mentally.

- — Learn something new or do things you haven't done before.
- — Improve your mental fitness (read newspapers/magazines/books, acquire a new hobby, play memory games).
- — Break the routine of your life (take a cooking class, try new recipes, make a new friend).

"An intelligent heart acquires knowledge, and the ear of the wise seeks knowledge" (PROVERBS 18:15 ESV).

Cultivate your brain . . . spiritually.

- — Practice gratitude.
- — Practice wonder. Pay attention to what is present all around you and be astonished by it.
- — Practice prayer.[21]
- — Practice releasing.
- — Practice connecting.

"For physical training is of some value, but godliness has value for all things, holding promise for both the present life and the life to come" (1 TIMOTHY 4:8).

How to Make a Connection with Someone Who Has Dementia

1. **Reminisce over childhood toys.** Ask questions about how they played with them, or in the case of construction toys, build something together.

2. **Look through photo albums.** Photo albums with pictures from their childhood or young adulthood are best.

3. **Read out loud to them.** Reading poetry aloud works especially well.

4. **Create a memory bag.** Fill a cloth bag with items that remind your loved one of childhood memories.

5. **Watch an old movie or TV show.**

6. **Look through old cookbooks.**

7. **Go on a nature walk.** Ask your loved ones what their favorite outdoor activities were.

These days should be remembered and observed
in every generation by every family.
(Esther 9:28)

My Personalized Plan

In the process of living in the here and now, **I will . . .**

Learn to adjust.

— Modify my activities and adapt them to fit my changing abilities.

— Count on God's strength to replace my weakness.

"He gives strength to the weary and increases the power of the weak" (Isaiah 40:29).

Learn to accept help.

— Rely on my doctors' advice for treatment, regular exercise or activity, and nutrition.

— Work up a plan with my loved ones and professionals that best meets my needs.

Key Passage to Read

Psalm 23

"Plans fail for lack of counsel, but with many advisers they succeed" (Proverbs 15:22).

Learn to grieve.

— Acknowledge that dementia brings with it many deep losses I need to grieve.

— Allow myself to cry as often as necessary, knowing tears offer me a cleansing emotional outlet and that God is acutely aware of all my tears.

"You keep track of all my sorrows. You have collected all my tears in your bottle. You have recorded each one in your book" (Psalm 56:8 NLT).

Learn to let go.

— Let go of any expectations that life will go back to the way it once was.

— Trust God with my present and my future, walk in obedience to Him, and follow His leading.

"Trust in the Lord with all your heart and lean not on your own understanding; in all your ways submit to him, and he will make your paths straight" (Proverbs 3:5–6).

Learn to laugh.

— Make the decision to not take myself (or my condition) too seriously, acknowledging God's sovereignty and the brevity of my earthly life.

— Enjoy the humorous things that happen in life and look for the joy each day holds.

"A cheerful heart is good medicine, but a crushed spirit dries up the bones" (PROVERBS 17:22).

Learn to give thanks.

— Show gratitude to family and friends who help and support me.

— Praise God daily for who He is and for His love and care for me.

"Give thanks in all circumstances; for this is God's will for you in Christ Jesus" (1 THESSALONIANS 5:18).

Questions & Answers

Question: "Is dementia an automatic part of aging?"

Answer: No. Although some memory loss is a normal part of aging, conditions and diseases of the brain like Alzheimer's and other forms of dementia are not. Otherwise, everyone who lives past a certain age would develop it. Thankfully, this is not true. Many people retain their mental abilities well into their eighties and nineties. Just because someone suffers from an occasional "senior moment" or a bout of forgetfulness from time to time doesn't automatically mean that person has or will get Alzheimer's or dementia.

None of us knows the number of days we have to live. But what we do know from God's Word is that we are to live sensibly and purposefully for as long as He gives us.

Teach us to number our days, that we may gain a heart of wisdom.
(PSALM 90:12)

Question: "Is there anything I can do to prevent Alzheimer's and other dementias?"

Answer: Yes and no. While many factors can influence your risk of dementia that are out of your control, there are steps you can take to lower your risk.

More recent practical data says you can potentially decrease your risk of developing Alzheimer's and other dementias by managing contributing factors, such as controlling high blood pressure, maintaining a healthy weight, eating a healthy diet, keeping physically active, staying mentally active, maintaining good relationships with family and friends, getting a good night's sleep, avoiding or limiting alcohol, and not smoking.[22]

Preserve sound judgment and discretion.
(PROVERBS 3:21)

ANGER

Facing the Fire Within

God's Heart on Anger

Anger is a God-given emotion. God Himself experiences anger.

"The LORD, the LORD, the compassionate and gracious God, slow to anger, abounding in love and faithfulness, maintaining love to thousands, and forgiving wickedness, rebellion and sin" (EXODUS 34:6-7).

Anger itself is not a sin, but what you do with it can lead to sin.

"Be angry and do not sin" (EPHESIANS 4:26 ESV).

Anger can propel you to action—to correct an injustice.

"He [Jesus] *looked around at them angrily and was deeply saddened by their hard hearts. Then he said to the man, 'Hold out your hand.' So the man held out his hand, and it was restored!"* (MARK 3:5 NLT).

Anger can be learned behavior, so be careful who you choose as friends.

"Do not make friends with a hot-tempered person, do not associate with one easily angered, or you may learn their ways and get yourself ensnared" (PROVERBS 22:24-25).

Anger can lead to abusive language.

"You must also rid yourselves of all such things as these: anger, rage, malice, slander, and filthy language from your lips" (COLOSSIANS 3:8).

Anger can lead to fighting.

"An angry person starts fights; a hot-tempered person commits all kinds of sin" (PROVERBS 29:22 NLT).

God wants you to be slow to anger.

"Everyone should be quick to listen, slow to speak and slow to become angry, because human anger does not produce the righteousness that God desires" (JAMES 1:19-20).

God wants you to refrain from anger.

"Refrain from anger and turn from wrath; do not fret—it leads only to evil" (PSALM 37:8).

God wants you to deal with your anger quickly.

"Do not let the sun go down while you are still angry" (EPHESIANS 4:26).

God wants you to be free from anger.

"Get rid of all bitterness, rage and anger, brawling and slander, along with every form of malice" (EPHESIANS 4:31).

God wants you to talk to Him about your anger.

"In my distress I prayed to the LORD, and the LORD answered me and set me free" (PSALM 118:5 NLT).

God wants you to be saved through faith in Christ so you do not experience His anger.

"God did not appoint us to suffer wrath but to receive salvation through our Lord Jesus Christ" (1 THESSALONIANS 5:9).

"To God belong wisdom and power;
counsel and understanding are his."
(JOB 12:13)

Anger Cues Checklist

- ☐ Do you have a decreased appetite?
- ☐ Do you have tense muscles?
- ☐ Do you feel unusually hot or cold?
- ☐ Do you have increased perspiration or sweaty palms?
- ☐ Do you feel flushed?
- ☐ Do you clench your teeth?
- ☐ Do you clench your fists?
- ☐ Do you experience dry mouth?
- ☐ Do you become silent, shutting down verbally?
- ☐ Do you use loud, rapid, or high-pitched speech?
- ☐ Do you breathe faster and harder than normal?
- ☐ Do you experience an upset, churning stomach?
- ☐ Do you walk hard and fast or pace back and forth?
- ☐ Do you twitch or exhibit anxious behavior (tapping a pencil, shaking a foot)?
- ☐ Do you use harsh, coarse, or inappropriate language (gossip, sarcasm, profanity)?
- ☐ Do you feel your heart racing or pounding?

"I will call to you whenever I'm in trouble,
and you will answer me."
(PSALM 86:7 NLT)

The Four Sources of Anger

1. **Hurt**: Your heart is wounded.[23]

   Everyone has a God-given inner need for *unconditional love.*[24] When you experience rejection or emotional pain of any kind, anger can become a protective wall keeping people, pain, and *hurt* away.

   Biblical Example: The Sons of Jacob

   "Israel [Jacob] *loved Joseph more than any of his other sons, because he had been born to him in his old age; and he made an ornate robe for him. When his brothers saw that their father loved him more than any of them, they hated him and could not speak a kind word to him"* (GENESIS 37:3–4).

2. **Injustice**: Your right is violated.[25]

   Everyone has a sense of right and wrong, fair and unfair, just and *unjust.* When you perceive that an *injustice* has occurred against you or others (especially those you love), you may feel angry. If you hold on to the offense, the unresolved anger can begin to take root in your heart.

   Biblical Example: King Saul

   "'Why should he be put to death? What has he done?' Jonathan asked his father. But Saul hurled his spear at him to kill him [Jonathan]. *Then Jonathan knew that his father intended to kill David. Jonathan got up from the table in fierce anger"* (1 SAMUEL 20:32–34).

3. **Fear**: Your future is threatened.[26]

   Everyone is created with a God-given inner need for *security.*[27] When you begin to worry, feel threatened, or get angry because of a change in circumstances, you may be responding to *fear.* A fearful heart reveals a lack of trust in God's perfect plan for your life.

   Biblical Example: King Saul

   "Saul was very angry . . . 'They have credited David with tens of thousands,' he thought, 'but me with only thousands.' . . . Saul was afraid of David, because the LORD was with David but had departed from Saul" (1 SAMUEL 18:8, 12).

4. **Frustration**: Your effort is not accepted.[28]

   Everyone has an inner need for *significance.*[29] When your efforts are thwarted or do not meet your own personal expectations, your sense of significance can be threatened. *Frustration* over unmet expectations of yourself or of others is a major source of anger.

   Biblical Example: Cain

"In the course of time Cain brought some of the fruits of the soil as an offering to the LORD. And Abel also brought an offering—fat portions from some of the firstborn of his flock. The LORD looked with favor on Abel and his offering, but on Cain and his offering he did not look with favor. So Cain was very angry, and his face was downcast. . . . Now Cain said to his brother Abel, 'Let's go out to the field.' While they were in the field, Cain attacked his brother Abel and killed him" (GENESIS 4:3–5, 8).

The Quick Answer to Anger

The effort to resolve anger can be reduced to two basic steps. These two steps involve one question and one action response.

Step 1. Ask: Can I change this situation?

Step 2. Action: If you can, change it. If you can't, release it.

Let's go back to the first step: Think of a situation that angers you. Can you change it? Answer *yes* or *no*—that's it.

Now consider the second step: If you answered *yes*, you are angry about something you can change—so change it.

If the door squeaks, oil it.

If the faucet leaks, fix it.

If you answered *no*, you are angry about something you cannot change—so release it. How do you release your anger? First, list what angers you—every person, every situation. Then, humbly go to God, reject any thought of revenge, and surrender the situation and yourself to the Lord. Although you may feel powerless, in reality you have the power to release your pain and anger to Him.

Prayer to Release Your Anger

"Lord Jesus, thank you for loving me.
Thank you for caring about me.
Since you know everything,
you know the strong sense of
(hurt, injustice, fear, and/or frustration)
I have felt about (name or situation).
Thank you for understanding my anger.
Right now, I release all of my anger to you.
I trust you with my future.
In Jesus' name I pray. Amen."

Alleviate Your Anger

Acknowledge your anger.

Realize, *"Whoever conceals their sins does not prosper, but the one who confesses and renounces them finds mercy"* (Proverbs 28:13).

Ascertain your style.

As you seek to identify the way you express your anger, pray, *"Test me, LORD, and try me, examine my heart and my mind"* (PSALM 26:2).

Assess the source.

Commit to total honesty before God: *"I know, my God, that you test the heart and are pleased with integrity"* (1 CHRONICLES 29:17).

Key Verses to Memorize

Everyone should be quick to listen, slow to speak and slow to become angry, because human anger does not produce the righteousness that God desires.
(JAMES 1:19–20)

Appraise your thinking.

Remember, *"The wicked put up a bold front, but the upright give thought to their ways"* (PROVERBS 21:29).

Admit your needs.[30]

Rest assured, *"My God will meet all your needs according to the riches of his glory in Christ Jesus"* (PHILIPPIANS 4:19).

Abandon your demands.

Constantly remind yourself that *"God is able to bless you abundantly, so that in all things at all times, having all that you need, you will abound in every good work"* (2 CORINTHIANS 9:8).

Address your anger.

"Through patience a ruler can be persuaded, and a gentle tongue can break a bone" (PROVERBS 25:15).

Alter your attitudes.

"Then make my joy complete by being like-minded, having the same love, being one in spirit and of one mind. Do nothing out of selfish ambition or vain conceit. Rather, in humility value others above yourselves, not looking to your own interests but each of you to the interests of the others. In your relationships with one another, have the same mindset as Christ Jesus: Who, being in very nature God, did not consider equality with God something to be used to his own advantage; rather, he made himself nothing by taking the very nature of a servant, being made in human likeness. And being found in appearance as a man, he humbled himself by becoming obedient to death—even death on a cross!" (PHILIPPIANS 2:2–8).

As charcoal to embers and as wood to fire,
so is a quarrelsome person for kindling strife.
(PROVERBS 26:21)

Communicate Your Anger

Choose to be proactive.

Choose a time and place to talk.

Choose to communicate your desires for open and honest communication and resolution.

My Personalized Plan

As I seek to control my anger, **I will:**

Believe that God can help me.
"I will instruct you and teach you in the way you should go; I will counsel you with my loving eye on you" (PSALM 32:8).

Respond to upsetting situations appropriately.
"Everyone should be quick to listen, slow to speak and slow to become angry" (JAMES 1:19).

Watch my words carefully.
"Set a guard over my mouth, LORD*; keep watch over the door of my lips"* (PSALM 141:3).

Be accountable to God and others.
"Two people are better off than one, for they can help each other succeed" (ECCLESIASTES 4:9 NLT).

Give thanks in every situation.
"Give thanks in all circumstances; for this is God's will for you in Christ Jesus" (1 THESSALONIANS 5:18).

Forgive and seek forgiveness.
"Bear with each other and forgive one another if any of you has a grievance against someone. Forgive as the Lord forgave you" (COLOSSIANS 3:13).

Key Passage to Read

Ephesians 4:26–27, 29–32

Questions & Answers

Question: "Is it a sin for me to be angry?"

Answer: No. Anger is a God-given emotion. In fact, Jesus felt and expressed anger, yet He did not sin (Mark 3:5; Hebrews 4:15). The way you handle or *express* your anger determines whether it leads to sin.

In your anger do not sin.
(Ephesians 4:26)

Question: "How can a God of love be a God of wrath at the same time?"

Answer: Consider the person you love the most. If they make harmful choices, it is natural to feel concerned. If they refuse to change and continue to make harmful choices, it is natural to feel anger. In the same way, the Bible is clear that God is loving (1 John 4:8). However, when people make harmful and sinful choices and refuse to change their ways, God's anger is ignited. He knows what is best and cares about our well-being. His anger is not opposed to His love—it is an expression of His love.

His anger lasts only a moment, but his favor lasts a lifetime.
(Psalm 30:5)

Question: "What should I do when I feel my anger getting out of control?"

Answer: When you feel irrational and unbridled behavior take the place of reason and self-control, put on the brakes and take a time-out. Unless you do something to intervene in the process, the direction of the conversation is not likely to change but will probably escalate.

Show proper respect to everyone.
(1 Peter 2:17)

ANOREXIA & BULIMIA

Control That Is Out of Control

God's Heart on Anorexia & Bulimia

God created you uniquely and wonderfully.

"You created my inmost being; you knit me together in my mother's womb. I praise you because I am fearfully and wonderfully made; your works are wonderful, I know that full well" (PSALM 139:13–14).

God sees you as precious and beloved.

"You are precious to me. You are honored, and I love you" (ISAIAH 43:4 NLT).

God wants you to find your identity in Christ—as His beloved child.

"See what great love the Father has lavished on us, that we should be called children of God! And that is what we are!" (1 JOHN 3:1).

God accepts you in Christ.

"Christ has accepted you so that God will be given glory" (ROMANS 15:7 NLT).

God gives us food as an expression of His love for us.

"He gives food to every creature. His love endures forever" (PSALM 136:25).

God provides food for our nourishment and enjoyment.

"God . . . richly provides us with everything for our enjoyment" (1 TIMOTHY 6:17).

God does not want you to be controlled by or addicted to anything—including food or your appearance.

"People are slaves to whatever has mastered them" (2 PETER 2:19).

God wants you to replace negative thoughts about yourself with the truth of His Word.

"We take captive every thought to make it obedient to Christ" (2 CORINTHIANS 10:5).

God instructs you to take care of your body.

"Do you not know that your bodies are temples of the Holy Spirit, who is in you, whom you have received from God? You are not your own; you were bought at a price. Therefore honor God with your bodies" (1 CORINTHIANS 6:19–20).

God heals damaged emotions that lead to and perpetuate unhealthy eating habits.

"He heals the brokenhearted and binds up their wounds" (PSALM 147:3).

God offers help and wise counsel for your recovery.

"Plans fail for lack of counsel, but with many advisers they succeed" (PROVERBS 15:22).

God longs for you to have compassion and help others who struggle with anorexia and bulimia.

"Be sympathetic, love one another, be compassionate and humble" (1 PETER 3:8).

This is what the LORD Almighty says:
"Give careful thought to your ways."
(HAGGAI 1:5)

Characteristics of Those with Eating Disorders

— **Confusion** over values
— **Deception** of self and others
— **Depression** over feeling "fat" (although weight is normal or far below)
— **Compulsion** for some feeling of control
— **Loneliness** because of the desire to avoid discovery
— **Low self-worth** because personal value is based on appearance
— **Perfectionism** because they believe that everything must fit just right, or it's horrible
— **People-pleasing** with an excessive desire for approval

Guide me in your truth and teach me.
(PSALM 25:5)

Situational Causes

— **Feeling worthless** because of abuse in the home
— **Feeling inadequate** because of unrealistic expectations of others
— **Feeling driven** in a high-performance atmosphere
— **Feeling hopeless** as a result of depression from past behaviors
— **Feeling powerless** because of obesity or other eating disorder in the family
— **Feeling angry** because of past mistreatment
— **Feeling anxious** due to stressful life changes

"I loathe my very life; therefore I will give free rein
to my complaint and speak out in the
bitterness of my soul."
(Job 10:1)

How to First Acknowledge 7 Key Needs

1. **Agree** to get a thorough medical checkup. This condition is life-threatening!

   "The prudent see danger and take refuge, but the simple keep going and pay the penalty" (Proverbs 27:12).

2. **Acquire** as much knowledge about eating disorders as possible—for yourself and for those close to you.

   "Plans fail for lack of counsel, but with many advisers they succeed" (Proverbs 15:22).

3. **Attend** weekly (or regular) sessions with a knowledgeable, professional, Christian counselor.

   "Apply your heart to instruction and your ears to words of knowledge" (Proverbs 23:12).

4. **Admit** your inability to control your eating pattern.

   "I do not understand what I do. For what I want to do I do not do, but what I hate I do" (Romans 7:15).

Key Verse to Memorize

"The Lord himself goes before you
and will be with you;
he will never leave you nor forsake you.
Do not be afraid; do not be discouraged."
(Deuteronomy 31:8)

5. **Abandon** the idea that you just need more willpower. This is not a diet or willpower problem, but a battle to address strongholds.

   "The weapons we fight with are not the weapons of the world. On the contrary, they have divine power to demolish strongholds. We demolish arguments and every pretension that sets itself up against the knowledge of God, and we take captive every thought to make it obedient to Christ" (2 Corinthians 10:4–5). (Also read 2 Corinthians 12:9–10.)

6. **Allow** yourself to forgive those who have hurt you . . . and even to forgive yourself.

   "Bear with each other and forgive one another if any of you has a grievance against someone. Forgive as the Lord forgave you" (Colossians 3:13).

7. **Act** in total faith on God's power to rescue you.

   "In you, LORD, I have taken refuge; let me never be put to shame. In your righteousness, rescue me and deliver me; turn your ear to me and save me. Be my rock of refuge, to which I can always go; give the command to save me, for you are my rock and my fortress" (PSALM 71:1–3).

My God will meet all your needs according to
the riches of his glory in Christ Jesus.
(PHILIPPIANS 4:19)

The Way to Freedom

— **Recognize** that you have an eating disorder.
— **Acknowledge** your need.
— **Get** professional help.
— **Discover** your past predispositions.
— **Identify** your present stressors.
— **Avoid** your destructive patterns.
— **Flee** your enticing triggers.
— **Resist** your compelling urges.

The Way to Sustained Freedom

Yield yourself to God.
"Submit yourselves, then, to God. Resist the devil, and he will flee from you" (JAMES 4:7).

Claim your victory in Christ.
"Do not offer any part of yourself to sin as an instrument of wickedness, but rather offer yourselves to God as those who have been brought from death to life; and offer every part of yourself to him as an instrument of righteousness" (ROMANS 6:13).

Picture your success.
"Our citizenship is in heaven. And we eagerly await a Savior from there, the Lord Jesus Christ, who, by the power that enables him to bring everything under his control, will transform our lowly bodies so that they will be like his glorious body" (PHILIPPIANS 3:20–21).

Replace lies with truth.

"Now it is God who makes both us and you stand firm in Christ. He anointed us, set his seal of ownership on us, and put his Spirit in our hearts as a deposit, guaranteeing what is to come. . . . Since we have these promises, dear friends, let us purify ourselves from everything that contaminates body and spirit, perfecting holiness out of reverence for God" (2 CORINTHIANS 1:21–22; 7:1).

Devise a plan for daily success.

"As long as he sought the LORD, God gave him success" (2 CHRONICLES 26:5).

Enlist the support of others.

"Two are better than one . . . If either of them falls down, one can help the other up. But pity anyone who falls and has no one to help them up" (ECCLESIASTES 4:9–10).

"Perfume and incense bring joy to the heart, and the pleasantness of a friend springs from their heartfelt advice" (PROVERBS 27:9).

Throw away your scales.

"See to it that no one takes you captive through hollow and deceptive philosophy, which depends on human tradition and the elemental spiritual forces of this world rather than on Christ" (COLOSSIANS 2:8).

Journal your journey.

"Fix these words of mine in your hearts and minds; tie them as symbols on your hands and bind them on your foreheads. Teach them to your children, talking about them when you sit at home and when you walk along the road, when you lie down and when you get up. Write them on the doorframes of your houses and on your gates" (DEUTERONOMY 11:18–20).

Key Passage to Read

Psalm 139:1–18, 23–24

It is for freedom that Christ has set us free.
Stand firm, then, and do not let yourselves
be burdened again by a yoke of slavery.
(GALATIANS 5:1)

My Personalized Plan

Embrace my identity in Christ.

- I will remember my identity is in Christ, not in how I look.
- I will learn to see myself through God's eyes—as His beloved, precious child.

"You are precious to me. You are honored, and I love you" (ISAIAH 43:4 NLT).

Care for my body.

— I will talk with a doctor and address any physical issues.

— I will develop healthy eating habits and take care of my body with proper rest and exercise.

"Do you not know that your bodies are temples of the Holy Spirit, who is in you, whom you have received from God? You are not your own; you were bought at a price. Therefore honor God with your bodies" (1 CORINTHIANS 6:19–20).

Address my emotions.

— I will identify the emotions that lead me to unhealthy eating habits—guilt, shame, fear, low self-worth, or other negative emotions.

— I will journal and/or talk with trusted friends or a counselor to process my emotions.

"I sought the LORD, and he answered me; he delivered me from all my fears" (PSALM 34:4).

Correct negative thoughts.

— I will identify any repeated, negative thoughts I have, especially about myself and how I look.

— I will replace those thoughts and lies with the truth of God's Word.

"Don't copy the behavior and customs of this world, but let God transform you into a new person by changing the way you think" (ROMANS 12:2 NLT).

Seek support.

— I will seek help from a support or recovery group.

— I will be open and honest about my struggles and my progress.

"Two people are better off than one, for they can help each other succeed. If one person falls, the other can reach out and help. But someone who falls alone is in real trouble" (ECCLESIASTES 4:9–10 NLT).

Help others.

— I will pray about sharing my story to help others who have struggled with anorexia and/or bulimia.

— I will celebrate my progress and ask God to use me to give others hope.

"He comforts us in all our troubles so that we can comfort others" (2 CORINTHIANS 1:4 NLT).

Questions & Answers

Question: "Isn't it good to eliminate all food until I lose all the weight I want?"

Answer: No, because not eating *enough* hurts your metabolism by slowing it down!

When you drop your calories too low, you lose weight, but that weight is certainly not all excess. You will also lose muscle weight. Your muscle is what burns the fat in your body.

How much better is a *healthy, balanced, disciplined diet* that results in appropriate weight loss and eliminates only surplus weight?

Those who disregard discipline despise themselves,
but the one who heeds correction
gains understanding.
(PROVERBS 15:32)

Question: "What roles do ego and vanity play in anorexia?"

Answer: None. Anorexics eat less and less in an effort to become smaller and smaller because of their self-effacing desire to simply disappear. Deep-seated insecurity, not vanity, is at the root of anorexia.

"Oh, that I had the wings of a dove!
I would fly away and be at rest."
(PSALM 55:6)

Question: "Why do anorexics seem so determined to destroy themselves?"

Answer: The negative thinking patterns of anorexics have convinced them that . . .

— They don't deserve to live.

— Their natural longing for love is not realistic.

— They have made too many mistakes.

Hope deferred makes the heart sick.
(PROVERBS 13:12)

ANXIETY

Calming the Fearful Heart

God's Heart on Anxiety

God wants you to remember that He is good and gracious—and compassionately cares about you.

"The LORD is gracious and compassionate, slow to anger and rich in love. The LORD is good to all; he has compassion on all he has made" (PSALM 145:8–9).

God wants you to remember He is with you when you're fearful.

"So do not fear, for I am with you; do not be dismayed, for I am your God. I will strengthen you and help you; I will uphold you with my righteous right hand" (ISAIAH 41:10).

God wants you to pray and experience His peace when you're feeling anxious.

"Do not be anxious about anything, but in every situation, by prayer and petition, with thanksgiving, present your requests to God. And the peace of God, which transcends all understanding, will guard your hearts and your minds in Christ Jesus" (PHILIPPIANS 4:6–7).

God wants you to look to Him and His Word when you're filled with anxiety.

"When anxiety was great within me, your consolation brought me joy" (PSALM 94:19).

God wants you to align your thoughts with His truth when you feel anxious.

"Whatever is true, whatever is noble, whatever is right, whatever is pure, whatever is lovely, whatever is admirable—if anything is excellent or praiseworthy—think about such things" (PHILIPPIANS 4:8).

God wants you to trust Him when you're anxious—to have faith and not fear.

"When I am afraid, I put my trust in you" (PSALM 56:3).

God wants you to talk to Him about all that causes you to feel anxious.

"Cast all your anxiety on him because he cares for you" (1 PETER 5:7).

God wants you to talk to others about your fears and anxieties.

"Where there is no guidance the people fall, but in abundance of counselors there is victory" (PROVERBS 11:14 NASB).

God wants you to take care of yourself physically and spiritually.

"For physical training is of some value, but godliness has value for all things, holding promise for both the present life and the life to come" (1 TIMOTHY 4:8).

God wants you to encourage others who struggle with anxiety.

"Anxiety weighs down the heart, but a kind word cheers it up" (PROVERBS 12:25).

God is our refuge and strength,
an ever-present help in trouble.
(PSALM 46:1)

Personal Anxiety Checklist[31]

Assess the following list to determine if any of these trigger anxiety in you. Notice not only those that lead specifically to anxiety, but also those that you tend to avoid.

- ☐ Anger/disapproval from others
- ☐ Appearing nervous
- ☐ Being in charge
- ☐ Cats/dogs
- ☐ Closed places
- ☐ Confronting people
- ☐ Criticism
- ☐ Crowds
- ☐ Driving automobiles
- ☐ Elevators
- ☐ Failure
- ☐ Fainting
- ☐ Fire
- ☐ Flying
- ☐ Heights
- ☐ Injections
- ☐ Loss of control
- ☐ Lovemaking with spouse
- ☐ Meeting new people
- ☐ Mice/snakes/spiders
- ☐ Mistakes
- ☐ Open spaces
- ☐ Public speaking
- ☐ Rejection
- ☐ Sharp instruments
- ☐ Sight of blood
- ☐ Talking on the phone
- ☐ Tests
- ☐ Thunderstorms

Myths and Misconceptions About Anxiety[32]

Myth: "Because I have an anxiety disorder, I should always avoid whatever makes me feel anxious."

Truth: Avoiding what makes you anxious can actually make you feel even more anxiety. You will likely find that you can ultimately work through an anxious situation when you face it.

"In my distress I called to the LORD; I cried to my God for help. From his temple he heard my voice; my cry came before him, into his ears" (PSALM 18:6).

Myth: "I'm afraid of passing out if I have a panic attack."

Truth: Fainting is unlikely because it's often caused by a sudden drop in blood pressure. During a panic attack, blood pressure doesn't fall; it rises slightly.

"You wearied yourself by such going about, but you would not say, 'It is hopeless.' You found renewal of your strength, and so you did not faint" (ISAIAH 57:10).

Key Verse to Memorize

Cast all your anxiety on him
because he cares for you.
(1 PETER 5:7)

Myth: "Medication is the only treatment available for anxiety."

Truth: Research shows that medication is helpful, but cognitive-behavioral therapy (CBT) may be just as effective or produce even better results when used in conjunction with medication.

"Plans fail for lack of counsel, but with many advisers they succeed" (PROVERBS 15:22).

Myth: "Some people are just 'naturally' anxious, neurotic, or worrywarts. Nothing really makes a difference."

Truth: While some people may have a predisposition to worry and exhibit anxious thoughts, regardless of temperament, beneficial therapy can reduce anxiety.

"Search me, God, and know my heart; test me and know my anxious thoughts" (PSALM 139:23).

Guide me in your truth and teach me,
for you are God my Savior,
and my hope is in you all day long.
(PSALM 25:5)

God's Word Can Calm an Anxious Heart

If You Say: "I'm afraid that my situation is impossible."

The Lord Says: *I can make all things possible.*

"What is impossible with man is possible with God" (LUKE 18:27).

If You Say: "I'm overwhelmed with fear."

The Lord Says: *I will give you My strength when you're afraid.*

"Do not fear, for I am with you; do not be dismayed, for I am your God. I will strengthen you and help you; I will uphold you with my righteous right hand" (ISAIAH 41:10).

If You Say: "I'm so worried and anxious over the wrongs I've done, and I can't forgive myself."

The Lord Says: *Let go of your worries and anxieties. I will forgive you.*

"If we confess our sins, he is faithful and just and will forgive us our sins and purify us from all unrighteousness" (1 JOHN 1:9).

If You Say: "I'm anxious and worried that my loved ones might leave me."

The Lord Says: *Once you've come to Me, I will never leave you.*

"The LORD himself goes before you and will be with you; he will never leave you nor forsake you. Do not be afraid; do not be discouraged" (DEUTERONOMY 31:8).

If You Say: "I'm anxious about dying."

The Lord Says: *I will give you eternal life.*

"For God so loved the world that he gave his one and only Son, that whoever believes in him shall not perish but have eternal life" (JOHN 3:16).

If You Say: "I'm anxious and I can't rest."

The Lord Says: *I will give you My rest.*

"Come to me, all of you who are weary and carry heavy burdens, and I will give you rest. Take my yoke upon you. Let me teach you, because I am humble and gentle at heart, and you will find rest for your souls. For my yoke is easy to bear, and the burden I give you is light." (MATTHEW 11:28-30 NLT).

How to Control Anxious Thoughts

Use this exercise to help focus and control your thoughts when you're anxious. Think through and answer the questions related to the eight characteristics listed in Philippians 4:8.

"Fix your thoughts on what is true, and honorable, and right,
and pure, and lovely, and admirable.
Think about things that are excellent and worthy of praise."
(PHILIPPIANS 4:8 NLT)

What is true?

— Ask yourself: *What is true and accurate about my situation? What does God say I should do (or not do)? What promises of God or attribute of God can speak to my situation?*

"I have chosen the way of truth; I have set Your ordinances before me" (PSALM 119:30 HCSB).

What is honorable?

— Ask yourself: *What is the respectful thing to do in my situation? Is there someone I trust and respect who I can talk to about my anxiety? What can I do that will honor the Lord?*

"Call on me in the day of trouble; I will deliver you, and you will honor me" (PSALM 50:15).

What is right?

— Ask yourself: *What does God say is the right thing to do in my circumstance? What will happen if I do what is right—and what will happen if I do what is wrong or unwise? Who can help me do what's right?*

"Do what is right and good in the LORD's sight" (DEUTERONOMY 6:18).

What is pure?

— Ask yourself: *Is my anxiety leading me to pursue holiness—to seek God's presence, His Word, His people? In what ways is my anxiety leading me away from God—tempting me to doubt God, control others, or sin?*

"I want you to understand what really matters, so that you may live pure and blameless lives until the day of Christ's return" (PHILIPPIANS 1:10 NLT).

What is lovely?

— Ask yourself: *In what ways has the Lord shown His love to me? What do I love about God? How can I show love to God, to others, and to myself?*

"May you have the power to understand, as all God's people should, how wide, how long, how high, and how deep his love is. May you experience the love of Christ, though it is too great to understand fully. Then you will be made complete with all the fullness of life and power that comes from God" (EPHESIANS 3:18–19 NLT).

What is admirable?

— Ask yourself: *Who can I speak well of or compliment? What aspects of my situation are good or commendable? Who has helped me (or is currently helping me) and deserves to be thanked?*

"Anxiety weighs down the heart, but a kind word cheers it up" (PROVERBS 12:25).

What is excellent?

— Ask yourself: *Are there any immoral thoughts or actions I need to confess and change? What morals, virtues, or godly characteristics do I need to work on, with God's help?*

"Make every effort to respond to God's promises. Supplement your faith with a generous provision of moral excellence, and moral excellence with knowledge, and knowledge with self-control, and self-control with patient endurance, and patient endurance with godliness, and godliness with brotherly affection, and brotherly affection with love for everyone" (2 PETER 1:5–7 NLT).

What is praiseworthy?

— Ask yourself: *What am I thankful for in my situation? What things can I praise God for (relationships, spiritual and material blessings, knowledge, health, etc.)?*

"I will praise the Lord at all times. I will constantly speak his praises . . . I prayed to the Lord, and he answered me. He freed me from all my fears" (PSALM 34:1, 4 NLT).

Key Passage to Read

Philippians 4:4–9

When seeking to control your anxious thoughts, remember that Jesus is the greatest thought you can have. That is why God's Word says to *"fix your thoughts on Jesus"* (Hebrews 3:1). Jesus is the most true, honorable, right, pure, lovely, admirable, excellent, and praiseworthy person in the world. And the great news is that Jesus is *for* you. He is *with* you. And He even dwells *in* you. When anxiety weighs you down, Jesus can lift you up and raise your thoughts to Him and the glorious future He has for you.

"Set your minds on things above, not on earthly things.
For you died, and your life is now hidden with Christ in God.
When Christ, who is your life, appears,
then you also will appear with him in glory."
(COLOSSIANS 3:2–4)

My Personalized Plan

As I seek God's help with my anxiety, **I will . . .**

Remember God's character

— I will believe that God is good, that He is with me, and that He will help me—and trust that He is in control and has my best interests at heart.

"The LORD is gracious and compassionate, slow to anger and rich in love. The LORD is good to all; he has compassion on all he has made. . . . The LORD is trustworthy in all he promises and faithful in all he does" (PSALM 145:8–9, 13).

Address physical issues

— I will seek to maintain a healthy lifestyle by eating well, exercising regularly, getting plenty of rest, staying hydrated, avoiding harmful substances, and learning relaxation techniques to manage stress and anxiety.

"I discipline my body and keep it under control" (1 CORINTHIANS 9:27 ESV).

Talk with others

— I will seek the help of a professional counselor, supportive group of people in my church or community, and/or talk with trusted friends and family members.

"Where there is no guidance the people fall, but in abundance of counselors there is victory" (PROVERBS 11:14 NASB).

Reorient my thoughts

— I will seek to align my thoughts with God's Word, identifying thoughts that are based on lies and replacing them with God's truth.

"Whatever is true, whatever is noble, whatever is right, whatever is pure, whatever is lovely, whatever is admirable—if anything is excellent or praiseworthy—think about such things" (PHILIPPIANS 4:8).

Be in community

— I will look into joining a local church, small group, Bible study, or community support group.

"Two people are better off than one, for they can help each other succeed. If one person falls, the other can reach out and help" (ECCLESIASTES 4:9-10 NLT).

Stay active spiritually

— I will constantly seek to grow in my relationship with Christ, who loves me and gives me grace each day.

"Grow in the grace and knowledge of our Lord and Savior Jesus Christ" (2 PETER 3:18).

Hang on to hope

— I will remember that true, lasting hope is found not in my circumstances but in God and His Word.

"Everything that was written in the past was written to teach us, so that through the endurance taught in the Scriptures and the encouragement they provide we might have hope" (ROMANS 15:4).

Questions & Answers

Question: "What is the difference between worry and anxiety?"

Answer: People often use the words *worry* and *anxiety* interchangeably. However, there are key differences between the two:

Worry is typically understood to be a *mental* process—ruminating on what-if scenarios that may or may not come to fruition. It is often anticipating an outcome, attempting to solve a problem, or avoiding a deeper issue.

— Although worry is not an emotion, it can lead to feeling anxious.

Anxiety is a present physiological feeling, usually an emotional response to a current or possible future threat (real or perceived).

— Excessive, obsessive worry can *lead* to anxiety. Likewise, stress can lead to worry or anxiety. Anxiety can also make an appearance all on its own.

Guide me in your truth and teach me,
for you are God my Savior,
and my hope is in you all day long.
(PSALM 25:5)

Question: "I am anxious all the time. Does my anxiety mean I'm not a good Christian?"

Answer: No. God doesn't qualify or quantify your status as a Christian by comparing you with others. You may experience anxiety at the thought of speaking in public or face an irrational fear of snow even if you live in a desert, but God doesn't expect everyone to have the boldness of Daniel facing the lions' den or his three friends entering the fiery furnace. Can you imagine the anxious dread they may have felt? Even Jesus was *"deeply distressed and troubled . . . overwhelmed with sorrow"* as he was praying in the garden of Gethsemane before His arrest and betrayal, leading to His death on the cross (Mark 14:33–34).

May God himself, the God of peace, sanctify you through and through.
May your whole spirit, soul and body be kept
blameless at the coming of our Lord Jesus Christ.
The one who calls you is faithful, and he will do it.
(1 THESSALONIANS 5:23–24)

ASSURANCE OF SALVATION

Safe, Sealed, and Secure

God's Heart on Assurance of Salvation

God wants believers in Christ to know they cannot lose their salvation—to know they have eternal life in Christ.

"I write these things to you who believe in the name of the Son of God so that you may know that you have eternal life" (1 JOHN 5:13).

God wants believers in Christ to know that nothing can snatch them out of His hand.

"I give them eternal life, and they shall never perish; no one will snatch them out of my hand" (JOHN 10:28).

God wants believers in Christ to know that they have passed from death to life.

"Very truly I tell you, whoever hears my word and believes him who sent me has eternal life and will not be judged but has crossed over from death to life" (JOHN 5:24).

God wants believers in Christ to know they will live forever with Christ in heaven after they die.

"I am the resurrection and the life. The one who believes in me will live, even though they die; and whoever lives by believing in me will never die" (JOHN 11:25–26).

God wants believers in Christ to know that nothing can separate them from His love.

"I am convinced that neither death nor life, neither angels nor demons, neither the present nor the future, nor any powers, neither height nor depth, nor anything else in all creation, will be able to separate us from the love of God that is in Christ Jesus our Lord" (ROMANS 8:38–39).

God wants you to know He completes the work He begins in believers.

"Being confident of this, that he who began a good work in you will carry it on to completion until the day of Christ Jesus" (PHILIPPIANS 1:6).

God wants you to rest in the finished work of Christ.

"Know that a person is not justified by the works of the law, but by faith in Jesus Christ. So we, too, have put our faith in Christ Jesus that we may be justified by faith in Christ and not by the works of the law, because by the works of the law no one will be justified" (GALATIANS 2:16).

God wants you to know your salvation is based on His grace, not on your works.

"It is by grace you have been saved, through faith—and this is not from yourselves, it is the gift of God—not by works, so that no one can boast" (EPHESIANS 2:8-9).

God gives believers in Christ His Holy Spirit as a seal, guaranteeing their salvation.

"You also were included in Christ when you heard the message of truth, the gospel of your salvation. When you believed, you were marked in him with a seal, the promised Holy Spirit, who is a deposit guaranteeing our inheritance until the redemption of those who are God's possession—to the praise of his glory" (EPHESIANS 1:13-14).

Key Verse to Memorize

I write these things to you who believe
in the name of the Son of God
so that you may know that
you have eternal life.
(1 JOHN 5:13)

God wants you to know that you are not saved by the strength of your faith but by the object of your faith—Jesus Christ.

"We are made right with God by placing our faith in Jesus Christ. And this is true for everyone who believes, no matter who we are" (ROMANS 3:22 NLT).

God will never leave you nor forsake you.

"I will never leave you nor forsake you" (HEBREWS 13:5 NKJV).

God offers salvation to all through faith in Christ, but those who reject Him will experience His judgment.

"Whoever believes in the Son has eternal life, but whoever rejects the Son will not see life, for God's wrath remains on them" (JOHN 3:36).

There is now no condemnation for those who are in Christ Jesus.
(ROMANS 8:1)

The Difference Between Anxiety over Salvation and Assurance of Salvation

Anxiety over Salvation: Guilty conscience

Assurance of Salvation: Clear conscience

"Let us draw near to God with a sincere heart and with the full assurance that faith brings, having our hearts sprinkled to cleanse us from a guilty conscience and having our bodies washed with pure water" (HEBREWS 10:22).

Anxiety over Salvation: Confusion about God's judgment

Assurance of Salvation: Confidence in God's mercy

"We do not have a high priest who is unable to empathize with our weaknesses, but we have one who has been tempted in every way, just as we are—yet he did not sin. Let us then approach God's throne of grace with confidence, so that we may receive mercy and find grace to help us in our time of need" (HEBREWS 4:15–16).

Anxiety over Salvation: Works-orientation

Assurance of Salvation: Grace-orientation

"It is by grace you have been saved, through faith—and this is not from yourselves, it is the gift of God—not by works, so that no one can boast" (EPHESIANS 2:8–9).

Anxiety over Salvation: Legalistic lifestyle

Assurance of Salvation: Liberty in lifestyle

"It is for freedom that Christ has set us free. Stand firm, then, and do not let yourselves be burdened again by a yoke of slavery" (GALATIANS 5:1).

Anxiety over Salvation: Insecurity about God's view of you

Assurance of Salvation: Security about God's view of you

"Now he has reconciled you by Christ's physical body through death to present you holy in his sight, without blemish and free from accusation" (COLOSSIANS 1:22).

Anxiety over Salvation: Fear of the future

Assurance of Salvation: Faith in the God of the future

"That is why I am suffering as I am. Yet this is no cause for shame, because I know whom I have believed, and am convinced that he is able to guard what I have entrusted to him until that day" (2 TIMOTHY 1:12).

Anxiety over Salvation: Feelings determining decisions

Assurance of Salvation: Facts determining decisions

"There is now no condemnation for those who are in Christ Jesus" (ROMANS 8:1).

This is no cause for shame,
because I know whom I have believed,
and am convinced that he is able
to guard what I have entrusted
to him until that day.
(2 TIMOTHY 1:12)

Salvation Checklist

From the Book of 1 John

☐ **Do I live by the truth, rejecting deeds done in darkness?**

"If we claim to have fellowship with him and yet walk in the darkness, we lie and do not live out the truth" (1:6).

☐ **Do I enjoy fellowship with other believers?**

"If we walk in the light, as he is in the light, we have fellowship with one another, and the blood of Jesus, his Son, purifies us from all sin" (1:7).

☐ **Do I have a love for God's Word and seek to obey it?**

"We know that we have come to know him if we keep his commands. Whoever says, 'I know him,' but does not do what he commands is a liar, and the truth is not in that person. But if anyone obeys his word, love for God is truly made complete in them. This is how we know we are in him" (2:3–5).

☐ **Do I reject the values I see in the world system?**

"Do not love the world or anything in the world. If anyone loves the world, love for the Father is not in them. For everything in the world—the lust of the flesh, the lust of the eyes, and the pride of life—comes not from the Father but from the world. The world and its desires pass away, but whoever does the will of God lives forever" (2:15–17).

☐ **Do I look forward to the return of Christ?**

"Dear friends, now we are children of God, and what we will be has not yet been made known. But we know that when Christ appears we shall be like him, for we shall see him as he is. All who have this hope in him purify themselves, just as he is pure" (3:2–3).

☐ **Do I sin less than I did before I claimed to become a Christian?**

"No one who lives in him keeps on sinning. No one who continues to sin has either seen him or known him" (3:6).

☐ **Do I experience opposition because of my love for Christ?**

"Do not be surprised, my brothers and sisters, if the world hates you" (3:13).

☐ **Do I genuinely love other Christians?**

"We know that we have passed from death to life, because we love each other. Anyone who does not love remains in death" (3:14).

☐ **Do I truly believe in Jesus by fully relying on Him for my salvation and my future?**

"Whoever believes in the Son of God accepts this testimony. Whoever does not believe God has made him out to be a liar, because they have not believed the testimony God has given about his Son. And this is the testimony: God has given us eternal life, and this life is in his Son" (5:10–11).

☐ **Do I experience answered prayer?**

"Dear friends, if our hearts do not condemn us, we have confidence before God and receive from him anything we ask, because we keep his commands and do what pleases him. . . . This is the confidence we have in approaching God: that if we ask anything according to his will, he hears us. And if we know that he hears us—whatever we ask—we know that we have what we asked of him" (3:21–22; 5:14–15).

Key Passage to Read

John 10:27–29

☐ **Do I have discernment of spiritual truth?**

"We are from God, and whoever knows God listens to us; but whoever is not from God does not listen to us. This is how we recognize the Spirit of truth and the spirit of falsehood" (4:6).

I write these things to you who believe in the name of the Son of God so that you may know that you have eternal life.
(1 JOHN 5:13)

Common Causes of Insecurity

— **Questioning** a childhood decision
— **Failing** to forgive an offender
— **Continuing** in unrepentance of sin
— **Lacking** the willingness to change sinful patterns
— **Depending** on church membership
— **Relying** on personal effort and works
— **Lacking** faith in Scripture
— **Expecting** feelings or emotions to confirm salvation
— **Intellectualizing** spiritual truths
— **Confusing** *backsliding* with *loss of salvation*

Examine yourselves to see
whether you are in the faith; test yourselves.
Do you not realize that Christ Jesus is in you
—unless, of course, you fail the test?
(2 CORINTHIANS 13:5)

My Personalized Plan

Remember God's grace.

- I will remember that my salvation is not based on my works but on God's grace.
- I will reflect on God's grace regularly and reject my works as a means of salvation.

"We believe it is through the grace of our Lord Jesus that we are saved" (ACTS 15:11).

Rest in Christ.

- I will remember that Jesus Christ came to save sinners.
- I will rest in the finished work of Christ to cover all my sins and secure my salvation.

"Here is a trustworthy saying that deserves full acceptance: Christ Jesus came into the world to save sinners—of whom I am the worst. But for that very reason I was shown mercy so that in me, the worst of sinners, Christ Jesus might display his immense patience as an example for those who would believe in him and receive eternal life" (1 TIMOTHY 1:15–16).

Pursue obedience.

- I will confess when I sin, and rest knowing that God forgives me of all my sin through Christ.
- I will seek to obey God, not out of fear of losing my salvation but out of love for saving me.

"We love because he first loved us" (1 JOHN 4:19).

Study God's Word.

- I will rest in what God's Word says—not what man says—about my salvation in Christ.
- I will memorize and meditate on passages that remind me of my salvation in Christ.

"They delight in the law of the LORD, meditating on it day and night" (PSALM 1:2 NLT).

Assure fellow believers.

- I will identify passages of Scripture (such as John 5:24, 10:28; Romans 8:38–39) that I can share with fellow believers.
- I will encourage my brothers and sisters in Christ through Scripture, prayer, listening, and finding answers together.

"Encourage one another and build each other up, just as in fact you are doing" (1 THESSALONIANS 5:11).

Questions & Answers

Question: "What happens to someone who is genuinely born again, experiences a changed life, but later disbelieves . . . at least for a period of time? If a person stops believing, doesn't that person also stop being saved?"

Answer: No, the Bible says once you are truly born again—once you receive the new birth—you receive an *"inheritance that can never perish, spoil or fade . . . kept in heaven for you"* (1 Peter 1:4). Every honest believer experiences periods of doubt. Doubt is not the opposite of faith; it is the flip side of the same coin. Sincere doubt signifies a search—a search that God honors.

Praise be to the God and Father
of our Lord Jesus Christ! In his great mercy
he has given us new birth into a living hope
through the resurrection of Jesus Christ
from the dead, and into an inheritance
that can never perish, spoil or fade.
This inheritance is kept in heaven for you.
(1 PETER 1:3–4)

Question: "I accept the Bible's assurance that no one can snatch a true believer out of Jesus' hand. However, because of my own sin, can't I snatch myself out of His hand of protection, as well as out of His very presence?"

Answer: No, Jesus specifically said in John's gospel that *"no one"*—not "no one except yourself"—can snatch you out of His hand . . . and that includes you! In addition, notice just before those words, He said, *"They shall never perish."*

"I give them eternal life, and they shall never perish;
no one will snatch them out of my hand.
My Father, who has given them to me,
is greater than all; no one can snatch them
out of my Father's hand."
(JOHN 10:28–29)

ATHEISM & AGNOSTICISM

The Great Debate

God's Heart on Atheism & Agnosticism

God is real and can be known.

"For ever since the world was created, people have seen the earth and sky. Through everything God made, they can clearly see his invisible qualities—his eternal power and divine nature. So they have no excuse for not knowing God" (Romans 1:20 NLT).

God reveals Himself through His Word.

"All Scripture is God-breathed and is useful for teaching, rebuking, correcting and training in righteousness" (2 Timothy 3:16).

God reveals Himself through creation.

"The heavens declare the glory of God; the skies proclaim the work of his hands" (Psalm 19:1).

God is fully revealed in the person of Jesus Christ.

"No one has ever seen God, but the one and only Son, who is himself God and is in closest relationship with the Father, has made him known" (John 1:18).

God says it is foolish to deny His existence.

"The fool says in his heart, 'There is no God'" (Psalm 14:1).

God promises to be found by those who seek Him.

"You will seek me and find me when you seek me with all your heart" (Jeremiah 29:13).

God is patient and desires all people to come to Him.

"The Lord is not slow in keeping his promise, as some understand slowness. Instead he is patient with you, not wanting anyone to perish, but everyone to come to repentance" (2 Peter 3:9).

God offers salvation through faith in Christ to all people.

"God our Savior . . . wants all people to be saved and to come to a knowledge of the truth. For there is one God and one mediator between God and mankind, the man Christ Jesus" (1 Timothy 2:3–5).

God wants you to be merciful to those who doubt.

"Be merciful to those who doubt" (Jude v. 22).

God urges you to pray for those who do not believe—that they would come to know Him.

"I urge you, first of all, to pray for all people . . . This is good and pleases God our Savior, who wants everyone to be saved and to understand the truth" (1 TIMOTHY 2:1, 3-4 NLT).

The LORD is the true God; he is the living God, the eternal King.
(JEREMIAH 10:10)

Answers to the Arguments of Atheists

Cause and Effect: If everything needs a cause, then so does God. If God does not need a cause, then neither does the world, then there is no need of God. —Bertrand Russell[33]

Answer: Only effects need a cause. If you theorize that even God is an effect and needs a cause, then you can never find a "first cause" for the creation of the universe.

"In the beginning you laid the foundations of the earth, and the heavens are the work of your hands" (PSALM 102:25).

Moral Incompatibilities: If God is all good and all powerful, He could and would defeat evil. Evil is not defeated; therefore, there is no God. —Pierre Bayle[34]

Answer: God did not create a puppet state in which people have no choice over their actions. He allows everyone freedom to choose good or evil now, yet He guarantees the destruction of all evil in the end.

"'He will wipe every tear from their eyes. There will be no more death' or mourning or crying or pain, for the old order of things has passed away. . . . But the cowardly, the unbelieving, the vile, the murderers, the sexually immoral, those who practice magic arts, the idolaters and all liars—they will be consigned to the fiery lake of burning sulfur. This is the second death" (REVELATION 21:4, 8).

Unjustifiable Suffering: Unjustifiable suffering is incompatible with a just God. —Albert Camus[35]

Answer: Our perspective of justice is limited in view of God's redeeming process, which produces a greater good. Example: The mother whose son is killed by a drunk driver becomes active in a program that saves thousands of lives (Mothers Against Drunk Driving or MADD).

"Whenever you face trials of many kinds . . . you know that the testing of your faith produces perseverance. Let perseverance finish its work so that you may be mature and complete, not lacking anything" (JAMES 1:2-4).

Incompatible Attributes: How can God possess attributes such as love and wrath, which are incompatible?

Answer: Love and wrath are not incompatible. Love is an attribute of God that never changes. God is never without agape love for you, which means He always seeks your highest good. Wrath is God's response to sin. Wrath seeks to avenge wrongs. God's wrath—like a refiner's fire—is born out of His pure love.

"He will sit as a refiner and purifier of silver; he will . . . refine them like gold and silver" (MALACHI 3:3).

"The Big Bang Theory": The universe is a result of a chance combination of particles in motion. The chance theory is also the explanation of human life.[36] —David Hume, atheist

Answer: A completely random universe that runs by chance defies intricate design, reliability, and intelligence, which is clearly visible. Example: If all the parts of your watch were put in a box and shaken for a million years, an intricate watch would not be created.

"Where were you when I laid the earth's foundation? Tell me, if you understand. Who marked off its dimensions? Surely you know! Who stretched a measuring line across it? On what were its footings set, or who laid its cornerstone—while the morning stars sang together and all the angels shouted for joy?" (JOB 38:4–7).

Wishful Thinking: Belief in God is based on a wish fulfillment, a childhood neurosis that seeks a protector.[37] —Sigmund Freud

Answer: The fact that people in all cultures, whether primitive or advanced, feel a great need for God and worship God is universal proof for the existence of a God.

"The wrath of God is being revealed from heaven against all the godlessness and wickedness of people, who suppress the truth by their wickedness, since what may be known about God is plain to them, because God has made it plain to them. For since the creation of the world God's invisible qualities—his eternal power and divine nature—have been clearly seen, being understood from what has been made, so that people are without excuse" (ROMANS 1:18–20).

Key Verse to Memorize

"You will seek me and find me when you seek me with all your heart." (JEREMIAH 29:13)

Physical Liabilities: God cannot be seen, heard, or touched.

Answer: God is not limited to making Himself known through physical attributes. He increasingly reveals Himself through the conscience as a person increasingly grows in faith.

"Though you have not seen him, you love him; and even though you do not see him now, you believe in him and are filled with an inexpressible and glorious joy" (1 PETER 1:8).

What may be known about God is plain to them,
because God has made it plain to them.
For since the creation of the world God's invisible qualities—
his eternal power and divine nature—have been clearly seen,
being understood from what has been made,
so that people are without excuse.
(ROMANS 1:19–20)

Two Types of Atheists

The Absolute Atheist: The classic or traditional atheist believes that to suggest the evidence of a supreme being is utterly ridiculous. God is simply a creation of the human imagination.

The Allegorical Atheist: This adaptable atheist believes that deity may have been helpful to primitive humans but is no longer necessary because society has evolved to a higher level of sophistication.

See to it, brothers and sisters, that none of you
has a sinful, unbelieving heart that
turns away from the living God.
(HEBREWS 3:12)

Two Types of Agnostics

The Antagonistic Agnostic: This "hard" agnostic does not know whether God exists and, therefore, states that no one can ever know.

The Accessible Agnostic: The "soft" agnostic does not know whether God exists, but could be willing to investigate.

Seek the LORD while he may be found;
call on him while he is near. . . .
"For my thoughts are not your thoughts,
neither are your ways my ways,"
declares the LORD.
"As the heavens are higher than the earth,
so are my ways higher than your ways
and my thoughts than your thoughts."
(ISAIAH 55:6, 8–9)

My Personalized Plan

For those who do not believe . . .

Investigate honestly.

— I will not simply dismiss the claims of Christianity as false.

— I will ask questions, read books, talk with others, and genuinely seek to learn the truth.

"Intelligent people are always ready to learn. Their ears are open for knowledge" (Proverbs 18:15 NLT).

Read Scripture.

— I will read the Bible for myself and not merely rely on what others have said about it.

— I will read about the life of Jesus in the Gospels—Matthew, Mark, Luke, and John.

"Open my eyes to see the wonderful truths in your instructions" (Psalm 119:18 NLT).

Consider praying.

— I will be open to praying and ask God to reveal Himself to me.

— I will allow God to reveal Himself to me in His time and His way.

"The Lord is near to all who call on him, to all who call on him in truth" (Psalm 145:18).

For those helping someone who does not believe . . .

Be patient.

— I will trust the Lord to reveal Himself to my loved one.

— I will not force my faith on my loved one but will be patient as God reveals Himself to them.

Key Passage to Read

Romans 1:18–2:29

"Always be humble and gentle. Be patient with each other, making allowance for each other's faults because of your love" (Ephesians 4:2 NLT).

Pray consistently.

— I will pray for my loved one regularly, asking the Lord to save them.

— I will pray for myself as well, to be an effective witness by reflecting God's love.

"Pray in the Spirit on all occasions with all kinds of prayers and requests" (Ephesians 6:18).

Serve lovingly.

— I will help my loved one find answers to their questions about the Christian faith.

— I will meet their practical needs and serve them as a reflection of Christ's love for them.

"Serve one another humbly in love" (GALATIANS 5:13).

Questions & Answers

Question: "How can a logical person believe in the existence of God?"

Answer: A logical person would not make such illogical statements.

To state, "I know there is no God" communicates, "I know all there is to know—nothing exists beyond my knowledge." However, no one knows everything. Therefore, if something is not known, that something might be God.

To state, "God does not exist" communicates, "I have been everywhere in the universe." Because you haven't been everywhere, you can't say God doesn't exist here.

"Do not I fill heaven and earth?" declares the LORD.
(JEREMIAH 23:24)

Question: "How can I intellectually accept God by faith?"

Answer: You frequently live by faith. When you board an elevator, you don't first inspect the cables and the flooring. You get in and push a button. And how much more will the One who created you be faithful to you? Faith is your choice.

We live by faith, not by sight.
(2 CORINTHIANS 5:7)

Question: "Does it even matter whether God exists?"

Answer: If God didn't care about your existence or was too weak to do anything about it, then *no*, it wouldn't matter. But if God is all-powerful yet personal, if He is concerned about you, and if He has a personalized plan for your life, then *yes*, it does matter.

In their hearts humans plan their course,
but the LORD establishes their steps.
(PROVERBS 16:9)

To the skeptic who says, "I've never seen or heard God," I offer these thoughts: Just because the blind never see a star and the deaf never hear a harp doesn't mean that stars and harps do not exist. With faith you can see His footprints. With an open heart you will hear His voice. —June Hunt

THE BIBLE: IS IT RELIABLE?

Truth on Trial

God's Heart on the Bible

The Bible is the Word of God—inspired by God, written by human authors, with the Holy Spirit being its ultimate author.

"All Scripture is God-breathed and is useful for teaching, rebuking, correcting and training in righteousness" (2 TIMOTHY 3:16).

The Bible is inerrant—completely true, eternal, and without error.

"All your words are true; all your righteous laws are eternal" (PSALM 119:160).

The Bible is infallible—completely trustworthy; it accomplishes everything it promises to accomplish.

"So is my word that goes out from my mouth: It will not return to me empty, but will accomplish what I desire and achieve the purpose for which I sent it" (ISAIAH 55:11).

The Bible is the final authority for the Christian's life, belief, and practice.

"Man shall not live on bread alone, but on every word that comes from the mouth of God" (MATTHEW 4:4).

The Bible is ultimately about Jesus—it is properly understood with respect to the person and work of the Lord Jesus Christ.

"He [Jesus] *said to them, 'This is what I told you while I was still with you: Everything must be fulfilled that is written about me in the Law of Moses, the Prophets and the Psalms'"* (LUKE 24:44).

The Holy Spirit gives understanding to the Word of God.

"When he, the Spirit of truth, comes, he will guide you into all the truth" (JOHN 16:13).

The Word of God will endure forever—it cannot be destroyed.

"The grass withers and the flowers fall, but the word of our God endures forever" (ISAIAH 40:8).

The Bible was written to give us hope.

"Everything that was written in the past was written to teach us, so that through the endurance taught in the Scriptures and the encouragement they provide we might have hope" (ROMANS 15:4).

The Bible is read by more people, translated into more languages, and published in more countries than any other book throughout history. No book has been more bought or more banned, more loved or more loathed, more memorized or more maligned than the Bible.

I am not ashamed of the gospel, because it is the power of God
that brings salvation to everyone who believes.
(Romans 1:16)

What Is the Bible?

In order to better understand what it is, we need to know the following overview of the Bible:

Title: The English word *Bible* is from the Latin word *biblia*, which means "books."[38]

Purpose: The Bible is the record that God has given us . . . of creation, of His work in the lives of people, and of the final destination—heaven or hell—for every person ever born.

Structure: The Bible is one book consisting of sixty-six smaller books containing a continuous, coordinated, congruent story of God's plan of salvation.

Revelation: The Bible is God's revealed truth in written form to all people. It is God's written self-disclosure of His will, His works, and His ways.

Author: The Bible is authored by God Himself.

Writers: The Bible was written by more than forty men who were inspired by God's Spirit to write.

Languages: The Bible was written in three different languages: Hebrew, Greek, and Aramaic.

Location: The Bible was written on three continents: Asia, Africa, and Europe.

Date: The Bible was written over a span of approximately 1,500–1,600 years.

Topics: The Bible addresses theology, history, and science, as well as many difficult subjects: the origin of the universe and life, the nature of God, the nature of sin and the plan for human redemption, and the future—including heaven, hell, and eternity.

Theme: The Bible contains one central theme: salvation through faith in Jesus Christ.

God chose you as firstfruits to be saved
through the sanctifying work of the Spirit
and through belief in the truth.
(2 THESSALONIANS 2:13)

What Is Scripture?

Scripture means sacred or holy writings.[39]

Scripture is God's Word; therefore, to quote Scripture is to quote God.

Scripture in the New Testament has equal authority with Scripture in the Old Testament.

Paul also wrote you with the wisdom that
God gave him. . . . His letters contain some things
that are hard to understand, which ignorant and
unstable people distort, as they do the other
Scriptures, to their own destruction.
(2 PETER 3:15–16)

What Is the Canon?

The *Canon of Scripture* refers to the collection of sixty-six officially accepted books of the Bible.

The Canon of the Bible meets the following tests for divine inspiration and authority.

> **Key Verse to Memorize**
>
> *All Scripture is God-breathed*
> *and is useful for teaching, rebuking,*
> *correcting and training in righteousness.*
> (2 TIMOTHY 3:16)

1. **Was the book written by a prophet of God or an apostle of Christ?**

   "We also have the prophetic message as something completely reliable, and you will do well to pay attention to it, as to a light shining in a dark place, until the day dawns and the morning star rises in your hearts" (2 PETER 1:19).

2. **Was the writing confirmed by an act of God or an affirmation from God?**

   "God also testified to it [the gospel of salvation] *by signs, wonders and various miracles, and by gifts of the Holy Spirit distributed according to his will"* (HEBREWS 2:4).

3. **Does the message reveal truth from or about God?**

   "He who forms the mountains, who creates the wind, and who reveals his thoughts to mankind, who turns dawn to darkness, and treads on the heights of the earth—the LORD God Almighty is his name" (AMOS 4:13).

4. **Did the writing arise from the Lord's divine initiative with edifying power?**

   "The word of God is alive and active. Sharper than any double-edged sword, it penetrates even to dividing soul and spirit, joints and marrow; it judges the thoughts and attitudes of the heart" (HEBREWS 4:12).

5. **Was it accepted as Scripture by the people of God—particularly the contemporaries of the writing?**

   "Our gospel came to you not simply with words but also with power, with the Holy Spirit and deep conviction. You know how we lived among you for your sake. You became imitators of us and of the Lord for you welcomed the message in the midst of severe suffering with the joy given by the Holy Spirit" (1 THESSALONIANS 1:5–6).

6. **Does it pass the test of "the history of theology"—presenting a contiguous and even progressive revelation?**

   "In the past God spoke to our ancestors through the prophets at many times and in various ways, but in these last days he has spoken to us by his Son, whom he appointed heir of all things, and through whom also he made the universe" (HEBREWS 1:1–2).

7. **Did Jesus Christ endorse the writing as Scripture?**

   "You study the Scriptures diligently because you think that in them you have eternal life. These are the very Scriptures that testify about me [Jesus]*"* (JOHN 5:39).

The Bible Has Authority Because It Is . . .

Inspired: The Bible is supernaturally inspired. It comes from God Himself. In fact, the Bible is the precise message God wanted recorded.

"All Scripture is God-breathed and is useful for teaching, rebuking, correcting and training in righteousness" (2 TIMOTHY 3:16).

Infallible: The Bible is incapable of deception. It is totally trustworthy. In fact, the Bible is totally truthful.[40]

"The law of the LORD is perfect, refreshing the soul. The statutes of the LORD are trustworthy, making wise the simple" (PSALM 19:7).

Inerrant: The Bible tells the truth and does so without error. It is absolutely accurate. In fact, the Bible contains no mistake, falsehood, or flaw.[41]

"The words of the LORD are flawless, like silver purified in a crucible, like gold refined seven times" (PSALM 12:6).

Inclusive: The Bible is all-inclusive. It encompasses all truth necessary for life.[42] In fact, the Bible contains everything we need for . . .

— Salvation

"By this gospel you are saved" (1 CORINTHIANS 15:2).

— Instruction

"Preach the word . . . correct, rebuke and encourage—with great patience and careful instruction" (2 TIMOTHY 4:2).

— Hope

"Everything that was written in the past was written to teach us, so that through the endurance taught in the Scriptures and the encouragement they provide we might have hope" (ROMANS 15:4).

Key Passage to Read

Psalm 119

"As the rain and the snow
come down from heaven,
and do not return to it
without watering . . .
so is my word that goes out from my mouth:
It will not return to me empty."
(ISAIAH 55:10–11)

My Personalized Plan

I will . . .

Recognize the Bible is God's Word.

— I will remember that the Bible alone is God's Word.

— I will remember that the Bible is inspired, infallible, and inerrant.

"All Scripture is God-breathed and is useful for teaching, rebuking, correcting and training in righteousness, so that the servant of God may be thoroughly equipped for every good work" (2 TIMOTHY 3:16–17).

Read God's Word regularly.

— I will read and study God's Word daily.

— I will find a Bible reading plan and commit to it.

"Blessed is the one who reads aloud the words of this prophecy, and blessed are those who hear it and take to heart what is written in it, because the time is near" (REVELATION 1:3).

Remember God's Word.

— I will memorize passages of Scripture each week.

— I will meditate on God's Word, thinking through what it means for my life.

"I meditate on your precepts and consider your ways" (PSALM 119:15).

Rejoice in God's Word.

— I will thank God regularly for giving me His Word.

— I will delight in God's many great promises to me.

"I rejoice in your word like one who discovers a great treasure" (PSALM 119:162 NLT).

Respond to God's Word.

— I will believe what God says in His Word.

— I will respond to God's commands with obedience.

"Do not merely listen to the word, and so deceive yourselves. Do what it says" (JAMES 1:22).

This command is a lamp,
this teaching is a light,
and correction and instruction
are the way to life.
(PROVERBS 6:23)

Questions & Answers

Question: "Isn't the Bible full of contradictions?"

Answer: A contradiction occurs when two statements directly oppose each other and cannot both be true at the same time. The Bible contains no such contradictions.

While some passages may appear confusing at first glance, these are often resolved by understanding the context, cultural background, and/or original language.

Far from being unreliable, the Bible is remarkably consistent, even though it was written by more than forty authors across fifteen hundred years. Its unity points to a divine author.

Rather than contradictions, the Bible offers a cohesive message of God's love, truth, and redemption for humanity.

Every word of God is flawless.
(PROVERBS 30:5)

Question: "How do we know the Bible we have today is the same as the original manuscripts? Hasn't it changed over time?"

Answer: The Bible we have today is one of the most well-preserved texts in history. This is proven by the sheer number of ancient manuscripts and the rigorous process of copying and verifying texts over centuries.

While there are minor differences between manuscripts, such as spelling or word order, none affect the core teachings or essential truths of the Bible. We can, therefore, have strong confidence that the Bible we read today reflects the original writings.

Your word, Lord, is eternal;
it stands firm in the heavens.
(Psalm 119:89)

THE BLENDED FAMILY

God's Recipe for Success

God's Heart on the Blended Family

God desires that a household be established upon His wisdom.

"By wisdom a house is built, and through understanding it is established" (PROVERBS 24:3).

God desires that you make a fresh start with your blended family without dwelling on the past.

"Forget the former things; not dwell on the past" (ISAIAH 43:18).

God desires that your blended family be filled with peace and encouragement.

"Let us therefore make every effort to do what leads to peace and to mutual edification" (ROMANS 14:19).

God desires unity within your blended family.

"How good and pleasant it is when God's people live together in unity!" (PSALM 133:1).

God desires that your blended family exhibit godly characteristics.

"As God's chosen people, holy and dearly loved, clothe yourselves with compassion, kindness, humility, gentleness and patience" (COLOSSIANS 3:12).

God desires that your blended family be wise and speak truth in love.

"The wise in heart are called discerning, and gracious words promote instruction" (PROVERBS 16:21).

God desires that your blended family resolve difficulties through forgiveness and love.

"Bear with each other and forgive one another if any of you has a grievance against someone. Forgive as the Lord forgave you" (COLOSSIANS 3:13).

God desires that your blended family grow in grace and persevere through trials together.

"Since we are surrounded by such a great cloud of witnesses, let us throw off everything that hinders and the sin that so easily entangles. And let us run with perseverance the race marked out for us" (HEBREWS 12:1).

God desires that your blended family honor the biblical parental roles.

"Honor your father and your mother, so that you may live long in the land the LORD your God is giving you" (EXODUS 20:12).

God desires that peace and gratitude rule in your blended family as a whole and as individuals.

"Let the peace of Christ rule in your hearts, since as members of one body you were called to peace. And be thankful" (COLOSSIANS 3:15).

"At the beginning the Creator 'made them male and female,' and said, 'For this reason a man will leave his father and mother and be united to his wife, and the two will become one flesh.'"
(MATTHEW 19:4–5)

Stages of Blended-Family Adjustments

1. **Fantasy Stage**—unrealistic expectations.
   - **The dream** of gaining happiness and wholeness through a new marriage.[43]
   - **The dream** of marrying a model parent who will love my children[44] and replace their absent parent.
   - **The dream** that I will love my spouse's children as my own.[45]
   - **The dream** that love is enough to conquer all problems.[46]
2. **Factual Stage**—reality sets in.
   - **The dream** of a unified family life is not reality.[47]
   - **The children are mourning** their lost parent and are not accepting the stepparent.[48]
   - **The transition** to a new family becomes more difficult than expected.
   - **The problems** seem too difficult, with a strong temptation to give up.
3. **Fruitful Stage**—growth and maturity.
   - **The realization** that a blended family is not ideal.
   - **The realization** that it is going to take the cooperation of both partners to make the marriage work.
   - **The realization** that it may be years before there are any signs of unity or smooth-functioning relationships.
   - **The realization** that God will use this blended family as a source of spiritual growth, a means of healing the past, and a demonstration of His unconditional love.

A blended family is like a jagged jigsaw puzzle. If you force the pieces to fit, you destroy the potential design. If you wait for God to work it, the picture comes—in time.

—June Hunt

Let the peace of Christ rule in your hearts,
since as members of one body you were
called to peace. And be thankful.
(COLOSSIANS 3:15)

Insights for the Instant Parent

Realize that becoming an instant parent is a challenging task.[49]

Remember that you're not replacing a parent; you're offering a new relationship.[50]

Rebuild a gradual authority system to function by biblical guidelines.[51]

Reflect the love of God by providing security for each child.[52]

Refuse to judge or criticize the missing parent.[53]

Resist the temptation to withdraw emotionally if you are not immediately accepted.

Key Verse to Memorize

Let us therefore make every effort to do what leads to peace and to mutual edification.
(ROMANS 14:19)

Resolve to pray for each child and for your marriage.[54]

Relinquish your right to be respected and loved.[55]

Preparing Children

Meet alone with your own children.

Communicate your unconditional love for them.

State your belief that remarriage is God's direction for your life.

Share the positive future you see for them.

Encourage them to be open and to share their feelings.

Explain that the stepparent *will not* replace their natural parent.

Make your marriage commitment clear.

Ask for their help in this transition.

Communicate their secure position.

Let them know that Christ will be the center of their new family.

Gracious words are a honeycomb,
sweet to the soul and healing to the bones.
(PROVERBS 16:24)

Blended-Family Bonding

B—Build a solid relationship with your spouse.

"That is why a man leaves his father and mother and is united to his wife, and they become one flesh" (GENESIS 2:24).

O—Observe family traditions and holidays with flexibility.[56]

"Be devoted to one another in love. Honor one another above yourselves" (ROMANS 12:10).

N—Nurture the children's nuclear family relationships.[57]

"Honor your father and your mother, so that you may live long in the land the LORD your God is giving you" (EXODUS 20:12).

D—Determine to stand firm.

"A rod and a reprimand impart wisdom, but a child left undisciplined disgraces its mother. . . . Discipline your children, and they will give you peace; they will bring you the delights you desire" (PROVERBS 29:15, 17).

I—Initiate family structure.[58]

"The LORD disciplines those he loves, as a father the son he delights in" (PROVERBS 3:12).

N—Negotiate mutual ground.[59]

"I appeal to you, brothers and sisters, in the name of our Lord Jesus Christ, that all of you agree with one another in what you say and that there may be no divisions among you, but that you be perfectly united in mind and thought" (1 CORINTHIANS 1:10).

G—Grow in dependence upon Christ.

"Just as you received Christ Jesus as Lord, continue to live your lives in him, rooted and built up in him, strengthened in the faith as you were taught, and overflowing with thankfulness" (COLOSSIANS 2:6–7).

The Shared Custody Shuffle

If you share custody, remember to do the following when a child returns to your home:

Stop what you are doing and greet with a warm hug.

Allow reentry time, then give focused attention.

Ask nonthreatening questions.

Expect children to try to manipulate your feelings.

Don't assume all they say is true.

Distance yourself emotionally from any anger.

My Personalized Plan

Grow in my dependence upon Christ.

— I will find my personal identity in Christ.

— I will not depend on others for my happiness.

"I have been crucified with Christ and I no longer live, but Christ lives in me. The life I now live in the body, I live by faith in the Son of God, who loved me and gave himself for me" (GALATIANS 2:20).

Build a solid relationship with my spouse.

— I will keep Christ at the center of the relationship.

— I will face difficulties with a united front.

"That is why a man leaves his father and mother and is united to his wife, and they become one flesh" (GENESIS 2:24).

Nurture the children's nuclear family relationships.

— I will respect the other parent's rights.

— I will encourage communication with all grandparents and relatives.

"Show proper respect to everyone" (1 PETER 2:17).

Key Passage to Read

Colossians 3:12–15

Maintain family structure.

— I will honor the God-given roles of husband, wife, parents, and children.

— I will establish well-defined boundaries and maintain consistent discipline.

"Wives, submit yourselves to your husbands, as is fitting in the Lord. Husbands, love your wives and do not be harsh with them. Children, obey your parents in everything, for this pleases the Lord. Fathers, do not embitter your children, or they will become discouraged" (COLOSSIANS 3:18–21).

Negotiate mutual ground.

— I will encourage open and honest communication.

— I will have frequent family meetings and devotions.

"If it is possible, as far as it depends on you, live at peace with everyone" (ROMANS 12:18).

Observe family traditions and holidays with flexibility.

— I will be aware of various family expectations.

— I will be considerate of children who are caught in the middle.

"Be devoted to one another in love. Honor one another above yourselves" (ROMANS 12:10).

Choose to love firmly with godly values.

— I will not expect a problem-free family but will anticipate trials.

— I will choose to love my family as Christ has loved me.

"A new command I give you: Love one another. As I have loved you, so you must love one another" (JOHN 13:34).

Questions & Answers

Question: "I have two children from a previous marriage, and my husband has three. His teenage son lives with us, along with my teenage daughter and preteen son. We constantly disagree on discipline. My husband rarely disciplines his son but is very critical of my children. This is causing a lot of anger, and I'm not sure our relationship will survive. How can we overcome these serious differences?"

Answer: It's common for spouses to prioritize their own children, but when their interests come before those of the marriage and family unit, division follows. Though blended families are complex, there is hope. You and your husband must agree on acceptable behavior and discipline for all children. Do nothing until you have a shared policy. As you learn to take each other's feelings into account and agree in other areas, you'll begin acting in the best interest of the entire family.[60]

Let each of you should look not only to his own interests,
but also to the interests of others.
(PHILIPPIANS 2:4 ESV)

BOUNDARIES

How to Set Them—How to Keep Them

God's Heart on Boundaries

Treat one another with respect.

"Show proper respect to everyone" (1 PETER 2:17).

Listen to one another and consider our words before we speak.

"Everyone should be quick to listen, slow to speak" (JAMES 1:19).

Do not lie, but speak truthfully from the heart.

"Each of you must put off falsehood and speak truthfully to your neighbor" (EPHESIANS 4:25).

Say *yes* or *no* without lengthy justification or feeling guilty.

"All you need to say is simply 'Yes' or 'No'" (MATTHEW 5:37).

Give and accept correction while refraining from flattery.

"Whoever rebukes a person will in the end gain favor rather than one who has a flattering tongue" (PROVERBS 28:23).

Confront one another with love, grace, and truth when we sin against one other.

"If your brother or sister sins, go and point out their fault, just between the two of you. If they listen to you, you have won them over" (MATTHEW 18:15).

Express anger in a helpful, not hurtful manner.

"In your anger do not sin" (EPHESIANS 4:26).

Take responsibility for doing wrong and forgive others when we've been wronged.

"Be kind and compassionate to one another, forgiving each other, just as in Christ God forgave you" (EPHESIANS 4:32).

Encourage one another—verbally, emotionally, and spiritually.

"Let us not neglect our meeting together . . . but encourage one another" (HEBREWS 10:25 NLT).

Practice mutual submission.

"Submit to one another out of reverence for Christ" (EPHESIANS 5:21).

Remove ourselves from abusive situations.

"Do not make friends with a hot-tempered person, do not associate with one easily angered" (PROVERBS 22:24).

Refuse to stay in a relationship if either of us is negatively influencing the other.

"Do not be misled: 'Bad company corrupts good character'" (1 CORINTHIANS 15:33).

Live in harmony with one another.
Do not be proud. . . . Do not be conceited.
(ROMANS 12:16)

Checklist for Broken Boundaries

- ☐ I have difficulty making decisions and sticking with them.
- ☐ I feel like I must seek the opinions of others before acting on a decision.
- ☐ I fear expressing what I really feel.
- ☐ I lack confidence in my own convictions.
- ☐ I avoid certain people because I fear I might be embarrassed.
- ☐ I am reluctant to ask others for help.
- ☐ I dread losing the love and affection of others.
- ☐ I do favors for others even when I know I shouldn't.
- ☐ I avoid asking people to return overdue items they've borrowed.
- ☐ I need a great deal of assurance from others.
- ☐ I ignore untruthfulness in others by failing to correct them.
- ☐ I have difficulty opposing unfair situations.
- ☐ I typically listen to a telemarketer even when I want to say, "No, thank you."
- ☐ I feel compelled to send money when I receive solicitations or requests for donations.
- ☐ I feel guilty when I say *no* to someone who is asking for my time.
- ☐ I sometimes accept the blame for the mistakes of others.
- ☐ I feel guilty when someone suffers a repercussion for breaking a boundary I set.

What Experiences Help Us Learn Boundaries?

We learn boundaries as we observe and experience the natural laws of God's created world.

We learn boundaries from parents and other authorities who model boundaries as they teach, encourage, and correct in love.[61]

We learn boundaries in our relationships with family, friends, and others.

Key Verse to Memorize

The Spirit God gave us does not make us timid, but gives us power, love and self-discipline.
(2 Timothy 1:7)

We learn boundaries as we understand that we are to reflect God's character.

We learn boundaries from making mistakes and from the consequences of our own poor choices.

We learn boundaries from the wisdom we gain from our own interactions, then by applying what really works.

"Forget the former things;
do not dwell on the past.
See, I am doing a new thing!"
(Isaiah 43:18–19)

Five Biblical Truths About Boundaries

1. **Loving others** requires boundaries.
   "We love because he first loved us" (1 John 4:19).

2. **Obeying God** demands boundaries.
   "There is no fear in love. But perfect love drives out fear, because fear has to do with punishment. The one who fears is not made perfect in love" (1 John 4:18).

3. **Serving others** necessitates boundaries.
   "Carry each other's burdens, and in this way you will fulfill the law of Christ. . . . For each one should carry their own load" (Galatians 6:2, 5).

4. **Submission** depends on boundaries.
   "You know that the household of Stephanas . . . devoted themselves to the service of the Lord's people. I urge you . . . submit to such people and to everyone who joins in the work and labors at it" (1 Corinthians 16:15–16).

5. **Selfishness** cannot survive boundaries.

"Follow God's example, therefore, as dearly loved children and walk in the way of love, just as Christ loved us and gave himself up for us as a fragrant offering and sacrifice to God" (EPHESIANS 5:1–2).

Six Steps for Success

1. **Admit** you have a problem and need a solution.
   "Search me, God, and know my heart; test me and know my anxious thoughts. See if there is any offensive way in me, and lead me in the way everlasting" (PSALM 139:23–24).

2. **Be aware** there will be times when you want to resist the hard work of change.
   "You desired faithfulness even in the womb; you taught me wisdom in that secret place" (PSALM 51:6).

3. **Care** about yourself.
   "With minds that are alert and fully sober, set your hope on the grace to be brought to you when Jesus Christ is revealed at his coming" (1 PETER 1:13).

4. **Don't try to set** new boundaries all at once.
   "Consider it pure joy, my brothers and sisters, whenever you face trials of many kinds, because you know that the testing of your faith produces perseverance. Let perseverance finish its work so that you may be mature and complete, not lacking anything" (JAMES 1:2–4).

5. **Enforce** your boundaries consistently.
   "Physical training is good, but training for godliness is much better, promising benefits in this life and in the life to come" (1 TIMOTHY 4:8 NLT).

6. **Face** the future and resist the urge to fall back into old, unhealthy patterns.
   "You need to persevere so that when you have done the will of God, you will receive what he has promised" (HEBREWS 10:36).

Those who hope in the LORD
will renew their strength.
They will soar on wings like eagles;
they will run and not grow weary,
they will walk and not be faint.
(ISAIAH 40:31)

Maintaining Boundaries

Pay attention to your feelings and watch for early warning signs that you are beginning to lose sight of your boundaries.

"Be on your guard; stand firm in the faith; be courageous; be strong. Do everything in love" (1 CORINTHIANS 16:13–14).

Plan ahead by role-playing with a friend or even by yourself in front of a mirror on how to say *no.*

"The fruit of the Spirit is love, joy, peace, forbearance, kindness, goodness, faithfulness, gentleness and self-control. Against such things there is no law" (GALATIANS 5:22–23).

Recognize that the guilty feelings you may have over setting appropriate boundaries is false guilt. It is healthy for you to establish and maintain personal boundaries.

"Whoever disregards discipline comes to poverty and shame, but whoever heeds correction is honored" (PROVERBS 13:18).

Rejoice as you continue to keep your personal boundaries and find yourself set free.

"Rejoice always . . . give thanks in all circumstances; for this is God's will for you in Christ Jesus" (1 THESSALONIANS 5:16, 18).

Key Passage to Read

Romans 13:1–14

My Personalized Plan

B—Build healthy boundaries.

"The LORD is my strength and my shield; my heart trusts in him, and he helps me" (PSALM 28:7).

O—Overcome the fear of others' disapproval of my boundaries.

"We are not trying to please people but God, who tests our hearts" (1 THESSALONIANS 2:4).

U—Understand that boundaries are biblical.

"I am the LORD your God; consecrate yourselves and be holy, because I am holy" (LEVITICUS 11:44).

N—Notify others of my boundaries (family, friends, coworkers).

"Speaking the truth in love, we will grow to become in every respect the mature body of him who is the head, that is, Christ" (EPHESIANS 4:15).

D—Develop relationships with people who have healthy boundaries.

"Walk with the wise and become wise, for a companion of fools suffers harm" (PROVERBS 13:20).

A—Admit my limitations and keep on trying.

"Bear with each other and forgive one another if any of you has a grievance against someone. Forgive as the Lord forgave you" (COLOSSIANS 3:13).

R—Realize my need to set and maintain new boundaries.

"Forget the former things; do not dwell on the past. See, I am doing a new thing! Now it springs up; do you not perceive it? I am making a way in the wilderness and streams in the wasteland" (ISAIAH 43:18–19).

I—Identify healthy boundaries for myself and commit to maintaining them.

"My words come from an upright heart; my lips sincerely speak what I know" (JOB 33:3).

E—Encourage my family members to establish and honor boundaries.

"May the God who gives endurance and encouragement give you the same attitude of mind toward each other that Christ Jesus had" (ROMANS 15:5).

S—See my identity in Christ.

"He chose us in him before the creation of the world. . . . In love he predestined us for adoption to sonship through Jesus Christ, in accordance with his pleasure and will. . . . In him [Christ] *we have redemption through his blood, the forgiveness of sins, in accordance with the riches of God's grace"* (EPHESIANS 1:4–5, 7).

Questions & Answers

Question: "As a Christian, I'm taught to be unselfish, patient, and generous—to love others as much as I love myself. Given those parameters, how do I maintain healthy boundaries?"

Answer: Appropriate boundaries are not selfish or unloving. As a Christian, you can continue to be generous with your time and attention without having to be available to anyone and everyone all of the time.

With boundaries, we are able to juggle togetherness and separateness by creating and maintaining that delicate balance in our relationships. We do this by keeping our relationship with God in the proper place of *priority*, others in a proper place of *importance*, and ourselves in a proper place of *perspective*. When God comes first and people come second, we have godly *companionship* with one another.

Jesus replied: "'Love the Lord
your God with all your heart
and with all your soul and with all your mind.'
This is the first and greatest commandment.
And the second is like it:
'Love your neighbor as yourself.'"
(MATTHEW 22:37-39)

Question: "Why do I as a parent need to set boundaries for my children?"

Answer: Boundaries demonstrate your loving care. As a parent, you should not feel guilty when setting and maintaining boundaries. You are loving well when you hold the line on limits.

Discipline your children, and they will give you peace;
they will bring you the delights you desire.
(PROVERBS 29:17)

BULLYING

Bullied—No More

God's Heart on Bullying

God sees your pain and cares about your suffering.

"You have seen my troubles, and you care about the anguish of my soul" (Psalm 31:7 NLT).

God understands the pain of being bullied, harassed, and abused.

"He [Jesus] *was despised and rejected by mankind, a man of suffering, and familiar with pain. Like one from whom people hide their faces he was despised, and we held him in low esteem"* (Isaiah 53:3).

God offers healing to those who have been hurt by bullying.

"He heals the brokenhearted and binds up their wounds" (Psalm 147:3).

God can redeem your painful experiences and use them for His good purposes.

"You intended to harm me, but God intended it for good to accomplish what is now being done, the saving of many lives" (Genesis 50:20).

God calls for bullies to change their abusive, violent ways.

"Give up your violence and oppression and do what is just and right" (Ezekiel 45:9).

God offers complete forgiveness to those who turn to Him in repentance.

"If we confess our sins, he is faithful and just and will forgive us our sins and purify us from all unrighteousness" (1 John 1:9).

God wants bystanders to intervene and help those who are being hurt by bullies.

"Do not withhold good from those to whom it is due, when it is in your power to act" (Proverbs 3:27).

God does not want bystanders to turn a blind eye to those being bullied and treated unjustly.

"Rescue those being led away to death; hold back those staggering toward slaughter. If you say, 'But we knew nothing about this,' does not he who weighs the heart perceive it? Does not he who guards your life know it? Will he not repay everyone according to what they have done?" (Proverbs 24:11–12).

God will hold each person accountable for their actions, including bullies and bystanders.

"Nothing in all creation is hidden from God's sight. Everything is uncovered and laid bare before the eyes of him to whom we must give account" (HEBREWS 4:13).

God wants you to defend and stand up for the oppressed, weak, and bullied.

"Defend the weak and the fatherless; uphold the cause of the poor and the oppressed" (PSALM 82:3).

Types of Bullying

Bullies target their victims in multiple categories:

School bullying is commonly committed by (1) stronger students or peers targeting weaker students, (2) occasionally, coaches and teachers targeting certain vulnerable students, and (3) least frequently, students targeting a teacher.

Home or domestic bullying is usually committed by (1) husbands targeting wives, (2) wives targeting husbands, and (3) fathers, mothers, or older siblings targeting a younger child.

Cyberbullying is most frequently committed by young persons who use electronic media—such as email, text messages, and social media—to intentionally target others.

Workplace bullying is typically committed by employers or employees who intimidate others.

Disabled bullying is committed by anyone who targets those with mental, psychological, or physical disabilities.

Elder bullying, called "elder abuse," is usually committed by (1) family members who target dependent elders living at home or (2) caregivers in facilities, such as retirement and nursing homes.

Spiritual bullying, called "spiritual abuse," is committed by religious leaders who misuse their position to target people under their authority. The Bible refers to these leaders as false shepherds and false teachers.

Key Verses to Memorize

For the Bully

"God opposes the proud
but shows favor to the humble."
Humble yourselves, therefore,
under God's mighty hand,
that he may lift you up in due time.
(1 PETER 5:5–6)

For the Bullied

He heals the brokenhearted
and binds up their wounds.
(PSALM 147:3)

Not a word from their mouth can be trusted;
their heart is filled with malice.
Their throat is an open grave;
with their tongues they tell lies.
(PSALM 5:9)

Fallacies vs. Facts of Bullying

Top 10 Fallacies About Bullying[62]

1. **Bullying** is normal—simply a rite of passage.
2. **Bullying** doesn't do any real harm.
3. **Bullying** is blatant.
4. **Bullying** is quickly stopped because it draws so much attention.
5. **Bullying** is a rare occurrence.
6. **Bullies** are underachievers with low self-worth.
7. **Bullies** are noticeable and easily recognized.
8. **Bullies** aren't popular or highly regarded by others.
9. **Bullies** eventually mature and grow out of bullying behavior.
10. **Bullies** will always be bullies and victims will always be victims.

Top 10 Facts About Bullying

1. **Bullying** is inexcusable and can never be dismissed as just "kids being kids."
2. **Bullying** causes great emotional and psychological pain.
3. **Bullying** is subtle and sinister—it mostly happens out of the sight of adults—in school hallways, cafeterias, bathrooms, and on school buses.
4. **Bullying** often goes undetected because victims feel too much shame and embarrassment to report it, feeling it is an indictment of their own inadequacies.
5. **Bullying** is experienced by about one in five school children (19.2%) among ages twelve through eighteen.[63]

6. **Bullies** carefully hone their arsenal of attack and deliberately develop their destructive demeanor. They gain notice through notoriety and often think they are superior to others.

7. **Bullies** appear "normal" and can hide behind a mask of friendship.

8. **Bullies** perceive and project popularity through power.

9. **Bullies** are more likely to engage in risky or harmful behavior in adulthood (abusive behaviors as a spouse or parent, criminal behavior, alcohol or drug abuse).[64]

10. **Bullies** can change. The reality is *not* "once a bully, always a bully." For those willing to change, the Bible says, *"I will give you a new heart and put a new spirit in you; I will remove from you your heart of stone and give you a heart of flesh. And I will put my Spirit in you and move you to follow my decrees and be careful to keep my laws"* (Ezekiel 36:26–27).

Seeking Help

1. **Find** someone you trust.

2. **Be** completely honest.

3. **Learn** to say *no.*

4. **Ask** about what kinds of social skills or techniques might help overcome or prevent bullying.

5. **Remain** calm.

6. **Finally, never give up!** If you look for help but don't find it, keep looking. Tell your story to others until you find the help that you need.

"Be strong and courageous. Do not be afraid;
do not be discouraged, for the LORD your God
will be with you wherever you go."
(JOSHUA 1:9)

My Personalized Plan

As the bully, **I will . . .**

Assess personal pain from my past.

— I will determine if I have buried pain from being a victim of bullying myself.

— I will evaluate how pain from my past affects my present behavior.

— I will consider how my bullying others attempts to illegitimately meet my unmet needs.

"If your brother or sister sins, go and point out their fault, just between the two of you. If they listen to you, you have won them over" (MATTHEW 18:15).

Choose to obey God's commands.

— I will be kind to the weak and oppressed.

— I will value those who are bullied because they are made in God's image.

— I will defend those who cannot defend themselves.

Key Passage to Read

Proverbs 6:16–19

"Be devoted to one another in love. Honor one another above yourselves" (ROMANS 12:10).

Seek forgiveness and restoration.

— I will confess the sin of bullying to God, asking Him to change my heart.

— I will ask forgiveness from those I've bullied.

— I will attempt to build a relationship with those whom I have hurt.

"If it is possible, as far as it depends on you, live at peace with everyone" (ROMANS 12:18).

As the one bullied, I will . . .

Grasp the immeasurable worth of every person.

— I will recognize that God does not favor the strong over the weak.

— I will remember that God uniquely gifts every person and has a unique plan for my life.

— I will find peace and hope in the unconditional love of God.

"But he [Jesus] *said to me, 'My grace is sufficient for you, for my power is made perfect in weakness'"* (2 CORINTHIANS 12:9).

Enlist help from God and others.

— I will avoid any tendencies to isolate based on my fear and shame.

— I will pray continually for God's intervention and resolution when I'm in a bullying situation.

— I will share troubling incidents with those who can be trusted to offer compassionate, biblical counsel.

"Trust in him at all times, you people; pour out your hearts to him, for God is our refuge" (Psalm 62:8).

Examine the need for forgiveness.

— I will meditate on Jesus' words and follow His example concerning forgiveness.

— I will pray for those who have bullied me and ask for God's healing in their lives.

— I will ask others for help with accountability in sustaining a forgiving heart.

"Bear with each other and forgive one another if any of you has a grievance against someone. Forgive as the Lord forgave you" (Colossians 3:13).

Questions & Answers

Question: "What is bullycide?"

Answer: "Bullycide" refers to "the act or an instance of killing oneself intentionally as a result of bullying."[65]

Some studies have suggested that those who experience bullying are more at risk for developing suicidal thoughts or feelings, as bullying can affect a person's mental, emotional, and physical health.[66] This underscores the importance of not being a bystander, but getting involved, knowing the warning signs of bullying and suicide, and helping those who are being bullied.

Learn to do good. Seek justice. Help the oppressed.
(Psalm 116:3 NLT)

Question: "One of my daughter's friends posted a mean message about another girl. My daughter says it's only a joke, but I'm concerned. What should I do?"

Answer: Don't assume the incident is not a "big deal." Explain to your daughter when she uses email, texts, or social media to intentionally intimidate, shame, or hurt others, it is *cyberbullying*, which is abusive, unacceptable, and can be considered a crime.

Though a cyberbully may hide behind a computer screen, God sees the wrong deeds done in secret and knows the wrong motives in each person's heart.

There is no deep shadow, no utter darkness,
where evildoers can hide.
(Job 34:22)

CAREGIVING

A Blessing, Not a Burden

God's Heart on Caregiving

God cares for you every day—throughout your lifetime.

"I have cared for you since you were born. Yes, I carried you before you were born. I will be your God throughout your lifetime—until your hair is white with age. I made you, and I will care for you. I will carry you along and save you" (ISAIAH 46:3–4 NLT).

God wants you to care for others.

"Take tender care of those who are weak. Be patient with everyone" (1 THESSALONIANS 5:14 NLT).

God will strengthen and sustain you as you care for others.

"Do not fear, for I am with you; do not be dismayed, for I am your God. I will strengthen you and help you; I will uphold you with my righteous right hand" (ISAIAH 41:10).

God wants you to care for others with the strength He provides.

"Do you have the gift of helping others? Do it with all the strength and energy that God supplies. Then everything you do will bring glory to God through Jesus Christ" (1 PETER 4:11 NLT).

God wants you to care for and serve others as if you were serving Christ.

"Whatever you do, work at it with all your heart, as working for the Lord, not for human masters, since you know that you will receive an inheritance from the Lord as a reward. It is the Lord Christ you are serving" (COLOSSIANS 3:23–24).

God wants you to recognize your limits and set boundaries.

"Above all else, guard your heart, for everything you do flows from it" (PROVERBS 4:23).

God wants you not to grow weary in your caregiving.

"Let us not become weary in doing good, for at the proper time we will reap a harvest if we do not give up" (GALATIANS 6:9).

God wants you not to neglect your own needs but to care for them as much as you address the needs of others.

"No one hates his own body but feeds and cares for it, just as Christ cares for the church" (EPHESIANS 5:29 NLT).

God wants to bear your burdens and take care of you when you feel overwhelmed.

"Give your burdens to the L*ORD, and he will take care of you. He will not permit the godly to slip and fall"* (PSALM 55:22 NLT).

God notices even the smallest acts of care—and He will reward them.

"If you give even a cup of cold water to one of the least of my followers, you will surely be rewarded" (MATTHEW 10:42 NLT).

For God is not unjust. He will not forget
how hard you have worked for him
and how you have shown your love to him
by caring for other believers, as you still do.
(HEBREWS 6:10 NLT)

Reflecting God's Heart through Caregiving

When you care for someone, you reflect the heart of God who *"cares for you"* (1 Peter 5:7).

When you help someone, you reflect the heart of God who is called *"my helper"* (Psalm 54:4 NLT).

When you welcome someone into your home, you reflect the heart of God who *"has welcomed you"* (Romans 15:7 ESV).

When you give someone food or help them eat, you reflect the heart of God who *"gives food to every creature"* (Psalm 136:25).

When you help someone find rest, you reflect the heart of God who *"gives rest to his loved ones"* (Psalm 127:2 NLT).

When you help someone get dressed, you reflect the heart of God who *"has dressed me with the clothing of salvation"* (Isaiah 61:10 NLT).

When you provide medical care to someone, you reflect the heart of God who *"heals the brokenhearted and binds up their wounds"* (Psalm 147:3).

When you help someone who has fallen, you reflect the heart of God who *"upholds all who fall and lifts up all who are bowed down"* (Psalm 145:14).

When you offer a gentle touch or supportive hand, you reflect the heart of God who *"takes hold of your right hand and says to you, Do not fear; I will help you"* (Isaiah 41:13).

When you help someone bathe or help clean their home, you reflect the heart of God who promises, *"I will sprinkle clean water on you, and you will be clean"* (Ezekiel 36:25).

When you help someone who is in danger or troubling circumstances, you reflect the heart of God who is *"always ready to help in times of trouble"* (Psalm 46:1 NLT).

When you help someone find a place to live and feel safe, you reflect the heart of God who is *"a shelter for the oppressed, a refuge in times of trouble"* (Psalm 9:9 NLT).

Key Verse to Memorize

"Let us not become weary in doing good, for at the proper time we will reap a harvest if we do not give up."
(GALATIANS 6:9)

When you listen to someone tell their story or share a memory, you reflect the heart of God who *"bends down to listen"* (Psalm 116:2 NLT).

When you sympathize with someone grieving or crying in pain, you reflect the heart of God who promises to *"wipe away every tear"* (Revelation 21:4).

When you provide loving, wise counsel to someone, you reflect the heart of God who *"counsel[s] you with my loving eye on you"* (Psalm 32:8).

When you simply sit with someone and keep them company, you reflect the heart of God who says, *"I am with you"* (Isaiah 41:10).

Characteristics of Unhealthy vs. Healthy Caregiving

Unhealthy Caregiving	Healthy Caregiving
Unreliable care	Dependable care
Rushed care	Planned and scheduled care
Burdened caregiver	Honored-to-serve caregiver
Stressed caregiving	Strengthened in caregiving
Exhausted caregiver	Well-rested caregiver
Overwhelmed caregiving	Shared responsibilities in caregiving
Martyr-like caregiver	Christlike caregiver

The Prison of Resentment

P—Physically exhausted—fatigued

R—Resentful—bitter and angry

I—Isolated—lonely and misunderstood

S—Stressed—guilty and torn

O—Overwhelmed—helpless

N—Neglected—unappreciated

"I cannot carry all these people by myself;
the burden is too heavy for me."
(NUMBERS 11:14)

The Caregiver's Crisis Checklist

- ☐ I get easily agitated with those I love.
- ☐ I become increasingly critical of others.
- ☐ I have difficulty laughing or having fun.
- ☐ I turn down most invitations to be with others.
- ☐ I feel depressed about my situation.
- ☐ I feel hurt when my efforts go unnoticed.
- ☐ I am resentful when other family members do not help.
- ☐ I feel trapped by all the responsibilities of caregiving.
- ☐ I feel manipulated by my care receiver.
- ☐ I miss sleep and regular exercise.
- ☐ I become so overwhelmed that my caregiving begins to suffer.
- ☐ I lose myself in the constant demands of caregiving.
- ☐ I frequently forfeit personal quiet time with God for my caregiving responsibilities.
- ☐ I feel guilty when I take time for myself.
- ☐ I am anxious due to feelings of inadequacy and fear of failure.

If you feel your stress has turned to distress, the Word of God says, "Cast all your anxiety on him because he cares for you" (1 Peter 5:7). Since God does care, He will empower you to change the behaviors that are hurting you.

Humble yourselves, therefore, under God's mighty hand,
that he may lift you up in due time.
Cast all your anxiety on him because he cares for you.
(1 PETER 5:6–7)

10 Practical Ways to Be a Healthier Caregiver[67]

1. **Be proactive.**

   "The prudent see danger and take refuge, but the simple keep going and pay the penalty" (PROVERBS 27:12).

2. **Find helpful resources.**

   "Let the wise hear and increase in learning, and the one who understands obtain guidance" (PROVERBS 1:5 ESV).

3. **Educate yourself.**

   "Instruct the wise and they will be wiser still; teach the righteous and they will add to their learning" (PROVERBS 9:9).

4. **Reach out to others.**

   "Two people are better off than one, for they can help each other succeed. If one person falls, the other can reach out and help. But someone who falls alone is in real trouble" (ECCLESIASTES 4:9–10 NLT).

5. **Know your limits.**

   "Guard your heart above all else, for it determines the course of your life" (PROVERBS 4:23 NLT).

6. **Pay attention to your stress level.**

   "As pressure and stress bear down on me, I find joy in your commands" (PSALM 119:143 NLT).

7. **Prepare for change.**

   "Do your planning and prepare your fields before building your house" (PROVERBS 24:27 NLT).

8. **Address legal and financial issues from the start.**

   "Plans fail for lack of counsel, but with many advisers they succeed" (PROVERBS 15:22).

9. **Give yourself grace, not guilt.**

   "By the grace of God I am what I am, and his grace to me was not without effect. No, I worked harder than all of them—yet not I, but the grace of God that was with me" (1 CORINTHIANS 15:10).

10. **Stay physically and spiritually healthy.**

"Do you not know that your bodies are temples of the Holy Spirit, who is in you, whom you have received from God? You are not your own; you were bought at a price. Therefore honor God with your bodies" (1 CORINTHIANS 6:19-20).

A heart at peace gives life to the body.
(PROVERBS 14:30)

My Personalized Plan

I will not try to do it all alone.

— **I will** learn to delegate to others.

— **I will** ask for help from family and friends or engage an outside support person.

"The LORD said to Moses: 'Bring me seventy of Israel's elders who are known to you as leaders and officials among the people. Have them come to the tent of meeting, that they may stand there with you. I will come down and speak with you there, and I will take some of the power of the Spirit that is on you and put it on them. They will share the burden of the people with you so that you will not have to carry it alone'" (NUMBERS 11:16-17).

I will not take things too seriously.

— **I will** focus on the positives of the situation.

— **I will** learn to laugh at little things and at myself.

"A cheerful heart is good medicine, but a crushed spirit dries up the bones" (PROVERBS 17:22).

I will not think my identity is found in meeting another's needs—to do so can quickly develop into codependency.

— **I will** realize that my identity is in Christ.

— **I will** know that God will meet my needs for meaning and purpose in my life.

"My old self has been crucified with Christ. It is no longer I who live, but Christ lives in me. So I live in this earthly body by trusting in the Son of God, who loved me and gave himself for me" (GALATIANS 2:20 NLT).

I will not repress my feelings of hurt and frustration.

— **I will** share my pain with a trusted friend.

— **I will** pour out my heart to the Lord.

"Trust in him at all times, you people; pour out your hearts to him, for God is our refuge" (PSALM 62:8).

I will not let myself become physically exhausted. Lack of rest is a setup for emotional vulnerability.

— **I will** set aside time to be alone—to exercise, pray, and do whatever revives and restores my spirit.

— **I will** set my own personal boundaries.

"Because so many people were coming and going that they did not even have a chance to eat, he said to them, 'Come with me by yourselves to a quiet place and get some rest.' So they went away by themselves in a boat to a solitary place" (MARK 6:31-32).

Key Passage to Read

Luke 10:25-37

I will not become spiritually depleted.

— **I will** thank God regularly for His blessings. I will call on Him for strength when I feel weak.

— **I will** increase the amount of time I spend in God's Word to gain hope and encouragement for the long haul.

"'My grace is sufficient for you, for my power is made perfect in weakness.' Therefore I will boast all the more gladly about my weaknesses, so that Christ's power may rest on me. That is why, for Christ's sake, I delight in weaknesses, in insults, in hardships, in persecutions, in difficulties. For when I am weak, then I am strong" (2 CORINTHIANS 12:9-10).

Questions & Answers

Question: "How should I treat a loved one who is stubborn and controlling?"

Answer: Apply the Golden Rule. Try to see the issue from the perspective of your loved one, and seek to understand the strong feelings being expressed. Try to determine what is behind the stubbornness. Then compassionately address these powerful underlying emotions.

"Do to others as you would have them do to you."
(LUKE 6:31)

Question: "Is affection important to a person receiving care?"

Answer: The need to feel loved, valued, and accepted is universal. Hugs, kisses, and loving touches communicate affection. If someone you care about is not comfortable with physical affection, then communicate your love in a nonphysical manner—with smiles, a gentle tone of voice, and caring words.

Do everything in love.
(1 CORINTHIANS 16:14)

CHILD EVANGELISM

Sharing the Savior with a Child

God's Heart on Child Evangelism

God loves all children and invites them to come to Him.

"Jesus called the children to him and said, 'Let the little children come to me, and do not hinder them, for the kingdom of God belongs to such as these'" (LUKE 18:16).

God loved us first.

"We love because he first loved us" (1 JOHN 4:19).

God made a way to take care of our sin.

"We all, like sheep, have gone astray, each of us has turned to our own way; and the LORD has laid on him the iniquity of us all" (ISAIAH 53:6).

God redeems and restores us through Jesus.

"God so loved the world that he gave his one and only Son, that whoever believes in him shall not perish but have eternal life" (JOHN 3:16).

God forgives our sins and makes us righteous through Christ.

"If we confess our sins, he is faithful and just and will forgive us our sins and purify us from all unrighteousness" (1 JOHN 1:9).

God promises to be with us always, so we don't have to be afraid.

"The LORD himself goes before you and will be with you; he will never leave you nor forsake you. Do not be afraid; do not be discouraged" (DEUTERONOMY 31:8).

God is near, so we can always come to Him.

"Come near to God and he will come near to you" (JAMES 4:8).

God knows each and every person.

"You have searched me, LORD, and you know me" (PSALM 139:1).

God is worthy of all our love.

"Love the LORD your God with all your heart and with all your soul and with all your strength" (DEUTERONOMY 6:5).

God is trustworthy, and promises to lead us well.

"Trust in the LORD with all your heart and lean not on your own understanding; in all your ways submit to him, and he will make your paths straight" (PROVERBS 3:5–6).

Children Are READY to Hear the Gospel When They Are . . .

R—Reaping consequences from their own behavior

E—Expressing worry about the future

A—Asking a lot of questions

D—Drastically changing their behavior

Y—Yielding to positive authority

Evangelism

The gospel is the good message of salvation available to us through faith in Christ and His finished work on the cross.

— **The gospel** comes from the Greek word *euaggelion*, which means "good message, good news."[68]

Child evangelism is sharing with a child the good news of how to receive the full forgiveness of God by entering into a personal relationship with Christ Jesus.

— ***Evangelism*** is the Greek word *euaggelizo*, which means "to bring good news."[69]

How to Present the Good News

G—God: "God created everything in this world, including you. He loves you and will always love you."

"In the beginning God created the heavens and the earth" (GENESIS 1:1).

O—Original Sin: "There is a problem between you and God, and it is called sin. Sin is anything you think or do that does not please God. Sin is going your own way instead of God's way."

"Surely I was sinful at birth, sinful from the time my mother conceived me" (PSALM 51:5).

O—Offering for Sin: "Jesus came from heaven to earth, lived in a body and grew . . . just like you and I grow."

"God so loved the world that he gave his one and only Son, that whoever believes in him shall not perish but have eternal life" (JOHN 3:16).

D—Death and Resurrection: "The Lord Jesus Christ died for your sins, but He also did something no one else has ever done—He came back to life!"

"Christ died for our sins according to the Scriptures . . . he was buried . . . he was raised on the third day according to the Scriptures, and . . . he appeared to Cephas [Peter], *and then to the Twelve. After that, he appeared to more than five hundred of the brothers and sisters at the same time, most of whom are still living, though some have fallen asleep. Then he appeared to James, then to all the apostles, and last of all he appeared to me also, as to one abnormally born"* (1 CORINTHIANS 15:3–8).

N—Need: "We all need a Savior because our sin is a problem."

"God did not send his Son into the world to condemn the world, but to save the world through him. Whoever believes in him is not condemned, but whoever does not believe stands condemned already because they have not believed in the name of God's one and only Son" (JOHN 3:17–18).

E—Eternal Life: "God's part is found in three promises to us."

— "We will not be condemned to hell for our sins."

"There is now no condemnation for those who are in Christ Jesus" (ROMANS 8:1).

— "We will live forever in heaven."

"Whoever lives by believing in me will never die" (JOHN 11:26).

— "Meanwhile, God will cause us to live a different kind of life now while we live on earth."

"He who began a good work in you will carry it on to completion" (PHILIPPIANS 1:6).

W—Word of God: "The Bible was supernaturally written by God."

"All Scripture is God-breathed and is useful for teaching, rebuking, correcting and training in righteousness" (2 TIMOTHY 3:16).

S—Salvation Prayer: "God invites us all to come to Him."

— Give an invitation for the child to receive Christ.

— Remind them again of their need for a Savior.

"If we confess our sins, he is faithful and just and will forgive us our sins and purify us from all unrighteousness" (1 JOHN 1:9).

— Review what Christ has done.

"Christ also suffered once for sins, the righteous for the unrighteous, to bring you to God. He was put to death in the body but made alive in the Spirit" (1 PETER 3:18).

— Ask, "Would you like Jesus to be your personal Lord and Savior?"

"If you declare with your mouth, 'Jesus is Lord,' and believe in your heart that God raised him from the dead, you will be saved" (ROMANS 10:9).

"Dear God, I know I do things You tell me not to do, and You call that sin. I realize that my sin has separated me from You. Please forgive me for my sins. Lord Jesus, thank You for taking the punishment that I should have had—You paid the price for my sins by dying on the cross for me. Right now I ask You to come into my life to be my Lord and my Savior. I want to be what You want me to be. And I want to do what You want me to do. Amen."

Preparing a Child's Heart

Portray the character of Christ.

"In everything set them an example by doing what is good. In your teaching show integrity, seriousness and soundness of speech that cannot be condemned" (TITUS 2:7–8).

Praise God in the presence of your child for specific blessings.

"I will extol the LORD at all times; his praise will always be on my lips" (PSALM 34:1).

Play and sing Christian songs with your child.

"Shout with joy to God, all the earth! Sing the glory of his name; make his praise glorious!" (PSALM 66:1–2).

Place pictures with a spiritual emphasis throughout your home.

"Love the LORD your God with all your heart and with all your soul and with all your strength. These commandments that I give you today are to be on your hearts. Impress them on your children. . . . Write them on the doorframes of your houses and on your gates" (DEUTERONOMY 6:5–7, 9).

Provide a regular time to read and talk about Scripture.

"Continue in what you have learned and have become convinced of, because you know those from whom you learned it, and how from infancy you have known the Holy Scriptures, which are able to make you wise for salvation through faith in Christ Jesus" (2 TIMOTHY 3:14–15).

Prepare Scripture memory verses on cutout forms or cards.

"I have hidden your word in my heart that I might not sin against you" (PSALM 119:11).

Pray out loud with and for your child.

"We have not stopped praying for you. We continually ask God to fill you with the knowledge of his will through all the wisdom and understanding that the Spirit gives, so that you may live a life worthy of the Lord and may please him in every way: bearing fruit in every good work, growing in the knowledge of God" (COLOSSIANS 1:9–10).

Prioritize regular spiritual programs for your child.

"Start children off on the way they should go, and even when they are old they will not turn from it" (PROVERBS 22:6).

Play creative games that bring God into focus.

"I have no greater joy than to hear that my children are walking in the truth" (3 JOHN V. 4).

I am reminded of your sincere faith,
which first lived in your grandmother Lois
and in your mother Eunice and, I am persuaded,
now lives in you also.
(2 TIMOTHY 1:5)

Vocabulary for Kids

Death, physical: when the real you—your spirit—leaves your body

Death, eternal: when a person is separated from God forever in a place of darkness and punishment

Faith: believing God will do what He says He will do

Saved/Salvation: trusting Jesus to forgive your sin, which means He won't punish you for doing wrong. He lives with you now and you will live with Him forever in heaven.

Key Verse to Memorize

"Truly I tell you, unless you change
and become like little children,
you will never enter the kingdom of heaven."
(MATTHEW 18:3)

My Personalized Plan

I will . . .

Consider the importance of children to Jesus.

— I will be a good example of Christ's love to the children in my life, listening to them and developing a relationship with them.

— I will provide space for questions, always keeping the lines of communication open, being patient and kind in my responses.

"At that time the disciples came to Jesus and asked, 'Who, then, is the greatest in the kingdom of heaven?' He called a little child to him, and placed the child among them. And he said: 'Truly I tell you, unless you change and become like little children, you will never enter the kingdom of heaven. Therefore, whoever takes the lowly position of this child is the greatest in the kingdom of heaven. And whoever welcomes one such child in my name welcomes me'" (MATTHEW 18:1–5).

Key Passage to Read

Psalm 78:2–7

Cover my children in daily prayer, paying close attention to their readiness and responsiveness to receive Jesus as their Savior.

— I will pray daily for and with my children, remembering they often model what they see the adults in their lives doing.

— I will tell my children Bible stories, remembering God has given them vivid imaginations to visualize the biblical truths I am sharing.

"Pray in the Spirit on all occasions with all kinds of prayers and requests" (EPHESIANS 6:18).

Cultivate my children's faith by modeling a Christ-centered life and teaching them to love Jesus.

— I will help them memorize Scripture, prioritize church and spiritual community, and let them experience life among fellow believers.

— I will always protect them, remembering their value to Jesus and ensuring I never cause them to stumble.

"I have no greater joy than to hear that my children are walking in the truth" (3 JOHN V. 4).

Commit my ways to the Lord and be open to sharing the love of Christ with all children.

— I will admit that while I may feel inadequate, the Holy Spirit will give me the power I need to share His truth.

— I will always find positive ways of sharing Christ's love with children, diverting from using fear or negative tactics.

"Let your conversation be gracious and attractive so that you will have the right response for everyone" (COLOSSIANS 4:6 NLT).

Coach and challenge my children to share Christ's love with others, growing in their walk with the Lord.

- — I will encourage my children to serve others, using their God-given gifts to serve the Lord.
- — I will encourage my children to follow Jesus, even when they experience difficulties and trials.

"Serve one another humbly in love" (GALATIANS 5:13).

Questions & Answers

Question: "At what age is a child old enough to understand the need and means of salvation?"

Answer: The Bible does not specify a minimum age for salvation. A child is ready when they recognize their sin, understand that Jesus paid the penalty for their sin through His death, and personally trust Him as their Savior.

Salvation is not based on knowing every doctrine but on a simple, genuine faith in Christ. When a child understands that they are a sinner and that Jesus saves those who believe in Him, they can repent, trust in Christ, and be saved.

Just as a newborn grows physically, those who are spiritually "born again" mature in their faith over time. Parents and mentors play a vital role in nurturing that growth.

Jesus called the children to him and said,
"Let the little children come to me,
and do not hinder them, for the kingdom of God
belongs to such as these."
(LUKE 18:16)

CHILDHOOD SEXUAL ABUSE

The Secret Storm

God's Heart on Childhood Sexual Abuse

God cares deeply about children—He welcomes them with open arms and blesses them.

"[Jesus] *said to them, 'Let the little children come to me, and do not hinder them, for the kingdom of God belongs to such as these.' . . . And he took the children in his arms, placed his hands on them and blessed them"* (Mark 10:14, 16).

God wants everyone to protect and defend the weak—especially children.

"Defend the weak and the fatherless; uphold the cause of the poor and the oppressed. Rescue the weak and the needy; deliver them from the hand of the wicked" (Psalm 82:3–4).

God wants survivors of abuse to know there is hope.

"There is surely a future hope for you, and your hope will not be cut off" (Proverbs 23:18).

God cares about your pain.

"You have seen my troubles, and you care about the anguish of my soul" (Psalm 31:7 NLT).

God can heal the wounds of abuse.

"He heals the brokenhearted and binds up their wounds" (Psalm 147:3).

God sees you as precious in His sight.

"You are precious and honored in my sight, and . . . I love you" (Isaiah 43:4).

God Himself is with you—to help and uphold you each day.

"Don't be afraid, for I am with you. Don't be discouraged, for I am your God. I will strengthen you and help you. I will hold you up with my victorious right hand" (Isaiah 41:10 NLT).

God uses counselors and other wise, helpful people to bring healing and victory over abuse.

"Where there is no guidance the people fall, but in abundance of counselors there is victory" (Proverbs 11:14 NASB).

God wants you to help others who have experienced abusive treatment.

"The Father of compassion and the God of all comfort . . . comforts us in all our troubles, so that we can comfort those in any trouble with the comfort we ourselves receive from God" (2 CORINTHIANS 1:3–4).

God will judge and hold accountable every abuser for every act of abuse.

"For we must all stand before Christ to be judged. We will each receive whatever we deserve for the good or evil we have done in this earthly body" (2 CORINTHIANS 5:10 NLT).

God calls for the abuser to change.

"Let the wicked change their ways and banish the very thought of doing wrong. Let them turn to the LORD" (ISAIAH 55:7 NLT).

God will one day end all abuse and pain.

"He will wipe every tear from their eyes, and there will be no more death or sorrow or crying or pain. All these things are gone forever" (REVELATION 21:4 NLT).

You are a refuge from the storm.
(ISAIAH 25:4 NLT)

Checklist for Childhood Sexual Abuse

As a child, did you experience . . . ?

- ☐ **Voyeurism**
- ☐ **Exhibitionism**
- ☐ **Lewdness**
- ☐ **Pornography**
- ☐ **Child Pornography**
- ☐ **Masturbation**
- ☐ **Psychological Abuse**
- ☐ **Fondling**
- ☐ **Intimate Kissing**
- ☐ **Oral Sex**
- ☐ **Penetration/Rape**
- ☐ **Child Prostitution**
- ☐ **Satanic Ritual Abuse**

What the wicked dread will overtake them;
what the righteous desire will be granted.
When the storm has swept by, the wicked are gone,
but the righteous stand firm forever.
(Proverbs 10:24-25)

Profile of Child Abusers[70]

A—**Alcohol** or drug abuse

B—**Background** of abuse

U—**Unresolved** anger

S—**Sexual** addiction to pornography

E—**Emotional** immaturity

R—**Rigid,** religious background

S—**Stepfamilies** or family problems

Surface the Secret[71]

Pray for supernatural wisdom from God.

Provide a safe atmosphere, away from people and places that could be upsetting or intimidating.

Ask, "Have you been experiencing something uncomfortable or confusing? Has anyone ever touched you in ways that made you uncomfortable?"

Listen carefully, repeat what is said, and ask, "Did I get it right?"

Be cautious about asking leading questions, such as, "Did he do ____________ to you?"

Let authorities with an expertise in childhood sexual abuse ask most of the questions in order to determine the truth.

Communicate that you believe the child.

Key Verse to Memorize

"Be strong and courageous.
Do not be afraid or terrified because of them,
for the Lord your God goes with you;
he will never leave you nor forsake you."
(Deuteronomy 31:6)

Acknowledge that the offender is wrong.

Give assurance that the child is not to blame.

Confirm that "telling" is the right thing to do.

Resist reaching out with physical affection unless you ask permission: "Would you like for me to hold your hand?" . . . "Can I give you a hug?" Even if the answer is yes, if you sense a hesitation, slowly withdraw.

Provide a safe atmosphere by displaying genuine love and compassion.

The purposes of a person's heart are deep waters,
but one who has insight draws them out.
(PROVERBS 20:5)

Replace Lies with Truth

Lie: "I am worthless and unlovable."
Truth: You are loved and precious in God's sight.
"You are precious to me. You are honored, and I love you" (ISAIAH 43:4 NLT).

Lie: "I am dirty and unacceptable."
Truth: You are holy and accepted in Christ.
"Even before he made the world, God loved us and chose us in Christ to be holy and without fault in his eyes. God decided in advance to adopt us into his own family by bringing us to himself through Jesus Christ. This is what he wanted to do, and it gave him great pleasure" (EPHESIANS 1:4–5 NLT).

Lie: "What happened to me is my fault."
Truth: It's not your fault. Abuse is never the victim's fault. Your abuser is completely responsible.
"We are each responsible for our own conduct" (GALATIANS 6:5 NLT).

Lie: "My abuse defines me. I am a victim."
Truth: God defines you—you are His child.
"See what great love the Father has lavished on us, that we should be called children of God! And that is what we are!" (1 JOHN 3:1).

Lie: "God doesn't care about me or what happened to me."
Truth: God cares deeply about you and everything that happens to you.
"Cast all your anxiety on him because he cares for you" (1 PETER 5:7).

Lie: "God wasn't there for me and He isn't there for me now."

Truth: God is always with you. He will never leave you.

"The LORD himself goes before you and will be with you; he will never leave you nor forsake you. Do not be afraid; do not be discouraged" (DEUTERONOMY 31:8).

Dos and Don'ts of Awareness[72]

- **Do** be aware that child abuse is illegal, a crime that must be reported.
- **Do** be aware that children are usually abused by people they know.
- **Do** be aware that children seldom lie about abuse.
- **Do** be aware that most often physical abuse is violent, but sexual abuse is usually not violent.
- **Do** be aware that children may deny or change their stories because of fear.
- **Do** be aware that sexual abuse is progressive and will get worse if not stopped.
- **Don't** be in denial, no matter how difficult it is to believe.
- **Don't** assume that if it happened only once, it is not serious.
- **Don't** minimize the abuse.
- **Don't** let the offender go without confrontation.
- **Don't** blame other family members.
- **Don't** keep abuse a "family secret."

Key Passage to Read

Psalm 55

My Personalized Plan

As I seek to overcome the abuse I've experienced, **I will . . .**

Acknowledge there is hope.

"There is surely a future hope for you, and your hope will not be cut off" (PROVERBS 23:18).

Decide who to tell.

"Two people are better off than one, for they can help each other succeed. If one person falls, the other can reach out and help" (ECCLESIASTES 4:9–10 NLT).

Find support.

"In abundance of counselors there is victory" (PROVERBS 24:6 ESV).

Address physical problems.

"For physical training is of some value, but godliness has value for all things, holding promise for both the present life and the life to come" (1 TIMOTHY 4:8).

Replace lies with truth.

"You will know the truth, and the truth will set you free" (JOHN 8:32).

Help others.

"The Father of compassion and the God of all comfort . . . comforts us in all our troubles, so that we can comfort those in any trouble with the comfort we ourselves receive from God" (2 CORINTHIANS 1:3–4).

Look to the Lord.

"Look to the LORD and his strength; seek his face always" (1 CHRONICLES 16:11).

Questions & Answers

Question: "I prayed for God to stop the abuse—why didn't He?"

Answer: The question of why God allows suffering might be the most frequently asked question about God. Even the writers of Scripture boldly asked God about it. One prophet cried out, *"How long, LORD, must I call for help, but you do not listen? Or cry out to you, 'Violence!' but you do not save? . . . Why do you tolerate wrongdoing?"* (Habakkuk 1:2–3). Even Jesus, in His final excruciating moments on the cross, cried out, *"My God, my God, why have you forsaken me?"* (Mark 15:34).

One reason abuse or any kind of suffering occurs is free will. God gives every person free will. And at times we are all victims of the wrong choices and sins others commit.

However, the fact that the abuse occurred does not mean God condones it. The Bible repeatedly speaks of God's hatred of violence and abusive behavior (Psalm 11:3; Proverbs 6:16–19). The Lord is also not indifferent to your suffering. Jesus is described as *"a man of suffering, and familiar with pain"* (Isaiah 53:3). God enters into our suffering, carries our burdens, and helps us through our pain.

While no one is protected from every storm in life, know that the Lord will walk with you through the waters. He will comfort and guide you. He will strengthen and sustain you. He will even use the storms of life to deepen your relationship with Him.

"When you pass through the waters, I will be with you;
and when you pass through the rivers, they will not sweep over you.
When you walk through the fire, you will not be burned;
the flames will not set you ablaze."
(ISAIAH 43:2)

CHRONIC ILLNESS & DISABILITIES

God's Peace in the Midst of Pain

God understands your pain.

"He was despised and rejected by mankind, a man of suffering, and familiar with pain" (ISAIAH 53:3).

God speaks to you in your suffering.

"Those who suffer he delivers in their suffering; he speaks to them in their affliction" (JOB 36:15).

God draws near to you when you are hurting.

"The LORD is close to the brokenhearted and saves those who are crushed in spirit" (PSALM 34:18).

God gives rest when you are weary and burdened.

"Come to me, all you who are weary and burdened, and I will give you rest" (MATTHEW 11:28).

God gives you peace in your suffering.

"Peace I leave with you; my peace I give you. I do not give to you as the world gives. Do not let your hearts be troubled and do not be afraid" (JOHN 14:27).

God promises hope.

"There is surely a future hope for you, and your hope will not be cut off" (PROVERBS 23:18).

God will relieve your pain and restore your body in heaven.

"'He will wipe every tear from their eyes. There will be no more death' or mourning or crying or pain, for the old order of things has passed away. He who was seated on the throne said, 'I am making everything new!'" (REVELATION 21:4–5).

God wants you to be compassionate to others who suffer.

"Be sympathetic, love one another, be compassionate and humble" (1 PETER 3:8).

Can Any Blessings Come from Afflictions?

Suffering can soften your heart so that you want to obey God's Word.

"Before I was afflicted I went astray, but now I obey your word" (PSALM 119:67).

Suffering can open your heart to make you more teachable.

"It was good for me to be afflicted so that I might learn your decrees" (PSALM 119:71).

Suffering can mellow your heart to make you more compassionate.

"Praise be to the God and Father of our Lord Jesus Christ, the Father of compassion and the God of all comfort, who comforts us in all our troubles, so that we can comfort those in any trouble with the comfort we ourselves receive from God" (2 CORINTHIANS 1:3–4).

Suffering can strengthen your heart to make you more mature.

"Consider it pure joy, my brothers and sisters, whenever you face trials of many kinds, because you know that the testing of your faith produces perseverance. Let perseverance finish its work so that you may be mature and complete, not lacking anything" (JAMES 1:2–4).

Suffering can humble your heart to keep you from becoming conceited.

"To keep me from becoming conceited, I was given a thorn in my flesh, a messenger of Satan, to torment me" (2 CORINTHIANS 12:7).

Key Verse to Memorize

"My grace is sufficient for you,
for my power is made perfect in weakness."
Therefore I will boast all the more gladly
about my weaknesses,
so that Christ's power may rest on me.
(2 CORINTHIANS 12:9)

Suffering can reveal your heart's weaknesses so that Christ can strengthen your heart and be your sufficiency.

"'My grace is sufficient for you, for my power is made perfect in weakness.' Therefore I will boast all the more gladly about my weaknesses, so that Christ's power may rest on me" (2 CORINTHIANS 12:9).

Suffering can give you a desire for eternal glory rather than temporal glory.

"I consider that our present sufferings are not worth comparing with the glory that will be revealed in us" (ROMANS 8:18).

Blessed is the one who perseveres under trial
because, having stood the test,
that person will receive the crown of life
that the Lord has promised to those who love him.
(JAMES 1:12)

God does not delight in your suffering, but He uses it to refine your faith and to develop Christ's character in you. His delight is in making you a blessing to those around you, and He does that by conforming you to the character of Christ. He tests your faith in order to prove it to be genuine, thus resulting in the praise, glory, and honor of Jesus Christ.

These [trials] *have come so that the proven genuineness of your faith . . . may result in praise, glory and honor when Jesus Christ is revealed.*
(1 Peter 1:7)

Dos & Don'ts for Family and Friends

Don't assume all illnesses are life-threatening—some are benign.

Do educate yourself by researching and asking questions like, "What have the doctors said? What do you know about this illness?"

Don't dispense unsolicited advice, presuming to know everything that should be done.

Do offer appropriate assistance. "How can I help? With meals, errands, transportation, or something else?"

Don't expect one doctor to have all the answers.

Do extend an offer to take notes. "Would it be helpful for you if I went to the doctor with you and took notes?"

Don't belittle or patronize the one suffering.

Do say, "Please let me know if things become a struggle so that we can find ways to help."

Don't fail to meet personal needs (but do so privately and unobtrusively). However, allow them to do as much as they can for as long as they can.

Do say privately, "Please know that I'm here if you need me to assist in any way."

Don't demand answers and explanations from God.

Do pray. Realize, every step of the way, He promises to direct your path.

Trust in the Lord with all your heart
and lean not on your own understanding;
in all your ways submit to him,
and he will make your paths straight.
(Proverbs 3:5–6)

Keys to Accepting Affliction

Your troubles are temporary—your glory is eternal.

"We do not lose heart. Though outwardly we are wasting away, yet inwardly we are being renewed day by day. For our light and momentary troubles are achieving for us an eternal glory that far outweighs them all. So we fix our eyes not on what is seen, but on what is unseen, since what is seen is temporary, but what is unseen is eternal" (2 CORINTHIANS 4:16–18).

Your body is designed to experience decay.

"By the sweat of your brow you will eat your food until you return to the ground, since from it you were taken; for dust you are and to dust you will return" (GENESIS 3:19).

Your afflictions are allowed by God in order to teach you.

"But those who suffer he delivers in their suffering; he speaks to them in their affliction" (JOB 36:15).

Your temptations are made bearable by God.

"No temptation has overtaken you except what is common to mankind. And God is faithful; he will not let you be tempted beyond what you can bear. But when you are tempted, he will also provide a way out so that you can endure it" (1 CORINTHIANS 10:13).

Your suffering enables you to see God.

"My ears had heard of you but now my eyes have seen you" (JOB 42:5).

Your life is being conformed to the image of Christ through your affliction.

"We know that in all things God works for the good of those who love him, who have been called according to his purpose" (ROMANS 8:28).

Your crushed spirit will be sustained when you are indwelled by the Spirit of God.

"The human spirit can endure in sickness, but a crushed spirit who can bear?" (PROVERBS 18:14).

Your transformation will be completed by God.

"He who began a good work in you will carry it on to completion until the day of Christ Jesus" (PHILIPPIANS 1:6).

The 5 Stages of Sorrow

1. **Denial**—avoiding the painful reality

   "Surely God does not reject one who is blameless or strengthen the hands of evildoers" (Job 8:20).

2. **Anger**—opening up honest emotions

   "I loathe my very life; therefore I will give free rein to my complaint and speak out in the bitterness of my soul" (Job 10:1).

3. **Bargaining**—attempting to change reality

   "Only grant me these two things, God, and then I will not hide from you: Withdraw your hand far from me, and stop frightening me with your terrors" (Job 13:20–21).

4. **Depression**—feeling despair over the situation

   "I despise my life; I would not live forever. Let me alone; my days have no meaning" (Job 7:16).

5. **Acceptance**—gaining a positive outlook

   "God is able to bless you abundantly, so that in all things at all times, having all that you need, you will abound in every good work" (2 Corinthians 9:8).

Key Passage to Read

2 Corinthians 12:7–10

My Personalized Plan

I will . . .

Learn to cry.

— Crying is *not* a sign of weakness, but a much-needed cleansing emotional outlet.

"Record my misery; list my tears on your scroll—are they not in your record?" (Psalm 56:8).

Learn to let go.

— Trust God with my future.

"Trust in the Lord with all your heart and lean not on your own understanding; in all your ways submit to him, and he will make your paths straight" (Proverbs 3:5–6).

Learn to rest.

— Rest in the adequacy of God.

"Let the beloved of the LORD rest secure in him, for he shields him all day long, and the one the LORD loves rests between his shoulders" (DEUTERONOMY 33:12).

Learn to adjust.

— Modify my activities and adapt them to fit my needs.

"He gives strength to the weary and increases the power of the weak" (ISAIAH 40:29).

Learn to laugh.

— Refuse to take myself or my condition too seriously.

"A cheerful heart is good medicine, but a crushed spirit dries up the bones" (PROVERBS 17:22).

Learn to be disciplined.

— Rely on my doctor's advice to develop the habit of regular exercise or activity.

"Plans fail for lack of counsel, but with many advisers they succeed" (PROVERBS 15:22).

Learn to give thanks.

— Show gratitude to family and friends who help and support me and praise God daily.

"Give thanks in all circumstances; for this is God's will for you in Christ Jesus" (1 THESSALONIANS 5:18).

I have been crucified with Christ
and I no longer live, but Christ lives in me.
The life I now live in the body, I live by faith in the Son of God,
who loved me and gave himself for me.
(GALATIANS 2:20)

Questions & Answers

Question: "Is a physical affliction the result of sin?"

Answer: Sometimes yes; sometimes no. Based on the Bible, sickness can be the consequence of sin or can be permitted by God to accomplish His higher purpose.

— A consequence of sin:

"Whoever eats the bread or drinks the cup of the Lord in an unworthy manner will be guilty of sinning against the body and blood of the Lord. Everyone ought to examine themselves before they eat of the bread and drink from the cup. For those who eat and drink without discerning the body of Christ eat and drink judgment on themselves. That is why many among you are weak and sick, and a number of you have fallen asleep" (1 CORINTHIANS 11:27–30).

— Not a consequence of sin:

"As he [Jesus] *went along, he saw a man blind from birth. His disciples asked him, 'Rabbi, who sinned, this man or his parents, that he was born blind?' 'Neither this man nor his parents sinned,' said Jesus, 'but this happened so that the works of God might be displayed in him'"* (John 9:1–3).

Question: "Is it okay to pray for miraculous healing?"

Answer: Yes. Absolutely! It is biblical to present your request to God for full restoration. It is also biblical to pray as Jesus did, *"Yet not my will, but yours be done"* (Luke 22:42). If it is God's will, you will receive what you asked . . . but, again, only if it is God's will. It is for us to submit our will to His will since He is God and worthy of our obedience. Yes, it is biblical that we ask, but always on the condition that our will lines up with His will and not vice versa.

I desire to do your will, my God; your law is within my heart.
(Psalm 40:8).

Question: "Is it okay to take medication when you are suffering with an illness, or does that demonstrate a lack of faith in God?"

Answer: Using medicine is biblical. Our Creator, God, placed medicinal qualities within His creation . . . within nature. You can certainly exercise faith in God and at the same time take medicine as prescribed. Though not all people who use medicine are healed, the Bible clearly states that God made *"leaves for healing"* (Ezekiel 47:12).

CODEPENDENCY

The Need to Be Needed

God's Heart on Codependency

Lie: I need people I can trust and depend on to feel good about myself.

Truth: I need to put my trust and confidence completely in the Lord.

"This is what the L*ORD says: 'Cursed is the one who trusts in man, who draws strength from mere flesh and whose heart turns away from the* L*ORD. But blessed is the one who trusts in the* L*ORD, whose confidence is in him'"* (JEREMIAH 17:5, 7).

Lie: I need the approval of others to feel good about myself.

Truth: I am to desire the approval of God, not men.

"They loved human praise more than praise from God" (JOHN 12:43).

Lie: I need to change who I am.

Truth: I am a new person in Christ, and He is changing me from the inside out and is making me into the person He created me to be.

"If anyone is in Christ, the new creation has come: The old has gone, the new is here!" (2 CORINTHIANS 5:17).

Lie: I can expect people to meet all my needs.

Truth: I am to look to God alone to meet my needs.

"And my God will meet all your needs according to the riches of his glory in Christ Jesus" (PHILIPPIANS 4:19).

Lie: My thinking does not need to change.

Truth: I am to use God's Word to transform my thinking.

"Whatever is true, whatever is noble, whatever is right, whatever is pure, whatever is lovely, whatever is admirable—if anything is excellent or praiseworthy—think about such things" (PHILIPPIANS 4:8).

Lie: I need someone to lead me.

Truth: I must rely on the Lord to lead me.

"He guides me along the right paths for his name's sake" (PSALM 23:3).

Lie: Everything I need for life and happiness can be found in a relationship with a significant person.

Truth: I have everything I need to live a godly life through my relationship with God alone.

"His divine power has given us everything we need for a godly life through our knowledge of him who called us by his own glory and goodness. Through these he has given us his very great and precious promises, so that through them you may participate in the divine nature, having escaped the corruption in the world caused by evil desires" (2 PETER 1:3–4).

Lie: My security and safety come from my relationships with others.

Truth: I must depend on God for my security and safety.

"You are my hiding place; you will protect me from trouble and surround me with songs of deliverance" (PSALM 32:7).

Common Codependent Relationships

A **wife** is excessively helpless around her **husband** . . . and the husband needs his wife to stay helpless.

A **husband** is excessively needy in the way he relates to his **wife** . . . and the wife needs him to stay needy.

A **student** is excessively tied to a **teacher** . . . and the teacher needs the student to stay tied to him/her.

A **child** is excessively pampered by the **parent** . . . and the parent needs the child to stay in need of pampering.

Key Verse to Memorize

Am I now trying to win the approval of human beings, or of God? Or am I trying to please people? If I were still trying to please people, I would not be a servant of Christ. (GALATIANS 1:10)

A **parent** is excessively protected by the **child** . . . and the child needs the parent to stay in need of protection.

An **employee** is excessively entangled with an **employer** . . . and the employer needs the employee to stay entangled.

A **friend** is excessively fixated on another **friend** . . . and that person needs the friend to stay fixated.

A **counselee** is excessively clinging to a **counselor** . . . and the counselor needs the counselee to continue clinging.

A **disciple** is excessively dependent on a **discipler** . . . and the discipler needs the disciple to stay dependent.

A **victim** is excessively vulnerable to a **victimizer** . . . and the victimizer needs the victim to stay vulnerable.

A **spiritual seeker** is excessively leaning on a **spiritual leader** . . . and the leader needs the seeker to continue leaning.

God Wants You to Depend on Him

To totally rely on Him, not on people or things or self-effort.

"My flesh and my heart may fail, but God is the strength of my heart and my portion forever" (PSALM 73:26).

To believe He will meet all of your needs. You can safely reveal your hurts, your fears, and your needs to God. He will be your Need-Meeter.

"The LORD will guide you always; he will satisfy your needs in a sun-scorched land and will strengthen your frame. You will be like a well-watered garden, like a spring whose waters never fail" (ISAIAH 58:11).

To trust Him to take care of your loved ones.

"Trust in him at all times, you people; pour out your hearts to him, for God is our refuge" (PSALM 62:8).

To rely on Christ, whose life in you will enable you to overcome any destructive dependency.

"The one [Christ] *who is in you is greater than the one* [Satan] *who is in the world"* (1 JOHN 4:4).

The LORD is my rock, my fortress and my deliverer;
my God is my rock, in whom I take refuge, my
shield and the horn of my salvation, my stronghold.
(PSALM 18:2)

The Codependent Relationship Profile[73]

Both people . . .

— Are in denial
— Have difficulty setting boundaries
— Have a false sense of security
— Become jealous and possessive
— Control and manipulate
— Struggle with low self-worth
— Violate their consciences
— Experience extreme ups and downs
— Fear abandonment

— Feel trapped in the relationship

I find more bitter than death the [person]
who is a snare, whose heart is a trap and
whose hands are chains.
(Ecclesiastes 7:26)

Finding the Road to Freedom

R—Recognize that you are overly dependent on another person, then choose to place your dependency on God.

"Love the Lord your God with all your heart and with all your soul and with all your mind and with all your strength" (Mark 12:30).

E—Examine your patterns of codependent thinking.

"I strive always to keep my conscience clear before God and man" (Acts 24:16).

L—Let go of your "super responsible" mindset.

"What you are doing is not good. You and these people who come to you will only wear yourselves out. The work is too heavy for you; you cannot handle it alone" (Exodus 18:17–18).

E—Extend forgiveness to those who have caused you pain.

"Bear with each other and forgive one another if any of you has a grievance against someone. Forgive as the Lord forgave you" (Colossians 3:13).

A—Appropriate your identity in Christ.

"I have been crucified with Christ and I no longer live, but Christ lives in me. The life I now live in the body, I live by faith in the Son of God, who loved me and gave himself for me" (Galatians 2:20).

S—Set healthy boundaries.

"The prudent see danger and take refuge, but the simple keep going and pay the penalty" (Proverbs 27:12).

E—Exchange your emotional focus for a spiritual focus.

"Direct me in the path of your commands, for there I find delight. Turn my heart toward your statutes and not toward selfish gain. Turn my eyes away from worthless things; preserve my life according to your word" (Psalm 119:35–37).

"My grace is sufficient for you,
for my power is made perfect in weakness."
(2 Corinthians 12:9)

Indicators That Signal a Backslide into Codependence

Compulsive thoughts

A sense of desperation accompanying the pursuit of a new relationship

Acting on impulse rather than praying, seeking counsel, and analyzing true motives

Key Passage to Read

Galatians 6:1–5

A growing disinterest in healthy, reformed ways of relating

A preoccupation with saving, changing, or healing the partner in the new relationship

The resurgence of codependent feelings and behaviors reminiscent of former relationships[74]

My Personalized Plan

I will . . .

Confront the fact that I am codependent.[75]

Confront the consequences of my codependency.

"Whoever conceals their sins does not prosper, but the one who confesses and renounces them finds mercy" (PROVERBS 28:13).

Confront my painful emotions.

"The pleasantness of a friend springs from their heartfelt advice" (PROVERBS 27:9).

Confront my "secondary addictions."[76]

"The heart of the discerning acquires knowledge, for the ears of the wise seek it out" (PROVERBS 18:15).

Confront my current codependent relationship.[77]

"Those God foreknew he also predestined to be conformed to the image of his Son" (ROMANS 8:29).

Confront my codependent focus.

"The wisdom of the prudent is to give thought to their ways, but the folly of fools is deception" (PROVERBS 14:8).

Confront my codependent conflicts.[78]
"Don't have anything to do with foolish and stupid arguments, because you know they produce quarrels" (2 TIMOTHY 2:23).

Confront my codependent responses.[79]
"Do not repay evil with evil or insult with insult. On the contrary, repay evil with blessing, because to this you were called so that you may inherit a blessing. . . . But do this with gentleness and respect, keeping a clear conscience, so that those who speak maliciously against your good behavior in Christ may be ashamed of their slander" (1 PETER 3:9, 15–16).

Confront what I need to *leave* in order to receive.[80]
"Wounds from a friend can be trusted, but an enemy multiplies kisses" (PROVERBS 27:6).

Confront my need to build mature, nondependent relationships.[81]
"Let us . . . be taken forward to maturity" (HEBREWS 6:1).

Questions & Answers

Question: "How can I know whether I'm an enabler?"

Answer: You are an *enabler* if you perpetuate another's destructive behavior by protecting that person from painful consequences that could actually serve as a motivation for change. Ask yourself, *How many lies have I told to protect the reputation of someone with a destructive habit?* The Bible has strong words to say about those who protect the guilty:

Whoever says to the guilty, "You are
innocent," will be cursed by peoples
and denounced by nations.
(PROVERBS 24:24)

Question: "What is wrong with people depending on people?"

Answer: We should have a healthy *interdependence*—valuing, loving, and learning from one another—but not total dependence. A healthy relationship involves mutual give-and-take, where neither person relies on the other to meet every need. Many people, however, have a *misplaced dependence* on others. These relationships are unhealthy, for God calls us to live in total dependence on Him. Over and over, the Bible portrays how godly people learn to have a *strong dependence* on the Lord rather than a *weak dependence* on each other. The apostle Paul said:

"But this happened that we might
not rely on ourselves but on God, who raises the dead."
(2 CORINTHIANS 1:9)

COMMUNICATION

The Heart of the Matter

God's Heart on Communication

God wants our communication to be encouraging.

"Do not let any unwholesome talk come out of your mouths, but only what is helpful for building others up according to their needs, that it may benefit those who listen" (EPHESIANS 4:29).

God can help guard our speech.

"Set a guard over my mouth, LORD; keep watch over the door of my lips" (PSALM 141:3).

God wants us to listen before we speak.

"To answer before listening—that is folly and shame" (PROVERBS 18:13).

God warns about speaking rashly.

"Those who guard their lips preserve their lives, but those who speak rashly will come to ruin" (PROVERBS 13:3).

God cautions us about anger and conflict.

"A hot-tempered person stirs up conflict, but the one who is patient calms a quarrel" (PROVERBS 15:18).

God reminds us sometimes less is more.

"Sin is not ended by multiplying words, but the prudent hold their tongues" (PROVERBS 10:19).

God points out the difference between gossip and confidentiality.

"A gossip goes around telling secrets, but those who are trustworthy can keep a confidence" (PROVERBS 11:13 NLT).

God is truth and He expects us to be truthful.

"Each of you must put off falsehood and speak truthfully to your neighbor, for we are all members of one body" (EPHESIANS 4:25).

God exposes our hearts in what we communicate.

"Whatever is in your heart determines what you say" (MATTHEW 12:34 NLT).

God wants our speech to be gracious and attractive to unbelievers.

"Let your conversation be gracious and attractive so that you will have the right response for everyone" (COLOSSIANS 4:6 NLT).

Don'ts for Listening

1. **Don't** feel you must do the talking.

   "There is . . . a time to tear and a time to mend, a time to be silent and a time to speak" (ECCLESIASTES 3:1, 7).

2. **Don't** give premature advice.

   "The heart of the righteous weighs its answers" (PROVERBS 15:28).

3. **Don't** become defensive.

   "Fools show their annoyance at once, but the prudent overlook an insult" (PROVERBS 12:16).

4. **Don't** become hot-tempered.

   "A hot-tempered person stirs up conflict, but the one who is patient calms a quarrel" (PROVERBS 15:18).

5. **Don't** laugh at others.

   "Whoever derides their neighbor has no sense, but the one who has understanding holds their tongue" (PROVERBS 11:12).

6. **Don't** hold on to hatred.

   "Hatred stirs up conflict, but love covers over all wrongs" (PROVERBS 10:12).

7. **Don't** break a confidence.

   "A gossip betrays a confidence, but a trustworthy person keeps a secret" (PROVERBS 11:13).

The "Ten Commandments" of Godly Communication

1. **God wants you to listen well.**

   "Everyone should be quick to listen, slow to speak and slow to become angry" (JAMES 1:19).

2. **God wants you to be silent at times.**

   "Even fools are thought wise if they keep silent, and discerning if they hold their tongues" (PROVERBS 17:28).

3. **God wants you to guard your mouth.**

   "Those who guard their mouths and their tongues keep themselves from calamity" (PROVERBS 21:23).

4. **God wants you to tell the truth—and not lie.**

   "The LORD detests lying lips, but he delights in those who tell the truth" (PROVERBS 12:22 NLT).

5. **God wants you to communicate gratitude—and not impurity.**

   "Let there be no filthiness nor foolish talk nor crude joking, which are out of place, but instead let there be thanksgiving" (EPHESIANS 5:4 ESV).

6. **God wants your words to encourage others—not put them down.**

   "Don't use foul or abusive language. Let everything you say be good and helpful, so that your words will be an encouragement to those who hear them" (EPHESIANS 4:29 NLT).

7. **God does not want you to vent your anger at others.**

   "Fools give full vent to their rage, but the wise bring calm in the end" (PROVERBS 29:11).

8. **God does not want you to gossip about others.**

   "A gossip betrays a confidence, but a trustworthy person keeps a secret" (PROVERBS 11:13).

9. **God wants your words to be loving.**

   "We will speak the truth in love, growing in every way more and more like Christ" (EPHESIANS 4:15 NLT).

10. **God wants your words to be wise and just.**

    "The mouths of the righteous utter wisdom, and their tongues speak what is just" (PSALM 37:30).

Key Verse to Memorize

Do not let any unwholesome talk
come out of your mouths,
but only what is helpful
for building others up
according to their needs,
that it may benefit those who listen.
(EPHESIANS 4:29)

Words That Wound

Degrading Words

"The words of the reckless pierce like swords" (PROVERBS 12:18).

Demanding Words

"Anger is cruel and fury overwhelming" (PROVERBS 27:4).

Demeaning Words

"You love any words that destroy, you treacherous tongue!" (PSALM 52:4 HCSB).

Destructive Words

"With their mouths the godless destroy their neighbors" (PROVERBS 11:9).

Deceitful Words

"A deceitful tongue crushes the spirit" (PROVERBS 15:4 NLT).

Wisdom will save you from the ways of wicked men,
from men whose words are perverse.
(PROVERBS 2:12)

How to COMMUNICATE Well (An acrostic)

C—Communicate care.
"I really care about your feelings. Are you okay?"

O—Open the door on the past.
"I would like to know how you felt about what happened."

M—Move away from manipulation.
"When is a good time for us to talk?"

M—Mirror the message back.
"I hear you saying that you feel I have rejected you. Is that right?"

U—Use "I" messages instead of "you" messages.
"I'm struggling with feeling that I am of little value to you."

N—Never say "never."
"I feel at times that my opinions are not respected."

I—Invest yourself in the other person's security.
"Have I made it safe for you to respond?"

C—Clarify when confused.

"Would it be better if I were not here at this time?"

A—Avoid arguments.

"Help me understand your reasons for this decision."

T—Trust the Lord's timing.

"Let's talk when it's convenient for you."

Key Passage to Read

Ephesians 4

E—Eliminate expectations.

"I love you and am committed to our relationship."

The tongue has the power of life and death,
and those who love it will eat its fruit.
(PROVERBS 18:21)

Listening to God

Listening to God is based on a belief that God loves me and desires to communicate with me.

"The LORD appeared to us in the past, saying: 'I have loved you with an everlasting love; I have drawn you with unfailing kindness'" (JEREMIAH 31:3).

Listening to God is consistently reading, studying, and meditating on His living Word—the Bible.

"My word that goes out from my mouth: It will not return to me empty, but will accomplish what I desire and achieve the purpose for which I sent it" (ISAIAH 55:11).

Listening to God is regularly getting alone and giving Him my undivided attention.

"He went up on a mountainside by himself to pray. Later that night, he was there alone" (MATTHEW 14:23).

Listening to God is opening my heart and letting God point His finger of truth on the real me.

"Search me, God, and know my heart; test me and know my anxious thoughts.
See if there is any offensive way in me, and lead me in the way everlasting"
(PSALM 139:23–24).

Listening to God is also listening carefully to others, realizing that God may be using them to communicate His personal message to me.

"Where there is strife, there is pride, but wisdom is found in those who take advice" (PROVERBS 13:10).

Listening to God is recognizing the presence of the Holy Spirit within me and responding to His guidance for communicating with others.

"The Advocate, the Holy Spirit, whom the Father will send in my name, will teach you all things and will remind you of everything I have said to you" (JOHN 14:26).

Let the wise listen and add to their learning,
and let the discerning get guidance.
(PROVERBS 1:5)

My Personalized Plan

I will . . .

Strengthen my ability to engage in fruitful communications by being a good listener and a kind responder.

— I will fully focus on what other people say to me, truly listening to them and not thinking about what I will say next.

— I will avoid interrupting someone to interject my opinion or story.

"Everyone should be quick to listen, slow to speak and slow to become angry" (JAMES 1:19).

Seek understanding and not fall into destructive or damaging communication styles.

— I will not use thoughtless, insensitive, teasing, critical, or degrading words when speaking to others.

— I will not demand, order, threaten, curse, or accuse others when communicating.

"A gentle answer turns away wrath, but a harsh word stirs up anger" (PROVERBS 15:1).

Strive to communicate effectively, staying calm and collected when confronted or in stressful situations.

— I will recognize when I start to feel upset, and take a moment to breathe deeply and regain my composure.

— I will be gracious and willing to compromise, remembering that God calls me to communicate with kindness and patience.

"Those who guard their mouths and their tongues keep themselves from calamity" (PROVERBS 21:23).

Sharpen my nonverbal communication.

— I will make sure that I maintain friendly eye contact and be mindful of my facial expressions and body language.

— I will be aware of my tone of voice and the volume I use when I speak.

"Let your conversation be always full of grace, seasoned with salt, so that you may know how to answer everyone" (Colossians 4:6).

Speak with grace and truth.

- — I will remember that God speaks to me with gracious love and firm truth.
- — I will ask the Lord for wisdom to balance grace and truth in my communication.

"The Word became flesh and made his dwelling among us. We have seen his glory, the glory of the one and only Son, who came from the Father, full of grace and truth" (John 1:14).

Questions & Answers

Question: "Why is it often difficult to have healthy communication within close relationships?"

Answer: Healthy, mature communication is the revelation of our true selves to someone who cares about us. Risk of rejection can be so intense that we learn different ways to hide our fears and self-doubts. We may not be aware of the destructive habits often formed in childhood that stay with us into adulthood. Yet they remain established responses that block honest and sincere communication with others.

Fix your thoughts on what is true, and honorable,
and right, and pure, and lovely, and admirable.
Think [and speak] *about things that are*
excellent and worthy of praise.
(Philippians 4:8 NLT)

Question: "How can I communicate with others in a way that is most pleasing to God?"

Answer: The method of communication most pleasing to God is one that reflects Jesus Christ in all you say and do. That means allowing Jesus Christ to be Lord of your life . . . allowing Him to express His words and actions through you.

Let the message of Christ dwell among you richly
as you teach and admonish one another
with all wisdom through psalms, hymns,
and songs from the Spirit, singing to God
with gratitude in your hearts. And whatever you do, whether in word
or deed, do it all in the name of the Lord Jesus,
giving thanks to God the Father through him.
(Colossians 3:16-17)

CONFLICT RESOLUTION

Solving Your People Problems

God's Heart on Conflict Resolution

Conflicts can be used to accomplish God's purpose.

"We know that in all things God works for the good of those who love him, who have been called according to his purpose" (ROMANS 8:28).

Conflicts cannot always be avoided.[82]

"I have told you these things, so that in me you may have peace. In this world you will have trouble. But take heart! I have overcome the world" (JOHN 16:33).

Conflicts that are resolved require advance preparation and planning.

"The plans of the diligent lead to profit as surely as haste leads to poverty" (PROVERBS 21:5).

Conflicts are not necessarily bad—they can actually sharpen us if we respond correctly.[83] Handled well, they provide an opportunity for role modeling.

"Blessed is the one who perseveres under trial because, having stood the test, that person will receive the crown of life that the Lord has promised to those who love him" (JAMES 1:12).

Conflicts can sometimes be settled through negotiation.

"Listen to advice and accept discipline, and at the end you will be counted among the wise" (PROVERBS 19:20).

Conflicts that are resolved require action toward peace.

"Let us therefore make every effort to do what leads to peace and to mutual edification" (ROMANS 14:19).

Different Types of Conflict[84]

1. **Intrapersonal Conflict**

   A struggle within a person to decide *between two or more choices.*

   "All the king's officials and the people of the royal provinces know that for any man or woman who approaches the king in the inner court without being summoned the king has but one law: that they be put to death unless the king extends the gold scepter to them and spares their lives. But thirty days have passed since I was called to go to the king" (ESTHER 4:11).

2. **Interpersonal Conflict**

   A clash of ideas or interests *between two or more people.*

   "When Haman saw that Mordecai would not kneel down or pay him honor, he was enraged" (Esther 3:5).

3. **Intraorganizational Conflict**

   A competitive or opposing action *within a group* (a family, department, church, political party, state, or nation).

   "The king got up in a rage, left his wine and went out into the palace garden. But Haman, realizing that the king had already decided his fate, stayed behind to beg Queen Esther for his life" (Esther 7:7).

4. **Interorganizational Conflict**

   A battle or opposing action *between two or more groups* (families, companies, religions, or countries).

   "Dispatches were sent by couriers to all the king's provinces with the order to destroy, kill and annihilate all the Jews—young and old, women and children—on a single day, the thirteenth day of the twelfth month, the month of Adar, and to plunder their goods" (Esther 3:13).

Root Cause of Negative Conflict

Wrong Belief for Attackers: "I have the right to have my way by whatever means. To feel significant, I must attack and conquer. Everyone is out for himself."

Wrong Belief for Avoiders: "I am afraid of conflict because it makes me feel insecure. To feel secure, I must find some way to avoid it or get rid of it. If I stand up for myself, I won't be loved."

Right Belief: "I know that conflict is a natural result of living with different types of people. My sense of significance and security are based on the fact that God loves me, He created me with a plan and purpose, and Jesus willingly died for me."

There is no fear in love. But perfect love drives out fear,
because fear has to do with punishment.
The one who fears is not made perfect in love.
(1 John 4:18)

First Things First

1. **Who?** Who is involved in the conflict?
2. **What?** What is your goal?
3. **Why?** Why do you want to take action?
4. **Where?** Where will it happen?
5. **When?** When do you want it done?
6. **How?** How do you want it to be done?

The heart of the discerning acquires knowledge,
for the ears of the wise seek it out.
(PROVERBS 18:15)

When Others Are Critical of You

Be discerning regarding the accuracy of the critical words of others.

"The wise in heart are called discerning, and gracious words promote instruction" (PROVERBS 16:21).

Be open to the slightest kernel of truth when you are criticized.

"A rebuke impresses a discerning person more than a hundred lashes a fool" (PROVERBS 17:10).

Be willing to consider the criticism. If it is true, this person is God's megaphone to get your attention.

"The way of fools seems right to them, but the wise listen to advice" (PROVERBS 12:15).

Key Verse to Memorize

Let us therefore make every effort
to do what leads to peace
and to mutual edification.
(ROMANS 14:19)

Be able to receive criticism without being defensive. Admit to any truth in the criticism—agreeing when you are in error and then asking for further correction.

"If you listen to constructive criticism, you will be at home among the wise" (PROVERBS 15:31 NLT).

Be determined to speak well of your critic.

"Bless those who persecute you; bless and do not curse" (ROMANS 12:14).

Be dependent on the Lord's perspective, not on the opinion of others, to determine your worth and value.

"Am I now trying to win the approval of human beings, or of God? Or am I trying to please people? If I were still trying to please people, I would not be a servant of Christ" (GALATIANS 1:10).

Do not be overcome by evil, but overcome evil with good.
(ROMANS 12:21)

Turn Foes into Friends

F—Find ways to compliment your opposer.

"The mouths of the righteous utter wisdom, and their tongues speak what is just" (PSALM 37:30).

R—Repay your opposer's evil with good.

"Do not repay anyone evil for evil. Be careful to do what is right in the eyes of everyone" (ROMANS 12:17).

I—Intercede in prayer for your opposer.

"As for me, far be it from me that I should sin against the LORD by failing to pray for you. And I will teach you the way that is good and right" (1 SAMUEL 12:23).

E—Empathize with your opposer.

"Finally, all of you, be like-minded, be sympathetic, love one another, be compassionate and humble" (1 PETER 3:8).

N—Nurture a forgiving heart toward your opposer.

"Be kind and compassionate to one another, forgiving each other, just as in Christ God forgave you" (EPHESIANS 4:32).

D—Decide to love your opposer.

"Let no debt remain outstanding, except the continuing debt to love one another, for whoever loves others has fulfilled the law" (ROMANS 13:8).

S—Seek to reach out to your opposer.

"If your enemy is hungry, feed him; if he is thirsty, give him something to drink. In doing this, you will heap burning coals on his head" (ROMANS 12:20).

Principles for Facing Conflict

1. **Appreciation:** Acknowledge attributes and actions.

   "I always thank my God as I remember you in my prayers, because I hear about your love for all his holy people and your faith in the Lord Jesus. I pray that your partnership with us in the faith may be effective in deepening your understanding of every good thing we share for the sake of Christ. Your love has given me great joy and encouragement, because you, brother, have refreshed the hearts of the Lord's people" (PHILEMON VV. 4–7).

2. **Humility:** Don't speak from a position of power but of equality.

   "In Christ I could be bold and order you to do what you ought to do" (PHILEMON V. 8).

3. **Love:** Appeal for a resolution on the basis of love.

   "I prefer to appeal to you on the basis of love. It is as none other than Paul—an old man and now also a prisoner of Christ Jesus" (PHILEMON V. 9).

4. **Integrity:** Be absolutely honest about the problems.

   "I appeal to you for my son Onesimus, who became my son while I was in chains. Formerly he was useless to you, but now he has become useful both to you and to me" (PHILEMON VV. 10–11).

5. **Vulnerability:** Share your feelings and your heart's desire.

   "I am sending him—who is my very heart—back to you. I would have liked to keep him with me so that he could take your place in helping me while I am in chains for the gospel" (PHILEMON VV. 12–13).

6. **Mutuality:** Don't force or coerce but defer and seek agreement.

   "But I did not want to do anything without your consent" (PHILEMON V. 14).

7. **Optimism:** Expect the best.

   "So that any favor you do would not seem forced but would be voluntary" (PHILEMON V. 14).

8. **Faith:** Recognize and trust the sovereign hand of God.

   "Perhaps the reason he was separated from you for a little while was that you might have him back forever—no longer as a slave, but better than a slave, as a dear brother. He is very dear to me but even dearer to you, both as a fellow man and as a brother in the Lord" (PHILEMON VV. 15–16).

9. **Forgiveness:** Release the past and receive God's plan for the future.

   "So if you consider me a partner, welcome him as you would welcome me. If he has done you any wrong or owes you anything, charge it to me. I, Paul, am writing this with my own hand. I will pay it back—not to mention that you owe me your very self. I do wish, brother, that I may have some benefit from you in the Lord; refresh my heart in Christ" (PHILEMON VV. 17–20).

10. **Exhortation:** Express confidence in God's ability to bring resolution.

    "Confident of your obedience, I write to you, knowing that you will do even more than I ask" (PHILEMON V. 21).

Steps to Conflict Resolution

Confront your offender. The struggler feels hurt, frustrated, or angry toward the offender and needs to plan a time to get these feelings out.

Communicate your feelings. Express your feelings in a way that doesn't accuse.

Commit to listening. Be willing to listen to your offender, actively and attentively.

Confirm by repeating. Try to understand the offender's perspective, consider their words, and repeat it back for clarification.

Choose possible changes. The offender offers several possible changes in behavior, and the struggler will choose one of the changes.

Convey compassionate care. After the change in behavior has been agreed on, both parties extend appreciation for the opportunity to resolve the problem.

Consider your own condition. The struggler should consider that the offender could also have been offended.

Whoever refreshes others will be refreshed.
(PROVERBS 11:25)

My Personalized Plan

As I prepare to walk the road to resolution of a conflict, **I will remember to . . .**

Pledge my commitment.

"If it is possible, as far as it depends on you, live at peace with everyone" (ROMANS 12:18).

Pray for everyone involved in the conflict.

"Search me, God, and know my heart; test me and know my anxious thoughts. See if there is any offensive way in me, and lead me in the way everlasting" (PSALM 139:23–24).

Prepare before I ask for a meeting.

"Let us examine our ways and test them, and let us return to the LORD*"* (LAMENTATIONS 3:40).

Propose a time to talk face-to-face.

"Make every effort to keep the unity of the Spirit through the bond of peace" (EPHESIANS 4:3).

Provide a private place.

"If your brother or sister sins, go and point out their fault, just between the two of you. If they listen to you, you have won them over" (MATTHEW 18:15).

Purpose to be honest.[85]

"An honest witness tells the truth, but a false witness tells lies" (PROVERBS 12:17).

Permit total forgiveness.

"Bear with each other and forgive one another if any of you has a grievance against someone. Forgive as the Lord forgave you. And over all these virtues put on love, which binds them all together in perfect unity" (COLOSSIANS 3:13–14).

Key Passage to Read

The letter to Philemon

Perceive a future harvest.

"Let us not become weary in doing good, for at the proper time we will reap a harvest if we do not give up" (GALATIANS 6:9).

Present the present conflict.

"It [love] *. . . keeps no record of wrongs"* (1 CORINTHIANS 13:5).

Promote fairness and objectivity.

"Do not pervert justice; do not show partiality to the poor or favoritism to the great, but judge your neighbor fairly" (LEVITICUS 19:15).

Protect my privacy.

"A gossip betrays a confidence, but a trustworthy person keeps a secret" (PROVERBS 11:13).

Preserve individuality.

"I too will have my say; I too will tell what I know" (JOB 32:17).

Project openness and optimism.

"Therefore encourage one another and build each other up, just as in fact you are doing" (1 THESSALONIANS 5:11).

Practice love.

"A friend loves at all times, and a brother is born for a time of adversity" (PROVERBS 17:17).

I appeal to you . . . that all of you agree with one another.
(1 CORINTHIANS 1:10)

Questions & Answers

Question: "Is forgiveness the same as reconciliation?"

Answer: No. Forgiveness is not the same as reconciliation.

- — Forgiveness focuses on the *offense*; reconciliation focuses on the *relationship.*
- — Forgiveness requires *no relationship,* while reconciliation requires *nurturing a relationship.*
- — Forgiveness involves a change in *thinking about* the offender; reconciliation involves a change in *behavior by* the offender.
- — Forgiveness is *extended even if it is never earned*; reconciliation is *offered to the offender only if it has been earned.*

Do two walk together unless they have agreed to do so?
(AMOS 3:3)

CONFRONTATION

Challenging Others to Change

God's Heart on Confrontation

God declares you are to show respect and are to be treated with respect.

"Show proper respect to everyone . . ." (1 PETER 2:17).

God declares you are to speak truthfully from your heart and others are to speak truthfully to you.

"Each of you must put off falsehood and speak truthfully to your neighbor" (EPHESIANS 4:25).

God declares you are to listen to others and others should listen to you.

"Everyone should be quick to listen, slow to speak and slow to become angry" (JAMES 1:19).

God declares you are to express appropriate anger and to have anger appropriately expressed toward you.

"'In your anger do not sin'" (EPHESIANS 4:26).

God declares you are to value and protect your conscience by treating others in a Christlike way.

"I strive always to keep my conscience clear before God and man" (ACTS 24:16).

God declares you are to say *no* to selfish or self-serving motives or actions.

"Say 'No' to ungodliness and worldly passions" (TITUS 2:12).

God declares you are to remove yourself from an any hostile or harmful confrontation.

"Do not make friends with a hot-tempered person, do not associate with one easily angered" (PROVERBS 22:24).

God declares you are to both seek and give emotional and spiritual support.

"Let us consider how we may spur one another on toward love and good deeds, not giving up meeting together . . . but encouraging one another" (HEBREWS 10:24–25).

God declares you are to appeal to a higher authority when necessary.

"If the charges brought against me by these Jews are not true, no one has the right to hand me over to them. I appeal to Caesar!" (ACTS 25:11).

God declares you are to confront and to be confronted with all wisdom.

"Let the message of Christ dwell among you richly as you teach and admonish one another with all wisdom through psalms, hymns, and songs from the Spirit, singing to God with gratitude in your hearts" (COLOSSIANS 3:16).

The way of fools seems right to them,
but the wise listen to advice.
(PROVERBS 12:15)

When You Should Confront

When someone is in danger.

"Rescue those being led away to death; hold back those staggering toward slaughter. If you say, 'But we knew nothing about this,' does not he who weighs the heart perceive it? Does not he who guards your life know it? Will he not repay everyone according to what they have done?" (PROVERBS 24:11–12).

When a relationship is threatened.

"I plead with Euodia and I plead with Syntyche to be of the same mind in the Lord. Yes, and I ask you, my true companion, help these women since they have contended at my side in the cause of the gospel, along with Clement and the rest of my co-workers, whose names are in the book of life" (PHILIPPIANS 4:2–3).

When division exists within a group.

"Let us therefore make every effort to do what leads to peace and to mutual edification" (ROMANS 14:19).

When someone sins against you.

"If your brother or sister sins, go and point out their fault, just between the two of you. If they listen to you, you have won them over" (MATTHEW 18:15).

Key Verses to Memorize

Brothers and sisters,
if someone is caught in a sin,
you who live by the Spirit
should restore that person gently.
But watch yourselves,
or you also may be tempted.
Carry each other's burdens,
and in this way
you will fulfill the law of Christ.
(GALATIANS 6:1–2)

When someone is caught in a sin.

"When I [God] *say to a wicked person, 'You will surely die,' and you do not warn them or speak out to dissuade them from their evil ways in order to save their life, that wicked person will die for their sin, and I will hold you accountable for their blood"* (EZEKIEL 3:18).

When others are offended.

"I opposed him to his face, because he stood condemned. For before certain men came from James, he used to eat with the Gentiles. But when they [the Jews] *arrived, he began to draw back and separate himself from the Gentiles because he was afraid of those who belonged to the circumcision group. The other Jews joined him in his hypocrisy, so that by their hypocrisy even Barnabas was led astray"* (GALATIANS 2:11–13).

There is a proper time and procedure for every matter.
(ECCLESIASTES 8:6)

When You Should Not Confront

When you are not the right person to confront.

"Like one who grabs a stray dog by the ears is someone who rushes into a quarrel not their own" (PROVERBS 26:17).

When it's not the right time to confront.

"There is a time for everything . . . a time to be silent and a time to speak" (ECCLESIASTES 3:1, 7).

When you are uncertain of the facts.

"To answer before listening—that is folly and shame" (PROVERBS 18:13).

When the consequences of the confrontation outweigh those of the offense.

"Better a dry crust with peace and quiet than a house full of feasting, with strife" (PROVERBS 17:1).

When the person you want to confront has a habit of foolishness and quarreling.

"Don't have anything to do with foolish and stupid arguments, because you know they produce quarrels. And the Lord's servant must not be quarrelsome but must be kind to everyone, able to teach, not resentful" (2 TIMOTHY 2:23–24).

When the person who offended you is your enemy.

"Love your enemies and pray for those who persecute you, that you may be children of your Father in heaven. He causes his sun to rise on the evil and the good, and sends rain on the righteous and the unrighteous" (MATTHEW 5:44–45).

When confrontation will be ineffective and reprisal severe.

"Whoever corrects a mocker invites insults; whoever rebukes the wicked incurs abuse" (PROVERBS 9:7).

Do not rebuke an older man harshly,
but exhort him as if he were your father.
(1 TIMOTHY 5:1)

The Root Cause for Confusion

Wrong Beliefs about Confronting: The **passive** person says: "If I confront others, the end result will be bad. I will hurt, they will hurt, and our relationship will be hurt. By avoiding confrontation, I can protect my basic needs from being threatened. The only way I can please those around me is to keep silent."

The **aggressive** person says: "If I don't strongly confront others, the end result will be bad. I will lose, they will win, and my goals will not succeed. By strongly confronting, I can ensure that my basic needs are met. The only way I can reach my goals is to dominate others."

The **passive-aggressive** person says: "If I confront, I could be rejected. If I don't confront, I could be belittled. By masking my discontent, I can still find ways to make my point without risking personal loss. The only way I can reach my goals is to avoid direct confrontation but covertly attack from a safe distance."

Right Belief about Confronting: The **assertive** person says: "I will neither be afraid of nor exaggerate opportunities to confront. Knowing I am deeply loved, eternally secure, and truly significant, I will be willing to confront with confidence, knowing that confrontation can produce positive growth and change. I will also keep uppermost in my mind that my goal is to please God, not myself or someone else."

Am I now trying to win the approval
of human beings, or of God?
Or am I trying to please people?
If I were still trying to please people,
I would not be a servant of Christ.
(Galatians 1:10)

The Sandwich Technique

Bread of Appreciation: Begin with a positive statement, a sincere compliment, or a genuine statement of loving care. Accentuate the positive aspect of the situation.

"The wise in heart are called discerning, and gracious words promote instruction" (Proverbs 16:21).

Meat of the Matter: Clarify the desired goal. Objectively recount the chain of events that led up to the present problem, examining what might have gone wrong and why. Problem-solve by brainstorming about possible options presently available for correcting the situation. Then determine a future course of action.

"Whoever loves discipline loves knowledge, but whoever hates correction is stupid" (PROVERBS 12:1).

Bread of Encouragement: Conclude with a statement expressing confidence and assurance of future success.

"Encourage one another and build each other up, just as in fact you are doing" (1 THESSALONIANS 5:11).

My Personalized Plan

Before establishing a plan for confronting someone else, plan to confront yourself. Honest self-examination is necessary before you can build a strong case for confronting another person's behavior.

By the grace God has given me,
I laid a foundation as a wise builder. . . .
But each one should build with care.
(1 CORINTHIANS 3:10)

I will . . .

Make sure my heart is right.[86]

"Search me, God, and know my heart; test me and know my anxious thoughts. See if there is any offensive way in me, and lead me in the way everlasting" (PSALM 139:23–24).

Look at the conflict from the offender's perspective.

"Do nothing out of selfish ambition or vain conceit. Rather, in humility value others above yourselves, not looking to your own interests but each of you to the interests of the others. In your relationships with one another, have the same mindset as Christ Jesus" (PHILIPPIANS 2:3–5).

Key Passage to Read

Matthew 18:15–17

Listen in order to gain insight into thoughts, feelings, and concerns.

"My dear brothers and sisters, take note of this: Everyone should be quick to listen, slow to speak and slow to become angry" (JAMES 1:19).

Take responsibility for my emotional reactions.

"Better a patient person than a warrior, one with self-control than one who takes a city" (PROVERBS 16:32).

Keep my tongue under control.

"A good man brings good things out of the good stored up in his heart, and an evil man brings evil things out of the evil stored up in his heart. For the mouth speaks what the heart is full of" (LUKE 6:45).

Ask forgiveness of my offender.

"Confess your sins to each other" (JAMES 5:16).

Forgive my offender.

"Bear with each other and forgive one another if any of you has a grievance against someone. Forgive as the Lord forgave you" (COLOSSIANS 3:13).

Pray for my offender.

"Far be it from me that I should sin against the LORD by failing to pray for you. And I will teach you the way that is good and right" (1 SAMUEL 12:23).

Care about my offender.

"Administer true justice; show mercy and compassion to one another" (ZECHARIAH 7:9).

Be sensitive to the pain of my offender.

"Mourn with those who mourn" (ROMANS 12:15).

Make the level of the confrontation match the level of the offense.

"He has shown you, O mortal, what is good. And what does the LORD require of you? To act justly and to love mercy and to walk humbly with your God" (MICAH 6:8).

Complete the task and comfort my offender.

"The punishment inflicted on him by the majority is sufficient. Now instead, you ought to forgive and comfort him, so that he will not be overwhelmed by excessive sorrow . . . reaffirm your love for him" (2 CORINTHIANS 2:6–8).

Questions & Answers

Question: "Why can't I just forgive and forget? Why do I have to confront someone when they offend me?"

Answer: Undisclosed forgiveness benefits you by keeping you from becoming bitter, but it does not necessarily benefit your offender, who is in need of correction. Yes, you need to forgive and not dwell on the offense, but you also need to confront in order to make your offender aware of a problem area in need of being addressed.

Forgiving without confronting can later result in your offender resenting you for not caring enough to make the offense known so that the bad behavior could be changed. Your offender could then develop a bitter root that later bears bitter fruit.[87]

See to it that . . . no bitter root grows up to
cause trouble and defile many.
(HEBREWS 12:15)

Question: "If I have a Christian friend who is continuing to live in sin, am I obligated to confront my friend?"

Answer: You are not obligated, but God might lead you to confront in love. Realize that you may be His agent to help your friend change and then grow to become more Christlike. If you care enough to confront, God can use you to encourage and support different loved ones to overcome habits that enslave them or alienate them from others. At times He will call you to directly and lovingly intervene in the lives of fellow believers who have wandered from the truth and have become ensnared by sin.

Whoever turns a sinner from the error of their way
will save them from death and cover
over a multitude of sins.
(JAMES 5:20)

CONSIDERING MARRIAGE

Are You Fit to Be Tied?

God's Heart on Considering Marriage

God wants you to seek His will and His Word when making a decision about marriage.

"I desire to do your will, my God; your law is within my heart" (PSALM 40:8).

God wants you to understand His design for marriage—a union between husband and wife.

"For this reason a man will leave his father and mother and be united to his wife, and the two will become one flesh" (EPHESIANS 5:31).

God will be faithful to guide you to make a wise and informed decision about marriage.

"I will instruct you and teach you in the way you should go; I will counsel you with my loving eye on you" (PSALM 32:8).

God wants you to enter a marriage that adheres to biblical guidelines for a Christian marriage.

"The precepts of the LORD are right, giving joy to the heart. The commands of the LORD are radiant, giving light to the eyes" (PSALM 19:8).

God wants you to consider counsel from parents, wise friends, and church leaders.

"Plans fail for lack of counsel, but with many advisers they succeed" (PROVERB 15:22).

God wants your decision about marriage to please Him above pleasing people.

"We are not trying to please people but God, who tests our hearts" (1 THESSALONIANS 2:4).

God wants you to pursue purity before marriage—and focus on building your character.

"Run from anything that stimulates youthful lusts. Instead, pursue righteous living, faithfulness, love, and peace. Enjoy the companionship of those who call on the Lord with pure hearts" (2 TIMOTHY 2:22 NLT).

God does not want you to marry an unbeliever.

"Do not be yoked together with unbelievers. For what do righteousness and wickedness have in common? Or what fellowship can light have with darkness?" (2 CORINTHIANS 6:14).

God wants you to focus on character, not just appearance, in a future spouse.
"Charm is deceptive, and beauty is fleeting; but a woman who fears the LORD is to be praised" (PROVERBS 31:30).

God wants your marriage to display Christ's love for the church.
"Husbands, love your wives, just as Christ loved the church and gave himself up for her to make her holy, cleansing her by the washing with water through the word, and to present her to himself as a radiant church, without stain or wrinkle or any other blemish, but holy and blameless" (EPHESIANS 5:25–27).

There is no fear in love. But perfect love drives out fear,
because fear has to do with punishment.
The one who fears is not made perfect in love.
(1 JOHN 4:18)

Preparation for Partnership

A couple needs to have an accurate understanding of each other's expectations and desires. Preparation for Partnership is an excellent exercise for opening the door to meaningful communication. Both parties should complete each sentence in writing and then talk through each point.

My definition of love is . . .

My reason for marriage is . . .

My way of handling conflict is . . .

My way of dealing with anger is . . .

My preference for spending free time is . . .

My concept of the role and responsibilities of a husband is . . .

My concept of the role and responsibilities of a wife is . . .

My views on sex within marriage are . . .

My commitments to my extended family are . . .

My commitments to my future in-laws are . . .

My expectation regarding time with friends (following marriage) is . . .

My position on the use of alcohol is . . .

My experience with illegal drugs is . . .

My priorities for spending money are . . .

My priorities for saving money are . . .

My goals for marriage are . . .

My desires regarding children are . . .

My commitment to be actively involved in a church fellowship is . . .

My spiritual goals and desires are . . .

How much better to get wisdom than gold,
to get insight rather than silver!
(PROVERBS 16:16)

Wrong Motives for Marriage[88]

"I want to marry because all of my friends are getting married."

"I want to be married so I won't feel like a failure."

"I want to fulfill my romantic dreams."

"I want to get out of my painful homelife."

"I want to get even with the person who rejected me."

"I want a better family life than I had while growing up."

"I want to prove that I'm stable and can make a commitment."

"I want to prove that I'm not struggling with homosexuality."

"I want the wholesome family ideal."

"I want to please my family."

"I want to please my friends."

"I want to please the person I'm dating."

"I want to please God, who said, 'It is not good for the man to be alone'" (Genesis 2:18).

Key Verses to Memorize

And this is my prayer:
that your love may abound
more and more in knowledge
and depth of insight, so that
you may be able to discern what is best
and may be pure and blameless
for the day of Christ.
(PHILIPPIANS 1:9–10)

"I want to have sex whenever I desire."

"I want to have children."

"I want my children to grow up in a two-parent home."

"I want someone so I won't be alone."

"I want someone to benefit my career/ministry."

"I want someone to need me."

"I want someone to make me happy."

"I want someone to take care of me financially."

"I want someone to take care of me emotionally."

"I want someone with whom I can grow old."

A person may think their own ways are right,
but the LORD weighs the heart.
(PROVERBS 21:2)

Our Commitment to Grow Together Spiritually[89]

We commit our lives to Jesus Christ and submit to His control.

"Whoever wants to be my disciple must deny themselves and take up their cross daily and follow me" (LUKE 9:23).

We commit our home to God and pledge to make it Christ-centered.

"Choose for yourselves this day whom you will serve. . . . But as for me and my household, we will serve the LORD" (JOSHUA 24:15).

We commit our bodies to each other and vow to be sexually faithful.

"Marriage should be honored by all, and the marriage bed kept pure, for God will judge the adulterer and all the sexually immoral" (HEBREWS 13:4).

Key Passage to Read

1 Corinthians 13:4–7

We commit our finances to God and will honor Him with our tithe.

"'Bring the whole tithe into the storehouse, that there may be food in my house. Test me in this,' says the LORD Almighty, 'and see if I will not throw open the floodgates of heaven and pour out so much blessing that there will not be room enough to store it'" (MALACHI 3:10).

We commit to reading the Bible and praying with each other daily.

"Your word is a lamp for my feet, a light on my path. I have taken an oath and confirmed it, that I will follow your righteous laws" (PSALM 119:105–106).

We commit to not go to bed while still angry with one another.

"'In your anger do not sin': Do not let the sun go down while you are still angry" (EPHESIANS 4:26).

We commit to nurturing each other through loving encouragement.

"And let us consider how we may spur one another on toward love and good deeds" (HEBREWS 10:24).

We commit to admitting our weaknesses and to seeking prayer support in order to change.

"Confess your sins to each other and pray for each other so that you may be healed. The prayer of a righteous person is powerful and effective" (JAMES 5:16).

We commit to growing with each other into a deeper relationship with the Lord.

"Let us draw near to God with a sincere heart and with the full assurance that faith brings, having our hearts sprinkled to cleanse us from a guilty conscience and having our bodies washed with pure water. Let us hold unswervingly to the hope we profess, for he who promised is faithful" (HEBREWS 10:22–23).

Submit to one another out of reverence for Christ.
(EPHESIANS 5:21)

My Personalized Plan

I will . . .

Seek God's will.

- I will study what God's Word says about His heart and design for marriage.
- I will consider God's guidelines for choosing a spouse and His warnings about becoming unequally yoked.

"Do not be yoked together with unbelievers. For what do righteousness and wickedness have in common? Or what fellowship can light have with darkness?" (2 CORINTHIANS 6:14).

Pray regularly.

- I will pray throughout my decision-making process while considering marriage.

— I will tell God about my fears, concerns, hopes, and dreams about being married.

"Do not be anxious about anything, but in every situation, by prayer and petition, with thanksgiving, present your requests to God. And the peace of God, which transcends all understanding, will guard your hearts and your minds in Christ Jesus" (PHILIPPIANS 4:6–7).

Seek wise counsel.

— Talk to my family, friends, and trusted counselors about my decision to get married.

— I will talk with husbands, wives, and/or married couples who can provide wisdom and guidance on making the decision about who and when to marry.

"In an abundance of counselors there is safety" (PROVERBS 11:14 ESV).

Focus on character.

— I will look for godly characteristics in a spouse, not just appearances.

— I will prioritize purity and focus on becoming more Christlike as I date and consider marriage.

"Pursue righteousness and a godly life, along with faith, love, perseverance, and gentleness" (1 TIMOTHY 6:11 NLT).

Trust God's plan.

— I will trust in God's timing for marriage, and submit to His will as His Spirit leads me.

— I will look to the Lord to help me make decisions about marriage that will honor Him and display Christ's love.

"Trust in the LORD with all your heart and lean not on your own understanding; in all your ways submit to him, and he will make your paths straight" (PROVERBS 3:5–6).

Questions & Answers

Question: "How can I be 100 percent sure that the person I marry will remain committed to me?"

Answer: You can't be 100 percent sure about the commitment of any other person, but you can commit 100 percent of yourself to the marriage.

She is your partner, the wife of your marriage covenant.
. . . So be on your guard, and do not be unfaithful
to the wife [or husband] *of your youth.*
(MALACHI 2:14–15)

Question: "I cannot financially afford to marry my fiancé. Isn't it okay for us to live together without marrying?"

Answer: No. In the second chapter of the Bible, God says a man is to leave his parents, enter into marriage, and then enjoy the sexual union. If the order is wrong, the results will be wrong. Before you enter into marriage, you need to have wisdom and discipline about money, both income and expenses.

My God will meet all your needs
according to the riches of his glory in Christ Jesus.
(PHILIPPIANS 4:19)

Question: "My fiancé has difficulty talking about his feelings. How can I help him open up and share his hopes, dreams, and expectations for marriage?"

Answer: Seek advice from an older, mature couple. Find a church that offers premarital counseling. Make a list of topics for both of you to address. Ask married couples which issues they wish they had discussed prior to marriage.

The heart of the discerning acquires knowledge,
for the ears of the wise seek it out.
(PROVERBS 18:15)

CRISIS & TRAUMA

Finding Help, Healing & Hope

God's Heart on Crisis & Trauma

God is with you in times of crisis and trauma.

"God is our refuge and strength, an ever-present help in trouble" (PSALM 46:1).

God offers peace in times of crisis and trauma.

"I have told you these things, so that in me you may have peace. In this world you will have trouble. But take heart! I have overcome the world" (JOHN 16:33).

God is the ultimate source of safety and protection in times of crisis and trauma.

"The LORD is my rock, my fortress, and my savior; my God is my rock, in whom I find protection. He is my shield, the power that saves me, and my place of safety" (PSALM 18:2 NLT).

God can use counselors, ministers, and trusted friends to help during times of crisis and trauma.

"Where there is no guidance the people fall, but in abundance of counselors there is victory" (PROVERBS 11:14 NASB).

God can redeem traumatic experiences.

"Put your hope in the LORD, for with the LORD is unfailing love and with him is full redemption" (PSALM 130:7).

God can heal the wounds of trauma.

"He heals the brokenhearted and binds up their wounds" (PSALM 147:3).

God can help me forgive others who have wounded me, just as He has forgiven me.

"Be kind and compassionate to one another, forgiving each other, just as God through Christ has forgiven you" (EPHESIANS 4:32).

God can be trusted.

"For the word of the LORD holds true, and we can trust everything he does" (PSALM 32:2 NLT).

God will never abandon or reject you.

"For the LORD will not reject his people; he will never forsake his inheritance" (PSALM 94:14).

God invites us to lament and mourn our difficult experiences.

"How long must I struggle with anguish in my soul, with sorrow in my heart every day? . . . But I trust in your unfailing love. I will rejoice because you have rescued me. I will sing to the LORD because he is good to me" (PSALM 13:2, 5-6 NLT).

God can comfort you in your pain and use you to comfort others.

"The Father of compassion and the God of all comfort . . . comforts us in all our troubles, so that we can comfort those in any trouble with the comfort we ourselves receive from God" (2 CORINTHIANS 1:3–4).

God gives grace and strength when we are weak and overwhelmed.

"But he said to me, 'My grace is sufficient for you, for my power is made perfect in weakness.' Therefore I will boast all the more gladly about my weaknesses, so that Christ's power may rest on me" (2 CORINTHIANS 12:9).

Crisis & Trauma Definitions

Trauma is defined as "any disturbing experience that results in significant fear, helplessness, dissociation, confusion, or other disruptive feelings intense enough to have a long-lasting negative effect on a person's attitudes, behavior, and other aspects of functioning."[90]

A crisis is defined as "a situation that produces significant cognitive or emotional stress in those involved in it."[91]

The difference between trauma and a crisis is that a crisis refers to an *event* (a temporary stressful situation that usually resolves in time), while trauma tends to be more long-lasting and refers to the physical, psychological, emotional, or spiritual impact that the event has on an individual.

The word *crisis* comes from the Greek *krisis,* meaning *decision, turning point,* or *sudden change,* and was often used in a medical context to describe a turning point or critical stage of an illness or disease.[92]

The word trauma also has its origins in Greek, meaning "wound" or "injury."[93]

Taking the origins of the words together, a crisis can be considered a stressful event that becomes a turning point in which we have the opportunity to look to God for help. The trauma, or wounds, we experience in life can likewise be an opportunity to grow in our faith as we seek the Lord for healing.

He heals the brokenhearted and binds up their wounds.
(PSALM 147:3)

What is a Crisis?

A crisis can be:

— Real: an event that actually happened (accidents, a death, drug overdose, suicide, child running away, etc.)

— Imagined: fears, drug-induced psychosis, delusions, etc.

— Anticipated: an unwanted pregnancy, expected legal troubles, potential job loss, pending divorce, terminal illness, etc.

A crisis can be the result of:

— The reality of living in a fallen, sinful, and broken world

— The sinful choices of another person

— Making unwise, unsafe, or sinful choices

— Spiritual warfare and spiritual attacks

Help me, LORD my God; save me according to your unfailing love.
(PSALM 109:26)

The Impact of Trauma

1. **Trauma** can cause us to get stuck in a cycle of shame and unhealthy coping mechanisms.

2. **Trauma** can impact the way we cope with life and develop relationships.

3. **Trauma** can impact intimacy, attachment, and our ability to trust other people.

4. **Trauma** can impact our ability to look toward a hopeful future.

5. **Trauma** can impact our ability to trust or believe that God loves us and that we have value in His eyes.

6. **Trauma** is not automatically healed with time.

7. **Trauma**, if unresolved, can lead down a path of hopelessness and self-destruction.

8. **Trauma** affects the body, mind, emotions, and spirit, leading to physical symptoms (such as fatigue, headaches, or muscle tension), cognitive struggles (like flashbacks, poor concentration, or intrusive thoughts), emotional distress (such as anxiety, fear, or shame), behavioral changes (including withdrawing from others, sleep disturbances, or increased substance use), and spiritual unbalance (distorted, false, and unhealthy views or beliefs about God and His Word).

9. **Trauma** affects people differently, with varying levels of impact on their mind, body, and emotions.

10. **Trauma**, suffering, and times of crisis can be used by God to transform us.

My soul is in deep anguish. How long, LORD, how long?
Turn, LORD, and deliver me; save me because of your unfailing love.
(PSALM 6:3–4)

Causes & Contributors of Trauma

Accidents (car crash, serious injury, burn, fall, etc.)

Acts of war, terrorism, displacement, being trafficked

Emotional abuse (neglect, being threatened, constant verbal abuse, bullying)

Natural disaster (flood, earthquake, hurricane, tornado, wildfire)

Physical abuse (assault, violence, domestic abuse)

Sexual assault, rape, childhood sexual abuse

Sudden and/or dramatic life change (significant loss, being in the hospital, miscarriage, terminal diagnosis, etc.)

Chronic, ongoing stress or instability (divorce, financial instability, drug addiction, incarceration)

Turn to me and have mercy, for I am alone and in deep distress.
(PSALM 25:16 NLT)

The ABCs of Crisis Care[94]

A–Achieve a connection with the other person.

— Instill confidence by demonstrating a strong positive voice and a strong positive attitude.

— Understand the power of presence in the moment.

— Be calm and control yourself.

— Listen! Listen! Listen!

— Encourage the expression of feelings.

— Be empathetic as opposed to sympathetic.

— Do not minimize, devalue, or underestimate the situation.

- Begin where the other person is (spiritually, emotionally, cognitively, relationally, etc.).
- Accept the person as and where they are. (This does not necessarily mean you are accepting their choices/behaviors.)
- Be confidential unless the person or someone else is endangered.

B-Break down the problem.

- Look for the major issue(s) or theme(s).
- Assess how critical the situation or crisis really is in terms of thoughts, feelings, behaviors, experiences, incidents, etc.
    - Use a 10-point Self-Report Scale similar to the typical pain scale used by doctors and in emergency rooms.
    - Be aware of the tendency to deny, minimize, and/or underreport.
    - Determine frequency, intensity, duration, variability.
- Consider the impact of how the crisis affects the whole person:
    - Physical needs and issues
    - Emotional needs and issues
    - Family/Social/Relational needs and issues
    - Mental/Psychological needs and issues
    - Financial/Vocational, or Other/Practical needs and issues
    - Spiritual needs and issues

Key Verse to Memorize

The Lord is close to the brokenhearted and saves those who are crushed in spirit.
(Psalm 34:18)

- Pinpoint the priorities for effective intervention and/or care, especially any life-threatening or other critical decisions that need to be made—***safety first!***
- Look for those issues that can be attended to easily and quickly.
- Examine what has been tried already.
- Look at new alternatives and directions that can be considered.
- Examine any potential consequences of actions that may be taken.
- Work toward appropriate ownership of the problem or situation.

C-Commit to a plan of action.

- Identify all potential support systems and resources.
- Encourage the formulation of a plan and utilize the following principles in doing so. Build a plan:
    - Using the person's strengths.
    - With two to three primary/initial goals.

    - With specific objectives (smaller steps) to meet those goals.
    - With goals and objectives that are attainable.
    - With goals and objectives that are behavioral.
    - With goals and objectives that are measurable.
    - Set time limits to initiate the plan.
- Be firm and supportive in working through resistance.
- Know when you are in over your head. Have referral sources available and be ready to use them.
- Contact a supervisor, member of the leadership team, and/or pastor as appropriate.

D–Document the interaction

- Write down any identifying information.
- Document the important points of what you discussed, said, did, or recommended.
- Note any issues or concerns, especially those that may have legal, ethical, or liability-related implications.
- Keep the documentation confidential.

E–Explain the plan of action

- Make sure the person understands exactly what the next steps are.
- Consider writing down the plan of action and/or contact names and phone numbers.
- Have the person repeat the plan of action back to you verbally.
- Notify a family member, close friend, pastor, etc., and explain the plan as appropriate.
- Tell the person that you will follow up with them and give them the day/time.

F–Follow up as soon as possible

- Contact the person the next day if possible, or as agreed upon.
- Verify that the action plan has been implemented/started.
- Provide ongoing support and accountability.
- Assess the ongoing level of isolation and the proactive/consistent commitment to stay connected to available/recommended support systems (both within the church and the community at large).
- Check progress utilizing the same four assessment markers as in B: Step 2 (Frequency, Intensity, Duration, and Variability).

But you, Lord, do not be far from me.
You are my strength; come quickly to help me.
(PSALM 22:19)

When to Refer Someone to Professional Help[95]

Supervision with additional wise counsel or appropriate referrals should be sought:

When the person presents an actual or imminent danger to themselves (severe depression, suicidal intent/behaviors, running away, excessive drug abuse, eating disorders, etc.)

When the person presents an actual or imminent danger to others (extreme hostility, aggression, violence or threats thereof; perpetration of child, domestic, or elder abuse, etc.)

When the person has experienced a marked decline in the ability to care for themselves and function in day-to-day life, whether at home, school, or in the workplace (extreme anxiety, panic attacks, severe depression, severe phobias, obsessive-compulsive disorders, uncontrollable and excessive addictive behaviors, etc.)

When the person's reality testing/perception of reality is severely impaired to the extent that judgment, emotions, memory, and/or orientation is disordered (delusions, visual/auditory hallucinations, dissociative identity disorder, severe bipolar cycles, etc.)

When the person's excessive alcohol or substance abuse will require detoxification and the possibility of medical intervention

When the caregiver feels that the problem or situation is beyond his/her abilities, training, experience, competence, availability, or comfort level

When the person is not responding to short-term support and interventions and may require more in-depth or extensive professional help

When there is a strong transference or countertransference dynamic that seems at an impasse despite attempts to address the issue

When the possibility of a dual relationship exists that may negatively affect the caregiving process

When the person asks for a referral to another caregiver

In abundance of counselors there is victory.
(PROVERBS 24:6 ESV)

Crisis Hotlines

NOTE: *If you are ever in immediate danger or having suicidal thoughts and intend to harm yourself, call 911 immediately.* You can also call or text one of the following suicide prevention hotlines anytime. These free, confidential services are available 24/7 and exist to help and support you. Remember, you're not alone. Help is available—and there is hope.

Suicide & Crisis Lifeline

— Call 988

— Available for Deaf + Hard of Hearing individuals

— Help available in Spanish (Ayuda disponible en Español)

— www.988lifeline.org

Crisis Text Line

— Text HOME to 741741 to connect with a volunteer Crisis Counselor

— Help available in Spanish (Ayuda disponible en Español)

— www.crisistextline.org

National Domestic Violence Hotline

— 1-800-799-SAFE (7233)

— Text START to 88788

— Available for Deaf + Hard of Hearing individuals

— Help available in Spanish (Ayuda disponible en Español)

— www.thehotline.org (Live chat available)

National Drug Helpline

— 1-844-289-0879

— https://drughelpline.org/

My Personalized Plan

Find safety

— I will focus on the immediate, most critical needs

— I will seek physical safety for myself and loved ones when facing a crisis.

— I will keep a list of names and numbers I can call or text when in a crisis.

"A prudent person foresees danger and takes precautions" (PROVERBS 27:12 NLT).

Get help

- I will ask my friends, family, church, and/or community for help in a crisis situation.
- I will seek help from a pastor or professional counselors as needed.
- I will keep a list of contact numbers to call or text, including a crisis hotline (see below).

"Where there is no guidance, a people falls, but in an abundance of counselors there is safety" (PROVERBS 11:14 ESV).

Learn relaxation techniques

- I will do deep breathing exercises to calm my body down.
- I will use grounding techniques (strategies to shift my focus away from distress) to promote stability.
- I will focus on what I can control.

"I have calmed and quieted myself, I am like a weaned child with its mother; like a weaned child I am content" (PSALM 131:2).

Develop healthy coping mechanisms

- I will write down the ways I currently deal with stress and difficult situations.
- I will avoid using drugs, alcohol, or other substances to cope with my experience(s).
- I will find healthy ways to cope such as prayer, journaling, exercise, talking with someone, art/music, and similar activities that uplift my spirit.

Key Passage to Read

Lamentations 3:19-26

"Give your burdens to the LORD, and he will take care of you" (PSALM 55:22 NLT).

Maintain routines

- I will seek to maintain a sense of normalcy in my life with regular routines.
- I will not make sudden, drastic changes.
- I will try to keep normal routines of sleep, work, exercise, prayer spiritual disciplines, and leisure.

"In peace I will lie down and sleep, for you alone, LORD, make me dwell in safety" (PSALM 4:8).

Process my thoughts and emotions

- I will accept how I feel and not minimize or ignore my emotions.
- I will not isolate, but I will find someone whom I can talk with, in a safe space, about my experience(s).

— I will consider a creative outlet to express my feelings such as journaling, painting, or playing music.

"Pour out your heart to him, for God is our refuge" (PSALM 62:8 NLT).

Look to the Lord

— I will seek the Lord each day through prayer and reading the Bible.

— I will remember that God is always with me.

— I will remember that He wants to help and heal me from past pain.

"So do not fear, for I am with you; do not be dismayed, for I am your God. I will strengthen you and help you; I will uphold you with my righteous right hand" (ISAIAH 41:10).

Hang onto hope

— I will remember that healing is a process, and it will take time to recover from my crisis and/or traumatic experience.

— I will take things one day at a time.

— I will remember that God gives me hope for the future.

"There is surely a future hope for you, and your hope will not be cut off" (PROVERBS 23:18).

Help Others

— I can be present, listen, pray for, and love others.

— I can practice the ministry of presence with others who are experiencing difficulties even if I don't know exactly what to say or do.

— I can assist others in finding additional help such as a professional counselor, minister, or other resource.

"Carry each other's burdens, and in this way you will fulfill the law of Christ" (GALATIANS 6:2).

Questions & Answers

Question: What is complex trauma?

Answer: Complex trauma is "the exposure to multiple, often interrelated forms of traumatic experiences *and* the difficulties that arise as a result of adapting to or surviving these experiences."[96] Unlike a single traumatic event, like a car accident, complex trauma refers to repeated and prolonged exposure to stressful, dangerous, unsafe, or unstable environments. These experiences often occur in childhood, and impact our mind, body, emotions, and relationships in profound ways.[97] Complex trauma is typically the result of direct harm that is interpersonal (e.g., premeditated, planned, and caused by other people).

In the Psalms, we see how King David's distressing circumstances had a deep effect on his mind, body, and emotions. *"Be merciful to me, Lord, for I am in distress; my eyes grow weak with sorrow, my soul and body with grief. My life is consumed by anguish and my years by groaning; my strength fails because of my affliction, and my bones grow weak"* (Psalm 31:9-10).

God's Word acknowledges the painful reality of traumatic experiences, yet also points us to the reality of hope and restoration.

Though you have made me see troubles, many and bitter,
you will restore my life again;
from the depths of the earth you will again bring me up.
(Psalm 71:20)

Question: What's the difference between stress and trauma?

Answer: Stress is a normal part of life. It is a physical or emotional reaction to the demands of life—taking a test, finishing a project at work, raising children, or planning a wedding. Stress typically goes away after the situation is over.

Trauma, on the other hand, has a much deeper, persistent, and long-lasting effect. People experience trauma not due to the normal demands of life like stress, but due to a sudden, chronic, dangerous, or life-threatening event. Trauma can also develop from a series of events or circumstances, or chronic, ongoing instability such as profound neglect in childhood, ongoing abuse at home, financial instability, or combat in war. The effects of trauma can last for years after the traumatic event.

Whether facing day-to-day stress or the deep wounds from a traumatic experience, the Lord invites us to come to Him for healing, hope, and peace.

In my distress I prayed to the Lord,
and the Lord answered me and set me free.
(Psalm 118:5)

> (Psalm 71:20)

> (Psalm 118:5)

CRITICAL SPIRIT

Confronting the Heart of a Critic

God's Heart on a Critical Spirit

In **Matthew 7:1–5,** Jesus spoke unforgettable words with unforgettable imagery . . .

Don't be judgmental or you, too, will be judged.

"Do not judge, or you too will be judged" (v. 1).

Don't judge or you will be judged in the same way and measured by the same standard.

"For in the same way you judge others, you will be judged, and with the measure you use, it will be measured to you" (v. 2).

Don't focus on the small faults of others before focusing on your own big faults.

"Why do you look at the speck of sawdust in your brother's eye and pay no attention to the plank in your own eye?" (v. 3).

Don't talk to others about their faults while ignoring your own.

"How can you say to your brother, 'Let me take the speck out of your eye,' when all the time there is a plank in your own eye?" (v. 4).

Don't be hypocritical—correct your own faults first! Then you can correct someone else's faults!

"You hypocrite, first take the plank out of your own eye, and then you will see clearly to remove the speck from your brother's eye" (v. 5).

Luke, one of the gospel writers, records Jesus saying very similar words:

"Do not judge, and you will not be judged.
Do not condemn, and you will not be condemned.
Forgive, and you will be forgiven."
(Luke 6:37)

Differences Between a Critical Spirit and a Caring Spirit

A critical spirit condemns the person as well as the action.

A caring spirit condemns the action, but not the person.
"The words of the reckless pierce like swords, but the tongue of the wise brings healing" (PROVERBS 12:18).

A critical spirit focuses on the faults of others.

A caring spirit focuses on their own faults.
"Why do you look at the speck of sawdust in your brother's eye and pay no attention to the plank in your own eye?" (LUKE 6:41).

A critical spirit makes judgments based on appearances.

A caring spirit makes judgments based on facts.
"Stop judging by mere appearances, but instead judge correctly" (JOHN 7:24).

A critical spirit assumes the worst without first hearing from the accused.

A caring spirit assumes the best while waiting to hear from the accused.
"Does our law condemn a man without first hearing him to find out what he has been doing?" (JOHN 7:51).

A critical spirit tears others down without seeing their unmet needs.

A caring spirit builds others up according to their inner needs.
"Do not let any unwholesome talk come out of your mouths, but only what is helpful for building others up according to their needs, that it may benefit those who listen" (EPHESIANS 4:29).

A critical spirit publicly criticizes those who have wronged them—without first going to them.

A caring spirit privately confronts those who have wronged them—going to them first.

"If your brother or sister sins, go and point out their fault, just between the two of you. If they listen to you, you have won them over" (MATTHEW 18:15).

Walk in the way of love, just as Christ loved us
and gave himself up for us as a fragrant offering
and sacrifice to God.
(EPHESIANS 5:2)

Childhood Wounds

H—Harshness, which communicates "You're not worthy of any consideration."

U—Unconcern, which communicates "You have no value."

R—Rejection, which communicates "You're not acceptable."

T—Taunting, which communicates "You deserve to be insulted."

The Root Cause

Wrong Belief: "My sense of significance is increased when I point out the wrongs of others. The fact that I believe I am right justifies my criticism of others."

But the Bible says, *"You, therefore, have no excuse, you who pass judgment on someone else, for at whatever point you judge another, you are condemning yourself, because you who pass judgment do the same things"* (Romans 2:1).

Key Verse to Memorize

Let your conversation be always full of grace, seasoned with salt, so that you may know how to answer everyone.
(COLOSSIANS 4:6)

Right Belief: "When I am critical of others, I am actually exposing my own sin. Because Christ lives in me, and He continually extends His mercy toward me, I will reflect His compassion by caring about others rather than by criticizing them."

The Bible says, *"Encourage the disheartened, help the weak, be patient with everyone. Make sure that nobody pays back wrong for wrong, but always strive to do what is good for each other and for everyone else"* (1 Thessalonians 5:14–15).

How to Respond to Criticism

1. **Be assured**, you can accept others in the same way Christ accepts you.

   "Accept one another, then, just as Christ accepted you, in order to bring praise to God" (ROMANS 15:7).

2. **Be open** to the slightest kernel of truth when you are criticized.

   "A rebuke impresses a discerning person more than a hundred lashes a fool" (PROVERBS 17:10).

3. **Be willing** to consider that the criticism may be true. Your critic may be God's megaphone to get your attention.

   "The way of fools seems right to them, but the wise listen to advice" (PROVERBS 12:15).

4. **Be diligent** about receiving criticism without becoming defensive.[98]

   "Mockers resent correction, so they avoid the wise" (PROVERBS 15:12).

5. **Be determined** not to speak ill of your critic.

   "Set a guard over my mouth, LORD; keep watch over the door of my lips" (PSALM 141:3).

6. **Be committed** to pray for your critic.

   "Love your enemies and pray for those who persecute you" (MATTHEW 5:44).

7. **Be aware** that as a follower of Christ, you will be criticized.

   "Blessed are you when people insult you, persecute you and falsely say all kinds of evil against you because of me" (MATTHEW 5:11).

8. **Be encouraged** that you will be disciplined by God because you are His child.

   "And have you completely forgotten this word of encouragement that addresses you as a father addresses his son? It says, 'My son, do not make light of the Lord's discipline, and do not lose heart when he rebukes you, because the Lord disciplines the one he loves, and he chastens everyone he accepts as his son'" (HEBREWS 12:5–6).

9. **Be dependent** on the Lord's perspective to determine your worth and value, not on the opinions of others.

   "Am I now trying to win the approval of human beings, or of God? Or am I trying to please people? If I were still trying to please people, I would not be a servant of Christ" (GALATIANS 1:10).

10. **Be discerning** regarding the accuracy of the critical words of others.

    "The wise in heart are called discerning, and gracious words promote instruction" (PROVERBS 16:21).

My Personalized Plan

Let's examine how a critical heart can become a caring heart. Consider the biblical truths below, and ask the Lord how you can start taking steps today to demonstrate a caring heart toward others.

A caring heart sees its own shortcomings.

"Search me, God, and know my heart; test me and know my anxious thoughts. See if there is any offensive way in me, and lead me in the way everlasting" (PSALM 139:23–24).

A caring heart has active compassion for others.

"As God's chosen people, holy and dearly loved, clothe yourselves with compassion, kindness, humility, gentleness and patience" (COLOSSIANS 3:12).

A caring heart draws out the heartfelt needs of others.

"The purposes of a person's heart are deep waters, but one who has insight draws them out" (PROVERBS 20:5).

A caring heart offers acceptance to others.

"Accept the one whose faith is weak, without quarreling over disputable matters . . . for God has accepted them" (ROMANS 14:1, 3).

Key Passage to Read

James 3:1–12

A caring heart sees God-given worth in others.

"Are not five sparrows sold for two pennies? Yet not one of them is forgotten by God. Indeed, the very hairs of your head are all numbered. Don't be afraid; you are worth more than many sparrows" (LUKE 12:6–7).

A caring heart praises the positives in others.

"The wisdom that comes from heaven is first of all pure; then peace-loving, considerate, submissive, full of mercy and good fruit, impartial and sincere" (JAMES 3:17).

A caring heart doesn't wound others with words.

"Let the message of Christ dwell among you richly as you teach and admonish one another with all wisdom" (COLOSSIANS 3:16).

A caring heart sees the unmet needs of others.

"My God will meet all your needs according to the riches of his glory in Christ Jesus" (PHILIPPIANS 4:19).

A caring heart relies on God's Word and God's Spirit for wisdom.

"This is what we speak, not in words taught us by human wisdom but in words taught by the Spirit, explaining spiritual realities with Spirit-taught words" (1 CORINTHIANS 2:13).

If you have any encouragement from being united with Christ,
if any comfort from his love, if any common sharing in the Spirit,
if any tenderness and compassion, then make my joy complete
by being like-minded, having the same love,
being one in spirit and of one mind.
(PHILIPPIANS 2:1–2)

Questions & Answers

Question: "Several leaders in my church seem to have judgmental spirits and continually criticize other members. I try to be pleasant and forgiving, but is this the way the leaders in church should act?"

Answer: For a spiritual leader to be critical is contrary to Scripture. The Bible says the "shepherds of God's flock" are to be humble examples of Christ. Examine yourself and the other people in your church. You could be in a church that is legalistic, and therefore one that doesn't allow the grace of God or the love of Christ to flourish. Ask the Lord to lead you in either bringing the matter to a church leader whom you respect, or in finding a new church.

To the elders among you. . . .
Be shepherds of God's flock that is
under your care, watching over them . . .
not pursuing dishonest gain, but eager to serve;
not lording it over those entrusted to you,
but being examples to the flock.
(1 PETER 5:1–3)

Question: "What can I say to friends who bad-mouth my husband? The things they say about him keep me focused on his faults."

Answer: Set boundaries with your friends as to what you will and will not listen to in regard to your husband.

Explain that you have determined to switch your focus from your husband's faults to his needs . . . and to pray that your husband would let the Lord meet his deepest inner needs.

Above all, love each other deeply, because
love covers over a multitude of sins.
(1 PETER 4:8)

CULTS

The Truth Twisters

God's Heart on Cults

God desires that we know Him and His Word, the Bible. Any teaching that contradicts His Word draws us away from God.

"This is eternal life: that they know you, the only true God, and Jesus Christ, whom you have sent" (JOHN 17:3).

God desires that we know Him as our heavenly Father, the one true God.

"See what great love the Father has lavished on us, that we should be called children of God! And that is what we are! The reason the world does not know us is that it did not know him" (1 JOHN 3:1).

God desires that we know the authority and sufficiency of His inerrant, infallible Word.

"All your words are true; all your righteous laws are eternal" (PSALM 119:160).

God desires that we follow His Word, not any distortion, twisting, or perversion of His Word, so we will be equipped to do His will.

"All Scripture is God-breathed and is useful for teaching, rebuking, correcting and training in righteousness, so that the servant of God may be thoroughly equipped for every good work" (2 TIMOTHY 3:16–17).

God desires that no one perishes. He has provided salvation through faith in Christ alone.

"This is good, and pleases God our Savior, who wants all people to be saved and to come to a knowledge of the truth. For there is one God and one mediator between God and mankind, the man Christ Jesus, who gave himself as a ransom for all people" (1 TIMOTHY 2:3–6).

God desires that we choose to serve Him alone. Cults often manipulate people into following false gods.

"If serving the LORD seems undesirable to you, then choose for yourselves this day whom you will serve, whether the gods your ancestors served beyond the Euphrates, or the gods of the Amorites, in whose land you are living. But as for me and my household, we will serve the LORD" (JOSHUA 24:15).

God desires that all come to know Him. A cult will isolate followers from family and friends.

"The Lord is not slow in keeping his promise, as some understand slowness. Instead he is patient with you, not wanting anyone to perish, but everyone to come to repentance" (2 Peter 3:9).

God desires Christlike humility in spiritual leaders. False apostles often lack humility, possessing authoritarian, graceless gospels.

"Don't be selfish; don't try to impress others. Be humble, thinking of others as better than yourselves. Don't look out only for your own interests, but take an interest in others, too. You must have the same attitude that Christ Jesus had" (Philippians 2:3–5 nlt).

God desires that no one be deceived by false religion or pagan practices.

"See to it that no one takes you captive through hollow and deceptive philosophy, which depends on human tradition and the elemental spiritual forces of this world rather than on Christ" (Colossians 2:8).

God desires that no one be abused; He hates violence. Cults have been known to use violence to coerce those within their sect.

"The Lord examines the righteous, but the wicked, those who love violence, he hates with a passion" (Psalm 11:5).

God desires that all know of the deity of Jesus. Cults often deny or distort Christ's divinity.

"In Christ all the fullness of the Deity lives in bodily form" (Colossians 2:9).

God desires that we experience His great love and that we believe in the true gospel of Christ's death and resurrection for our sins.

"God demonstrates his own love for us in this: While we were still sinners, Christ died for us" (Romans 5:8).

How Cults Vary from Orthodox Christianity

Every cult varies in its teachings from one or more of six fundamental doctrines of the Christian faith.

V—Virgin Birth—Jesus Christ was conceived by the Holy Spirit and born of a virgin.

"This is how the birth of Jesus the Messiah came about: His mother Mary was pledged to be married to Joseph, but before they came together, she was found to be pregnant through the Holy Spirit. . . . 'The virgin will conceive and will give birth to a son, and they will call him Immanuel' (which means, 'God with us')" (Matthew 1:18, 23).

A—Atonement—Only the shed blood of Jesus Christ pays the penalty for our personal sin.

"God demonstrates his own love for us in this: While we were still sinners, Christ died for us. Since we have now been justified by his blood, how much more shall we be saved from God's wrath through him!" (ROMANS 5:8-9).

Key Verse to Memorize

Do your best to present yourself
to God as one approved,
a worker who does not need to be ashamed
and who correctly handles the word of truth.
(2 TIMOTHY 2:15)

R—Resurrection—Jesus Christ was raised from the dead in bodily form and was seen on earth by many.

"Christ died for our sins according to the Scriptures, that he was buried, that he was raised on the third day according to the Scriptures, and that he appeared to Cephas [Peter], *and then to the Twelve. After that, he appeared to more than five hundred of the brothers and sisters at the same time"* (1 CORINTHIANS 15:3-6).

I—Incarnation—Jesus Christ, who is God, took on human form and was fully God and fully man.

"In the beginning was the Word, and the Word was with God, and the Word was God. He was with God in the beginning. Through him all things were made; without him nothing was made that has been made. . . . The Word became flesh and made his dwelling among us. We have seen his glory, the glory of the one and only Son, who came from the Father, full of grace and truth" (JOHN 1:1-3, 14).

E—Eschatology—After Jesus Christ visibly returns to earth during the end times, a final judgment is a certainty, sending the unrighteous to eternal punishment and the righteous to eternal life.

"Just as people are destined to die once, and after that to face judgment, so Christ was sacrificed once to take away the sins of many; and he will appear a second time, not to bear sin, but to bring salvation to those who are waiting for him" (HEBREWS 9:27-28).

"Then they will go away to eternal punishment, but the righteous to eternal life" (MATTHEW 25:46).

S—Scripture—The Bible is wholly inspired by God, is without error in the original writings and revelation, and is the only authority for righteous living.

"All Scripture is God-breathed and is useful for teaching, rebuking, correcting and training in righteousness" (2 TIMOTHY 3:16).

"Every word of God is flawless;
he is a shield to those who take refuge in him.
Do not add to his words,
or he will rebuke you and prove you a liar."
(PROVERBS 30:5–6)

Mathematical Formula[99]

Does it:

+ **Add** to God's Word?

Mormons add three other books of Scripture, including the Book of Mormon, what they call "the most correct book on earth."

Rosicrucians include, along with the Bible, the *Egyptian Book of the Dead* and *The Lost Books of Jesus* as their holy books.

"Every word of God is flawless; he is a shield to those who take refuge in him. Do not add to his words, or he will rebuke you and prove you a liar" (PROVERBS 30:5–6).

- **Subtract** from the person of Jesus Christ?

Jehovah's Witnesses teach that Jesus was actually Michael the Archangel, not God in the flesh.

The Unification Church ("Moonies") teaches that Jesus failed in His mission on earth and that Reverend Moon is the second coming of the Messiah.

"The Son is the image of the invisible God. . . . For in him all things were created: things in heaven and on earth, visible and invisible, whether thrones or powers or rulers or authorities; all things have been created through him and for him" (COLOSSIANS 1:15–16).

× **Multiply** Salvation requirements?

The New Age Movement denies Jesus' sacrifice on the cross for salvation and substitutes reincarnation as the means of perfecting the soul.

Scientology teaches that "engrams" (subconscious negative impressions) have developed for seventy-four trillion years, causing health and psychological problems. Only through countless therapeutic sessions, at costly fees, can people achieve the ultimate state to become "theta clear." The goal of an "operating thetan" is to be clear from the necessity of having a body and to live with "supernatural power" outside the body.

"It is by grace you have been saved, through faith—and this is not from yourselves, it is the gift of God—not by works, so that no one can boast" (EPHESIANS 2:8–9).

÷ **Divide** the follower's loyalty?

Heaven's Gate taught that one must renounce family ties and all sexual relations in order to enter the Level Beyond Human (heaven).

Branch Davidians taught that one cannot be loyal to God without being loyal to David Koresh.

"You shall have no other gods before me" (EXODUS 20:3).

How Cults Cloak Themselves with Twists on Truth

Can you imagine a neighbor saying, "I have joined a wonderful cult. Would you like me to tell you about it?" Of course not! Cults are much more subtle in their approach, using deceptive statements like these:[100]

— "Join us for a free dinner and discussion group about current events."

— "You can reach your true potential by attending this course on self-awareness."

— "Come with me to our retreat this weekend—you have to be present to experience its power."

— "Would you be interested in helping us bring love and unity to all mankind?"

— "This seminar will teach you a new technique for handling stress in your life."

— "We have a new Bible study that reveals ancient secrets unknown to most Christians."

Key Passage to Read

John 1:1-18

Those people are zealous to win you over, but for no good.
What they want is to alienate you from us,
so that you may have zeal for them.
(GALATIANS 4:17)

My Personalized Plan

I will . . .

Acknowledge that cults are real and dangerous, bringing those involved in them under the control of others and away from the one true God.

— I will acknowledge that participation in a cult clouds and confuses judgment of what is true.

— I will acknowledge that cults lead to a path of destruction.

"There is a way that appears to be right, but in the end it leads to death" (PROVERBS 14:12).

Abandon all aspects of any cult, realizing that teaching contradicting God's Word is false and cannot be taken as truth.

— I will abandon any involvement in a cult. Following a cult leads to bondage, secrecy, exclusion, danger, abuse, and loss of self, family, friends, and possibly even life.

— I recognize cult followers are convinced of "their truth," and no matter how many errors are uncovered in their beliefs, they may fiercely defend and remain loyal to its leader.

"Turn away from godless chatter and the opposing ideas of what is falsely called knowledge, which some have professed and in so doing have departed from the faith" (1 TIMOTHY 6:20-21).

Ask God to forgive my involvement in cult activity and show me how to live in the light and freedom of His love and grace.

— I will confess and turn away from any and all cult activity, trusting that Jesus forgives me and accepts me on the basis of His grace.

— I will ask God to free me from confusion so that I can follow Him, live according to His Word, and be free from the grip of deception.

"I have been crucified with Christ. It is no longer I who live, but Christ who lives in me. And the life I now live in the flesh I live by faith in the Son of God, who loved me and gave himself for me" (GALATIANS 2:20 ESV).

Adjust my life to replace old thoughts and habits with new and healthy ones.

— I will identify the lies I've been led to believe about God, myself, others, and the world.

— I will replace those lies with the truth of God's Word.

"Guide me in your truth and teach me, for you are God my Savior, and my hope is in you all day long" (PSALM 25:5).

Questions & Answers

Question: "Didn't the apostle Paul start a heretical sect—Christianity—which Christ never intended?"

Answer: No. Jesus Christ was the promised Messiah, who fulfilled all the Old Testament prophesies about the "Anointed One" who was to come. Christianity is not a perversion of truth, but the perfection of truth. Christ did not come to create a new teaching, but rather to fulfill the old.

"Do not think that I have come to abolish the Law or the Prophets; I have not come to abolish them but to fulfill them."
(MATTHEW 5:17)

Question: "Are all cults basically the same?"

Answer: Yes and no. Cults can differ, but exhibit similar psychological patterns.

- **Closed-mindedness**—not interested in a rational evaluation of the facts
- **Blind obedience to authority**—the dogma of the leader or founder is supreme
- **Controlled living**—details of daily life are dictated by the leader
- **Contempt for outsiders**—intolerance for any belief system other than their own

There will be false teachers among you.
They will secretly introduce destructive heresies,
even denying the sovereign Lord
who bought them—bringing swift
destruction on themselves.
(2 PETER 2:1)

Question: "Is complete recovery possible?"

Answer: Yes!

"For nothing will be impossible with God."
(LUKE 1:37 ESV)

DATING

Great Relating When Dating

God's Heart on Dating

God desires that Christians date only those who have yielded their lives to Christ and are in right relationship with Him.

"Do not be yoked together with unbelievers. For what do righteousness and wickedness have in common? Or what fellowship can light have with darkness? . . . Or what does a believer have in common with an unbeliever?" (2 CORINTHIANS 6:14–15).

God desires that you know the meaning of genuine love and choose prospective dates with these attributes.

"Love is patient, love is kind. It does not envy, it does not boast, it is not proud. It does not dishonor others, it is not self-seeking, it is not easily angered, it keeps no record of wrongs. Love does not delight in evil but rejoices with the truth. It always protects, always trusts, always hopes, always perseveres" (1 CORINTHIANS 13:4–7).

God desires that you date those who are committed to purity and live according to His Word.

"How can a young person stay on the path of purity? By living according to your word" (PSALM 119:9).

God desires that you pursue godly qualities in your life and date those who are like-minded.

"Pursue righteousness, faith, love and peace, along with those who call on the Lord out of a pure heart" (2 TIMOTHY 2:22).

God desires that you and those you date honor each other with self-control toward each other.

"Each of you should learn to control your own body in a way that is holy and honorable" (1 THESSALONIANS 4:4).

God desires that you and those you date speak the truth in love to each other and grow in Christian maturity before each other.

"Speaking the truth in love, we will grow to become in every respect the mature body of him who is the head, that is, Christ" (EPHESIANS 4:15).

God desires that, as you date, you encourage one another and build each other up.

"Encourage one another and build each other up, just as in fact you are doing" (1 THESSALONIANS 5:11).

God desires that your dating relationship be a means of sharpening one another in character.

"As iron sharpens iron, so one person sharpens another" (PROVERBS 27:17).

God desires that in your dating relationship you seek to please Him above all others.

"'Love the Lord your God with all your heart and with all your soul and with all your strength and with all your mind'; and, 'Love your neighbor as yourself'" (LUKE 10:27).

Teach me to do your will,
for you are my God;
may your good Spirit
lead me on level ground.
(PSALM 143:10)

Checklist for Dating

Does your prospective date . . .

- ☐ Act fairly and justly in all areas of life?
- ☐ Extend forgiveness and mercy?
- ☐ Demonstrate humility before God and others?
- ☐ Display wisdom and discernment?
- ☐ Exercise discipline and self-control?
- ☐ Express genuine respect toward authority?
- ☐ Follow through by meeting obligations?
- ☐ Have a heart to do what is in your best interest?
- ☐ Have a reputation as someone who keeps commitments?
- ☐ Interact with consistent kindness and thoughtfulness?
- ☐ Live in a way that displays integrity?
- ☐ Maintain eye contact when talking with people?
- ☐ Manage money well?
- ☐ Meet the approval of the significant people in your life?
- ☐ Possess a sensitive conscience in regard to right and wrong?
- ☐ Present a positive outlook on life?
- ☐ Refuse to use you or others to gain status?
- ☐ Reveal an active Bible study and prayer life?
- ☐ Share your personal values?
- ☐ Show evidence of the fruit of the Spirit?

The fruit of the Spirit is love, joy, peace,
forbearance, kindness,
goodness, faithfulness, gentleness
and self-control.
(GALATIANS 5:22–23)

Self-Centered Dating vs. Christ-Centered Dating[101]

Self-Centered Dating	Christ-Centered Dating
Focuses on *finding* the right person	Focuses on *being* the right person
Focuses on romance	Focuses on friendship
Spends much one-on-one time together	Limits one-on-one time together
Spends most time with each other, not in groups	Spends time together with others, often in groups
Expects sexual involvement	Respects sex as sacred; purity is paramount
Prioritizes pleasing self	Prioritizes pleasing the Lord
Relies on self and feelings for guidance	Relies on prayer, wise counsel, and accountability
Pursues pleasure as ultimate goal	Pursues marriage as ultimate goal
Views marriage as a contract	Views marriage as a covenant
Sees parental approval as unimportant	Seeks parental approval of relationship
Heavy emotional and physical involvement	Spiritually connected
Focuses on each other for fulfillment	Focuses first on Christ and then on each other for fulfillment

Let the wise listen and add to their learning,
and let the discerning get guidance.
(PROVERBS 1:5)

Purity

The following acrostic on **purity** can help you maintain a godly perspective in your dating relationship.

P—Prioritize God's standard for purity in your dating.

"Marriage should be honored by all, and the marriage bed kept pure, for God will judge the adulterer and all the sexually immoral" (HEBREWS 13:4).

U—Undertake personal accountability for how you treat your date's body.

"But among you there must not be even a hint of sexual immorality, or of any kind of impurity, or of greed, because these are improper for God's holy people" (EPHESIANS 5:3).

R—Refrain from activities that arouse sexual desires and violate God's standard. Repent and recommit to sexual purity if these standards are violated.

"And this is my prayer: that your love may abound more and more in knowledge and depth of insight, so that you may be able to discern what is best and may be pure and blameless for the day of Christ, filled with the fruit of righteousness that comes through Jesus Christ—to the glory and praise of God" (PHILIPPIANS 1:9–11).

Key Verse to Memorize

In your relationships with one another, have the same mindset as Christ Jesus.
(PHILIPPIANS 2:5)

I—Implement goals that are pleasing to God.

"We make it our goal to please him, whether we are at home in the body or away from it. For we must all appear before the judgment seat of Christ, so that each of us may receive what is due us for the things done while in the body, whether good or bad" (2 CORINTHIANS 5:9–10).

T—Trust in God's timing.

"Jacob served seven years to get Rachel, but they seemed like only a few days to him because of his love for her" (GENESIS 29:20).

Y—Yield your life to the Lord.

"Seek first his kingdom and his righteousness, and all these things will be given to you as well" (MATTHEW 6:33).

The wisdom of the prudent is to give thought to their ways,
but the folly of fools is deception.
(PROVERBS 14:8)

My Personalized Plan

Be wise—I will ask the Lord to . . .

— Guide my decision to date

— Guide the decisions of my date

— Guard my heart, mind, body, and soul during the dating process

Be safe—To ensure I am safe, I will . . .

— Allow trusted friends and family to introduce me to those who share my beliefs and interests

— Spend time together with new dates in a group setting as we get to know each other

— Meet in public places as we build trust and observe character

Be real—Seeking to get to know the person I am dating by being real, I will . . .

— Share the basics: faith, family, friends, background, education

— Not be afraid to go deeper: talk about previous relationships, career, and financial stability

— Discuss our expectations for the dating relationship: both share what we hope to give *and* get from the relationship

Key Passage to Read

1 Thessalonians 4:4–6

Be honest—Talking to my date about what I do not enjoy or appreciate, I will . . .

— Set boundaries rather than go along with whatever my date wants

— Speak up if my date says or does something that makes me uncomfortable

— Stand up to peer pressure and say *no* when I know I should say *no*

Kings take pleasure in honest lips;
they value the one who speaks what is right.
(Proverbs 16:13)

Questions & Answers

Question: "How do I know when I've met the 'right' person?"

Answer: Instead of only asking, "Is this the right person for me?" why not also ask, "Am I becoming the right person?" Being the "right person" is coming to a relationship with love to share, not seeking love and validation in another person.

If you continually learn about yourself—growing emotionally, socially, and spiritually, and taking responsibility for your own feelings of safety, security, and worth—you will not be attracted to someone who is manipulative and controlling or who just wants to be loved but not give love in return.

To discover whether the person you're dating is who they say they are, you need to see them in a variety of situations and settings. How a person handles conflict is one of the best ways to see the real person. A "right" person is open to learning from conflict, not just wanting to win at all costs. Invest adequate time in the relationship to see each other as you truly are.

Other characteristics to watch for in "Mr. Right" or "Ms. Right" are . . .

— Closely matched levels of emotional and spiritual maturity

— Commitment to lifelong marriage

— Common interests and values

— Compatible long-term goals

— Comparable health and fitness standards

— Common money management practices

— Chemistry—at least a spark of attraction

Teach me good discernment and knowledge,
for I believe in Your commandments.
(Psalm 119:66 nasb)

DEATH & HEAVEN

The Doorway to Your Destiny

God's Heart on Death and Heaven

God lives in heaven, ruling all things from His heavenly throne.

"The LORD has established his throne in heaven, and his kingdom rules over all" (PSALM 103:19).

God destroyed death through the life, death, and resurrection of Jesus Christ.

"It has now been revealed through the appearing of our Savior, Christ Jesus, who has destroyed death and has brought life and immortality to light through the gospel" (2 TIMOTHY 1:10).

God offers eternal life to everyone through faith in Jesus Christ.

"God so loved the world that he gave his one and only Son, that whoever believes in him shall not perish but have eternal life" (JOHN 3:16).

God will judge each person after they die.

"People are destined to die once, and after that to face judgment" (HEBREWS 9:27).

God promises believers they will be with the Lord when they die.

"As long as we are at home in the body we are away from the Lord. . . . We are confident, I say, and would prefer to be away from the body and at home with the Lord" (2 CORINTHIANS 5:6, 8).

God will resurrect everyone on the last day—believers to eternal life in heaven and unbelievers to eternal punishment in hell.

"Multitudes who sleep in the dust of the earth will awake: some to everlasting life, others to shame and everlasting contempt" (DANIEL 12:2).

God does not delight in the death of the unbelieving.

"Do you think that I like to see wicked people die? says the Sovereign LORD. Of course not! I want them to turn from their wicked ways and live" (EZEKIEL 18:23 NLT).

God will make a new heaven and new earth at the end of time.

"See, I will create new heavens and a new earth. The former things will not be remembered, nor will they come to mind" (ISAIAH 65:17).

God promises that heaven will be free of suffering and death.

"He will wipe every tear from their eyes, and there will be no more death or sorrow or crying or pain. All these things are gone forever" (REVELATION 21:4 NLT).

God wants you to focus on the realities of heaven.

"Since you have been raised to new life with Christ, set your sights on the realities of heaven, where Christ sits in the place of honor at God's right hand. Think about the things of heaven, not the things of earth" (COLOSSIANS 3:1–2 NLT).

God wants you to encourage others with the hope of eternal life with Him.

"We want you to know what will happen to the believers who have died so you will not grieve like people who have no hope. For since we believe that Jesus died and was raised to life again, we also believe that when Jesus returns, God will bring back with him the believers who have died . . . Then we will be with the Lord forever. So encourage each other with these words" (1 THESSALONIANS 4:13–14, 17–18 NLT).

God wants you to share the gospel and lead people to their eternal home in heaven.

"We are therefore Christ's ambassadors, as though God were making his appeal through us. We implore you on Christ's behalf: Be reconciled to God" (2 CORINTHIANS 5:20).

"I am the resurrection and the life.
The one who believes in me will live,
even though they die; and whoever
lives by believing in me will never die.
Do you believe this?"
(JOHN 11:25–26)

Myths and Truths About Heaven

Myth: All religions lead people to heaven.

Truth: No. Jesus said, "I am the way and the truth and the life. No one comes to the Father except through me" (John 14:6). The Bible is clear that *"salvation is found in no one else, for there is no other name under heaven given to mankind by which we must be saved"* (Acts 4:12).

Myth: You cannot know for sure whether you will go to heaven.

Truth: Jesus told the repentant thief on the cross, *"Truly I tell you, today you will be with me in paradise"* (Luke 23:43). He assured Martha, *"Anyone who believes in me will live, even after dying"* (John 11:25 NLT). You can know for sure that you will go to heaven. Jesus said that those who believe in Him already have eternal life: *"I tell you the truth, those who listen to my message and believe in God who sent me have eternal life. They will never be condemned for their sins, but they have already passed from death into life"* (John 5:24 NLT).

Myth: Heaven will be boring.

Truth: Heaven is a place of unending joy, peace, and blessing. Jesus described the joy of feasting in God's kingdom, saying, *"Blessed is the one who will eat at the feast in the kingdom of God"* (Luke 14:15). Elsewhere, the Bible describes the joy of being in God's presence: *"You make known to me the path of life; you will fill me with joy in your presence, with eternal pleasures at your right hand"* (Psalm 16:11).

Myth: Heaven will be unending choir practice.

Truth: Indeed, heaven will be filled with wonderful music and worship. The Bible also describes heaven as a place of feasting (Luke 14:15), serving and reigning with Christ (Revelation 22:3-5), and living in the most beautiful, magnificent city—the New Jerusalem—with God forever (Revelation 21-22).

"No longer will there be any curse. The throne of God and of the Lamb will be in the city, and his servants will serve him. They will see his face, and his name will be on their foreheads. There will be no more night. They will not need the light of a lamp or the light of the sun, for the Lord God will give them light. And they will reign for ever and ever" (REVELATION 22:3-5).

We are confident, yes, well pleased rather
to be absent from the body
and to be present with the Lord.
(2 CORINTHIANS 5:8 NKJV)

Myths and Truths about Hell

Myth: Talking about hell is "unloving."

Truth: Warning someone of certain danger is actually a very loving act. Jesus speaks more about hell than anything else in the Bible, and He provides the only hope of escaping the certainty of hell. Why would anyone not sound the alarm if they also knew the only way of escape?

"Serve the LORD with fear and celebrate his rule with trembling. Kiss his son, or he will be angry and your way will lead to your destruction, for his wrath can flare up in a moment. Blessed are all who take refuge in him" (PSALM 2:11-12).

Key Verse to Memorize

Jesus said to her, "I am the
resurrection and the life.
The one who believes in me will live,
even though they die."
(JOHN 11:25)

Myth: A loving God would never send anyone to hell.

Truth: Rather than *sending* people to hell, our loving God offers opportunities to avoid the judgment of hell, through the redemption offered in Christ.

Since God is a just and righteous and holy God, the penalty for sin must be paid. Jesus paid the penalty for all sin, but we must accept His merciful gift. If anyone does not accept that free gift of salvation, that person has already been condemned by their own sin and will face God's judgment.

"Do not be afraid of those who kill the body and after that can do no more. But I will show you whom you should fear: Fear him who, after your body has been killed, has authority to throw you into hell" (LUKE 12:4–5).

Myth: Hell won't be so bad—all the "fun" people will be there to party.

Truth: Hell is not a place of celebration. No, the Bible describes it as a place of torment—a place of isolation from God, absent of all things good, where its inhabitants are thrown into utter *"darkness, where there will be weeping and gnashing of teeth"* (Matthew 25:30).

"The Son of Man will send out his angels, and they will weed out of his kingdom everything that causes sin and all who do evil. They will throw them into the blazing furnace, where there will be weeping and gnashing of teeth" (MATTHEW 13:41–42).

Myth: Hell won't last forever—eventually the punishment of hell will end.

Truth: God's Word says there will be no end—literally—to the torment of those who inhabit hell. Jesus said hell is a place of *"eternal fire"* (Matthew 25:41) and *"eternal punishment"* (25:46).

"They will be punished with eternal destruction, forever separated from the Lord and from his glorious power" (2 THESSALONIANS 1:9 NLT).

Living with an Eternal Perspective

Remember your days are numbered.

"Teach us to number our days, that we may gain a heart of wisdom" (PSALM 90:12).

Reflect on the reality of heaven.

"Since you have been raised to new life with Christ, set your sights on the realities of heaven, where Christ sits in the place of honor at God's right hand. Think about the things of heaven, not the things of earth" (COLOSSIANS 3:1–2 NLT).

Live to please God.

"We urge you in the name of the Lord Jesus to live in a way that pleases God" (1 THESSALONIANS 4:1 NLT).

Pray for the lost.

"My heart's desire and prayer to God for them is that they may be saved" (ROMANS 10:1 ESV).

Steward your resources well.

"Command those who are rich in this present world not to be arrogant nor to put their hope in wealth, which is so uncertain, but to put their hope in God, who richly provides us with everything for our enjoyment. Command them to do good, to be rich in good deeds, and to be generous and willing to share" (1 TIMOTHY 6:17–18).

View your suffering in light of eternity.

"Therefore we do not lose heart. Though outwardly we are wasting away, yet inwardly we are being renewed day by day. For our light and momentary troubles are achieving for us an eternal glory that far outweighs them all. So we fix our eyes not on what is seen, but on what is unseen, since what is seen is temporary, but what is unseen is eternal" (2 CORINTHIANS 4:16–18).

Key Passage to Read

Psalm 23

Love others deeply.

"The end of all things is near. Therefore be alert and of sober mind so that you may pray. Above all, love each other deeply" (1 PETER 4:7–8).

Take time to enjoy life.

"I decided there is nothing better than to enjoy food and drink and to find satisfaction in work. Then I realized that these pleasures are from the hand of God" (ECCLESIASTES 2:24 NLT).

> *Be very careful, then, how you live—not as unwise but as wise, making the most of every opportunity, because the days are evil.*
> (EPHESIANS 5:15–16)

Overcoming the Fear of Death

Remember God's promises.

"I will listen to what God the LORD says; he promises peace to his people" (PSALM 85:8).

Reflect on heaven's joys.

"Think about the things of heaven, not the things of earth. For you died to this life, and your real life is hidden with Christ in God. And when Christ, who is your life, is revealed to the whole world, you will share in all his glory" (COLOSSIANS 3:2–4 NLT).

Rejoice in your salvation.

"I will greatly rejoice in the LORD; my soul shall exult in my God, for he has clothed me with the garments of salvation; he has covered me with the robe of righteousness" (ISAIAH 61:10 ESV).

My Personalized Plan

I will . . .

Consider my own death and take seriously my own mortality.

"Show me, LORD, my life's end and the number of my days; let me know how fleeting my life is" (PSALM 39:4).

Address and take care of end-of-life matters.

"This is what the LORD says: Put your house in order, because you are going to die" (2 KINGS 20:1).

Honestly evaluate my life and legacy.

"Let us examine our ways and test them, and let us return to the LORD" (LAMENTATIONS 3:40).

Accept the sovereignty of God over my life and death.

"You ought to say, 'If the Lord wills, we will live and do this or that'" (JAMES 4:15 ESV).

Live with the hope of heaven—even when I'm suffering.

"I consider that our present sufferings are not worth comparing with the glory that will be revealed in us" (ROMANS 8:18).

Tell others about Christ and how they can have eternal life.

"Whoever believes in the Son has eternal life, but whoever rejects the Son will not see life, for God's wrath remains on them" (JOHN 3:36).

Seek to honor God in my life and in my death.

"We make it our goal to please him, whether we are at home in the body or away from it" (2 CORINTHIANS 5:9).

"You will be secure, because there is hope."
(JOB 11:18)

Questions & Answers

Question: "My loved one is dying and I feel like there's nothing I can do about it. What can I do?"

Answer: You may not be able to save them physically, but there are many meaningful things you can do to comfort them spiritually and emotionally.

— Spend time with them.
— Share your favorite memories together.

— Read comforting passages of God's Word.
— Share God's plan of salvation with them if they don't know the Lord.
— Pray with them.
— Tell them what they mean to you, expressing gratitude for your relationship.
— When you're ready, say goodbye . . . and trust the Lord that their life is in His hands.

The Father of compassion . . . comforts us in all our troubles.
(2 CORINTHIANS 1:3–4)

Question: "It seems unfair that people, who live for a relatively short amount of time, should be punished for all eternity for a finite amount of sin. How is that fair?"

Answer: The question shouldn't be "Why do people deserve to go to hell?" but rather "Why should sinners ever be allowed in heaven?" If we wanted God to treat us in total fairness, *everyone* would be in hell. But thanks be to God, He is gracious and does not treat us as our sins deserve.

[God] *does not treat us as our sins deserve*
or repay us according to our iniquities.
(PSALM 103:10)

DECISION-MAKING

Discerning the Will of God

God's Heart on Decision-Making

God is the ultimate source for true wisdom and guidance.
"The Lord gives wisdom; from his mouth come knowledge and understanding" (Proverbs 2:6).

God wants you to seek His will.
"I desire to do your will, my God; your law is within my heart" (Psalm 40:8).

God is faithful to lovingly guide you.
"I will instruct you and teach you in the way you should go; I will counsel you with my loving eye on you" (Psalm 32:8).

God wants you to look to His Word for guidance.
"Your word is a lamp to my feet and a light to my path" (Psalm 119:105 ESV).

God can use wise counselors to help you make decisions.
"Plans fail for lack of counsel, but with many advisers they succeed" (Proverbs 15:22).

God wants you to desire His will above your own.
"Father, if you are willing, take this cup from me; yet not my will, but yours be done" (Luke 22:42).

God wants your decisions to please Him above pleasing people.
"We are not trying to please people but God, who tests our hearts" (1 Thessalonians 2:4).

I lift up my eyes to the mountains—
where does my help come from?
My help comes from the Lord,
the Maker of heaven and earth.
(Psalm 121:1–2)

God's Will in God's Word

1. **God's *perfect* will**
   — God has an ideal plan that is pleasing and good.

"Do not conform to the pattern of this world, but be transformed by the renewing of your mind. Then you will be able to test and approve what God's will is—his good, pleasing and perfect will" (ROMANS 12:2).

2. God's *permissive* will

— God permits each person to exercise free will, yet is *ultimately sovereign over all that He permits.*

"Let us move beyond the elementary teachings about Christ and be taken forward to maturity. . . . And God permitting, we will do so" (HEBREWS 6:1, 3).

3. God's *prevailing* will

— God's plans cannot be thwarted because He is sovereign.

"Many are the plans in a person's heart, but it is the LORD's purpose that prevails" (PROVERBS 19:21).

Decision-Making Checklist[102]

- ☐ Do I know all the facts about the decision I need to make? Ask: Who? What? When? Where? Why? How? How much?
- ☐ Have I given myself at least twenty-four hours to let a decision settle in my mind?
- ☐ Am I mentally tired or thinking with a clear head?
- ☐ Are my emotions driving my decision?
- ☐ Have I considered how this decision will impact others?
- ☐ Have I checked references, reviews, and/or reputations regarding this decision?
- ☐ What difference will my decision make in five, ten, fifteen, twenty, or more years?
- ☐ What key assumptions am I making? Do I know the true costs and benefits?
- ☐ How will this decision affect my long-term strategy?
- ☐ Have I sought outside advice?
- ☐ Have I done due diligence (research and analysis)?
- ☐ Have I narrowed my choices to the top two or three options?
- ☐ Have I broken down big decisions into smaller parts?
- ☐ Is this the best time to make this decision? If not now, when?
- ☐ If an immediate choice is necessary, what would I decide right now? Why?

God gave Solomon wisdom and very great insight,
and a breadth of understanding
as measureless as the sand on the seashore.
(1 KINGS 4:29)

Why Is Decision-Making Complicated?

Common reasons decision-making can become complicated and confusing include . . .

Not having pure motives

"When you ask, you do not receive, because you ask with wrong motives, that you may spend what you get on your pleasures" (JAMES 4:3).

Not surrendering self-will

"Going a little farther, he fell with his face to the ground and prayed, 'My Father, if it is possible, may this cup be taken from me. Yet not as I will, but as you will'" (MATTHEW 26:39).

Not seeking God's will through His Word

"The LORD gives wisdom; from his mouth come knowledge and understanding" (PROVERBS 2:6).

Not repenting of known sin

"If I had cherished sin in my heart, the Lord would not have listened" (PSALM 66:18).

Not praying continually and earnestly

"If you call out for insight and cry aloud for understanding, and if you look for it as for silver and search for it as for hidden treasure, then you will . . . find the knowledge of God. For the LORD gives wisdom; from his mouth come knowledge and understanding" (PROVERBS 2:3–6).

Not expecting God to answer

"If any of you lacks wisdom, you should ask God, who gives generously to all without finding fault, and it will be given to you. But when you ask, you must believe and not doubt, because the one who doubts is like a wave of the sea, blown and tossed by the wind. That person should not expect to receive anything from the Lord" (JAMES 1:5–7).

Not patiently waiting for God's timing

"After waiting patiently, Abraham received what was promised" (HEBREWS 6:15).

Not willing to suffer for the glory of Christ

"Since Christ suffered in his body, arm yourselves also with the same attitude, because whoever suffers in the body is done with sin. As a result, they do not live the rest of their earthly lives for evil human desires, but rather for the will of God" (1 PETER 4:1–2).

"The Son of Man did not come
to be served, but to serve, and to give
his life as a ransom for many."
(MARK 10:45)

Common Obstacles to Good Decision-Making[103]

— Cognitive Bias
— Decision Fatigue
— False Sense of Urgency
— Loss Aversion
— Overoptimism
— Procrastination
— Unmanaged Emotions

"Build up, build up, prepare the road!
Remove the obstacles out of the way of my people."
(ISAIAH 57:14)

Don'ts of Decision-Making

Don't wait until all else fails before seeking God's will.

"First seek the counsel of the LORD" (1 KINGS 22:5).

Don't seek just the plan but rather seek the Lord, who reveals the plan.

"Trust in the LORD with all your heart and lean not on your own understanding; in all your ways submit to him, and he will make your paths straight" (PROVERBS 3:5–6).

Don't pray for permission regarding something God has forbidden.

"I have taken an oath and confirmed it, that I will follow your righteous laws" (PSALM 119:106).

Don't make decisions based solely on feelings.

"Above all else, guard your heart, for everything you do flows from it" (PROVERBS 4:23).

Don't assume that God's will is too difficult for you to do.

"This is love for God: to keep his commands. And his commands are not burdensome" (1 JOHN 5:3).

Don't have divided loyalty and allow money alone to dictate your decision.

"No one can serve two masters. Either you will hate the one and love the other, or you will be devoted to the one and despise the other. You cannot serve both God and money" (MATTHEW 6:24).

Don't test God by seeking visible signs.

"Do not put the LORD your God to the test" (DEUTERONOMY 6:16).

Don't think trials and adversity indicate you are out of God's will.

"Those who suffer according to God's will should commit themselves to their faithful Creator and continue to do good" (1 PETER 4:19).

8 Tests of Decision-Making

Scriptural Test: "Has God already spoken about it in His Word?"

"All Scripture is God-breathed and is useful for teaching, rebuking, correcting and training in righteousness" (2 TIMOTHY 3:16).

Secrecy Test: "Would it bother me if everyone knew this was my choice?"

"The integrity of the upright guides them, but the unfaithful are destroyed by their duplicity" (PROVERBS 11:3).

Survey Test: "What if everyone followed my example?"

"Set an example for the believers in speech, in conduct, in love, in faith and in purity" (1 TIMOTHY 4:12).

Spirit Test: "Am I being people-pressured or Spirit-led?"

"Am I now trying to win the approval of human beings, or of God? Or am I trying to please people? If I were still trying to please people, I would not be a servant of Christ" (GALATIANS 1:10).

Key Verses to Memorize

I urge you, brothers and sisters,
in view of God's mercy,
to offer your bodies as living sacrifices,
holy and pleasing to God—
this is your true and proper worship.
Do not conform to the pattern of this world,
but be transformed
by the renewing of your mind.
Then you will be able to test
and approve what God's will is—
his good, pleasing and perfect will.
(ROMANS 12:1–2)

Stumbling Test: "Could this cause another person to stumble?"

"It is better not to eat meat or drink wine or to do anything else that will cause your brother or sister to fall" (ROMANS 14:21).

Serenity Test: "Have I prayed and received peace about this decision?"

"Do not be anxious about anything, but in every situation, by prayer and petition, with thanksgiving, present your requests to God. And the peace of God, which transcends all understanding, will guard your hearts and your minds in Christ Jesus" (PHILIPPIANS 4:6-7).

Sanctification Test: "Will this keep me from growing in the character of Christ?"

"Whoever claims to live in him must live as Jesus did" (1 JOHN 2:6).

Supreme Test: "Does this glorify God?"

"Whether you eat or drink or whatever you do, do it all for the glory of God" (1 CORINTHIANS 10:31).

My Personalized Plan

Seek God's will first and foremost.

— Pray fervently for wisdom and direction in all I do.
— Search Scripture, asking, "What has God's Word said about this issue?"
— Discern how God might be using this circumstance to direct me.

"Get wisdom, get understanding; do not forget my words or turn away from them" (PROVERBS 4:5).

Be *decisive* about being decisive.

— Allow faith, not fear, to prevail by memorizing verses that strengthen my faith.
— Avoid procrastination by making a weekly schedule for taking care of specific responsibilities.
— Refrain from making decisions solely to please others.

"God is faithful, who has called you into fellowship with his Son, Jesus Christ our Lord" (1 CORINTHIANS 1:9).

Let personal values lead the way.[104]

— Identify my highest priorities (saving for retirement, making more time for family, etc.).
— Create a core list of personal values (compassion, dependability, honesty, etc.).
— Determine how to make future decisions based on core values.

"Choose my instruction instead of silver, knowledge rather than choice gold" (PROVERBS 8:10).

Flee from false, ungodly counsel.

— Renounce all counsel from occult sources, such as astrologers and psychics.

— Reject any counsel that advises relying solely on intuition or instinct.

— Rebuff all counsel that violates biblical principles.

"Blessed is the one who does not walk in step with the wicked or stand in the way that sinners take or sit in the company of mockers" (PSALM 1:1).

Key Passage to Read

1 Thessalonians 4:1–12

Practice sound judgment.

— Commit to never let feelings alone be the driving force in decision-making.

— Assess any personal motives behind the decisions I need to make.

— Carefully weigh all sides of an issue before making a decision.

"The fear of the LORD is the beginning of wisdom, and knowledge of the Holy One is understanding" (PROVERBS 9:10).

Questions & Answers

Question: "Has God already determined His will for me?"

Answer: Yes. God's will for you was prepared in advance.

We are God's handiwork, created in Christ Jesus
to do good works, which God prepared
in advance for us to do.
(EPHESIANS 2:10)

Question: "Can I actually know God's will for my life?"

Answer: Yes. God desires to reveal His will to you in a personal way.

"The God of our ancestors has chosen you to know
his will and to see the Righteous One and
to hear words from his mouth."
(ACTS 22:14)

Question: "What if God's will seems undesirable?"

Answer: Aspects of God's will may seem undesirable and unpleasant when your heart is following your own desires and not trusting God, but the outcome will be the fulfillment of your deepest desires when your heart trusts and is yielded to Him.

Take delight in the LORD,
and he will give you the desires of your heart.
(PSALM 37:4)

Question: "Why does God's will for me sometimes include sorrow and suffering?"

Answer: Suffering allows you to see God's sufficiency as you learn to depend on Him. As we experience sorrow and suffering, we can better empathize with others who are experiencing pain, sorrow, and suffering.

It was good for me to be afflicted
so that I might learn your decrees.
(PSALM 119:71)

DEPRESSION

Walking from Darkness into the Dawn

God's Heart on Depression

God is with us in our depression.

"Do not fear, for I am with you; do not be dismayed, for I am your God. I will strengthen you and help you; I will uphold you with my righteous right hand" (ISAIAH 41:10).

God sees our pain and suffering.

"You, God, see the trouble of the afflicted; you consider their grief and take it in hand" (PSALM 10:14).

God hears our cries and listens to us in our pain.

"The LORD has heard my weeping" (PSALM 6:8).

God wants to give us light in our darkness.

"It is you who light my lamp; the LORD my God lightens my darkness" (PSALM 18:28 ESV).

God wants to lift us up when we're feeling down.

"The LORD upholds all who fall and lifts up all who are bowed down" (PSALM 145:14).

God wants us to talk to Him when we're depressed.

"Trust in him at all times, you people; pour out your hearts to him, for God is our refuge" (PSALM 62:8).

God wants to comfort us.

"I, yes I, am the one who comforts you" (ISAIAH 51:12 NLT).

God wants to give us peace.

"Peace I leave with you; my peace I give you. I do not give to you as the world gives. Do not let your hearts be troubled and do not be afraid" (JOHN 14:27).

God wants to give us hope.

"'I know the plans I have for you,' declares the LORD, 'plans to prosper you and not to harm you, plans to give you hope and a future'" (JEREMIAH 29:11).

God wants us to trust Him.

"The LORD is my strength and my shield; my heart trusts in him, and he helps me" (PSALM 28:7).

God wants us to comfort others who are depressed.

"The Father of compassion and the God of all comfort . . . comforts us in all our troubles, so that we can comfort those in any trouble with the comfort we ourselves receive from God" (2 CORINTHIANS 1:3–4).

God will one day wipe away all our tears—and there will be no more sorrow or suffering.

"He will wipe every tear from their eyes, and there will be no more death or sorrow or crying or pain. All these things are gone forever" (REVELATION 21:4 NLT).

The LORD is God,
and he has made his light shine on us.
(PSALM 118:27)

Signs and Symptoms of Depression[105]

- **Persistent feelings** of sadness, anxiousness, or "emptiness" most or all of the time
- **Feelings** of hopelessness
- **Feelings** of irritability, frustration, or restlessness
- **Feelings** of worthlessness or disappointment in oneself
- **Complete or near-complete loss** of interest or pleasure in activities that were once enjoyable
- **Significant change** in appetite or weight
- **Difficulty** sleeping most nights or sleeping too much
- **Agitated thoughts and movements** (i.e., fidgeting, pacing, tapping fingers or feet) or slowed responses (i.e., pausing more when talking; speaking slower, more quietly, or infrequently; moving slowly)
- **Chronically fatigued**, easily decreased energy
- **Lack of concentration**, focus, memory retention, or inability to make decisions
- **Physical aches** and pains, headaches, cramps, or digestive problems
- **Recurring thoughts** of death or suicide or suicide attempts

Note: Regarding diagnosing depression, always consult a doctor or mental health professional (psychiatrist, psychologist, licensed professional counselor) who can give you an educated assessment after conducting a detailed analysis of your situation and symptoms.

Dear friend, I pray that you may enjoy good health and that all
may go well with you, even as your soul is getting along well.
(3 JOHN 1:2)

Emotional and Situational Contributors of Depression

Repressed *anger* over:

Loss of a relationship	Loss of expectations
Loss of self-esteem	Loss of respect of others
Loss of control	Loss of health or abilities
Loss of possessions	Loss of accomplishments

Get rid of all bitterness, rage and anger, brawling and slander, along with every form of malice.
(EPHESIANS 4:31)

Suppressed *fear* of:

Job loss	Abandonment
Dying	Growing old
Empty nest	Being alone
Failure	Rejection

"Do not fear, for I am with you;
do not be dismayed, for I am your God.
I will strengthen you and help you;
I will uphold you with my righteous right hand."
(ISAIAH 41:10)

Unresolved *guilt* from:

Past moral failure(s)	Unconfessed sin
Poor treatment of others	Unfaithfulness
Failed expectations	Broken promises
Habits and addictions	Harbored secrets

There is now no condemnation for those who are in Christ Jesus.
(ROMANS 8:1)

Internalized *stress* over:

Work difficulties	Financial obligations
Health issues	Family responsibilities
Marital problems	Troubled child
Friendship struggles	School problems

Cast all your anxiety on him because he cares for you.
(1 PETER 5:7)

Spiritual Contributors of Depression[106]

Unconfessed sin
"Then I acknowledged my sin to you and did not cover up my iniquity. I said, 'I will confess my transgressions to the LORD.' And you forgave the guilt of my sin" (PSALM 32:5).

Longing for God
"As the deer pants for streams of water, so my soul pants for you, my God. My soul thirsts for God, for the living God" (PSALM 42:1–2).

Spiritual attack
"Be strong in the Lord and in his mighty power. Put on all of God's armor so that you will be able to stand firm against all strategies of the devil. For we are not fighting against flesh-and-blood enemies, but against evil rulers and authorities of the unseen world, against mighty powers in this dark world, and against evil spirits in the heavenly places. . . . Take the sword of the Spirit, which is the word of God. Pray in the Spirit at all times and on every occasion. Stay alert and be persistent in your prayers for all believers everywhere" (EPHESIANS 6:10–12, 17–18 NLT).

Yes, my soul, find rest in God; my hope comes from him.
(PSALM 62:5)

Discerning God's Purpose in Depression

God may have allowed depression in order to . . .

Bring you closer to Him.
"Let us then approach God's throne of grace with confidence, so that we may receive mercy and find grace to help us in our time of need" (HEBREWS 4:16).

Reveal to you His grace and strength in your weakness.

"My grace is all you need. My power works best in weakness" (2 CORINTHIANS 12:9 NLT).

Slow you down and cause you to reflect inwardly.

"Search me, God, and know my heart; test me and know my anxious thoughts. See if there is any offensive way in me, and lead me in the way everlasting" (PSALM 139:23–24).

Warn you that something is wrong and put you on the right path.

"Before I was afflicted I went astray, but now I obey your word" (PSALM 119:67).

Begin a healing process for damaged emotions.

"Heal me, LORD, and I will be healed; save me and I will be saved, for you are the one I praise" (JEREMIAH 17:14).

Cause you to pour out your heart to Him.

"I cry aloud to the LORD; I lift up my voice to the LORD for mercy. I pour out before him my complaint; before him I tell my trouble. When my spirit grows faint within me, it is you who watch over my way" (PSALM 142:1–3).

Key Verse to Memorize

Why am I so depressed?
Why this turmoil within me?
Put your hope in God, for I will still praise Him,
my Savior and my God.
(PSALM 42:5 HCSB)

Show you that He hears you and wants to encourage you.

"You, LORD, hear the desire of the afflicted; you encourage them, and you listen to their cry" (PSALM 10:17).

Develop your trust in Him.

"Why, my soul, are you downcast? Why so disturbed within me? Put your hope in God, for I will yet praise him, my Savior and my God" (PSALM 43:5).

Confirm your worth and the value of your life.

"Are not five sparrows sold for two pennies? Yet not one of them is forgotten by God. Indeed, the very hairs of your head are all numbered. Don't be afraid; you are worth more than many sparrows" (LUKE 12:6–7).

Teach you to rely on His resources.

"But this happened that we might not rely on ourselves but on God, who raises the dead. . . . On him we have set our hope that he will continue to deliver us" (2 CORINTHIANS 1:9–10).

Develop your perseverance and maturity.

"Consider it pure joy . . . whenever you face trials of many kinds, because you know that the testing of your faith produces perseverance. Let perseverance finish its work so that you may be mature and complete, not lacking anything" (JAMES 1:2–4).

Increase your compassion and understanding for others.

"The Father of compassion and the God of all comfort . . . comforts us in all our troubles, so that we can comfort those in any trouble with the comfort we ourselves receive from God" (2 CORINTHIANS 1:3–4).

Conquer Depression

C—Confront the losses in your life. Allow yourself to grieve.

"[There is] *a time to weep and a time to laugh, a time to mourn and a time to dance"* (ECCLESIASTES 3:4).

O—Offer your heart to Christ and give Him control. Pour your heart out to God and trust Him.

"Trust in him at all times, you people; pour out your hearts to him, for God is our refuge" (PSALM 62:8).

N—Nurture the thoughts of God's love for you. Remember: His love will never end.

"I have loved you with an everlasting love; I have drawn you with unfailing kindness" (JEREMIAH 31:3).

Q—Quit all negative thinking. Replace negative self-talk by focusing on the positive.

"Whatever is true, whatever is noble, whatever is right, whatever is pure, whatever is lovely, whatever is admirable—if anything is excellent or praiseworthy—think about such things" (PHILIPPIANS 4:8).

U—Understand God's purpose for allowing pain. God promises to use your heartaches for your ultimate good.

"We know that in all things God works for the good of those who love him, who have been called according to his purpose" (ROMANS 8:28).

E—Exchange your hurt for thanksgiving. Choose to give thanks even when you don't feel thankful.

"Give thanks in all circumstances; for this is God's will for you in Christ Jesus" (1 THESSALONIANS 5:18).

R—Remember God is sovereign over your life. He promises hope for your future.

"You have been my hope, Sovereign LORD. . . . You are my strong refuge. . . . I will always have hope" (PSALM 71:5, 7, 14).

"Let the one who walks in the dark,
who has no light,
trust in the name of the LORD
and rely on their God."
(ISAIAH 50:10)

Choices You Can Make

Listen to uplifting and inspirational music.

Read a passage of Scripture or an inspiring, helpful book.

Set and achieve small, attainable goals each day.

Make a nutritious meal.

Go for a walk outside or exercise at the gym.

Keep your living environment clean, uncluttered, and cheerful.

Resist spending long periods of time on your phone or tablet or in front of the TV.

Refuse to introduce negative or evil activities into your life.

Write notes of appreciation or encouragement to others.

Look for something thoughtful and kind to do for someone each day.

My Personalized Plan

As I walk through the darkness of depression into the light of dawn, **I will . . .**

Recognize that my depression is real.
"I am suffering and in pain. Rescue me, O God, by your saving power" (PSALM 69:29 NLT).

Remember that my pain is temporary.
"He will wipe every tear from their eyes, and there will be no more death or sorrow or crying or pain. All these things are gone forever" (REVELATION 21:4 NLT).

Reaffirm the importance of caring for my physical needs.

"Physical training is of some value, but godliness has value for all things, holding promise for both the present life and the life to come" (1 TIMOTHY 4:8).

Restrict the amount of stress in my life.

"Give me relief from my distress; have mercy on me and hear my prayer" (PSALM 4:1).

Reveal my emotional needs.

"I call to you, LORD, every day; I spread out my hands to you" (PSALM 88:9).

Restrain negative thought patterns.

"Whatever is true, whatever is noble, whatever is right, whatever is pure, whatever is lovely, whatever is admirable—if anything is excellent or praiseworthy—think about such things" (PHILIPPIANS 4:8).

Key Passage to Read

Lamentations 3:19–26

Renew my commitment to get my spiritual needs met.

"All the believers devoted themselves to the apostles' teaching, and to fellowship, and to sharing in meals (including the Lord's Supper), and to prayer" (ACTS 2:42 NLT).

There is surely a future hope for you,
and your hope will not be cut off.
(PROVERBS 23:18)

Questions & Answers

Question: "Is there any objective, medical proof to substantiate the need for medication?"

Answer: Yes. With the aid of PET scans (positron emission tomography), physicians can see the difference between the function of a normal brain and a depressed brain.[107]

- PET scans map how the brain functions.
- They also display changes in the brain after antidepressant medication has been taken.

Antidepressants can provide a temporary or extended neurological advantage by increasing brain functioning and decreasing depression.

How wonderful that the God of creation made the brain with the capacity to respond to appropriate medication in order to alleviate debilitating depression.

I am fearfully and wonderfully made.
(PSALM 139:14)

Question: "Does taking medicine for depression show a lack of faith?"

Answer: No. Some people may be able to manage their depression and overcome it without medication, others might take medication temporarily to relieve severe symptoms, and still others might need to take certain medications long term to make up for a biochemical imbalance.

The decision of whether to use medication is one best made with the recommendation of a qualified physician who closely monitors and manages its administration.

Every good and perfect gift is from above,
coming down from the Father of the heavenly lights.
(JAMES 1:17)

DIVORCE

Beginning Again—From Brokenness

God's Heart on Divorce[108]

God hates divorce. *"'I hate divorce,' says the* L*ORD, the God of Israel"* (Malachi 2:16 NASB). God does not view divorce favorably, as it dissolves the "one flesh" spiritual bond of marriage.

"Anyone who divorces his wife and marries another woman commits adultery against her. And if she divorces her husband and marries another man, she commits adultery" (MARK 10:11–12).

God hates divorce, but He also hates sexual immorality and violence: *"Those who love violence, he* [God] *hates with a passion"* (Psalm 11:5); therefore, God allows for the possibility of separation in such cases.

"Do not make friends with a hot-tempered person, do not associate with one easily angered" (PROVERBS 22:24).

"I tell you that anyone who divorces his wife, except for sexual immorality, and marries another woman commits adultery" (MATTHEW 19:9).

God may close His ears to the prayers of one who breaks a marriage covenant through infidelity.

"You flood the L*ORD's altar with tears. You weep and wail because he no longer looks with favor on your offerings or accepts them with pleasure from your hands. You ask, 'Why?' It is because the* L*ORD is the witness between you and the wife of your youth. You have been unfaithful to her, though she is your partner, the wife of your marriage covenant"* (MALACHI 2:13–14).

God's heart is for reconciliation, even if there has been a divorce.

"To the married I give this command (not I, but the Lord): A wife must not separate from her husband. But if she does, she must remain unmarried or else be reconciled to her husband. And a husband must not divorce his wife" (1 CORINTHIANS 7:10–11).

God's Heart on Remarriage after Divorce

God allows remarriage in cases where divorce occurred before the person became a Christian; the person was divorced without biblical grounds and the former mate has died or has had sexual relations with another; the person divorced an adulterous mate; or the person's former unbelieving spouse left the marriage.

"If the unbeliever leaves, let it be so. The brother or the sister is not bound in such circumstances" (1 CORINTHIANS 7:15).

God guards and protects the faithful and just, without regard to marital status.

"He guards the course of the just and protects the way of his faithful ones" (PROVERBS 2:8).

God heals the brokenhearted, and He will still accomplish His ultimate purpose for you.

"We know that in all things God works for the good of those who love him, who have been called according to his purpose" (ROMANS 8:28).

God promises to meet your needs, whether you remain divorced or you remarry.

"My God will meet all your needs according to the riches of his glory in Christ Jesus" (PHILIPPIANS 4:19).

Stable vs. Stagnant Marriages

Stable Marriage: Good communication
Stagnant Marriage: Poor communication/anger or silence

Stable Marriage: Sexual intimacy
Stagnant Marriage: Sexual apathy or infidelity

Stable Marriage: Time together
Stagnant Marriage: Time apart

Stable Marriage: Honesty
Stagnant Marriage: Deception

Stable Marriage: Conflict resolution
Stagnant Marriage: Conflict escalation

Stable Marriage: Financial responsibility
Stagnant Marriage: Financial irresponsibility

Stable Marriage: Emotional connection
Stagnant Marriage: Emotional distance, isolation, or abuse

Divorce Danger Signs

- ☐ Do you often align yourself with another person against your mate?
- ☐ Do you avoid sexual intimacy with your spouse?
- ☐ Do you disagree about important decisions?
- ☐ Do you disrespect each other?
- ☐ Do you dread being alone with your mate?
- ☐ Do you fail to maintain your marriage vows?
- ☐ Do you find yourself avoiding your mate?
- ☐ Do you often go through periods of silence?
- ☐ Do you have the same fights over and over?
- ☐ Do you hide things from your mate?
- ☐ Do you sleep in separate bedrooms?
- ☐ Do you spend less time together than ever before?
- ☐ Do your thoughts about your mate often turn negative?

Common Causes for Divorce

Uncommitted view of marriage

"Some Pharisees came to him to test him [Jesus]. *They asked, 'Is it lawful for a man to divorce his wife for any and every reason?'"* (MATTHEW 19:3).

Unrealistic view of marriage

"Have nothing to do with godless myths and old wives' tales; rather, train yourself to be godly. For physical training is of some value, but godliness has value for all things, holding promise for both the present life and the life to come" (1 TIMOTHY 4:7–8).

Key Verse to Memorize

"When you pass through the waters,
I will be with you;
and when you pass through the rivers,
they will not sweep over you."
(ISAIAH 43:2)

Unbiblical view of marriage

"The time will come when people will not put up with sound doctrine. Instead, to suit their own desires, they will gather around them a great number of teachers to say what their itching ears want to hear. They will turn their ears away from the truth and turn aside to myths" (2 TIMOTHY 4:3–4).

Unresolved problems from the past

"So I tell you this . . . you must no longer live as the Gentiles do, in the futility of their thinking. They are darkened in their understanding and separated from the life of God because of the ignorance that is in them due to the hardening of their hearts" (EPHESIANS 4:17–18).

Unsolved conflicts within the marriage

"As obedient children, do not conform to the evil desires you had when you lived in ignorance. But just as he who called you is holy, so be holy in all you do; for it is written: 'Be holy, because I am holy'" (1 PETER 1:14–16).

You, my brothers and sisters, were called to be free.
But do not use your freedom to indulge the flesh;
rather, serve one another humbly in love.
(GALATIANS 5:13)

Enticements That Easily Entangle

According to God's Word, worldly desires can be divided into three categories:

Lust of the Flesh

— **Privilege**

"In your relationships with one another, have the same mindset as Christ Jesus: Who, being in very nature God, did not consider equality with God something to be used to his own advantage; rather, he made himself nothing by taking the very nature of a servant, being made in human likeness. And being found in appearance as a man, he humbled himself by becoming obedient to death—even death on a cross!" (PHILIPPIANS 2:5–8).

— **Pleasure**

"The heart of the wise is in the house of mourning, but the heart of fools is in the house of pleasure" (ECCLESIASTES 7:4).

— **Prosperity**

"Keep falsehood and lies far from me; give me neither poverty nor riches, but give me only my daily bread. Otherwise, I may have too much and disown you and say, 'Who is the LORD?' Or I may become poor and steal, and so dishonor the name of my God" (PROVERBS 30:8–9).

Lust of the Eyes

— **Possessions**

"Sell your possessions and give to the poor. Provide purses for yourselves that will not wear out, a treasure in heaven that will never fail, where no thief comes near and no moth destroys" (LUKE 12:33).

— **Property**

"You suffered along with those in prison and joyfully accepted the confiscation of your property, because you knew that you yourselves had better and lasting possessions" (HEBREWS 10:34).

— **Prestige**

"Live in harmony with one another. Do not be proud, but be willing to associate with people of low position. Do not be conceited" (ROMANS 12:16).

Pride of Life

— **Position**

"Therefore, whoever takes the lowly position of this child is the greatest in the kingdom of heaven" (MATTHEW 18:4).

— **Popularity**

"Am I now trying to win the approval of human beings, or of God? Or am I trying to please people? If I were still trying to please people, I would not be a servant of Christ" (GALATIANS 1:10).

— **Power**

"Though the pride of the godless person reaches to the heavens and his head touches the clouds, he will perish forever, like his own dung" (JOB 20:6–7).

"Do not store up for yourselves treasures on earth,
where moths and vermin destroy,
and where thieves break in and steal.
But store up for yourselves treasures in heaven,
where moths and vermin do not destroy,
and where thieves do not break in and steal.
For where your treasure is, there your heart will be also."
(MATTHEW 6:19–21)

How to Mend a Marriage

Before you seek to renew your commitment to your spouse, rekindle your love for the Lord.

Concentrate on making Jesus Christ the sole source of your fulfillment in life.

Become the whole person God created you to be (caring for your body, soul, and spirit).

Recognize your need for God's help and the support of others.

As the Lord leads you to try to mend your marriage . . .

Eliminate dishonoring actions and attitudes (e.g., anger, sarcasm, unfair criticism, inconsistency, selfishness, arrogance).

Focus on finding solutions that will renew and enrich your relationship with your spouse.

Make an effort to open your spouse's heart if it has been closed to you.

Become a more effective communicator.

Be devoted to one another in love.
Honor one another above yourselves.
(ROMANS 12:10)

My Personalized Plan

As I struggle through the turmoil of divorce and seek to heal, I will renew my personal identity. I will embrace the reality that I am deeply rooted in Christ and firmly fixed in these eight essential biblical truths:

1. My identity (whether married or single) is in Christ, not in a role or in another person.

   "I have been crucified with Christ and I no longer live, but Christ lives in me. The life I now live in the body, I live by faith in the Son of God, who loved me and gave himself for me" (GALATIANS 2:20).

2. I am complete in Christ, not an incomplete single if I don't remarry.

   "For in Christ all the fullness of the Deity lives in bodily form, and in Christ you have been brought to fullness. He is the head over every power and authority" (COLOSSIANS 2:9–10).

3. My happiness comes from inner virtues and attitudes, not outer circumstances.

   "The fruit of the Spirit is love, joy, peace, forbearance, kindness, goodness, faithfulness, gentleness and self-control. Against such things there is no law" (GALATIANS 5:22–23).

4. My purpose in life, whether married or single, is to honor and glorify God.

   "Do you not know that your bodies are temples of the Holy Spirit, who is in you, whom you have received from God? You are not your own; you were bought at a price. Therefore honor God with your bodies. . . . Whatever you do, do it all for the glory of God" (1 CORINTHIANS 6:19–20, 10:31).

5. I choose to draw from my resources in Christ to continually walk in forgiveness with regard to myself, my ex-spouse, and others who may hurt me.

   "Bear with each other and forgive one another if any of you has a grievance against someone. Forgive as the Lord forgave you" (COLOSSIANS 3:13).

6. I choose to live in the power of Christ and to draw on His strength to overcome temptations.

   "No temptation has overtaken you except what is common to mankind. And God is faithful; he will not let you be tempted beyond what you can bear. But when you are tempted, he will also provide a way out so that you can endure it" (1 CORINTHIANS 10:13).

7. I am free to be concerned with the things of the Lord.

   "I would like you to be free from concern. An unmarried man is concerned about the Lord's affairs—how he can please the Lord. But a married man is concerned about the affairs of this world—how he can please his wife—and his interests are divided. An unmarried woman or virgin is concerned about the Lord's affairs: Her aim is to be devoted to the Lord in both body and spirit. But a married woman is concerned about the affairs of this world—how she can please her husband" (1 CORINTHIANS 7:32–34).

Key Passage to Read

Romans 8:38–39

8. I can be an even more effective witness in the lives of others because of my suffering.

   "Those who suffer according to God's will should commit themselves to their faithful Creator and continue to do good" (1 PETER 4:19).

So then, just as you received Christ Jesus as Lord,
continue to live your lives in him,
rooted and built up in him,
strengthened in the faith as you were taught,
and overflowing with thankfulness.
(COLOSSIANS 2:6–7)

Questions & Answers

Question: "The Bible says that God hates divorce (Malachi 2:16). Does God hate me because I've been divorced?"

Answer: Absolutely not! The Bible does say that God hates divorce, but nowhere does it say He hates the divorcée. God doesn't hate the people involved in divorce—He hates the pain involved in forsaking the covenant relationship that He intended to use as an illustration of His everlasting love and commitment to us.

God looks with compassion on all people everywhere and desires to save everyone from the brokenness in their lives and the wounds divorce inflicts.

"The LORD is good to all;
he has compassion on all he has made."
(PSALM 145:9)

Question: "I've been separated for more than a year. Some people have said dating would be good for me. Am I free to date now?"

Answer: Since you're not free to remarry, neither are you free to date. The fact is, you are still married, and the purpose of separation is to give both of you the opportunity to focus and work on the individual attitudes and actions that harm your marriage relationship. Your goal is to move toward reconciliation, not divorce or dating. Keep your focus on what God desires for you, not the opinions of others.

Those who live according to the flesh
have their minds set on what the flesh desires;
but those who live in accordance with the Spirit
have their minds set on what the Spirit desires.
(ROMANS 8:5)

DOMESTIC ABUSE

There's No Excuse for Abuse!

God's Heart on Domestic Abuse

God cares for those who have experienced abuse.

"You have seen my troubles, and you care about the anguish of my soul" (PSALM 31:7 NLT).

God understands the pain of abuse.

"He [Jesus] *was despised and rejected by mankind, a man of suffering, and familiar with pain"* (ISAIAH 53:3).

God hates violence and will judge the violent.

"The LORD examines the righteous, but the wicked, those who love violence, he hates with a passion. On the wicked he will rain fiery coals and burning sulfur; a scorching wind will be their lot" (PSALM 11:5–6).

God calls for the abuser to change.

"Give up your violence and oppression and do what is just and right" (EZEKIEL 45:9).

God does not want you to associate with those prone to anger and violence.

"Do not make friends with a hot-tempered person, do not associate with one easily angered" (PROVERBS 22:24).

God wants husbands to love their wives and not mistreat them.

"Husbands, love your wives and do not be harsh with them" (COLOSSIANS 3:19).

God wants husbands to treat their wives with honor, care, understanding, and respect.

"Husbands, in the same way be considerate as you live with your wives, and treat them with respect as the weaker partner and as heirs with you of the gracious gift of life, so that nothing will hinder your prayers" (1 PETER 3:7).

God offers healing for those who have experienced the pain of abuse.

"He heals the brokenhearted and binds up their wounds" (PSALM 147:3).

God wants you to help those who are experiencing abuse.

"Rescue the weak and the needy; deliver them from the hand of the wicked" (PSALM 82:4).

God will end all violence and abuse one day.

"No longer will violence be heard in your land, nor ruin or destruction within your borders. . . . The LORD will be your everlasting light, and your God will be your glory. . . . I am the LORD; in its time I will do this swiftly" (ISAIAH 60:18–19, 22).

God's Heart for the Victim of Violence

God hears the cry and keeps track of the tears of the victim.

"You keep track of all my sorrows. You have collected all my tears in your bottle. You have recorded each one in your book" (PSALM 56:8 NLT).

God sees the pain of the victim.

"'You are the God who sees me,' for she said, 'I have now seen the One who sees me'" (GENESIS 16:13).

God holds the hand of the victim.

"I am the LORD your God who takes hold of your right hand and says to you, Do not fear; I will help you" (ISAIAH 41:13).

God confirms the worth of the victim.

"Are not five sparrows sold for two pennies? Yet not one of them is forgotten by God. Indeed, the very hairs of your head are all numbered. Don't be afraid; you are worth more than many sparrows" (LUKE 12:6–7).

God avenges the victim.

"He who avenges blood remembers; he does not ignore the cries of the afflicted" (PSALM 9:12).

Biblical Bill of Rights

Within the marriage relationship . . .

I. **God's will is that you** treat one another with respect.

   "The wife must respect her husband" (EPHESIANS 5:33).

   "Husbands, in the same way be considerate as you live with your wives, and treat them with respect" (1 PETER 3:7).

II. **God's will is that you** experience mutual submission.

   "Submit to one another out of reverence for Christ" (EPHESIANS 5:21).

III. **God's will is that you** speak truth and have truth spoken to you in a loving manner.

"Speaking the truth in love, we will grow to become in every respect the mature body of him who is the head, that is, Christ" (EPHESIANS 4:15).

IV. **God's will is that you** express anger and have anger expressed toward you in appropriate ways.

"'In your anger do not sin': Do not let the sun go down while you are still angry" (EPHESIANS 4:26).

V. **God's will is that you** both spend personal time alone.

"Very early in the morning, while it was still dark, Jesus got up, left the house and went off to a solitary place, where he prayed" (MARK 1:35).

VI. **God's will is that you** use your unique talents and gifts to serve others.

"Each of you should use whatever gift you have received to serve others, as faithful stewards of God's grace in its various forms" (1 PETER 4:10).

VII. **God's will is that you** enjoy freedom from fear.

"I prayed to the LORD, and he answered me. He freed me from all my fears" (PSALM 34:4 NLT).

VIII. **God's will is that you** both seek emotional and spiritual support from others.

"Let us not neglect our meeting together . . . but encourage one another" (HEBREWS 10:25 NLT).

IX. **God's will is that you** report abuse to governmental authorities.

"Submit yourselves for the Lord's sake to every human authority . . . who are sent by him to punish those who do wrong and to commend those who do right" (1 PETER 2:13–14).

X. **God's will is that you** leave an abusive relationship to protect yourself from danger.

"The prudent see danger and take refuge, but the simple keep going and pay the penalty" (PROVERBS 27:12).

How to Prepare a Safety Plan for Leaving[109]

A violent spouse may enter a blind rage when he discovers a different dynamic in the relationship. The greatest danger can come when a husband learns his wife has intentions of leaving. A person who is wise will have prepared for the worst by having a safety plan for leaving.

The prudent see danger and take refuge,
but the simple keep going and pay the penalty.
(PROVERBS 22:3 NIV)

Create a list of phone numbers you may need for emergencies (police, hotline for domestic violence [911, 988, 1-800-799-SAFE (7233), County Registry of Protective Orders, etc.).

"Keep me safe, LORD, from the hands of the wicked" (PSALM 140:4).

Share the seriousness of your situation with trustworthy people.

"Blessed are those who have regard for the weak; the LORD delivers them in times of trouble" (PSALM 41:1).

Plan an escape route.

- — Identify the safest areas in your home as well as the risk areas (rooms with only one exit, where weapons are stored)
- — Identify which emergency exits you can use (doors, windows, elevator, stairwell) and practice getting out safely.
- — If an argument begins, move away from any room containing objects that could be used as weapons (such as the kitchen).
- — Move to a room that has an exit (not a bathroom, a closet, or a small space where the abuser could trap you).
- — Ensure your car is able to get out easily and has plenty of fuel.

"Give careful thought to the paths for your feet and be steadfast in all your ways" (PROVERBS 4:26).

Teach your children "safety secrets" (how to stay out of harm's way, how to call the police, when and how to escape, where to go for safety). Consider using a code word to signal to your children that you need help, to call the police, or to leave.

"Through knowledge the righteous escape" (PROVERBS 11:9).

Key Verse to Memorize

This is how we know what love is:
Jesus Christ laid down his life for us.
(1 JOHN 3:16)

Place physical evidence of violence with a trusted confidant or in a safety deposit box, and store digital evidence (texts, emails, photos) in a secure, password-protected location.

"They do not realize that I remember all their evil deeds. Their sins engulf them; they are always before me" (HOSEA 7:2).

Identify essential or meaningful items (children's favorite toys and blankets, medicines, pictures, sentimental items, your pets, etc.) you can gather quickly and safely.

"Gather up your belongings to leave the land, you who live under siege" (JEREMIAH 10:17).

Keep important papers and documents easily accessible and together in one place. Many of these items can be scanned or photographed and kept digitally. But remember, everything on this list can be replaced if needed.

"Wisdom reposes in the heart of the discerning" (PROVERBS 14:33).

Cover your bases before leaving.

— Accumulate some emergency cash and keep it hidden.

— Transfer important digital files to external media and then delete them from the computer.

— Hide an extra set of car and house keys.

— Open a checking and/or savings account in your name.

— Cancel any shared bank accounts or credit cards that do not require both parties' consent.

— Change passwords to online accounts that you'll need to access.

— Open a post office box in your name.

— Set aside jewelry, silver, or other valuables your husband would not likely miss that you can quickly sell for cash.

"If you are wise, your wisdom will reward you" (PROVERBS 9:12).

Consider creating a personalized safety plan with the help of online tools and worksheets. (For example, one is available at the National Domestic Violence Hotline's website, www.thehotline.org.)

"Keep me safe, my God, for in you I take refuge" (PSALM 16:1).

Safety Steps for Being Out

Change your regular travel habits and routes.

Try to get rides with different people.

Shop and bank in different places.

Keep your court order and emergency numbers with you at all times.

Notify your children's school or day care and ask for help in keeping you and your children safe.

Program a cell phone to call an emergency number or the police. (Keep it with you at all times.)

The LORD will keep you from all harm—
he will watch over your life.
(PSALM 121:7)

My Personalized Plan

Recognize that domestic violence is contrary to God's will. Mistreatment, hurt, or injury is never acceptable. Domestic violence and abuse should never be ignored or dismissed, but confronted and stopped.

"Love is patient, love is kind. It does not envy, it does not boast, it is not proud. It does not dishonor others, it is not self-seeking, it is not easily angered, it keeps no record of wrongs. Love does not delight in evil but rejoices with the truth. It always protects, always trusts, always hopes, always perseveres. . . . Love never fails" (1 CORINTHIANS 13:4–8).

Realize that it is healthy and appropriate to set healthy boundaries while seeking wisdom from the Word of God and a wise and well-trained counselor.

"My people will live in peaceful dwelling places, in secure homes, in undisturbed places of rest" (ISAIAH 32:18).

Relinquish any shame I feel to God, recognizing that it comes from wrong beliefs and not from Him.

"We put our hope in the LORD. He is our help and our shield" (PSALM 33:20 NLT).

Key Passage to Read

Psalm 91:1–4, 9, 11, 14–15

Recognize my worth.

"You are precious and honored in my sight, and . . . I love you" (ISAIAH 43:4).

Rebuild my life in the light and knowledge of what is good and healthy. I will rely on the Lord to guide my steps and my life.

"He heals the brokenhearted and binds up their wounds" (PSALM 147:3).

Rest in the Lord continually.

"He lifted me out of the slimy pit, out of the mud and mire; he set my feet on a rock and gave me a firm place to stand. He put a new song in my mouth, a hymn of praise to our God. Many will see and fear the LORD and put their trust in him" (PSALM 40:2–3).

Questions & Answers

Question: "Would God condone my husband's abusing me in order to punish me for my sins?"

Answer: No. There is no instance in Scripture where God used the violence of one mate to punish the other mate. God hates sin, and abuse is sin.

Do no wrong or violence.
(JEREMIAH 22:3)

Question: "I am angry at God. If He is just and hates violence, why does He allow abuse?"

Answer: Beware of misplacing anger or blame. While God loves righteousness and hates violence and all other forms of sin, He allows people to choose how they will behave, whether it be righteously or violently. God gives all people free will—the freedom to choose right or wrong—even those who go against His will.

Rest assured, God is just and He will deal rightly with those who abuse you.

God is just: He will pay back trouble
to those who trouble you.
(2 THESSALONIANS 1:6)

Question: "If a wife separates from her abusive husband, is she not ultimately divorcing her husband or at least opening the door to divorce?"

Answer: No, the husband is the one who has opened the door to separation by his violence, not the wife. Separation is not divorce and does not necessarily open the door to divorce, but instead opens the door to safety and obedience to God.

Do not make friends with a hot-tempered person,
do not associate with one easily angered.
(PROVERBS 22:24)

THE DYSFUNCTIONAL FAMILY

Making Peace with Your Past

God's Heart on the Significance of Family

Represents the relationship believers have with Christ

"Both the one who makes people holy and those who are made holy are of the same family. So Jesus is not ashamed to call them brothers and sisters" (HEBREWS 2:11).

Provides a solid foundation for discipleship

"I am reminded of your sincere faith, which first lived in your grandmother Lois and in your mother Eunice and, I am persuaded, now lives in you also" (2 TIMOTHY 1:5).

Confirms that it is worthy of protection

"Remember the Lord, who is great and awesome, and fight for your families, your sons and your daughters, your wives and your homes" (NEHEMIAH 4:14).

Verifies the lineage of Jesus Christ

"Joseph also went up from the town of Nazareth in Galilee to Judea, to Bethlehem the town of David, because he belonged to the house and line of David. He went there to register with Mary, who was pledged to be married to him and was expecting a child" (LUKE 2:4–5).

Forms the basis for recording ancestral connections

"My God put it into my heart to assemble the nobles, the officials and the common people for registration by families" (NEHEMIAH 7:5).

God's Heart on the Role of Family

Rejoices together in God's blessings

"There, in the presence of the LORD your God, you and your families shall eat and shall rejoice in everything you have put your hand to, because the LORD your God has blessed you" (DEUTERONOMY 12:7).

Declares God's works to the next generation

"One generation commends your works to another; they tell of your mighty acts" (PSALM 145:4).

Supports the local church

"Then the leaders of families . . . gave willingly. They gave toward the work on the temple of God" (1 CHRONICLES 29:6–7).

Provides for individual family members

"Anyone who does not provide for their relatives, and especially for their own household, has denied the faith and is worse than an unbeliever" (1 TIMOTHY 5:8).

Loves God's family

"And in fact, you do love all of God's family throughout Macedonia. Yet we urge you, brothers and sisters, to do so more and more" (1 THESSALONIANS 4:10).

God's Heart on the Purpose of Family

Praises the attributes of God

"Ascribe to the LORD, all you families of nations, ascribe to the LORD glory and strength" (PSALM 96:7).

Practices Christianity

"If a widow has children or grandchildren, these should learn first of all to put their religion into practice by caring for their own family and so repaying their parents and grandparents, for this is pleasing to God" (1 TIMOTHY 5:4).

Participates in regularly scheduled group Bible studies

"On the second day of the month, the heads of all the families, along with the priests and the Levites, gathered around Ezra the teacher to give attention to the words of the Law" (NEHEMIAH 8:13).

Portrays humility before God

"All the ends of the earth will remember and turn to the LORD, and all the families of the nations will bow down before him" (PSALM 22:27).

Protects against loneliness

"God sets the lonely in families" (PSALM 68:6).

Checklist for Unresolved Conflicts from Your Past

- ☐ Do you fear personal criticism?
- ☐ Do you constantly seek approval?
- ☐ Do you suppress your emotions?
- ☐ Do you lie when you could easily tell the truth?
- ☐ Do you feel you must rescue others?
- ☐ Do you confuse pity with love?
- ☐ Do you judge yourself too harshly?
- ☐ Do you find yourself easily manipulated?

- ☐ Do you assume too much responsibility?
- ☐ Do you have unresolved anger toward any family member(s)?
- ☐ Do you avoid taking personal responsibility for your actions?
- ☐ Do you fear abandonment?
- ☐ Do you violate your own conscience in order to please others?
- ☐ Do you feel you need to control others?

Test me, LORD, and try me,
examine my heart and my mind.
(PSALM 26:2)

Dominant Traits of Dysfunctional Families

1. **Chaos**—drama and confusion reign with emotions ruling decision-making. Reasoning and self-restraint take a back seat.

2. **Control**—keeping members in compliance with family rules and ideology is critical. Maintaining and supporting the hierarchy is essential to family preservation.

3. **Denial**—obvious family problems are unacknowledged, unaddressed, and unchanged. Lies are accepted as truth, and inappropriate behavior is often ignored.

4. **Inconsistency**—what was said one day is retracted the next. Expectations constantly change, and commitments are easily broken.

Key Verses to Memorize

"If you hold to my teaching,
you are really my disciples.
Then you will know the truth,
and the truth will set you free."
(JOHN 8:31-32)

5. **Indifference**—emotional support of family members is blatantly lacking unless challenged by outsiders. Children are valued for their devotion and contribution to the family system.

6. **Instability**—emotions quickly fluctuate from happy to sad, pleased to angry. Change is constant and unforeseeable; insecurity runs rampant among family members.

7. **Shame**—members serve as emotional punching bags for each other, with shame being the most effective way of hurting, manipulating, and obtaining compliance.

8. **Unpredictability**—keeping each other guessing is everyone's specialty; therefore, what is allowed one day is forbidden the next day and what pleases someone today displeases them tomorrow.

Satisfy us in the morning with your unfailing love,
that we may sing for joy and be glad all our days.
(Psalm 90:14)

What Causes Dysfunction to Develop in Some Families?

Presence of chemical addiction results in maladaptive behavior

Existence of emotional, physical, or psychological disturbances damages family members

Tolerance of abusive behavior within the family prevents healthy interaction

Adherence to a rigid, dogmatic belief system leads to bondage

Unexpected death of a significant family member creates a crisis of faith that causes chaos

Now the Lord is the Spirit, and where the Spirit
of the Lord is, there is freedom.
(2 Corinthians 3:17)

The Root Cause for a Dysfunctional Family

Wrong Belief: "My parents did not give me the unconditional love, significance, and security I needed as a child. Since my past is unchangeable, I can't change who I am today."

Right Belief: "My need for unconditional love, significance, and security can be met by Christ. Although I can't change my past, I can change my attitude about my past. I will depend on God to empower me to learn healthy ways of relating to my family."

Bear with each other and forgive one another
if any of you has a grievance against someone.
Forgive as the Lord forgave you.
(Colossians 3:13)

How to Be a Healthy Family[110]

Emphasize the uniqueness of each individual family member.

"Even so the body is not made up of one part but of many. Now if the foot should say, 'Because I am not a hand, I do not belong to the body,' it would not for that reason stop being part of the body. And if the ear should say, 'Because I am not an eye, I do not belong to the body,' it would not for that reason stop being part of the body. If the whole body were an eye, where would the sense of hearing be? If the whole body were an ear, where would the sense of smell be?" (1 CORINTHIANS 12:14–17).

Seek togetherness, but also encourage individuality.[111]

"There are different kinds of gifts, but the same Spirit distributes them. There are different kinds of service, but the same Lord. There are different kinds of working, but in all of them and in everyone it is the same God at work. Now to each one the manifestation of the Spirit is given for the common good" (1 CORINTHIANS 12:4–7).

Maintain consistency in the messages you communicate.

"Out of the same mouth come praise and cursing. My brothers and sisters, this should not be. Can both fresh water and salt water flow from the same spring? My brothers and sisters, can a fig tree bear olives, or a grapevine bear figs? Neither can a salt spring produce fresh water. Who is wise and understanding among you? Let them show it by their good life, by deeds done in the humility that comes from wisdom" (JAMES 3:10–13).

Practice immediate but appropriate discipline.

"Whoever spares the rod hates their children, but the one who loves their children is careful to discipline them" (PROVERBS 13:24).

Allow a generous margin for mistakes.

"Be kind and compassionate to one another, forgiving each other, just as in Christ God forgave you" (EPHESIANS 4:32).

Encourage the appropriate expression of feelings.

"The purposes of a person's heart are deep waters, but one who has insight draws them out" (PROVERBS 20:5).

Promote and develop natural talents and abilities.

"Start children off on the way they should go, and even when they are old they will not turn from it" (PROVERBS 22:6).

Require family members to take responsibility for their own attitudes and actions.

"Each one should test their own actions. Then they can take pride in themselves alone, without comparing themselves to someone else, for each one should carry their own load" (GALATIANS 6:4–5).

Treat everyone with love and respect.

"Love never fails" (1 CORINTHIANS 13:8).

Nurture a dependence on the Lord.

"Trust in the LORD with all your heart and lean not on your own understanding; in all your ways submit to him, and he will make your paths straight" (PROVERBS 3:5–6).

My Personalized Plan[112]

To overcome the pain in my past and move forward to a brighter future, I will:

Give myself time to grieve the past.[113]

"Very truly I tell you, you will weep and mourn while the world rejoices. You will grieve, but your grief will turn to joy" (JOHN 16:20).

Give up my need to control.

"Cast your cares on the LORD and he will sustain you; he will never let the righteous be shaken" (PSALM 55:22).

Give Christ first place in my heart.

"Whoever wants to be my disciple must deny themselves and take up their cross daily and follow me. For whoever wants to save their life will lose it, but whoever loses their life for me will save it" (LUKE 9:23–24).

Give God thanks for my past.

"Give thanks in all circumstances; for this is God's will for you in Christ Jesus" (1 THESSALONIANS 5:18).

Give attention to how I responded to my circumstances as a child.

"The heart of the discerning acquires knowledge, for the ears of the wise seek it out" (PROVERBS 18:15).

Give thought to my present dysfunctional characteristics.

"Search me, God, and know my heart; test me and know my anxious thoughts. See if there is any offensive way in me, and lead me in the way everlasting" (PSALM 139:23–24).

Give consideration to my God-given rights.

"We must obey God rather than human beings!" (ACTS 5:29).

Give myself boundaries.[114]

"Am I now trying to win the approval of human beings, or of God? Or am I trying to please people? If I were still trying to please people, I would not be a servant of Christ" (GALATIANS 1:10).

Give up resentment.

"Be kind and compassionate to one another, forgiving each other, just as in Christ God forgave you" (EPHESIANS 4:32).

Give time to restoring healthy family relationships.

"If you are offering your gift at the altar and there remember that your brother or sister has something against you, leave your gift there in front of the altar. First go and be reconciled to them; then come and offer your gift" (MATTHEW 5:23–24).

Key Passage to Read

Genesis chapter 37

And we know that in all things God works
for the good of those who love him,
who have been called according to his purpose.
(ROMANS 8:28)

Questions & Answers

Question: "I grew up in an unhealthy family, and I am now repeating many patterns from the past. What should I do?"

Answer: Ask the Lord to give you discernment in identifying which patterns need to be changed and wisdom in selecting action steps that will enable you to move toward emotional health. Tell those closest to you that you want to give up these unhealthy childhood ways of thinking, reasoning, and acting from the past. Ask them to help hold you accountable.

When I was a child, I talked like a child,
I thought like a child, I reasoned like a child.
When I became a man,
I put the ways of childhood behind me.
(1 CORINTHIANS 13:11)

EMPLOYMENT

Getting the Right Job . . . and Keeping It!

God's Heart on the Dignity of Work

God is constantly working to fulfill His purposes.

"My Father is always at his work to this very day, and I too am working" (JOHN 5:17).

God created work in the beginning, so it is to be viewed as good—not as a curse.

"The LORD God took the man and put him in the Garden of Eden to work it and take care of it" (GENESIS 2:15).

God wants you to enjoy your work.

"People should eat and drink and enjoy the fruits of their labor, for these are gifts from God" (ECCLESIASTES 3:13 NLT).

God wants you to enjoy the benefits of your work.

"You will eat the fruit of your labor; blessings and prosperity will be yours" (PSALM 128:2).

God wants you to work hard, knowing that you are ultimately working for Him.

"Whatever you do, work at it with all your heart, as working for the Lord, not for human masters" (COLOSSIANS 3:23).

God wants you to do the work He has prepared for you.

"We are God's handiwork, created in Christ Jesus to do good works, which God prepared in advance for us to do" (EPHESIANS 2:10).

God wants you to work without complaining.

"Do everything without grumbling or arguing" (PHILIPPIANS 2:14).

God wants you to acknowledge those who work hard.

"Now we ask you, brothers and sisters, to acknowledge those who work hard among you, who care for you in the Lord and who admonish you" (1 THESSALONIANS 5:12).

God wants you to work to receive a wage.

"Scripture says, 'Do not muzzle an ox while it is treading out the grain' and 'The worker deserves his wages'" (1 TIMOTHY 5:18).

God wants your work to meet your needs and the needs of others.

"You yourselves know that these hands of mine have supplied my own needs and the needs of my companions. In everything I did, I showed you that by this kind of hard work we must help the weak, remembering the words the Lord Jesus himself said: 'It is more blessed to give than to receive'" (ACTS 20:34–35).

God wants you to regularly rest from work.

"There are six days when you may work, but the seventh day is a day of sabbath rest, a day of sacred assembly. You are not to do any work; wherever you live, it is a sabbath to the LORD" (LEVITICUS 23:3).

God wants you to work for His glory and give thanks to Him for your work.

"Whatever you do, whether in word or deed, do it all in the name of the Lord Jesus, giving thanks to God the Father through him" (COLOSSIANS 3:17).

It is God who works in you to will and to act in order to fulfill his good purpose.
(PHILIPPIANS 2:13)

Job Dissatisfaction

Use the following questions to evaluate your current level of job satisfaction:

Y / N "Is the pay adequate for my job?"

Y / N "Is there a chance for advancement?"

Y / N "Are benefits sufficient?"

Y / N "Is the stress level something I can live with?"

Y / N "Are the hours satisfactory?"

Y / N "Is the work sufficiently challenging?"

Y / N "Is the location convenient?"

Y / N "Is there enough responsibility to keep me challenged?"

Y / N "Is there too much responsibility?"

Y / N "Is the boss reasonable?"

Y / N "Are working conditions satisfactory?"

Y / N "Are coworkers pleasant/cooperative?"

Y / N "Is there a sense of accomplishment?"

Y / N "Is there job security?"

"In this world you will have trouble.
But take heart! I have overcome the world."
(John 16:33)

Qualities of a Great Employee

Adaptable

— Quick to make needed changes

Self-starter

— Doesn't have to be told what to do

Listener

— Attentive, doesn't have to have instructions repeated over and over again

Problem Solver

— Turns problems into opportunities for improvement and making needed changes

Committed

— Stays focused on work and is not easily distracted from the task at hand

Present

— Focuses on the work at hand and establishes healthy boundaries between work and personal life

Key Verse to Memorize

Whatever you do,
work at it with all your heart,
as working for the Lord,
not for human masters.
(Colossians 3:23)

Grounded

— Maintains logic and controls emotions under pressure

Trustworthy

— Speaks the truth; follows through on spoken and written agreements and commitments

Assertive

— Expresses opinions and ideas with strength, but not in a condescending or belligerent manner

Correctable

— Accepts constructive criticism without defensiveness or blame-shifting

The Lord . . . *delights in people who are trustworthy.*
(Proverbs 12:22)

Steps to Success at Work

See your work from God's perspective.

"Whatever you do, work at it with all your heart, as working for the Lord, not for human masters, since you know that you will receive an inheritance from the Lord as a reward. It is the Lord Christ you are serving. Anyone who does wrong will be repaid for their wrongs, and there is no favoritism" (Colossians 3:23–25).

Accept the fact that God is directing the events of your life.

*"*Lord*, I know that people's lives are not their own; it is not for them to direct their steps"* (Jeremiah 10:23).

Begin each morning in prayer, committing the day to God.

"This is the day that the Lord *has made; let us rejoice and be glad in it"* (Psalm 118:24 esv).

Pray for your employer and fellow employees.

"As for me, far be it from me that I should sin against the Lord *by failing to pray for you. And I will teach you the way that is good and right"* (1 Samuel 12:23).

Allow Christ to reflect Himself through you each day.

"It is God who works in you to will and to act in order to fulfill his good purpose" (Philippians 2:13).

Develop positive attitudes.

"Whatever is true, whatever is noble, whatever is right, whatever is pure, whatever is lovely, whatever is admirable—if anything is excellent or praiseworthy—think about such things" (Philippians 4:8).

Display a servant's heart.

"God is not unjust; he will not forget your work and the love you have shown him as you have helped his people and continue to help them" (Hebrews 6:10).

Defuse difficult people.

"Make every effort to live in peace with everyone and to be holy; without holiness no one will see the Lord" (Hebrews 12:14).

Discover His power in your weaknesses.

"He said to me, 'My grace is sufficient for you, for my power is made perfect in weakness.' Therefore I will boast all the more gladly about my weaknesses, so that Christ's power may rest on me" (2 Corinthians 12:9).

Put your future in the hands of God.

"I tell you, do not worry about your life, what you will eat or drink; or about your body, what you will wear. Is not life more than food, and the body more than clothes? Look at the birds of the air; they do not sow or reap or store away in barns, and yet your heavenly Father feeds them. Are you not much more valuable than they? Can any one of you by worrying add a single hour to your life?" (Matthew 6:25–27).

My heart says of you, "Seek his face!"
Your face, Lord, I will seek.
(Psalm 27:8)

My Personalized Plan

In my work, I will . . .

— Be confident.
— Be dependable, predictable.
— Be myself, be real.
— Be purposeful in my performance.
— Be thorough.
— Be what I expect others to be.

I will . . .

— Demonstrate patience.
— Develop credibility.
— Do what I am asked and do it well.
— Do what I am expected to do.
— Do what I expect others to do.
— Do things outside of my comfort zone.

Key Passage to Read

The book of Nehemiah

I will . . .

— Purposefully improve my self-esteem.
— Pursue excellence.
— Persist in acquiring new skills and learning new information.
— Pay attention to detail.
— Practice living a balanced life.
— Project a can-do attitude.

I will . . .

— Seek to be creative and open-minded.
— Stay calm in the midst of discord.

— Stay positive in the midst of discouragement.
— Stimulate hearts and minds.
— Stretch myself and grow.
— Strive to be a model employee.

In everything he did he had great success,
because the LORD was with him.
(1 SAMUEL 18:14)

Questions & Answers

Question: "I'm a single parent. Should I change jobs in order to spend more time with my preschooler?"

Answer: As a parent, one of your primary purposes is that of training your child in godly living, and that requires both time and effort. Deuteronomy 6:5–9 expresses God's instructions to parents, and your role is definitely one of modeling, character building, and instilling truth in your child. But as a single parent, you also need to provide for your child.

Choose employment that still allows you the time and opportunity to build character and a heart for God into the life of your child.

These commandments that I give you today
are to be on your hearts.
Impress them on your children.
(DEUTERONOMY 6:6–7)

Question: "One of my coworkers continues to make lewd comments toward me. If I report this harassment, I'm afraid I will lose my job. Wouldn't it be best to just ignore this behavior?"

Answer: No. Not only do these behaviors break the law, but they also lead to a hostile work environment. Allowing wrong behavior to continue without addressing the issue only prolongs the abuse and could subject other victims to the same behavior.

Acknowledge your feelings and determine how to respond appropriately. If at times you wonder whether you did something to cause this treatment, remember no one makes another person behave inappropriately.

Nothing in all creation is hidden from God's sight.
(HEBREWS 4:13)

ENVY & JEALOUSY

Taming the Terrible Twins

God's Heart on Envy

God instructs us:

— **Don't** yearn for anything that belongs to another person.

"You shall not covet . . . anything that belongs to your neighbor" (EXODUS 20:17).

— **Don't** desire what the ungodly have, and don't seek their friendship.

"Do not envy the wicked, do not desire their company" (PROVERBS 24:1).

— **Don't** allow yourself to crave more and more, but rather to give more and more.

"All day long he craves for more, but the righteous give without sparing" (PROVERBS 21:26).

— **Don't** obsess over what others have; instead focus on how you can express love to others.

"The commandments, 'You shall not commit adultery . . . murder . . . steal . . . covet,' and whatever other command there may be, are summed up in this one command: 'Love your neighbor as yourself'" (ROMANS 13:9).

God's Heart on Jealousy

God instructs us:

— **Jealousy** over someone straying from devotion to Christ is godly jealousy.

"I am jealous for you with a godly jealousy. I promised you to one husband, to Christ, so that I might present you as a pure virgin to him" (2 CORINTHIANS 11:2).

— **Jealousy** can be a fierce protector.

"Place me like a seal over your heart, like a seal on your arm; for love is as strong as death, its jealousy unyielding as the grave. It burns like blazing fire, like a mighty flame" (SONG OF SONGS 8:6).

— **Jealousy** that is marked by sin, worldliness, and fighting should not control our lives.

"For you are still controlled by your sinful nature. You are jealous of one another and quarrel with each other. Doesn't that prove you are controlled by your sinful nature? Aren't you living like people of the world?" (1 CORINTHIANS 3:3 NLT).

— **Jealousy** that is worldly reveals selfishness, a life out of order, and ungodly actions—and must be rooted out of our hearts.

"Jealousy and selfishness are not God's kind of wisdom. Such things are earthly, unspiritual, and demonic. For wherever there is jealousy and selfish ambition, there you will find disorder and evil of every kind" (James 3:15–16 NLT).

When you follow the desires of your sinful nature,
the results are very clear . . .
hostility, quarreling, jealousy,
outbursts of anger, selfish ambition,
dissension, division, envy.
(Galatians 5:19–21 NLT)

The Envy and Jealousy Checklists

The Envy Checklist

- ☐ Do you resent a relationship that someone else enjoys?
- ☐ Do you feel unhappy over someone's happiness?
- ☐ Do you secretly resent another's abilities?
- ☐ Do you feel provoked over another person's elevated position?
- ☐ Do you feel bothered by another person's possessions?
- ☐ Do you ever feel angry over someone else's success?
- ☐ Do you pout about another person's popularity?
- ☐ Do you secretly rejoice when someone suffers a setback?

The Jealousy Checklist

- ☐ Do you feel overly possessive of someone or something?
- ☐ Do you attempt to control others?
- ☐ Do you want an exclusive relationship with someone?
- ☐ Do you feel anxious over any potential loss of someone or something?
- ☐ Do you assume your worth is tied to someone or something?
- ☐ Do you feel emotionally dependent on someone?
- ☐ Do you feel distrustful of others concerning someone (or something)?
- ☐ Do you feel unable to trust God with the future regarding someone (or something)?

Causes of Being DISCONTENT

D—Desiring the approval of others, and failing to be satisfied with the approval of God

"Am I now trying to win the approval of human beings, or of God? Or am I trying to please people? If I were still trying to please people, I would not be a servant of Christ" (GALATIANS 1:10).

I—Insisting on God doing things *our* way, and failing to do things *His* way

"Let us examine our ways and test them, and let us return to the LORD" (LAMENTATIONS 3:40).

S—Seeking personal significance, and failing to be humble before God

"When pride comes, then comes disgrace, but with humility comes wisdom" (PROVERBS 11:2).

C—Comparing ourselves with others, and failing to seek to be Christlike

"We do not dare to classify or compare ourselves with some who commend themselves. When they measure themselves by themselves and compare themselves with themselves, they are not wise" (2 CORINTHIANS 10:12).

Key Verses to Memorize

I know what it is to be in need,
and I know what it is to have plenty.
I have learned the secret of being content
in any and every situation,
whether well fed or hungry,
whether living in plenty or in want.
I can do all this through him [Christ]
who gives me strength.
(PHILIPPIANS 4:12–13)

O—Opposing the success of others, and failing to acknowledge the achievements of others

"Do not withhold good from those to whom it is due, when it is in your power to act" (PROVERBS 3:27).

N—Nurturing selfish gain, and failing to make righteousness our goal

"Seek first his kingdom and his righteousness, and all these things will be given to you as well" (MATTHEW 6:33).

T—Thinking too highly of ourselves, and failing to accurately judge ourselves and walk in humility

"By the grace given me I say to every one of you: Do not think of yourself more highly than you ought, but rather think of yourself with sober judgment, in accordance with the faith God has distributed to each of you" (ROMANS 12:3).

E—Expecting to impress others by praising ourselves, and failing to credit God for working through us

"Let someone else praise you, and not your own mouth; an outsider, and not your own lips" (PROVERBS 27:2).

N—Needing to hear praise from others. and failing to keep our focus on serving others and pleasing God

"We were not looking for praise from people, not from you or anyone else" (1 THESSALONIANS 2:6).

T—Taking delight in the misfortune of another, and failing to minister to our enemies through prayer

"Do not gloat when your enemy falls; when they stumble, do not let your heart rejoice" (PROVERBS 24:17).

Where you have envy and selfish ambition,
there you find disorder and every evil practice.
(JAMES 3:16)

How to Eliminate Envy

Face your feelings of resentment and use them as indicators of your need to change.

"Get rid of all bitterness, rage, anger, harsh words, and slander, as well as all types of evil behavior" (EPHESIANS 4:31 NLT).

Recognize the source of the self-centered emotion of envy.

"Turn my heart toward your statutes and not toward selfish gain" (PSALM 119:36).

Eliminate the emotion of envy.

"The love of Christ controls us, because we have concluded this: that one has died for all, therefore all have died" (2 CORINTHIANS 5:14 ESV).

Be sure your thinking lines up with God's thinking—now and in the future.

"You were taught, with regard to your former way of life, to put off your old self, which is being corrupted by its deceitful desires; to be made new in the attitude of your minds; and to put on the new self, created to be like God in true righteousness and holiness" (EPHESIANS 4:22–24).

Turn your focus from *receiving from* others to *giving to* others.

"It is more blessed to give than to receive" (ACTS 20:35).

Let the message about Christ, in all its richness, fill your lives.
Teach and counsel each other with all the wisdom he gives.
Sing psalms and hymns and spiritual songs
to God with thankful hearts.
(COLOSSIANS 3:16 NLT)

My Personalized Plan[115]

I will fight . . .

Arrogance: "I humbly acknowledge that everything I have is actually a gift from God."

"What do you have that God hasn't given you? And if everything you have is from God, why boast as though it were not a gift?" (1 CORINTHIANS 4:7 NLT).

Comparison: "I will remember that God reveals His strength through my weakness."

"He said to me, 'My grace is sufficient for you, for my power is made perfect in weakness.' Therefore I will boast all the more gladly about my weaknesses, so that Christ's power may rest on me" (2 CORINTHIANS 12:9).

Competition: "I will choose to care about others rather than compete with them."

"Do nothing out of selfish ambition or vain conceit. Rather, in humility value others above yourselves, not looking to your own interests but each of you to the interests of the others" (PHILIPPIANS 2:3–4).

Covetousness: "I'll be thankful for what I have in this life."

"Since we are receiving a kingdom that cannot be shaken, let us be thankful" (HEBREWS 12:28).

Denial: "I will change my thoughts and ask God to purify my heart from all that is not right in His sight."

"If we claim to be without sin, we deceive ourselves and the truth is not in us. If we confess our sins, he is faithful and just and will forgive us our sins and purify us from all unrighteousness" (1 JOHN 1:8–9).

Key Passage to Read

Matthew 20:1–16

Discontent: "I will be content with everything God has provided me."

"The LORD God is a sun and shield; the LORD bestows favor and honor; no good thing does he withhold from those whose walk is blameless" (PSALM 84:11).

Dissatisfaction: "I will be satisfied that God will meet my needs."

"The LORD will guide you always; he will satisfy your needs in a sun-scorched land and will strengthen your frame. You will be like a well-watered garden, like a spring whose waters never fail" (ISAIAH 58:11).

Fear: "I will trust God to help me and calm my fear."

"Do not fear, for I am with you; do not be dismayed, for I am your God. I will strengthen you and help you; I will uphold you with my righteous right hand" (ISAIAH 41:10).

Insecurity: "I will not put my trust in what I have, but will entrust my life to the Lord."

"Let the morning bring me word of your unfailing love, for I have put my trust in you. Show me the way I should go, for to you I entrust my life" (PSALM 143:8).

Pride: "I will acknowledge that I cannot control everything in my life, but I can trust and bow down to the Lord who can."

"You shall have no other gods before me . . . for I, the LORD your God, am a jealous God" (EXODUS 20:3, 5).

Do not conform to the pattern of this world,
but be transformed by the renewing of your mind.
Then you will be able to test and approve what
God's will is—his good, pleasing and perfect will.
(ROMANS 12:2)

Questions & Answers

Question: "Is envy ever right?"

Answer: No. Envy is an expression of self-centered pride, and, as such, is always wrong. To envy is to covet—which is expressly prohibited by God in His Ten Commandments. Envy is often accompanied by entitlement: "I'm entitled to have what you have." The Bible never speaks of envy in a positive light. God's Word says that love does not envy. Since the greatest commands are to love God and love our neighbors—and love does not envy—it can never be loving or right to be envious.

Love . . . does not envy.
(1 CORINTHIANS 13:4)

Question: "Isn't jealousy always wrong?"

Answer: No, sometimes jealousy is wrong and sometimes right.

Ungodly jealousy arises from selfishness and insecurity or the belief that one person owns another person. This worldly jealousy is not based on love but on self-centered desires.

Godly jealousy surfaces when a covenant relationship is threatened (such as in a marriage or in our relationship with God). Out of His great love for us, God jealously guards His special relationship with us. God, in giving the Ten Commandments, describes Himself as a "jealous God": "I, the LORD your God, am a jealous God" (Exodus 20:5).

"Do not worship any other god,
for the LORD, whose name is Jealous,
is a jealous God."
(EXODUS 34:14)

ETHICS & INTEGRITY

The Foundation for All Your Decisions

God's Heart on Ethics & Integrity

To truthfully portray the character of Christ, we must live with integrity, displaying the hallmarks of His character in our walk, in our talk, with each acquaintance, with each encounter—in the daylight and in the dark—always reflecting the heart of Christ.

Challenge yourself to raise the bar of integrity in your own life by adopting these divine and distinctive character traits seen in the Bible:

Avoids Evil

"Abstain from every form of evil" (1 THESSALONIANS 5:22 NKJV).

Blameless Behavior

"Now he has reconciled you by Christ's physical body through death to present you holy in his sight, without blemish and free from accusation" (COLOSSIANS 1:22).

Commendable Communication

"Do not let any unwholesome talk come out of your mouths, but only what is helpful for building others up according to their needs, that it may benefit those who listen" (EPHESIANS 4:29).

Decidedly Disciplined

"No discipline seems pleasant at the time, but painful. Later on, however, it produces a harvest of righteousness and peace for those who have been trained by it" (HEBREWS 12:11).

Earnest Encourager

"Encourage the disheartened, help the weak, be patient with everyone" (1 THESSALONIANS 5:14).

Ethically Honorable

"We are sure that we have a clear conscience and desire to live honorably in every way" (HEBREWS 13:18).

Gentle and Respectful

"In your hearts revere Christ as Lord. Always be prepared to give an answer to everyone who asks you to give the reason for the hope that you have. But do this with gentleness and respect" (1 PETER 3:15).

Humble Heart

"Do nothing out of selfish ambition or vain conceit. Rather, in humility value others above yourselves" (PHILIPPIANS 2:3).

Legitimate Leadership

"Since an overseer manages God's household, he must be blameless—not overbearing, not quick-tempered, not given to drunkenness, not violent, not pursuing dishonest gain. Rather, he must be hospitable, one who loves what is good, who is self-controlled, upright, holy and disciplined" (TITUS 1:7–8).

Pursuer of Peace

"Blessed are the peacemakers, for they will be called children of God" (MATTHEW 5:9).

Truth Teller

"These are the things you are to do: Speak the truth to each other" (ZECHARIAH 8:16).

Uncompromising Confidentiality

"Argue your case with your neighbor himself, and do not reveal another's secret" (PROVERBS 25:9 ESV).

Wholehearted Worker

"Whatever you do, work at it with all your heart, as working for the Lord, not for human masters" (COLOSSIANS 3:23).

What does the LORD require of you?
To act justly and to love mercy
and to walk humbly with your God.
(MICAH 6:8)

Six Systems of Ethics

1. **Relativism**: Moral standards for right and wrong are determined by the majority.

   Biblical Conclusion: Society can be wrong. Truth is determined only by God's moral laws.

   "We must obey God rather than human beings!" (ACTS 5:29).

2. **Utilitarianism**: Moral standards for right and wrong are determined by what is considered "most loving" or for the greatest good in a given situation.

   Biblical Conclusion: People show love best by following God's will.

   "This is love: that we walk in obedience to his commands. . . . His command is that you walk in love" (2 JOHN V. 6).

3. **Existentialism**: Moral standards for right and wrong do not exist. Actions are determined by personal preference.

   Biblical Conclusion: Emotions are not a dependable gauge for actions. God does set limits on human behavior.

   "The heart is deceitful above all things and beyond cure. Who can understand it?" (JEREMIAH 17:9).

4. **Behaviorism**: Moral standards for right and wrong do not exist. All behavior is determined by environment or heredity.

   Biblical Conclusion: God has instilled His moral laws within the human heart and has given all people free will to choose their behaviors.

   "The requirements of the law are written on their hearts" (ROMANS 2:15).

Key Verse to Memorize

The integrity of the upright guides them,
but the unfaithful are destroyed
by their duplicity.
(PROVERBS 11:3)

5. **Legalism**: Moral absolutes for right and wrong are universal, unchangeable, and determined by a supreme moral or legal authority.

   Biblical Conclusion: People eventually fail to meet the demands of an objective legal authority, always striving for, yet never attaining, absolute perfection.

   "You experts in the law . . . load people down with burdens they can hardly carry, and . . . will not lift one finger to help them" (LUKE 11:46).

6. **Christianity**: Moral absolutes for right and wrong are universal, unchangeable, and determined by the revealed will of God.

   Biblical Conclusion: Christ empowers Christians to live out His grace and truth.

   "I have been crucified with Christ and I no longer live, but Christ lives in me" (GALATIANS 2:20).

The Root Cause of a Lack of Integrity

Wrong Belief: "Following an ancient book of laws is not intellectually honest. God has given me a mind, and He expects me to use it for making my own decisions about right and wrong."

There is a way that appears to be right,
but in the end it leads to death.
(PROVERBS 14:12)

Right Belief: "God established the world with scientific and moral laws. Adopting an alternative set of morals through which I can rationalize sin is not intellectually honest. God has given me His Spirit that I might know what is wrong and do what is right based on His eternal principles."

Your word, LORD, is eternal;
it stands firm in the heavens. . . .
Your laws endure to this day,
for all things serve you.
If your law had not been my delight,
I would have perished in my affliction.
I will never forget your precepts,
for by them you have preserved my life.
(PSALM 119:89, 91–93)

Speaking Truth When Facing a Dilemma

W—Worth—Speak positively about the ***worth*** of the person or organization.

I—Integrity—Explain why you are committed to ***integrity*** and what you will or will not do.

N—Nurture—Use encouraging words to ***nurture*** the other person.

Virtue

Just as fuel in your car engine produces power for movement, the virtue of Jesus Christ in the believer produces power for a changed life.

V—Value the importance of moral purity.

"Just as he who called you is holy, so be holy in all you do; for it is written: 'Be holy, because I am holy'" (1 PETER 1:15–16).

I—Instill God's Word in your heart.

"I meditate on your precepts and consider your ways. I delight in your decrees; I will not neglect your word" (PSALM 119:15–16).

R—Recognize your dependence on God's grace.

"Let us then approach God's throne of grace with confidence, so that we may receive mercy and find grace to help us in our time of need" (HEBREWS 4:16).

T—Trust in Christ for your identity.

"God has chosen to make known among the Gentiles the glorious riches of this mystery, which is Christ in you, the hope of glory" (COLOSSIANS 1:27).

U—Understand that your strength is in Christ.

"Being strengthened with all power according to his glorious might so that you may have great endurance and patience" (COLOSSIANS 1:11).

E—Expect testing and temptation.

"Consider it pure joy, my brothers and sisters, whenever you face trials of many kinds" (JAMES 1:2).

His divine power has given us everything
we need for a godly life
through our knowledge of him
who called us by his own
glory and goodness.
(2 PETER 1:3)

My Personalized Plan

The Ethics Exam

Before I make a decision over an ethical issue of right or wrong, I will ask myself these questions:

Key Passage to Read

Psalm 101:1–8

Is there a principle about it in the Bible?

"Since through God's mercy we have this ministry, we do not lose heart. Rather, we have renounced secret and shameful ways; we do not use deception, nor do we distort the word of God. On the contrary, by setting forth the truth plainly we commend ourselves to everyone's conscience in the sight of God" (2 CORINTHIANS 4:1–2).

Is it beneficial?

"'I have the right to do anything,' you say—but not everything is beneficial" (1 CORINTHIANS 10:23).

Is it self-serving at someone else's expense?

"No one should seek their own good, but the good of others" (1 CORINTHIANS 10:24).

Is it setting an example I would want others to follow?

"Follow my example, as I follow the example of Christ" (1 CORINTHIANS 11:1).

Examine yourselves to see whether
you are in the faith; test yourselves.
(2 CORINTHIANS 13:5)

The Integrity Interrogation

Before I act on my decisions, I will check my motives by asking myself these questions:

Am I choosing to do this to look good in the eyes of others?

"Am I now trying to win the approval of human beings, or of God? Or am I trying to please people? If I were still trying to please people, I would not be a servant of Christ" (GALATIANS 1:10).

Am I doing this only to receive financial gain?

"Better a little with the fear of the LORD than great wealth with turmoil" (PROVERBS 15:16).

Am I willing to do this even if I don't get the credit?

"All those who exalt themselves will be humbled, and those who humble themselves will be exalted" (LUKE 14:11).

Am I doing something unethical because I don't think I'll be found out?

"Nothing in all creation is hidden from God's sight. Everything is uncovered and laid bare before the eyes of him to whom we must give account" (HEBREWS 4:13).

All a person's ways seem pure to them,
but motives are weighed by the LORD.
(PROVERBS 16:2)

Questions & Answers

Question: "Is there truly a difference between right and wrong? Isn't it just a matter of opinion?"

Answer: Everyone has sincere opinions, but opinions aren't necessarily right. In fact, at times we've all been sincere, yet sincerely *wrong*! That is why we need to ask ourselves, *What is my foundation for truth?* The Bible must be your foundation for truth. If your thinking doesn't line up with God's thinking, you need to align your thoughts with God's thoughts.

Consider these questions:

— Do you want to make mistakes? (Of course not.)
— Do you want to give wise counsel? (Who wouldn't?)
— What is the actual source of wisdom? (God Himself.)
— If you could think like God thinks, would you be wise? (Undoubtedly.)
— Where can you find God's thoughts? (In the Bible.)

Conclusion: The more you know God's Word, the more you will know what God wants you to do. When talking with a person about a problem, first ask yourself, *Has God already spoken directly about this in His Word?* If so, what has He said? If not, is there a general biblical principle that needs to be considered?

When your deepest dependence is on the Word of God, you will be wise and will have greater confidence in knowing the true difference between right and wrong.

A person of understanding delights in wisdom.
(Proverbs 10:23)

EVIL & SUFFERING . . . WHY?

Is God Fair?

God's Heart on Evil & Suffering

God understands the pain of evil and suffering.

"He was despised and rejected by mankind, a man of suffering, and familiar with pain. Like one from whom people hide their faces he was despised, and we held him in low esteem" (ISAIAH 53:3).

God allows evil and suffering for the time being because He has given humanity free will.

"The LORD God commanded the man, 'You are free to eat from any tree in the garden; but you must not eat from the tree of the knowledge of good and evil, for when you eat from it you will certainly die'" (GENESIS 2:16-17).

God is the pure essence of goodness, holiness, and righteousness. Everything good comes from Him.

"Dear friend, do not imitate what is evil but what is good. Anyone who does what is good is from God. Anyone who does what is evil has not seen God" (3 JOHN V. 11).

God wants your words and actions to be marked by goodness, not evil.

"Whoever of you loves life and desires to see many good days, keep your tongue from evil and your lips from telling lies. Turn from evil and do good; seek peace and pursue it" (PSALM 34:12–14).

God promises to never stop doing good to His people.

"I will make an everlasting covenant with them: I will never stop doing good to them" (JEREMIAH 32:40).

God does not want you to take part in evil deeds but rather bring them to the light.

"Take no part in the worthless deeds of evil and darkness; instead, expose them" (EPHESIANS 5:11 NLT).

God wants you to clearly distinguish between what is good and evil.

"Woe to those who call evil good and good evil, who put darkness for light and light for darkness, who put bitter for sweet and sweet for bitter" (ISAIAH 5:20).

God helps us overcome evil with good.

"Do not be overcome by evil, but overcome evil with good" (ROMANS 12:21).

God uses the testing of trials to produce perseverance and maturity.

"Consider it pure joy, my brothers and sisters, whenever you face trials of many kinds, because you know that the testing of your faith produces perseverance. Let perseverance finish its work so that you may be mature and complete, not lacking anything" (JAMES 1:2–4).

God can use even the hard and difficult things of life for good.

"We know that in all things God works for the good of those who love him, who have been called according to his purpose" (ROMANS 8:28).

God is near to all those who suffer.

"The LORD is close to the brokenhearted and saves those who are crushed in spirit" (PSALM 34:18).

God will one day end all evil and suffering.

"He will wipe every tear from their eyes, and there will be no more death or sorrow or crying or pain. All these things are gone forever" (REVELATION 21:4 NLT).

"Shall we accept good from God, and not trouble?"
(JOB 2:10)

God's Purpose for Pain

Suffering—when we are being disciplined—is a great demonstration of God's fatherly love.

"The Lord disciplines the one he loves, and chastises every son whom he receives" (HEBREWS 12:6 ESV).

Suffering disciplines us—just as children are disciplined—for our good, to conform us to His character.

"They [our fathers] *disciplined us for a little while as they thought best; but God disciplines us for our good, in order that we may share in his holiness"* (HEBREWS 12:10).

Suffering—when we respond the right way—brings us into right relationship with God and produces supernatural peace.

"No discipline seems pleasant at the time, but painful. Later on, however, it produces a harvest of righteousness and peace for those who have been trained by it" (HEBREWS 12:11).

Suffering brings glory to God—amazing, spectacular glory—when He performs a miraculous healing.

"Jesus said, 'This sickness will not end in death. No, it is for God's glory so that God's Son may be glorified through it'" (JOHN 11:4).

Suffering keeps us humble—preventing us from becoming conceited. The apostle Paul said:

"In order to keep me from becoming conceited, I was given a thorn in my flesh, a messenger of Satan, to torment me" (2 CORINTHIANS 12:7).

Key Verse to Memorize

Those who suffer according to God's will should commit themselves to their faithful Creator and continue to do good.
(1 PETER 4:19)

Suffering requires us to live our lives being dependent on God's power—we would not do so otherwise!

"My grace is sufficient for you, for my power is made perfect in weakness" (2 CORINTHIANS 12:9).

The Sovereignty of God

S—Seek God in prayer for discernment in your circumstances.

"Is anyone among you in trouble? Let them pray" (JAMES 5:13).

O—Open your heart to God with complete honesty about your feelings.

"Cast your cares on the LORD and he will sustain you; he will never let the righteous be shaken" (PSALM 55:22).

V—Verify your belief in God's love for you.

"Though he brings grief, he will show compassion, so great is his unfailing love" (LAMENTATIONS 3:32).

E—Expect God to change your life through the truth He reveals to you.

"It was good for me to be afflicted so that I might learn your decrees" (PSALM 119:71).

R—Realize that God is all-powerful and sovereign over your circumstances.

"'Don't you realize I have power either to free you or to crucify you?' Jesus answered, 'You would have no power over me if it were not given to you from above'" (JOHN 19:10–11).

E—Expect God to work through all things to prove your faith and to bring Him praise, glory, and honor.

"The God of all grace, who called you to his eternal glory in Christ, after you have suffered a little while, will himself restore you and make you strong, firm and steadfast" (1 PETER 5:10).

I—Invest time in studying Scripture and in prayer.

"I meditate on your precepts and consider your ways. I delight in your decrees; I will not neglect your word" (PSALM 119:15–16).

G—Gain an eternal perspective of God's purposes for your present pain.

"'Neither this man nor his parents sinned,' said Jesus, 'but this happened so that the works of God might be displayed in him'" (JOHN 9:3).

N—Never allow bitterness to grow in your heart.

"Though the fig tree does not bud and there are no grapes on the vines, though the olive crop fails and the fields produce no food, though there are no sheep in the pen and no cattle in the stalls, yet I will rejoice in the LORD, I will be joyful in God my Savior" (HABAKKUK 3:17–18).

T—Turn to the indwelling Christ, who provides you with His power for victory.

"I can do all this through him who gives me strength" (PHILIPPIANS 4:13).

Y—Yield to God's sovereignty. You may never understand or have any answers for your suffering.

"Trust in the LORD with all your heart and lean not on your own understanding; in all your ways submit to him, and he will make your paths straight" (PROVERBS 3:5–6).

He changes times and seasons;
he deposes kings and raises up others.
He gives wisdom to the wise
and knowledge to the discerning.
(DANIEL 2:21)

The Cause of Evil & Suffering

There is no single clear cause for the evil and suffering in the world. However, it is clear that evil and suffering are the result of at least five different elements that may occur independently or in conjunction with one another.

1. **The result of our choices**

   "The LORD God banished him from the Garden of Eden to work the ground from which he had been taken" (GENESIS 3:23).

2. **The result of the choices of others**

   "Just as one trespass resulted in condemnation for all people, so also one righteous act resulted in justification and life for all people" (ROMANS 5:18).

3. **The result of Satan and evil spirits**

   "'You will not certainly die,' the serpent said to the woman. 'For God knows that when you eat from it your eyes will be opened, and you will be like God, knowing good and evil.' When the woman saw that the fruit of the tree was good for food and pleasing to the eye, and also desirable for gaining wisdom, she took some and ate it. She also gave some to her husband, who was with her, and he ate it" (GENESIS 3:4–6).

4. **The result of natural order**

   "To the woman he said, 'I will make your pains in childbearing very severe; with painful labor you will give birth to children. Your desire will be for your husband, and he will rule over you.' To Adam he said, 'Because you listened to your wife and ate from the tree about which I commanded you, "You must not eat from it," cursed is the ground because of you; through painful toil you will eat food from it all the days of your life'" (GENESIS 3:16–17).

Key Passage to Read

Romans 8:18–25

5. **The result of God's permissive will**

   "The LORD God commanded the man, 'You are free to eat from any tree in the garden; but you must not eat from the tree of the knowledge of good and evil, for when you eat from it you will certainly die'" (GENESIS 2:16–17).

God Cares About Your Suffering

He is close to you when you are brokenhearted.

"The LORD is close to the brokenhearted and saves those who are crushed in spirit" (PSALM 34:18).

He stays around you in the midst of trouble.

"The angel of the LORD encamps around those who fear him, and he delivers them" (PSALM 34:7).

He keeps a record of your grief and keeps hold of your tears.

"You have kept count of my tossings; put my tears in your bottle. Are they not in your book?" (PSALM 56:8 ESV).

My Personalized Plan

I will . . .

Dwell on God's character, purposes, and promises so that, when evil and suffering touch my life, I can fully trust Him with my future.

— I will not blame God for the choices of others but will accept that I live in a world where good and evil both exist, and can touch my life.

— I will look to the Lord in my pain, and trust that He is working for my good—even when He permits suffering in my life.

"Those who suffer according to God's will should commit themselves to their faithful Creator and continue to do good" (1 PETER 4:19).

Develop a biblical understanding of evil and suffering.

— I will remember that Jesus understands and empathizes with my pain, for He is called a "man of suffering, and familiar with pain" (Isaiah 53:3).

— I will remember that suffering and pain can be used by God to accomplish good for myself and others.

"You intended to harm me, but God intended it for good to accomplish what is now being done, the saving of many lives" (GENESIS 50:20).

Deepen my walk with the Lord by honestly confronting my pain.

— I will allow myself to grieve the loss I am experiencing, so that I can work through the pain and suffering.

— I will seek support from God, His Word, encouraging believers and/or support groups, so I can be whole and free.

"I cry aloud to the LORD; I lift up my voice to the LORD for mercy. I pour out before him my complaint; before him I tell my trouble" (PSALM 142:1–2).

Display a heart of forgiveness.

— I will receive God's forgiveness and grace for things I have done wrong that have caused others and me pain.

— I will forgive those who have hurt or wounded me and will continue to grow in my relationship with Christ.

"Bear with each other and forgive one another if any of you has a grievance against someone. Forgive as the Lord forgave you" (COLOSSIANS 3:13).

Determine to live with an eternal perspective of God's purposes in regards to my present pain.

— I will be open to the good that comes out of my pain and be willing to accept a new normal for my life.

— I will share my heart with others who are in pain, using my experiences to help them.

"Praise be to the God and Father of our Lord Jesus Christ, the Father of compassion and the God of all comfort, who comforts us in all our troubles, so that we can comfort those in any trouble with the comfort ourselves receive from God" (2 CORINTHIANS 1:3–4).

The LORD is righteous in all his ways
and faithful in all he does.
(PSALM 145:17)

Questions & Answers

Question: "Doesn't the existence of evil prove that God is not a good God?"

Answer: The existence of evil does not negate the existence of a good God any more than darkness negates light or death negates life. Some things are better defined by the contrast of their opposites.

Since both good and evil clearly exist, a good God must necessarily exist. What else is the source of good?

God in His goodness and in His timing will deal with evil and those who promote evil.

The evildoer has no future hope,
and the lamp of the wicked will be snuffed out.
(PROVERBS 24:20)

Question: "Why do Christians sometimes suffer for doing good?"

Answer: Evil is always in opposition to good. By its very nature, evil will seek to harm and destroy those who do good. The only real peace to be found in the midst of suffering is in the One who has made us to be at peace with God.

In His time, this Prince of Peace, Jesus, will do away with evil and thereby secure total peace for all eternity for His followers. He Himself suffered for doing good. As His followers, we at times will also experience suffering for doing good.

"If the world hates you, keep in mind that it hated me first. . . .
If they persecuted me, they will persecute you also.
If they obeyed my teaching, they will obey yours also."
(JOHN 15:18, 20)

FEAR

No Longer Afraid

God's Heart on Fear

He is with you and will never leave you.

"The LORD himself goes before you and will be with you; he will never leave you nor forsake you. Do not be afraid; do not be discouraged" (DEUTERONOMY 31:8).

He is your light, salvation, and stronghold.

"The LORD is my light and my salvation—whom shall I fear? The LORD is the stronghold of my life—of whom shall I be afraid?" (PSALM 27:1).

He keeps you safe as you trust in Him.

"Fear of man will prove to be a snare, but whoever trusts in the LORD is kept safe" (PROVERBS 29:25).

He has His hand on you.

"You hem me in behind and before, and you lay your hand upon me" (PSALM 139:5).

He guides and holds you.

"Even there your hand will guide me, your right hand will hold me fast" (PSALM 139:10).

He delivers you.

"I sought the LORD, and he answered me; he delivered me from all my fears" (PSALM 34:4).

He cares for you.

"Cast all your anxiety on him because he cares for you" (1 PETER 5:7).

He strengthens, helps, and upholds you.

"Do not fear, for I am with you; do not be dismayed, for I am your God. I will strengthen you and help you; I will uphold you with my righteous right hand" (ISAIAH 41:10).

He works in all things for your good.

"We know that in all things God works for the good of those who love him, who have been called according to his purpose" (ROMANS 8:28).

He says nothing can separate you from His love.

"I am convinced that neither death nor life, neither angels nor demons, neither the present nor the future, nor any powers, neither height nor depth, nor anything else in all creation, will be able to separate us from the love of God that is in Christ Jesus our Lord" (Romans 8:38–39).

He has plans to give you hope and a future.

"'I know the plans I have for you,' declares the Lord, 'plans to prosper you and not to harm you, plans to give you hope and a future'" (Jeremiah 29:11).

He has made you more than a conqueror.

"In all these things we are more than conquerors through him who loved us" (Romans 8:37).

Three Levels of Anxiety

The level of anxiety people experience is generally identified as either moderate or intense. One can actually prove to be an asset, but the other is always a liability.

Normal anxiety—normal, fearful concern can be healthy and helpful:

- — It motivates us and leads to increased efficiency.
- — It forces us out of our "comfort zone."
- — It helps us avoid dangerous situations.
- — It causes us to live dependently on the Lord.

When you see him again you may be glad
and I may have less anxiety.
(Philippians 2:28)

Mild to moderate anxiety—becomes limiting and begins to interfere with daily living:

- — It makes concentration difficult.
- — It causes forgetfulness.
- — It hinders performance.
- — It blocks communication with others.

Banish anxiety from your heart.
(Ecclesiastes 11:10)

Intense anxiety—abnormal fearful obsession is more profound and problematic:

- — It becomes a severe preoccupation with fears.

— It requires tremendous effort to avoid triggers.
— It impacts physical health to an alarming degree.
— It harms relationships in many areas—professionally and personally.

When anxiety was great within me, your consolation brought me joy.
(PSALM 94:19)

Fear vs. Fact

Fear: "I can't help this feeling of intense fear!"

Fact: "This feeling is misleading. It is not grounded in truth."

"So we say with confidence, 'The Lord is my helper; I will not be afraid. What can mere mortals do to me?'" (HEBREWS 13:6).

Fear: "I have this feeling of doom—the feeling that I'm going to die."

Fact: "The time of my death is in God's hands. I will choose to trust Him."

"From one man he [God] *made all the nations . . . and he marked out their appointed times in history and the boundaries of their lands"* (ACTS 17:26).

Key Verse to Memorize

"Do not fear, for I am with you;
do not be dismayed, for I am your God.
I will strengthen you and help you;
I will uphold you
with my righteous right hand."
(ISAIAH 41:10)

Fear: "I'm afraid of what others are thinking about me."

Fact: "My peace comes from pleasing God, not in pleasing others."

"We make it our goal to please him" (2 CORINTHIANS 5:9).

Fear: "I am hopeless and can never change."

Fact: "In Christ, I am a new person. Nothing is hopeless."

"If anyone is in Christ, the new creation has come: The old has gone, the new is here!" (2 CORINTHIANS 5:17).

Fear: "I am so nervous, I can't think clearly."

Fact: "God will guard my mind and give me peace."

"The peace of God, which transcends all understanding, will guard your hearts and your minds in Christ Jesus" (PHILIPPIANS 4:7).

Fear: "To be safe, I have to be in control."

Fact: "God is in control of my life, and He is with me step by step."

"The LORD himself goes before you and will be with you; he will never leave you nor forsake you. Do not be afraid; do not be discouraged" (DEUTERONOMY 31:8).

My Personalized Plan

Be honest about my fear

— I will acknowledge my fears and how they impact my life, relationships, and walk with God.

— I will tell God about my fears and consider talking with a trusted friend, pastor, or counselor as well.

"I sought the LORD, and he answered me; he delivered me from all my fears" (PSALM 34:4).

Acknowledge God's presence

— I will remember that God is always with me, so I never face my fears alone.

— I will ask the Lord for help to overcome my fear.

"Even though I walk through the valley of the shadow of death, I will fear no evil, for you are with me; your rod and your staff, they comfort me" (PSALM 23:4 ESV).

Trust in God's sovereignty

— I will remember that God is in control of everything when I am afraid of the unknown.

— I will rest in God's sovereignty over my life and future.

"When I am afraid, I put my trust in you" (PSALM 56:3).

Identify root causes

— I will consider whether my fear is real or imagined, whether based on reality or based on my thoughts and imagination.

— I will consider the root of my fear (past experience, childhood, trauma, etc.) and address those underlying issues.

"Search me, God, and know my heart; test me and know my anxious thoughts. See if there is any offensive way in me, and lead me in the way everlasting" (PSALM 139:23–24).

Consider outcomes

— I will consider what will happen if I never deal with my fear(s) and how it could impact my life.

— I will imagine what my life could be like if I do overcome my fears and the opportunities this freedom can give me.

"Now this is what the LORD Almighty says: "Give careful thought to your ways" (HAGGAI 1:5).

Take small steps

— I will break down overcoming my fear into small, manageable steps.

— I will determine what is the first step to take, asking others to help, if needed.

"For I am the LORD your God who takes hold of your right hand and says to you, Do not fear; I will help you" (ISAIAH 41:13).

Choose faith over fear

— I will choose to walk in faith and not let fear control my life or decisions.

— I will acknowledge the steps I have taken to overcome my fear, and thank God for His help and provision.

"We walk by faith, not by sight" (2 CORINTHIANS 5:7).

Questions & Answers

Question: "Throughout the Bible we are told not to fear, and yet we are told to have 'the fear of the Lord.' How can I love and trust a God I'm told to fear?"

Answer: The biblical phrase "the fear of the Lord" depicts *reverential awe* for our all-powerful God, a deep-seated respect for our all-seeing God based on His sovereignty. Realize, the Creator of the universe is still the all-knowing God and He has the right to rule over you.

The fear of the Lord can be compared to a child relating to a loving father. The child expresses delight and deep, abiding trust in the father. At the same time, he feels a respect for his authority. Unconditional love is never questioned, but the child also learns that his father will exert discipline to quell disobedience.

Key Passage to Read

Psalm 23

Let us . . . worship God acceptably with reverence and awe,
for our "God is a consuming fire."
(HEBREWS 12:28–29)

Question: "What is the difference between fear and worry?

Answer: Worry is *mentally* dwelling on a possible, undesired happening in the *future*. Fear, on the other hand, is a strong *emotional* reaction to a perceived, *imminent* danger. Worry is distracting and can lead to distress and even depression. In addition, worry is unproductive because it concerns unknown future events. Fear focuses on present events, is energizing, and can prove to be productive by propelling a person to action that can remove or lessen any real danger.

"Call on me in the day of trouble;
I will deliver you, and you will honor me."
(PSALM 50:15)

FINANCIAL FREEDOM

How to Manage Your Money—Wisely

God's Heart on Financial Freedom

God provides for our needs.

"My God will meet all your needs according to the riches of his glory in Christ Jesus" (PHILIPPIANS 4:19).

God instructs us to count the cost of our plans and financial decisions.

"Suppose one of you wants to build a tower. Won't you first sit down and estimate the cost to see if you have enough money to complete it?" (LUKE 14:28).

God calls us to wise stewardship and generosity.

"Each of you should give what you have decided in your heart to give, not reluctantly or under compulsion, for God loves a cheerful giver" (2 CORINTHIANS 9:7).

God warns us about the love of money.

"The love of money is a root of all kinds of evil" (1 TIMOTHY 6:10).

God encourages diligent work.

"All hard work brings a profit, but mere talk leads only to poverty" (PROVERBS 14:23).

God teaches us to wisely save and manage our resources.

"The wise store up choice food and olive oil, but fools gulp theirs down" (PROVERBS 21:20).

God cautions against borrowing money.

"The rich rule over the poor, and the borrower is slave to the lender" (PROVERBS 22:7).

God encourages us to live without debt.

"Give to everyone what you owe them: If you owe taxes, pay taxes; if revenue, then revenue; if respect, then respect; if honor, then honor. Let no debt remain outstanding, except the continuing debt to love one another, for whoever loves others has fulfilled the law" (ROMANS 13:7–8).

God desires that we serve Him rather than money.

"No one can serve two masters. Either you will hate the one and love the other, or you will be devoted to the one and despise the other. You cannot serve both God and money" (MATTHEW 6:24).

God commands us to honor Him with the firstfruits of our wealth.

"Honor the L*ORD with your wealth, with the firstfruits of all your crops; then your barns will be filled to overflowing, and your vats will brim over with new wine"* (PROVERBS 3:9–10).

God wants us to be content and rest in His constant presence.

"Keep your lives free from the love of money and be content with what you have, because God has said, 'Never will I leave you; never will I forsake you'" (HEBREWS 13:5).

God wants our hope to be in Him, not in money.

"Command those who are rich in this present world not to be arrogant nor to put their hope in wealth, which is so uncertain, but to put their hope in God, who richly provides us with everything for our enjoyment" (1 TIMOTHY 6:17).

> *"You may say to yourself, 'My power and the strength of my hands have produced this wealth for me.' But remember the* L*ORD your God, for it is he who gives you the ability to produce wealth."*
> (DEUTERONOMY 8:17–18)

Financial Discontentment Checklist

☐ Do you pine after money?

"Whoever loves money never has enough; whoever loves wealth is never satisfied with their income" (ECCLESIASTES 5:10).

☐ Do you prioritize money over God?

"No one can serve two masters. Either you will hate the one and love the other, or you will be devoted to the one and despise the other. You cannot serve both God and money" (MATTHEW 6:24).

☐ Can you be trusted to manage God's money wisely?

"Now it is required that those who have been given a trust must prove faithful" (1 CORINTHIANS 4:2).

☐ Are you in financial bondage to credit lenders?

"Let no debt remain outstanding, except the continuing debt to love one another, for whoever loves others has fulfilled the law" (ROMANS 13:8).

The Cords of Financial Bondage

B—Bitterness: When we are discontent with God or others over our finances, our anger spreads a deep root of underlying bitterness, affecting both us and those around us.

"See to it that no one falls short of the grace of God and that no bitter root grows up to cause trouble and defile many" (HEBREWS 12:15).

O—Overcommitment: Overcommitment to work leads to a life out of balance with what God desires. This workaholic lifestyle is centered around business to the exclusion of rest, relaxation, and relationships. Many Christians fall into this kind of bondage.

"The blessing of the LORD brings wealth, without painful toil for it" (PROVERBS 10:22).

N—Naiveté: To be naive is to be gullible and easily fooled by deception and dishonesty. To remain naive is to shun wise counsel and refuse to gain the knowledge needed to stop falling prey to dishonest deceivers.

"The wisdom of the prudent is to give thought to their ways, but the folly of fools is deception" (PROVERBS 14:8).

Key Verses to Memorize

"Whoever can be trusted with very little can also be trusted with much,
and whoever is dishonest with very little will also be dishonest with much.
So if you have not been trustworthy in handling worldly wealth,
who will trust you with true riches?"
(LUKE 16:10–11)

D—Dishonesty: Deceitfulness in finances is a subtle evil. It's usually the little, unseen deceptions that reveal a heart of insincerity, hypocrisy, lying, cheating, fraud, and stealing.

"If you have not been trustworthy with someone else's property, who will give you property of your own?" (LUKE 16:12).

A—Anxiety: Anxiety involves uneasy feelings, apprehension, fear, worry, or emotional tension.

"Anxiety weighs down the heart" (PROVERBS 12:25).

G—Greed: Greed is an insatiable thirst for *more*. To harbor greed is to reject God's right to rule and reign in your life and be the resource from which your every need is supplied. God is to be your Provider, the One you seek out to meet your needs, not material wealth.

"Then he said to them, 'Watch out! Be on your guard against all kinds of greed; life does not consist in an abundance of possessions'" (LUKE 12:15).

E—Envy: Envy is a resentful desire to have that which belongs to another. Envy grabs hold of a discontented heart by promising an increasing sense of worth but only causes pain.

"A heart at peace gives life to the body, but envy rots the bones" (PROVERBS 14:30).

Financial Bondage Checklist

- ☐ Do you get cash advances from credit cards to pay other expenses?
- ☐ Do you pay only the minimum on balances?
- ☐ Do you overdraw your bank account?
- ☐ Do you ignore the importance of having a savings account steadily accruing money?
- ☐ Do you use savings to pay credit card bills?
- ☐ Do you send in payments past the due dates?

The World's Mindset for Money vs. God's Mindset

The world's mindset for money: to get what you want

God's mindset for money: to give you what you need

"Do not worry, saying, 'What shall we eat?' or 'What shall we drink?' or 'What shall we wear?' For the pagans run after all these things, and your heavenly Father knows that you need them. But seek first his kingdom and his righteousness, and all these things will be given to you as well" (MATTHEW 6:31–33).

The world's mindset for money: to be used in whatever way you wish

God's mindset for money: to be used only in trustworthy ways

"Whoever can be trusted with very little can also be trusted with much, and whoever is dishonest with very little will also be dishonest with much. So if you have not been trustworthy in handling worldly wealth, who will trust you with true riches?" (LUKE 16:10–11).

The world's mindset for money: to gain temporary treasures

God's mindset for money: to gather eternal treasures

"Do not store up for yourselves treasures on earth, where moths and vermin destroy, and where thieves break in and steal. But store up for yourselves treasures in heaven, where moths and vermin do not destroy, and where thieves do not break in and steal" (MATTHEW 6:19–20).

"For my thoughts are not your thoughts,
neither are your ways my ways," declares the LORD.
(ISAIAH 55:8)

Checklist for Trustworthy Spending

- ☐ "Is this purchase a need or a mere desire?"
- ☐ "Do I have adequate funds to purchase this without using credit?"
- ☐ "Have I compared the cost of competitive products?"
- ☐ "Have I prayed about this purchase?"
- ☐ "Have I been patient in waiting on God's provision?"
- ☐ "Do I have God's peace regarding this purchase?"
- ☐ "Does this purchase conform to the purpose God has for me?"
- ☐ "Does my spouse agree with me [if you are married] about this purchase?"

"Well done, my good servant!" his master replied. "Because you have been trustworthy in a very small matter, take charge of ten cities."
(LUKE 19:17)

My Personalized Plan

I will . . .

Seek help from others.

- I will read books and look into classes or online resources that can help me learn how to manage my finances.
- I ask for help from trusted friends and family who manage their finances wisely.

"Get all the advice and instruction you can, so you will be wise the rest of your life" (PROVERBS 19:20 NLT).

Key Passage to Read

Matthew 6:25–34

Learn contentment.

- I will be content with what God has given me in terms of my time, talent, and treasure.
- I will be content in my situation and circumstances, making the most of what God gives me.

"I know what it is to be in need, and I know what it is to have plenty. I have learned the secret of being content in any and every situation, whether well fed or hungry, whether living in plenty or in want. I can do all this through him who gives me strength" (PHILIPPIANS 4:12–13).

Steward my resources.

— I will remember that everything I have comes from God.

— I will view my money, time, and resources as things to be stewarded faithfully.

"Each of you should use whatever gift you have received to serve others, as faithful stewards of God's grace in its various forms" (1 PETER 4:10).

Practice self-control.

— I will count the cost of my purchases and financial decisions before I make transactions.

— I will ask God to help me with self-control, so I can say no to things I don't need.

"The Holy Spirit produces this kind of fruit in our lives: love, joy, peace, patience, kindness, goodness, faithfulness, gentleness, and self-control" (GALATIANS 5:22–23 NLT).

Give generously.

— I will remember that God calls me to honor Him with my money.

— I will faithfully share God's blessings and provision.

"Honor the LORD with your wealth and with the best part of everything you produce" (PROVERBS 3:9 NLT).

Whoever loves money never has enough;
whoever loves wealth is never satisfied with their income.
(ECCLESIASTES 5:10)

Questions & Answers

Question: "Is God against being rich or accumulating wealth?"

Answer: Not at all. The Bible tells us that God gave riches to Abraham, as well as to many others. Job experienced a severe trial in which he lost everything, but God restored and even doubled Job's wealth because of his faithfulness. God is infinitely more interested in the kind of heart you have than in the amount of money you have.

After Job had prayed for his friends, the LORD restored his fortunes
and gave him twice as much as he had before.
(JOB 42:10)

Question: "If I give money to God, can I expect Him to bless me with financial gain?"

Answer: Many Christians secretly "give to get." The truth is, if we want to imitate God, we need to give as He gives—unconditionally—not out of a selfish heart desiring our own gain. God desires that we amass spiritual riches. He alone will judge and reward our true motives.

All a person's ways seem pure to them,
but motives are weighed by the LORD.
(PROVERBS 16:2)

Question: "How important is the amount of my gift to my church?"

Answer: The issue is not how big your gift is, but how big your faith is. One of the most famous gifts came from a widow—the poorest person of all by the world's standards. (Read Mark 12:41–44.)

"They all gave out of their wealth; but she, out of her poverty,
put in everything—all she had to live on."
(MARK 12:44)

FORGIVENESS

Releasing You Is Freeing Me

God's Heart on Forgiveness

God wants us to forgive each other because He has forgiven us.

"Be kind and compassionate to one another, forgiving each other, just as in Christ God forgave you" (EPHESIANS 4:32).

God wants us to see unforgiveness as sin.

"If anyone, then, knows the good they ought to do and doesn't do it, it is sin for them" (JAMES 4:17).

God wants us to get rid of unforgiveness and have a heart of mercy.

"Blessed are the merciful, for they will be shown mercy" (MATTHEW 5:7).

God wants us to do our part to live in peace with everyone.

"If it is possible, as far as it depends on you, live at peace with everyone" (ROMANS 12:18).

God wants us to overcome evil with good.

"Do not be overcome by evil, but overcome evil with good" (ROMANS 12:21).

God wants us to forgive others so we will not become bitter.

"See to it that no one falls short of the grace of God and that no bitter root grows up to cause trouble and defile many" (HEBREWS 12:15).

God wants us to forgive others so we will accurately reflect the character of Jesus.

"Follow God's example, therefore, as dearly loved children and walk in the way of love, just as Christ loved us and gave himself up for us as a fragrant offering and sacrifice to God" (EPHESIANS 5:1–2).

In him [Jesus] *we have redemption*
through his blood, the forgiveness of sins,
in accordance with the riches of God's grace.
(EPHESIANS 1:7)

What Forgiveness Is Not

Forgiveness is not forgetting.
It is necessary to remember before you can forgive.

Forgiveness is not denying the hurt.
It is feeling the hurt and releasing it to God.

Forgiveness is not the same as reconciliation.
It takes two to reconcile, but it takes only one to forgive.

Forgiveness is not circumventing God's justice.
It is allowing God to execute His justice in His time and in His way.

Forgiveness is not excusing wrong behavior.
It is acknowledging that the behavior was wrong and shouldn't happen again.

Forgiveness is not waiting for "time to heal all wounds."
It is clear that time doesn't always heal wounds; some people will not allow healing.

Forgiveness is not letting the guilty "off the hook."
It is moving the guilty from your hook to God's hook.

Forgiveness is not explaining away the hurt.
It is working through the hurt.

Forgiveness is not stuffing your anger.
It is resolving your anger by releasing the offense to God.

Forgiveness is not a feeling.
It is a choice—an act of the will.

Forgiveness vs. Reconciliation[116]

Forgiveness is directed one-way.
Reconciliation is reciprocal, occurring two ways.

Forgiveness is a decision to release the offender.
Reconciliation is the effort to rejoin the offender.

Forgiveness is a free gift to the one who has broken trust.
Reconciliation is a restored relationship based on restored trust.

Forgiveness is unconditional, regardless of a lack of repentance.

Reconciliation is conditional, based on repentance.

Unforgiveness vs. Forgiveness[117]

Unforgiveness allows a root of bitterness to grow.

Forgiveness keeps a root of bitterness from growing.

"See to it that no one falls short of the grace of God and that no bitter root grows up to cause trouble and defile many" (HEBREWS 12:15).

Unforgiveness opens a door to Satan in your life.

Forgiveness closes the door to Satan in your life.

"I have forgiven in the sight of Christ for your sake, in order that Satan might not outwit us. For we are not unaware of his schemes" (2 CORINTHIANS 2:10–11).

Unforgiveness causes you to walk in darkness.

Forgiveness brings you into the light.

Key Verse to Memorize

Bear with each other
and forgive one another if any of you
has a grievance against someone.
Forgive as the Lord forgave you.
(COLOSSIANS 3:13)

"Anyone who claims to be in the light but hates a brother or sister is still in the darkness. . . . Anyone who hates a brother or sister is in the darkness and walks around in the darkness. They do not know where they are going, because the darkness has blinded them" (1 JOHN 2:9, 11).

Unforgiveness makes you captive to sin.

Forgiveness frees you.

"I see that you are full of bitterness and captive to sin" (ACTS 8:23).

Unforgiveness grieves the Spirit of God.

Forgiveness is empowered by the Spirit of God.

"Do not grieve the Holy Spirit of God, with whom you were sealed for the day of redemption. Get rid of all bitterness, rage and anger, brawling and slander, along with every form of malice" (EPHESIANS 4:30–31).

Cast all your anxiety on him
because he cares for you.
(1 PETER 5:7)

Spiritual Strongholds

When you refuse to forgive your offender, you develop *unresolved anger.*

Unresolved anger, in turn, allows Satan to set up a stronghold in your mind, giving him opportunity to tempt you into greater sin.

This stronghold gives Satan more room to operate in your life, which means you will face more *"flaming arrows of the evil one"* (Ephesians 6:16).

These flaming arrows of accusation and unforgiveness can continue to burn in your heart and keep you *captive* to do the Enemy's will.

The Root Cause of Unforgiveness

Wrong Belief: "It's natural for me to resent those who have wronged me. If I forgive them, they will get away with it. My offenders need to pay for the wrongs committed against me."

Result: This belief reflects an attitude of pride that sets you up as a judge higher than God, who is willing to forgive and chooses to forget.

"I, even I, am he who blots out your transgressions,
for my own sake, and remembers your sins no more."
(Isaiah 43:25)

Right Belief: "Because God has totally forgiven me, I can release my resentment and choose to forgive others. I will rely on Christ, who lives in me, to enable me to forgive."

Result: This belief reflects a heart of humility that results in a desire to forgive others in the same way God forgives you.

Be kind and compassionate to one another, forgiving
each other, just as in Christ God forgave you.
(Ephesians 4:32)

The Four Stages of Forgiveness

1. **Face** the offense.
   "Have nothing to do with the fruitless deeds of darkness, but rather expose them" (Ephesians 5:11).

2. **Feel** the offense.[118]

   "The Lord *is close to the brokenhearted and saves those who are crushed in spirit"* (Psalm 34:18).

3. **Forgive** the offender.[119]

   "When you stand praying, if you hold anything against anyone, forgive them, so that your Father in heaven may forgive you your sins" (Mark 11:25).

4. **Find** oneness—if appropriate.

   "If you have any encouragement from being united with Christ, if any comfort from his love, if any common sharing in the Spirit, if any tenderness and compassion, then make my joy complete by being like-minded, having the same love, being one in spirit and of one mind" (Philippians 2:1-2).

"Do not seek revenge or bear a grudge
against anyone among your people,
but love your neighbor as yourself."
(Leviticus 19:18)

How to Truly Forgive

Make a list of all the offenses caused by your offender.

Imagine a meat hook hanging around your neck and a burlap bag hanging from the hook, laying against your chest. Then imagine all the pain caused by the offenses represented as one hundred pounds of rocks dropped into the burlap bag. Now you have one hundred pounds of heavy rocks—rocks of resentment—hanging from the hook around your neck.

Ask yourself: *Do I really want to carry all this pain with me for the rest of my life?*

Are you willing to take the pain from the past and release it into the hands of the Lord? If so, lift up your pain and release it all to Jesus.

Key Passage to Read

Matthew 18:23-35

Visualize taking the one who hurt or offended you off of your "emotional hook" and placing that person onto God's hook.

Remember, the Lord knows how to deal with your offender in His time and in His way. God says, "It is mine to avenge; I will repay" (Romans 12:19).

Finally, pray to release your offender to God.

Prayer to Forgive Your Offender

"Lord Jesus, thank You for caring about how much my heart has been hurt.
You know the pain I have felt because of (list every offense).
Right now I release all that pain into Your hands.
Thank You, Lord, for dying on the cross for me
and extending Your forgiveness to me.
As an act of my will, I choose to forgive (name).
Right now, I move (name) off of my emotional hook to Your hook.
I refuse all thoughts of revenge.
I trust that in Your time and in Your way
You will deal with (name) as You see fit.
And Lord, thank You for giving me Your power to forgive
so that I can be set free.
In Your precious name I pray. Amen."

My Personalized Plan

In choosing to seek forgiveness from God . . .

I will invite Jesus into my life as Lord and Savior, if I haven't received Him and His free gift of salvation.

I will make a list of my wrongdoings against God and individual people as He brings them to mind.

I will ask God to forgive me for my sins against Him and against others.

I will allow Jesus to take control of my life and to live His life through me.

The L*ORD gives wisdom;*
from his mouth come knowledge and understanding,
He holds success in store for the upright,
he is a shield to those whose walk is blameless,
for he guards the course of the just
and protects the way of his faithful ones.
(PROVERBS 2:6–8)

In choosing to seek forgiveness from others . . .

I will ask the Lord to go before me and soften the hearts of those I have offended.

I will humble myself before each person and acknowledge the offenses I have committed against them.

I will acknowledge the pain others have suffered as a result of my offenses.

I will ask each person to forgive the wrongful acts I have committed against them.

I will demonstrate true repentance by proving myself to be consistently trustworthy.

"If you are offering your gift at the altar
and there remember that your brother or sister
has something against you,
leave your gift there in front of the altar.
First go and be reconciled to them;
then come and offer your gift."
(Matthew 5:23–24)

In choosing to forgive others . . .

I will make a list of wrongs done to me by each person I have not forgiven.

I will forgive each offense and each offender.

I will take each offense and each offender off my emotional hook and put them onto God's hook.

I will ask God to bring good from each offense I have suffered.

I will seek oneness and restoration with each offender, without resentment, if reconciliation is appropriate and possible.

"We are taking pains to do what is right,
not only in the eyes of the Lord
but also in the eyes of man."
(2 Corinthians 8:21)

Questions & Answers

Question: "Is it possible to sin beyond God's ability to forgive?"

Answer: No. God's grace is greater than our sin. God promises to forgive and purify us from *all* unrighteousness, not just specific sins, but we are still called to confess our sins. And if we agree with God about our sin, we not only admit we have sinned, but we also turn from our sins and turn to Jesus, entrusting our lives to the One who died for our sins.

I acknowledged my sin to you
and did not cover up my iniquity. . . .
And you forgave
the guilt of my sin.
(Psalm 32:5)

Question: "How do I know if I have truly forgiven someone?"

Answer: Over time, as you go through the process of forgiveness, you may find old thoughts and feelings resurfacing. You may wonder if you've really forgiven your offender. It's completely normal. Ask yourself the following questions:

— "Do I still expect my offender 'to pay' for the wrong done to me?"

— "Do I still have bitter feelings toward my offender?"

— "Do I still have vengeful thoughts toward my offender?"

— "Do I desire that my offender will one day come to have a saving relationship with Jesus Christ and experience a changed life?"

— "When is the last time I prayed for my offender?"

Remember, forgiving someone does not in any way mean that you do not want justice. It simply means that you are leaving the offense entirely in God's hands. You are refusing to harbor hateful feelings toward your offender. Forgiveness is an ongoing process which requires that you choose to forgive every time the offense comes to mind. Likewise, you choose to pray for the offender every time the offense crosses your mind.

"Pray for those who hurt you."
(Luke 6:28 NLT)

FRIENDSHIP

Iron Sharpening Iron

God's Heart on Friendship

God demonstrates perfect love and friendship in Christ.

"Greater love has no one than this: to lay down one's life for one's friends" (JOHN 15:13).

God calls you His friend.

"I no longer call you servants, because a servant does not know his master's business. Instead, I have called you friends, for everything that I learned from my Father I have made known to you" (JOHN 15:15).

God wants to have a close relationship with you, as one has with a friend.

"The LORD would speak to Moses face to face, as one speaks to a friend" (EXODUS 33:11).

God is a friend to those who fear Him, learn from Him, and look to Him.

"The LORD is a friend to those who fear him. He teaches them his covenant. My eyes are always on the LORD, for he rescues me from the traps of my enemies" (PSALM 25:14–15 NLT).

God reveals that friendship is marked by constant, consistent love.

"A friend loves at all times, and a brother is born for a time of adversity" (PROVERBS 17:17).

God gives us friends to provide mutual help and support to one another.

"Two people are better off than one, for they can help each other succeed. If one person falls, the other can reach out and help. But someone who falls alone is in real trouble" (ECCLESIASTES 4:9–10 NLT).

God wants you to have godly friends who will help you grow in wisdom.

"Walk with the wise and become wise, for a companion of fools suffers harm" (PROVERBS 13:20).

God wants you to listen to friends who will hold you accountable and speak the truth in love.

"Faithful are the wounds of a friend, but the kisses of an enemy are deceitful" (PROVERBS 27:6 NKJV).

God wants your friendships to be marked by encouragement, pointing one another to the Lord.

"I long to visit you so I can bring you some spiritual gift that will help you grow strong in the Lord. When we get together, I want to encourage you in your faith, but I also want to be encouraged by yours" (ROMANS 1:11-12 NLT).

God wants you to pray for your friends regularly.

"Pray in the Spirit at all times and on every occasion. Stay alert and be persistent in your prayers for all believers everywhere" (EPHESIANS 6:18 NLT).

If either of them [a friend] *falls down,*
one can help the other up.
But pity anyone who falls
and has no one to help them up.
(ECCLESIASTES 4:10)

The Codependency Checklist

- ☐ Do you struggle with feeling loved, and therefore look for ways to be needed?
- ☐ Do you throw all of your energy into helping another person?
- ☐ Do you feel compelled to take charge of another person's crisis?
- ☐ Do you feel drawn to a person whom you think needs to be rescued?
- ☐ Do you have difficulty setting and keeping boundaries with another person?
- ☐ Do you find it difficult to identify and express your true feelings?
- ☐ Do you rely on another person to make most of the decisions?
- ☐ Do you feel lonely, sad, and empty when you are alone?
- ☐ Do you feel threatened when the person closest to you spends time with someone else?
- ☐ Do you refrain from speaking in order to keep peace?
- ☐ Do you fear conflict because it could cause you to be abandoned?
- ☐ Do you feel "stuck" in your relationship with another person?
- ☐ Do you feel you have lost your personal identity in order to "fit into" another person's world?
- ☐ Do you feel controlled and manipulated by another person?
- ☐ Do you feel used and taken advantage of by another person?
- ☐ Do you prioritize your relationship with another person over your relationship with the Lord?

How to Initiate Possible Friendships

Look for opportunities to meet other people who share your same values and interests.

"Make the most of every opportunity" (COLOSSIANS 4:5).

Be friendly and sociable by smiling, introducing yourself to people in close proximity to you, and inviting people to your home.

"Offer hospitality to one another without grumbling. Each of you should use whatever gift you have received to serve others, as faithful stewards of God's grace in its various forms. If anyone speaks, they should do so as one who speaks the very words of God. If anyone serves, they should do so with the strength God provides" (1 PETER 4:9–11).

Key Verse to Memorize

A friend loves at all times,
and a brother is born for a time of adversity.
(PROVERBS 17:17)

Relax and be yourself. Trust God to make you a person of interest to whomever would be a positive person in your life.

"The righteous hate what is false" (PROVERBS 13:5).

Eliminate expectations of any kind.

"In everything, do to others what you would have them do to you, for this sums up the Law and the Prophets" (MATTHEW 7:12).

Five Levels of Communication

Level 1 communication is for easy, fun, or casual times—keeping the conversation light and refraining from talking about anything personally revealing.

Level 2 contains somewhat personal information but remains fairly simple—moving from general conversation to sharing on a slightly deeper level.

Level 3 begins the self-revealing stage—progressing to more personal information, but not anything too hard to handle.

Level 4 is talking about issues that could be fairly uncomfortable—taking your friendship into a more vulnerable stage, requiring more time and emotional investment.

Level 5 is for the deepest form of intimacy—plunging into personal discussions about deep desires and devastating disappointments, thereby demanding supreme trust and total commitment.

How to RELEASE from a Codependent Friendship

R—Recognize that you are overly dependent on another person, then choose to place your dependency on God.

"Love the Lord your God with all your heart and with all your soul and with all your mind and with all your strength" (MARK 12:30).

E—Examine your patterns of codependent thinking.

"Each of you must put off falsehood and speak truthfully to your neighbor" (EPHESIANS 4:25).

L—Let go of your "super-savior" mentality.

"What you are doing is not good. You and these people who come to you will only wear yourselves out. The work is too heavy for you; you cannot handle it alone" (EXODUS 18:17–18).

E—Extend forgiveness to those who have caused you pain.

"Be kind and compassionate to one another, forgiving each other, just as in Christ God forgave you" (EPHESIANS 4:32).

A—Affirm your identity in Christ.

"Not that we are competent in ourselves to claim anything for ourselves, but our competence comes from God" (2 CORINTHIANS 3:5).

S—Set healthy boundaries.

"The prudent see danger and take refuge, but the simple keep going and pay the penalty" (PROVERBS 27:12).

E—Exchange your emotional focus for spiritual focus.

"Direct me in the path of your commands, for there I find delight. Turn my heart toward your statutes and not toward selfish gain. Turn my eyes away from worthless things; preserve my life according to your word" (PSALM 119:35–37).

"In this world you will have trouble.
But take heart! I have overcome the world."
(JOHN 16:33)

My Personalized Plan

I will . . .

Focus on the benefits of friendship.

— I will remember that friendships keep me involved in community with others.

— I will remember that God desires for me to have positive interactions with others.

"As iron sharpens iron, so one person sharpens another" (PROVERBS 27:17).

Foster my friendships with acceptance and encouragement.

— I will be honest with my friends, always with kindness.

— I will encourage my friends in their successes and support them through their struggles.

"The pleasantness of a friend springs from their heartfelt advice" (PROVERBS 27:9).

Face the reality that not all people will like me and that some relationships are not healthy.

— I will set healthy boundaries for myself and not engage in codependent or one-sided relationships.

— I will remember that in healthy relationships, friends appreciate each other's differences.

"Bad company corrupts good character" (1 CORINTHIANS 15:33).

Key Passage to Read

Philippians 2:1–8

Fortify my friendships when times get tough.

— I will listen and seek to understand my friends when they face difficulties.

— I will look out for my friends and keep their best interest in mind as I pray for them.

"Be joyful in hope, patient in affliction, faithful in prayer" (ROMANS 12:12).

Form a deep and abiding friendship with Christ.

— I will remember that when I feel alone, Christ is with me and interceding for me with His Father.

— I will remember that Christ laid down His life for me; therefore, I can trust Him to be my most faithful friend.

"Greater love has no one than this: to lay down one's life for one's friends" (JOHN 15:13).

Questions & Answers

Question: "Is there a physiological benefit to having friendships?"

Answer: Yes. For example, while studying the effects of stress, researchers stumbled upon the benefits of friendship for women in times of stress. They found that while all people generally possess a flight-or-fight response to stressful situations, women also tend to exhibit a "tend or befriend" response, which drives them to look after children or spend extra time with friends.[120] Women who gather with their friends more frequently or spend more time caring for their children also experience the added benefit of increased oxytocin production, which helps to further provide a sense of calm and well-being.[121]

"If one person falls,
the other can reach out and help."
(ECCLESIASTES 4:10 NLT)

Question: "How can I deal with feeling so friendless and insecure? I hate not being accepted!"

Answer: Feeling friendless and insecure is painful. First, realize the deeper your dependence on the Lord, the less desperate you are to search for your security and acceptance in people.

And second, applying these action steps will make a significant difference:

— **Look** for others around you who need a friend.

— **Ask** the Lord to make you into an encourager to them.

— **Reach out** to them with compassion and practice generosity toward them.

Encourage one another and build each other up.
(1 THESSALONIANS 5:11)

GAMBLING

Betting Your Life Away

God's Heart on Gambling

The World of Gambling focuses on the temporal, acquiring material things.

The Word of God focuses on the eternal, storing up treasure in heaven.

"Do not store up for yourselves treasures on earth, where moths and vermin destroy, and where thieves break in and steal. But store up for yourselves treasures in heaven, where moths and vermin do not destroy, and where thieves do not break in and steal" (MATTHEW 6:19–20).

The World of Gambling promotes the pursuit of exhilaration.

The Word of God promotes the pursuit of peace.

"Make it your ambition to lead a quiet life: You should mind your own business and work with your hands" (1 THESSALONIANS 4:11).

The World of Gambling encourages careless financial stewardship.

The Word of God encourages wise financial stewardship.

"A good person leaves an inheritance for their children's children" (PROVERBS 13:22).

The World of Gambling focuses on winning whatever you can.

The Word of God focuses on working with all your heart as if you are working for the Lord.

"Whatever you do, work at it with all your heart, as working for the Lord, not for human masters" (COLOSSIANS 3:23).

The World of Gambling promotes a "get rich quick" mentality.

The Word of God promotes a "get to work" mentality.

"The one who is unwilling to work shall not eat" (2 THESSALONIANS 3:10).

The World of Gambling prioritizes making a living through luck.

The Word of God prioritizes making a living though labor.

"You will eat the fruit of your labor; blessings and prosperity will be yours" (PSALM 128:2).

The World of Gambling presents an attempt to survive through winning.

The Word of God presents our means of survival through working.

"The LORD God took the man and put him in the Garden of Eden to work it and take care of it" (GENESIS 2:15).

The World of Gambling points to the neglect of providing for the family.

The Word of God points to the need of providing for the family.

"Anyone who does not provide for their relatives, and especially for their own household, has denied the faith and is worse than an unbeliever" (1 TIMOTHY 5:8).

The World of Gambling concentrates on selfish greed as the fastest way to prosper.

The Word of God concentrates on trusting God as the only way to prosper.

"The greedy stir up conflict, but those who trust in the LORD will prosper" (PROVERBS 28:25).

General Characteristics of Problem Gamblers

Cannot seem to muster the willpower to stop gambling

Consider gambling a viable means of adding to their income

Convince family and friends to gamble even when they have no desire to do so

Consume hours of their time gambling alone

Customarily visit casinos, race tracks, betting shops, or amusement arcades with slot machines numerous times over the course of a week

Key Verse to Memorize

"Watch out! Be on your guard against all kinds of greed; life does not consist in an abundance of possessions." (LUKE 12:15)

Convince themselves that their excessive use of Internet gambling is normal

Constantly purchase lottery tickets they cannot afford

Commit crimes to support their gambling habit or to pay off gambling debts

Continuously make comments about "others" having gambling problems

Commonly carry around betting slips, scratch cards, or tokens for slot machines

Signs of Problem Gambling

— **Extreme** emotional ups and downs
— **Frequent** requests for money
— **Pawning**/selling of possessions
— **Increasing** debt
— **Neglect** of loved ones
— **Secret** activity with bills and bank statements
— **Sleep** difficulties
— **Stealing** or other criminal activities
— **Unexplainable** times of generosity
— **Worry**, anxiety, depression, and shame

10 Common Causes for Attraction to Gambling

The lures into the world of gambling are many. People gamble . . .

1. **To enjoy** the thrill and excitement of gambling.
2. **To experience** a new sensation or "high."
3. **To improve** their self-image.
4. **To be lured** by the process of playing the odds.
5. **To feel** the passion grow.
6. **To avoid** growing up.
7. **To escape** responsibility.
8. **To dream** great dreams.
9. **To socialize** and gain attention from peers.
10. **To get** something for nothing.

Those who trust in their riches will fall,
but the righteous will thrive like a green leaf.
(PROVERBS 11:28)

My Personalized Plan

Through the strength of Christ, I will take the necessary steps to stop gambling permanently.

1. **Admit**: "I will admit I have an addiction to gambling."
2. **Tell**: "I will tell my family and friends that I have a gambling problem and am working toward my recovery."
3. **Break**: "I will break my patterns of when I most often gambled."
4. **Avoid**: "I will avoid looking at gambling ads."
5. **Discard**: "I will throw away all gambling memorabilia and gambling paraphernalia."
6. **Refuse**: "I will refuse to dwell on the 'excitement' of gambling."
7. **Replace**: "I will do another preplanned activity when I want to gamble."
8. **Eliminate**: "I will eliminate all unnecessary activities that cause me to want to gamble."
9. **Be accountable**: "I will make myself accountable to someone who can and will help me."
10. **Submit**: "I will temporarily give over my checkbook, credit cards, and family finances to my spouse or another close loved one, and I will use direct deposit for my paycheck."
11. **Commit**: "I will return home immediately after work, making no stops. I won't go to gambling establishments—I will change my driving route if necessary."
12. **Cut off**: "I will cut off all communication with 'gambling buddies' because the Bible says, 'Bad company corrupts good character'!" (1 Corinthians 15:33).
13. **Call**: "When tempted, I will call a supportive friend or family member."
14. **Shift**: "I will shift my attention to something else when the urge to gamble strikes. I will make a list of other choices that I need to . . . or want to do. I will begin new activities and hobbies (including church activities, especially small group Bible studies)."
15. **Evaluate**: "I will make a list of how my gambling has negatively affected my life."

16. **Divide**: "I will divide my list into six categories: social, emotional, spiritual, mental, physical, and financial. I will consider what impact my addiction has had on my life and will review the list when I feel the urge to gamble."

17. **Visualize**: "I will write out what I want my life to look like once gambling is no longer part of my life."

18. **Abstain**: "I will eliminate alcohol, which lowers my resistance."

19. **Invest**: "I will invest time daily reading the Bible to find strength for overcoming my addiction."

20. **Seek**: "I will seek counsel and support from those who have found freedom from their gambling addiction."

21. **Thank**: "I will thank God each day for the restraint to not gamble."

22. **Track**: "I will track the days on a calendar since I last gambled and will use it as a source of encouragement and strength when I am tempted."

Key Passage to Read

1 Timothy 6:6–11

Questions & Answers

Question: "What could be wrong with trying to supplement my earned income with occasionally gambling if I can control my impulses?"

Answer: Gambling is the effort to quickly increase your income by putting your confidence in luck rather than consistently entrusting your life to the sovereign Lord. God's Word encourages us to work diligently instead of relying on luck or hasty methods of gaining money:

The plans of the diligent lead to profit
as surely as haste leads to poverty.
(Proverbs 21:5)

Question: "Is it considered gambling if I'm risking money on raising crops or cattle, investing in commodities, stocks, or a new start-up business—especially when the outcome is uncertain?"

Answer: No. Gambling is a win-lose situation. Someone has to lose money in order for someone to win. However, investing is intended to be a win-win situation. For example, by starting a small restaurant, you have the opportunity to . . .

— Prepare food for the public

— Produce income for employees

— Purchase food, furniture, and supplies from vendors
— Provide income for yourself or your family
— Participate in economic growth and value of a community

"Whoever has will be given more,
and they will have an abundance."
(MATTHEW 25:29)

GOD: WHO IS HE?

Who Do You Say That He Is?

God's Heart on Who He Is

God exists outside of time and space.

"Before the mountains were born or you brought forth the whole world, from everlasting to everlasting you are God" (PSALM 90:2).

God is one being, eternally existing in three persons: Father, Son, and Holy Spirit.

"May the grace of the Lord Jesus Christ, and the love of God, and the fellowship of the Holy Spirit be with you all" (2 CORINTHIANS 13:14).

God is our Creator.

"In the beginning God created the heavens and the earth" (GENESIS 1:1).

God has one and only Son, Jesus Christ, the Word made flesh.

"In the beginning was the Word, and the Word was with God, and the Word was God. . . . The Word became flesh and made his dwelling among us. We have seen his glory, the glory of the one and only Son, who came from the Father, full of grace and truth" (JOHN 1:1, 14).

God created all things, and all things were created for Him.

"In him all things were created: things in heaven and on earth, visible and invisible, whether thrones or powers or rulers or authorities; all things have been created through him and for him" (COLOSSIANS 1:16).

God is faithful and holy.

"Know therefore that the LORD your God is God; he is the faithful God, keeping his covenant of love to a thousand generations of those who love him and keep his commandments" (DEUTERONOMY 7:9).

God is trustworthy.

"Those who know your name trust in you, for you, LORD, have never forsaken those who seek you" (PSALM 9:10).

God is omnipresent—present everywhere at once.

"Where can I go from your Spirit? Where can I flee from your presence? If I go up to the heavens, you are there; if I make my bed in the depths, you are there" (PSALM 139:7–8).

God is the righteous ruler and judge.

"Nothing in all creation is hidden from God's sight. Everything is uncovered and laid bare before the eyes of him to whom we must give account" (Hebrews 4:13).

God is love.

"We know and rely on the love God has for us. God is love. Whoever lives in love lives in God, and God in them" (1 John 4:16).

Know therefore that the Lord your God is God;
he is the faithful God, keeping his covenant
of love to a thousand generations of those
who love him and keep his commandments.
(Deuteronomy 7:9)

Names of God Containing *El*

Elohim—God as Creator[122]

"In the beginning God [Elohim] *created the heavens and the earth"* (Genesis 1:1).

El Elyon—"God Most High"

"He [Melchizedek] *was priest of God Most High* [El Elyon], *and he blessed Abram, saying, 'Blessed be Abram by God Most High, Creator of heaven and earth. And praise be to God Most High* [El Elyon], *who delivered your enemies into your hand'"* (Genesis 14:18–20).

El Roi—"The God Who Sees"

"She gave this name to the Lord who spoke to her: 'You are the God who sees [El Roi] *me,' for she said, 'I have now seen the One who sees* [El Roi] *me'"* (Genesis 16:13).

El Shaddai—"God Almighty"[123]

"When Abram was ninety-nine years old, the Lord appeared to him and said, 'I am God Almighty [El Shaddai]; *walk before me faithfully and be blameless'"* (Genesis 17:1).

El Olam—"God Everlasting"

"Abraham planted a tamarisk tree in Beersheba, and there he called upon the name of the Lord, the Eternal God [El Olam]*"* (Genesis 21:33).

The Hebrew Names of God Involving Jehovah

Jehovah means "the Self-Existent One"—the name *Jehovah* emphasizes His covenant-keeping role.

Jehovah—"Lord, the Self-Existent One, Yahweh"

"This is the account of the heavens and the earth when they were created, when the LORD God made the earth and the heavens" (GENESIS 2:4).

Jehovah-Jireh—"the Lord, my Provider"

"Abraham called that place The LORD Will Provide. And to this day it is said, 'On the mountain of the LORD it will be provided'" (GENESIS 22:14).

Jehovah-Rapha—"the Lord who Heals"

"He said, 'If you listen carefully to the LORD your God and do what is right in his eyes, if you pay attention to his commands and keep all his decrees, I will not bring on you any of the diseases I brought on the Egyptians, for I am the LORD, who heals you'" (EXODUS 15:26).

Jehovah-Nissi—"the Lord my Banner"

"Moses built an altar and called it The LORD is my Banner" (EXODUS 17:15).

Jehovah-M'Kaddesh—"the Lord who Sanctifies, who makes holy"

"Say to the Israelites, 'You must observe my Sabbaths. This will be a sign between me and you for the generations to come, so you may know that I am the LORD, who makes you holy'" (EXODUS 31:13).

Jehovah-Shalom—"the Lord is Peace"

"The LORD said to him, 'Peace! Do not be afraid. You are not going to die.' So Gideon built an altar to the LORD there and called it The LORD Is Peace" (JUDGES 6:23–24).

Key Verse to Memorize

Acknowledge and take to heart this day that the LORD is God in heaven above and on the earth below. There is no other.
(DEUTERONOMY 4:39)

Jehovah-Sabaoth—"the Lord of Hosts"

"As for our Redeemer, the LORD of hosts is His name, the Holy One of Israel" (ISAIAH 47:4 NKJV).

Jehovah-Ra'ah—"the Lord my Shepherd"

"The LORD is my shepherd, I lack nothing" (PSALM 23:1).

Jehovah-Tsidkenu—"the Lord our Righteousness"

"In His days Judah will be saved, and Israel will dwell securely; and this is His name by which He will be called, 'The LORD our righteousness'" (JEREMIAH 23:6 NASB).

Jehovah-Shammah—"the Lord is There"

"The distance all around will be 18,000 cubits. And the name of the city from that time on will be: THE LORD IS THERE" (EZEKIEL 48:35).

"I am God, and there is no other;
I am God, and there is none like me.
I make known the end from the beginning,
from ancient times, what is still to come.
I say, 'My purpose will stand,
and I will do all that I please.'
From the east I summon a bird of prey;
from a far-off land, a man to fulfill my purpose.
What I have said, that I will bring about;
what I have planned, that I will do."
(ISAIAH 46:9–11)

Natural Attributes . . . the Essential Being of God

Omniscient—all-knowing
"You have searched me, LORD, and you know me. You know when I sit and when I rise; you perceive my thoughts from afar. You discern my going out and my lying down; you are familiar with all my ways. Before a word is on my tongue you, LORD, know it completely" (PSALM 139:1–4).

Omnipotent—all-powerful
"I am the LORD, the God of all mankind. Is anything too hard for me?" (JEREMIAH 32:27).

Omnipresent—present everywhere
"'Am I only a God nearby,' declares the LORD, 'and not a God far away? Who can hide in secret places so that I cannot see them?' declares the LORD. 'Do not I fill heaven and earth?' declares the LORD" (JEREMIAH 23:23–24).

Eternal—not bound by time
"I live forever" (DEUTERONOMY 32:40).

Immutable—unchanging
"I the LORD do not change" (MALACHI 3:6).

Incomprehensible—unfathomable and mysterious
"Oh, the depth of the riches of the wisdom and knowledge of God! How unsearchable his judgments, and his paths beyond tracing out!" (ROMANS 11:33).

Self-existent—life in Himself
"As the Father has life in himself, so he has granted the Son also to have life in himself" (JOHN 5:26).

Self-sufficient—God's ability within Himself to act

"From him and through him and for him are all things" (Romans 11:36).

Infinite—boundless

"Where can I go from your Spirit? Where can I flee from your presence? If I go up to the heavens, you are there; if I make my bed in the depths, you are there. If I rise on the wings of the dawn, if I settle on the far side of the sea, even there your hand will guide me, your right hand will hold me fast. If I say, 'Surely the darkness will hide me and the light become night around me,' even the darkness will not be dark to you; the night will shine like the day, for darkness is as light to you" (Psalm 139:7–12).

Transcendent—above all

"As the heavens are higher than the earth, so are my ways higher than your ways and my thoughts than your thoughts" (Isaiah 55:9).

Sovereign—supreme ruler

"All the peoples of the earth are regarded as nothing. He does as he pleases with the powers of heaven and the peoples of the earth. No one can hold back his hand or say to him: 'What have you done?'" (Daniel 4:35).

Moral Attributes . . . the Character of God

Holy—pure, set apart from sin

"Just as he who called you is holy, so be holy in all you do; for it is written: 'Be holy, because I am holy'" (1 Peter 1:15–16).

Righteous—absolute good

"You are righteous, Lord, and your laws are right" (Psalm 119:137).

Just—fair

"Righteousness and justice are the foundation of your throne" (Psalm 89:14).

Merciful—compassionate

"The Lord is gracious and righteous; our God is full of compassion" (Psalm 116:5).

Long-suffering—patient

"The Lord is not slow in keeping his promise, as some understand slowness. Instead he is patient with you, not wanting anyone to perish, but everyone to come to repentance" (2 Peter 3:9).

Wise—perfect in choices

"How many are your works, Lord! In wisdom you made them all; the earth is full of your creatures" (Psalm 104:24).

Good—pure in motive

"Do you show contempt for the riches of his kindness, forbearance and patience, not realizing that God's kindness is intended to lead you to repentance?" (ROMANS 2:4).

Wrathful—hatred for sin

"The wrath of God is being revealed from heaven against all the godlessness and wickedness of people, who suppress the truth by their wickedness" (ROMANS 1:18).

Truthful—pure in word

"This truth gives them confidence that they have eternal life, which God—who does not lie—promised them before the world began" (TITUS 1:2 NLT).

Key Passage to Read

John chapter 14

Faithful—true to promises

"If we are faithless, he remains faithful, for he cannot disown himself" (2 TIMOTHY 2:13).

Jealous—unwilling to share what is rightfully His

"Do not worship any other god, for the LORD, whose name is Jealous, is a jealous God" (EXODUS 34:14).

Loving—seeking another's best, doing the most positive, selfless, and redemptive act possible for another

"The LORD appeared to us in the past, saying: 'I have loved you with an everlasting love; I have drawn you with unfailing kindness'" (JEREMIAH 31:3).

The God of All Comfort

Thank You, God, that You . . .

C—Care for me with compassion

"Because of the LORD's great love we are not consumed, for his compassions never fail" (LAMENTATIONS 3:22).

O—Offer strength when I am weak

"I can do all things through him [Christ] *who strengthens me"* (PHILIPPIANS 4:13 ESV).

M—Meet all my needs

"My God will meet all your needs according to the riches of his glory in Christ Jesus" (PHILIPPIANS 4:19).

F—Forget my sins and mistakes

"I will forgive their wickedness and will remember their sins no more" (HEBREWS 8:12).

O—Offer hope for the future

"'I know the plans I have for you,' declares the LORD, 'plans to prosper you and not to harm you, plans to give you hope and a future'" (JEREMIAH 29:11).

R—Reassure me of Your love

"But from everlasting to everlasting the LORD's love is with those who fear him, and his righteousness with their children's children" (PSALM 103:17).

T—Turn my pain into joy

"Weeping may stay for the night, but rejoicing comes in the morning" (PSALM 30:5).

Five Ways God Reveals Himself

Through Creation—General Revelation

"Since the creation of the world God's invisible qualities—his eternal power and divine nature—have been clearly seen, being understood from what has been made, so that people are without excuse" (ROMANS 1:20).

Through Conscience—Moral Awareness

"Gentiles, who do not have the law, do by nature things required by the law" (ROMANS 2:14).

Through Communication—Prophetic Word

"Prophecy never had its origin in the human will, but prophets, though human, spoke from God as they were carried along by the Holy Spirit" (2 PETER 1:21).

Through Canon—The Bible

"All Scripture is God-breathed and is useful for teaching, rebuking, correcting and training in righteousness, so that the servant of God may be thoroughly equipped for every good work" (2 TIMOTHY 3:16–17).

Through Christ—God Incarnate

"Anyone who has seen me [Jesus] *has seen the Father"* (JOHN 14:9).

My Personalized Plan

I will . . .

Grow in my relationship with God—He gives me grace and knowledge.
"Grow in the grace and knowledge of our Lord and Savior Jesus Christ" (2 PETER 3:18).

Rest in God's unchanging nature—He never changes.
"Jesus Christ is the same yesterday and today and forever" (HEBREWS 13:8).

Release my worries to God—He cares for me.
"Cast all your anxiety on him because he cares for you" (1 PETER 5:7).

Focus on studying God's Word—He provides me with His truth.
"Sanctify them by the truth; your word is truth" (JOHN 17:17).

Forgive the way God forgives—He showers me with His mercy.
"If you, LORD, kept a record of sins, Lord, who could stand? But with you there is forgiveness, so that we can, with reverence, serve you" (PSALM 130:3–4).

Trust God in all things—He knows what is best for me.
"Trust in the LORD with all your heart and lean not on your own understanding; in all your ways submit to him, and he will make your paths straight" (PROVERBS 3:5–6).

Tell others about God's goodness to me—He blesses me again and again.
"Return home and tell how much God has done for you" (LUKE 8:39).

Love by God's example—God is love.
"Follow God's example, therefore, as dearly loved children and walk in the way of love, just as Christ loved us and gave himself up for us as a fragrant offering and sacrifice to God" (EPHESIANS 5:1–2).

Remember God's faithfulness—He is always faithful to keep His promises.
"I will sing of the steadfast love of the LORD, forever; with my mouth I will make known your faithfulness to all generations" (PSALM 89:1 ESV).

Give God all the glory—He alone is worthy.
"You are worthy, our Lord and God, to receive glory and honor and power, for you created all things, and by your will they were created and have their being" (REVELATION 4:11).

Questions & Answers

Question: "Outside the Bible are there any explanations for the existence of God?"

Answer: There are at least four logical arguments for God's existence.[124]

Cosmological Argument: For every effect there must be a cause. The world exists. Something cannot come from nothing. Someone had to cause the universe to come into being. For example, if you see a painting, there must have been an artist.

"Every house is built by someone, but God is the builder of everything" (HEBREWS 3:4).

Teleological Argument: There is an order and design in the universe, from the galaxies to the smallest microbe, implying an intelligent master designer. For example, if you hold a watch, you assume there was a watchmaker.

"This is what the LORD says—he who created the heavens, he is God; he who fashioned and made the earth, he founded it; he did not create it to be empty, but formed it to be inhabited—he says: 'I am the LORD, and there is no other'" (ISAIAH 45:18).

Anthropological (or Moral) Argument: People have an awareness of right and wrong with the long-term consequences of their actions. Each person has a conscience, an intellect, emotions, and a will. All humanity has a sense of fair play, justice, right and wrong. Thus, guilt is a common human factor. In fact, every culture, from primitive to advanced, has a system of moral justice. For example, in no culture is it ever right to take another man's wife. The source of this awareness is in God.

"They show that the requirements of the law are written on their hearts, their consciences also bearing witness, and their thoughts sometimes accusing them and at other times even defending them" (ROMANS 2:15).

Ontological Argument: The concept of God is universal in all cultures. God must have placed this idea within man.

"What may be known about God is plain to them, because God has made it plain to them. For since the creation of the world God's invisible qualities—his eternal power and divine nature—have been clearly seen, being understood from what has been made, so that people are without excuse" (ROMANS 1:19–20).

GRIEF

Living at Peace with Loss

God's Heart on Grief

God empathizes with your grief because He has experienced grief Himself.

"He [Jesus] *was despised and rejected—a man of sorrows, acquainted with deepest grief"* (Isaiah 53:3 NLT).

God is with you in your grief.

"Do not fear, for I am with you; do not be dismayed, for I am your God. I will strengthen you and help you; I will uphold you with my righteous right hand" (Isaiah 41:10).

God sees your grief and suffering.

"You, God, see the trouble of the afflicted; you consider their grief and take it in hand" (Psalm 10:14).

God hears your cries and listens to you in your pain.

"The Lord has heard my weeping" (Psalm 6:8).

God wants you to process your grief with Him.

"Cast your cares on the Lord and he will sustain you; he will never let the righteous be shaken" (Psalm 55:22).

God wants you to have hope even in your grief.

"Dear brothers and sisters, we want you to know what will happen to the believers who have died so you will not grieve like people who have no hope" (1 Thessalonians 4:13 NLT).

God wants to give you joy even in your grief.

"You have turned my mourning into joyful dancing. You have taken away my clothes of mourning and clothed me with joy" (Psalm 30:11 NLT).

God wants to comfort you with His presence.

"I, yes I, am the one who comforts you" (Isaiah 51:12 NLT).

God wants to comfort you through others.

"God, who comforts the downcast, comforted us by the coming of Titus" (2 Corinthians 7:6).

God wants to comfort you with His Word.

"I have suffered much; preserve my life, LORD, *according to your word"* (PSALM 119:107).

God wants to use your grief to comfort others.

"Praise be to the God and Father of our Lord Jesus Christ, who comforts us in all our troubles, so that we can comfort those in any trouble with the comfort we ourselves receive from God" (2 CORINTHIANS 1:3–4).

God will one day wipe away your tears—and there will be no more death or mourning or grief.

"He will wipe every tear from their eyes, and there will be no more death or sorrow or crying or pain. All these things are gone forever" (REVELATION 21:4 NLT)

God is our refuge and strength,
an ever-present help in trouble.
(PSALM 46:1)

What Complicates the Grieving Process?

Logistics—dealing with immediate concerns surrounding a loss (phone calls; funeral plans; writing an obituary; notifying insurance; processing a will/probate; coordinating meetings, work schedule, childcare, meal planning).

Housing/property/finances—dividing assets; cleaning out a home; having to relocate; dealing with insurance payments or status, hospital bills, funeral expenses, taxes, debts, adjustments to change in income.

Busyness—being consumed by daily life and responsibilities to the extent that you do not have adequate time to process your thoughts and emotions.

Support system/remaining family—not having people who can comfort you and be there for you; adjusting to new family dynamics; handling conflicts.

Circumstances surrounding the loss or death—not recognizing how the unique circumstances of the loss or cause of death will impact survivors (for example: grieving over a miscarriage, suicide, drug overdose, terminal illness, violent death, sudden or accidental death, losing multiple people at once).

Length/type of relationship—not understanding how the duration or type of relationship can intensify the grief (parent/child, spouse, grandparent, friend, church member, coworker/boss, pet, student/teacher).

Memories—being confronted with memories of your loved one (often in unexpected ways or at unexpected times) through various people, places, songs, meals, smells, etc.

Emotional complexity/inexperience with grief—not knowing what to do with the depth and range of emotions or what to expect or how to cope.

Spiritual needs—not having a spiritual foundation or community to understand and process grief

Physical needs—neglecting physical needs, such as sleeping, eating, or exercising.

Regret/guilt—wishing you had said or done something differently before the loss; feeling responsible for wrongdoing toward the person you've lost.

Denial/refusal—living as if the loss has not occurred; choosing to ignore the loss.

The LORD is good,
a refuge in times of trouble.
He cares for those who trust in him.
(NAHUM 1:7)

Stages of Healthy Grieving

Crisis Stage: This initial stage can typically last a few days or a number of weeks. In this stage of grief, you mechanically go through daily activities and experience many of the following symptoms:

Anxiety/fear	Appetite/sleep loss	Confusion
Denial	Exhaustion	Feeling trapped
Shock/numbness	Uncontrollable crying	

My eyes will flow unceasingly,
without relief.
(LAMENTATIONS 3:49)

Crucible Stage: This stage can last for months or a few years, perhaps even for a lifetime if the grief is not resolved. This time of sorrow can feel all-consuming and will often be accompanied by many of the following characteristics:

Anger/resentment	Anguish	Bargaining with God
Depression/sadness	Helplessness/lethargy	Impaired judgment
Loneliness/isolation	Self-pity	

My soul is in deep anguish.
(PSALM 6:3)

Comforted Stage: This stage accepts the loss, leaving it in the past. This stage not only accepts that the present offers stability, but also accepts that the future offers new and promising hope. As this time approaches, the following characteristics will become more and more apparent:

— New ability to leave the loss behind

— Greater contentment in all circumstances

— Fuller dependence on the Lord

— Restored purpose in life

Come and hear, all you who fear God;
let me tell you what he has done for me.
(PSALM 66:16)

Dos & Don'ts of Healthy Grieving

Don't let self-pity dominate your thoughts.

Do learn to find contentment in Christ.

"I have learned to be content whatever the circumstances" (PHILIPPIANS 4:11).

Don't become consumed with regret.

Do learn from and accept the past.

"Look straight ahead, and fix your eyes on what lies before you" (PROVERBS 4:25 NLT).

Don't ignore memories and feelings—both positive and negative.

Do allow yourself to feel your emotions and to reflect on your memories.

"I thank my God every time I remember you" (PHILIPPIANS 1:3).

Don't isolate yourself.

Do seek the support of others and look to the Lord to meet your needs.

"Two people are better off than one, for they can help each other succeed. If one person falls, the other can reach out and help" (ECCLESIASTES 4:9–10 NLT).

Don't compare your circumstances to the circumstances of others.

Do focus on what God wants you to do in your situation.

"Teach me to do your will, for you are my God; may your good Spirit lead me on level ground" (PSALM 143:10).

Don't busy yourself with distractions in an effort to avoid your grief.

Do set aside time to process your grief through prayer, journaling, conversations, etc.

"In my distress I prayed to the LORD, and the LORD answered me and set me free" (PSALM 118:5 NLT).

Don't make major decisions while grieving.

Do establish priorities and seek wise counsel.

"The wisdom of the prudent is to give thought to their ways" (PROVERBS 14:8).

Don't define yourself by your grief.

Do find your identity in Christ as a beloved child of God.

"See what great love the Father has lavished on us, that we should be called children of God! And that is what we are!" (1 JOHN 3:1).

God Can Use Your Grief

God can use grief and suffering to . . .

Cause you to cry out to Him.

"I cry aloud to the LORD; I lift up my voice to the LORD for mercy, I pour out before him my complaint; before him I tell my trouble. When my spirit grows faint within me, it is you who watch over my way" (PSALM 142:1–3).

Speak to you in your pain.

"Those who suffer he delivers in their suffering; he speaks to them in their affliction" (JOB 36:15).

Give you an opportunity to trust Him.

"Let those who suffer according to God's will entrust their souls to a faithful Creator while doing good" (1 PETER 4:19 ESV).

Key Verses to Memorize

Praise be to the God and Father
of our Lord Jesus Christ,
the Father of compassion
and the God of all comfort,
who comforts us in all our troubles,
so that we can comfort
those in any trouble with the comfort
we ourselves receive from God.
(2 CORINTHIANS 1:3–4)

Develop dependence on Him.

"The widow who is really in need and left all alone puts her hope in God and continues night and day to pray and to ask God for help" (1 TIMOTHY 5:5).

Comfort you with His presence.

"Even though I walk through the darkest valley, I will fear no evil, for you are with me; your rod and your staff, they comfort me" (PSALM 23:4).

Show His strength in your weaknesses.

"I will boast all the more gladly of my weaknesses, so that the power of Christ may rest upon me. For the sake of Christ, then, I am content with weaknesses, insults, hardships, persecutions, and calamities. For when I am weak, then I am strong" (2 CORINTHIANS 12:9–10 ESV).

Produce endurance, character, and hope.

"We rejoice in our sufferings, knowing that suffering produces endurance, and endurance produces character, and character produces hope, and hope does not put us to shame, because God's love has been poured into our hearts through the Holy Spirit who has been given to us" (ROMANS 5:3–5 ESV).

Teach you to love others as Christ loves.

"Live a life filled with love, following the example of Christ" (EPHESIANS 5:2 NLT).

Make you a conduit of comfort to others.

"[God] *comforts us in all our troubles, so that we can comfort those in any trouble with the comfort we ourselves receive from God"* (2 CORINTHIANS 1:4).

Bring glory to God.

"Our light and momentary troubles are achieving for us an eternal glory that far outweighs them all" (2 CORINTHIANS 4:17).

How to Help the Grieving

Pray. Remind yourself to pray regularly for the grieving and, as appropriate, pray with them.

Be there. Don't feel the need to fill the silence. Sometimes the most meaningful way to show compassion is simply to be present. Offer a hug when appropriate.

Listen. Give the one grieving opportunities to talk about the loss. Expect tears and emotional extremes. Accept emotional or verbal responses without judgment.

Offer to help with phone calls. Depending on the loss, there may be a lot of phone calls to make. Offer to help answer phone calls and relay information, if needed.

Bring a meal. Cook a warm meal and deliver it to the one grieving. Use disposable containers if possible. Be aware of any dietary needs/restrictions or allergies.

Run an errand. Offer to go to the grocery store, post office, dry cleaners, etc.

Send gift cards. Buy them a gift card for a restaurant, grocery store, movie theater, online store, etc.

Send a card or flowers. Immediately following the loss, send a card or flowers to let them know you're thinking of them. Stay in touch by writing a letter or sharing a story or memory.

Encourage a change of scenery. Take them out to lunch, dinner, shopping, or just for a walk.

Travel with them. Offer to drive them somewhere or join them in running errands so they are not alone.

Help around the house. Offer to clean, mow the lawn, do laundry, etc.

Offer to house-sit, babysit, take care of pets. This can help the grieving person get some rest or attend to errands or personal responsibilities.

Gather information and identify helpful networks. Depending on the loss, you can help find available jobs, houses, or services. Reach out to others who may be able to help the grieving individual or family as well.

Show hospitality. Depending on the loss and your availability, open up your home as a place for people to meet, have a meal, or spend a night.

When God's people are in need, be ready to help them.
Always be eager to practice hospitality.
(ROMANS 12:13)

My Personalized Plan

Acknowledge my feelings

— I will remember that God welcomes my lament, tears, and sorrow—so I do not need to hide or minimize my feelings.

— I will express my feelings to God, to other trusted people, and consider journaling as an outlet to express my emotions.

"Trust in him at all times, you people; pour out your hearts to him, for God is our refuge" (PSALM 62:8).

Key Passage to Read

Lamentations 3:19-26

Receive God's comfort

— I will read God's Word and meditate on His promises to find comfort and peace.

— I will remember that God often uses people to comfort me.

"My comfort in my suffering is this: Your promise preserves my life (PSALM 119:50).

Give myself time and grace

— I will remember that grieving is a process, and I may experience feelings of grief months or years after the loss.

— I will take things one day at a time, remembering the Lord is always with me in my grief.

"For everything there is a season, a time for every activity under heaven . . . a time to cry and a time to laugh. A time to grieve and a time to dance" (ECCLESIASTES 3:1, 4 NLT).

Honor my loved one

— I will find ways to honor my loved one's memory, being mindful of important anniversaries, and consider how these days might affect me.

— I will acknowledge that healing and moving forward does not mean I am dishonoring or forgetting my loved one.

"I thank my God every time I remember you" (PHILIPPIANS 1:3).

Remember God's promises

— I will rejoice in the promise that I will see my brothers and sisters in Christ in heaven.

— I will remember that one day God will wipe away all my tears.

"He will wipe every tear from their eyes, and there will be no more death or sorrow or crying or pain. All these things are gone forever" (REVELATION 21:4 NLT).

Reach out to others

— I will prayerfully consider how God can use me to comfort others.

— I will reach out to others who are grieving and find ways to support and comfort them.

"The Father of compassion and the God of all comfort . . . comforts us in all our troubles, so that we can comfort those in any trouble with the comfort we ourselves receive from God" (2 CORINTHIANS 1:3–4).

Move forward with hope

— I will learn to be grateful for the past and the time I had with my loved one.

— I will acknowledge my present new reality and establish new patterns and habits, while maintaining hope for the future.

"Now may our Lord Jesus Christ himself and God our Father, who loved us and by his grace gave us eternal comfort and a wonderful hope, comfort you and strengthen you in every good thing you do and say" (2 THESSALONIANS 2:16-17 NLT).

Questions & Answers

Question: "I have been told that the death of my young daughter from cancer was a result of my lack of faith. Could this be true?"

Answer: Absolutely not. Your daughter did not die because of a lack of faith. Sadly, in our broken world, unspeakable tragedies happen. The Bible is filled with stories of people who had tremendous faith yet experienced suffering and loss. The apostle Paul prayed three times that his "thorn in the flesh" would be removed, yet God did not remove it. Paul's suffering was not because of a lack of faith and neither is yours. Know that in your suffering, God is not punishing you, but He extends grace to you.

He [the Lord] *said to me, "My grace is sufficient for you,*
for my power is made perfect in weakness."
(2 CORINTHIANS 12:9)

Question: "I'm having a hard time getting over the death of my Christian father. What can I do?"

Answer: Take comfort in knowing that your father is in heaven and that you will see him again because of your own faith in Christ. Consider what you can do to honor his memory. The greatest way you can honor your father is to live out your faith in Christ and reflect His character. Your dad's greatest joy would be for you to follow in his godly footsteps, to live a Christlike life, and to grow in your faith. Such a life would honor both your earthly father and your heavenly Father.

I have no greater joy than to hear that
my children are walking in the truth.
(3 JOHN V. 4)

GUILT & SHAME

Living Guilt-Free Through Grace

God's Heart on Guilt

God is gracious and forgiving, yet He does not overlook or excuse the guilty.

"The LORD! The God of compassion and mercy! I am slow to anger and filled with unfailing love and faithfulness. I lavish unfailing love to a thousand generations. I forgive iniquity, rebellion, and sin. But I do not excuse the guilty" (EXODUS 34:6–7 NLT).

God declares that all people are guilty of sin.

"All have sinned and fall short of the glory of God" (ROMANS 3:23).

God placed our sin and guilt on Christ so we could be forgiven.

"He was pierced for our transgressions, he was crushed for our iniquities; the punishment that brought us peace was on him, and by his wounds we are healed" (ISAIAH 53:5).

God does not condemn those who are in Christ—who have received Jesus as their Lord and Savior.

"The result of God's gracious gift is very different from the result of that one man's sin. For Adam's sin led to condemnation, but God's free gift leads to our being made right with God, even though we are guilty of many sins" (ROMANS 5:16 NLT).

God will judge those who reject Christ and His free gift of salvation.

"Whoever believes in the Son has eternal life, but whoever rejects the Son will not see life, for God's wrath remains on them" (JOHN 3:36).

God doesn't want you to hide your sin and guilt, but to confess it and receive His grace.

"People who conceal their sins will not prosper, but if they confess and turn from them, they will receive mercy" (PROVERBS 28:13 NLT).

God wants you to repent with godly sorrow, not worldly sorrow.

"The kind of sorrow God wants us to experience leads us away from sin and results in salvation. There's no regret for that kind of sorrow. But worldly sorrow, which lacks repentance, results in spiritual death" (2 CORINTHIANS 7:10 NLT).

God completely forgives and cleanses you of all sin.

"If we confess our sins to him, he is faithful and just to forgive us our sins and to cleanse us from all wickedness" (1 JOHN 1:9 NLT).

God calls you by His grace to leave sin behind you.

"'Neither do I condemn you,' Jesus declared. 'Go now and leave your life of sin'" (JOHN 8:11).

God wants you to forgive others who are guilty of wronging you.

"Bear with each other and forgive one another if any of you has a grievance against someone. Forgive as the Lord forgave you" (COLOSSIANS 3:13).

Because of his great love for us, God,
who is rich in mercy, made us alive with Christ
even when we were dead in transgressions—
it is by grace you have been saved.
(EPHESIANS 2:4–5)

God's Heart on Shame

God wants you to remember He does not subject His children to shame.

"In you our ancestors put their trust; they trusted and you delivered them. To you they cried out and were saved; in you they trusted and were not put to shame" (PSALM 22:4–5).

God wants you to know that no one who hopes in Him will ever be put to shame.

"I trust in you; do not let me be put to shame, nor let my enemies triumph over me. No one who hopes in you will ever be put to shame" (PSALM 25:2–3).

God wants you to reflect His light with a face never covered with shame.

"Those who look to him are radiant; their faces are never covered with shame" (PSALM 34:5).

God wants you to find refuge from shame in Him.

"In you, LORD, I have taken refuge; let me never be put to shame" (PSALM 71:1).

God wants you to display God's goodness as proof of His help and comfort.

"Give me a sign of your goodness, that my enemies may see it and be put to shame, for you, LORD, have helped me and comforted me" (PSALM 86:17).

God wants your worship—and warns that idol worship leads only to shame and disappointment.

"All who worship images are put to shame, those who boast in idols—worship him, all you gods!" (PSALM 97:7).

God wants you to be wise.

"The wise inherit honor, but fools get only shame" (PROVERBS 3:35).

God wants the righteous to reject what is false and remain free from shame.
"The righteous hate what is false, but the wicked make themselves a stench and bring shame on themselves" (PROVERBS 13:5).

God wants us to accept discipline and correction.
"Whoever disregards discipline comes to poverty and shame, but whoever heeds correction is honored" (PROVERBS 13:18).

God wants us to remember hope does not put us to shame.
"Hope does not put us to shame, because God's love has been poured out into our hearts through the Holy Spirit, who has been given to us" (ROMANS 5:5).

Key Verse to Memorize

I acknowledged my sin to you
and did not cover up my iniquity.
I said, "I will confess
my transgressions to the LORD.*"*
And you forgave
the guilt of my sin.
(PSALM 32:5)

God wants us to remember Jesus disregarded the shame of the cross for us.
"We do this by keeping our eyes on Jesus, the champion who initiates and perfects our faith. Because of the joy awaiting him, he endured the cross, disregarding its shame. Now he is seated in the place of honor beside God's throne" (HEBREWS 12:2 NLT).

"He himself bore our sins" in his body on the cross,
so that we might die to sins and live for righteousness;
"by his wounds you have been healed."
(1 PETER 2:24)

The Difference Between Guilt and Shame

Guilt and shame are not the same. Guilt focuses on your behavior; **shame** focuses on you.

Shame can be a response to what was done to you, but **guilt** is a response to something you have done.

Shame is a painful emotion of disgrace caused by a strong sense of real or imagined **guilt**.

Shame focuses on who you *are*, but **guilt** focuses on what you've *done*.

Shame is experienced when your **guilt** moves from knowing you have done something bad to feeling that you are bad.

Shame creates an inner desire to maintain rigid control over emotions and behavior; **guilt** can motivate a desire to change—or justify emotions and behavior.

Shame produces feelings of loneliness that foster unhealthy dependencies, but **guilt** produces inner longings that foster healthy repentance in relationships.

Shame steals the joy of your salvation; **guilt** confessed restores joy in salvation.

Restore to me the joy of your salvation and grant me a willing spirit, to sustain me. (PSALM 51:12)

The Difference Between True and False Guilt

True guilt is based on fact.

False guilt is based on feelings.

"If anyone, then, knows the good they ought to do and doesn't do it, it is sin for them" (JAMES 4:17).

True guilt results in a godly sorrow over sin.

False guilt results in a worldly sorrow over consequences.

"Godly sorrow brings repentance that leads to salvation and leaves no regret, but worldly sorrow brings death. See what this godly sorrow has produced in you: what earnestness, what eagerness to clear yourselves, what indignation, what alarm, what longing, what concern, what readiness to see justice done. At every point you have proved yourselves to be innocent in this matter" (2 CORINTHIANS 7:10–11).

True guilt brings conviction.

False guilt brings condemnation.

"There is a time for everything . . . a time to love and a time to hate, a time for war and a time for peace" (ECCLESIASTES 3:1, 8).

True guilt results in repentance.

False guilt results in retreating.

"I will give you a new heart and put a new spirit in you; I will remove from you your heart of stone and give you a heart of flesh. And I will put my Spirit in you and move you to follow my decrees and be careful to keep my laws" (EZEKIEL 36:26–27).

True guilt accepts forgiveness.

False guilt attempts to earn forgiveness.

"All the prophets testify about him that everyone who believes in him receives forgiveness of sins through his name" (ACTS 10:43).

True guilt focuses on Christ's works.

False guilt focuses on personal good works.

"It is by grace you have been saved, through faith—and this is not from yourselves, it is the gift of God—not by works, so that no one can boast" (EPHESIANS 2:8-9).

True guilt brings reconciliation with God and others.

False guilt brings rejection from God and others.

"I have loved you with an everlasting love; I have drawn you with unfailing kindness" (JEREMIAH 31:3).

Possible Symptoms of Unresolved Guilt

Anxiety
Body shakes
Depression
Easily fatigued
Inability to relax
Muscle tension
Phobias
Sexual impotency
Sleeplessness
Ulcers

How to Break Free from Guilt and Shame

If you are experiencing true guilt (feeling bad about what you've done), confess your sins to God and receive His forgiveness.

"I confessed all my sins to you and stopped trying to hide my guilt. I said to myself, 'I will confess my rebellion to the Lord.' And you forgave me! All my guilt is gone" (PSALM 32:5 NLT).

If you are experiencing false guilt (feeling bad although you've done no wrong), reject the false guilt and replace the lies you've been led to believe with the truth of God's Word.

"Lead me by your truth and teach me, for you are the God who saves me. All day long I put my hope in you" (PSALM 25:5 NLT).

If you are experiencing shame (feeling bad about who you are), embrace God's love for you and meditate regularly on your identity in Christ as a chosen, beloved child of God.

"See what great love the Father has lavished on us, that we should be called children of God! And that is what we are!" (1 JOHN 3:1).

The powerful emotions of guilt and shame can take time to untangle and overcome. In addition to believing the truth of God's Word, talk with a wise friend, counselor, or pastor to help you gain victory over these feelings.

"In abundance of counselors there is victory."
(Proverbs 11:14 NASB)

My Personalized Plan

I will acknowledge . . . the existence and prevalence of guilt and/or shame in my life.

- Identify specific areas in which I am prone to experience guilt or shame
- Clarify how often and the degree to which I feel guilt or shame

"Troubles without number surround me; my sins have overtaken me, and I cannot see. They are more than the hairs of my head, and my heart fails within me" (Psalm 40:12).

I will ascertain . . . the sources of my guilt and/or shame.

- Discern if my feelings of guilt or shame are related to rules and regulations from childhood, church, or culture
- Determine if my guilt and/or shame is the result of failing to meet God's, someone else's, or my own expectations of me

"Do not bring your servant into judgment, for no one living is righteous before you" (Psalm 143:2).

I will admit . . . the ineffective ways I sometimes address my guilt and/or shame.

- Honestly evaluate if I constantly deny, analyze, ignore, mask, suppress, cover, disguise, or surrender to my feelings of guilt or shame
- Realistically assess if I deal with guilt or shame by justifying it, pretending it doesn't exist, getting angry, avoiding people and places, blaming others, becoming legalistic, or doing good deeds in an attempt to atone for my sins

"The heart of the discerning acquires knowledge, for the ears of the wise seek it out" (Proverbs 18:15).

I will differentiate . . . between true guilt, false guilt, and shame.

- Read, study, memorize, and meditate on God's Word so I might know Him well enough to recognize when I have sinned against Him, and then experience true guilt
- Examine possible wrong beliefs I have that might produce false feelings of guilt or shame

"I have hidden your word in my heart that I might not sin against you" (Psalm 119:11).

I will reject . . . shame.

- Replace wrong beliefs leading to shame with new beliefs based on biblical truth
- Ask God to keep me alert to feelings of shame operating in me and to point out areas where I am vulnerable to accepting misplaced blame

"See if there is any offensive way in me, and lead me in the way everlasting" (PSALM 139:24).

Key Passage to Read

Hebrews 10:1–23

I will respond . . . to true guilt.

- Identify the sin leading to guilt feelings, respond to the Holy Spirit's conviction, repent and renounce my sin, acknowledge and confess my sin to God and relevant others, seek forgiveness from God and others
- Make restitution when possible, seek reconciliation when appropriate, commit to make needed changes in attitude and/or behavior, accept forgiveness, and make a God-directed plan to establish a new behavior pattern

"I will instruct you and teach you in the way you should go; I will counsel you with my loving eye on you" (PSALM 32:8).

Questions & Answers

Question: "I struggle with false guilt. What can I do when I can't stop thinking about sins I've confessed and no longer do?"

Answer: The next time your mind begins to replay your repented sins, realize this taunting trick comes from Satan to discourage you. Ask yourself:

- *What am I hearing?* (False accusation.)
- *What am I feeling?* (False guilt.)
- *What are the facts?* (I am no longer guilty because I have confessed and been fully forgiven of this sin.)

Use Scripture as your standard to distinguish between true guilt and false guilt. If Jesus Christ is your Savior and Lord, He took away your sins when He died on the cross.

There is now no condemnation for those who are in Christ Jesus.
(ROMANS 8:1)

Question: "How can I know if the inner voice I'm hearing is God's loving conviction of sin or Satan's false accusations?"

Answer: Be willing to search out both the behavior and your motives for the behavior that produced your guilt. Ask God to give you insight and to help you recognize what is truly from the Holy Spirit. God has given you His Word to reveal His thoughts and ways to you. The more you study His Word, the more likely you will correctly identify His voice when He speaks to you.

Whether you turn to the right or to the left,
your ears will hear a voice behind you, saying,
"This is the way; walk in it."
(Isaiah 30:21)

HABITS & ADDICTIONS

Success in Self-Control

God's Heart on Habits and Addictions

Habits can be beneficial and profitable.

"Blessed are those who keep my ways" (PROVERBS 8:32).

Habits can be evil and destructive.

"They get into the habit of being idle and going about from house to house. And not only do they become idlers, but also busybodies who talk nonsense, saying things they ought not to" (1 TIMOTHY 5:13).

Habits can be passed down from generation to generation.

"The LORD was with Jehoshaphat because he followed the ways of his father David before him" (2 CHRONICLES 17:3).

Habits can reflect devotion to God and God's character.

"I have kept the ways of the LORD; I am not guilty of turning from my God" (PSALM 18:21).

Habits can increase consistency and strengthen character.

"The righteous will hold to their ways, and those with clean hands will grow stronger" (JOB 17:9).

Habits are a choice—a function of the will—but they can also be influenced by the mind and emotions.

"What you decide on will be done, and light will shine on your ways" (JOB 22:28).

Habits can be a positive witness to others.

"Let your light shine before others, that they may see your good deeds and glorify your Father in heaven" (MATTHEW 5:16).

Addictions are not just a choice, but the result of a bad choice that has been repeatedly made over an extended period of time.

"They promise them freedom, while they themselves are slaves of depravity—for 'people are slaves to whatever has mastered them'" (2 PETER 2:19).

Addictions lead hearts astray and hurt the cause of Christ.

"Many will follow their depraved conduct and will bring the way of truth into disrepute" (2 PETER 2:2).

Addictions hold people captive and cover them with a canopy of darkness.

"I will keep you and will make you . . . to open eyes that are blind, to free captives from prison and to release from the dungeon those who sit in darkness" (ISAIAH 42:6–7).

Addictions enslave people, but freedom comes from the Lord, who delights in breaking the yoke of slavery.

"They will know that I am the LORD, when I break the bars of their yoke and rescue them from the hands of those who enslaved them" (EZEKIEL 34:27).

Addictions hold mastery over us, but God is to be our only Master.

"'I have the right to do anything'—but I will not be mastered by anything" (1 CORINTHIANS 6:12).

Positive habits can be developed and addictions overcome through Christ.

"You, dear children, are from God and have overcome them, because the one [Jesus] *who is in you is greater than the one* [Satan] *who is in the world"* (1 JOHN 4:4).

Whoever fears God will avoid all extremes.
(ECCLESIASTES 7:18)

What Is Characteristic of All Habits and Addictions?

H—Habitual: They occur with regularity.

A—Automatic: They happen without thinking.

B—Behavioral: They outwardly reflect inner morals and character.

I—Intense: They grow stronger and more ingrained with repetition.

T—Tenacious: They persist and become hard to change over time.

S—Satisfying: They are purposeful and provide a degree of pleasure.

"No one can serve two masters.
Either you will hate the one and love the other,
or you will be devoted to the one
and despise the other."
(LUKE 16:13)

Four Categories of Habits

Harmless Habits: Some habits are common to many but cause injury to none. They are at best innocuous and at worst irritants.

"Fools show their annoyance at once, but the prudent overlook an insult" (PROVERBS 12:16).

Heart Habits: The heart that is not right in God's sight produces wrong attitudes and emotions that result in ungodly "heart habits."

"Out of the heart come evil thoughts" (MATTHEW 15:19).

Hidden Habits: Good behaviors done to excess become bad behaviors and "hidden habits."

"Whoever fears God will avoid all extremes" (ECCLESIASTES 7:18).

Hard Habits/Addictions: Destructive habits create a damaging climate for everyone, making them "hard habits."

"The acts of the flesh are obvious: sexual immorality, impurity and debauchery; idolatry and witchcraft; hatred, discord, jealousy, fits of rage, selfish ambition, dissensions, factions and envy; drunkenness, orgies, and the like" (GALATIANS 5:19–21).

Key Verse to Memorize

I can do all things through Christ who strengthens me.
(PHILIPPIANS 4:13 NKJV)

Addictive Habits Checklist

- ☐ Are my thoughts consumed with it?
- ☐ Is my time scheduled around it?
- ☐ Could my health be harmed by it?
- ☐ Does my guilt increase because of it?
- ☐ Are my finances affected by it?
- ☐ Am I defensive when asked about it?
- ☐ Are my relationships hurt by it?
- ☐ Am I upset when I can't do it?
- ☐ Is my spiritual growth hindered by it?
- ☐ Do I hide it from others?
- ☐ Would Jesus avoid doing it?
- ☐ Does it diminish my witness for Christ?

The Cycle of Addiction

Past pain: You are motivated to find a way to ease the continual hurt of past experiences.

"Even in laughter the heart may ache, and rejoicing may end in grief" (PROVERBS 14:13).

Mood-altering activity: You attempt to temporarily relieve emotional or psychological pain.

"How long must I wrestle with my thoughts and day after day have sorrow in my heart?" (PSALM 13:2).

Key Passages to Read

Galatians 5:13–17

Addiction: You participate in unbridled mood-altering activities on a regular basis.

"When you were slaves to sin, you were free from the control of righteousness. What benefit did you reap at that time from the things you are now ashamed of? Those things result in death!" (ROMANS 6:20–21).

Violating values: You disregard your own convictions by engaging in mood-altering addictive behaviors.

"Our parents were unfaithful; they did evil in the eyes of the LORD our God and forsook him. They turned their faces away from the LORD's dwelling place and turned their backs on him" (2 CHRONICLES 29:6).

Guilt: You feel conscience-struck for having wrong attitudes and committing wrong actions.

"My guilt has overwhelmed me like a burden too heavy to bear" (PSALM 38:4).

Shame: You believe you are a bad person who is without worth or hope because of your addictions.

"I live in disgrace all day long, and my face is covered with shame" (PSALM 44:15).

Present pain: You are motivated to find a way to ease the continual pain produced by the shame that accompanies addictive behaviors.

"LORD, hear my prayer, listen to my cry for mercy; in your faithfulness and righteousness come to my relief" (PSALM 143:1).

Excuses Checklist

- ☐ "This makes me feel better; and, besides, I deserve it."
- ☐ "This habit is caused by my past. I really can't help it."
- ☐ "I can control this anytime. I'll change when I'm ready."
- ☐ "I don't want to try to quit and risk finding out I can't."
- ☐ "Doing it one last time won't make any difference."

- ☐ "What I'm doing is not really that bad. A lot of people do worse things."
- ☐ "I've not been able to change before, so why try now?"
- ☐ "Everyone deserves at least one vice."
- ☐ "If I give this up, something worse will just take its place."
- ☐ "This is not a good time for me to try to change."
- ☐ "I don't have the time to focus on this right now."
- ☐ "As soon as I have a sign from God, I'll change."

My Personalized Plan

I will . . .

Seek to do God's will.

— Commit my will to God.

"I desire to do your will, my God; your law is within my heart" (Psalm 40:8).

Ask God for wisdom to know and accomplish His will.

— Discern God's priorities and plans for breaking the bad habits in my life.

"If any of you lacks wisdom, you should ask God, who gives generously to all without finding fault, and it will be given to you" (James 1:5).

Accept by faith that God will give me the wisdom I need.

— Reject any thoughts that suggest I may not be able to break my habit.

"This is the confidence we have in approaching God: that if we ask anything according to his will, he hears us" (1 John 5:14).

Write out the strategy that God has placed on my heart.

— Write down the first particular habit I plan to change and make a list of the reasons I want to change it.

"I know that you can do all things; no purpose of yours can be thwarted" (Job 42:2).

Identify the wrong beliefs supporting my habit.

— Replace each wrong belief with a biblically accurate belief.

"The simple believe anything, but the prudent give thought to their steps" (Proverbs 14:15).

Plan ways to remove possible reinforcements of my bad habit.

— Negate rewards for the bad behavior by replacing them with negative repercussions. Institute rewards for engaging in a desired behavior.

"The faithless will be fully repaid for their ways, and the good rewarded for theirs" (Proverbs 14:14).

Share my plan with an accountability partner.

— Enlist the help of a mature Christian to help strengthen and support me in my efforts and to correct me when I get off course.

"Plans fail for lack of counsel, but with many advisers they succeed" (PROVERBS 15:22).

Resolve to stay the course.

— Have no expectation that my fleshly desires will die or will accept defeat quietly, quickly, or easily.

"Put on the full armor of God, so that you can take your stand against the devil's schemes" (EPHESIANS 6:11).

Questions & Answers

Question: "What is the difference between a habit and an addiction?"

Answer: With any behavior, repetition leads to the forming of a habit that can then develop into an addiction. The difference between a repeated habit and an enslaving addiction is the amount of time it takes from your life, the power it has over your life, and the negative impact it has on your life.

If you are determined to allow only God to have mastery over you, He will give you the power to either gain and maintain mastery over the behavior or to have victory over it and stop it.

Sin shall no longer be your master, because you
are not under the law, but under grace.
(ROMANS 6:14)

Question: "When I became a Christian, shouldn't that have changed my addictions and my tendency to sin?"

Answer: When you put your trust in Christ, you did indeed receive a new life. The Spirit of God inside you now enables you to overcome sin. While you have been saved from the penalty of sin and while the power of sin over you has been broken, you still have tendencies to think, feel, and act in sinful ways. You must still choose not to sin when you are tempted.

You were taught, with regard to your
former way of life, to put off your old self,
which is being corrupted by its deceitful desires;
to be made new in the attitude of your minds;
and to put on the new self, created to be like God
in true righteousness and holiness.
(EPHESIANS 4:22–24)

THE HOLY SPIRIT

Living Free in the Power and Peace of the Spirit

God's Heart on the Holy Spirit

God wants you to know the Holy Spirit is fully God, the third member of the Trinity.

"Go and make disciples of all nations, baptizing them in the name of the Father and of the Son and of the Holy Spirit" (MATTHEW 28:19).

God gives you the Holy Spirit when you believe in Christ for your salvation.

"You also were included in Christ when you heard the message of truth, the gospel of your salvation. When you believed, you were marked in him with a seal, the promised Holy Spirit, who is a deposit guaranteeing our inheritance until the redemption of those who are God's possession—to the praise of his glory" (EPHESIANS 1:13–14).

God gives you the Holy Spirit to dwell within you forever.

"I will ask the Father, and he will give you another advocate to help you and be with you forever—the Spirit of truth. The world cannot accept him, because it neither sees him nor knows him. But you know him, for he lives with you and will be in you" (JOHN 14:16–17).

God gives you the Holy Spirit to help you understand the truth of His Word.

"When he, the Spirit of truth, comes, he will guide you into all the truth. He will not speak on his own; he will speak only what he hears, and he will tell you what is yet to come" (JOHN 16:13).

God gives you the Holy Spirit to make you more like Christ.

"We all, who with unveiled faces contemplate the Lord's glory, are being transformed into his image with ever-increasing glory, which comes from the Lord, who is the Spirit" (2 CORINTHIANS 3:18).

God gives you the Holy Spirit to help you in your weakness.

"The Spirit helps us in our weakness. We do not know what we ought to pray for, but the Spirit himself intercedes for us through wordless groans" (ROMANS 8:26).

God does not want you to grieve the Holy Spirit by willful disobedience.

"Do not grieve the Holy Spirit of God, with whom you were sealed for the day of redemption" (EPHESIANS 4:30).

God wants you to be filled with the Holy Spirit.

"Don't be drunk with wine, because that will ruin your life. Instead, be filled with the Holy Spirit, singing psalms and hymns and spiritual songs among yourselves, and making music to the Lord in your hearts" (EPHESIANS 5:18–19 NLT).

God wants you to walk in step with the Spirit.

"Since we are living by the Spirit, let us follow the Spirit's leading in every part of our lives" (GALATIANS 5:25 NLT).

God wants to develop the fruit of the Spirit in your life.

"The fruit of the Spirit is love, joy, peace, patience, kindness, goodness, faithfulness, gentleness, self-control; against such things there is no law" (GALATIANS 5:22–23 ESV).

Who Is the Holy Spirit?

The Holy Spirit is the third person of the Trinity—the triune God. God the Spirit is coequal in power and glory with God the Father and God the Son. He is the active presence and power of God in the life of an individual (Ephesians 3:16).[125]

What Is the Evidence of Being Filled with the Spirit?

Love: Am I seeking the highest and best for others or seeking to serve my own needs?

Joy: Am I living with gladness over what I have or fretting over what I don't have?

Peace: Am I resting in the strength and security of God or worrying about my circumstances?

Forbearance (patience): Am I enduring difficult trials calmly or complaining and becoming bitter?

Kindness: Am I exhibiting a benevolent heart by helping others or resenting having to meet the needs of others?

Goodness: Am I displaying godly character with purity of heart or adopting the world's standards of morality?

Faithfulness: Am I trusting God in the midst of suffering and sorrow or doubting His perfect and persistent love?

Gentleness: Am I treating others with tenderness and respect or being harsh and short-tempered?

Self-control: Am I rising to God's call to do what is right in His sight or giving in to my feelings and selfish desires?

The fruit of the Spirit is love, joy, peace,
forbearance, kindness, goodness, faithfulness,
gentleness and self-control.
(GALATIANS 5:22–23)

What Are Spiritual Gifts?

Spiritual gifts are supernatural abilities that the Holy Spirit bestows on each believer at the time of salvation for the purpose of strengthening the church.

These are unearned, undeserved gifts from the Spirit of God.

The Gifts of the Spirit

Following are two passages that list spiritual gifts and how to use them.

Romans 12:6–8

Prophecy: a supernatural ability to proclaim or reveal God's truth

Serving (ministry): a supernatural ability to recognize and meet the needs of others

Teaching: a supernatural ability to communicate and clarify truth

Encouragement (exhorting): a supernatural ability to inspire and stimulate the faith of others

Giving: a supernatural ability to entrust assets where they are most needed

Key Verse to Memorize

The mind governed by the flesh is death,
but the mind governed by
the Spirit is life and peace.
(ROMANS 8:6)

Leadership: a supernatural ability to organize, and coordinate efforts

Mercy: a supernatural ability to reach out with active compassion to comfort others

1 Corinthians 12:7–11

Wisdom: a supernatural application of knowledge

Knowledge: a supernatural revelation

Faith: a supernatural ability to believe that God will provide

Healing: a supernatural ability to believe that God will cure human illness

Miraculous powers: a supernatural ability to perform feats outside the laws of nature

Prophecy: a supernatural ability to proclaim or reveal what is hidden

Discernment: a supernatural ability to distinguish between truth and error, as well as good and evil spirits

Tongues: a supernatural ability to speak in a language that the speaker has never learned

Interpretation of tongues: a supernatural ability to understand and interpret messages in tongues

How Do You Discern Your Spiritual Gifts?[126]

Make sure you have come into a saving relationship with Jesus Christ.

Pray for the Holy Spirit to lead you to the truth about your personal spiritual gift(s).

With a humble heart, desire only the gift(s) that the Spirit has given you to serve others. Don't covet the gifts of others.

Evaluate, in light of spiritual gifts, the times when you as a Christian knew that God successfully used you to help others.

Be aware of God's confirmation through your own joy and fulfillment when helping others.

Ask one or more mature Christians who know you well for their observations regarding your spiritual strengths and giftedness.

Listen to advice and accept discipline,
and at the end you will be counted among the wise.
(PROVERBS 19:20)

Are You Self-Centered or Spirit-Controlled?

Self-Centered People . . .	Spirit-Controlled People . . .
Misuse their freedom	**Are called** to freedom
Are self-indulgent	**Are self-sacrificing**
Destroy one another	**Love** one another
Live by sinful desires	**Live** by the Spirit
Desire what is sinful	**Desire** what is spiritual
Display the acts of sin (Galatians 5:19–21)	**Display** the fruit of the Spirit (Galatians 5:22–23)

The acts of the flesh are obvious: sexual immorality, impurity and debauchery; idolatry and witchcraft; hatred, discord, jealousy, fits of rage, selfish ambition, dissensions, factions and envy; drunkenness, orgies, and the like. I warn you, as I did before, that those who live like this will not inherit the kingdom of God.

But the fruit of the Spirit is love, joy, peace, forbearance, kindness, goodness, faithfulness, gentleness and self-control.
Against such things there is no law.
Those who belong to Christ Jesus have crucified the flesh with its passions and desires.
Since we live by the Spirit, let us keep in step with the Spirit.
Let us not become conceited, provoking and envying each other.
(Galatians 5:19–25)

My Personalized Plan

I will . . .

Ask God to fill me with His Spirit so I can fulfill His purposes.

"Be filled with the Spirit, speaking to one another with psalms, hymns, and songs from the Spirit. Sing and make music from your heart to the Lord, always giving thanks to God the Father for everything, in the name of our Lord Jesus Christ" (Ephesians 5:18–20).

Walk by the Spirit in order to fight temptation and fleshly desires.

"Walk by the Spirit, and you will not gratify the desires of the flesh. for the flesh desires what is contrary to the Spirit, and the Spirit what is contrary to the flesh. They are in conflict with each other, so that you are not to do whatever you want" (GALATIANS 5:16–17).

Read God's Word and ask the Holy Spirit to teach me the truth.

"When he, the Spirit of truth, comes, he will guide you into all the truth. He will not speak on his own; he will speak only what he hears, and he will tell you what is yet to come" (JOHN 16:13).

Key Passage to Read

Galatians 5:13–25

Not grieve the Holy Spirit by engaging in willful, unrepentant sin.

"Do not grieve the Holy Spirit of God, with whom you were sealed for the day of redemption" (EPHESIANS 4:30).

Use the spiritual gifts God has given me to serve others.

"A spiritual gift is given to each of us so we can help each other" (1 CORINTHIANS 12:7 NLT).

Seek unity with my brothers and sisters in the Lord.

"Make every effort to keep the unity of the Spirit through the bond of peace" (EPHESIANS 4:3).

Allow the Spirit to produce fruit in my life.

"The Holy Spirit produces this kind of fruit in our lives: love, joy, peace, patience, kindness, goodness, faithfulness, gentleness, and self-control" (GALATIANS 5:22–23 NLT).

Questions & Answers

Question: "When does a person receive the Holy Spirit?"

Answer: At the moment of salvation, every true believer receives the Holy Spirit.

> *You also were included in Christ when you heard*
> *the message of truth, the gospel of your salvation.*
> *When you believed, you were marked in him*
> *with a seal, the promised Holy Spirit.*
> (EPHESIANS 1:13)

Question: "If I sin after receiving the Holy Spirit, will I lose my salvation?"

Answer: No, the Bible says that at the time of salvation every authentic Christian is sealed with the promised Holy Spirit, who is a guarantee—a promise from God that we will be physically redeemed in heaven.

He anointed us, set his seal of ownership on us,
and put his Spirit in our hearts as a deposit,
guaranteeing what is to come.
(2 CORINTHIANS 1:21–22)

Question: "Can I be an authentic Christian and not have the Holy Spirit?"

Answer: No. You cannot have Christ without having the Spirit of Christ.

If anyone does not have the Spirit of Christ, they do not belong to Christ.
(ROMANS 8:9)

Question: "Can I choose a spiritual gift?"

Answer: No. Each person's gift is chosen by the Spirit of God.

He distributes them to each one, just as he determines.
(1 CORINTHIANS 12:11)

HOMOSEXUALITY & SSA

The Struggle with Same-Sex Attraction

God's Heart on Homosexuality

The Scriptural Standard

Genesis 19:4–7—*"All the men from every part of the city of Sodom . . . surrounded the house. They called to Lot, 'Where are the men who came to you tonight? Bring them out to us so that we can have sex with them.' Lot . . . said, 'No, my friends. Don't do this wicked thing.'"*

Leviticus 18:22—*"Do not have sexual relations with a man as one does with a woman; that is detestable."*

Leviticus 20:13—*"If a man has sexual relations with a man as one does with a woman, both of them have done what is detestable."*

Judges 19:22–23—*"'Bring out the man who came to your house so we can have sex with him.' The owner of the house . . . said to them, 'No, my friends, don't be so vile. Since this man is my guest, don't do this outrageous thing.'"*

Romans 1:26–27—*"Because of this, God gave them over to shameful lusts. Even their women exchanged natural sexual relations for unnatural ones. In the same way the men also abandoned natural relations with women and were inflamed with lust for one another. Men committed shameful acts with other men, and received in themselves the due penalty for their error."*

1 Corinthians 6:9–10—*"Do you not know that wrongdoers will not inherit the kingdom of God? Do not be deceived: Neither the sexually immoral nor idolaters nor adulterers nor men who have sex with men . . . will inherit the kingdom of God."*

"Be holy because I, the LORD your God, am holy."
(LEVITICUS 19:2)

The Scriptural Solution

1 Corinthians 6:11—*"And that* [homosexual] *is what some of you were. But you were washed, you were sanctified, you were justified in the name of the Lord Jesus Christ and by the Spirit of our God."*

1 Corinthians 6:13—*"The body, however, is not meant for sexual immorality but for the Lord, and the Lord for the body."*

1 Corinthians 6:18—*"Flee from sexual immorality. All other sins a person commits are outside the body, but whoever sins sexually, sins against their own body."*

1 Corinthians 6:19–20—*"Do you not know that your bodies are temples of the Holy Spirit, who is in you, whom you have received from God? You are not your own; you were bought at a price. Therefore honor God with your bodies."*

1 Corinthians 10:13—*"No temptation has overtaken you except what is common to mankind. And God is faithful; he will not let you be tempted beyond what you can bear. But when you are tempted, he will also provide a way out so that you can endure it."*

James 1:21—*"Get rid of all moral filth and the evil that is so prevalent and humbly accept the word planted in you, which can save you."*

How can a young person stay on the path of purity?
By living according to your word.
I seek you with all my heart;
do not let me stray from your commands.
I have hidden your word in my heart
that I might not sin against you.
(PSALM 119:9–11)

Factors That Frequently Lead to Homosexuality in Men

1. **Failure to identify** with his father, whom he perceives as absent or weak, while seeing women as undesirable

   "There are those who curse their fathers and do not bless their mothers" (PROVERBS 30:11).

2. **Failure to bond** with his father, whom he views as non-affirming

   "Fathers, do not exasperate your children; instead, bring them up in the training and instruction of the Lord" (EPHESIANS 6:4).

3. **Failure to emotionally attach** to a positive, healthy male because of abuse by a significant male

   "You, Sovereign LORD, help me for your name's sake; out of the goodness of your love, deliver me. For I am poor and needy, and my heart is wounded within me" (PSALM 109:21–22).

My son, do not let wisdom and understanding out of your sight,
preserve sound judgment and discretion;
they will be life for you,
an ornament to grace your neck.
Then you will go on your way in safety,
and your foot will not stumble.
(PROVERBS 3:21–23)

Factors That Frequently Lead Females into Lesbianism

1. **Failure to identify with her mother**, whom she perceives as absent or weak

   "Heartache crushes the spirit" (PROVERBS 15:13).

2. **Failure to bond with her mother**, whom she views as non-nurturing

   "The wise woman builds her house, but with her own hands the foolish one tears hers down" (PROVERBS 14:1).

3. **Failure to be drawn to males** because of her abusive father or mistreatment from other males

   "Fathers, do not embitter your children, or they will become discouraged" (COLOSSIANS 3:21).

Key Verses to Memorize

For Convicting the Heart

God did not call us to be impure,
but to live a holy life.
(1 THESSALONIANS 4:7)

For Conquering the Hurt

"I am the LORD, the God of all mankind.
Is anything too hard for me?"
(JEREMIAH 32:27)

Charm is deceptive, and beauty is fleeting;
but a woman who fears the LORD is to be praised.
(PROVERBS 31:30)

How to Change Patterns of the Past

Focus on God's love for you.

"As obedient children, do not conform to the evil desires you had when you lived in ignorance. But just as he who called you is holy, so be holy in all you do; for it is written: 'Be holy, because I am holy'" (1 PETER 1:14–16).

Take responsibility for your negative emotions.

"Whoever conceals their sins does not prosper, but the one who confesses and renounces them finds mercy" (PROVERBS 28:13).

Refuse to act on your emotions.

"I have hidden your word in my heart that I might not sin against you" (PSALM 119:11).

Key Passage to Read

1 Corinthians 6:9–20

Make forgiveness your priority.

"Do not judge, and you will not be judged. Do not condemn, and you will not be condemned. Forgive, and you will be forgiven" (LUKE 6:37).

Understand your triggers to sexual temptation.[127]

"Each person is tempted when they are dragged away by their own evil desire and enticed" (JAMES 1:14).

Embrace your true identity.

"See what great love the Father has lavished on us, that we should be called children of God! And that is what we are!" (1 JOHN 3:1).

Establish healthy boundaries in relationships.

"I have been crucified with Christ and I no longer live, but Christ lives in me. The life I now live in the body, I live by faith in the Son of God, who loved me and gave himself for me" (GALATIANS 2:20).

Holy brothers and sisters, who share in the heavenly calling,
fix your thoughts on Jesus, whom we acknowledge
as our apostle and high priest.
(HEBREWS 3:1)

My Personalized Plan

Renounce the homosexual lifestyle and **regard** engaging in sexual activity with someone of my same gender as sin.

Renounce my "mistaken identity" as a homosexual and **recognize** and live out of my true identity in Christ.

Renounce a codependent lifestyle and **remove** myself from codependent relationships.

Renounce my fear-based thinking and **replace** my fear with a new walk of faith.

Renounce old vows to my gay partner(s) and **renew** my vow to God.

Renounce "one flesh" gay relationships and emotional "soul ties" and **remove** every keepsake that keeps me emotionally tied.

Renounce all my sexual sin and **relinquish** all parts of my body to Christ to be used by Him to accomplish His purposes for me.

Renounce prioritizing my partner(s) above the Lord and **repent** by giving Christ first place in my heart and life.

Renounce all unforgiveness toward those who have hurt me and **rid** my heart of the "right" to revenge.

Renounce unhealthy responses to my wounded emotions and **receive** emotional healing by working through the pain of my past.

Renounce self-hatred and shame because of my guilt and **realize** that Jesus died to forgive my sin and remove my guilt.

Renounce any bitterness against God and **repent** by thanking God for the gender He gave me.

Heal me, LORD, and I will be healed;
save me and I will be saved,
for you are the one I praise.
(JEREMIAH 17:14)

Questions & Answers

Question: "Is homosexual behavior a sin?"

Answer: Yes, according to numerous passages in the Bible. The law of God states:

"Do not have sexual relations with a man as
one does with a woman; that is detestable."
(LEVITICUS 18:22)

Question: "Is homosexuality the worst sin?"

Answer: No. Based on the Bible, if we commit *any sin*, we are guilty of breaking the whole law.

Whoever keeps the whole law and yet stumbles
at just one point is guilty of breaking all of it.
(JAMES 2:10)

Question: "Is a person born a homosexual?"

Answer: No, homosexuality is a *behavior, not* an *identity.*[128] No scientific study has identified a gay gene or any other cause for homosexuality.[129] And God would never specifically *create* someone to be (or *cause* someone to do) that which He forbids. However, because Adam and Eve chose to sin, everyone is now born with a personal inclination or "bent" to sin, which expresses itself uniquely in each of us (Romans 3:10–18).

Apart from a child's natural *bent to sin,* two other significant factors leading to homosexuality are the childhood *environment* and the child's *responses* to that environment.

Do not conform to the pattern of this world,
but be transformed by the renewing of your mind.
Then you will be able to test and approve what God's will is—
his good, pleasing and perfect will.
(Romans 12:2)

HOPE

The Anchor for Your Soul

God's Heart on Hope

God is the God of hope.

"I pray that God, the source of hope, will fill you completely with joy and peace because you trust in him. Then you will overflow with confident hope through the power of the Holy Spirit" (ROMANS 15:13 NLT).

God is the only lasting hope for everyone.

"You are the hope of everyone on earth, even those who sail on distant seas" (PSALM 65:5 NLT).

God wants your hope to be in Him.

"O Lord, you alone are my hope" (PSALM 71:5 NLT).

God wants His Word and His promises to be your source of hope.

"You are my refuge and my shield; your word is my source of hope" (PSALM 119:114 NLT).

God does not want you to put your hope in people or leaders.

"It is better to take refuge in the LORD than to trust in humans. It is better to take refuge in the LORD than to trust in princes" (PSALM 118:8–9).

God does not want your hope to be in money or wealth.

"Command those who are rich in this present world not to be arrogant nor to put their hope in wealth, which is so uncertain, but to put their hope in God, who richly provides us with everything for our enjoyment" (1 TIMOTHY 6:17).

God has a plan for your life that is filled with hope.

"'I know the plans I have for you,' declares the LORD, 'plans to prosper you and not to harm you, plans to give you hope and a future'" (JEREMIAH 29:11).

God wants you to have hope all day—every day.

"Guide me in your truth and teach me, for you are God my Savior, and my hope is in you all day long" (PSALM 25:5).

God gives you hope during times of trouble and suffering.

"Why, my soul, are you downcast? Why so disturbed within me? Put your hope in God, for I will yet praise him, my Savior and my God" (PSALM 42:5).

God strengthens you with His hope.

"Those who hope in the LORD will renew their strength. They will soar on wings like eagles; they will run and not grow weary, they will walk and not be faint" (ISAIAH 40:31).

God keeps you anchored with His hope.

"We have this hope as an anchor for the soul, firm and secure" (HEBREWS 6:19).

God wants you to know that no matter what happens—there is always hope.

"There is surely a future hope for you, and your hope will not be cut off" (PROVERBS 23:18).

"In his name the nations will put their hope."
(MATTHEW 12:21)

What Is Hope?

Cultural hope is an ***optimistic desire*** that something will be fulfilled. This is *not* a *guaranteed* hope because it is subject to changeable people and circumstances.[130]

Christian hope is an ***optimistic assurance*** that something will be fulfilled. This is a *guaranteed hope* not subject to change, but rather anchored in Christ and every promise in the Word of God.[131]

Inner Feelings of Hopelessness

Do you feel . . .

— **Deceived?** Duped by someone you trusted
— **Disliked?** Deeming yourself unwanted
— **Dejected?** Despairing/emotionally sunk
— **Deadened?** Desensitized and numb
— **Disqualified?** Discounting your true value
— **Degraded?** Demeaned/belittled by others
— **Detached?** Discarded/isolated
— **Doomed?** Determined there's no way out
— **Deprived?** Discriminated against
— **Downcast?** Downhearted

Let us hold unswervingly to the hope we profess,
for he who promised is faithful.
(HEBREWS 10:23)

Are You Anchored in Hope?

When you have Christ, you have . . .

Contentment: being patient because of what you hope for
"If we hope for what we do not yet have, we wait for it patiently" (ROMANS 8:25).

Courage: being bold because of God's hope within you
"Since we have such a hope, we are very bold" (2 CORINTHIANS 3:12).

Confidence: being assured because God is your hope
"You have been my hope, Sovereign LORD, my confidence since my youth" (PSALM 71:5).

Cheerfulness: being joyful because your hope is in God
"Be joyful in hope, patient in affliction, faithful in prayer" (ROMANS 12:12).

Comfort: being encouraged because of God's unfailing love for you
"May your unfailing love be with us, LORD, even as we put our hope in you" (PSALM 33:22).

Conviction: being anchored in hope because of God's Word within you
"May those who fear you rejoice when they see me, for I have put my hope in your word" (PSALM 119:74).

Christlikeness: being conformed to the character of Christ because of God's hope for you
"I eagerly expect and hope that I will in no way be ashamed, but will have sufficient courage so that now as always Christ will be exalted in my body, whether by life or by death" (PHILIPPIANS 1:20).

Key Verse to Memorize

"I know the plans I have for you,"
declares the LORD,
"plans to prosper you and not to harm you,
plans to give you hope and a future."
(JEREMIAH 29:11)

Unreliable Anchors

Anchoring hope in **politics**
"The nations have fallen into the pit they have dug; their feet are caught in the net they have hidden" (PSALM 9:15).

Anchoring hope in **economics**

"When times are good, be happy; but when times are bad, consider this: God has made the one as well as the other. Therefore, no one can discover anything about their future" (ECCLESIASTES 7:14).

Anchoring hope in **society**

"In those days Israel had no king; everyone did as they saw fit" (JUDGES 17:6).

Anchoring hope in **law**

"Justice—do you rulers know the meaning of the word? Do you judge the people fairly? No! You plot injustice in your hearts. You spread violence throughout the land" (PSALM 58:1–2 NLT).

Anchoring hope in **vocation**

"There was a man all alone; he had neither son nor brother. There was no end to his toil, yet his eyes were not content with his wealth. 'For whom am I toiling,' he asked, 'and why am I depriving myself of enjoyment?' This too is meaningless—a miserable business!" (ECCLESIASTES 4:8).

Anchoring hope in **health**

"My back is filled with searing pain; there is no health in my body" (PSALM 38:7).

Anchoring hope in **money**

"Riches do not endure forever, and a crown is not secure for all generations" (PROVERBS 27:24).

Anchoring hope in **marriage**

"The LORD is the witness between you and the wife of your youth. You have been unfaithful to her, though she is your partner, the wife of your marriage covenant" (MALACHI 2:14).

Anchoring hope in **friendship**

"Even my close friend, someone I trusted, one who shared my bread, has turned against me" (PSALM 41:9).

Anchoring hope in **children**

"A foolish son brings grief to his father and bitterness to the mother who bore him" (PROVERBS 17:25).

Anchoring hope in **longevity**

"There is a time for everything, and a season for every activity under the heavens: a time to be born and a time to die" (ECCLESIASTES 3:1–2).

Anchoring hope in **religion**

"[God] *saved us and called us to a holy calling, not because of our works but because of his own purpose and grace*" (2 TIMOTHY 1:9 ESV).

Anchoring hope in **possessions**

"Do not be afraid, little flock, for your Father has been pleased to give you the kingdom. Sell your possessions and give to the poor. Provide purses for yourselves that will not wear out, a treasure in heaven that will never fail, where no thief comes near and no moth destroys. For where your treasure is, there your heart will be also" (LUKE 12:32–34).

"Everyone who hears these words of mine and does not put them into practice is like a foolish man who built his house on sand."
(MATTHEW 7:26)

Root Cause of Hopelessness

Wrong Belief: "I can take charge of my life and make it what I want it to be. I can look to myself, to others, and to other things to give me hope. I don't need God to give me purpose, meaning, or hope—or to help me weather the storms of life."

Right Belief: "I refuse to base my hope on anything that can be taken away from me, including my own abilities and resources. My hope is in everything God promises and in Jesus Christ. He alone provides everything I need for my present, my future, and for eternity."

The Benefits of God's Hope

Provides you joy in living

"Be joyful in hope, patient in affliction, faithful in prayer" (ROMANS 12:12).

Generates faith and love in you

"We have heard of your faith in Christ Jesus and of the love you have for all God's people—the faith and love that spring from the hope stored up for you in heaven and about which you have already heard in the true message of the gospel" (COLOSSIANS 1:4–5).

Causes you to live a pure life

"All who have this hope in him purify themselves, just as he is pure" (1 JOHN 3:3).

Inspires you to persevere with endurance

"We remember before our God and Father your work produced by faith, your labor prompted by love, and your endurance inspired by hope in our Lord Jesus Christ" (1 THESSALONIANS 1:3).

Lifts up your downcast soul

"Why, my soul, are you downcast? Why so disturbed within me? Put your hope in God, for I will yet praise him, my Savior and my God" (PSALM 43:5).

Causes you to praise God

"As for me, I will always have hope; I will praise you more and more" (PSALM 71:14).

Anchors your soul

"We have this hope as an anchor for the soul, firm and secure" (HEBREWS 6:19).

Generates boldness in you

"Since we have such a hope, we are very bold" (2 CORINTHIANS 3:12).

Develops your patience

"If we hope for what we do not yet have, we wait for it patiently" (ROMANS 8:25).

Gives you reason to rejoice

"Through whom we have gained access by faith into this grace in which we now stand. And we boast in the hope of the glory of God" (ROMANS 5:2).

Establishes your security and safety

"You will be secure, because there is hope; you will look about you and take your rest in safety" (JOB 11:18).

Guarantees your eternal life

"He saved us, not because of righteous things we had done, but because of his mercy. He saved us through the washing of rebirth and renewal by the Holy Spirit, whom he poured out on us generously through Jesus Christ our Savior, so that, having been justified by his grace, we might become heirs having the hope of eternal life" (TITUS 3:5–7).

Helping Those Who Feel Hopeless

Know your limits. Don't think you can "do it all."

Learn the warning signs. Despairing people can be suicidal. Therefore, learn the warning signs of suicide.

Be present and available. Call, visit, and check in on them regularly.

Listen with compassion. Don't feel like you have to say something to "fix it."

Suggest activities that engage them and could prove beneficial.

Encourage them to pursue professional help. Help them find a local counselor or clinic.

Don't hesitate to call for help.

My Personalized Plan

I will . . .

Remember that true hope is anchored in God.

"And so, Lord, where do I put my hope? My only hope is in you" (PSALM 39:7 NLT).

Recognize that when I feel hopeless, God calls me to trust Him.

"May the God of hope fill you with all joy and peace as you trust in him, so that you may overflow with hope by the power of the Holy Spirit" (ROMANS 15:13).

Key Passage to Read

Lamentations 3:19–25

Realize that there is always hope and God will help me overcome the obstacles in my life.

"Though I walk in the midst of trouble, you preserve my life; . . . The LORD will fulfill his purpose for me; your steadfast love, O LORD, endures forever" (PSALM 138:7–8 ESV).

Rely on the Lord and others for support and help when I feel hopeless.

"Where there is no guidance the people fall, but in abundance of counselors there is victory" (PROVERBS 11:14 NASB).

Recount my blessings, thanking God for them.

"Put your hope in the LORD, for with the LORD is unfailing love and with him is full redemption" (PSALM 130:7).

Reach out to others and share the hope of Christ.

"Encourage one another and build each other up, just as in fact you are doing" (1 THESSALONIANS 5:11).

I am counting on the LORD; yes, I am counting on him.
I have put my hope in his word.
(PSALM 130:5 NLT)

Questions & Answers

Question: "Where is God when I need Him the most? I don't see Him at work in my life."

Answer: Have you ever seen an anchor on the deck of a ship? It's impressive! But it's serving little purpose just sitting there on deck. If the anchor is doing its job, you won't see it.

Likewise, when Jesus is "doing His job," you often won't "see" Him either. But He is there. Keep looking to Him and to His Word, trusting Him to help you.

There is wonderful joy ahead, even though
you must endure many trials for a little while. . . .
Though you do not see him now, you trust him;
and you rejoice with a glorious, inexpressible joy.
The reward for trusting him will be
the salvation of your souls.
(1 PETER 1:6, 8–9 NLT)

Question: "As a Christian, how can I be certain hope is guaranteed and God will fulfill His promises?"

Answer: Christian hope can sound beyond belief, unreal, far-fetched. But there are reasons to have assurance in God's promises. Consider:

— **The character of God**: You can have absolute confidence in the promises of the Bible because they are the promises of *God*.

— **The fulfillment of His Word**: He has proven Himself time and time again—the Lord always fulfills His Word.

The LORD is trustworthy in all he promises
and faithful in all he does.
(PSALM 145:13)

IDENTITY & SELF-IMAGE

Knowing What's True About You

God's Heart on Your Identity

You are loved.

"God loves you and has chosen you to be his own people" (1 THESSALONIANS 1:4 NLT).

You are chosen.

"Even before he made the world, God loved us and chose us in Christ to be holy and without fault in his eyes" (EPHESIANS 1:4 NLT).

You are accepted.

"Christ has accepted you so that God will be given glory" (ROMANS 15:7 NLT).

You are redeemed.

"This is what the LORD says—he who created you . . . he who formed you . . . 'Do not fear, for I have redeemed you; I have summoned you by name; you are mine'" (ISAIAH 43:1).

You are precious.

"You are precious to me. You are honored, and I love you" (ISAIAH 43:4 NLT).

You are forgiven.

"You were dead because of your sins and because your sinful nature was not yet cut away. Then God made you alive with Christ, for he forgave all our sins" (COLOSSIANS 2:13 NLT).

You are cleansed.

"You were cleansed; you were made holy; you were made right with God by calling on the name of the Lord Jesus Christ and by the Spirit of our God" (1 CORINTHIANS 6:11 NLT).

You are renewed.

"Anyone who belongs to Christ has become a new person. The old life is gone; a new life has begun!" (2 CORINTHIANS 5:17 NLT).

You are empowered.

"His divine power has given us everything we need for a godly life through our knowledge of him who called us by his own glory and goodness" (2 PETER 1:3).

You are gifted.

"In his grace, God has given us different gifts for doing certain things well" (ROMANS 12:6 NLT).

You are useful.

"We are God's handiwork, created in Christ Jesus to do good works, which God prepared in advance for us to do" (EPHESIANS 2:10).

You are blessed.

"All praise to God, the Father of our Lord Jesus Christ, who has blessed us with every spiritual blessing in the heavenly realms because we are united with Christ" (EPHESIANS 1:3 NLT).

Just as you accepted Christ Jesus as your Lord,
you must continue to follow him.
Let your roots grow down into him,
and let your lives be built on him.
Then your faith will grow strong
in the truth you were taught,
and you will overflow with thankfulness.
(COLOSSIANS 2:6–7 NLT)

What Is an Identity Crisis?

A period of difficult transition, such as adolescence or midlife, when the *outer you* severely conflicts with the *inner you*—causing pain, distress, and a desire for change.

A period of severe disillusionment when your identity is based on a *role* or a *relationship* that has been changed or removed.[132]

As water reflects the face,
so one's life reflects the heart.
(PROVERBS 27:19)

Common False Identities

Controller: Some seek to control every situation and the people around them. Instead of trusting God, who is in control of all things, they become obsessive, anxious, and overstressed.

Defender: Some stand in the gap to save others when their own world is falling apart. They find significance in rescuing others. While this is a noble effort, defenders may only see weaknesses in others while neglecting to see their own.

Dependent: Some look to people, positions, and possessions to identify who they are. The things they depend on for their identity could be removed, lost, or taken away—resulting in a devastating blow to their identity.

Excuser: Some refuse to accept responsibility for their own actions and beliefs. They sit on the fence and fail to make decisions.

Failure: Some surrender to setbacks as if failure is always inevitable. Instead of learning from a failure, they define themselves by it and avoid new opportunities to learn, grow, and change.

Fixer: Some attempt to solve problems they encounter all on their own. They usually attach their own value and identity to accolades they expect by "fixing" others.

Key Verse to Memorize

I have been crucified with Christ
and I no longer live, but Christ lives in me.
The life I now live in the body,
I live by faith in the Son of God,
who loved me and gave himself for me.
(GALATIANS 2:20)

Performer: Some seek praise and affirmation by putting on a show or doing a task as perfectly as possible. They don't know who they are unless they are immersed in a project, task, or role.

Pleaser: Some try to prove value and worth by pleasing other people. They struggle to set boundaries with others and all too often end up doing tasks that others should be doing.

Sufferer: Some play the martyr when trials come. They may see themselves as righteous and altruistic, yet they may be neglecting their own faults.

Misplaced Identity Checklist

- ☐ Do you always need to receive praise for your efforts?
- ☐ Do you need to have everything perfectly in place?
- ☐ Do you expect others to do things your way?
- ☐ Do you believe making mistakes is unacceptable?
- ☐ Do you consider your way to be the *right* way?
- ☐ Do you find it impossible to let go of a mistake?
- ☐ Do you think you must perform perfectly to receive God's love?
- ☐ Do you avoid taking a risk for fear of failure?
- ☐ Do you avoid conflict at all costs?
- ☐ Do you think other people are always trying to find fault with you?

- ☐ Do you set higher standards for yourself than you do for others?
- ☐ Do you think people would not respect you if they learned you have struggles in life?
- ☐ Do you set such high goals that you are continually under stress?
- ☐ Do you think that making a mistake makes you less valuable as a person?
- ☐ Do you wonder whether people would love you if they really knew you?
- ☐ Do you feel responsible for someone else's happiness?
- ☐ Do you believe you must please everyone, all of the time?
- ☐ Do you refuse to take a rest for fear of failure or disapproval?

Replacing Self-Perception with God's Perspective

Do you think . . . you are unacceptable?

God says . . . you are accepted by Him.

"Accept one another, then, just as Christ accepted you, in order to bring praise to God" (ROMANS 15:7).

Do you think . . . you are alone?

God says . . . He will never leave you nor forsake you.

"The LORD himself goes before you and will be with you; he will never leave you nor forsake you. Do not be afraid; do not be discouraged" (DEUTERONOMY 31:8).

Do you think . . . you are incompetent, a failure?

God says . . . He has made you competent.

"Not that we are competent in ourselves to claim anything for ourselves, but our competence comes from God" (2 CORINTHIANS 3:5).

Do you think . . . you are bad, not good enough?

God says . . . He sees you through the lens of His mercy.

"He saved us, not because of righteous things we had done, but because of his mercy" (TITUS 3:5).

Do you think . . . you are a mistake?

God says . . . you are wonderfully made.

"I praise you because I am fearfully and wonderfully made; your works are wonderful, I know that full well" (PSALM 139:14).

Do you think . . . you are unloved?

God says . . . He has great love for you.

"Because of his great love for us, God, who is rich in mercy, made us alive with Christ even when we were dead in transgressions—it is by grace you have been saved" (EPHESIANS 2:4-5).

Do you think . . . you can't be forgiven?

God says . . . your sins are forgiven and are gone.

"As far as the east is from the west, so far has he removed our transgressions from us" (PSALM 103:12).

My Personalized Plan

Embrace my identity in Christ.

— I will study God's Word regularly to remind myself of who God is and who He says I am.

— I will look to Christ to find my primary identity.

"For you died, and your life is now hidden with Christ in God" (COLOSSIANS 3:3).

Put my old self and old ways behind me.

— I will remember that I am not defined by my past or my sins.

— I will seek to overcome the sins that have previously entrapped me.

"We know that our old sinful selves were crucified with Christ so that sin might lose its power in our lives. We are no longer slaves to sin. . . . So you also should consider yourselves to be dead to the power of sin and alive to God through Christ Jesus" (ROMANS 6:6, 11 NLT).

Key Passage to Read

Colossians 3:1-17

Acknowledge my background.

— I will acknowledge the people, places, and positions that have influenced my identity (for good or bad), but remember they are not where my ultimate identity lies.

— I will reflect on and be thankful for the positive influences that shaped who I am today—my family, culture, education, friends, jobs, and life experiences.

"Give thanks for everything to God the Father in the name of our Lord Jesus Christ" (EPHESIANS 5:20 NLT).

Honestly evaluate myself.

— I will not think of myself too highly—remembering that I am a sinner saved by grace.

— I will not think of myself too lowly—remembering that I am made in God's image and loved.

"Don't think you are better than you really are. Be honest in your evaluation of yourselves, measuring yourselves by the faith God has given us" (Romans 12:3 NLT).

Correct faulty thinking and emotions.

— I will identify the lies I've believed about myself, about others, about life, and about God.

— I will look to God's Word to replace those lies with the truth.

"You will know the truth, and the truth will set you free" (John 8:32).

Encourage others.

— I will reach out to those struggling with identity and self-image issues and help them see their God-given worth.

— I will embrace my identity as an ambassador of Christ and share the life-changing identity others can also have in Christ.

"We are therefore Christ's ambassadors, as though God were making his appeal through us. We implore you on Christ's behalf: Be reconciled to God" (2 Corinthians 5:20).

By the grace of God I am what I am,
and his grace to me was not without effect.
(1 Corinthians 15:10)

Questions & Answers

Question: How do I overcome my tendency to always want to please people?

Answer: You're not alone. Many struggle with people-pleasing. They may be a peace-at-any-price type of person who generally avoids confrontation. They may fear sticking up for themselves or making their opinions known—or they may have never learned how to set boundaries with others. Deep down, they may seek the approval of others as a way to meet an inner need for love, significance, or security.

Address your fears. You may have underlying fears about not meeting others' approval. Pray, journal, and talk with someone you trust to help you address those fears. Whatever the reason for people-pleasing in your life, it can feel like an inescapable trap—but you can be set free with God's help. (Proverbs 29:25)

Set boundaries. It's okay to say *no* to others. Sometimes you need to say *no* to people so you can say *yes* to God. Setting boundaries can help guard you from excessively doing things for others in an attempt to gain approval. (Proverbs 4:23)

Trust God to meet your needs. Only God can meet your deep needs for love, significance, and security. Even if you receive the approval of others, it won't satisfy the deepest longings in your heart. Look to Christ to meet those needs and seek God's approval above all.

Am I now trying to win the approval
of human beings, or of God?
Or am I trying to please people?
If I were still trying to please people,
I would not be a servant of Christ.
(GALATIANS 1:10)

INFERTILITY

Building Hope from Broken Dreams

God's Heart on Infertility

God gave us the desire for children from the beginning.

"God blessed them and said to them, 'Be fruitful and increase in number; fill the earth and subdue it'" (GENESIS 1:28).

God understands the hope of your heart.

"Hope deferred makes the heart sick, but a longing fulfilled is a tree of life" (PROVERBS 13:12).

God has unfailing love and compassion for you.

"'Though the mountains be shaken and the hills be removed, yet my unfailing love for you will not be shaken nor my covenant of peace be removed,' says the LORD, who has compassion on you" (ISAIAH 54:10).

God understands the pain of grief.

"He was despised and rejected by mankind, a man of suffering, and familiar with pain" (ISAIAH 53:3).

God heals the brokenhearted.

"He heals the brokenhearted and binds up their wounds" (PSALM 147:3).

God offers comfort and rest.

"Come to me, all you who are weary and burdened, and I will give you rest. Take my yoke upon you and learn from me, for I am gentle and humble in heart, and you will find rest for your souls. For my yoke is easy and my burden is light" (MATTHEW 11:28–30).

God gives peace, even in the midst of pain.

"Peace I leave with you; my peace I give you. I do not give to you as the world gives. Do not let your hearts be troubled and do not be afraid" (JOHN 14:27).

God hears your cries.

"I cry aloud to the LORD; I lift up my voice to the LORD for mercy. I pour out before him my complaint; before him I tell my trouble" (PSALM 142:1–2).

We know that in all things God works
for the good of those who love him,
who have been called according to his purpose.
(ROMANS 8:28)

Women in the Bible Who Experienced Infertility

— **Sarah** (Genesis 11:30, 16:1–4, 18:13–14, 21:1–3)
— **Rachel** (Genesis 29:31, 30:1, 3, 22)
— **Hannah** (1 Samuel 1:2, 5, 7–8, 11, 20)
— **Elizabeth** (Luke 1:6–7, 25, 58)

Myths About Infertility

Myth: "Infertility is rare."

Truth: One in six couples of childbearing age is infertile.[133]

Myth: "Once you have given birth to a child, you can always have another."

Truth: Secondary infertility is more common than primary infertility due to onset of medical problems and the lessening of fertility as the couple ages.[134]

Myth: "Infertility is synonymous with sterility."

Truth: Sterility is an *irreversible condition*. Infertility is a *current condition* that can possibly be altered.[135]

Myth: "My highest calling is to bear and raise children."

Truth: Your highest calling is to be conformed to the character of Christ.

"Those God foreknew he also predestined to be conformed to the image of his Son" (ROMANS 8:29).

Myth: "I could love only a child that is my own."

Truth: An adoptive child can be loved just as deeply as a birth child.

"Now then, your two sons born to you in Egypt before I came to you here will be reckoned as mine; Ephraim and Manasseh will be mine, just as Reuben and Simeon are mine" (GENESIS 48:5).

Myth: "My infertility is a punishment from God."
Truth: Infertility is not a punishment, but is rather a physical condition with a variety of causes and treatments.[136]

"There is now no condemnation for those who are in Christ Jesus" (ROMANS 8:1).

Myth: "If we adopt a child, then we'll probably have our own biological child."

Truth: Adoption is not a cure for infertility, and there is no guarantee that adopting will lead to pregnancy.

"All a person's ways seem pure to them, but motives are weighed by the LORD" (PROVERBS 16:2).

The LORD is close to the brokenhearted
and saves those who are crushed in spirit.
(PSALM 34:18)

Coping for Couples[137]

Communicate the love you have for your spouse.

"No one ever hated their own body, but they feed and care for their body, just as Christ does the church—for we are members of his body. 'For this reason a man will leave his father and mother and be united to his wife, and the two will become one flesh'" (EPHESIANS 5:29–31).

Confess the fears and feelings you have regarding childlessness.

"An honest answer is like a kiss on the lips" (PROVERBS 24:26).

Key Verse to Memorize

"The LORD is close to the brokenhearted and saves those who are crushed in spirit."
(PSALM 34:18)

Compliment, affirm, and support your spouse verbally.

"Do not let any unwholesome talk come out of your mouths, but only what is helpful for building others up according to their needs, that it may benefit those who listen" (EPHESIANS 4:29).

Confront difficulties and differences directly.

"Better is open rebuke than hidden love" (PROVERBS 27:5).

Commit each day to the sovereignty of the Lord Jesus Christ.

"This is the day that the LORD has made; let us rejoice and be glad in it" (PSALM 118:24 ESV).

Crucify selfish desires and become a living sacrifice for your spouse.

"I urge you, brothers and sisters, in view of God's mercy, to offer your bodies as a living sacrifice, holy and pleasing to God—this is your true and proper worship" (ROMANS 12:1).

Bear one another's burdens, and so fulfill the law of Christ.
(GALATIANS 6:2 ESV)

Evaluate the Options

O—Open your heart to accepting a marriage without children.[138]

"Godliness with contentment is great gain" (1 TIMOTHY 6:6).

P—Participate in infertility tests to help identify possible alternatives.[139]

"All who are prudent act with knowledge" (PROVERBS 13:16).

T—Trade parenting for other roles in life that can be just as rewarding.

"In their hearts humans plan their course, but the LORD establishes their steps" (PROVERBS 16:9).

I—Invest your life in the lives of others.[140]

"Enlarge the place of your tent, stretch your tent curtains wide, do not hold back; lengthen your cords, strengthen your stakes" (ISAIAH 54:2).

O—Offer long-term relationships to nieces, nephews, and other young people.

"'Sing, barren woman, you who never bore a child; burst into song, shout for joy, you who were never in labor; because more are the children of the desolate woman than of her who has a husband,' says the LORD" (ISAIAH 54:1).

N—Nurture a deep marital relationship with your spouse.

"That is why a man leaves his father and mother and is united to his wife, and they become one flesh" (GENESIS 2:24).

S—Seek adoption as an option.[141]

"When the child grew older, she took him to Pharaoh's daughter and he became her son. She named him Moses, saying, 'I drew him out of the water'" (EXODUS 2:10).

Pathway from Pain to Peace[142]

Assumption: "Naturally, I'll have children."

Anxiety: "Is something wrong?"

Denial: "It's just a matter of time."

Shock: "I never dreamed this would happen to me!"

Anger: "It's not fair that this could happen to me!"

Bargaining: "God, give me a child, and I'll be a better person."

Guilt: "This must be punishment for sin."

Isolation and Depression: "I'll never be like others. I'll never be happy."

Apathy: "It doesn't really matter."

Grief: "The desire of my life is destroyed."

Seeking: "God, please help me understand my pain."

Acceptance and Growth: "I'll seek God's desire for my life and focus on serving others."

Peace: "Thank You, God, for revealing Yourself to me through my pain."

Don'ts for Friends and Relatives[143]

Don't assume that every couple without children chooses not to have children.

Don't underestimate the grief a couple without children may be experiencing.

Don't ask why a couple does not have children.

Don't be afraid to discuss the problem if they know that you really love them and care about them.

Perfume and incense bring joy to the heart,
and the pleasantness of a friend
springs from their heartfelt advice.
(PROVERBS 27:9)

My Personalized Plan

I will . . .

Bring my burdens to God in prayer.
"Praise be to the Lord, to God our Savior, who daily bears our burdens" (PSALM 68:19)

Trust God even when I can't understand.
"Trust in the LORD with all your heart and lean not on your own understanding; in all your ways submit to him, and he will make your paths straight" (PROVERBS 3:5–6).

Believe that God has a plan and purpose for me, whether I have children or not.
"The LORD will fulfill his purpose for me; your steadfast love, O LORD, endures forever" (PSALM 138:8 ESV).

Seek comfort in God's Word.

"Everything that was written in the past was written to teach us, so that through the endurance taught in the Scriptures and the encouragement they provide we might have hope" (Romans 15:4).

Key Passage to Read

Isaiah 54:1–8

Talk with my spouse about our situation and how to move forward, sharing my hopes and burdens.

"Carry each other's burdens, and in this way you will fulfill the law of Christ" (Galatians 6:2).

Consider finding a support group and/or talking with trusted friends about my situation and emotions.

"In an abundance of counselors there is safety" (Proverbs 11:14 esv).

Put my hope in God, not in my circumstances.

"Put your hope in the Lord, for with the Lord is unfailing love and with him is full redemption" (Psalm 130:7).

Thank God for His faithfulness and compassion.

"Because of the Lord's great love we are not consumed, for his compassions never fail. They are new every morning; great is your faithfulness" (Lamentations 3:22–23).

Questions & Answers

Question: "How can I better understand infertility so I can pray for and encourage others?"

Answer: Here are a few ideas for understanding those struggling with infertility:

— **Understand** that while many couples want children, not all plan to have a family.

— **Understand** that a couple experiencing infertility may be facing grief, especially if they have experienced a miscarriage or failed infertility treatments.

— **Understand** that it is loving and appropriate to respect people's privacy. You can pray for them and be ready to listen and encourage, if they choose to share.

— **Understand** that couples experiencing infertility and other issues in their marriage would most often prefer not to receive unsolicited advice. Pray for them and ask God to give you a compassionate, loving heart toward them.

- **Understand** that infertility impacts both men and women.
- **Understand** that you don't need to focus every conversation on children. It is good to focus conversations on topics other than having children when people are experiencing infertility.
- **Be ready** and willing to talk with people about infertility if they bring it up. Let them know you love and care about them and ask how you can pray for them.

"By this everyone will know that you are
my disciples, if you love one another."
(JOHN 13:35)

INTIMACY

The Road to Deeper Relationships

God's Heart on Intimacy

God knows you completely.

"Your ways are in full view of the LORD, and he examines all your paths" (PROVERBS 5:21).

God loves you deeply.

"I have loved you with an everlasting love; I have drawn you with unfailing kindness" (JEREMIAH 31:3).

God wants you to know Him intimately.

"Now this is eternal life: that they know you, the only true God, and Jesus Christ, whom you have sent" (JOHN 17:3).

God wants you to be vulnerable with him, trusting Him with your innermost thoughts and feelings.

"Trust in him at all times, you people; pour out your hearts to him, for God is our refuge" (PSALM 62:8).

God wants you to know that you'll find grace when you come to Him for help.

"Let us then approach God's throne of grace with confidence, so that we may receive mercy and find grace to help us in our time of need" (HEBREWS 4:16).

God wants you to be a trustworthy person, one whom others can trust with their thoughts and feelings.

"A gossip goes around telling secrets, but those who are trustworthy can keep a confidence" (PROVERBS 11:13 NLT).

God wants you to have a close and intimate relationship with your spouse.

"'For this reason a man will leave his father and mother and be united to his wife, and the two will become one flesh.' So they are no longer two, but one flesh" (MARK 10:7–8).

God wants you to have close, intimate, honest relationships with fellow believers.

"Each of you must put off falsehood and speak truthfully to your neighbor, for we are all members of one body" (EPHESIANS 4:25).

God wants you to have close, intimate, committed friendships.

"There are 'friends' who destroy each other, but a real friend sticks closer than a brother" (PROVERBS 18:24 NLT).

God wants you to exercise appropriate caution when establishing intimate relationships.

"Above all else, guard your heart, for everything you do flows from it" (PROVERBS 4:23).

God wants you to tell others that they can have a close, personal relationship with God.

"We are therefore Christ's ambassadors, as though God were making his appeal through us. We implore you on Christ's behalf: Be reconciled to God" (2 CORINTHIANS 5:20).

God wants you to look forward to the day when you will see Jesus face-to-face and know Him fully.

"Now we see only a reflection as in a mirror; then we shall see face to face. Now I know in part; then I shall know fully, even as I am fully known" (1 CORINTHIANS 13:12).

Roads Toward Intimacy[144]

Agreement—Choose a relationship with someone who has the same basic beliefs and values.

"Do not be yoked together with unbelievers. For what do righteousness and wickedness have in common? Or what fellowship can light have with darkness? . . . Or what does a believer have in common with an unbeliever? . . . Come out from them and be separate" (2 CORINTHIANS 6:14–15, 17).

Commitment—Pledge to maintain the relationship as an act of the will.

"When a man makes a vow to the LORD or takes an oath to obligate himself by a pledge, he must not break his word but must do everything he said" (NUMBERS 30:2).

Encouragement—Compliment and build others up.

"Encourage one another and build each other up, just as in fact you are doing" (1 THESSALONIANS 5:11).

Faithfulness—Maintain lasting loyalty, regardless of the circumstances.

"Let love and faithfulness never leave you; bind them around your neck, write them on the tablet of your heart" (PROVERBS 3:3).

Forgiveness—Give up personal rights and release hurts and offenses to God.

"Bear with each other and forgive one another if any of you has a grievance against someone. Forgive as the Lord forgave you" (COLOSSIANS 3:13).

Gentleness—Communicate with kind, tender words and actions.

"A gentle answer turns away wrath, but a harsh word stirs up anger" (PROVERBS 15:1).

Honesty—Respond truthfully with a willingness to accept mutual correction.

"Wounds from a friend can be trusted, but an enemy multiplies kisses" (PROVERBS 27:6).

Humility—Know your own faults and weaknesses.

"Be completely humble and gentle; be patient, bearing with one another in love" (EPHESIANS 4:2).

Love—Take the most redemptive, edifying, and constructive action possible on behalf of another.

"This is how we know what love is: Jesus Christ laid down his life for us. And we ought to lay down our lives for our brothers and sisters" (1 JOHN 3:16).

Key Verses to Memorize

I pray that you,
being rooted and established in love,
may have power, together with
all the Lord's holy people, to grasp
how wide and long and high and deep
is the love of Christ, and to know
this love that surpasses knowledge—
that you may be filled to the measure
of all the fullness of God.
(EPHESIANS 3:17–19)

Patience—Be self-controlled, calm, and slow to anger.

"Whoever is patient has great understanding, but one who is quick-tempered displays folly" (PROVERBS 14:29).

Respect—Honor and put others above yourself.

"Be devoted to one another in love. Honor one another above yourselves" (ROMANS 12:10).

Spiritual Maturity—Grow and deepen your personal relationship with the Lord.

"Grow in the grace and knowledge of our Lord and Savior Jesus Christ" (2 PETER 3:18).

Avenues of Avoiding Intimacy[145]

Attitudes and behaviors that hinder intimacy include:

Alcoholism	Dishonesty	Overeating
Aloofness	Distrust	Restlessness
Apathy	Drug addictions	Sarcasm

Busyness	Faultfinding	Unforgiveness
Defensiveness	Frequent absence	Unresolved anger
Depression	Guilt	Workaholism

Ways That Past Pain Detours Intimacy[146]

Avoiding risk
— Due to negative messages

Evading personal disclosure
— Unwilling to reveal failures and weaknesses

Resisting vulnerability
— Fearing the loss of independence and self-determination

Living with guilt
— Failing to accept forgiveness and receive freedom

Remembering past rejection
— Rejection from others and/or self

"Forget the former things;
do not dwell on the past."
(ISAIAH 43:18)

Intimacy with God

An intimate relationship with God . . .

Is to be your desire as a Christian.

"I consider everything a loss because of the surpassing worth of knowing Christ Jesus my Lord. . . . I want to know Christ—yes, to know the power of his resurrection and participation in his sufferings" (PHILIPPIANS 3:8, 10).

Includes an awareness of His Son, Jesus Christ, living within your heart.

"Christ will make his home in your hearts as you trust in him" (EPHESIANS 3:17 NLT).

Involves studying His Word.

"All Scripture is God-breathed and is useful for teaching, rebuking, correcting and training in righteousness, so that the servant of God may be thoroughly equipped for every good work" (2 TIMOTHY 3:16–17).

Involves rejoicing in Him, praying to Him, and thanking Him.

"Rejoice always, pray continually, give thanks in all circumstances; for this is God's will for you in Christ Jesus" (1 THESSALONIANS 5:16–18).

Involves seeking to obey Him in all things.

"Teach these new disciples to obey all the commands I have given you. And be sure of this: I am with you always, even to the end of the age" (MATTHEW 28:20 NLT).

Involves trusting Him and seeking His direction for your life.

"Trust in the LORD with all your heart and lean not on your own understanding; in all your ways submit to him, and he will make your paths straight" (PROVERBS 3:5–6).

Involves telling others about Jesus.

"My friends, I want you to know that through Jesus the forgiveness of sins is proclaimed to you" (ACTS 13:38).

My Personalized Plan

In nurturing deeper intimacy with God, I will prioritize the time I spend with Him in:

- — Studying, memorizing, personalizing, and meditating on His Word
- — Praying and listening closely to His Word
- — Applying biblical principles to my life and keeping a journal of my journey with Him
- — Being actively involved in a local church body

In nurturing deeper intimacy within my committed relationships, I will prioritize time together:

- — Sharing fun experiences as well as doubts, hurts, fears, and disappointments
- — Revealing struggles, challenges, failures, hopes, longings, and deep desires
- — Expressing spiritual, physical, and emotional encouragement and appreciation
- — Focusing on growing spiritually, mentally, and emotionally and holding one another accountable

Key Passages to Read

Intimacy with God
Psalm 73:23–28

Intimacy in Friendship
Ecclesiastes 4:8–12

Intimacy in Marriage
Ephesians 5:25–28

In nurturing moderate intimacy within my casual relationships, I will make time for:

- — Engaging in dialogue regarding their interests, friends, family, and life goals
- — Creating safety by not judging or being defensive and by maintaining honesty
- — Reaching out emotionally by sharing relevant life experiences
- — Offering spiritual and emotional encouragement and opportunities for growth

Follow God's example, therefore,
as dearly loved children and walk in the way of love,
just as Christ loved us and gave himself up for us
as a fragrant offering and sacrifice to God.
(EPHESIANS 5:1–2)

Questions & Answers

Question: "Won't an intimate relationship with one special person provide all the love, significance, and security I need?"[147]

Answer: No one person, except for God Himself, can meet all your needs for love, significance, and security. But when God is in your relationship, the bond between the three of you will be strong enough to weather the storms of life.

Though one may be overpowered,
two can defend themselves.
A cord of three strands is not quickly broken.
(ECCLESIASTES 4:12)

Question: "If I reveal my true self, won't I just be hurt?"

Answer: Being vulnerable does open the door to the possibility of pain, but it also opens the door to the opportunity of developing a deep relationship, one with true heart-to-heart intimacy.

Dear friends, let us love one another, for love comes from God.
(1 JOHN 4:7)

JESUS: IS HE GOD?

Is the Deity of Christ Defendable?

God's Heart on Jesus

God declares that Jesus is His beloved Son.

"A voice from heaven said, 'This is my Son, whom I love; with him I am well pleased'" (MATTHEW 3:17).

God reveals Himself fully in the person of Jesus Christ.

"God was pleased to have all his fullness dwell in him" (COLOSSIANS 1:19).

God is honored by honoring Jesus.

"The Father judges no one, but has entrusted all judgment to the Son, that all may honor the Son just as they honor the Father. Whoever does not honor the Son does not honor the Father, who sent him" (JOHN 5:22–23).

God reconciles all things through Christ.

"Through him God reconciled everything to himself. He made peace with everything in heaven and on earth by means of Christ's blood on the cross" (COLOSSIANS 1:20 NLT).

God will judge the world through Jesus Christ.

"He has set a day when he will judge the world with justice by the man he has appointed. He has given proof of this to everyone by raising him from the dead" (ACTS 17:31).

God justifies believers in Christ—declaring them righteous in His sight.

"Know that a person is not justified by the works of the law, but by faith in Jesus Christ. So we, too, have put our faith in Christ Jesus that we may be justified by faith in Christ and not by the works of the law, because by the works of the law no one will be justified" (GALATIANS 2:16).

God sanctifies believers in Christ—helping them grow into His character.

"All of us who have had that veil removed can see and reflect the glory of the Lord. And the Lord—who is the Spirit—makes us more and more like him as we are changed into his glorious image" (2 CORINTHIANS 3:18 NLT).

God will glorify believers in Christ—making them like Christ when He returns.

"We know that when Christ appears, we shall be like him, for we shall see him as he is" (1 JOHN 3:2).

God wants you to believe in Jesus Christ for salvation—to receive eternal life.

"God so loved the world that he gave his one and only Son, that whoever believes in him shall not perish but have eternal life" (JOHN 3:16).

God wants you to grow in your knowledge of Jesus Christ.

"Grow in the grace and knowledge of our Lord and Savior Jesus Christ. To him be glory both now and forever! Amen" (2 PETER 3:18).

God wants you to make disciples of Jesus Christ.

"Jesus came to them and said, 'All authority in heaven and on earth has been given to me. Therefore go and make disciples of all nations, baptizing them in the name of the Father and of the Son and of the Holy Spirit, and teaching them to obey everything I have commanded you. And surely I am with you always, to the very end of the age'" (MATTHEW 28:18–20).

God wants you to love others just as Christ loved you.

"A new command I give you: Love one another. As I have loved you, so you must love one another. By this everyone will know that you are my disciples, if you love one another" (JOHN 13:34–35).

"What about you?" he asked. "Who do you say I am?"
(MATTHEW 16:15)

Old and New Testaments Present Jesus as God

Jesus is the First and the Last.

"This is what the LORD says—Israel's King and Redeemer, the LORD Almighty: I am the first and I am the last; apart from me there is no God" (ISAIAH 44:6).

"When I saw him, I fell at his feet as though dead. Then he placed his right hand on me and said: 'Do not be afraid. I am the First and the Last'" (REVELATION 1:17).

Jesus is the Lord, who provides salvation.

"Everyone who calls on the name of the LORD will be saved; for on Mount Zion and in Jerusalem there will be deliverance, as the LORD has said, even among the survivors whom the LORD calls" (JOEL 2:32).

"Everyone who calls on the name of the Lord will be saved" (ROMANS 10:13).

Jesus is the Creator.

"Do you not know? Have you not heard? The LORD is the everlasting God, the Creator of the ends of the earth. He will not grow tired or weary, and his understanding no one can fathom" (ISAIAH 40:28).

"Through him all things were made; without him nothing was made that has been made" (JOHN 1:3).

Jesus is the originator and sustainer of the universe.

"You alone are the LORD. *You made the heavens, even the highest heavens, and all their starry host, the earth and all that is on it, the seas and all that is in them. You give life to everything, and the multitudes of heaven worship you"* (NEHEMIAH 9:6).

"In him all things were created: things in heaven and on earth, visible and invisible, whether thrones or powers or rulers or authorities; all things were created through him and for him. He is before all things, and in him all things hold together" (COLOSSIANS 1:16–17).

"I [Jesus] *and the Father are one."*
(JOHN 10:30)

How to Love God & Others Like Jesus

Love God Like Jesus

"'Love the Lord your God with all your heart and with all your soul and with all your mind.' This is the first and greatest commandment."
(MATTHEW 22:37–38)

Obey completely.

"I have come down from heaven to do the will of God who sent me, not to do my own will" (JOHN 6:38 NLT).

Pray reverently.

"During the days of Jesus' life on earth, he offered up prayers and petitions with fervent cries and tears to the one who could save him from death, and he was heard because of his reverent submission" (HEBREWS 5:7).

Work heartily.

"Whatever you do, work at it with all your heart, as working for the Lord, not for human masters, since you know that you will receive an inheritance from the Lord as a reward. It is the Lord Christ you are serving" (COLOSSIANS 3:23–24).

Deny yourself daily.

"If any of you wants to be my follower, you must give up your own way, take up your cross daily, and follow me" (LUKE 9:23 NLT).

Key Verses to Memorize

"In the beginning was the Word,
and the Word was with God,
and the Word was God. . . .
The Word became flesh
and made his dwelling among us.
We have seen his glory, the glory of the one and only Son, who came from the Father,
full of grace and truth."
(JOHN 1:1, 14)

Suffer willingly.

"God called you to do good, even if it means suffering, just as Christ suffered for you. He is your example, and you must follow in his steps" (1 PETER 2:21 NLT).

Give thanks consistently.

"Give thanks in all circumstances; for this is God's will for you in Christ Jesus" (1 THESSALONIANS 5:18).

Love Others Like Jesus

"And the second is like it: 'Love your neighbor as yourself.'
All the Law and the Prophets hang on these two commandments."
(MATTHEW 22:39–40)

Love sacrificially.

"My command is this: Love each other as I have loved you. Greater love has no one than this: to lay down one's life for one's friends" (JOHN 15:12–13).

Serve humbly.

"Now that I, your Lord and Teacher, have washed your feet, you also should wash one another's feet. I have set you an example that you should do as I have done for you" (JOHN 13:14–15).

Forgive completely.

"Be kind and compassionate to one another, forgiving each other, just as in Christ God forgave you" (EPHESIANS 4:32).

Build up others spiritually.

"We must not just please ourselves. We should help others do what is right and build them up in the Lord. For even Christ didn't live to please himself" (ROMANS 15:1–3 NLT).

Accept others graciously.

"Accept each other just as Christ has accepted you so that God will be given glory" (ROMANS 15:7 NLT).

Help others practically.

"This is how we know what love is: Jesus Christ laid down his life for us. And we ought to lay down our lives for our brothers and sisters. If anyone has material possessions and sees a brother or sister in need but has no pity on them, how can the love of God be in that person?" (1 JOHN 3:16–17).

"As I have loved you, so you must love one another.
By this everyone will know that you are my disciples,
if you love one another."
(JOHN 13:34–35)

Did Jesus Claim to Be God?

According to His own claim . . .
Jesus and the heavenly Father both have:

Equality in activity, both doing the same work

"Jesus gave them this answer: 'Very truly I tell you, the Son can do nothing by himself; he can do only what he sees his Father doing, because whatever the Father does the Son also does'" (JOHN 5:19).

Equality in knowledge; nothing is hidden

"The Father loves the Son and shows him all he does. Yes, and he will show him even greater works than these, so that you will be amazed" (JOHN 5:20).

Equality in giving people life after death

"Just as the Father raises the dead and gives them life, even so the Son gives life to whom he is pleased to give it" (JOHN 5:21).

Equality in passing judgment on people

"The Father judges no one, but has entrusted all judgment to the Son" (JOHN 5:22).

Key Passage to Read

The Gospel of John

Equality in receiving honor from people

"That all may honor the Son just as they honor the Father. Whoever does not honor the Son does not honor the Father, who sent him" (JOHN 5:23).

Equality in bestowing eternal life to people

"Very truly I tell you, whoever hears my word and believes him who sent me has eternal life and will not be judged but has crossed over from death to life" (JOHN 5:24).

Equality in being self-existent—both always in existence

"As the Father has life in himself, so he has granted the Son also to have life in himself" (JOHN 5:26).

For this reason they tried all the more to kill him;
not only was he breaking the Sabbath,
but he was even calling God his own Father,
making himself equal with God.
(JOHN 5:18)

My Personalized Plan

I will . . .

Learn about Jesus.

— I will read the Bible for myself to discover the life and teachings of Jesus.

— I will read books and talk with a pastor to understand who Jesus is.

"He said to them, 'This is what I told you while I was still with you: Everything must be fulfilled that is written about me in the Law of Moses, the Prophets and the Psalms.' Then he opened their minds so they could understand the Scriptures" (LUKE 24:44–45).

Receive Jesus.

— I will pray to receive Jesus as my personal Lord and Savior, if I have not already received Him and His free gift of salvation.

— I will receive His love and grace for me each day.

"To all who did receive him, to those who believed in his name, he gave the right to become children of God" (JOHN 1:12).

Abide in Jesus.

— I will spend time with Jesus each day through prayer and reading the Bible.

— I will meditate and memorize Bible verses, so His Word is always in my heart.

"Abide in me, and I in you. As the branch cannot bear fruit by itself, unless it abides in the vine, neither can you, unless you abide in me. I am the vine; you are the branches. Whoever abides in me and I in him, he it is that bears much fruit, for apart from me you can do nothing. . . . As the Father has loved me, so have I loved you. Abide in my love" (JOHN 15:4–5, 9 ESV).

Follow Jesus.

— I will ask Jesus for guidance to lead me in all the areas of my life.

— I will follow Jesus all the days of my life, even when it is difficult.

"My sheep listen to my voice; I know them, and they follow me" (JOHN 10:27).

Love Jesus.

— I will reflect on Jesus' love for me each day, thanking Him for His grace.

— I will strive to love Jesus through my words, actions, and decisions.

"We love because he first loved us" (1 JOHN 4:19).

Tell others about Jesus.

— I will share the good news of Jesus' salvation with those around me.

— I will share my testimony as a source of hope for others.

"We are therefore Christ's ambassadors, as though God were making his appeal through us. We implore you on Christ's behalf: Be reconciled to God" (2 CORINTHIANS 5:20).

"Anyone who has seen me has seen the Father."
(JOHN 14:9)

Questions & Answers

Question: "If Jesus was God, how could He possibly have been human at the same time?"

Answer: Jesus did not lose His deity by becoming a human being. The incarnation means that Jesus, being the eternal Son of God, took on human flesh. The apostle John wrote, *"In the beginning was the Word, and the Word was with God, and the Word was God.... The Word became flesh and made his dwelling among us"* (John 1:1, 14).

By taking on humanity, He did not lose His divinity. During His life, Jesus performed many miracles to show His deity. Yet as a human being, He experienced hunger (Matthew 21:18) and thirst (John 4:7). He got tired at times and slept (Mark 4:38). He wept (John 11:35) and rejoiced (Luke 10:21).

Jesus had to be both God and man to be the perfect sacrifice for sin. As God, He was sinless. As man, He was flesh and blood and had a body to be sacrificed. The apostle Paul wrote, *"in Christ all the fullness of the Deity lives in bodily form"* (Colossians 2:9). Being human, He qualified to be the substitute for humanity and to die the death we deserved because of sin. Being God, He qualified to be an acceptable sacrifice.

Since the children have flesh and blood,
he too shared in their humanity so that by his death
he might break the power of him who holds
the power of death—that is, the devil....
For this reason he had to be made like them,
fully human in every way, in order that he
might become a merciful and faithful high priest
in service to God, and that he might make
atonement for the sins of the people.
Because he himself suffered when he was tempted,
he is able to help those who are being tempted.
(HEBREWS 2:14, 17–18).

LEADERSHIP

Unleashing the Leader in You

God's Heart on Leadership

God leads us with His truth.

"Lead me by your truth and teach me, for you are the God who saves me. All day long I put my hope in you" (PSALM 25:5 NLT).

God calls leaders to be caring, watchful, servant-hearted shepherds.

"Be shepherds of God's flock that is under your care, watching over them—not because you must, but because you are willing, as God wants you to be; not pursuing dishonest gain, but eager to serve; not lording it over those entrusted to you, but being examples to the flock" (1 PETER 5:2–3).

God gives us different gifts to lead in different areas.

"We have different gifts, according to the grace given to each of us. If your gift is prophesying, then prophesy in accordance with your faith; if it is serving, then serve; if it is teaching, then teach; if it is to encourage, then give encouragement; if it is giving, then give generously; if it is to lead, do it diligently; if it is to show mercy, do it cheerfully" (ROMANS 12:6–8).

God encourages servant leadership.

"Those who are the greatest among you should take the lowest rank, and the leader should be like a servant" (LUKE 22:26 NLT).

God gives us godly leaders as examples to follow.

"Remember your leaders, who spoke the word of God to you. Consider the outcome of their way of life and imitate their faith" (HEBREWS 13:7).

God gives leaders to raise up more leaders.

"The things you have heard me say in the presence of many witnesses entrust to reliable people who will also be qualified to teach others" (2 TIMOTHY 2:2).

God wants leaders to have integrity and skill to shepherd others.

"David shepherded them with integrity of heart; with skillful hands he led them" (PSALM 78:72).

God desires leaders to exhibit godly characteristics.

"As God's chosen people, holy and dearly loved, clothe yourselves with compassion, kindness, humility, gentleness and patience" (COLOSSIANS 3:12).

God wants leaders to set a good example.

"Be an example to all believers in what you say, in the way you live, in your love, your faith, and your purity" (1 TIMOTHY 4:12 NLT).

God wants leaders to be grateful and honor Christ in all they do.

"Whatever you do, whether in word or deed, do it all in the name of the Lord Jesus, giving thanks to God the Father through him" (COLOSSIANS 3:17).

God wants leaders to seek His wisdom when making decisions.

"If any of you lacks wisdom, you should ask God, who gives generously to all without finding fault, and it will be given to you" (JAMES 1:5).

God wants leaders to delegate and not be overburdened as a leader.

"You're going to wear yourself out—and the people, too. This job is too heavy a burden for you to handle all by yourself. . . . Select from all the people some capable, honest men who fear God and hate bribes. Appoint them as leaders over groups of one thousand, one hundred, fifty, and ten" (EXODUS 18:18, 21 NLT).

We know that in all things God works
for the good of those who love him,
who have been called according to his purpose.
(ROMANS 8:28)

Leadership Principles from the Book of Proverbs

Don't allow yourself to be isolated or insulated from others.

Do let others know they are free to come to you with their advice and perspective on new and different ideas.

"The way of fools seems right to them, but the wise listen to advice" (12:15).

Don't feel you must appear perfect.

Do confess your failures, and you will receive mercy.

"Whoever conceals their sins does not prosper, but the one who confesses and renounces them finds mercy" (28:13).

Don't think others can't see when you act inconsistently.

Do follow through with whatever you've promised, as long as it's just and right.

"To do what is right and just is more acceptable to the LORD than sacrifice" (21:3).

Don't brag about your own accomplishments.

Do wait for someone else to shine the spotlight on you.

"Let someone else praise you, and not your own mouth; an outsider, and not your own lips" (27:2).

Don't fail to hold others accountable.

Do explain your expectations, provide each person with responsibilities, and set deadlines for completion.

"The hearts of the wise make their mouths prudent, and their lips promote instruction" (16:23).

Don't allow yourself to become prideful.

Do maintain a heart of humility, understanding your own limitations and weakness, and depending on the Lord's leadership in your life.

"Pride goes before destruction, a haughty spirit before a fall" (16:18).

Humble yourselves, therefore, under God's mighty hand,
that he may lift you up in due time.
(1 PETER 5:6)

What Is a Cycle of Christian Leadership?

The Christian leader . . .

1. **Receives** a calling from God.
2. **Reveals** God's possible plan for the people.
3. **Resolves** to help others envision the fulfillment of God's plan for them.
4. **Relies** on the Holy Spirit to delineate the new mission.
5. **Rallies** the people to move forward to accomplish the new mission.

Key Verse to Memorize

Follow my example,
as I follow the example of Christ.
(1 CORINTHIANS 11:1)

How Can You Be a More Effective Leader?

My life aligns with God's direction.

"Jesus often withdrew to the wilderness for prayer" (LUKE 5:16 NLT).

I daily receive my assignment from God.

"Seek the LORD and his strength; seek his presence continually!" (1 CHRONICLES 16:11 ESV).

I depend on God to live a life of action.

"It is God who is at work in you, both to will and to work for His good pleasure" (PHILIPPIANS 2:13 NASB).

My life is designed to follow God and assist in how He is working.

"You call me Teacher and Lord, and you are right, for so I am. If I then, your Lord and Teacher, have washed your feet, you also ought to wash one another's feet" (JOHN 13:13–14 ESV).

I allow myself to be held accountable.

"Encourage one another and build each other up" (1 THESSALONIANS 5:11).

How Can a Servant Leader Improve?

A servant leader needs development in . . .

Peacemaking

"Blessed are the peacemakers, for they will be called children of God" (MATTHEW 5:9).

Steadfastness

"Blessed are those who have been persecuted for the sake of righteousness, for theirs is the kingdom of heaven" (MATTHEW 5:10 NASB).

Surrender to the Lord

"Blessed are you when people insult you and persecute you, and falsely say all kinds of evil against you because of Me. Rejoice and be glad, for your reward in heaven is great; for in the same way they persecuted the prophets who were before you" (MATTHEW 5:11–12 NASB)

Effective Leadership

R—Relational—Leaders realize that relationships built with those they lead form the basis on which they move forward in accomplishing the goals or tasks that God has given them. Each relationship is forged on a foundation of trust and integrity.

E—Expectations—Communication is the lifeline to leadership. Unspoken or poorly communicated expectations can quickly lead to conflict, and unresolved conflict can create a breach of trust in the relationship. Broken trust attacks and weakens the very foundation on which the relationship is built.

A—Accountability—Leaders know that accountability is essential to cohesion in a team. To answer to no one or to no overriding principles leaves a leader ungrounded and untethered, disconnected from those being led.

L—Learning—Accomplishment of any goal falls short of full completion if the experience is not assessed and eventually applied. Known as *reflective learning,* leaders evaluate the experience: What worked, what challenges were faced, and what can be learned from problems encountered and overcome to help reach future goals?

My Personalized Plan

I will . . .

Model integrity

— I will remember that those I lead are watching to see if I have integrity.

— I will strive to be the same in the dark as I am in the light—the same in private as I am in public.

"The integrity of the upright guides them, but the unfaithful are destroyed by their duplicity" (PROVERBS 11:3).

Live with conviction

— I will know what I believe and settle my convictions.

— I will write down my core values so that I am clear about what is most important to me.

"Let love and faithfulness never leave you; bind them around your neck, write them on the tablet of your heart" (PROVERBS 3:3).

Help others succeed

— I will build up those I lead, focusing on their growth.

— I will help meet the needs of those I lead.

"Encourage one another and build each other up, just as in fact you are doing" (1 THESSALONIANS 5:11).

Key Passage to Read

Philippians 2:1-11

Master strategic planning

— I will commit my plans to the Lord, asking for His guidance.

— I will help those I lead see the big picture of what is ahead for them.

"Commit to the LORD whatever you do, and he will establish your plans" (PROVERBS 16:3).

Demonstrate effectiveness and efficiency

— I will focus on getting the right tasks done, not simply every task done.

— I will manage my time and others' time well.

"There is a proper time and procedure for every matter" (ECCLESIASTES 8:6).

Share the vision

— I will cast vision, clearly communicating plans and goals.

— I will help people see how they fit into the big picture and how they help fulfill the larger plan.

"Where there is no vision, the people perish" (PROVERBS 29:18 KJV).

Persevere through difficulties

— I will remember my priorities when things get tough.

— I will weather the storms that come my way, looking to God for help.

"May the Lord direct your hearts into God's love and Christ's perseverance" (2 THESSALONIANS 3:5)

Give encouragement

— I will look for character traits to compliment in those I lead.

— I will be on the alert to "catch" others doing something good.

"Encourage one another daily" (HEBREWS 3:13).

Make difficult decisions

— I will strive to do what is right even when it is hard, painful, or unpopular.

— I will aim to please God above pleasing people.

"Am I now trying to win the approval of human beings, or of God? Or am I trying to please people? If I were still trying to please people, I would not be a servant of Christ" (GALATIANS 1:10).

Display courage

— I will ask God to help me lead with courage and conviction.

— I will remember that God is with me, calling me to lead without fear.

"Have I not commanded you? Be strong and courageous. Do not be afraid; do not be discouraged, for the LORD your God will be with you wherever you go" (JOSHUA 1:9).

Questions & Answers

Question: "How do I know if God is calling me into leadership?"

Answer: The question is not whether God is calling you to be a leader—but rather, what type of leadership God may have for you. How is He asking you to demonstrate leadership?

Leadership starts within the leader. The character of the leader will determine how God will use them. Character based on integrity means being the same in the dark as you are in the light—the same in private as you are in public.

As you respond to God's calling on your life into leadership, remember that there can be a long span of time between the initial call and its fulfillment. In other words, God may first want to train you so you grow as a leader.

God's "leadership training" is often intensive and extensive. In our culture, we often look to speed—but God looks for heart adjustment and discernment. For example, prior to ruling as king, David was anointed by the prophet Samuel. Then David killed Goliath, but spent years running from King Saul in the wilderness before actually serving as king.

Wandering in the desert is not typically a popular choice for leadership training, but God's ways are different from our own. God's training ground is often in a desertlike environment. Moses spent years in the desert before encountering God in the burning bush, and Jesus Himself spent forty days in the wilderness to be tested before His ministry officially began.

I will instruct you and teach
you in the way you should go;
I will counsel you with my loving eye on you.
(Psalm 32:8)

LONELINESS

From Longing to Belonging

God's Heart for the Lonely

God is always with you.

"Surely I am with you always, to the very end of the age" (MATTHEW 28:20).

God will never leave you.

"The LORD himself goes before you and will be with you; he will never leave you nor forsake you. Do not be afraid; do not be discouraged" (DEUTERONOMY 31:8).

God says it is not good to be alone.

"The LORD God said, 'It is not good for the man to be alone. I will make a helper suitable for him'" (GENESIS 2:18).

God wants you to turn to Him when you're lonely to find grace.

"Turn to me and be gracious to me, for I am lonely and afflicted. Relieve the troubles of my heart and free me from my anguish" (PSALM 25:16–17).

God calls you into relationship with Him and His Son, Jesus Christ.

"God is faithful, who has called you into fellowship with his Son, Jesus Christ our Lord" (1 CORINTHIANS 1:9).

God gives you His Spirit to be with you and live in you.

"The Spirit of truth. The world cannot accept him, because it neither sees him nor knows him. But you know him, for he lives with you and will be in you" (JOHN 14:17).

God wants you to be involved in a local church for fellowship and spiritual growth.

"They devoted themselves to the apostles' teaching and to fellowship, to the breaking of bread and to prayer" (ACTS 2:42).

God emphasizes the value of relationships.

"Two people are better off than one, for they can help each other succeed. If one person falls, the other can reach out and help. But someone who falls alone is in real trouble" (ECCLESIASTES 4:9–10 NLT).

God gives us family and friendships to protect against loneliness.

"God sets the lonely in families" (PSALM 68:6).

God wants you to pursue meaningful friendships.

"As iron sharpens iron, so a friend sharpens a friend" (Proverbs 27:17 NLT).

God wants you to reach out to others who feel burdened and alone.

"Carry each other's burdens, and in this way you will fulfill the law of Christ" (Galatians 6:2).

God promises to be with His people forever in heaven.

"I heard a loud shout from the throne, saying, 'Look, God's home is now among his people! He will live with them, and they will be his people. God himself will be with them. He will wipe every tear from their eyes, and there will be no more death or sorrow or crying or pain. All these things are gone forever'" (Revelation 21:3–4 NLT).

You have searched me, Lord,
and you know me. . . .
Where can I go from your Spirit?
Where can I flee from your presence?
(Psalm 139:1, 7)

Loneliness Inventory

Check (✓) each statement that applies to you.

- ☐ "I feel all alone."
- ☐ "I don't believe anyone understands the way I feel."
- ☐ "I don't really matter to anyone."
- ☐ "I don't have any good qualities that draw people to me."
- ☐ "I have nothing to offer to a relationship."
- ☐ "I can't seem to connect with other people."
- ☐ "I will never find anyone to love me."
- ☐ "I don't feel like I fit in with anyone."
- ☐ "I'm tired of trying to make people like me. I always fail."
- ☐ "I'm empty on the inside."
- ☐ "I'm always left out."
- ☐ "I'm too messed up for anyone to like me or want to be around me."
- ☐ "I'm just a born loser."
- ☐ "I feel like I've been deserted."
- ☐ "I don't deserve to be loved or to have friends."
- ☐ "I think I'm the only one who feels like this."

If you checked five or more of these statements, evaluate how you might be experiencing loneliness. In the biblical book of Job, this godly man experienced and expressed his loneliness:

"My relatives have gone away;
my closest friends have forgotten me."
(Job 19:14)

The Difference Between Being Alone and Being Lonely

Part of the difference between being alone and being lonely involves the sense of being in control.

Solitude is being alone by choice.[148] It is deliberately seeking quiet, private time alone to reflect, to be in prayer, or simply to be still and listen for God's voice. As Psalm 37:7 says: *"Be still before the Lord and wait patiently for him."*

Loneliness, on the other hand, is the emotion that arises when you feel you have little control over being alone.[149] You feel isolated and abandoned, and wish your circumstances were different. Often this is a consequence of a change in your life—a move, a death, a broken relationship, or any situation where you find yourself wishing for attachments you once enjoyed.

Key Verse to Memorize

"The Lord himself goes before you
and will be with you;
he will never leave you nor forsake you.
Do not be afraid; do not be discouraged."
(Deuteronomy 31:8)

Other distinctions between being alone and being lonely include:[150]

Being alone refers to the *physical* . . . the state of being separated from others.

Being lonely refers to the *emotional* . . . the state of feeling isolated, rejected, or desolate.

Being alone can be a *positive experience* . . . a time of creativity and communion with the Lord.

Being lonely is always a *negative feeling* . . . often accompanied by feelings of hopelessness.

Look and see, there is no one at my right hand;
no one is concerned for me.
I have no refuge;
no one cares for my life.
(PSALM 142:4)

What Leads to Loneliness?

Feelings of loneliness are often associated with changes that occur as a normal part of life, such as . . .

C—Circumstances—divorce, death of a loved one, empty nest, loss of a job or home, major move

H—Holidays—unfulfilled expectations, separation from family or friends, memories of the past, lack of plans, singleness

A—Affliction—physical impairment, compromised mental or emotional wellness, chronic or terminal illness, aging, abuse

N—Naiveté—lack of experience in new areas of decision-making, taking on new responsibilities previously performed by another person

G—Goals—career change, retirement, job advancement, pursuit of higher education

E—Estrangement—cheating spouse, marital separation, rebellious children, conflict with friends or coworkers

10 Ways to Be a True Friend

1. **Accept invitations**

   "Make the most of every opportunity in these evil days" (EPHESIANS 5:16 NLT).

2. **Be positive and proactive**

   "Gracious words are a honeycomb, sweet to the soul and healing to the bones" (PROVERBS 16:24).

3. **Focus on being open and real**

   "An honest answer is like a kiss of friendship" (PROVERBS 24:26 NLT).

4. **Have a heart of acceptance**

   "Accept one another, then, just as Christ accepted you, in order to bring praise to God" (ROMANS 15:7).

5. **Be flexible and humble**

   "If you are wise and understand God's ways, prove it by living an honorable life, doing good works with the humility that comes from wisdom" (JAMES 3:13 NLT).

6. **Extend empathy**

   "Finally, all of you, be like-minded, be sympathetic, love one another, be compassionate and humble" (1 PETER 3:8).

7. **Commit to mutuality**

   "Make every effort to do what leads to peace and to mutual edification" (ROMANS 14:19).

8. **Look for ways to love and serve**

   "Greater love has no one than this: to lay down one's life for one's friends" (JOHN 15:13).

9. **Practice forgiveness**

   "Be kind and compassionate to one another, forgiving each other, just as in Christ God forgave you" (EPHESIANS 4:32).

10. **Express gratitude often**

    "I have not stopped giving thanks for you, remembering you in my prayers" (EPHESIANS 1:16).

My Personalized Plan

When my life is void of meaningful relationships and I am feeling all alone and lonely, **I will** . . .

Temper the negative feelings that often accompany my loneliness with the reality that even Jesus felt discouraged, sad, lonely, and grieved at times.

"What, then, shall we say in response to these things? If God is for us, who can be against us? He who did not spare his own Son, but gave him up for us all—how will he not also, along with him, graciously give us all things?" (ROMANS 8:31–32).

Talk to a trained professional such as a pastor, doctor, or counselor when my loneliness and isolation become overwhelming or when it leads to low self-worth, disillusionment, depression, or thoughts of self-harm.

"Turn to me and be gracious to me, for I am lonely and afflicted" (PSALM 25:16).

Turn to Christ to find comfort in my relationship with Him.

"Be strong and courageous. Do not be afraid or terrified because of them, for the LORD your God goes with you; he will never leave you nor forsake you" (DEUTERONOMY 31:6).

Key Passage to Read

Psalm 63:1-8

Thank God that I am His child and have a forever family in the body of Christ.

"Let us continually offer to God a sacrifice of praise—the fruit of lips that openly profess his name. And do not forget to do good and to share with others, for with such sacrifices God is pleased" (HEBREWS 13:15–16).

Think about how God can use me to encourage others when I am willing to be real with them about my struggles.

"A father to the fatherless, a defender of widows, is God in his holy dwelling. God sets the lonely in families, he leads out the prisoners with singing; but the rebellious live in a sun-scorched land" (PSALM 68:5–6).

Take steps to continue growing in my relationships with God, myself, and others.

"He heals the brokenhearted and binds up their wounds" (PSALM 147:3).

Questions & Answers

Question: "My life is full and I'm very active. So why do I often feel lonely?"

Answer: Activity alone does not prevent loneliness. If you are interacting with other people, but only at a superficial level, it could be that you are craving closeness in deeper, more meaningful relationships. Simply being over-involved in activities is not an antidote to loneliness.

If you stay busy in a flurry of activity without truly connecting with others, this can be an attempt to avoid a longing in your heart, certainly for relationships, but especially a longing for God.

"Yes, my soul, find rest in God;
my hope comes from him."
(PSALM 62:5)

Question: "At times I feel like I must get away by myself. Is there something wrong with me wanting to spend time alone?"

Answer: No, solitude is time spent physically apart from others, which can be good for you.

Many people believe that being alone is the same thing as being lonely. However, they usually base their thinking on their own painful experiences.

Healthy solitude is:[151]

— A chosen separation from the press of people

— A healthy haven from unhealthy emotions

— A positive time alone apart from the needs of others

— A respite during grief to process a loss

— A private sanctuary to rest, pray, and meditate

At daybreak, Jesus went out to a solitary place.
(LUKE 4:42)

LYING VS. TRUTHFULNESS

How to Stop Truth Decay

God's Heart on Lying and Telling the Truth

Lying is a sin detested by God.
"The LORD detests lying lips, but he delights in people who are trustworthy" (PROVERBS 12:22).

Lying is contrary to the character of God.
"It is impossible for God to lie" (HEBREWS 6:18).

Lying to others is lying to God.
"You have not lied just to human beings but to God" (ACTS 5:4).

Lying disrupts the unity of Christians.
"Each of you must put off falsehood and speak truthfully to your neighbor, for we are all members of one body" (EPHESIANS 4:25).

Lying, if allowed by leaders, corrupts those who listen.
"If a ruler listens to lies, all his officials become wicked" (PROVERBS 29:12).

Liars go from one sin to another.
"They [the unfaithful] *make ready their tongue like a bow, to shoot lies; it is not by truth that they triumph in the land. They go from one sin to another; they do not acknowledge me* [the Lord]*"* (JEREMIAH 9:3).

Liars who mask their lies as "jokes" are deceptive.
"Like a maniac shooting flaming arrows of death is one who deceives their neighbor and says, 'I was only joking!'" (PROVERBS 26:18–19)

Liars listen attentively to other liars.
"A wicked person listens to deceitful lips; a liar pays attention to a destructive tongue" (PROVERBS 17:4).

Lying tongues won't last forever.
"Truthful lips endure forever, but a lying tongue lasts only a moment" (PROVERBS 12:19).

Lying people will not go unpunished.
"A false witness will not go unpunished, and whoever pours out lies will not go free" (PROVERBS 19:5).

The truth brings delight to the Lord.

"Behold, you delight in truth in the inward being, and you teach me wisdom in the secret heart" (PSALM 51:6 ESV).

The truth is a way of life we can choose.

"I have chosen the way of truth; Your judgments I have laid before me" (PSALM 119:30 NKJV).

The truth brings us into the light.

"Whoever lives by the truth comes into the light, so that it may be seen plainly that what they have done has been done in the sight of God" (JOHN 3:21).

The truth is what we speak from the heart.

"LORD, who may dwell in your sacred tent? Who may live on your holy mountain? The one whose walk is blameless, who does what is righteous, who speaks the truth from their heart" (PSALM 15:1–2).

Key Verse to Memorize

"Set a guard over my mouth, LORD; keep watch over the door of my lips." (PSALM 141:3)

The truth is what will guide us.

"Send out your light and your truth; let them guide me. Let them lead me to your holy mountain, to the place where you live" (PSALM 43:3 NLT).

The truth purifies us.

"Now that you have purified yourselves by obeying the truth so that you have sincere love for each other, love one another deeply, from the heart" (1 PETER 1:22).

The truth is what we should walk in.

"Your lovingkindness is before my eyes, and I have walked in Your truth" (PSALM 26:3 NKJV).

The truth is what we should correctly handle.

"Do your best to present yourself to God as one approved, a worker who does not need to be ashamed and who correctly handles the word of truth" (2 TIMOTHY 2:15).

The truth is what we should be faithful to honor.

"It gave me great joy when some believers came and testified about your faithfulness to the truth, telling how you continue to walk in it" (3 JOHN V. 3).

The truth is Jesus, who shows us the way to live life.

"Jesus answered, 'I am the way and the truth and the life'" (JOHN 14:6).

Lies We Tell Other People

We lie to avoid humiliation. ("Yes, Doctor, I floss every day"—when we don't.)

We lie about how we feel. ("I'm fine"—when we're not.)

We lie with excuses. ("I have other plans"—when we don't.)

We lie in denial. ("I am not an alcoholic"—when we have a problem.)

We lie out of kindness. ("This meatloaf is delicious!"—when we don't like it.)

We lie to protect ourselves. ("No, Officer, I had no idea I was speeding"—when we know we were.)

We lie by procrastinating. ("The doctor is booked all week"—when we didn't even check.)

We lie to cover our wrongdoing. ("I had to work late"—when we really went shopping.)

We lie to carry out traditions. ("Yes, the tooth fairy is real"—and we don't know why we lie.)

We lie to save time. ("I have read and agreed to the above terms and conditions"—when we wouldn't understand it anyway.)

We lie to get our child out of school. ("My son is sick today"—when he really isn't, we just want to leave early for vacation.)

We lie to manipulate a situation. ("His birth father has never paid a dime of support"—when we know he has.)

We lie to fellow Christians. ("I'm praying for you"—when we have no intention of doing so.)

Nothing in all creation is hidden from God's sight.
Everything is uncovered and laid bare before
the eyes of him to whom we must give account.
(Hebrews 4:13)

Lies We Tell Ourselves

"Dieting doesn't work for me because I have a slow metabolism."

"When I find the perfect mate, then I'll be complete."

"Her behavior drives me to drink!"

"When I get the perfect job, then I'll be happy."

"I can't" . . . can't get out of bed before 8:00 a.m., can't exercise, can't learn.

"I'm not" . . . not good enough, not attractive enough, not smart enough.

"My life is harder than anyone else's." "My childhood was worse than yours."

"I'm too" . . . too young, too old, too qualified, too fat, too dumb, etc.

"I'm not judgmental. I'm discerning."

"He's not perfect, but he's good enough." "She's not perfect, but she'll do."

"I need lots of money if I'm ever going to be truly happy."

"I'm a bad wife/husband." . . . "I'm a bad mother/father." . . . "I'm a bad friend."

"I'm too overweight and unattractive to go to the gym."

"I don't make enough money to be a good husband and provider."

"I'll start my diet tomorrow."

"I'll never find someone to love me."

But he [Jesus] *said to me, "My grace is sufficient for you,*
for my power is made perfect in weakness."
(2 CORINTHIANS 12:9)

12 Common Causes for Lying

To save face
"Keep your tongue from evil and your lips from telling lies" (PSALM 34:13).

To make us seem more interesting
"All the words of my mouth are righteous; there is nothing twisted or crooked in them" (PROVERBS 8:8 ESV).

To shift blame
"The man said, 'The woman whom you gave to be with me, she gave me fruit of the tree, and I ate.' Then the LORD God said to the woman, 'What is this that you have done?' The woman said, 'The serpent deceived me, and I ate'" (GENESIS 3:12–13 ESV).

To control a response
"The integrity of the upright guides them, but the unfaithful are destroyed by their duplicity" (PROVERBS 11:3).

To give a false impression

"Pray for us, for we are sure that we have a clear conscience, desiring to act honorably in all things" (HEBREWS 13:18 ESV).

To avoid confrontation

"Everyone lies to their neighbor; they flatter with their lips but harbor deception in their hearts" (PSALM 12:2).

To cover up mistakes

"Blessed is the one whose sin the LORD does not count against them and in whose spirit is no deceit" (PSALM 32:2).

To replace pain temporarily

"Do not deceive yourselves. If any of you think you are wise by the standards of this age, you should become 'fools' so that you may become wise" (1 CORINTHIANS 3:18).

To escape accountability

"Each one should test their own actions. Then they can take pride in themselves alone, without comparing themselves to someone else, for each one should carry their own load" (GALATIANS 6:4–5).

To create a fantasy

"Do not let anyone who delights in false humility and the worship of angels disqualify you. Such a person also goes into great detail about what they have seen; they are puffed up with idle notions by their unspiritual mind" (COLOSSIANS 2:18).

To avoid punishment

"There are those who hate the one who upholds justice in court and detest the one who tells the truth" (AMOS 5:10).

To exploit others

"In their greed these teachers will exploit you with fabricated stories. Their condemnation has long been hanging over them, and their destruction has not been sleeping" (2 PETER 2:3).

How to Tell the Truth[152]

Know that you cannot please everyone.

"Am I now trying to win the approval of human beings, or of God? Or am I trying to please people? If I were still trying to please people, I would not be a servant of Christ" (GALATIANS 1:10).

Know that you are not responsible for everyone's feelings.

"Whoever corrects a mocker invites insults; whoever rebukes the wicked incurs abuse. Do not rebuke mockers or they will hate you; rebuke the wise and they will love you. Instruct the wise and they will be wiser still; teach the righteous and they will add to their learning" (PROVERBS 9:7–9).

Know that you can speak the truth in a loving way.

"Speaking the truth in love, we will grow to become in every respect the mature body of him who is the head, that is, Christ" (EPHESIANS 4:15).

Know that you are not a perfect person—no one is perfect.

"We all, like sheep, have gone astray, each of us has turned to our own way; and the LORD has laid on him the iniquity of us all" (ISAIAH 53:6).

Know that you are not accountable for how others respond to the truth.

"Each of us will give an account of ourselves to God" (ROMANS 14:12).

Deliverance from Deceit[153]

Discover God's consequences for lying and His hatred for deceit.

"You [God] *destroy those who tell lies. The bloodthirsty and deceitful you, LORD, detest"* (PSALM 5:6).

Demand complete honesty with myself and examine my motives.

"Create in me a pure heart, O God, and renew a steadfast spirit within me" (PSALM 51:10).

Decide that I want my life to reflect Christ, if He truly lives in me.

"For those God foreknew he also predestined to be conformed to the image of his Son" (ROMANS 8:29).

Depend on the strength of Christ within me to enable me to change.

"I can do all this through him who gives me strength" (PHILIPPIANS 4:13).

Delight in the truth, which is more rewarding than lies.

"Whoever conceals their sins does not prosper, but the one who confesses and renounces them finds mercy" (PROVERBS 28:13).

Desire to please the Lord and bring honor to Him in all that I do.

"For you were once darkness, but now you are light in the Lord. Live as children of light (for the fruit of the light consists in all goodness, righteousness and truth) and find out what pleases the Lord" (EPHESIANS 5:8–10).

My Personalized Plan

I will . . .

Understand God's disdain for deceit.

"You [God] *destroy those who tell lies. The bloodthirsty and deceitful you,* LORD, *detest"* (PSALM 5:6).

Ask God to help me become completely honest with myself and examine my motives.

"Create in me a pure heart, O God, and renew a steadfast spirit within me" (PSALM 51:10).

Make the decision to be totally honest with God and admit my sin and failures.

"If we claim to be without sin, we deceive ourselves and the truth is not in us" (1 JOHN 1:8).

Key Passage to Read

Proverbs 6:16–19

Pause and think about what I am about to say and discern if it is truthful.

"Those who guard their mouths and their tongues keep themselves from calamity" (PROVERBS 21:23).

Commit to a life that reflects Christ, who embodies the truth.

"I was born and came into the world to testify to the truth. All who love the truth recognize that what I say is true" (JOHN 18:37 NLT).

Depend on the strength of Christ within me to enable me to change.

"I can do all this through him who gives me strength" (PHILIPPIANS 4:13).

Delight in the truth, which is more rewarding than lies.

"Love does not delight in evil but rejoices with the truth" (1 CORINTHIANS 13:6).

Seek to please the Lord and bring honor to Him in all that I think, do, and say.

"For you were once darkness, but now you are light in the Lord. Live as children of light (for the fruit of the light consists in all goodness, righteousness and truth) and find out what pleases the Lord" (EPHESIANS 5:8–10).

Questions & Answers

Question: "Is it ever right to tell a lie?"

Answer: Not according to the example Jesus set for us. Even with all the trap questions asked of Him and the life-threatening snares set for Him, Jesus never lied. While He did not directly answer every question, He never lied to protect Himself or others. Instead, He entrusted Himself to His heavenly Father, who cannot lie, and spoke as the Father directed Him to speak. Then upon His earthly departure, He explained that all of His followers would be given His Spirit of truth to guide us "into all truth."

"When he, the Spirit of truth, comes, he will guide you into all the truth.
He will not speak on his own; he will speak only what he hears,
and he will tell you what is yet to come."
(JOHN 16:13)

Question: "How do I teach my child to distinguish what is real from what is make-believe?"

Answer: Just as you teach your child every other virtue, you must demonstrate the value of truth. As you reward your children for truth telling, they will learn that lying results in a loss for them. As they develop and grow, they will also be able to distinguish and discern the difference between a fib and a fairy tale.

Be certain that you, too, lead by example.

If you are convinced that you are a guide for the blind,
a light for those who are in the dark,
an instructor of the foolish, a teacher of little children,
because you have in the law the embodiment of knowledge and truth—
you, then, who teach others, do you not teach yourself?
(ROMANS 2:19–21)

MANIPULATION

Cutting the Strings That Control You

God's Heart on Manipulation

The world says there is no God, but God says He has made Himself plainly known to everyone.

"They know the truth about God because he has made it obvious to them. For ever since the world was created, people have seen the earth and sky. Through everything God made, they can clearly see his invisible qualities—his eternal power and divine nature. So they have no excuse for not knowing God" (ROMANS 1:19–20 NLT).

The world says follow your heart, but God says guard your heart.

"Guard your heart above all else, for it determines the course of your life" (PROVERBS 4:23 NLT).

The world says make your own plans, but God says that He has good plans for you.

"'I know the plans I have for you,' declares the LORD, 'plans to prosper you and not to harm you, plans to give you hope and a future'" (JEREMIAH 29:11).

The world says it's okay to do whatever you want, but God says if it causes your brother or sister to stumble, don't do it.

"If what I eat causes my brother or sister to fall into sin, I will never eat meat again, so that I will not cause them to fall" (1 CORINTHIANS 8:13).

The world says it's okay to "save your own skin" or lie to keep yourself out of trouble, but God says He detests lying and delights in truth.

"The LORD detests lying lips, but he delights in those who tell the truth" (PROVERBS 12:22 NLT).

The world says it's okay to shirk your responsibilities, but God says each of us must do our own part.

"Each one should carry their own load" (GALATIANS 6:5).

The world says it's okay to hold a grudge or get even when you're angry with someone, but God says to forgive as He forgives you.

"Bear with each other and forgive one another if any of you has a grievance against someone. Forgive as the Lord forgave you" (COLOSSIANS 3:13).

The world says that bitterness and slander are acceptable when you've been wronged, but God says to put away bitterness and slander and to be kind and compassionate.

"Get rid of all bitterness, rage and anger, brawling and slander, along with every form of malice. Be kind and compassionate to one another" (EPHESIANS 4:31–32).

The world says to get what you can any way you can, but God says ill-gotten gains profit nothing.

"Ill-gotten treasures have no lasting value, but righteousness delivers from death" (PROVERBS 10:2).

The world says to conform to its ways, but God says to be transformed and to seek His ways.

"Do not conform to the pattern of this world, but be transformed by the renewing of your mind. Then you will be able to test and approve what God's will is—his good, pleasing and perfect will" (ROMANS 12:2).

Fear of man will prove to be a snare,
but whoever trusts in the LORD is kept safe.
(PROVERBS 29:25)

Seven S's of Verbal Manipulation

1. **Scheming Shoulds**: "If you don't meet my expectations, you are guilty of neglect."
2. **Strident Screaming**:[154] "If you don't do what I want, I'll make you wish you had."
3. **Sarcastic Swords**:[155] "If you aren't what I want you to be, I will use words to wound you."
4. **Sexual Seduction**:[156] "If you don't buy what I'm selling, you are not going to be desirable."
5. **Showering Sentiments**:[157] "If you don't respond to my generosity by doing what I want you to do, you are ungrateful."
6. **Sly Suggestions**:[158] "You ought to meet my every desire, and if you don't, I'll make you feel guilty."
7. **Sympathy Seekers**:[159] "You should take care of my heart, and if you don't, you are callous and cruel."

Seven S's of Nonverbal Manipulation

1. **Situation Seizer**: "My wants and wishes supersede those of everyone else."
2. **Silent Treatment**:[160] "If you don't do what I want, you won't get my approval, my communication, or me."
3. **Stomping/Slamming**: "If you don't meet my expectations, you don't deserve any dialogue with me, but I'll make my point in other ways."
4. **Scornful Sneer**: "If you don't do what I want you to do, you don't deserve my respect."
5. **Suppressed Support**:[161] "If you don't meet my standards, you will not get any attention whatsoever from me."
6. **Strategic Stalling**: "If you don't give me control, I'll take control in other ways."
7. **Sniveling Sobber**:[162] "If you don't meet my emotional needs, I'll get your attention and make you feel guilty by falling apart."

Key Verses to Memorize

For the One Manipulated

Am I now trying to win the approval of human beings, or of God? Or am I trying to please people? If I were still trying to please people, I would not be a servant of Christ.
(Galatians 1:10)

For the Manipulator

His divine power has given us everything we need for a godly life through our knowledge of him who called us by his own glory and goodness. Through these he has given us his very great and precious promises, so that through them you may participate in the divine nature, having escaped the corruption in the world caused by evil desires.
(2 Peter 1:3–4)

Why People Manipulate Others

People manipulate to[163] **. . .**

- — **Get** their own way
- — **Avoid** responsibilities
- — **Protect** themselves
- — **Present** reality the way they want others to see it
- — **Confuse** others with unclear messages
- — **Control** others' beliefs, thoughts, emotions, and actions
- — **Entice** others to do what they would not otherwise do themselves
- — **Make** others feel guilty or feel sorry for them

— **Force** others to take responsibility for them
— **Rescue** themselves or have someone else clean up after their problems
— **Maintain** a dependent relationship even when the relationship is unhealthy
— **Appear** positive when they actually feel negative toward someone

The heart is deceitful above all things
and beyond cure.
Who can understand it?
(JEREMIAH 17:9)

Why Do Some Succumb to Manipulation?

Misplaced Dependence on the Manipulator[164]

"Stop trusting in mere humans, who have but a breath in their nostrils. Why hold them in esteem?" (ISAIAH 2:22).

Misplaced Priorities[165]

"I strive always to keep my conscience clear before God and man" (ACTS 24:16).

Fear of Disapproval

"Do not fear the reproach of mere mortals or be terrified by their insults. For the moth will eat them up like a garment; the worm will devour them like wool. But my righteousness will last forever, my salvation through all generations" (ISAIAH 51:7–8).

Performance-Based Acceptance

"The very hairs of your head are all numbered. Don't be afraid; you are worth more than many sparrows" (LUKE 12:7).

Defensiveness About the Relationship

"Fear of man will prove to be a snare, but whoever trusts in the LORD is kept safe" (PROVERBS 29:25).

Loss of Independence

"My salvation and my honor depend on God; he is my mighty rock, my refuge" (PSALM 62:7).

Loss of Confidence

"Encourage one another and build each other up, just as in fact you are doing" (1 THESSALONIANS 5:11).

Loss of Identity

"It is for freedom that Christ has set us free. Stand firm, then, and do not let yourselves be burdened again by a yoke of slavery" (GALATIANS 5:1).

Loss of Objectivity

"Better is open rebuke than hidden love" (PROVERBS 27:5).

Key Passage to Read

1 Thessalonians 2:3–8

Manipulative Maneuvers

Have you ever been told . . .

— You are manipulative or controlling?
— You are too possessive or confining?
— You do not take responsibility?
— You are always "nicer" to others?
— You tend to overreact?
— You usually insist on getting your way?
— You use anger or blame to motivate others?
— You have a destructive style of interaction?

How to Stop Being Spiritually Manipulated

Submit yourself to God's authority.

"We must obey God rather than human beings!" (ACTS 5:29).

Talk about your concerns with spiritual leaders who are not involved in your manipulative situation.

"[We are to] *be completely humble and gentle; be patient, bearing with one another in love. Make every effort to keep the unity of the Spirit through the bond of peace"* (EPHESIANS 4:2–3).

Consider how the spiritually manipulative attitude of others is impacting your spiritual life, your relationships with family members and friends, and your sense of personal value.

"As iron sharpens iron, so one person sharpens another" (PROVERBS 27:17).

Separate yourself from manipulative situations and seek out people who are encouraging.

"Encourage one another daily . . . so that none of you may be hardened by sin's deceitfulness" (HEBREWS 3:13).

My Personalized Plan

I will . . .

1. **State** clearly what I am willing to accept and not willing to accept from the manipulator.

   "The one who has knowledge uses words with restraint, and whoever has understanding is even-tempered" (PROVERBS 17:27).

2. **Tell** the manipulator the consequences I will enforce if the manipulator violates my request.

   "A man reaps what he sows" (GALATIANS 6:7).

3. **Enforce** the consequence every single time manipulative behavior occurs.

   "All you need to say is a simple 'Yes' or 'No'" (JAMES 5:12).

4. **Absolutely** refuse to negotiate.

   "Sin is not ended by multiplying words, but the prudent hold their tongues" (PROVERBS 10:19).

5. **Never "react"** when my boundary is violated—I will only respond.

   "The end of a matter is better than its beginning, and patience is better than pride. Do not be quickly provoked in your spirit, for anger resides in the lap of fools" (ECCLESIASTES 7:8–9).

6. **Solicit** the support of one or two wise, objective people to help me through this process.

   "Listen to advice and accept discipline, and at the end you will be counted among the wise" (PROVERBS 19:20).

The words of the reckless pierce like swords,
but the tongue of the wise brings healing.
(PROVERBS 12:18)

Questions & Answers

Question: "What is the difference between manipulation and persuasion?"

Answer: There is a subtle yet profound difference between manipulation and persuasion.

Those who manipulate use dishonest emotions to achieve their goal.

Those who persuade use honest reasoning to achieve their goal.

The Bible speaks plainly about our need to appeal to others by using accurate reasoning.

Unlike so many. . . . in Christ we speak before God
with sincerity, as those sent from God. . . .
Rather, we have renounced secret
and shameful ways; we do not use deception.
(2 Corinthians 2:17; 4:2)

Question: "What is the difference between spiritual manipulation and biblical obedience?"

Answer: Obedience is the act of conforming outwardly to God's righteous standard and inwardly to the character of Christ through the enabling grace of God.

In manipulation, the resource is self-effort; the motive is self-promotion. Manipulation results in pride. God is approached on the basis of self-performance.

In obedience, the resource is the Spirit of God, the motive is to glorify God. Obedience results in humility. God is approached on the basis of Christ's performance.

The grace of God has appeared that
offers salvation to all people.
It teaches us to say "No" to ungodliness
and worldly passions, and to live self-controlled,
upright and godly lives in this present age.
(Titus 2:11–12)

MARRIAGE

To Have and to Hold

God's Heart on Marriage

The marriage relationship should . . .

Be honored and kept pure

"Marriage should be honored by all, and the marriage bed kept pure, for God will judge the adulterer and all the sexually immoral" (HEBREWS 13:4).

Provide companionship and intimacy

"Each one of you also must love his wife as he loves himself, and the wife must respect her husband" (EPHESIANS 5:33).

Exhibit unity

"'For this reason a man will leave his father and mother and be united to his wife, and the two will become one flesh.' So they are no longer two, but one flesh" (MARK 10:7–8).

Last a lifetime

"When a woman marries, the law binds her to her husband as long as he is alive. But if he dies, the laws of marriage no longer apply to her" (ROMANS 7:2 NLT).

Not end in divorce

"What God has joined together, let no one separate" (MARK 10:9).

Not be damaged by hardened hearts

"Jesus replied, 'Moses permitted you to divorce your wives because your hearts were hard. But it was not this way from the beginning'" (MATTHEW 19:8).

Display Christ's love for the church

"Husbands, love your wives, just as Christ loved the church and gave himself up for her to make her holy, cleansing her by the washing with water through the word, and to present her to himself as a radiant church, without stain or wrinkle or any other blemish, but holy and blameless" (EPHESIANS 5:25–27).

The commandments of the LORD are right,
bringing joy to the heart.
(PSALM 19:8 NLT)

God's Purpose for Marriage

Partnership: God has given you and your spouse to one another as partners for life. True companionship grows within the marriage relationship when there is emotional, spiritual, and physical unity.

"My beloved is mine and I am his" (Song of Songs 2:16).

Key Verse to Memorize

Submit to one another out of reverence for Christ.
(Ephesians 5:21)

Parenting: God's first command in Scripture was for Adam and Eve to *"be fruitful and multiply"* (Genesis 1:28 ESV). God desires that the earth be filled with godly offspring.

"Marry and have sons and daughters; find wives for your sons and give your daughters in marriage, so that they too may have sons and daughters. Increase in number there; do not decrease" (Jeremiah 29:6).

Pleasure: The marriage relationship and your mate are God's special gifts to you. True enjoyment of your spouse will grow out of a servant's heart.

"I belong to my beloved, and his desire is for me" (Song of Songs 7:10).

Perfecting: In the intimate relationship of marriage, spouses become well aware of one another's shortcomings. God uses the weaknesses and strengths of both spouses to sharpen and conform each of them into the image of Christ.

"As iron sharpens iron, so one person sharpens another" (Proverbs 27:17).

Misconceptions About Marriage Partners

Wife: "I'll get security."
Husband: "I'll get significance."

Wife: "I'll get to be queen of the castle."
Husband: "I'll get to be king of my castle."

Wife: "I'll get a home and manage it."
Husband: "I'll get to manage my wife."

Wife: "I'll get a husband to take care of me."
Husband: "I'll get a wife to take care of me."

Wife: "I'll get a husband who . . .
— "Will repair anything broken."

— "Will always take out the trash."
— "Will spend quality time with the children."
— "Will romance me every week."
— "Will treat me like we are dating."

Husband: "I'll get a wife who . . .
— "Will always cook perfect meals."
— "Will always keep a spotless house."
— "Will make the children obey perfectly."
— "Will always want to please me."
— "Will treat me like we are dating."

Wife: "I'll get unconditional love from my husband."
Husband: "I'll get unconditional love from my wife."

The Bible addresses a critical component to having valid expectations not only met, but exceeded.

And they exceeded our expectations:
They gave themselves first of all to the Lord,
and then by the will of God also to us.
(2 Corinthians 8:5)

What Priorities Help Marriages Last a Lifetime?

"**My marriage** is sacred before God."

"**My spouse** and I pray together daily."

"**My spouse** is my best friend."

"**My spouse** is someone I really like."

"**My spouse** and I have the same values and goals."

"**My spouse** is becoming more interesting as our marriage matures."

"**My spouse** and I deeply desire that our marriage succeed."

"**My marriage** is a long-term, lifelong commitment."

Whatever is true, whatever is noble,
whatever is right, whatever is pure,
whatever is lovely, whatever is admirable—
if anything is excellent or praiseworthy—
think about such things.
(PHILIPPIANS 4:8)

The Root Cause for Troubled Marriages

Wrong Belief: "I have the right to expect my marriage partner to meet all my needs."

Right Belief: "God will empower me to keep my marriage commitment. I will look to the Lord to provide my deepest needs and allow Christ to love and serve my spouse through me."

"The Son of Man did not come to be served, but to serve,
and to give his life as a ransom for many."
(MATTHEW 20:28)

How to Manage Mutual Submission

Choose to live under your God-given authorities.

"The authorities that exist have been established by God" (ROMANS 13:1).

Choose to pray for those in authority over you.

"I urge, then, first of all, that petitions, prayers, intercession and thanksgiving be made for all people—for kings and all those in authority, that we may live peaceful and quiet lives in all godliness and holiness" (1 TIMOTHY 2:1–2).

Choose to respect the position rather than the personality.

"Let everyone be subject to the governing authorities, for there is no authority except that which God has established" (ROMANS 13:1).

Choose to sacrificially submit to others out of reverence for Christ.

"Walk in the way of love, just as Christ loved us and gave himself up for us as a fragrant offering and sacrifice to God" (EPHESIANS 5:2).

Choose to please others rather than seeking your own way.

"Do nothing out of selfish ambition or vain conceit. Rather, in humility value others above yourselves" (PHILIPPIANS 2:3).

Choose to put your future in the hands of God.

"'I know the plans I have for you,' declares the Lord, 'plans to prosper you and not to harm you, plans to give you hope and a future'" (JEREMIAH 29:11).

Choose to be submissive, even if it means hardship and suffering.

"Suffering produces perseverance; perseverance, character; and character, hope" (ROMANS 5:3–4).

Choose to thank God, regardless of the end result.

"Give thanks in all circumstances; for this is God's will for you in Christ Jesus" (1 THESSALONIANS 5:18).

Make my joy complete by being like-minded, having the same love,
being one in spirit and of one mind.
(PHILIPPIANS 2:2)

How to Renew Your Vows—Yearly

If you desire to have a marriage that is pleasing to God, then yearly reinforce His four cornerstones for a healthy marriage—*lifetime, covenant, unconditional, commitment.* You don't have to make this renewal a public spectacle. It can be as simple as repeating your vows in private on your anniversary. Reminding each other of these fundamental principles can ground and strengthen your marriage. And remember: For what God has intended, He has provided!

My Personalized Plan

I will take the following steps to help strengthen my marriage . . .

Become aware of my vulnerability.

"The prudent see danger and take refuge, but the simple keep going and pay the penalty" (PROVERBS 22:3).

Guard the gateway to my mind against inappropriate thoughts.

"Whatever is true, whatever is noble, whatever is right, whatever is pure, whatever is lovely, whatever is admirable—if anything is excellent or praiseworthy—think about such things" (PHILIPPIANS 4:8).

Key Passage to Read

Ephesians 5:22–33

Focus on building up my mate.

"Encourage one another and build each other up, just as in fact you are doing" (1 THESSALONIANS 5:11).

Value and practice forgiveness.

"Be kind and compassionate to one another, forgiving each other, just as in Christ God forgave you" (EPHESIANS 4:32).

Keep the lines of communication open.

"If I speak in the tongues of men and of angels, but have not love, I am a noisy gong or a clanging cymbal" (1 CORINTHIANS 13:1 ESV).

Confide in another committed Christian for support and accountability.

"Plans fail for lack of counsel, but with many advisers they succeed" (PROVERBS 15:22).

Renew my commitments.

"Trust in the LORD with all your heart and lean not on your own understanding; in all your ways submit to him, and he will make your paths straight" (PROVERBS 3:5–6).

"But those who are considered worthy of taking part in the age to come and in the resurrection from the dead will neither marry nor be given in marriage."
(LUKE 20:35)

Questions & Answers

Question: "What is the difference between obedience and submission?"

Answer: Both obedience and submission are clear directives from God. However, consider the difference between conformity to the letter of the law and yielding to the spirit of the law. Mere outward compliance does not reflect God's heart. God's desire is that submission to His ordained authorities be done with inner attitudes of respect, loyalty, gentleness, and ultimate trust in Him for the outcome.

Submission is to *voluntarily yield* to the will of another.

— **Obedience** is to *comply* with the commands of another.

Submission is an *inner attitude* of the heart.

— **Obedience** is an *outer act* of conformity

"The LORD does not look at the things people look at. People look at the outward appearance, but the LORD looks at the heart."
(1 SAMUEL 16:7)

Question: "No one should submit to abuse, but are there other circumstances when a mate should not submit to the desires or demands of a spouse?"

Answer: Submission stops at the threshold of violating God's moral principles.

Do not submit when asked to violate God's Word.

You are to submit first to God and are never to violate a scriptural command.

"We must obey God rather than men."
(Acts 5:29 ESV)

Do not submit when asked to violate your conscience.

Your conscience is God-given, and you should obey it when you are in doubt.

"I strive always to keep my conscience
clear before God and man."
(Acts 24:16)

Do not submit to an action that does not glorify God.

In the Bible, a wife named Sarah submitted to her husband's (Abraham's) request to deceive Pharaoh and King Abimelek (Genesis 12:10–20; 20:1–10). You are not to engage in such deception. Abraham and Sarah failed to trust God for their safety. As a result, they were banished from the land and they brought dishonor to God.

Then Abimelek called Abraham in and said,
"What have you done to us? How have I wronged you
that you have brought such great guilt upon me
and my kingdom? You have done things
to me that should never be done."
(Genesis 20:9)

MENTORING, COACHING, AND DISCIPLING

Passing the Torch

God's Heart on Mentoring, Coaching, and Discipling

God gives us mentors, coaches, and disciple-makers to help us grow.

"Remember your leaders who taught you the word of God. Think of all the good that has come from their lives, and follow the example of their faith" (HEBREWS 13:7 NLT).

God wants us to be open to advice, correction, and guidance from others.

"Get all the advice and instruction you can, so you will be wise the rest of your life" (PROVERBS 19:20 NLT).

God commends planning with wise advisers.

"Plans fail for lack of counsel, but with many advisers they succeed" (PROVERBS 15:22).

God calls us to be discipled and to make disciples.

"Jesus came to them and said, 'All authority in heaven and on earth has been given to me. Therefore go and make disciples of all nations, baptizing them in the name of the Father and of the Son and of the Holy Spirit, and teaching them to obey everything I have commanded you. And surely I am with you always, to the very end of the age'" (MATTHEW 28:18–20).

God gives us gifts and abilities to mentor, coach, and disciple others.

Each of you should use whatever gift you have received to serve others, as faithful stewards of God's grace in its various forms" (1 PETER 4:10).

God calls us to abide in Christ, so leadership flows out of relationship with Jesus.

"Abide in me, and I in you. As the branch cannot bear fruit by itself, unless it abides in the vine, neither can you, unless you abide in me. I am the vine; you are the branches. Whoever abides in me and I in him, he it is that bears much fruit, for apart from me you can do nothing . . . As the Father has loved me, so have I loved you. Abide in my love" (JOHN 15:4–5, 9 ESV).

God wants us to mentor, coach, and disciple others with a servant's heart.
"Among you it will be different. Those who are the greatest among you should take the lowest rank, and the leader should be like a servant" (LUKE 22:26 NLT).

God wants us to seek His counsel as we lead others.
"First seek the counsel of the LORD" (1 KINGS 22:5).

God wants us to become good listeners—an essential skill of a good mentor, coach, or disciple-maker.
"To answer before listening—that is folly and shame" (PROVERBS 18:13).

God calls us to continually learn and seek guidance from Him and others.
"Let the wise listen and add to their learning, and let the discerning get guidance" (PROVERBS 1:5).

"The student is not above the teacher,
but everyone who is fully trained
will be like their teacher."
(LUKE 6:40)

What Are 10 Characteristics of Life Coaching?

Unlike counseling, life coaching doesn't center on what is broken in an effort to fix it, but rather on what's right, what works, and what the client can become. Contrary to counseling, in Christian coaching, change comes by choice—not through crisis. Coaches help their clients change in order to reach the next level of success.

1. **Coaches don't criticize**; they critique—and then they hold their clients accountable.
2. **Coaches help** clients articulate what they need in order to succeed.
3. **Coaches build** on clients' strengths instead of trying to fix their weaknesses.
4. **Coaches don't focus** on clients' problems, but on proactively producing results.
5. **Coaches encourage** by believing in clients until the clients believe in themselves.
6. **Coaches understand** each client's style of communication and endeavor to help develop that style.
7. **Coaches are active**, objective listeners and experts at asking questions.

8. **Coaches don't delve into past traumas**, but develop plans and strategies for future successes.

9. **Coaches encourage** clients to extend their capacity for success and to stretch their strengths.

10. **Coaches show clients how they are part of God's plan**—for both today and the future.

Dos and Don'ts of Reaching Out

Don't assume the role of savior.

Jesus said, "I am the vine; you are the branches. If you remain in me and I in you, you will bear much fruit; apart from me you can do nothing" (JOHN 15:5).

Don't have rigid thoughts that all disciples should be alike.

"There are different kinds of service, but the same Lord" (1 CORINTHIANS 12:5).

Don't have too many in a group.

"One of those days Jesus went out to a mountainside to pray, and spent the night praying to God. When morning came, he called his disciples to him and chose twelve of them, whom he also designated apostles" (LUKE 6:12–13).

Don't sacrifice personal devotional time.

"You, God, are my God, earnestly I seek you; I thirst for you, my whole being longs for you, in a dry and parched land where there is no water" (PSALM 63:1).

Key Verse to Memorize

"Go and make disciples of all nations, baptizing them in the name of the Father and of the Son and of the Holy Spirit."
(MATTHEW 28:19)

Don't become emotionally dependent on the person you are discipling.

"But Jesus would not entrust himself to them, for he knew all people. He did not need any testimony about mankind, for he knew what was in each person" (JOHN 2:24–25).

Don't think that you are a failure if the one you are discipling fails.

"Each of us will give an account of ourselves to God" (ROMANS 14:12).

Don't fail to mentor every child in your own family.

"He must manage his own family well and see that his children obey him, and he must do so in a manner worthy of full respect" (1 TIMOTHY 3:4).

Do make the development of people a major priority in your life.

"My goal is that they may be encouraged in heart and united in love, so that they may have the full riches of complete understanding, in order that they may know the mystery of God, namely, Christ" (COLOSSIANS 2:2).

Do focus on forming relationships from the beginning and getting to know one another's story, strengths, weaknesses, and temperaments.

"Make my joy complete by being like-minded, having the same love, being one in spirit and of one mind. Do nothing out of selfish ambition or vain conceit. Rather, in humility value others above yourselves, not looking to your own interests but each of you to the interests of the others" (PHILIPPIANS 2:2–4).

Do give of yourself and your unconditional support without any expectation of receiving in return.

"Always give yourselves fully to the work of the Lord, because you know that your labor in the Lord is not in vain" (1 CORINTHIANS 15:58).

Do include others when you engage in any activity you want to pass along to them.

"When Barnabas and Saul had finished their mission, they returned from Jerusalem, taking with them John, also called Mark" (ACTS 12:25).

Key Passage to Read

2 Timothy chapter 2

Do share personal knowledge and other resources to further develop personal and professional growth.

"I no longer call you servants, because a servant does not know his master's business. Instead, I have called you friends, for everything that I learned from my Father I have made known to you" (JOHN 15:15).

Do lend your presence, modeling Christlike attitudes and Christlike behaviors to be emulated until they can be accurately replicated without your presence.

"For this reason I have sent to you Timothy, my son whom I love, who is faithful in the Lord. He will remind you of my way of life in Christ Jesus, which agrees with what I teach everywhere in every church" (1 CORINTHIANS 4:17).

Do prepare those you have mentored to mentor others, just as you have mentored them.

"Therefore go and make disciples of all nations, baptizing them in the name of the Father and of the Son and of the Holy Spirit, and teaching them to obey everything I have commanded you. And surely I am with you always, to the very end of the age" (MATTHEW 28:19–20).

How to Set the Stage for Success

As you seek to shape the lives of those whom God places in your life, consider the ways you might set the stage for their success in living the life God has planned for them.

Believe in them.

Look at them not as they are now but as what they can become.

Transfer your belief in them to them.

Think the best of them.

Concentrate on the good they do.

Explore areas of potential growth.

Encourage employment and training that spotlights their strengths.

Always make it your goal to lead people to reach their highest potential—to become all God created them to be.

"Before I formed you in the womb I knew you,
before you were born I set you apart;
I appointed you as a prophet to the nations."
(JEREMIAH 1:5)

My Personalized Plan

I will . . .

Seek out a wise Christian to mentor, coach, and/or disciple me.

"Two people are better off than one, for they can help each other succeed. If one person falls, the other can reach out and help. But someone who falls alone is in real trouble" (ECCLESIASTES 4:9–10 NLT).

Remember that there are always areas where I can grow.

"Instruct the wise, and they will be even wiser. Teach the righteous, and they will learn even more" (PROVERBS 9:9 NLT).

Listen to advice, guidance, and correction.

"If you listen to constructive criticism, you will be at home among the wise" (PROVERBS 15:31 NLT).

Put into practice what I learn from those who lead me.

"Whatever you have learned or received or heard from me, or seen in me—put it into practice. And the God of peace will be with you" (PHILIPPIANS 4:9).

Lead by example.

"Set an example for the believers in speech, in conduct, in love, in faith and in purity" (1 TIMOTHY 4:12).

Fill my heart with God's Word and lead from the wisdom He provides.

"Let the message about Christ, in all its richness, fill your lives. Teach and counsel each other with all the wisdom he gives" (COLOSSIANS 3:16 NLT).

Pray regularly for those I mentor, coach, or disciple.

"Pray in the Spirit at all times and on every occasion. Stay alert and be persistent in your prayers for all believers everywhere" (EPHESIANS 6:18 NLT).

Help others form plans to reach their goals.

"Commit to the LORD whatever you do, and he will establish your plans" (PROVERBS 16:3).

Rejoice in the growth of others, and be empathetic to their struggles.

"Rejoice with those who rejoice, weep with those who weep" (ROMANS 12:15 ESV).

Always remember to point people to Christ and foster their maturity.

"He is the one we proclaim, admonishing and teaching everyone with all wisdom, so that we may present everyone fully mature in Christ" (COLOSSIANS 1:28).

"Go and make disciples of all nations,
baptizing them in the name of the Father
and of the Son and of the Holy Spirit,
and teaching them to obey
everything I have commanded you.
And surely I am with you always,
to the very end of the age."
(MATTHEW 28:19–20)

Questions & Answers

Question: "What is the difference between counseling and coaching?"

Answer: These two powerful professions have been lifesavers and "life-givers," but in very different ways. Counseling is "past oriented" and coaching is "future oriented." Counseling addresses dysfunction from the past to help people become whole today. Coaching endeavors to motivate people today to develop their potential for the future.

— Counseling pinpoints solving the *problem.*
— Coaching points to reaching the *potential.*
— Counseling provides welcomed *relief.*
— Coaching produces needed *results.*
— Counseling finds solutions for *stress.*
— Coaching plans the path for *success.*

May he give you the desire of your heart
and make all your plans succeed.
(PSALM 20:4)

Question: "How can I overcome the shame of my past if I want to become a mentor? I'm too afraid of being judged if I am ever found out."

Answer: There is absolutely nothing about your past that is not completely known to God. Whatever plan He has for using you in the lives of others, you can rest assured that He will *guard* your past or He will *use* your past—most likely, in time, He will do both, but only when you are ready.

There may be times when your past will be your platform for sharing His power to overcome and walk in victory.

There is now no condemnation
for those who are in Christ Jesus.
(ROMANS 8:1)

MIDLIFE CRISIS

Facing the Fork in the Road

God's Heart on Midlife Crisis

God is with you at every stage of life.

"That is what God is like. He is our God forever and ever, and he will guide us until we die" (PSALM 48:14 NLT).

God wants you to trust Him, knowing that your time is in His hands.

"I trust in you, LORD; I say, 'You are my God.' My times are in your hands" (PSALM 31:14–15).

God has a purpose for you in every season of life.

"There is a time for everything, and a season for every activity under the heavens" (ECCLESIASTES 3:1).

God wants you to remember your identity in Christ—you are His beloved child.

"See what great love the Father has lavished on us, that we should be called children of God! And that is what we are!" (1 JOHN 3:1).

God wants you to reflect on what He's done for you in the past.

"I will remember the deeds of the LORD" (PSALM 77:11).

God can redeem your past, your regrets, and your failures.

"Put your hope in the LORD, for with the LORD is unfailing love and with him is full redemption" (PSALM 130:7).

God wants you to live in the present and not worry about the future.

"Do not worry about tomorrow, for tomorrow will worry about itself. Each day has enough trouble of its own" (MATTHEW 6:34).

God wants you to take care of yourself physically and spiritually.

"Physical training is of some value, but godliness has value for all things, holding promise for both the present life and the life to come" (1 TIMOTHY 4:8).

God wants you to mentor and influence others with His truth.

"The things you have heard me say in the presence of many witnesses entrust to reliable people who will also be qualified to teach others" (2 TIMOTHY 2:2).

God wants you to tell the next generation about Him—about His character and His works.

"Even when I am old and gray, do not forsake me, my God, till I declare your power to the next generation, your mighty acts to all who are to come" (PSALM 71:18).

God wants you to look forward to the future as you continue the race and follow Jesus.

"I focus on this one thing: Forgetting the past and looking forward to what lies ahead, I press on to reach the end of the race and receive the heavenly prize for which God, through Christ Jesus, is calling us" (PHILIPPIANS 3:13–14 NLT).

God wants you to live with an eternal perspective.

"Therefore we do not lose heart. Though outwardly we are wasting away, yet inwardly we are being renewed day by day. For our light and momentary troubles are achieving for us an eternal glory that far outweighs them all. So we fix our eyes not on what is seen, but on what is unseen, since what is seen is temporary, but what is unseen is eternal" (2 CORINTHIANS 4:16–18).

Such a person is a double-minded and unstable in all they do.
(JAMES 1:8)

Characteristics of Midlife Crisis

Emotional

- — Anger
- — Anxiety
- — Depression
- — Fear of aging
- — Feeling trapped
- — "Now or never" mentality or sense of urgency
- — Self-pity
- — Self-doubt
- — Sense of loss

Hear my prayer, LORD;
let my cry for help come to you.
Do not hide your face from me
when I am in distress.
Turn your ear to me;
when I call, answer me quickly.
(PSALM 102:1–2)

Behavioral[166]

— Attempts to escape
— Dressing in a youthful manner
— Lack of church attendance and spiritual growth
— Negative outlook on life
— Personality changes
— Preoccupation with physical body
— Seeking to complete unfulfilled goals
— Strong desire for change
— Vulnerability to sexual attraction outside marriage
— Withdrawal from close relationships

Key Verse to Memorize

"Blessed is the one who trusts in the LORD, whose confidence is in him."
(JEREMIAH 17:7)

I said, "Oh, that I had the wings of a dove!
I would fly away and be at rest.
I would flee far away
and stay in the desert;
I would hurry to my place of shelter,
far from the tempest and storm."
(PSALM 55:6–8)

Midlife Crisis Checklist

☐ I feel trapped in my circumstances.
☐ I wish I could disappear.
☐ I feel I am getting old too fast.
☐ I feel I've never had the chance to do what I really wanted to do.
☐ I regret past decisions.
☐ I feel like a failure.
☐ I feel unappreciated.
☐ I don't have any real purpose for living.
☐ I have grown spiritually numb to the Lord and the church.
☐ I daydream and fantasize too much.
☐ I have little interest in sex with my spouse.
☐ I am easily angered.
☐ I mistrust the motives of those close to me.
☐ I feel that now is my last chance for happiness.

Surface Causes of Midlife Crisis[167]

T—**Thoughts** of one's own mortality

R—**Reassessment** of lifelong goals and values

A—**Achievement** of goals but not finding fulfillment

N—**Normal** biological and physiological changes

S—**Sexual drive** (diminishes in the male, increases in the female)

I—**Insufficient** financial resources

T—**Traumatic** illness or death of parents, family, or close friends

I—**Identity** misplaced (in a person, a job, or social status)

O—**Offspring** at difficult age and/or leaving home

N—**Narrowing** of job opportunities

S—**Social** emphasis on youth

There is a time for everything,
and a season for every activity under the heavens.
(ECCLESIASTES 3:1)

Move from Crisis to Christ

Who am I?

"What great love the Father has lavished on us, that we should be called children of God! And that is what we are! The reason the world does not know us is that it did not know him" (1 JOHN 3:1).

What is my purpose in life?

"I urge you . . . in view of God's mercy, to offer your bodies as living sacrifices, holy and pleasing to God—this is your true and proper worship. Do not conform to the pattern of this world, but be transformed by the renewing of your mind. Then you will be able to test and approve what God's will is—his good, pleasing and perfect will" (ROMANS 12:1–2).

In whom do I want to invest my life?

"Jesus replied: 'Love the Lord your God with all your heart and with all your soul and with all your mind.' This is the first and greatest commandment. And the second is like it: 'Love your neighbor as yourself'" (MATTHEW 22:37–39).

What do I want to do for the rest of my life?

"I desire to do your will, my God; your law is within my heart" (PSALM 40:8).

Where does God fit into my life?

"The LORD is my shepherd; I shall not want. He makes me lie down in green pastures. He leads me beside still waters. He restores my soul. He leads me in paths of righteousness for his name's sake. Even though I walk through the valley of the shadow of death, I will fear no evil, for you are with me; your rod and your staff, they comfort me. You prepare a table before me in the presence of my enemies; you anoint my head with oil; my cup overflows. Surely goodness and mercy shall follow me all the days of my life, and I shall dwell in the house of the LORD forever" (PSALM 23:1–6 ESV).

What does God do with my wrong choices?

"Because of the LORD's great love we are not consumed, for his compassions never fail. They are new every morning; great is your faithfulness" (LAMENTATIONS 3:22–23).

Where does my hope ultimately lie?

"Yes, my soul, find rest in God; my hope comes from him. Truly he is my rock and my salvation; he is my fortress, I will not be shaken. My salvation and my honor depend on God; he is my mighty rock, my refuge. Trust in him at all times, you people; pour out your hearts to him, for God is our refuge" (PSALM 62:5–8).

My Personalized Plan

I will . . .

Regard my current life stage as a valuable season of life.

"He has made everything beautiful in its time" (ECCLESIASTES 3:11).

Ask God to help me realize the advantages of aging.

"Is not wisdom found among the aged? Does not long life bring understanding?" (JOB 12:12).

Accept the physical changes that come with age, remembering that God will sustain me.

"I will be your God throughout your lifetime—until your hair is white with age. I made you, and I will care for you. I will carry you along and save you" (ISAIAH 46:4 NLT).

Consider talking with a pastor, counselor, life coach, or trusted friend to help me when I struggle with my stage of life.

"Without counsel plans fail, but with many advisers they succeed" (PROVERBS 15:22 ESV).

Evaluate my life purpose and seek God's direction through prayer and Bible study.

"I will instruct you and teach you in the way you should go; I will counsel you with my loving eye on you" (PSALM 32:8).

Set goals and challenge myself to grow.

"Commit to the LORD whatever you do, and he will establish your plans" (PROVERBS 16:3).

Develop strong, godly friendships that will encourage my growth.

"Walk with the wise and become wise, for a companion of fools suffers harm" (PROVERBS 13:20).

Key Passage to Read

2 Samuel 11:1–26

Look to the Lord to satisfy me—more than my job, dreams, or plans.

"Satisfy us in the morning with your unfailing love, that we may sing for joy and be glad all our days" (PSALM 90:14).

Determine to make the most of the time God gives me.

"Teach us to number our days, that we may gain a heart of wisdom" (PSALM 90:12).

Remember that God still has a purpose for me, and He will help me fulfill it.

"The LORD will fulfill his purpose for me; your steadfast love, O LORD, endures forever" (PSALM 138:8 ESV).

"When you pass through the waters,
I will be with you;
and when you pass through the rivers,
they will not sweep over you.
When you walk through the fire,
you will not be burned;
the flames will not set you ablaze."
(ISAIAH 43:2)

Questions & Answers

Question: "How can a husband help his wife through a difficult midlife crisis?"

Answer:

— Be a strong but gentle leader, walking with God. There is no greater cause for wifely respect than for a husband to assume spiritual servant headship in his household.

— Try to understand what she is feeling.
— Give her space and room to grow.
— Build her self-image with encouraging words.
— Be focused on strengthening her emotional security. Tell her every day that you love her, that she is your lifelong companion.

Husbands ought to love their wives as their own bodies.
(Ephesians 5:28)

Question: "How can a wife help her husband through a difficult midlife crisis?"

Answer:

— Be in daily prayer and study of God's Word. There is power in a praying wife who applies the truth and promises of God's Word to her own family, especially to her husband.
— Try to understand what he is battling emotionally.
— Be prepared if his anger is directed toward you.
— Find ways to gently encourage him to discuss his feelings.
— Be focused on strengthening his self-image.

Wives, in the same way submit yourselves
to your own husbands so that,
if any of them do not believe the word,
they may be won over without words
by the behavior of their wives.
(1 Peter 3:1)

NEW AGE SPIRITUALITY

A New Mask for an Old Message

God's Heart on New Age Spirituality

God reveals Himself as the only true God.

"I am the LORD, and there is no other; apart from me there is no God" (ISAIAH 45:5).

God reveals the truth about Himself, humanity, the world, sin, and salvation in His Word, the Bible.

"All your words are true; all your righteous laws are eternal" (PSALM 119:160).

God is the Creator, separate from creation.

"They exchanged the truth about God for a lie, and worshiped and served created things rather than the Creator—who is forever praised. Amen" (ROMANS 1:25).

God is opposed to occultic charms and deception.

"This is what the Sovereign LORD says: I am against all your magic charms, which you use to ensnare my people like birds" (EZEKIEL 13:20 NLT).

God forbids turning to mediums or spiritists.

"Do not turn to mediums or seek out spiritists, for you will be defiled by them. I am the LORD your God" (LEVITICUS 19:31).

God advises to test every spirit to determine if they are from God.

"Dear friends, do not believe every spirit, but test the spirits to see whether they are from God, because many false prophets have gone out into the world" (1 JOHN 4:1).

God confirms humanity experiences one physical death, not reincarnation, before facing judgment.

"Just as people are destined to die once, and after that to face judgment" (HEBREWS 9:27).

God establishes His plans and reigns sovereignly over humans.

"In their hearts humans plan their course, but the LORD establishes their steps" (PROVERBS 16:9).

God does not want you to be involved with any worldview or philosophy that is not rooted in Christ.

"See to it that no one takes you captive through hollow and deceptive philosophy, which depends on human tradition and the elemental spiritual forces of this world rather than on Christ" (COLOSSIANS 2:8).

God warns that some people will turn from the truth and sound, biblical doctrine.

"The time will come when people will not put up with sound doctrine. Instead, to suit their own desires, they will gather around them a great number of teachers to say what their itching ears want to hear. They will turn their ears away from the truth and turn aside to myths" (2 TIMOTHY 4:3-4).

God wants you to hold fast to the gospel of Jesus Christ so you can teach it and refute unbiblical teaching.

"He must hold firmly to the trustworthy message as it has been taught, so that he can encourage others by sound doctrine and refute those who oppose it" (TITUS 1:9).

God provides one way to be saved—through faith in the Lord Jesus Christ.

"Salvation is found in no one else, for there is no other name under heaven given to mankind by which we must be saved" (ACTS 4:12).

The Appeal of the New Age[168]

Many people are deceptively drawn into New Age spirituality because . . .

It seemingly offers something positive for everyone (health enthusiasts, psychologists, ecologists).

It rejects moral absolutes (no distinction between good and evil).

It incorporates a broader view of unity to the point that all religions are the same.

It generates curiosity in the supernatural.

It increases one's sense of personal worth.

It preys on the spiritual vacuum in a person.

It abandons accountability for sin.

It targets those with little knowledge of sound biblical doctrine.

It satisfies one's desire to be like God.

It offers a deceptive alternative to those who will not accept the simple message of Christ.

It nourishes one's hope for a perfect world.

The Root Cause of New Age Deception

Wrong Belief: "My identity (significance) is found in fulfilling my divine potential to become God!"

Right Belief: "My identity (significance) is in Jesus Christ, whose sacrificial love enables me to have a personal relationship with God."

God so loved the world that he gave his one and only Son,
that whoever believes in him shall not perish but have eternal life.
For God did not send his Son into the world to condemn the world,
but to save the world through him.
(John 3:16–17)

How to Challenge New Age Reasoning

Be prepared to challenge New Age reasoning.

Pray that God will open the eyes of New Agers to see their illogical thinking.

Understand the illogical assumptions:

— New Agers state that reason is an illusion.

— New Agers state that there is no right or wrong.

Respectfully lead them to see the inconsistencies between the way they live and the worldview they declare by asking a series of questions:

— "May I ask you some questions?"

— "Have you ever moved your hand from a hot stove?" If they answer *yes*, continue with the following:

— "If you are honest, wasn't it your logic and reason that gave you the impetus to move your hand to keep it from being burned?"

— "Have you ever quickly moved out of the path of a moving car?" If they answer *yes*, continue with the following:

— "Wasn't it your logic and reason that made you move out of the path of a moving car so that you would not die?"

— "If death doesn't exist, why did you move?"

— "Do you believe pain exists?"

Key Verse to Memorize

See to it that no one
takes you captive through
hollow and deceptive philosophy,
which depends on human tradition and
the elemental spiritual forces of this world
rather than on Christ.
(Colossians 2:8)

— "Do you believe death exists?"

"Because you have moved away from pain and from potentially deadly situations, then I must conclude that you do live as though logic is real. Therefore, your New Age worldview is not working for you."

"Come now, let us reason together, says the LORD:
though your sins are like scarlet,
they shall be as white as snow;
though they are red like crimson,
they shall become like wool."
(ISAIAH 1:18 ESV)

Biblical Answers to New Age Arguments

Argument: "We can create reality from 'universal energy.'"

Answer: Only God can create reality. Only God can create something out of nothing (ex nihilo).

"This is what the LORD says—he who created the heavens, he is God; he who fashioned and made the earth, he founded it; he did not create it to be empty, but formed it to be inhabited—he says: 'I am the LORD, and there is no other'" (ISAIAH 45:18).

Argument: "Brahman, the impersonal god of which all things are a part, rules the universe."

Answer: Only God rules the universe.

"The LORD has established his throne in heaven, and his kingdom rules over all" (PSALM 103:19).

Key Passage to Read

Genesis chapter 3

Argument: "God enables everyone to be wealthy because 'whatever the mind of man can conceive and believe, it can achieve.'"[169]

Answer: Jesus says not to focus on earthly, temporal things, but instead to focus on eternal treasures.

"Do not store up for yourselves treasures on earth, where moths and vermin destroy, and where thieves break in and steal. But store up for yourselves treasures in heaven, where moths and vermin do not destroy, and where thieves do not break in and steal. For where your treasure is, there your heart will be also" (MATTHEW 6:19–21).

They exchanged the truth of God for a lie,
and worshiped and served created things rather than the Creator.
(ROMANS 1:25)

My Personalized Plan

I will . . .

Seek wisdom from God's Word alone.

"All Scripture is God-breathed and is useful for teaching, rebuking, correcting and training in righteousness" (2 TIMOTHY 3:16).

Stay rooted in the gospel of Jesus Christ.

"Remember Jesus Christ, raised from the dead, descended from David. This is my gospel" (2 TIMOTHY 2:8).

Test every spiritual claim against Scripture.

"Test everything that is said. Hold on to what is good" (1 THESSALONIANS 5:21 NLT).

Ask the Holy Spirit to help me discern the truth.

"When he, the Spirit of truth, comes, he will guide you into all the truth" (JOHN 16:13).

Talk with trusted, mature believers when I am confused about new ideas or teaching.

"Remember your leaders, who spoke the word of God to you. Consider the outcome of their way of life and imitate their faith" (HEBREWS 13:7).

Reject any practice or teaching that contradicts God's truth.

"Guard what has been entrusted to your care. Turn away from godless chatter and the opposing ideas of what is falsely called knowledge" (1 TIMOTHY 6:20).

Renew my mind daily with God's Word.

"Do not conform any longer to the pattern of this world, but be transformed by the renewing of your mind. Then you will be able to test and approve what God's will is—his good, pleasing and perfect will" (ROMANS 12:2).

Affirm Jesus as the only way to be saved.

"I am the way and the truth and the life. No one comes to the Father except through me" (JOHN 14:6).

Share the good news of Jesus with others.

"We are therefore Christ's ambassadors, as though God were making his appeal through us. We implore you on Christ's behalf: Be reconciled to God" (2 CORINTHIANS 5:20).

Speak lovingly and graciously when interacting with people who have different beliefs.

"Let your conversation be always full of grace, seasoned with salt, so that you may know how to answer everyone" (COLOSSIANS 4:6).

"The God who made the world and everything in it is the Lord of heaven and earth and does not live in temples built by human hands."
(ACTS 17:24)

Questions & Answers

Question: "What's wrong with being positive?"

Answer: Nothing is wrong with having a positive attitude. The error is in believing that you can change the future by the way you think. God wants us to have a positive outlook based on the hope we have in Christ's victory over the reality of sin and death, not based on how we choose to think about the future.

"Where, O death, is your victory?
Where, O death, is your sting?"...
Thanks be to God! He gives us the victory through our Lord Jesus Christ.
(1 CORINTHIANS 15:55, 57)

Question: "Does the Bible teach anything about reincarnation?"

Answer: Although the Bible does teach that a person's soul is everlasting, we are appointed to die only once, then to be resurrected.

Just as people are destined to die once, and after that to face judgment.
(HEBREWS 9:27)

Question: "What does the Bible say happens after I die?"

Answer: The Bible says that after we die, we face God's judgment (Hebrews 9:27). Those who accepted Jesus as their Lord and Savior will spend eternity with God in heaven. Those who have rejected Jesus and His free gift of salvation spend eternity separated from God in hell. Eternity is too long to be wrong. Jesus invites all to come to Him by to receive the gift of salvation. Jesus said . . .

"I am the resurrection and the life. The one who believes in me will live, even though they die; and whoever lives by believing in me will never die. Do you believe this?"
(JOHN 11:25–26)

THE OCCULT

Demystifying the Deeds of Darkness

God's Heart on Witchcraft

Witchcraft is forbidden by God.

"Let no one be found among you who sacrifices their son or daughter in the fire, who practices divination or sorcery, interprets omens, engages in witchcraft" (DEUTERONOMY 18:10).

Witchcraft angers God.

"He sacrificed his children in the fire in the Valley of Ben Hinnom, practiced divination and witchcraft, sought omens, and consulted mediums and spiritists. He did much evil in the eyes of the LORD, arousing his anger" (2 CHRONICLES 33:6).

Witchcraft will be destroyed by God.

"I will destroy your witchcraft and you will no longer cast spells" (MICAH 5:12).

Witchcraft destroys peace.

"'How can there be peace,' Jehu replied, 'as long as all the idolatry and witchcraft of your mother Jezebel abound?'" (2 KINGS 9:22).

Witchcraft enslaves people.

"The wanton lust of a prostitute, alluring, the mistress of sorceries . . . enslaved nations by her prostitution and peoples by her witchcraft" (NAHUM 3:4).

Witchcraft is a barrier to entering the kingdom of God.

"The acts of the flesh are obvious: sexual immorality, impurity and debauchery; idolatry and witchcraft; . . . those who live like this will not inherit the kingdom of God" (GALATIANS 5:19–21).

"The LORD is my rock, my fortress and my deliverer;
my God is my rock, in whom I take refuge,
my shield and the horn of my salvation.
He is my stronghold, my refuge and my savior."
(2 SAMUEL 22:2–3)

Five Openings into the Occult

1. **Superstition** is unfounded beliefs—based not on the Bible but on tradition—regarding items or practices assumed to have supernatural power.

2. **Divination** is an attempt to "divine" or foretell the future through: astrology, cartomancy, numerology, palmistry, psychic games (Ouija Board, Magic 8 Ball), rod and pendulum, scrying, sortilege, tasseography, water witching/dowsing.

3. **Spiritism** is an attempt to communicate with the unseen world through: channeling, familiar spirits, Halloween, materialization, necromancy, psychometry, reincarnation, seances, sexual spirits, shamanism, spirit writing, spirit guides.

4. **Magic and sorcery** are attempts to control the natural world by invoking supernatural power from the spirit world through various practices, such as witchcraft, Modern Magic, and Satanism.

5. **Supernatural phenomena** is the appearance or manifestation of something beyond the natural realm. Methods used in an attempt to give a scientific basis for occult phenomena may include: apports, clairaudience, clairvoyance, extrasensory perception (ESP), Kirlian effect, levitation, mental telepathy, parapsychology, precognition, psychic surgery, psychometry, telekinesis.

"Do not let the prophets and diviners
among you deceive you."
(Jeremiah 29:8)

Signs of Occult Involvement

O—**Occult** material

B—**Black** clothing, Gothic attire[170]

S—**Sexual** perversion

E—**Exclusivity**, extreme secrecy

S—**Stimulants**, drugs

S—**Satanic** fascination

E—**Evil**, violence, and suicide

D—**Disdain** for biblical truth and authority

Why do you boast of evil, you mighty hero?
Why do you boast all day long, you who
are a disgrace in the eyes of God?...
You love evil rather than good,
falsehood rather than speaking the truth.
(PSALM 52:1, 3)

The Relationship Between the Occult and Evil

Occult phenomena are real, but the source is not God.

Occult power is evil.

Occult involvement is progressive.

Occult participation brings a person under Satan's control.

Occult practices run counter to biblical commands.

Occult involvement breeds rebellion against God.

Occult practices and involvement in them are detestable to God.

The Pharisees said, "It is by the prince of demons
that he drives out demons."
(MATTHEW 9:34)

Repelling the Deeds of Darkness

Renounce any involvement with the occult.
"Many who became believers confessed their sinful practices" (ACTS 19:18 NLT).

Remove all objects related to the occult.
"A number who had practiced sorcery brought their scrolls together and burned them publicly" (ACTS 19:19).

Recognize your enemy as Satan.
"Be alert and of sober mind. Your enemy the devil prowls around like a roaring lion looking for someone to devour" (1 PETER 5:8).

Rely on your authority over evil.
"The one [Christ] *who is in you is greater than the one* [Satan] *who is in the world"* (1 JOHN 4:4).

Refuse fascination with the occult.

"Let no one be found among you who sacrifices their son or daughter in the fire, who practices divination or sorcery, interprets omens, engages in witchcraft, or casts spells, or who is a medium or spiritist or who consults the dead. Anyone who does these things is detestable to the LORD*. . . . You must be blameless before the* LORD *your God. . . . But as for you, the* LORD *your God has not permitted you to do so"* (DEUTERONOMY 18:10–14).

Reside in close fellowship with believers.

"Let us not neglect our meeting together, as some people do, but encourage one another, especially now that the day of his return is drawing near" (HEBREWS 10:25 NLT).

Realize the truth of Scripture.

"All Scripture is God-breathed and is useful for teaching, rebuking, correcting and training in righteousness" (2 TIMOTHY 3:16).

Read Scripture for wisdom and knowledge.

"My son, if you accept my words and store up my commands within you, turning your ear to wisdom and applying your heart to understanding—indeed, if you call out for insight and cry aloud for understanding, and if you look for it as for silver and search for it as for hidden treasure, then you will understand the fear of the LORD *and find the knowledge of God. For the* LORD *gives wisdom; from his mouth come knowledge and understanding"* (PROVERBS 2:1–6).

Key Verse to Memorize

Woe to those who call evil good
and good evil,
who put darkness for light
and light for darkness,
who put bitter for sweet
and sweet for bitter.
(ISAIAH 5:20)

Reap the benefit of earnest prayer.

"Confess your sins to each other and pray for each other so that you may be healed. The prayer of a righteous person is powerful and effective" (JAMES 5:16).

Remain clothed in the armor of God.

"Be strong in the Lord and in his mighty power. Put on the full armor of God, so that you can take your stand against the devil's schemes. For our struggle is not against flesh and blood, but against the rulers, against the authorities, against the powers of this dark world and against the spiritual forces of evil in the heavenly realms. Therefore put on the full armor of God, so that when the day of evil comes, you may be able to stand your ground, and after you have done everything, to stand. Stand firm then, with the belt of truth buckled around your waist, with the breastplate of righteousness in place, and with your feet fitted with the readiness that comes from the gospel of peace. In addition to all this, take up the shield of faith, with which you can extinguish all the flaming arrows of the evil one. Take the helmet of salvation and the sword of the Spirit, which

is the word of God. And pray in the Spirit on all occasions with all kinds of prayers and requests. With this in mind, be alert and always keep on praying for all the Lord's people" (EPHESIANS 6:10–18).

We have renounced secret and shameful ways;
we do not use deception,
nor do we distort the word of God.
(2 CORINTHIANS 4:2)

My Personalized Plan

I will . . .

Admit that the occult is real, evil, and dangerous, and it brings all those involved in it under the control of Satan.

- I will admit I have been under the control of evil, and God alone can help me turn from it.
- I will admit I am powerless against evil and the forces of darkness without the power of Christ operating within me.

"If anyone walks in the night, he stumbles, because the light is not in him" (JOHN 11:10 ESV).

Abandon all aspects of the occult—from superstition to supernatural phenomenon—as it all originates with Satan and leads to death.

- I will renounce, abandon, and leave behind all aspects of the occult, including objects, actions, beliefs, literature, amulets, and places associated with it.
- I will pledge to no longer associate with anyone involved in the occult or its practices.

"Submit yourselves, then, to God. Resist the devil, and he will flee from you" (JAMES 4:7).

Ask God to forgive me and show me how to live in the light and freedom of His love.

- I will confess, renounce, and repent (turn away) from my rebellion and ask Jesus for His forgiveness.
- I will continually rely on God's powerful Word, prayer, and the Holy Spirit to keep me from turning back to wrong beliefs and practices.

"If we confess our sins, he is faithful and just and will forgive us our sins and purify us from all unrighteousness" (1 JOHN 1:9).

Adjust my life to reflect the changes I am making—replacing old thoughts and habits with new and healthy ones.

— I will be open and honest when I feel under attack and ask for support from the church, other believers, and the Lord.

— I will remember that because of Jesus' incredible sacrifice I am never alone. I have His Holy Spirit to guide me, comfort me, and give me hope.

"Since you have heard about Jesus and have learned the truth that comes from him, throw off your old sinful nature and your former way of life, which is corrupted by lust and deception. Instead, let the Spirit renew your thoughts and attitudes. Put on your new nature, created to be like God—truly righteous and holy" (Ephesians 4:21–24 NLT).

Key Passage to Read

1 John 4:1–6, 9–10

Associate with fellow believers in Christ who will help me grow in my faith.

— I will find a Bible-believing church and fellowship with my brothers and sisters in the Lord.

— I will encourage others lost in darkness to turn to the light and love of Christ.

"Once you were full of darkness, but now you have light from the Lord. So live as people of light! For this light within you produces only what is good and right and true" (Ephesians 5:8–9 NLT).

Therefore, if anyone is in Christ, the new creation has come:
The old has gone, the new is here!
(2 Corinthians 5:17)

Questions & Answers

Question: "Does Satan have the power to affect a person's actions?"

Answer: Yes. Satan can influence a person's heart to do evil.

The evening meal was in progress,
and the devil had already prompted Judas,
the son of Simon Iscariot, to betray Jesus.
(John 13:2)

Question: "Can a person actually be possessed by Satan?"

Answer: Yes. Judas was possessed and used by Satan to betray Jesus.

As soon as Judas took the bread,
Satan entered into him.
(John 13:27)

Question: "Can Christians be demon possessed?"

Answer: No. The Bible never presents even one believer as being possessed by a demon. Their bodies are not their own—they belong to Christ.

Do you not know that your bodies are temples
of the Holy Spirit, who is in you,
whom you have received from God?
You are not your own; you were bought at a price.
Therefore honor God with your bodies.
(1 Corinthians 6:19-20)

OVEREATING

Freedom from Food Fixation

God's Heart on Overeating

God gives us food as an expression of His love for us.

"He gives food to every creature. His love endures forever" (PSALM 136:25).

God gives us food for our nourishment and enjoyment.

"God . . . richly provides us with everything for our enjoyment" (1 TIMOTHY 6:17).

God warns that overeating can lead to poverty and laziness.

"Do not carouse with drunkards or feast with gluttons, for they are on their way to poverty, and too much sleep clothes them in rags" (PROVERBS 23:20–21 NLT).

God does not want you to be controlled by or addicted to anything—including food.

"People are slaves to whatever has mastered them" (2 PETER 2:19).

God wants you to find satisfaction in Him.

"Man shall not live on bread alone, but on every word that comes from the mouth of God" (MATTHEW 4:4).

God wants to renew your mind to help change unhealthy eating patterns.

"Do not conform to the pattern of this world, but be transformed by the renewing of your mind. Then you will be able to test and approve what God's will is—his good, pleasing and perfect will" (ROMANS 12:2).

God wants you to take care of your body.

"Do you not know that your bodies are temples of the Holy Spirit, who is in you, whom you have received from God? You are not your own; you were bought at a price. Therefore honor God with your bodies" (1 CORINTHIANS 6:19–20).

God wants you to practice self-control.

"A person without self-control is like a city with broken-down walls" (PROVERBS 25:28 NLT).

God wants to heal the damaged emotions that lead to and perpetuate unhealthy eating habits.

"He heals the brokenhearted and binds up their wounds" (PSALM 147:3).

God can use counselors, coaches, mentors, trainers, and doctors to help you develop healthy eating habits.

"Plans fail for lack of counsel, but with many advisers they succeed" (PROVERBS 15:22).

God wants you to have compassion and help others who struggle with overeating.

"Be sympathetic, love one another, be compassionate and humble" (1 PETER 3:8).

God wants your eating habits to glorify Him.

"Whether you eat or drink or whatever you do, do it all for the glory of God" (1 CORINTHIANS 10:31).

I can do all this through
him [Jesus] *who gives me strength.*
(PHILIPPIANS 4:13)

Compulsive Overeater Checklist[171]

Place a ✓ if your answer is *yes*, or an × if your answer is *no*.

- ☐ Do you spend a lot of time thinking about food?
- ☐ Do you look forward to an event because of the food that will be available there?
- ☐ Do you eat when you are sad, angry, or depressed?
- ☐ Do you eat when you are bored or under stress?
- ☐ Do you eat certain foods as a personal reward?
- ☐ Do you eat even when you are not hungry?
- ☐ Do you ever feel ashamed of how much you eat?
- ☐ Do you ever feel embarrassed about your personal appearance?
- ☐ Do you ever eat secretly to prevent others from knowing what or how much you eat?
- ☐ Do you lose weight on diets, then gain the weight (and more) back again?
- ☐ Do you think you could control your weight if you really wanted to?
- ☐ Do you resent it when family or friends express concern over your weight?
- ☐ Do you find that food consumes your thoughts, your actions, your very life?

I do not understand what I do.
For what I want to do I do not do, but what I hate I do. . . .
Who will rescue me from this body that is subject to death?
Thanks be to God, who delivers me through Jesus Christ our Lord!
(ROMANS 7:15, 24–25)

Dos and Don'ts of Wise Weight Loss

Don't say, "I am dieting."

Do say, "I'm eating healthy foods."

Don't start a new eating plan during a crisis, illness, holiday, or high-stress situation.

Do consult a doctor before beginning any new eating plan.

Don't adopt a plan just because it worked for someone else.

Do adopt a personalized plan that will work for your individual lifestyle.

Don't fail to set goals.

Do set realistic, short-term, incremental goals.

Key Verse to Memorize

Whether you eat or drink or whatever you do, do it all for the glory of God.
(1 Corinthians 10:31)

Don't weigh yourself every day.

Do record your weight once a week.

Don't keep unhealthy food around you.

Do keep healthy food prepared, including snacks.

Don't shop for groceries on impulse or when you are hungry.

Do shop with a prepared list.

Don't buy packaged food without reading the labels.

Do notice the first ingredients listed; these have the highest percentage in the food.

Don't eat fast!

Do chew slowly. It takes twenty minutes for your brain to register that you are full.

Don't keep your new plan a secret.

Do share with your friends and ask for their support.

Don't get caught off guard by temptation.

Do have an alternate plan (call a friend, memorize Scripture, take a walk, enjoy a hobby).

Don't reward yourself with food.

Do focus on the rewards of self-control and a new, healthy lifestyle.

How to Think "Healthy"

Think of yourself as the person God created you to be.

"He has given us his very great and precious promises, so that through them you may participate in the divine nature, having escaped the corruption in the world caused by evil desires" (2 PETER 1:4).

Have the correct *motive* for losing weight.

"We make it our goal to please him, whether we are at home in the body or away from it" (2 CORINTHIANS 5:9).

Identify the real reasons you overeat.[172]

"Search me, God, and know my heart; test me and know my anxious thoughts" (PSALM 139:23).

Make a personal commitment to obey God.

"The one who keeps God's commands lives in him, and he in them. And this is how we know that he lives in us: We know it by the Spirit he gave us" (1 JOHN 3:24).

Know how to *listen* to the Lord.

"I will instruct you and teach you in the way you should go; I will counsel you with my loving eye on you" (PSALM 32:8).

Key Passage to Read

Daniel 1:8-21

Develop an exercise plan that will increase your metabolism. Vary the plan.

"Those who disregard discipline despise themselves, but the one who heeds correction gains understanding" (PROVERBS 15:32).

Eat only when you are hungry and only foods you should eat.

"Do not destroy the work of God for the sake of food. All food is clean, but it is wrong for a person to eat anything that causes someone else to stumble" (ROMANS 14:20).

Allow for flexibility and include some enjoyable foods in your diet.

"Take delight in the LORD, and he will give you the desires of your heart" (PSALM 37:4).

Let the Holy Spirit direct your plans and provide needed self-control.

"The Advocate, the Holy Spirit, whom the Father will send in my name, will teach you all things and will remind you of everything I have said to you" (JOHN 14:26).

Turn your focus to the healthy foods you need to eat.

"The wicked put up a bold front, but the upright give thought to their ways" (PROVERBS 21:29).

Have a thankful heart.

"Being confident of this, that he who began a good work in you will carry it on to completion until the day of Christ Jesus" (PHILIPPIANS 1:6).

We are God's handiwork,
created in Christ Jesus to do good works,
which God prepared in advance for us to do.
(EPHESIANS 2:10)

My Personalized Plan

I will . . .

Take care of my body.

— I will remember that God made my body and wants me to honor Him with it.

— I will make an intentional effort to eat healthy and exercise regularly.

"Do you not know that your bodies are temples of the Holy Spirit, who is in you, whom you have received from God? You are not your own; you were bought at a price. Therefore honor God with your bodies" (1 CORINTHIANS 6:19–20).

Plan my meals.

— I will learn about healthy nutrition and meal planning.

— I will prepare my meals and snacks in advance to avoid overeating.

"Commit to the LORD whatever you do, and he will establish your plans" (PROVERBS 16:3).

Identify root causes.

— I will identify the reasons why and the situations where I tend to overeat.

— I will consider how I use food to meet emotional needs.

"Search me, God, and know my heart; test me and know my anxious thoughts. See if there is any offensive way in me, and lead me in the way everlasting" (PSALM 139:23–24).

Form healthy coping mechanisms.

— I will find productive, healthy ways to process my emotions.

— I will consider journaling, prayer, exercising, or talking with someone to work through my emotions.

"Give your burdens to the LORD, and he will take care of you" (PSALM 55:22 NLT).

Practice self-control.

— I will ask God to help me practice self-control.

— I will plan ahead and/or avoid situations where I'm tempted to overeat.

"The fruit of the Spirit is love, joy, peace, patience, kindness, goodness, faithfulness, gentleness, self-control" (GALATIANS 5:22–23 ESV).

Seek accountability and support.

— I will seek guidance and encouragement from a trusted friend or mentor to help me stay on track.

— I will also seek professional or medical help when needed to address deeper issues behind my struggles.

"As iron sharpens iron, so one person sharpens another" (PROVERBS 27:17).

Look to the Lord.

— I will ask God for help and strength to change my relationship with food.

— I will thank God for giving me food as an expression of His love.

"He gives food to every creature. His love endures forever" (PSALM 136:25).

Questions & Answers

Question: "Can overeating be considered a sin?"

Answer: Yes, overeating is a pattern of yielding to fleshly desires instead of yielding to God. Those who habitually eat to excess are controlled by their natural appetites rather than controlled by the Spirit of God.

The wise store up choice food and olive oil,
but fools gulp theirs down.
(PROVERBS 21:20)

Question: "Spiritually, is there a difference between a food addiction and other addictions, such as smoking, gambling, or drinking?"

Answer: No, the Bible places them in the same category, although the physical ramifications can be more serious with certain addictions.

Do not join those who drink too much wine
or gorge themselves on meat,
for drunkards and gluttons become poor,
and drowsiness clothes them in rags.
(PROVERBS 23:20–21)

PARENTING

Steps for Successful Parenting

God's Heart on Parenting

God wants you to know Him as a loving Father.

"See what great love the Father has lavished on us, that we should be called children of God! And that is what we are!" (1 JOHN 3:1).

God wants to you to have a personal, loving relationship with Him—from which you can love your children well.

"Love the LORD your God with all your heart and with all your soul and with all your strength. These commandments that I give you today are to be on your hearts" (DEUTERONOMY 6:5–6).

God want you to constantly teach your children about Him—about His character, His Word, and His works.

"Impress them on your children. Talk about them when you sit at home and when you walk along the road, when you lie down and when you get up" (DEUTERONOMY 6:7).

God wants you to seek His guidance in parenting.

"Look to the LORD and his strength; seek his face always" (PSALM 105:4).

God wants you to convey to your children that they are deeply loved and immeasurably valued by both you and the Lord.

"I pray that you, being rooted and established in love, may have power, together with all the Lord's holy people, to grasp how wide and long and high and deep is the love of Christ" (EPHESIANS 3:17–18).

God wants you to lead your children into a personal, growing relationship with Jesus Christ.

"Continue in what you have learned and have become convinced of, because you know those from whom you learned it, and how from infancy you have known the Holy Scriptures, which are able to make you wise for salvation through faith in Christ Jesus" (2 TIMOTHY 3:14–15).

God wants you to teach your children to delight in the Lord—to enjoy Him, thank Him, and find great pleasure in Him.

"Take delight in the LORD, and he will give you the desires of your heart" (PSALM 37:4).

God wants you to teach your children that He is able to meet all of their needs.

"My God will meet all your needs according to the riches of his glory in Christ Jesus" (PHILIPPIANS 4:19).

God wants you to train your children to tell others about His character and His ways.

"He [the Lord] *commanded our ancestors to teach their children, so the next generation would know them, even the children yet to be born, and they in turn would tell their children. Then they would put their trust in God and would not forget his deeds but would keep his commands"* (PSALM 78:5–7).

God wants you to model repentance and forgiveness to your children.

"If we confess our sins, he is faithful and just and will forgive us our sins and purify us from all unrighteousness" (1 JOHN 1:9).

God wants you to lovingly discipline your children.

"Those who spare the rod of discipline hate their children. Those who love their children care enough to discipline them" (PROVERBS 13:24 NLT).

God wants you to honor your own parents.

"Honor your father and your mother" (EXODUS 20:12).

The Role of a Father

Fathers, biological or adoptive, raise their children or help in the raising of their children.

Fathering children means accepting responsibility for their needs and providing leadership, guidance, and protection.

Father in Greek is *pater,* derived from the root word *pa,* meaning "nourisher, protector, upholder."[173]

Fathers profoundly influence their children's concept of the heavenly Father. Jesus said . . .

"If you, then, though you are evil,
know how to give good gifts to your children,
how much more will your Father in heaven
give good gifts to those who ask him!"
(MATTHEW 7:11)

To determine your biblical accountability as a father, ask yourself how many of the following statements are true of you.

I demonstrate reverence for God before our children.

"Blessed are those who fear the L*ORD, who find great delight in his commands. Their children will be mighty in the land; the generation of the upright will be blessed"* (PSALM 112:1–2).

I take godly responsibility for the leadership of our home.

"He will direct his children and his household after him to keep the way of the LORD *by doing what is right and just"* (GENESIS 18:19).

I provide financial support for our family.

"Anyone who does not provide for their relatives, and especially for their own household, has denied the faith and is worse than an unbeliever" (1 TIMOTHY 5:8).

I take responsibility—without harshness—for the spiritual training of our children.

"Fathers, do not exasperate your children; instead, bring them up in the training and instruction of the Lord" (EPHESIANS 6:4).

I lovingly discipline our children.

"The LORD *disciplines those he loves, as a father the son he delights in"* (PROVERBS 3:12).

I teach our children to respectfully obey.

"He must manage his own family well and see that his children obey him, and he must do so in a manner worthy of full respect" (1 TIMOTHY 3:4).

Key Verse to Memorize

Train up a child in the way he should go, and when he is old he will not depart from it.
(PROVERBS 22:6 NKJV)

I comfort and encourage our children while urging them to live godly lives.

"You know that we dealt with each of you as a father deals with his own children, encouraging, comforting and urging you to live lives worthy of God, who calls you into his kingdom and glory" (1 THESSALONIANS 2:11–12).

I pray for our children and for godly wisdom in parenting them.

Then [Samson's father] *prayed to the* LORD*: "Pardon your servant, Lord. I beg you to let the man of God you sent to us come again to teach us how to bring up the boy who is to be born"* (JUDGES 13:8).

The Role of a Mother

Mothers give birth to and/or raise their biological or adopted children.

Mothering children means nurturing, protecting, and comforting children.

Mother in the Old Testament is the word *em* and is referred to as "a source of comfort, teaching, and discipline" who is worthy of respect.[174]

Mothers are often considered the "bond of the family" and a source of blessing.

Her children arise and call her blessed;
her husband also, and he praises her.
(PROVERBS 31:28)

To determine your biblical accountability as a mother, ask yourself how many of the following statements are true of you.

I have a gentle, caring spirit toward our children.

"We were gentle among you, like a nursing mother taking care of her own children" (1 THESSALONIANS 2:7 ESV).

I openly express motherly compassion toward our children.

"Can a mother forget the baby at her breast and have no compassion on the child she has borne?" (ISAIAH 49:15).

I demonstrate sincere faith in Christ Jesus as our Lord.

"I am reminded of your sincere faith, which first lived in your grandmother Lois and in your mother Eunice and, I am persuaded, now lives in you also" (2 TIMOTHY 1:5).

I give unconditional love to my husband and children.

"Teach the older women to be reverent in the way they live, not to be slanderers or addicted to much wine, but to teach what is good. Then they can urge the younger women to love their husbands and children" (TITUS 2:3–4).

I exhibit self-control, kindness, and a pure heart in our home.

"Urge the younger women . . . to be self-controlled and pure, to be busy at home, to be kind, and to be subject to their husbands, so that no one will malign the word of God" (TITUS 2:4–5).

I provide for the needs of our family to the best of my ability.

"She gets up while it is still night; she provides food for her family" (PROVERBS 31:15).

I set an example of strength and dignity and express optimism about the future.

"She is clothed with strength and dignity; she can laugh at the days to come" (PROVERBS 31:25).

I faithfully instruct our children with godly wisdom using carefully chosen words.

"She speaks with wisdom, and faithful instruction is on her tongue" (PROVERBS 31:26).

The Principles of Discipline

Discipline is essential.

"Have you completely forgotten this word of encouragement that addresses you as a father addresses his son? It says, 'My son, do not make light of the Lord's discipline'" (HEBREWS 12:5).

Discipline is positive and meant to encourage.

"Do not lose heart when he rebukes you" (HEBREWS 12:5).

Discipline is an expression of love and acceptance.

"The Lord disciplines the one he loves, and he chastens everyone he accepts as his son" (HEBREWS 12:6).

Discipline is a natural part of healthy parent/child relationships.

"Endure hardship as discipline; God is treating you as his children. For what children are not disciplined by their father?" (HEBREWS 12:7).

Key Passage to Read

1 Thessalonians 2:7-12

Discipline builds a sense of security.

"If you are not disciplined . . . then you are not legitimate, not true sons and daughters at all" (HEBREWS 12:8).

Discipline instills respect.

"Moreover, we have all had human fathers who disciplined us and we respected them for it" (HEBREWS 12:9).

Discipline develops godly character.

"God disciplines us for our good, in order that we may share in his holiness" (HEBREWS 12:10).

Discipline is painful.

"No discipline seems pleasant at the time, but painful" (HEBREWS 12:11).

Discipline produces right living and peace.

"Later on, however, it produces a harvest of righteousness and peace" (HEBREWS 12:11).

Discipline must be consistent.
"For those who have been trained by it" (HEBREWS 12:11).

Discipline, to be accepted, requires strength.
"Strengthen your feeble arms and weak knees" (HEBREWS 12:12).

Discipline, when willingly accepted and acted on, brings healing.
"So that the lame may not be disabled, but rather healed" (HEBREWS 12:13).

My Personalized Plan

I will . . .

Lead Wisely by Example

— **Walk** in total dependence on Christ.

— **Read** and discuss God's Word with my children on a daily basis.

— **Maintain** an active prayer life.

— **Project** a positive, joyful, hopeful, and thankful attitude with my children.

— **Attend** church faithfully and do volunteer work together as a family.

Implement Boundaries by Example

— **Establish** boundaries in my own life and begin setting boundaries early in the lives of my children.

— **Present** boundaries that are clearly understood.

— **Assure** boundaries are fair, age-appropriate, and within my child's ability to maintain.

— **Enforce** the stated repercussion when my child disobeys and grant the reward when my child obeys.

— **Help** my children learn the importance of not following the crowd if the crowd is engaging in wrong or questionable behavior. I will teach them instead to look to Jesus as their example to follow.

Encourage by Example

— **Communicate** confidence in the ability of my children to succeed.

— **Encourage** my children to be good workers.

— **Attend** school activities and regularly spend quality time with each child.

— **Make** kindness to others a priority.

— **Read** biographies of Christian heroes to my children.

Comfort by Example

— **Assure** my children that their feelings are important to me.

— **Show** my family members that they can trust me.

— **Allow** all of my children to speak freely.

— **Embrace** everyone in the family of God with open arms.

— **Provide** a listening ear, a shoulder to cry on, and reasons to laugh together.

Love by Example

— **Tell** my children daily how much they are loved.

— **Surrender** myself and my children to God daily.

— **Begin** a Scripture-memory program in my family.

— **Tell** my children about my personal love for God, my conversion experience with Christ, and the difference He and His love for me have made in my life. I will explain to them everyone's need for salvation and God's loving plan for salvation.

— **Obey** the Lord in every area of my life.

Whoever says, "I know him," but does not do what he commands
is a liar, and the truth is not in that person.
But if anyone obeys his word, love for God is truly made complete in them.
This is how we know we are in him:
Whoever claims to live in him must live as Jesus did.
(1 JOHN 2:4–6)

Questions & Answers

Question: "My son is rebellious and often gets into trouble. Sometimes I feel like giving up. Am I wasting my time trying to set him on the right course?"

Answer: No. Even if your son continues to make wrong choices, as a parent, you are responsible for communicating what is right—in a loving, encouraging way. You are not accountable for your son's wrong decisions, but you are accountable for your parenting. If you won't try to teach your son what is right, who will?

The teaching of the wise is a fountain of life,
turning a person from the snares of death.
(PROVERBS 13:14)

Question: "My wife doesn't want the two of us to spend time together apart from our teenage daughter, and she won't go on any trips with me. Shouldn't our marriage sometimes be a priority over our daughter?"

Answer: This sounds like an overly dependent mother-daughter relationship. When a parent primarily focuses on one child, sometimes that child becomes a barrier against intimacy with the marriage partner. One problem with this behavior is that the child realizes the relational dynamic and feels excessively responsible for the enmeshed parent. Additionally, healthy bonding in marriage is not being modeled for the child. An enmeshed parent feels that investing in the child is all-important, but there needs to be balance. No child is to be prioritized over a marriage partner.

Enjoy life with your wife, whom you love.
(ECCLESIASTES 9:9)

PERFECTIONISM

The Performance Trap

God's Heart on Perfectionism

God created you uniquely and wonderfully—so you don't need to compare yourself to others.

"You created my inmost being; you knit me together in my mother's womb. I praise you because I am fearfully and wonderfully made; your works are wonderful, I know that full well" (PSALM 139:13–14).

God accepts you completely in Christ—not based on your performance but on His grace.

"Accept one another, then, just as Christ accepted you, in order to bring praise to God" (ROMANS 15:7).

God loves you unconditionally and eternally—there is nothing you can do to increase or decrease His love for you.

"I have loved you with an everlasting love; I have drawn you with unfailing kindness" (JEREMIAH 31:3).

God does not expect you to "measure up" because no one is perfect.

"All have sinned and fall short of the glory of God, and all are justified freely by his grace through the redemption that came by Christ Jesus" (ROMANS 3:23).

God completely forgives our sin and failures through Christ.

"In him we have redemption through his blood, the forgiveness of sins, in accordance with the riches of God's grace" (EPHESIANS 1:7).

God can fully redeem past failures, so you do not have to live with regret.

"Put your hope in the LORD, for with the LORD is unfailing love and with him is full redemption" (PSALM 130:7).

God does not condemn you when you fail.

"There is now no condemnation for those who are in Christ Jesus" (ROMANS 8:1).

God wants you to enjoy life and be free from bondage to unrealistic, man-made standards of perfection.

"If the Son sets you free, you will be free indeed" (JOHN 8:36).

God does not want you to live with a constant fear of failure.

"God gave us a spirit not of fear but of power and love and self-control" (2 TIMOTHY 1:7 ESV).

God uses our weaknesses to show His strength.

"He said to me, 'My grace is sufficient for you, for my power is made perfect in weakness.' Therefore I will boast all the more gladly about my weaknesses, so that Christ's power may rest on me" (2 CORINTHIANS 12:9).

God promises salvation as a free gift from Him not based on what we deserve or earn.

"God saved us and called us to live a holy life. He did this, not because we deserved it, but because that was his plan from before the beginning of time—to show us his grace through Christ Jesus" (2 TIMOTHY 1:9 NLT).

God calls us to pursue growth by His grace, not our performance.

"Grow in the grace and knowledge of our Lord and Savior Jesus Christ" (2 PETER 3:18).

Checklist of Classic Perfectionists

Do you . . .

- ☐ **Anticipate** that others are always trying to find fault with you?
- ☐ **Assume** you must please everyone all the time?
- ☐ **Avoid** conflict at all costs, believing you must have done something wrong?
- ☐ **Believe** if you are less than perfect, then you can lose your salvation?
- ☐ **Consider** mistakes never to be permissible?
- ☐ **Establish** goals so high that you continually stress over trying to achieve them?
- ☐ **Find** it impossible to let go of a mistake?
- ☐ **Hold** back and not take any risks because you are afraid of failure?
- ☐ **Need** to have everything in its place—always?
- ☐ **Presume** you must perform perfectly in order to gain and keep God's love?
- ☐ **Put** all of your energy into living life to please others?
- ☐ **Question** whether people would still love you if they really knew you?
- ☐ **Set** a higher standard for yourself than you do for others?
- ☐ **Suppose** that making a mistake diminishes your value?

☐ **Wonder** why everyone doesn't act the same way you do . . . because your way is the "right" way?

"Come to me, all you who are weary and burdened, and I will give you rest." (MATTHEW 11:28)

How to Accept the Lord's Acceptance

Evaluate your extremes.

"Let your gentleness be evident to all" (PHILIPPIANS 4:5).

Expect discomfort.

"Put off your old self, which is being corrupted by its deceitful desires; to be made new in the attitude of your minds; and to put on the new self, created to be like God in true righteousness and holiness" (EPHESIANS 4:22–24).

Stop comparing.

"We do not dare to classify or compare ourselves with some who commend themselves. When they measure themselves by themselves and compare themselves with themselves, they are not wise" (2 CORINTHIANS 10:12).

Key Verse to Memorize

"Peace I leave with you; my peace I give you. I do not give to you as the world gives. Do not let your hearts be troubled and do not be afraid." (JOHN 14:27)

Abolish expectations.

"Be devoted to one another in love. Honor one another above yourselves" (ROMANS 12:10).

Laugh at your mistakes.

"All the days of the oppressed are wretched, but the cheerful heart has a continual feast. . . . A cheerful heart is good medicine, but a crushed spirit dries up the bones" (PROVERBS 15:15; 17:22).

Practice patience.

"Do not let any unwholesome talk come out of your mouths, but only what is helpful for building others up according to their needs, that it may benefit those who listen" (EPHESIANS 4:29).

Just say *no.*

"Jesus' brothers said to him, 'Leave Galilee and go to Judea, so that your disciples there may see the works you do.'... [Jesus answered] *'You go to the festival. I am not going up to this festival, because my time has not yet fully come'"* (JOHN 7:3, 8).

Grow in grace.

"Grow in the grace and knowledge of our Lord and Savior Jesus Christ. To him be glory both now and forever!" (2 PETER 3:18).

Don't be so demanding.

"A person is not justified by the works of the law, but by faith in Jesus Christ. So we, too, have put our faith in Christ Jesus that we may be justified by faith in Christ and not by the works of the law, because by the works of the law no one will be justified" (GALATIANS 2:16).

Be accepting.

"Accept one another, then, just as Christ accepted you, in order to bring praise to God" (ROMANS 15:7).

Condemn no more.

"There is now no condemnation for those who are in Christ Jesus" (ROMANS 8:1).

Cancel your performance-based behaviors.

"I have learned to be content whatever the circumstances. I know what it is to be in need, and I know what it is to have plenty. I have learned the secret of being content in any and every situation, whether well fed or hungry, whether living in plenty or in want. I can do all this through him who gives me strength" (PHILIPPIANS 4:11–13).

Find Freedom

F—Fulfill your God-given call to live under grace, not under law.

"Formerly, when you did not know God, you were slaves to those who by nature are not gods. But now that you know God—or rather are known by God—how is it that you are turning back to those weak and miserable forces? Do you wish to be enslaved by them all over again?" (GALATIANS 4:8–9).

R—Release your burden of guilt to God.

"Let us draw near to God with a sincere heart and with the full assurance that faith brings, having our hearts sprinkled to cleanse us from a guilty conscience and having our bodies washed with pure water" (HEBREWS 10:22).

E—Eliminate your need to please others and instead focus on pleasing God.

"What does the LORD require of you? To act justly and to love mercy and to walk humbly with your God" (MICAH 6:8).

E—Enlarge your time for rest, recreation, and communion with the Lord.

"The LORD replied, 'My Presence will go with you, and I will give you rest'" (EXODUS 33:14).

D—Decide to acknowledge your personal feelings honestly and release all resentment.

"The godless in heart harbor resentment; even when he fetters them, they do not cry for help" (JOB 36:13).

O—Obey your Savior's mandate to live by the law of love rather than by the law of fear and perfectionism.

"There is no fear in love. But perfect love drives out fear, because fear has to do with punishment. The one who fears is not made perfect in love" (1 JOHN 4:18).

M—Maintain your sense of significance and satisfy your need for security by finding and living out of your identity in Christ.

"I have been crucified with Christ and I no longer live, but Christ lives in me. The life I now live in the body, I live by faith in the Son of God, who loved me and gave himself for me" (GALATIANS 2:20).

Managing Time

Spend time with God . . . in His Word and in prayer.

"I delight in your decrees; I will not neglect your word" (PSALM 119:16).

Write a to-do list daily. Make it realistic and reflective of your priorities.

"To humans belong the plans of the heart, but from the LORD comes the proper answer of the tongue. . . . Commit to the LORD whatever you do, and he will establish your plans" (PROVERBS 16:1, 3).

List your detailed plans in order of importance. Remember the benefit of doing them with diligence.

"The plans of the diligent lead to profit as surely as haste leads to poverty" (PROVERBS 21:5).

Establish a starting and finishing time for each task. Stick to your time schedule so that one activity does not take time allotted to another.

"There is a time for everything, and a season for every activity under the heavens" (ECCLESIASTES 3:1).

Set parameters on having an open-door policy in order to ensure "alone time." Guard your time with God just as Jesus protected His time with the Father.

"After he had dismissed them, he went up on a mountainside by himself to pray. Later that night, he was there alone" (MATTHEW 14:23).

Set aside specific time for family, for friends, and for yourself.

"Those who plan what is good find love and faithfulness" (PROVERBS 14:22).

The wise heart will know the proper time and procedure.
For there is a proper time and procedure for every matter,
though a person may be weighed down by misery.
(ECCLESIASTES 8:5–6)

My Personalized Plan

I will . . .

Learn to see myself through God's eyes—as His beloved child.

"See what great love the Father has lavished on us, that we should be called children of God! And that is what we are!" (1 JOHN 3:1).

Ask God to forgive me for past failures and embrace His forgiveness.

"You, Lord, are forgiving and good, abounding in love to all who call to you" (PSALM 86:5).

Acknowledge and use the gifts and strengths God has given me to serve others.

"Each of you should use whatever gift you have received to serve others, as faithful stewards of God's grace in its various forms" (1 PETER 4:10).

Work wholeheartedly, not out of perfectionism, but out of a desire to serve the Lord.

"Whatever you do, work at it with all your heart, as working for the Lord, not for human masters, since you know that you will receive an inheritance from the Lord as a reward. It is the Lord Christ you are serving" (COLOSSIANS 3:23–24).

Seek to please God, not people, through my actions and work.

"Am I now trying to win the approval of human beings, or of God? Or am I trying to please people? If I were still trying to please people, I would not be a servant of Christ" (GALATIANS 1:10).

Seek God's help to relieve my troubled heart when I feel the need to be perfect.

"Relieve the troubles of my heart and free me from my anguish" (PSALM 25:17).

Look to God as my source for love and acceptance, remembering nothing can separate me from His love.

"I am convinced that neither death nor life, neither angels nor demons, neither the present nor the future, nor any powers, neither height nor depth, nor anything else in all creation, will be able to separate us from the love of God that is in Christ Jesus our Lord" (ROMANS 8:38–39).

Remember that my spiritual growth is not based on my performance but on God working in me.

"Being confident of this, that he who began a good work in you will carry it on to completion until the day of Christ Jesus" (PHILIPPIANS 1:6).

Key Passage to Read

Philippians 3:3–14

Remember that I am set free in Christ, and do not have to live controlled by rules and fear.

"It is for freedom that Christ has set us free. Stand firm, then, and do not let yourselves be burdened again by a yoke of slavery" (GALATIANS 5:1).

Thank God for His grace as I grow in maturity and walk in freedom from perfectionism.

"Give thanks in all circumstances; for this is God's will for you in Christ Jesus" (1 THESSALONIANS 5:18).

God is able to bless you abundantly,
so that in all things at all times,
having all that you need,
you will abound in every good work.
(2 CORINTHIANS 9:8)

Questions & Answers

Question: "Since the Bible says, 'Be perfect,' aren't we called to be sinless?"

Answer: God understands that all humans make mistakes and sin. The biblical word *perfect* typically means "mature and complete" as we surrender our will to God's will.

We are called to be perfect—not faultless, sinless, flawless; but rather mature, whole, complete.

If we claim to be without sin,
we deceive ourselves and the truth is not in us.
(1 JOHN 1:8)

Question: "Shouldn't all doctors, dentists, and other professionals be perfectionists?"

Answer: No. When new approaches are needed, perfectionists are often too fear-based to try new ideas or procedures. That means their perfectionism can actually hinder their performance.

The most successful and talented professionals push themselves to do their work faithfully with *excellence*, not *perfection*.

In Christ all the fullness of the Deity lives in bodily form,
and in Christ you have been brought to fullness.
(COLOSSIANS 2:9-10)

PREGNANCY . . . UNPLANNED

I'm Pregnant?

God's Heart on Unplanned Pregnancy

God is with you and will help you throughout your pregnancy.

"Do not fear, for I am with you; do not be dismayed, for I am your God. I will strengthen you and help you; I will uphold you with my righteous right hand" (ISAIAH 41:10).

God cares for the unborn.

"I have cared for you since you were born. Yes, I carried you before you were born" (ISAIAH 46:3 NLT).

God is the author and giver of life.

"He himself gives life and breath to everything, and he satisfies every need" (ACTS 17:26 NLT).

God opens and closes the womb.

"The LORD . . . opened her womb" (GENESIS 29:31 ESV).

"The LORD . . . closed her womb" (1 SAMUEL 1:5).

God ordains all pregnancies—regardless of the circumstances.

"This is what the LORD says—your Redeemer, who formed you in the womb: I am the LORD, the Maker of all things" (ISAIAH 44:24).

God creates every life.

"He is the Creator of everything that exists, including his people, his own special possession" (JEREMIAH 51:19 NLT).

God creates everyone for His glory.

"Bring my sons from afar and my daughters from the ends of the earth—everyone who is called by my name, whom I created for my glory, whom I formed and made" (ISAIAH 43:6–7).

God sustains every life.

"The life of every living thing is in his hand, and the breath of every human being" (JOB 12:10 NLT).

God cares for every person throughout their entire life.

"I will be your God throughout your lifetime—until your hair is white with age. I made you, and I will care for you. I will carry you along and save you" (ISAIAH 46:4 NLT).

God has plans for every life He creates.

"'I know the plans I have for you,' declares the L*ORD, 'plans to prosper you and not to harm you, plans to give you hope and a future'"* (JEREMIAH 29:11).

How to Weigh Your Options[175]

Are you afraid that the response of others will be ridicule or rejection?

Realize . . . it is wiser to fear the response of God than the response of people.

Are you being pressured, especially by your parents, the baby's father, or abortion counselors?

Realize . . . there is no easy way out, and doing what God says is more important than doing what people say.

Are you wanting to escape the reminder that you made a major mistake?

Realize . . . God wants your child to be a reminder of His sovereignty and His purposes, not of your mistake.

Are you reluctant to bring an unwanted child into this world?

Realize . . . every child is wanted by God, and you can choose to want to have your child.

Are you concerned about possible health problems of the baby?

Realize . . . the value of life is not related to the health of the baby but to the God-given value placed on this baby by the Creator of life.

Are you viewing abortion as a form of birth control?

Realize . . . abortion kills a life, which is different from preventing the conception of a life.

Are you wanting to get rid of a baby who is a result of a wrongful act such as rape or incest?

Realize . . . your baby is innocent of any wrongful act and is undeserving of the death penalty.

Terminating an innocent life will not end your grief but will rather compound grief with guilt.

There is a way that appears to be right,
but in the end it leads to death.
(PROVERBS 14:12)

Predictable Reactions[176]

Denial

"You will know the truth, and the truth will set you free" (JOHN 8:32).

Distress

"Do not hide your face from me when I am in distress. Turn your ear to me; when I call, answer me quickly" (PSALM 102:2).

Key Verse to Memorize

He will bless the fruit of your womb.
(DEUTERONOMY 7:13)

Depression

"Why, my soul, are you downcast? Why so disturbed within me? Put your hope in God, for I will yet praise him, my Savior and my God" (PSALM 42:5).

Dread

"Take away the disgrace I dread, for your laws are good" (PSALM 119:39).

Dilemma

"If any of you lacks wisdom, you should ask God, who gives generously to all without finding fault, and it will be given to you" (JAMES 1:5).

How to Walk with Wisdom

W—Write down your thoughts and feelings, admitting your anxiety, confessing any guilt, and casting your cares on the Lord.

"Humble yourselves, therefore, under God's mighty hand, that he may lift you up in due time. Cast all your anxiety on him because he cares for you" (1 PETER 5:6–7).

I—Imagine what life would be like for you and your baby in the next year and ten years from now if you followed each option (abortion, parenting, adoption).

"The wisdom of the prudent is to give thought to their ways" (PROVERBS 14:8).

S—Sort through your options in terms of what God has revealed about your baby's life and what is best for your child.

"Before I formed you in the womb I knew you, before you were born I set you apart" (JEREMIAH 1:5).

D—Develop a support structure of family and friends.

"A friend loves at all times, and a brother is born for a time of adversity" (PROVERBS 17:17).

O—Obtain godly counsel that lines up with what God says in His Word.

"I will instruct you and teach you in the way you should go; I will counsel you with my loving eye on you" (PSALM 32:8).

M—Make a decision to entrust your future and your baby's future to the Lord.

"Trust in the LORD with all your heart and lean not on your own understanding; in all your ways submit to him, and he will make your paths straight" (PROVERBS 3:5–6).

The advantage of knowledge is this:
Wisdom preserves those who have it.
(ECCLESIASTES 7:12)

For Family and Friends . . . Encouragement in Pain

Call the family and closest friends together, talk through the situation, share feelings, and pray for the entire family.

"Carry each other's burdens, and in this way you will fulfill the law of Christ" (GALATIANS 6:2).

Concentrate on the positive by keeping an ongoing list of every valuable aspect of the situation.

"Whatever is true, whatever is noble, whatever is right, whatever is pure, whatever is lovely, whatever is admirable—if anything is excellent or praiseworthy—think about such things" (PHILIPPIANS 4:8).

Key Passage to Read

Psalm 139

Count on various forms of rejection. Do not expect others to accept the circumstances or to support your decisions during this difficult time.

"Though my father and mother forsake me, the LORD will receive me. Teach me your way, LORD; lead me in a straight path because of my oppressors" (PSALM 27:10–11).

Cherish God's Word in your heart and meditate on Scripture for your source of strength and security.

"My comfort in my suffering is this: Your promise preserves my life" (PSALM 119:50).

Cast every care upon God in prayer, thanking Him for what He will do in your situation.

"Cast your cares on the LORD and he will sustain you; he will never let the righteous be shaken" (PSALM 55:22).

Cultivate consistency through a normal family routine—don't stop functioning as a family unit.

"God is not a God of disorder but of peace" (1 CORINTHIANS 14:33).

Choose forgiveness—letting go of the past and pursuing peace.

"Bear with each other and forgive one another if any of you has a grievance against someone. Forgive as the Lord forgave you" (COLOSSIANS 3:13).

Claim this as an opportunity to be used for God's glory and for the good of your family.

"If anyone is in Christ, the new creation has come: The old has gone, the new has come! All this is from God, who reconciled us to himself through Christ and gave us the ministry of reconciliation" (2 CORINTHIANS 5:17–18).

Come to accept that these changes in your life are permanent.

"The LORD will fulfill his purpose for me; your steadfast love, O LORD, endures forever" (PSALM 138:8 ESV).

Advice for Single Parents

When raising your child, reinforce the Father image of God with . . .

Scriptures of His guidance

"Show me your ways, LORD, teach me your paths. Guide me in your truth and teach me, for you are God my Savior, and my hope is in you all day long" (PSALM 25:4–5).

Songs of His sovereignty

"You are my strength, I sing praise to you; you, God, are my fortress, my God on whom I can rely" (PSALM 59:17).

Words of His watchful care

"The LORD watches over you—the LORD is your shade at your right hand; the sun will not harm you by day, nor the moon by night. The LORD will keep you from all harm—he will watch over your life; the LORD will watch over your coming and going both now and forevermore" (PSALM 121:5–8).

Prayers for His provision

"My God will meet all your needs according to the riches of his glory in Christ Jesus" (PHILIPPIANS 4:19).

My Personalized Plan

I will . . .

Seek wise advice and listen to the truth concerning this life in the womb.

"Before I formed you in the womb I knew you, before you were born I set you apart" (JEREMIAH 1:5).

Sacrifice my personal desires for what is best for this unborn child's future.

"Do nothing out of selfish ambition or vain conceit. Rather, in humility value others above yourselves, not looking to your own interests but each of you to the interests of the others" (PHILIPPIANS 2:3–4).

Strive to put the life of this unborn child above any perceived losses or fears I have.

"Children are a gift from the LORD" (PSALM 127:3 NLT).

Submit to God's will, recognizing that not everyone will support my decision.

"Commit to the LORD whatever you do, and he will establish your plans" (PROVERBS 16:3)

Serve my unborn child in ways that support and encourage.

"Serve one another humbly in love" (GALATIANS 5:13).

Surround myself with a strong positive support group to walk with me through the various stages of pregnancy.

"In an abundance of counselors there is safety" (PROVERBS 11:14 ESV).

Share my concerns with God and others, asking the Lord to guide my next steps.

"Trust in him at all times, you people; pour out your hearts to him, for God is our refuge" (PSALM 62:8).

Questions & Answers

Question: "In the midst of this unplanned pregnancy, will I ever have inner peace?"

Answer: With God, inner peace is always possible, even in the midst of your problems and fears. Jesus, as the Prince of Peace, wants to *be peace* for you. Regardless of your fears and problems, you can have His *inner peace* when you have His *inner presence.*

"In me you may have peace.
In this world you will have trouble.
But take heart! I have overcome the world."
(John 16:33)

Question: "Shouldn't every child be a wanted child?"

Answer: Although an unborn baby may not be wanted by the mother or the father, no baby is unwanted by God. The Bible says that God knows every child and has plans for every child—even before conception.

"Before I formed you in the womb I knew you,
before you were born I set you apart."
(Jeremiah 1:5)

Question: "What does God think of me for being sexually active and not married? How can He forgive me for becoming pregnant and bringing so much hurt to my family?"

Answer: Your pregnancy has not taken God by surprise. Although He knew this situation would occur in your life, He never has wavered nor will He ever waver in His love for you. If you allow Him, He will restore your life and give you new meaning and purpose.

[God] *redeems your life from the pit*
and crowns you with love and compassion.
(Psalm 103:4)

PREJUDICE

How to Be a Barrier Breaker

God's Heart on Prejudice

God created all people in His image.

"God created mankind in his own image, in the image of God he created them; male and female he created them" (GENESIS 1:27).

God does not favor one people over another.

"God does not show favoritism" (ROMANS 2:11).

God brings peace and unites people together through Christ.

"He himself is our peace, who has made the two groups one and has destroyed the barrier, the dividing wall of hostility" (EPHESIANS 2:14).

God sees prejudicial behavior as sinful.

"If you show favoritism, you sin and are convicted by the law as lawbreakers" (JAMES 2:9).

God understands the pain of prejudice.

"He [Jesus] *was despised and rejected by mankind, a man of suffering, and familiar with pain. Like one from whom people hide their faces he was despised, and we held him in low esteem"* (ISAIAH 53:3).

God extends the free gift of salvation to all through Christ.

"There is one God and one Mediator who can reconcile God and humanity—the man Christ Jesus. He gave his life to purchase freedom for everyone" (1 TIMOTHY 2:5–6 NLT).

God wants us to do good to all people.

"As we have opportunity, let us do good to all people" (GALATIANS 6:10).

God wants us to live peacefully and humbly with others, regardless of their status or position.

"Live in harmony with one another. Do not be proud, but be willing to associate with people of low position. Do not be conceited" (ROMANS 12:16).

God wants us to spread the good news of Jesus to all nations.

"It was also written that this message would be proclaimed in the authority of his name to all the nations, beginning in Jerusalem: 'There is forgiveness of sins for all who repent'" (LUKE 24:47 NLT).

God will fill heaven with people from every tongue, tribe, and nation.

"After this I looked, and there before me was a great multitude that no one could count, from every nation, tribe, people and language, standing before the throne and before the Lamb. They were wearing white robes and were holding palm branches in their hands. And they cried out in a loud voice: 'Salvation belongs to our God, who sits on the throne, and to the Lamb'" (REVELATION 7:9–10).

"I am praying not only for these disciples
but also for all who will ever believe in me through their message.
I pray that they will all be one, just as you and I are one. . . .
May they experience such perfect unity
that the world will know that you sent me
and that you love them as much as you love me."
(JOHN 17:20–21, 23 NLT)

Prejudicial Statements[177]

Assuming someone of another ethnicity is foreign-born
—"You're not from around here, are you?"

"'Nazareth! Can anything good come from there?' Nathanael asked. 'Come and see,' said Philip" (JOHN 1:46).

Ascribing conditional intelligence to a person based on ethnicity or gender
—"You are a credit to your race."

"Senseless people do not know, fools do not understand" (PSALM 92:6).

Asserting "color-blindness," implying you don't see the other person's unique differences
—"I don't see color when I look at you."

"After this I looked, and behold, a great multitude that no one could number, from every nation, from all tribes and peoples and languages" (REVELATION 7:9 ESV).

Attaching criminality to another race
—"I make sure my wallet is secure when I visit someone from the other side of town."

"One of Crete's own prophets has said it: 'Cretans are always liars, evil brutes, lazy gluttons'" (TITUS 1:12).

Attributing stereotypical, sexist language
—"Women are too emotional to be good leaders."

"Now Deborah, a prophet, the wife of Lappidoth, was leading Israel at that time. She held court under the Palm of Deborah between Ramah and Bethel in the hill country of Ephraim, and the Israelites went up to her to have their disputes decided" (JUDGES 4:4–5).

Avoiding personal acceptance of one's hidden prejudice

—"I'm not racist or prejudiced. Some of my neighbors are minorities and that doesn't bother me."

"Do not keep talking so proudly or let your mouth speak such arrogance, for the LORD is a God who knows, and by him deeds are weighed" (1 SAMUEL 2:3).

Associating achievement with unfair advantage

—"She got the job because she's a woman, and he was promoted to meet a minority quota."

"A good person produces good things from the treasury of a good heart, and an evil person produces evil things from the treasury of an evil heart. And I tell you this, you must give an account on judgment day for every idle word you speak"
(MATTHEW 12:35–36 NLT).

With the tongue we praise our Lord and Father,
and with it we curse human beings,
who have been made in God's likeness.
Out of the same mouth come praise and cursing.
My brothers and sisters, this should not be.
(JAMES 3:9–10)

Some Personal Beliefs That Promote Prejudice

Believing that cultural customs and traditions are sacred rather than flawed by human weaknesses when compared to God's Word and His standards.

Believing that blending different cultures and diverse life experiences is scary and threatening rather than an avenue for learning and edification.

Key Verse to Memorize

There is no longer Jew or Gentile,
slave or free, male and female.
For you are all one in Christ Jesus.
(GALATIANS 3:28–29 NLT)

Believing that certain ideologies are hostile and their proponents are to be feared and fought rather than logically examining and evaluating ideologies in light of God's Word.

Believing that one person or people group must make all the adjustments in developing or improving relations with other people groups rather than encouraging everyone to work together in finding ways to peacefully negotiate and establish equality with mutual give-and-take by all.

Believing that some groups of people are designed to dominate or subjugate another group based on color, sex, culture, education, physical strength, social status, intelligence, talents, etc., rather than to honor and serve all others knowing they have equal value and worth to God.

Believing that greatness is achieving success in the world, enjoying a higher standard of living, being respected and admired, rather than humbly serving others and sharing God's great love with everyone.

A person may think their own ways are right,
but the LORD weighs the heart.
(PROVERBS 21:2)

Equality in Your Heart

E—Express God's love for all people.

"The LORD is good to all; he has compassion on all he has made" (PSALM 145:9).

Q—Quit the tendency to stereotype any persons different from yourself.

"My brothers and sisters, believers in our glorious Lord Jesus Christ must not show favoritism" (JAMES 2:1).

U—Understand the God-given worth of all human beings.

"God created mankind in his own image, in the image of God he created them; male and female he created them" (GENESIS 1:27).

A—Acknowledge your need to be forgiven as well as your need to forgive.

"Forgive us our sins, for we also forgive everyone who sins against us" (LUKE 11:4).

L—Learn from people who are different from you.

"Let the wise listen and add to their learning" (PROVERBS 1:5).

I—Invest in others by having a servant's heart toward everyone.

"For even the Son of Man did not come to be served, but to serve, and to give his life as a ransom for many" (MARK 10:45).

T—Turn from critically judging others to self-examination.

"How can you say to your brother, 'Let me take the speck out of your eye,' when all the time there is a plank in your own eye?" (MATTHEW 7:4).

Y—Yield to Christ, whose power is at work in you.

"His divine power has given us everything we need for a godly life through our knowledge of him who called us by his own glory and goodness" (2 PETER 1:3).

My Personalized Plan

I will . . .

Pray for the Holy Spirit to convict and change my prejudiced heart.

"When he [the Holy Spirit] *comes, he will prove the world to be in the wrong about sin and righteousness and judgment"* (JOHN 16:8).

Prepare to challenge prejudice when it occurs.

"Be prepared, whether the time is favorable or not. Patiently correct, rebuke, and encourage your people with good teaching" (2 TIMOTHY 4:2 NLT).

Key Passage to Read

Ephesians 2:13–22

Persist in correcting false generalities made about others.

"Learn to do good; seek justice, correct oppression" (ISAIAH 1:17 ESV).

Purpose to keep conversations based on truth and facts rather than falsehoods and heated emotions.

"Each of you must put off falsehood and speak truthfully to your neighbor, for we are all members of one body" (EPHESIANS 4:25).

Put forward only true, factual information.

"We do not use deception . . . by setting forth the truth plainly we commend ourselves to everyone's conscience in the sight of God" (2 CORINTHIANS 4:2).

Profess the fact that I am not knowledgeable in certain areas and that I am willing to be vulnerable and teachable.

"Do not think of yourself more highly than you ought, but rather think of yourself with sober judgment" (ROMANS 12:3).

Present God's truth on the intrinsic value of all people.

"What is mankind that you are mindful of them, human beings that you care for them? You have made them a little lower than the angels and crowned them with glory and honor" (PSALM 8:4–5).

Pursue fellowship with others who are not prejudiced.

"Blessed is the one who does not walk in step with the wicked or stand in the way that sinners take or sit in the company of mockers" (PSALM 1:1).

Perceive the unmet needs that prejudicial attitudes are feeding.

"The wise in heart are called discerning, and gracious words promote instruction" (PROVERBS 16:21).

Plant the seeds of Christ's love and His ability to meet all our needs.

"I planted the seed in your hearts, and Apollos watered it, but it was God who made it grow" (1 CORINTHIANS 3:6 NLT).

Make every effort to live in peace
with everyone and to be holy;
without holiness no one will see the Lord.
See to it that no one falls short
of the grace of God and that
no bitter root grows up to cause
trouble and defile many.
(HEBREWS 12:14–15)

Questions & Answers

Question: "Is discernment different from discrimination?"

Answer: Yes, there is a world of difference between the two. Our immediate perceptions help simplify complex messages we receive about the world around us. This input gathered from our senses helps us process information easily and efficiently. But this rush to judgment can lead to unfair and inaccurate assessments.

To be discerning is to wisely evaluate a given situation, looking at the details in such a way as to correctly identify and understand the big picture and then to determine the best course of action.

To discriminate is to recognize a difference and then show partiality to one side, most often to the detriment of the other.

Knowledge comes easily to the discerning.
(PROVERBS 14:6)

Question: "What can I do to curb my biased thoughts?"

Answer: Known as implicit, unconscious, or cognitive bias, this refers to underlying attitudes or thought patterns that affect how we make decisions, process information, and interact with others. While we may not eliminate bias completely, we can reduce its negative influence: Challenge your thinking, listen to others, ask questions, reserve judgment, and take time to see things objectively. God's Word encourages us to think critically and seek truth.

I have chosen the way of truth.
(PSALM 119:30 NKJV)

PRIDE & HUMILITY

The Prescription for "I" Strain

God's Heart on Pride & Humility

God opposes the proud and gives grace to the humble.

"He gives grace generously. As the Scriptures say, 'God opposes the proud but gives grace to the humble'" (JAMES 4:6 NLT).

God wants you to follow Christ's example of humility.

"Don't be selfish; don't try to impress others. Be humble, thinking of others as better than yourselves. Don't look out only for your own interests, but take an interest in others, too. You must have the same attitude that Christ Jesus had" (PHILIPPIANS 2:3–5 NLT).

God lifts up those who are humble, and brings down those who are proud.

"Those who exalt themselves will be humbled, and those who humble themselves will be exalted" (MATTHEW 23:12).

God guides and teaches those who are humble.

"He guides the humble in what is right and teaches them his way" (PSALM 25:9).

God wants His people to be marked by humility toward one another.

"All of you, clothe yourselves with humility toward one another, because, 'God opposes the proud but shows favor to the humble'" (1 PETER 5:5).

God wants you to humble yourself, turn from sin, and seek His forgiveness.

"If my people, who are called by my name, will humble themselves and pray and seek my face and turn from their wicked ways, then I will hear from heaven, and I will forgive their sin and will heal their land" (2 CHRONICLES 7:14).

God will bring circumstances into your life to humble a prideful heart.

"He humbled you, causing you to hunger and then feeding you with manna, which neither you nor your ancestors had known, to teach you that man does not live on bread alone but on every word that comes from the mouth of the LORD" (DEUTERONOMY 8:3).

God will oppose the prideful.

"The LORD detests all the proud of heart. Be sure of this: They will not go unpunished" (PROVERBS 16:5).

God warns that pride leads to destruction.

"Pride goes before destruction, a haughty spirit before a fall" (PROVERBS 16:18).

God will not tolerate an unrepentant, prideful heart.

"Whoever slanders their neighbor in secret, I will put to silence; whoever has haughty eyes and a proud heart, I will not tolerate" (PSALM 101:5).

God will one day judge the prideful.

"Human pride will be brought down, and human arrogance will be humbled. Only the Lord will be exalted on that day of judgment" (ISAIAH 2:11 NLT).

God looks on the humble with favor.

"'Has not my hand made all these things, and so they came into being?' declares the LORD*. 'These are the ones I look on with favor: those who are humble and contrite in spirit, and who tremble at my word'"* (ISAIAH 66:2).

When pride comes, then comes disgrace,
but with humility comes wisdom.
(PROVERBS 11:2)

Characteristics of the Humble Nature of Christ vs. Human Nature

Performance—"How well I perform in all areas of my life determines the amount of pride I feel in my achievements and my abilities as a whole. For that reason I am committed to do whatever it takes to be the best."

By contrast, the Bible says about Jesus . . .

"The Son can do nothing by himself; he can do only what he sees his Father doing" (JOHN 5:19).

Pedigree—"Having a proper and prestigious family lineage definitely opens doors in society and business. Even if I do not have that lineage, I can make up for it by making a name for myself on my own merits."

By contrast, the Bible says about Jesus . . .

"Isn't this the carpenter's son?" (MATTHEW 13:55).

Personal Appearance—"Only pretty people are popular and prosperous today, so I must spare no expense in making myself physically attractive and desirable to others."

By contrast, the Bible says about Jesus . . .

"He had no beauty or majesty to attract us to him, nothing in his appearance that we should desire him" (ISAIAH 53:2).

Proficiency—"Excellence is the name of the game if I want to be successful and carve out a name and place for myself in the business world. I cannot afford to be anything less than an authority in my profession."

By contrast, the Bible says about Jesus . . .

"My teaching is not my own. It comes from the one who sent me" (JOHN 7:16).

Prestige—"One of my goals in life is to gain prestige and have a place of prominence in the business world among my colleagues and in society among my friends and neighbors."

By contrast, the Bible says about Jesus . . .

"He was despised and rejected by mankind" (ISAIAH 53:3).

Popularity—"I want to be a somebody, not a nobody. I want lots of friends. I want everyone who is anyone to like me and to want my name on their invitation lists and to view me as one of their top ten favorite people."

By contrast, the Bible says about Jesus . . .

"If the world hates you, keep in mind that it hated me first" (JOHN 15:18).

Praise—"Everyone wants recognition and to have their praises sung, especially by people who are held in high regard, and I am no exception. I love accolades and long to be held in high esteem by my peers."

By contrast, the Bible says about Jesus . . .

"I do not accept glory from human beings" (JOHN 5:41).

Key Verse to Memorize

"God resists the proud,
but gives grace to the humble."
(JAMES 4:6 NKJV)

Position—"In order to gain notoriety and to make a name for myself, I need to have a position that commands respect and special privileges."

By contrast, the Bible says about Jesus . . .

"Even the Son of Man did not come to be served, but to serve" (MARK 10:45).

Possessions—"Having a palatial home, acquiring impressive possessions, and gaining the admiration and envy of others is important to my self-esteem and enhances my confidence. It is nice to have beautiful things to show off."

By contrast, the Bible says about Jesus . . .

"The Son of Man has no place to lay his head" (MATTHEW 8:20).

Power—"Control is critical in today's economy, and only those who have power can exert their will over others and get their way. I don't want anyone to have enough power over me to dictate what I will or will not do."

By contrast, the Bible says about Jesus . . .
"Yet not as I will, but as you will" (MATTHEW 26:39).

Some Surface Causes of Pride

S—Selling out to the world's concept of success[178]

"Here now is the man who did not make God his stronghold but trusted in his great wealth and grew strong by destroying others!" (PSALM 52:7).

E—Elevating self-worth by attaining worldly goals

"My people come to you, as they usually do, and sit before you to hear your words, but they do not put them into practice. Their mouths speak of love, but their hearts are greedy for unjust gain. Indeed, to them you are nothing more than one who sings love songs with a beautiful voice and plays an instrument well, for they hear your words but do not put them into practice" (EZEKIEL 33:31–32).

L—Lifting the burden of guilt for sins through personal performance

"Since they did not know the righteousness of God and sought to establish their own, they did not submit to God's righteousness" (ROMANS 10:3).

F—Focusing on self[179]

"People will be lovers of themselves, lovers of money, boastful, proud, abusive, disobedient to their parents, ungrateful, unholy" (2 TIMOTHY 3:2).

Myths About Humility

Myth #1: Humble people are usually losers. They aren't as capable as others.
Truth: The humble are lifted up by the Lord.
"Humble yourselves before the Lord, and he will lift you up" (JAMES 4:10).

Myth #2: Humble people end up as failures. They aren't as important as others.
Truth: The humble will one day be exalted.
"Those who exalt themselves will be humbled, and those who humble themselves will be exalted" (MATTHEW 23:12).

Myth #3: Humble people won't be victorious. They aren't as successful as others.
Truth: The humble succeed in the end.
"For the LORD takes delight in his people; he crowns the humble with victory" (PSALM 149:4).

My Personalized Plan

I will . . .

Recognize humility as an essential characteristic of a follower of Christ.

"As God's chosen people, holy and dearly loved, clothe yourselves with compassion, kindness, humility, gentleness and patience" (COLOSSIANS 3:12).

Embrace God's perspective on pride.

"To fear the LORD is to hate evil; I hate pride and arrogance, evil behavior and perverse speech" (PROVERBS 8:13).

Listen to the correction and advice of others.

"Fools think their own way is right, but the wise listen to others" (PROVERBS 12:15 NLT).

Pray for all my blind spots to be revealed and removed by God.

"Search me, God, and know my heart; test me and know my anxious thoughts. See if there is any offensive way in me, and lead me in the way everlasting" (PSALM 139:23–24).

Respond with humility to God's influences in my life (the Word of God, authorities in my life, the counsel of family and friends, God's discipline).

"Do not despise the LORD's discipline, and do not resent his rebuke" (PROVERBS 3:11–12).

Key Passage to Read

Luke 18:9–14

Accept with gratitude everything God allows in my life.

"Give thanks in all circumstances; for this is God's will for you in Christ Jesus" (1 THESSALONIANS 5:18).

Develop a true and genuine servant's heart of love toward others.

"Serve one another humbly in love" (GALATIANS 5:13).

Be humble and patient with people who I find difficult.

"Be completely humble and gentle; be patient, bearing with one another in love" (EPHESIANS 4:2).

Not consider myself better than others but willing to associate with anyone God puts in my life.

"Live in harmony with one another. Do not be proud, but be willing to associate with people of low position. Do not be conceited" (ROMANS 12:16).

Look out not only for my interests but those of others.

"Be humble, thinking of others as better than yourselves. Don't look out only for your own interests, but take an interest in others, too" (PHILIPPIANS 2:3–4 NLT).

Do not think of yourself more highly
than you ought, but rather think of yourself
with sober judgment, in accordance with
the faith God has distributed to each of you.
(ROMANS 12:3)

Questions & Answers

Question: "What is the difference between self-esteem and self-worth?"

Answer: Self-esteem can mean two very different things. On one hand, it refers to a healthy recognition of your inherent value as God's creation—your true self-worth. Because God made you in His image, you possess immeasurable worth and dignity. Healthy self-worth means humbly recognizing this God-given value while also acknowledging your sin, your need for the Savior, and your reliance on Him every day. This balanced view prevents you from thinking too low (false humility) or too high (pridefulness).

As the apostle Paul said, *"For by the grace given me I say to every one of you: Do not think of yourself more highly than you ought, but rather think of yourself with sober judgment, in accordance with the faith God has distributed to each of you"* (Romans 12:3).

On the other hand, self-esteem can become an inflated sense of self—pridefulness—where you believe you are good enough on your own to meet your own needs. In this view, your value is based on personal achievements rather than on Christ's redeeming work. Jesus warns us:

"You are the ones who justify yourselves in the eyes of others,
but God knows your hearts.
What people value highly is detestable in God's sight."
(LUKE 16:15)

Question: "Is pride really that harmful?"

Answer: Pride distorts our view of God, ourselves, and others. Almost all lists of negative traits in the Bible contain the word or concept of *pride.*

People will be lovers of themselves, lovers of money, boastful, proud, abusive,
disobedient to their parents, ungrateful, unholy.
(2 TIMOTHY 3:2)

PROCRASTINATION

Preventing the Decay of Delay

God's Heart on Diligence

God's heart is that we work diligently, because diligence produces progress.
"Be diligent in these matters; give yourself wholly to them, so that everyone may see your progress" (1 TIMOTHY 4:15).

God's heart is that we be diligent to fulfill the promises we make to Him.
"When you make a promise to God, don't delay in following through, for God takes no pleasure in fools. Keep all the promises you make to him" (ECCLESIASTES 5:4 NLT).

God's heart is that we diligently encourage each other to do loving acts and good works.
"Let us think of ways to motivate one another to acts of love and good works" (HEBREWS 10:24 NLT).

God's heart is that we diligently do the works of God while we can.
"As long as it is day, we must do the works of him who sent me. Night is coming, when no one can work" (JOHN 9:4).

God's heart is that we be diligent in finishing the work God gives us to do.
"I have brought you glory on earth by finishing the work you gave me to do" (JOHN 17:4).

The Negligent vs. the Diligent

The negligent are never filled, but the diligent are fully filled.
"A sluggard's appetite is never filled, but the desires of the diligent are fully satisfied" (PROVERBS 13:4).

The negligent have a blocked way, but the path of the diligent is wide open.
"The way of the sluggard is blocked with thorns, but the path of the upright is a highway" (PROVERBS 15:19).

The negligent focus on fantasies, but the diligent focus on work.
"Those who work their land will have abundant food, but those who chase fantasies have no sense" (PROVERBS 12:11).

The negligent experience poverty, but the diligent experience profit.
"Hard work brings a profit, but mere talk leads only to poverty" (PROVERBS 14:23).

The negligent are filled with poverty, but the diligent are filled with food.
"Those who work their land will have abundant food, but those who chase fantasies will have their fill of poverty" (PROVERBS 28:19).

The Directive to Be Diligent

Diligently work to share with others.
"Anyone who has been stealing must steal no longer, but must work, doing something useful with their own hands, that they may have something to share with those in need" (EPHESIANS 4:28).

Diligently work as for the Lord, not others.
"Whatever you do, work at it with all your heart, as working for the Lord, not for human masters, since you know that you will receive an inheritance from the Lord as a reward. It is the Lord Christ you are serving" (COLOSSIANS 3:23–24).

Diligently work not to be a burden to others.
"Surely you remember, brothers and sisters, our toil and hardship; we worked night and day in order not to be a burden to anyone while we preached the gospel of God to you" (1 THESSALONIANS 2:9).

Diligently work with your hands.
"Make it your ambition to lead a quiet life: You should mind your own business and work with your hands, just as we told you" (1 THESSALONIANS 4:11).

Diligently work or you won't eat.
"Even when we were with you, we gave you this rule: 'The one who is unwilling to work shall not eat'" (2 THESSALONIANS 3:10).

Potholes of Procrastination

Place a ✓ if your answer is *yes*, or an × if your answer is *no*.

- ☐ Do you delay starting projects?
- ☐ Do you collect materials for projects but struggle to move forward?
- ☐ Do you hinder the efforts of others by delaying your part?
- ☐ Do you resent suggestions on how to be more productive?
- ☐ Do you avoid competition and other situations where you might not succeed?

- ☐ Do you act indecisively and force others to make decisions?
- ☐ Do you shirk responsibility by focusing on the faults of others?
- ☐ Do you dodge making or keeping commitments?
- ☐ Do you become irritable when asked to do something unpleasant?
- ☐ Do you find yourself consistently late for appointments?
- ☐ Do you pay bills and other financial obligations late?
- ☐ Do you fail to return phone calls?
- ☐ Do you postpone sending correspondence until it is too late?
- ☐ Do you live in a state of disorganization?
- ☐ Do you become addicted to time-wasting activities?
- ☐ Do you feel "spiritually bankrupt" yet reject the Bible's riches?
- ☐ Do you desperately need direction yet fail to pray for God's guidance?
- ☐ Do you resist God's correction by rejecting His conviction?

The heart of the discerning acquires knowledge,
for the ears of the wise seek it out.
(Proverbs 18:15)

The Procrastinator's Excuses

The Rationalizer

"I'm not ready to begin right now."

"I'll work better if I finish these other tasks first."

"I must wait until I'm truly inspired."

"I'll do a better job when I feel up to the task."

"It's too late in the week to start."

"I need a larger block of time."

"I don't have enough information yet."

"If I wait, I'll do a first-class job!"

"I've already done some of it. I'll finish it later."

"I still have time."

"I've really been working hard. I deserve a break."

"I can always stay up all night and finish it then."

"There is a way that appears to be right, but in the end it leads to death."
(PROVERBS 14:12)

The Dodger

"I sometimes focus on the tasks I can complete instead of the most important."

"It's easier to first tackle trivial tasks even if others have a higher priority."

"I know this project is time-sensitive, but I overslept and got to work late. I have lunch plans, so I'll work on it later."

"I was out with my friends, so I didn't have time to buy groceries or do laundry this weekend."

"I can't get some of my important work done because I have letters, phone calls, and emails to answer."

"I enjoy good entertainment but I end up feeling bad when I don't get other things done."

"I'm happy to serve at church, help the kids, and other charitable work, but I don't have time for my own responsibilities."

"When you make a vow to God, do not delay to fulfill it."
(ECCLESIASTES 5:4)

The Martyr

"I can't help that I am constantly interrupted."

"I haven't been given enough time to accomplish the task."

"I don't have what I need to do the work."

"I don't have working conditions that are conducive to doing the job."

"I just can't get others to cooperate with me!"

"I keep being asked to do other things."

"Do everything without grumbling or arguing, so that you may become blameless and pure, 'children of God without fault in a warped and crooked generation.' Then you will shine among them like stars in the sky."
(PHILIPPIANS 2:14–15)

How to Motivate a Procrastinator

Pray for the procrastinator.

"As for me, far be it from me that I should sin against the LORD by failing to pray for you" (1 SAMUEL 12:23).

Propose an accountability plan.

"As iron sharpens iron, so one person sharpens another" (PROVERBS 27:17).

Note the unmet needs.

"I cry out to God Most High . . . who fulfills his purpose for me" (PSALM 57:2 ESV).

Encourage the use of a daily calendar.

"Those who disregard discipline despise themselves, but the one who heeds correction gains understanding" (PROVERBS 15:32).

Properly order your priorities.

"A longing fulfilled is sweet to the soul" (PROVERBS 13:19).

Group similar goals.

"There will be a time for every activity" (ECCLESIASTES 3:17).

Key Verses to Memorize

Be very careful, then, how you live—
not as unwise but as wise,
making the most of every opportunity.
(EPHESIANS 5:15-16)

Limit the number of options.

"Let your eyes look straight ahead; fix your gaze directly before you. . . . Do not turn to the right or the left" (PROVERBS 4:25, 27).

Compliment small accomplishments.

"A word fitly spoken is like apples of gold in settings of silver" (PROVERBS 25:11 NKJV).

Use the "sandwich technique" to confront failure.

(Bread of Appreciation, Meat of the Matter, Bread of Encouragement)

"A person finds joy in giving an apt reply—and how good is a timely word!" (PROVERBS 15:23).

Establish and maintain boundaries.

"It is better not to make a vow than to make a vow and not fulfill it" (ECCLESIASTES 5:5).

Set flexible arrangements.

"Let us therefore make every effort to do what leads to peace and to mutual edification" (ROMANS 14:19).

Acknowledge your own mistakes.
"If I must boast, I will boast of the things that show my weakness" (2 CORINTHIANS 11:30).

Avoid being manipulated into accepting another's responsibility.
"Each one should carry their own load" (GALATIANS 6:5).

Present the ultimate purpose.
Say to the procrastinator, "Do you know God's purpose for your life? God's purpose for every Christian is to be conformed to the character of Christ. Romans 8:29 says that you are *'predestined to be conformed to the image of his Son.'* That means you can have the discipline and self-control of Christ."

My Personalized Plan

I will . . .

Acknowledge that procrastination smothers motivation.
"Despite their desires, the lazy will come to ruin, for their hands refuse to work" (PROVERBS 21:25 NLT).

Tell God that I am tired of fighting the clock. I will pray for wisdom and help in using the time He has given me.
"Teach us to number our days, that we may gain a heart of wisdom" (PSALM 90:12).

Keep a record of my time, tracking everything I need to do and checking off each task with the exact day and time I complete it.
"There will be a time for every activity, a time to judge every deed" (ECCLESIASTES 3:17).

Refuse to "major on the minors" but will keep the "main thing" the "main thing." I will prioritize the five most important tasks I need to do each day—then do them in order.
"He who follows worthless pursuits will have plenty of poverty" (PROVERBS 28:19 ESV).

Estimate the time needed to complete each project—being realistic. I will add additional time for unexpected interruptions and delays.
"Suppose one of you wants to build a tower. Won't you first sit down and estimate the cost to see if you have enough money to complete it? For if you lay the foundation and are not able to finish it, everyone who sees it will ridicule you" (LUKE 14:28–29).

Resist the temptation to feel guilty if an unforeseen situation arises, making it impossible for me to complete all my tasks in one day. I will continue to persevere the next day, again giving top priority to the five most important tasks.

"Do not throw away your confidence; it will be richly rewarded. You need to persevere so that when you have done the will of God, you will receive what he has promised" (HEBREWS 10:35-36).

Consider the impact of my negative self-talk when I get emotionally stuck. I will change my thoughts and internal dialogue to please God and to reflect His truth about me.

"May these words of my mouth and this meditation of my heart be pleasing in your sight, LORD, my Rock and my Redeemer" (PSALM 19:14).

Key Passage to Read

Proverbs 24:30-34

Ask a friend or someone wise to help me if I struggle with getting started.

"The way of fools seems right to them, but the wise listen to advice" (PROVERBS 12:15).

Trust God to help me and believe that He will direct my path.

"Trust in the LORD with all your heart and lean not on your own understanding; in all your ways submit to him, and he will make your paths straight" (PROVERBS 3:5-6).

Remember God's promise to provide for my needs.

"My God will meet all your needs according to the riches of his glory in Christ Jesus" (PHILIPPIANS 4:19).

Questions & Answers

Question: "Is there a difference between procrastination and laziness?"

Answer: Many people assume that procrastinators are always lazy. However, laziness is just one cause of procrastination. If you are lazy, you are negligent in handling your responsibilities because of choosing not to do what you need to do.

On the other hand, you may be highly productive and in no way lazy, but still procrastinate by failing to start a task on time or not accurately predicting how long it will take. This procrastinator desires to work and yet delays, whereas the lazy procrastinator lacks desire and refuses to work. Proverbs, the book of wisdom, warns us about the way of the sluggard:

The way of the sluggard is blocked with thorns,
but the path of the upright is a highway.
(PROVERBS 15:19)

Question: "Could I have a combination of causes for procrastination?"

Answer: Yes. One person could be both a *perfectionist* and *overwhelmed*, resulting in a major struggle with procrastination. Another person could delay needlessly because of both *low self-worth* and a *lack of goals*. Some people struggle with procrastination related to a learning or attention issue such as attention-deficit/hyperactivity disorder (ADHD) or a mental-health issue such as obsessive compulsive disorder (OCD). Whether your procrastination stems from one cause or several, each and every temptation to procrastinate can be overcome.

"Watch and pray so that you will not
fall into temptation.
The spirit is willing, but the flesh is weak."
(Matthew 26:41)

PROSPERITY THEOLOGY

False Teachers—False Hope!

God's Heart on Prosperity Theology

God wants you to look to Him, not money, as your source of hope.

"Command those who are rich in this present world not to be arrogant nor to put their hope in wealth, which is so uncertain, but to put their hope in God, who richly provides us with everything for our enjoyment" (1 TIMOTHY 6:17).

God wants you to put your trust in Him, not in your possessions.

"Some trust in chariots and some in horses, but we trust in the name of the LORD *our God"* (PSALM 20:7).

God wants you to seek Him above wealth and possessions.

"Seek the Kingdom of God above all else, and live righteously, and he will give you everything you need" (MATTHEW 6:33 NLT).

God warns against using religion and spirituality as a means of financial gain.

"These people always cause trouble. Their minds are corrupt, and they have turned their backs on the truth. To them, a show of godliness is just a way to become wealthy. Yet true godliness with contentment is itself great wealth" (1 TIMOTHY 6:5–6 NLT).

God wants you to be thankful for what He has given you.

"Give thanks in all circumstances; for this is God's will for you in Christ Jesus" (1 THESSALONIANS 5:18).

God does not promise a life free of problems, but He offers His peace in the midst of troubles.

"I have told you these things, so that in me you may have peace. In this world you will have trouble. But take heart! I have overcome the world" (JOHN 16:33).

God allows trials in our lives so that we grow and realize the sufficiency of His grace.

"He said to me, 'My grace is sufficient for you, for my power is made perfect in weakness.' Therefore I will boast all the more gladly about my weaknesses, so that Christ's power may rest on me" (2 CORINTHIANS 12:9).

God wants you to be on guard against greed and materialism.

"Then he said to them, 'Watch out! Be on your guard against all kinds of greed; life does not consist in an abundance of possessions'" (LUKE 12:15).

God wants you to invest in heavenly treasures, not earthly things.

"Do not store up for yourselves treasures on earth, where moths and vermin destroy, and where thieves break in and steal. But store up for yourselves treasures in heaven, where moths and vermin do not destroy, and where thieves do not break in and steal" (Matthew 6:19–20).

God wants you to avoid the traps of temptation that bring ruin and destruction.

"We brought nothing into the world, and we can take nothing out of it. But if we have food and clothing, we will be content with that. Those who want to get rich fall into temptation and a trap and into many foolish and harmful desires that plunge people into ruin and destruction" (1 Timothy 6:7–9).

God wants you to carefully steward what He entrusts to your care.

"Whoever can be trusted with very little can also be trusted with much, and whoever is dishonest with very little will also be dishonest with much" (Luke 16:10).

God wants you to know He will meet all your needs.

"Give me neither poverty nor riches, but give me only my daily bread" (Proverbs 30:8).

Six Primary Positions of Prosperity Theology

1. **Prosperity Position**: "Sickness is always the result of sin."

   Biblical Position: Directly refuted when the disciples asked Jesus about a man blind from birth.

   "'Rabbi, who sinned, this man or his parents, that he was born blind?' [Jesus answered] *'Neither this man nor his parents sinned . . . but this happened so that the works of God might be displayed in him'"* (John 9:2–3).

2. **Prosperity Position**: "Poverty is always the result of sin."

   Biblical Position: Directly refuted by Jesus when He said about Himself, "the Son of Man has no place to lay his head."

   "Foxes have dens and birds have nests, but the Son of Man has no place to lay his head" (Matthew 8:20).

3. **Prosperity Position**: "Sickness is a curse."

   Biblical Position: Directly refuted by the illness of Job, who was not cursed but was allowed by God to be physically afflicted by Satan.

   "The Lord said to Satan, 'Have you considered my servant Job? There is no one on earth like him; he is blameless and upright, a man who fears God and shuns evil. And he still maintains his integrity, though you incited me against him to ruin him without any reason'" (Job 2:3).

4. **Prosperity Position**: "Poverty is always a curse."

   Biblical Position: Directly refuted by the fact that Jesus honored a poor widow for her meager offering to God, something He would not have done had He considered her cursed. It should also be remembered that wealth does not solve every problem and may even contribute to certain difficulties.

   "He also saw a poor widow put in two very small copper coins. 'Truly I tell you,' he said, 'this poor widow has put in more than all the others'" (LUKE 21:2–3).

5. **Prosperity Position**: "Sickness is of the devil."

   Biblical Position: Directly refuted by Jesus when He responded to the illness of his good friend Lazarus.

   "Jesus said, 'This sickness will not end in death. No, it is for God's glory so that God's Son may be glorified through it'" (JOHN 11:4).

Key Verse to Memorize

Give me neither poverty nor riches,
but give me only my daily bread.
(PROVERBS 30:8)

6. **Prosperity Position**: "If you have enough faith, you will be healed."

   Biblical Position: Directly refuted by the experience and testimony of the apostle Paul.

   "I was given a thorn in my flesh, a messenger of Satan, to torment me. Three times I pleaded with the Lord to take it away from me. But he said to me, 'My grace is sufficient for you, for my power is made perfect in weakness.' Therefore I will boast all the more gladly about my weaknesses, so that Christ's power may rest on me. That is why, for Christ's sake, I delight in weaknesses, in insults, in hardships, in persecutions, in difficulties. For when I am weak, then I am strong" (2 CORINTHIANS 12:7–10).

Afflictions: A Blessing or a Curse?

Afflictions soften your heart toward obeying God's Word.

"Before I was afflicted I went astray, but now I obey your word" (PSALM 119:67).

Afflictions open your heart to make you more teachable.

"I know, LORD, that your laws are righteous, and that in faithfulness you have afflicted me" (PSALM 119:75).

Afflictions humble your heart to keep you from being conceited.

"In order to keep me from becoming conceited, I was given a thorn in my flesh, a messenger of Satan, to torment me" (2 CORINTHIANS 12:7).

Afflictions uncover your heart's weakness so that you may appropriate Christ as your strength.

"My grace is sufficient for you, for my power is made perfect in weakness." Paul then responds, *"Therefore I will boast all the more gladly about my weaknesses, so that Christ's power may rest on me"* (2 CORINTHIANS 12:9).

Is Divine Healing Guaranteed?

1. **The apostle Paul was not miraculously healed.**

   Paul records that he had a *"thorn in my flesh,"* and, *"Three times I pleaded with the Lord to take it away from me."* However, the Lord's answer was no. Instead, Jesus said, *"My grace is sufficient for you, for my power is made perfect in weakness"* (2 CORINTHIANS 12:7–9).

2. **Timothy was not miraculously healed.**

   Paul told Timothy, his son in the faith, *"Stop drinking only water, and use a little wine because of your stomach and your frequent illnesses"* (1 TIMOTHY 5:23).

3. **Epaphroditus was not miraculously healed.**

   Paul told the Philippian church, *"Epaphroditus . . . is distressed because you heard he was ill. Indeed he was ill, and almost died. But God had mercy on him. . . . He almost died for the work of Christ"* (PHILIPPIANS 2:25–27, 30).

4. **Trophimus was not miraculously healed.**

   Paul traveled with Trophimus. Paul wrote to Timothy, *"I left Trophimus sick in Miletus"* (2 TIMOTHY 4:20).

Participate in God's Plan

T—Thank God for what He has given to you.

> *"Sing and make music from your heart to the Lord, always giving thanks to God the Father for everything, in the name of our Lord Jesus Christ"* (EPHESIANS 5:19–20).

R—Rest in God as your Provider.

> *"Command those who are rich in this present world not to be arrogant nor to put their hope in wealth, which is so uncertain, but to put their hope in God, who richly provides us with everything for our enjoyment"* (1 TIMOTHY 6:17).

U—Uphold God's perspective on possessions.

> *"Watch out! Be on your guard against all kinds of greed; life does not consist in an abundance of possessions"* (LUKE 12:15).

S—Seek God's provision in each and every circumstance.

"The wild animals honor me, the jackals and the owls, because I provide water in the wilderness and streams in the wasteland, to give drink to my people, my chosen" (ISAIAH 43:20).

T—Trust in God, not in what you possess.

"Some trust in chariots and some in horses, but we trust in the name of the LORD *our God"* (PSALM 20:7).

H—Honor God with what He gives to you.

"All the believers were one in heart and mind. No one claimed that any of their possessions was their own, but they shared everything they had. . . . They sold property and possessions to give to anyone who had need" (ACTS 4:32; 2:45).

Key Passage to Read

1 Timothy 6:3–19

I—Invest in heavenly treasures, not in earthly things.

"You suffered along with those in prison and joyfully accepted the confiscation of your property, because you knew that you yourselves had better and lasting possessions" (HEBREWS 10:34).

M—Manage well what God entrusts to your care.

"Whoever can be trusted with very little can also be trusted with much, and whoever is dishonest with very little will also be dishonest with much" (LUKE 16:10).

The Right Focus on Faith

Our faith is to be placed in the Lord as we yield our will to His will.

Our faith is not to be in our faith!

Our prayer should be, "Not what I will, but what you will" (Mark 14:36).

My Personalized Plan

I will . . .

Seek the Lord first, rather than earthly things.

"Seek first his kingdom and his righteousness, and all these things will be given to you as well" (MATTHEW 6:33).

Trust God even when He does not answer my prayers for healing or provision in the way I desire.

"You will keep in perfect peace those whose minds are steadfast, because they trust in you. Trust in the LORD forever, for the LORD, the LORD himself, is the Rock eternal" (ISAIAH 26:3–4).

Ask God to help me wait on Him and His perfect timing.

"Those who hope in the LORD will renew their strength. They will soar on wings like eagles; they will run and not grow weary, they will walk and not be faint" (ISAIAH 40:31).

Expect trials as a normal part of living in a broken world.

"Dear friends, don't be surprised at the fiery trials you are going through, as if something strange were happening to you. Instead, be very glad—for these trials make you partners with Christ in his suffering, so that you will have the wonderful joy of seeing his glory when it is revealed to all the world" (1 PETER 4:12–13 NLT).

Remember that sickness and want are opportunities to grow in my faith and in reliance on God as my provider and ultimate healer.

"Indeed, we felt we had received the sentence of death. But this happened that we might not rely on ourselves but on God, who raises the dead" (2 CORINTHIANS 1:9).

Remember that God alone is my master, not money.

"No one can serve two masters. Either you will hate the one and love the other, or you will be devoted to the one and despise the other. You cannot serve both God and money" (MATTHEW 6:24).

Learn to be content, whether I have plenty or I am in need.

"I know what it is to be in need, and I know what it is to have plenty. I have learned the secret of being content in any and every situation, whether well fed or hungry, whether living in plenty or in want. I can do all this through him who gives me strength" (PHILIPPIANS 4:12–13).

Ask God to confirm when I hear false teaching.

"This is what the LORD Almighty says: 'Do not listen to what the prophets are prophesying to you; they fill you with false hopes. They speak visions from their own minds, not from the mouth of the LORD'" (JEREMIAH 23:16).

Be on guard against teaching that goes against the gospel truth.

"I am astonished that you are so quickly deserting the one who called you to live in the grace of Christ and are turning to a different gospel—which is really no gospel at all. Evidently some people are throwing you into confusion and are trying to pervert the gospel of Christ" (GALATIANS 1:6–7).

Study Scripture so I can discern whether God's truth is being twisted or taught accurately.

"Be diligent to present yourself approved to God, a worker who does not need to be ashamed, rightly dividing the word of truth" (2 Timothy 2:15 NKJV).

Give me neither poverty nor riches,
but give me only my daily bread.
(Proverbs 30:8)

Questions & Answers

Question: "Is it okay to pray for miraculous healing?"

Answer: Yes, absolutely. It is biblical to present your request to God for full restoration. It is also biblical to pray as Jesus prayed, *"Father . . . not my will, but yours be done"* (Luke 22:42). If it is God's will, you will receive what you asked.

If we ask anything according to his will, he hears us.
And if we know that he hears us—whatever we ask—
we know that we have what we asked of him.
(1 John 5:14-15)

Question: "Why would a loving God want me to suffer?"

Answer: God does not delight in your suffering, but He allows suffering in order to refine your faith, to develop Christ's character in you, and to bring glory to Himself.

In all this you greatly rejoice, though now for a little while you may have had to suffer grief in all kinds of trials. These have come so that the proven genuineness of your faith . . . may result in praise,
glory and honor when Jesus Christ is revealed.
(1 Peter 1:6-7)

Question: "If I pray with total faith, doesn't the Bible say that I will be blessed with health, wealth, and problem-free living?"

Answer: No. The Bible clearly reveals that Jesus, along with the apostles, did not experience health, wealth, and problem-free living. Scripture does state that when you share in the sufferings of Christ, you are blessed by God.

Rejoice inasmuch as you participate in
the sufferings of Christ, so that you may be
overjoyed when his glory is revealed.
(1 Peter 4:13)

PURPOSE IN LIFE

Pinpointing Your Priorities

God's Heart on Purpose in Life

God has plans and purposes for you.

"'I know the plans I have for you,' declares the LORD, *'plans to prosper you and not to harm you, plans to give you hope and a future'"* (JEREMIAH 29:11).

God had a purpose for you even before you were born.

"Before I formed you in the womb I knew you, before you were born I set you apart" (JEREMIAH 1:5).

God has good works that He prepared specifically for you.

"We are God's handiwork, created in Christ Jesus to do good works, which God prepared in advance for us to do" (EPHESIANS 2:10).

God is committed to fulfilling His purpose for you.

"The LORD *will fulfill his purpose for me; your steadfast love, O* LORD, *endures forever"* (PSALM 138:8 ESV).

God's purposes for you do not change based on shifting circumstances, cultural trends, or feelings.

"The plans of the LORD *stand firm forever, the purposes of his heart through all generations"* (PSALM 33:11).

God wants you to look to His Word to discover His purposes and the path He has for you.

"Your word is a lamp to my feet and a light to my path" (PSALM 119:105 ESV).

God can use wise, insightful people to help you understand your purpose.

"The purposes of a person's heart are deep waters, but one who has insight draws them out" (PROVERBS 20:5).

God gives you a specific spiritual gift to help fulfill your purpose and to serve others.

"God has given each of you a gift from his great variety of spiritual gifts. Use them well to serve one another" (1 PETER 4:10 NLT).

God's purpose in every circumstance and season of life is to make you more like Jesus.

"We know that in all things God works for the good of those who love him, who have been called according to his purpose. For those God foreknew he also predestined to be conformed to the image of his Son" (ROMANS 8:28–29).

God has purposes for your suffering—to reveal His compassion to you and equip you to comfort others.

"The Father of compassion and the God of all comfort . . . comforts us in all our troubles, so that we can comfort those in any trouble with the comfort we ourselves receive from God" (2 CORINTHIANS 1:3–4).

God's highest purpose and priority for you is to love the Lord and to love others.

"'Love the Lord your God with all your heart and with all your soul and with all your mind and with all your strength.' . . . 'Love your neighbor as yourself.' There is no commandment greater than these" (MARK 12:30–31).

God's purpose for you is to know Him and make Him known to others.

"We are therefore Christ's ambassadors, as though God were making his appeal through us. We implore you on Christ's behalf: Be reconciled to God" (2 CORINTHIANS 5:20).

20 Questions to Help Discover Your Purpose in Life

1. **What** activities have been the most fulfilling to you—ones that brought you great joy and satisfaction?
2. **When** do you feel like you're "in the zone" or "at your best"?
3. **What** has God clearly revealed to you in His Word about His purpose for you?
4. **What** would you like to spend more time doing?
5. **What** do you know should be a priority to you?
6. **What** is your greatest passion? What do you love doing the most?
7. **What** activities come naturally to you?
8. **What** activities/work have brought you success?
9. **What** have others noticed you're good at doing?
10. **What** dreams, desires, or goals do you often ponder?

11. **What** are your most important roles and responsibilities?
12. **What** are your God-given gifts and talents?
13. **What** current opportunities do you have?
14. **What** resources do you have at your disposal?
15. **What** do you really want out of life?
16. **What** problem in the world do you think needs to be solved?
17. **What** people do you have a heart for helping? Who needs help?
18. **When** have you felt like you've made a difference?
19. **What** would you like to be remembered for doing?
20. **What** do you want to accomplish before you die?

Develop a Personal Purpose Statement

Think. Make a list of activities you do best and enjoy the most. Consider how these activities can help benefit others.

Reflect. Pay attention to any desires you've held in the back of your mind. Write them down. Pray about each one. Ask God for wisdom to know if these strong desires reflect His will for you. Believe God's promise that anything is possible with Him.

Write. Commit to writing what you think your purpose statement could be. Don't worry about grammar or sentence structure at this point. Jot down what easily comes to mind. Reference your brainstorm lists as needed.

Key Verse to Memorize

We know that in all things God works for the good of those who love him, who have been called according to his purpose.
(Romans 8:28)

Refine. For a while, your purpose statement will be a work in progress. Continue to hone it, moving phrases around, eliminating words or phrases, making sure it flows logically, sounds good, and is short enough to be quoted.

Memorize. Once finalized, commit your purpose statement to memory. This will guide you, keep you on track, and help you evaluate what you are doing and where you are going in your life.

Display. Frame your purpose statement and hang it on your wall or place it on your desk—anywhere you will see it frequently. This will motivate you to "put feet" to purpose and keep you headed in the right direction.

Who is wise and understanding among you?
Let them show it by their good life,
by deeds done in the humility
that comes from wisdom.
(JAMES 3:13)

Prayer of Purpose

"Dear Lord, Thank You for having a unique plan and purpose for me.
Thank You for caring about every detail of my life.
It gives me hope to know that my life has meaning
and that You will accomplish Your purposes in my life
through the good times and even through the difficult times.
I ask that You reveal Your purposes for my life
as I study Your Word, talk to others, and pray for Your leading.
Help me discover Your specific goals and plans for my life.
Thank You, Father, for the gifts You have given me,
and that You will accomplish Your purposes in and through me.
In Jesus' name, amen."

I cry out to God Most High,
to God who will fulfill his purpose for me.
(PSALM 57:2 NLT)

My Personalized Plan

I will . . .

Seek God's will.

— I will read the Bible to understand God's clear purposes for me.

— I will seek God's will for every area of my life: physical, mental, emotional, relational, spiritual, and vocational.

"I desire to do your will, my God; your law is within my heart" (PSALM 40:8).

Talk with others.

— I will talk with those who know me well to help identify my calling and purpose.

— I will listen to their guidance and advice about my strengths and weaknesses.

"Get all the advice and instruction you can, so you will be wise the rest of your life" (PROVERBS 19:20 NLT).

Identify gifts and passion.

— I will discover and understand my God-given gifts, skills, and abilities.

— I will identify areas I'm passionate about and consider how to use my gifts.

"Each of you should use whatever gift you have received to serve others, as faithful stewards of God's grace in its various forms" (1 PETER 4:10).

Be aware of idols and pitfalls.

— I will be mindful of areas where I'm tempted to find my purpose in temporary things such as a job, possessions, or a relationship.

— I will fight temptations that distract me from fulfilling my purpose.

"Search me, God, and know my heart; test me and know my anxious thoughts. See if there is any offensive way in me, and lead me in the way everlasting" (PSALM 139:23–24).

Key Passage to Read

The book of Ecclesiastes

Distinguish between *purpose* and *roles.*

— I will remember that my purpose is deeper and different from the jobs or roles I have in life.

— I will adjust to changing circumstances, knowing my purpose goes beyond any job or relationship.

"The LORD will fulfill his purpose for me; your steadfast love, O LORD, endures forever" (PSALM 138:8 ESV).

Remember the main thing.

— I will remember that my main purpose is to glorify God and grow in Christlikeness.

— I will remember the greatest commandment—to love God and others.

"Love the Lord your God with all your heart and with all your soul and with all your mind and with all your strength.' The second is this: 'Love your neighbor as yourself.' There is no commandment greater than these" (MARK 12:30–31).

Questions & Answers

Question: "I don't feel like my life has any purpose. Is there any hope for me?"

Answer: Yes. You have hope—you were created by the God of hope. In the Bible, God says that He created you with a specific plan for your life. Your life can be filled with hope and purpose when you choose to follow God's will.

"I know the plans I have for you," declares
the LORD, "plans to prosper you and not to harm you,
plans to give you hope and a future."
(JEREMIAH 29:11)

Question: "Do I have only one purpose in life?"

Answer: No. You will have several purposes, depending on the major roles in your life.

Many are the plans in a person's heart,
but it is the LORD's purpose that prevails.
(PROVERBS 19:21)

Question: "Are purposes and goals the same?"

Answer: No. Purposes are different from goals; however, they are related. Your purposes answer, "Why am I here on earth?" Your goals answer, "What do I want to do here on earth?"[180]

For example, one of your purposes could be to *"honor your father and your mother"* (Exodus 20:12). Yet, if your father is painfully critical, your short-term goal could be to pray for him every time you are around him and every time you think of him.

"Pray for those who persecute you."
(MATTHEW 5:44)

Question: "What is God's purpose for my life?"

Answer: God's highest purpose for your life is to conform you to the character of Christ.

Those God foreknew he also predestined
to be conformed to the image of his Son.
(ROMANS 8:29)

RECONCILIATION

Restoring Broken Relationships

God's Heart on Reconciliation

Rejecting relationships leads to disunity and dysfunction.
Restoring relationships lets healing and harmony prevail.
"Live in harmony with one another. Do not be proud" (Romans 12:16).

Rejecting relationships grieves the heart of God.
Restoring relationships gladdens the heart of God.
"Make my joy complete by being like-minded, having the same love, being one in spirit and of one mind" (Philippians 2:2).

Rejecting relationships signals unforgiveness.
Restoring relationships signifies forgiveness.
"Forgive, and you will be forgiven" (Luke 6:37).

Rejecting relationships deepens guilt and drains joy.
Restoring relationships dissipates burdensome emotions.
"My guilt has overwhelmed me like a burden too heavy to bear" (Psalm 38:4).

Rejecting relationships breeds deep-seated anger and hostility.
Restoring relationships brings about peace.
"'In your anger do not sin': Do not let the sun go down while you are still angry" (Ephesians 4:26).

Rejecting relationships misses opportunities to show mercy.
Restoring relationships mirrors the character of God.
"Remember, Lord, your great mercy and love, for they are from of old" (Psalm 25:6).

Make every effort to be found spotless,
blameless and at peace with him.
(2 Peter 3:14)

Types of Reconciliation

Relational: to bring a broken relationship into harmony

Personal: to be at peace with our circumstances or with ourselves

Financial: to bring accounting records into agreement

Spiritual: to be at harmony with God

All this is from God, who reconciled us
to himself through Christ
and gave us the ministry of reconciliation.
(2 CORINTHIANS 5:18)

What Characterizes a Heart of Reconciliation?

Humility:[181] Do I focus on how much the Lord continues to forgive me?

Self-Examination:[182] Do I expect change only in others, or do I recognize my own need to change also?

Forgiveness:[183] Do I choose to release my personal rights and allow the Lord to empower me to forgive?

Confrontation:[184] Do I communicate my feelings without accusation?

Communication: Do I set aside quality time to share my heart and have personal interaction?

Risk-Taking: Do I risk rejection, knowing that God's love and acceptance will fulfill me?

Commitment: Do I set aside my personal hurt for the sake of the relationship?

Confidence: Do I trust God to heal my heartaches and to meet my needs?

The one who calls you is faithful, and he will do it.
(1 THESSALONIANS 5:24)

Reconciliation vs. Forgiveness

Reconciliation focuses on the relationship.
Forgiveness focuses on the offense.

Reconciliation requires at least two people.
Forgiveness requires only one person.

Reconciliation is necessarily reciprocal.
Forgiveness is not necessarily reciprocal but may be directed only one way.

Reconciliation is the choice to rejoin the offender.

Forgiveness is the choice to release the offender.

Reconciliation involves a change in behavior by the offender.
Forgiveness involves a change in thinking about the offender.

Reconciliation is a restored relationship based on restored trust.
Forgiveness is a free gift to the one who has broken trust.

Reconciliation is offered to the offender because it has been earned.
Forgiveness is extended even if it is never, ever earned.

Reconciliation is conditional, based on repentance.
Forgiveness is unconditional, regardless of a lack of repentance.

Reconciliation necessitates a relationship agreed on by both parties.
Forgiveness necessitates no relationship at all.

Do two walk together unless they
have agreed to do so?
(AMOS 3:3)

Key Verse to Memorize

Do not repay evil with evil or insult with insult.
On the contrary, repay evil with blessing,
because to this you were called
so that you may inherit a blessing.
(1 PETER 3:9)

The Heart Test

Place a ✓ if your answer is *yes*, or an × if your answer is *no*.

- ☐ Do my actions demonstrate love toward my offender?
  "Love your enemies" (MATTHEW 5:44).

- ☐ Do I speak well of my offender?
  "Bless those who curse you" (LUKE 6:28).

- ☐ Do I do what is right toward my offender?
  "Do not repay anyone evil for evil. Be careful to do what is right in the eyes of everyone" (ROMANS 12:17).

- ☐ Do I have a forgiving spirit toward my offender?
  "If you forgive other people when they sin against you, your heavenly Father will also forgive you. But if you do not forgive others their sins, your Father will not forgive your sins" (MATTHEW 6:14–15).

- ☐ Do I exhibit humility toward my offender?

  "God blesses those who are humble, for they will inherit the whole earth" (MATTHEW 5:5 NLT).

- ☐ Do I pray on behalf of my offender?

  "Pray for those who persecute you" (MATTHEW 5:44).

How to Respond When Reconciliation Is Refused[185]

If your heart has been repentant, you have God's total forgiveness.

"If we claim to be without sin, we deceive ourselves and the truth is not in us. If we confess our sins, he is faithful and just and will forgive us our sins and purify us from all unrighteousness" (1 JOHN 1:8–9).

Pray for the one who refuses reconciliation—there is an unmet need.

"Love your enemies and pray for those who persecute you" (MATTHEW 5:44).

God never leaves you when you suffer the loss of a close relationship.

"The LORD is close to the brokenhearted and saves those who are crushed in spirit" (PSALM 34:18).

Don't be vengeful—in time God will deal with those who do wrong.

"Do not take revenge, my dear friends, but leave room for God's wrath, for it is written: 'It is mine to avenge; I will repay,' says the Lord" (ROMANS 12:19).

My Personalized Plan

I will . . .

Prepare my heart for seeking reconciliation.

"Let the peace of Christ rule in your hearts, since as members of one body you were called to peace. And be thankful" (COLOSSIANS 3:15).

Know that refusal to seek reconciliation affects the intimacy of my fellowship with God.

"In anger his master handed him over to the jailers to be tortured, until he should pay back all he owed. This is how my heavenly Father will treat each of you unless you forgive your brother or sister from your heart" (MATTHEW 18:34-35).

Seek forgiveness and apologize for ways I have hurt the other person.

"If you are offering your gift at the altar and there remember that your brother or sister has something against you, leave your gift there in front of the altar. First go and be reconciled to them; then come and offer your gift" (MATTHEW 5:23-24).

Recognize the ground rules of communication.[186] Offer unconditional acceptance.

"My dear brothers and sisters, take note of this: Everyone should be quick to listen, slow to speak and slow to become angry" (JAMES 1:19).

Be kind and gentle, trusting God to work in the heart of the other person.[187]

"The Lord's servant must not be quarrelsome but must be kind to everyone, able to teach, not resentful. Opponents must be gently instructed, in the hope that God will grant them repentance leading them to a knowledge of the truth" (2 TIMOTHY 2:24-25).

Reflect the character of Christ in all that I do.

"I have been crucified with Christ and I no longer live, but Christ lives in me. The life I now live in the body, I live by faith in the Son of God, who loved me and gave himself for me" (GALATIANS 2:20).

Key Passage to Read

Luke 15:11-32

Enlist a mediator if necessary.[188] Pray for God to prepare the heart of my offender for mediation.

"If they will not listen [to you], *take one or two others along, so that 'every matter may be established by the testimony of two or three witnesses'"* (MATTHEW 18:16).

Not hold myself solely responsible for the outcome.[189] I cannot force reconciliation to occur.

"We know that in all things God works for the good of those who love him, who have been called according to his purpose" (ROMANS 8:28).

Rest in the knowledge that I have done all I can do to seek peace. Continue to show love and treat the other person with forgiveness.

"If it is possible, as far as it depends on you, live at peace with everyone" (ROMANS 12:18).

If anyone is in Christ, the new creation has come:
The old has gone, the new is here!
All this is from God, who reconciled us
to himself through Christ and
gave us the ministry of reconciliation.
(2 CORINTHIANS 5:17-18)

Questions & Answers

Question: "What do I do if I can't persuade someone with a stubborn heart to reconcile?"

Answer: You are not responsible for the response of another person, but you are accountable to God to seek reconciliation. Each person is directly accountable before God.

Each of us will give an account of ourselves to God.
(Romans 14:12)

Question: "Should I seek reconciliation even when I am still angry?"

Answer: Reconciliation will not take place if you have not dealt with your unresolved anger. Allow the Spirit of God to bring about true repentance on your part and an attitude that can soften the heart of the one wronged.

A brother wronged is more unyielding than a fortified city;
disputes are like the barred gates of a citadel.
(Proverbs 18:19)

Question: "How do I know if I am chasing an impossible dream by hoping for reconciliation in the future?"

Answer: You cannot know whether a broken relationship will truly be reconciled. No one but God has total knowledge of the future, and the Bible tells us that *"with God all things are possible"* (Matthew 19:26). But if you respond to the Lord and to the conflict in a Christlike manner, you can assuredly have God's peace for the future.

"Peace I leave with you; my peace I give you.
I do not give to you as the world gives.
Do not let your hearts be troubled
and do not be afraid."
(John 14:27)

REJECTION & ABANDONMENT

Healing a Wounded Heart

God's Heart on Rejection

God won't reject His people—those He made His own.

"For the sake of his great name the LORD will not reject his people, because the LORD was pleased to make you his own" (1 SAMUEL 12:22).

God won't reject our prayers or withhold His love from us . . . not ever.

"Praise be to God, who has not rejected my prayer or withheld his love from me!" (PSALM 66:20).

God knows the pain of rejection, for He Himself was rejected.

"He was despised and rejected by mankind, a man of suffering, and familiar with pain. Like one from whom people hide their faces he was despised, and we held him in low esteem" (ISAIAH 53:3).

God says those who reject His Word lack wisdom and will be dismayed, trapped, and shamed.

"The wise will be put to shame; they will be dismayed and trapped. Since they have rejected the word of the LORD, what kind of wisdom do they have?" (JEREMIAH 8:9).

God says those who reject His Son will not see eternal life.

"Whoever believes in the Son has eternal life, but whoever rejects the Son will not see life, for God's wrath remains on them" (JOHN 3:36).

God says those who reject the truth will receive anger and wrath.

"For those who are self-seeking and who reject the truth and follow evil, there will be wrath and anger" (ROMANS 2:8).

God equates the rejection of Christians as a rejection of Him.

"Whoever listens to you listens to me; whoever rejects you rejects me; but whoever rejects me rejects him who sent me" (LUKE 10:16).

God views rejection of His instruction as a direct rejection of Him.

"Anyone who rejects this instruction does not reject a human being but God, the very God who gives you his Holy Spirit" (1 THESSALONIANS 4:8).

God tells us to reject evil in all its forms.
"Reject every kind of evil" (1 THESSALONIANS 5:22).

God calls Christians blessed when we're rejected for carrying His name.
"Blessed are you when people hate you, when they exclude you and insult you and reject your name as evil, because of the Son of Man" (LUKE 6:22).

Love is patient, love is kind.
It does not envy, it does not boast, it is not proud.
It does not dishonor others, it is not self-seeking,
it is not easily angered, it keeps no record of wrongs.
Love does not delight in evil but rejoices with the truth.
It always protects, always trusts, always hopes,
always perseveres. Love never fails.
(1 CORINTHIANS 13:4–8)

Rejection vs. Acceptance

Rejection is the act of refusing to accept or consider a person or thing that is not wanted or not approved.[190]
"The stone the builders rejected has become the cornerstone" (MATTHEW 21:42).

To be rejected is to be cast aside, cast off, cast away—to be thrown away as having no value.[191]
"You have a fine way of setting aside the commands of God in order to observe your own traditions!" (MARK 7:9).

To reject someone means to despise, refuse, shun, turn away from.[192]
"Blessed are you when people hate you, when they exclude you and insult you and reject your name as evil, because of the Son of Man" (LUKE 6:22).

To accept someone means to approve or to receive that one favorably or willingly.[193] We should receive and value others because of their God-given worth.
"Accept one another, then, just as Christ accepted you, in order to bring praise to God" (ROMANS 15:7).

Three Levels of Acceptance[194]

1. **Zero acceptance**
   "No matter what I do, I'll never be accepted."
   "Get rid of all bitterness, rage and anger, brawling and slander, along with every form of malice" (EPHESIANS 4:31).

2. **Performance-based acceptance**

   "I feel accepted only when I perform perfectly."

   "Judgment without mercy will be shown to anyone who has not been merciful. Mercy triumphs over judgment" (JAMES 2:13).

3. **Unconditional acceptance**

   "No matter what I do, even when I fail, I always feel accepted."

   "Show mercy and compassion to one another" (ZECHARIAH 7:9).

Rejection Breeds Rejection[195]

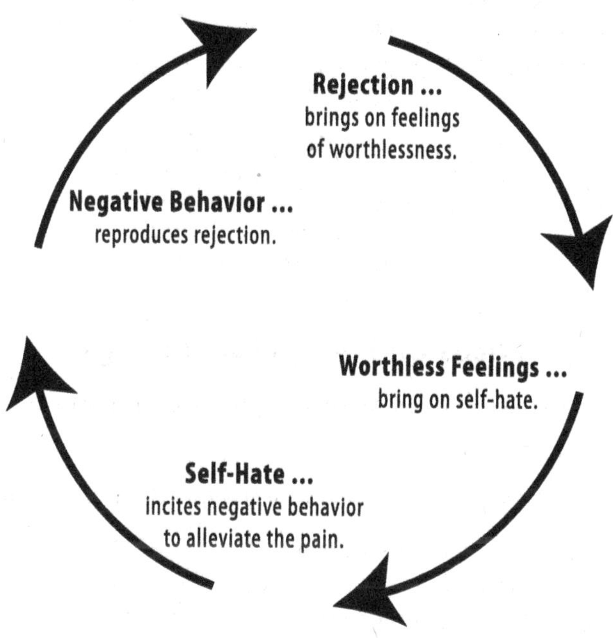

The Fear of Rejection Test[196]

Place a ✓ if your answer is *yes*, or an × if your answer is *no*.

☐ Do you avoid certain people out of fear that they will reject you?

☐ Do you become anxious when you think someone might not accept you?

☐ Do you feel awkward around others who are different from you?

- ☐ Do you feel disturbed when someone is not friendly toward you?
- ☐ Do you work hard at trying to determine what people think of you?
- ☐ Do you become depressed when others are critical of you?
- ☐ Do you consider yourself basically shy and unsociable around others?
- ☐ Do you look for the negative in others?
- ☐ Do you find yourself trying to impress others?
- ☐ Do you search for clues as to how others are responding to you in order to avoid the pain of rejection?
- ☐ Do you say *yes* when you should say *no* to others?
- ☐ Do you hear people saying that you are a "codependent person"?
- ☐ Do you experience hypersensitivity to the opinions of others but insensitivity to your own emotions?
- ☐ Do you struggle with anger and resentment toward others?
- ☐ Do you seem to be easily manipulated by others?

Am I now trying to win the approval of human beings,
or of God? Or am I trying to please people?
If I were still trying to please people,
I would not be a servant of Christ.
(GALATIANS 1:10)

Focus on Facts, Not Feelings

When you are tempted to feel defeated due to rejection, say to the Lord . . .

"Thank You, Lord, for loving me."
"This is how we know what love is: Jesus Christ laid down his life for us" (1 JOHN 3:16).

"Thank You, Lord, that You are with me."
"The LORD your God is with you, the Mighty Warrior who saves. He will take great delight in you; in his love he will no longer rebuke you, but will rejoice over you with singing" (ZEPHANIAH 3:17).

"Thank You, Lord, that You forgave me."
"I acknowledged my sin to you and did not cover up my iniquity. I said, 'I will confess my transgressions to the LORD.' And you forgave the guilt of my sin" (PSALM 32:5).

Key Verse to Memorize

"The LORD himself goes before you
and will be with you;
he will never leave you nor forsake you.
Do not be afraid; do not be discouraged."
(DEUTERONOMY 31:8)

"Thank You, Lord, that You adopted me."

"To all who did receive him, to those who believed in his name, he gave the right to become children of God" (JOHN 1:12).

"Thank You, Lord, that You will complete Your work in me."

"He who began a good work in you will carry it on to completion until the day of Christ Jesus" (PHILIPPIANS 1:6).

"Thank You, Lord, that You never leave me."

"God has said, 'Never will I leave you; never will I forsake you.' So we say with confidence, 'The Lord is my helper; I will not be afraid. What can mere mortals do to me?'" (HEBREWS 13:5–6).

"Thank You, Lord, that You care for me."

"Cast all your anxiety on him because he cares for you" (1 PETER 5:7).

"Thank You, Lord, that You have accepted me."

"He [God] *made us accepted in the Beloved"* (EPHESIANS 1:6 NKJV).

Key Passage to Read

Romans 8:28–39

"Thank You, Lord, that You live in me."

"It is because of him that you are in Christ Jesus, who has become for us wisdom from God—that is, our righteousness, holiness and redemption" (1 CORINTHIANS 1:30).

"Thank You, Lord, that You have given me everything I need to live a godly life."

"His divine power has given us everything we need for a godly life through our knowledge of him who called us by his own glory and goodness" (2 PETER 1:3).

When Rejection Is Deserved

Acknowledge to God the sinful behavior that led to your being rejected.

"If we confess our sins, he is faithful and just and will forgive us our sins and purify us from all unrighteousness" (1 JOHN 1:9).

Ask God to bring you to the point of seeing your sin as He sees it.

"Search me, God, and know my heart; test me and know my anxious thoughts. See if there is any offensive way in me, and lead me in the way everlasting" (PSALM 139:23–24).

Assume the responsibility of asking forgiveness from the person(s) you have offended.

"If you are offering your gift at the altar and there remember that your brother or sister has something against you, leave your gift there in front of the altar. First go and be reconciled to them; then come and offer your gift" (MATTHEW 5:23–24).

Act out of your identity in Christ.

"I have been crucified with Christ and I no longer live, but Christ lives in me. The life I now live in the body, I live by faith in the Son of God, who loved me and gave himself for me" (GALATIANS 2:20).

My Personalized Plan

I will . . .

A—Admit the rejection of the past and acknowledge its pain.

"I remember my affliction and my wandering, the bitterness and the gall. I well remember them, and my soul is downcast within me. Yet this I call to mind and therefore I have hope: Because of the LORD's great love we are not consumed, for his compassions never fail. They are new every morning; great is your faithfulness" (LAMENTATIONS 3:19–23).

C—Claim God's acceptance and unconditional love.

"'Though the mountains be shaken and the hills be removed, yet my unfailing love for you will not be shaken nor my covenant of peace be removed,' says the LORD, who has compassion on you" (ISAIAH 54:10).

C—Choose to forgive those who rejected me.

"Bear with each other and forgive one another if any of you has a grievance against someone. Forgive as the Lord forgave you" (COLOSSIANS 3:13).

E—Expect future rejection as natural in a fallen world.

"Dear friends, do not be surprised at the fiery ordeal that has come on you to test you, as though something strange were happening to you. But rejoice inasmuch as you participate in the sufferings of Christ, so that you may be overjoyed when his glory is revealed. If you are insulted because of the name of Christ, you are blessed, for the Spirit of glory and of God rests on you" (1 PETER 4:12–14).

P—Plant Scripture in my mind to produce new thought patterns.

"Do not conform to the pattern of this world, but be transformed by the renewing of your mind. Then you will be able to test and approve what God's will is—his good, pleasing and perfect will" (ROMANS 12:2).

T—Thank God for what I've learned through my rejection.

"It was good for me to be afflicted so that I might learn your decrees" (PSALM 119:71).

E—Encourage others as an expression of Christ's love.

"Encourage one another daily" (HEBREWS 3:13).

D—Draw on the power of Christ's life within me.

"I can do all this through him who gives me strength" (PHILIPPIANS 4:13).

"I will turn the darkness into light before them
and make the rough places smooth.
These are the things I will do;
I will not forsake them."
(ISAIAH 42:16)

Questions & Answers

Question: "Can an authentic Christian be rejected by God?"

Answer: No. Based on various verses in the Bible, an authentic Christian who has truly trusted in Christ will still sin but will never be rejected by God. If you find yourself fearful of being forsaken by God, claim the following truth from God's unchanging Word:

The LORD will not reject his people;
he will never forsake his inheritance.
(PSALM 94:14)

Question: "My father died six years ago, but I'm still struggling with anger toward him. He favored my brother and treated my sister, my mother, and me like second-class citizens. How can I stop being controlled by this anger?"

Answer: Anger often stems from hurt, fear, frustration, or injustice—yours likely involves all but fear. Rejection is painful, being dismissed is frustrating, and favoritism is unjust. But his behavior reflected his own brokenness, not your worth. Let go of expectations he never met. Accept that he couldn't give what he didn't have. Forgiveness isn't approval of his actions—it's freedom for your heart. Release him to God and move forward without bitterness. Reflecting on God's own loving and forgiving heart can help you forgive your father and let go of past pain.

"You, Lord, are forgiving and good,
abounding in love to all who call to you."
(PSALM 86:5)

SALVATION

Answering Arguments, Overcoming Objections

God's Heart on Salvation

God loves you.

"God so loved the world that he gave his one and only Son, that whoever believes in him shall not perish but have eternal life" (John 3:16).

God wants all people to be saved.

"[God] *wants all people to be saved and to come to a knowledge of the truth"* (1 Timothy 2:4).

God extends the loving grace of salvation as a free gift.

"He has saved us and called us to a holy life—not because of anything we have done but because of his own purpose and grace. This grace was given us in Christ Jesus before the beginning of time" (2 Timothy 1:9).

God provides only one way to be saved—through faith in the Lord Jesus Christ.

"Jesus answered, 'I am the way and the truth and the life. No one comes to the Father except through me'" (John 14:6).

God requires that you believe in Jesus to be saved.

"Whoever believes in the Son has eternal life" (John 3:36).

God saves and forgives people for all their sins.

"You were dead because of your sins and because your sinful nature was not yet cut away. Then God made you alive with Christ, for he forgave all our sins" (Colossians 2:13 NLT).

God wants you to be assured of your salvation.

"Very truly I tell you, whoever hears my word and believes him who sent me has eternal life and will not be judged but has crossed over from death to life" (John 5:24).

God wants you to tell others about His salvation.

"We are therefore Christ's ambassadors, as though God were making his appeal through us. We implore you on Christ's behalf: Be reconciled to God" (2 Corinthians 5:20).

Truly my soul finds rest in God;
my salvation comes from him.
(PSALM 62:1)

The Reason We Need Saving

We need to be saved because of our *sin.*

Many of us are reluctant to admit we're not good enough to please God. We can point to numerous people—friends, neighbors, family—who are clearly much "worse" than we are. But contrary to what we like to think about ourselves, we're not intrinsically "good" people.

We should not compare ourselves against others. We must examine ourselves against the standard God established for His creation. And all of humanity falls far short of the perfect goodness of God. Therefore, everyone needs salvation!

There is no one righteous, not even one.
(ROMANS 3:10)

A Salvation Checklist

Place a ✓ if your answer is *yes*, or an × if your answer is *no*.

☐ I recognize my need to be saved.
"He stands at the right hand of the needy, to save their lives from those who would condemn them" (PSALM 109:31).

☐ I realize I cannot earn my salvation.
"It is by grace you have been saved, through faith—and this is not from yourselves, it is the gift of God—not by works" (EPHESIANS 2:8–9).

☐ I know Jesus died for me and paid the penalty for my sin.
"My friends, I want you to know that through Jesus the forgiveness of sins is proclaimed to you" (ACTS 13:38).

☐ I believe God loves me and He will not reject me.
"Help me, LORD my God; save me according to your unfailing love" (PSALM 109:26).

☐ I feel genuine sorrow when I sin, but God is faithful to forgive me.
"Godly sorrow brings repentance that leads to salvation and leaves no regret, but worldly sorrow brings death" (2 CORINTHIANS 7:10).

☐ I know that my salvation does not depend on my performance.

"I was shown mercy so that in me, the worst of sinners, Christ Jesus might display his immense patience as an example for those who would believe in him and receive eternal life" (1 TIMOTHY 1:16).

☐ I can reject performance-based salvation and humbly receive God's gift of grace.

"Just as sin reigned in death, so also grace might reign through righteousness to bring eternal life through Jesus Christ our Lord" (ROMANS 5:21).

☐ I no longer fear God's judgment.

"There is no fear in love. But perfect love drives out fear, because fear has to do with punishment. The one who fears is not made perfect in love" (1 JOHN 4:18).

☐ I no longer expect God's punishment.

"He [the Messiah Jesus] *was pierced for our transgressions, he was crushed for our iniquities; the punishment that brought us peace was on him, and by his wounds we are healed"* (ISAIAH 53:5).

Key Verse to Memorize

"Believe in the Lord Jesus, and you will be saved."
(ACTS 16:31)

☐ I may not ever be totally "sinless" this side of heaven, but God helps me "sin less and less."

"My dear children, I write this to you so that you will not sin. But if anybody does sin, we have an advocate with the Father—Jesus Christ, the Righteous One" (1 JOHN 2:1).

☐ I know that once I'm saved, I cannot lose my salvation.

"By one sacrifice he has made perfect forever those who are being made holy" (HEBREWS 10:14).

☐ There is nothing I can do to make God love me *more* and nothing I can do to make Him love me *less.*

"The LORD is good and his love endures forever; his faithfulness continues through all generations" (PSALM 100:5).

We know also that the Son of God has come
and has given us understanding,
so that we may know him who is true.
And we are in him who is true
by being in his Son Jesus Christ.
He is the true God and eternal life.
(1 JOHN 5:20)

God's Plan for Salvation

1. God's Purpose for You: ***Salvation***

   What was God's motivation in sending Jesus Christ to earth? To express His love for you by saving you! The Bible says, "*God so loved the world that he gave his one and only Son, that whoever believes in him shall not perish but have eternal life. For God did not send his Son into the world to condemn the world, but to save the world through him*" (John 3:16–17).

   What was Jesus' purpose in coming to earth? To forgive your sins, to empower you to have victory over sin, and to enable you to live a fulfilled life! Jesus said, "*I have come that they may have life, and have it to the full*" (John 10:10).

2. The Problem: ***Sin***

   What exactly is sin? *Sin* is living independently of God's standard—knowing what is wrong and doing it anyway—also knowing what is right and choosing not to do it. The apostle Paul said, "*I know that nothing good lives in me, that is, in my sinful nature. I want to do what is right, but I can't. I want to do what is good, but I don't. I don't want to do what is wrong, but I do it anyway*" (Romans 7:18–19 NLT).

   What is the major consequence of sin? Spiritual death, eternal separation from God. The Bible says, "*Your iniquities* [sins] *have separated you from your God*" (Isaiah 59:2). Scripture also says, "*The wages of sin is death, but the gift of God is eternal life in Christ Jesus our Lord*" (Romans 6:23).

3. God's Provision for You: ***The Savior***

   Can anything remove the penalty for sin? Yes! Jesus died on the cross to personally pay the penalty for your sins. The Bible says, "*God demonstrates his own love for us in this: While we were still sinners, Christ died for us*" (Romans 5:8).

   What is the solution to being separated from God? Belief in (entrusting your life to) Jesus Christ as the only way to God the Father. Jesus said, "*I am the way and the truth and the life. No one comes to the Father except through me*" (John 14:6). The Bible says, "*Believe in the Lord Jesus, and you will be saved*" (Acts 16:31).

4. Your Part: ***Surrender***

   Give Christ control of your life, entrusting yourself to Him. Jesus said, "*Whoever wants to be my disciple must deny themselves and take up their cross and follow me. For whoever wants to save their life will lose it, but whoever loses their life for me will find it. What good will it be for someone to gain the whole world, yet forfeit their soul?*" (Matthew 16:24–26).

   Place your faith in (rely on) Jesus Christ as your personal Lord and Savior and reject your "good works" as a means of earning God's approval. The

Bible says, *"It is by grace you have been saved, through faith—and this is not from yourselves, it is the gift of God—not by works, so that no one can boast"* (Ephesians 2:8–9).

Prayer of Salvation

You can tell God that you want to surrender your life to Christ in a simple, heartfelt prayer like this:

"God, I want a real relationship with You.
I admit that many times I've chosen to go my own way
instead of Your way.
Please forgive me for my sins.
Jesus, thank You for dying on the cross
to pay the penalty for my sins.
Come into my life to be my Lord and my Savior.
Change me from the inside out and make me the person
You created me to be.
In Your holy name I pray. Amen."

"Truly I tell you, whoever hears my word
and believes him who sent me
has eternal life and will not be judged
but has crossed over from death to life."
(John 5:24)

Welcome to God's Family

You are completely forgiven and cleansed of all your sins.

"The law requires that nearly everything be cleansed with blood, and without the shedding of blood there is no forgiveness. . . . How much more, then, will the blood of Christ, who through the eternal Spirit offered himself unblemished to God, cleanse our consciences from acts that lead to death, so that we may serve the living God! . . . He [the Holy Spirit] *adds: 'Their sins and lawless acts I will remember no more'"* (Hebrews 9:22, 14; 10:17).

You are a new creation.

"For you died, and your life is now hidden with Christ in God. . . . Do not lie to each other, since you have taken off your old self with its practices and have put on the new self, which is being renewed in knowledge in the image of its Creator" (Colossians 3:3, 9–10).

You are declared righteous by God . . . right in God's sight.

"God made him who had no sin to be sin for us, so that in him we might become the righteousness of God" (2 CORINTHIANS 5:21).

You have received the gift of eternal life.

"My sheep hear my voice, and I know them, and they follow me. I give them eternal life, and they will never perish, and no one will snatch them out of my hand. My Father, who has given them to me, is greater than all, and no one is able to snatch them out of the Father's hand" (JOHN 10:27–29 ESV).

Key Passage to Read

John 3:1–6, 13–18

You have peace with God.

"Since we have been justified through faith, we have peace with God through our Lord Jesus Christ" (ROMANS 5:1).

You will never be condemned by God.

"There is now no condemnation for those who are in Christ Jesus" (ROMANS 8:1).

You will never be separated from God's love.

"I am convinced that neither death nor life, neither angels nor demons, neither the present nor the future, nor any powers, neither height nor depth, nor anything else in all creation, will be able to separate us from the love of God that is in Christ Jesus our Lord" (ROMANS 8:38–39).

Eternal Security Assured by God

Eternal security of every Christian is a true fact that is:

Initiated **by God the** ***Father***

"He chose us in him before the creation of the world to be holy and blameless in his sight" (EPHESIANS 1:4).

Accomplished **through God the** ***Son***

"In him we have redemption through his blood, the forgiveness of sins, in accordance with the riches of God's grace" (EPHESIANS 1:7).

Guaranteed **by God the** ***Holy Spirit***

"You also were included in Christ when you heard the message of truth, the gospel of your salvation. When you believed, you were marked in him with a seal, the promised Holy Spirit, who is a deposit guaranteeing our inheritance until the redemption of those who are God's possession—to the praise of his glory" (EPHESIANS 1:13–14).

You are receiving the end result of your faith,
the salvation of your souls.
(1 Peter 1:9)

Questions & Answers

Question: "I'm a good person, so why do I need to be saved?"

Answer: One of the most common roadblocks to salvation is the presumption that some of us don't need to be "saved." We see the severity of evil in the world. Clearly, people who commit *those* sins need to be saved. And we think, *But I'm a good person. Why do I need to be saved?*

Any sin is an affront to God.

Jesus addressed legalistic religious leaders who thought they had achieved sufficient righteousness on their own through their strict keeping of the Law. In His Sermon on the Mount, Jesus taught the crowd the error of such thinking. He showed that what we would consider a "major" sin, like murder, really originates in common sins like out-of-control anger, name-calling, or refusing to forgive (Matthew 5:21-26). Similarly, adultery begins in the mind, with impure thoughts about another person (Matthew 5:27-30). Surprisingly, it's these "little" sins He warns about that put us in danger of hell (Matthew 5:22, 30).

Even a so-called good person falls short of God's holy standard. Breaking one of God's commandments is no different than breaking them all (James 2:10).

You might protest: "It seems that God is holding us to an impossible standard!"

That's the point! But the Lord doesn't leave us alone to helplessly agonize over our sins with no way to remedy our sin problem. He has provided a Savior as a substitute for the penalty of our sin. We can count on Jesus for forgiveness.

Jesus answered, "I am the way and the truth
and the life. No one comes to the Father
except through me."
(John 14:6)

SATAN, DEMONS, AND SATANISM

A Sinister Reality

God's Heart on Satan's Power

Satan cannot be everywhere at once.

"The L*ORD said to Satan, 'Where have you come from?' Satan answered the* L*ORD, 'From roaming throughout the earth, going back and forth on it'"* (JOB 1:7).

Satan does not have power over a believer's possessions, body, or life.

"Have you [God] *not put a hedge around him* [Job] *and his household and everything he has? . . . The* L*ORD said to Satan, 'Very well, then, everything he has is in your power, but on the man himself do not lay a finger.' . . . The* L*ORD said to Satan, 'Very well, then, he is in your hands; but you must spare his life'"* (JOB 1:10, 12, 2:6).

Satan and demons must obey Jesus and those who speak with Jesus' authority.

"Jesus said to him, 'Away from me, Satan! For it is written: "Worship the Lord your God, and serve him only."' Then the devil left him, and angels came and attended him" (MATTHEW 4:10–11).

"The seventy-two returned with joy and said, 'Lord, even the demons submit to us in your name'" (LUKE 10:17).

Satan must ask permission to tempt a believer.

"Simon, Simon, Satan has asked to sift all of you as wheat" (LUKE 22:31).

Satan has to leave if he is resisted by believers.

"Submit yourselves, then, to God. Resist the devil, and he will flee from you" (JAMES 4:7).

Satan and his evil schemes can be overcome by believers.

"They triumphed over him [Satan] *by the blood of the Lamb and by the word of their testimony"* (REVELATION 12:11).

Satan cannot protect his demons, followers, or worshipers from God's judgment.

"Then he [Jesus, the King] *will say to those on his left, 'Depart from me, you who are cursed, into the eternal fire prepared for the devil and his angels'"* (MATTHEW 25:41).

Satan cannot prevent his own demise.

"The devil, who deceived them, was thrown into the lake of burning sulfur, where the beast and the false prophet had been thrown. They will be tormented day and night for ever and ever" (REVELATION 20:10).

Satan brings darkness and death and closes eyes, while God brings light and life and opens eyes.

"I am sending you [Paul] *to them to open their eyes and turn them from darkness to light, and from the power of Satan to God, so that they may receive forgiveness of sins and a place among those who are sanctified by faith in me"* (ACTS 26:17–18).

Satan will soon be crushed by God under the feet of believers.

"The God of peace will soon crush Satan under your feet" (ROMANS 16:20).

Who Is Satan?

Satan is the supreme adversary of God and the leader of the spiritual forces of evil.[197]

Satan is an angelic being created by God.

What Is Satanism?

Satanism is a religion that worships and declares *allegiance* to Satan.

Satanism is also a religion based on the *exaltation of evil* with no belief in a personal devil.[198]

What Is the Church of Satan?

A legal and highly organized religion that teaches that indulgence in sin is the path to freedom.

Founded in the United States on April 30, 1966, by Anton LaVey (a former carnival member).

The rituals mock Christianity.

The initiation rituals are sexual.

Teachings include

— No supernatural being exists.

— Satan is only a symbol of self-indulgence.

— No personal devil exists.

— Man is the epitome of existence.

Published *The Satanic Bible* in 1969.

The Spirit clearly says that in later times some will abandon the faith and follow deceiving spirits and things taught by demons.
(1 TIMOTHY 4:1)

What Are the Signs of Satanic Involvement?

Signs of Possible Satanic Curiosity[199]

Unexplained mood swings

Avoidance of family members

Intense rebelliousness

Change in friends

Black candles

Black clothing and jewelry

Hostility toward the church

Fixation on death

Preference for heavy metal rock music

Use of satanic paraphernalia

Drawing or displaying satanic symbols

Secret agendas and unexplained activities

Obsession with occult books, games, videos, movies

Key Verse to Memorize

Be alert and of sober mind. Your enemy the devil prowls around like a roaring lion looking for someone to devour.
(1 PETER 5:8)

Signs of Possible Satanic Captivity[200]

Wearing items such as an inverted cross, pentagram

Reading *The Satanic Bible*

Collection of bones and death items

Tattoos of satanic symbols

Cutting the body destructively

Witchcraft and occult practices

Puncture wounds on animals

Arson

Sexual abuse

Multiple personality disorder

Kidnapping and torture

Suicide attempts

Murder

The Diminishing Role of Demons

Demons know that Jesus Christ is the Holy One of God.

"A man . . . who was possessed by an impure spirit cried out, 'What do you want with us, Jesus of Nazareth? Have you come to destroy us? I know who you are—the Holy One of God!'" (MARK 1:23–24).

Demons shudder and tremble before God.

"You believe that there is one God. Good! Even the demons believe that—and shudder" (JAMES 2:19).

Demons must submit to Jesus.

"[Jesus] *has gone into heaven and is at God's right hand—with angels, authorities and powers in submission to him"* (1 PETER 3:22).

Demons cannot escape their final judgment.

"God did not spare angels when they sinned, but sent them to hell, putting them in chains of darkness to be held for judgment" (2 PETER 2:4).

Demons know that torture is their destiny.

"'What do you want with us, Son of God?' they shouted. 'Have you come here to torture us before the appointed time?'" (MATTHEW 8:29).

The great dragon was hurled down—
that ancient serpent called the devil, or Satan,
who leads the whole world astray.
He was hurled to the earth, and his angels with him.
(REVELATION 12:9)

Prevention and Protection

Be aware. Know that satanic influence can touch any family.

Be knowledgeable. Know what the Bible says about Satan.

Key Passage to Read

1 John 3:7–10

Be alert. Be quick to recognize signs and symptoms of satanic involvement.

Be loving. Listen for and hear feelings and emotions that are being communicated.

Be respectful. Do not be accusing or condemning.

Be involved. Attend a warm, Bible-believing, spiritually alert church.

Be tough. Realistically present the consequences of satanic involvement.

Be edifying. Plan activities and projects that build self-worth.

Be in contact. Get support from ministers, youth leaders, and police experts.

Be in prayer. Ask God for a hedge of protection around your family.

The Lord is faithful, and he will strengthen you
and protect you from the evil one.
(2 THESSALONIANS 3:3)

My Personalized Plan

I will . . .

Commit my entire life to Christ as Lord. Fully rely on Jesus Christ as my Lord and Savior.

"If you declare with your mouth, 'Jesus is Lord,' and believe in your heart that God raised him from the dead, you will be saved" (ROMANS 10:9).

Confess any past or present involvement with Satan. Recognize and renounce each evil practice I have experienced.

"If we confess our sins, he is faithful and just and will forgive us our sins and purify us from all unrighteousness" (1 JOHN 1:9).

Confront Satan as a liar. Refuse to believe any thought that Satan puts into my mind.

"He [Satan] *was a murderer from the beginning, not holding to the truth, for there is no truth in him. When he lies, he speaks his native language, for he is a liar and the father of lies"* (JOHN 8:44).

Command Satan to leave me. Base my command on the authority given to me in Christ.

"Submit yourselves, then, to God. Resist the devil, and he will flee from you" (JAMES 4:7).

Cleanse my home. Destroy all satanic and occult paraphernalia I possess.

"Reject every kind of evil" (1 THESSALONIANS 5:22).

Conform my thinking to God's thinking. Transform my mind by memorizing Scripture.

"Do not conform to the pattern of this world, but be transformed by the renewing of your mind. Then you will be able to test and approve what God's will is—his good, pleasing and perfect will" (ROMANS 12:2).

Concede my own weakness. I cannot resist evil in my own strength. I must rely on the indwelling power of Christ.

"I can do all things through Christ who strengthens me" (PHILIPPIANS 4:13 NKJV).

Clothe myself with the armor of God. Learn God's way of protecting myself against the devil's schemes.

"Put on the full armor of God, so that when the day of evil comes, you may be able to stand your ground" (EPHESIANS 6:13).

Prayer of Deliverance & Protection

"Lord Jesus, thank You for saving me
and adopting me into Your family.
I acknowledge that Your blood was the payment
that purchased the full forgiveness of my sins.
My testimony is that I truly am a child of God.
Right now, I take the authority that is mine in Christ
and renounce any satanic, demonic power that was or is coming against me.
When I sleep, I ask that the helmet of salvation protect my mind.
May the breastplate of righteousness deflect
any flaming arrows from the Evil One.
Put a hedge of protection around my mind and purify my dreams,
and may God get the glory.
In the powerful name of Jesus I pray. Amen."

Questions & Answers

Question: "If God is so powerful, why doesn't He destroy Satan and Satanism?"

Answer: He will. The day will come when Satan is cast forever into the lake of fire. The destiny of the devil is never-ending torment . . . eternal punishment . . . *"day and night for ever and ever."*

The devil, who deceived them,
was thrown into the lake of burning sulfur. . . .
[He] *will be tormented day and night for ever and ever.*
(REVELATION 20:10)

Question: "For several years, I have been having perverse sexual dreams. I can't seem to do anything about them. Although I recently became a Christian, our family was heavily involved in witchcraft and Satanism. What can I do to stop having these nightmares?"

Answer: Because your family was heavily involved in witchcraft and Satanism, your first line of defense is to enter into spiritual warfare against these powers. If satanic oppression is the cause of an involuntary, immoral dream invading your life, through prayer it can be overcome. Claim your position as a child of God by thanking Him for loving you and saving you. Speak audibly, for Satan cannot read your thoughts. Then, in the name of the Lord Jesus Christ and through the power of His blood, renounce and reject any influence of the occult or any evil presence attacking you.

They triumphed over him [Satan] *by the blood of the Lamb* [Jesus]
and by the word of their testimony.
(REVELATION 12:11)

SELF-WORTH

Discover Your God-Given Value

God's Heart on Self-Worth

God wants you to see yourself through His eyes—as His image-bearer with infinite worth.

"God created mankind in his own image, in the image of God he created them; male and female he created them. . . . God saw all that he had made, and it was very good" (GENESIS 1:27, 31).

God wants you to see yourself through His eyes—as precious and honored in His sight.

"You are precious and honored in my sight, and . . . I love you" (ISAIAH 43:4).

God wants you to see yourself through His eyes—as His beloved child.

"See what great love the Father has lavished on us, that we should be called children of God! And that is what we are!" (1 JOHN 3:1).

God wants you to know that you are fully accepted in Christ—not due to your performance but due to His grace.

"He made us accepted in the Beloved" (EPHESIANS 1:6 NKJV).

God will not reject His people, His beloved possession.

"The LORD will not reject his people; he will not abandon his special possession" (PSALM 94:14 NLT).

God understands the pain of being devalued and held in low esteem.

"He [Jesus] *was despised and rejected by mankind, a man of suffering, and familiar with pain. Like one from whom people hide their faces he was despised, and we held him in low esteem"* (ISAIAH 53:3).

God offers healing from past pain, guilt, and shame.

"LORD my God, I called to you for help, and you healed me" (PSALM 30:2).

God wants you to forgive those who hurt you and led you to feel worthless.

"Bear with each other and forgive one another if any of you has a grievance against someone. Forgive as the Lord forgave you" (COLOSSIANS 3:13).

God wants you to show respect to everyone because we all bear His image.

"Show proper respect to everyone" (1 PETER 2:17).

God wants you to encourage others who have low self-worth.

"Let everything you say be good and helpful, so that your words will be an encouragement to those who hear them" (EPHESIANS 4:29 NLT).

God wants you to look to Him and His Word to find your true worth.

"You are my refuge and my shield; your word is my source of hope" (PSALM 119:114 NLT).

When I consider your heavens,
the work of your fingers,
the moon and the stars,
which you have set in place,
what is mankind that you are mindful of them,
human beings that you care for them?
You have made them a little lower than the angels
and crowned them with glory and honor.
(PSALM 8:3–5)

Characteristics of Low Self-Worth

Emotional

— Ashamed of background
— Fearful of failure
— Feel inferior
— Feel incompetent in comparison to others
— Feel undeserving of help, compliments, or positive feedback
— Frequent depression
— Frequent guilt
— Self-critical
— Self-loathing/self-hate

Behavioral

— Argumentative
— Avoid taking risks
— Controlled by a victim mentality
— Neglect personal appearance
— Often afraid to defend oneself
— Overly critical of others
— Reluctant to express true feelings
— Resistant to authority
— Unable to set boundaries

Relational

- — Afraid to get close to people
- — Constantly comparing oneself to others
- — Defensive when confronted
- — Desperate for others' approval
- — Distrustful of others
- — Peace-at-any-price people pleaser
- — Strive to meet the expectations of others
- — Unable to accept compliments
- — Unforgiving of others

Key Verses to Memorize

"I have chosen you and have not rejected you.
So do not fear, for I am with you;
do not be dismayed, for I am your God.
I will strengthen you and help you;
I will uphold you
with my righteous right hand."
(Isaiah 41:9–10)

Self-Worth Substitutes Checklist

Sometimes people with low self-worth pursue a substitute to make up for an emotional deficit. Read the statements below, and place a ✓ if the statement is true of you, or an ✗ if it is not.

- ☐ "I am impressed with status symbols and often live beyond my income."
- ☐ "I am overly competitive and view losing as a reflection of my value and worth."
- ☐ "I am seeking approval or am envious of important people."
- ☐ "I am constantly striving for recognition."
- ☐ "I am perfectionistic in an attempt to earn approval."
- ☐ "I am addicted to substances, sex, food, and/or ______________________."
- ☐ "I am angry and intimidating at times in a zeal to accomplish my goals."
- ☐ "I am financially extravagant in an attempt to impress others."
- ☐ "I am obsessed with having certain possessions."
- ☐ "I am insistent on getting my way."

The Root Cause of Low Self-Worth

Wrong Belief: "My self-worth is based on how I see myself in comparison to others and how others view me."

Right Belief: "My self-worth is not based on how I see myself or how others see me, but on how *God* sees me, for I was created by Him in His image. Not only did Jesus pay the highest price for me by dying on the cross for my sins, but He also lives in me to fulfill His plan and purpose for me."

We are God's handiwork, created in Christ Jesus
to do good works, which God prepared
in advance for us to do.
(EPHESIANS 2:10)

Replace Lies with God's Truth

If you say: "I just can't do anything right."

The Lord says: "I'll give you My strength to do what is right."

"I can do all things through Christ who strengthens me" (PHILIPPIANS 4:13 NKJV).

If you say: "I feel that I'm too weak."

The Lord says: "My power is perfected in your weakness."

"My grace is sufficient for you, for my power is made perfect in weakness" (2 CORINTHIANS 12:9).

If you say: "I feel that I'm not able to measure up."

The Lord says: "Rely on Me. I am able to accomplish through you what you think you can't."

"God is able to bless you abundantly, so that in all things at all times, having all that you need, you will abound in every good work" (2 CORINTHIANS 9:8).

If you say: "I don't feel that anyone loves me."

The Lord says: "I love you."

"I have loved you with an everlasting love; I have drawn you with unfailing kindness" (JEREMIAH 31:3).

If you say: "I can't forgive myself."

The Lord says: "I forgive you."

"I, even I, am he who blots out your transgressions, for my own sake, and remembers your sins no more" (ISAIAH 43:25).

If you say: "I wish I'd never been born."

The Lord says: "Since before you were born, I've had plans for you."

"Before I formed you in the womb I knew you, before you were born I set you apart" (JEREMIAH 1:5).

If you say: "I feel my futvure is hopeless."

The Lord says: "I know the future I have for you . . . and it is good."

"Many, LORD my God, are the wonders you have done, the things you planned for us. None can compare with you; were I to speak and tell of your deeds, they would be too many to declare" (PSALM 40:5).

My Personalized Plan

W—Work on eliminating my negative attitudes and beliefs.

"I will not hide my feelings or refuse to face them."

"I will not wallow in feelings of self-pity or project my feelings onto others and become critical."

"Whatever is true, whatever is noble, whatever is right, whatever is pure, whatever is lovely, whatever is admirable—if anything is excellent or praiseworthy—think about such things" (PHILIPPIANS 4:8).

O—Obtain a biblical understanding of loving myself.

"I am not to love myself with conceited love (pride)."

"I am to love the truth that God loves me and has a purpose for me."

— *Agape love* for myself: seeking God's highest purpose for me

— *Agape love* for others: seeking the highest good of another

"Love your neighbor as yourself" (GALATIANS 5:14).

Key Passage to Read

Psalm 139

R—Refuse to compare myself with others.

"I will not measure myself by others."

"I will thank God for what He has given me and what He is making of me."

"We do not dare to classify or compare ourselves with some who commend themselves" (2 CORINTHIANS 10:12).

T—Thank God for His unconditional love for me.

"I will choose an attitude of thanksgiving even if I do not feel thankful."

"I will spend personal time with God, thanking Him for His unfailing love."

"We meditate on your unfailing love" (PSALM 48:9).

H—Hope with full assurance in God's promise to mold me into the character of Christ.

"I know that personal growth is a process."

"I know that God is committed to my growth."

"He who began a good work in you will carry it on to completion until the day of Christ Jesus" (PHILIPPIANS 1:6).

Y—Yield my talents and abilities to helping others.

"I will be generous with my God-given gifts."

"I will serve others and help them see their God-given worth."

"Each of you should use whatever gift you have received to serve others, as faithful stewards of God's grace in its various forms" (1 PETER 4:10).

Questions & Answers

Question: "In Luke 14:26, does the Bible really mean for me to hate my family and myself?"

Answer: Jesus was not promoting a lifestyle of personal hatred. Such a message is completely inconsistent with the heart of the Bible and the heart of the Lord.

Jesus instead appealed to His followers to hate anything—including anything in their own lives—that stood in the way of giving their relationship with Him absolute priority. If we are to be true disciples, Jesus must be *preeminent*—Jesus must occupy the place of highest priority. We should not let anyone take the place that He alone should have.

He is the head of the body, the church;
he is the beginning and the firstborn from
among the dead, so that in everything
he might have the supremacy.
(COLOSSIANS 1:18)

Question: "Since the Bible says, *'Love your neighbor as yourself,'* am I actually supposed to love myself, or is that being arrogant and prideful?"

Answer: The Bible says, *"God is love"* (1 John 4:8). The essence of God is *agape*—a love that always seeks the highest and best on behalf of others. If we are truly godly, then we will value what He values and love what He loves. You have godly *agape* love for yourself when you do what God says is best for you, cooperating with His perfect plan for your life. You have *agape* love for those around you by doing what is consistent with God's very best for them.

"Love your neighbor as yourself."
(MATTHEW 22:39)

SEX AND HUMAN TRAFFICKING

Taking a Stand—and Stopping It!

God's Heart on Human Trafficking

God sees the abuse and victimization of human trafficking.

"There is nothing hidden that will not be disclosed, and nothing concealed that will not be known or brought out into the open" (LUKE 8:17).

God is full of compassion toward those who are being exploited.

"The LORD is gracious and righteous; our God is full of compassion" (PSALM 116:5).

God protects and defends the vulnerable—especially children.

"The LORD secures justice for the poor and upholds the cause of the needy" (PSALM 140:12).

God will strengthen, help, and uphold those caught in human trafficking.

"Do not fear, for I am with you; do not be dismayed, for I am your God. I will strengthen you and help you; I will uphold you with my righteous right hand" (ISAIAH 41:10).

God hates abuse and violence of every kind.

"The LORD examines the righteous, but the wicked, those who love violence, he hates with a passion" (PSALM 11:5).

God desires to free those enslaved in bondage so they can live a holy life.

"Now that you have been set free from sin and have become slaves of God, the benefit you reap leads to holiness, and the result is eternal life" (ROMANS 6:22).

God will put an end to the violence of human trafficking one day.

"No longer will violence be heard in your land, nor ruin or destruction within your borders, but you will call your walls Salvation and your gates Praise" (ISAIAH 60:18).

God avenges those who trust in Him.

"The LORD lives! Praise be to my Rock! Exalted be my God, the Rock, my Savior! He is the God who avenges me" (2 SAMUEL 22:47–48).

God confirms the value and worth of every person.

"Are not five sparrows sold for two pennies? Yet not one of them is forgotten by God. Indeed, the very hairs of your head are all numbered. Don't be afraid; you are worth more than many sparrows" (LUKE 12:6–7).

God wants those violated by human trafficking to know He has plans for them that offer hope and a future.

"'I know the plans I have for you,' declares the Lord, 'plans to prosper you and not to harm you, plans to give you hope and a future'" (Jeremiah 29:11).

He upholds the cause of the oppressed
and gives food to the hungry.
The Lord sets prisoners free.
(Psalm 146:7)

Definitions of Sex Trafficking and Human Trafficking

Sex trafficking is "the recruitment, harboring, transportation, provision, or obtaining of a person for the purpose of a commercial sex act"[201]—the act of forcing a person to engage in sexual activity for profit.

Human trafficking is, simply put, the "act of recruiting, harboring, transporting, providing, or obtaining a person for compelled labor or commercial sex acts through the use of force, fraud, or coercion."[202]

Lures and Tactics Perpetrators Use

Perpetrators manipulate and control their victims through many of these lures of lies and trafficking tactics:

Controlling through violence and jealousy to threaten and intimidate

Creating an emotional seesaw of alternating threats and violence with apologies and promises of love and affection

Encouraging inappropriate sexual acts and behavior to desensitize victims

Giving expensive gifts and later demanding recompense

Insisting on or demanding sex

Luring younger victims with promises as an older or stronger protector

Lying about profession/career/job

Making victims feel an overwhelming financial obligation they are unable to repay

Promising impossible outcomes that are too good to be true

Urging illegal activities which later can be used for extortion

Do not trust in extortion
or put vain hope in stolen goods;
though your riches increase,
do not set your heart on them.
(PSALM 62:10)

Progression of Sex Trafficking

1. **Identify**—Traffickers visit places children and young people hang out and watch for those who show signs of vulnerability: isolating behaviors (sitting alone, walking alone, playing alone), low self-worth (little eye contact), easily intimidated (fearful), emotional neediness (indecisive).

2. **Groom**—Perpetrators draw their victims into a relationship by building an emotional connection with them to gain their trust for the purpose of sexual exploitation.

3. **Traumatize**—The perpetrator initiates some sort of trauma. Trauma bonding attaches the victim with the perpetrator more closely, thus ensuring the victim establishes a tight connection with the person who caused the most pain.

4. **Isolate**—The perpetrator uses various techniques to restrict victims' access to outside communication by taking away phones and personal identification documents, imposing physical punishment unless the trafficker's demands are met, and making threats of harm or even death to the victim or loved ones.

5. **Control**—The perpetrator sees the victim as having very little (if any) human significance or emotions and relies on physical forms of control to keep the victim doing just what he wants. The victim, feeling no choice but to bow to the supreme power of the perpetrator, slips quietly into enslavement. Then, when hopelessness reigns, the victim's soul is suppressed.

Key Verse

I will say to the prisoners,
"Come out in freedom,"
and to those in darkness,
"Come into the light."
(ISAIAH 49:9 NLT)

Like a lion in cover he lies in wait.
He lies in wait to catch the helpless;
he catches the helpless and drags them off in his net.
(PSALM 10:9)

Ways to Report Trafficking

Reporting possible sex trafficking in the United States can be done through a variety of means:

Local law enforcement

— **Call**: 911

National Human Trafficking Hotline

— **Call**: 1-888-373-7888

— **Text**: "HELP" or "INFO" to 233733

— **Visit**: www.humantraffickinghotline.org

The National Runaway Safeline

— **Call**: 1-800-RUNAWAY

— **Visit**: www.1800RUNAWAY.org

U.S. Immigration and Customs Enforcement

— **Call (In the U.S. and Canada)**: 1-866-347-2423

— **Visit**: www.ice.gov/tips/

FBI

— **Visit**: https://tips.fbi.gov

— **Visit**: www.fbi.gov/contact-us/field-offices (for local field offices)

If visa or passport fraud is suspected

— **Email**: TraffickingTips@state.gov

The Center for Missing or Exploited Children

— **Call**: 1-800-THE-LOST

— **Visit**: www.cybertipline.org

U.S. Department of Labor Wage and Hour Division

— **Call**: 1-866-4US-WAGE

My Personalized Plan for Healing

I will . . .

Acknowledge that I have pain in my life as a result of being victimized.

— I will ask God to help me salvage my life and live in peace as I learn to walk in His strength.

"The LORD is a refuge for the oppressed, a stronghold in times of trouble" (PSALM 9:9).

Accept that as a victim I was unable to defend myself. I will live my life in light of God's truth.

— I will remember that I am made pure and whole and restored when my identity is in Christ. By virtue of His death and resurrection, I can live in newness of life.

"Record my misery; list my tears on your scroll—are they not in your record?" (PSALM 56:8).

Conquer the past and create a new life.

— I will ask God to heal my low self-worth, replacing negative messages I received from my abuser, or even from myself, with positive statements and promises from God's Word.

"I praise you because I am fearfully and wonderfully made; your works are wonderful, I know that full well" (PSALM 139:14).

Deal with whatever information surfaces, knowing that some effects of trauma can surface many years after abuse has ended.

— I will lean on God, trusting Him to help me deal with the pain of the past, rather than turning to sexual riskiness, alcohol, drugs, food/eating disorders, or thoughts of suicide to cope.

"Come to me, all you who are weary and burdened, and I will give you rest" (MATTHEW 11:28).

Key Passage

Psalm 55

Embrace living in the truth and freedom of healing—building healthy and trust-filled relationships with those whom God has placed in my life.

— I will use what God has taught me through this journey of healing to help others going through similar situations.

"Defend the weak and the fatherless; uphold the cause of the poor and the oppressed" (PSALM 82:3).

Questions & Answers

Question: "How are victims marketed/sold?"

Answer: Trafficking victims may be marketed and sold by a variety of means. These methods can be overtly obvious or covertly inconspicuous, such as:

— Internet classified ads, pornographic websites, pop-up ads, spam emails, social media
— Magazine advertisements
— Printed fliers
— Sexually oriented businesses
— Direct prostitution
— Word of mouth

"Do not degrade your daughter by making her a prostitute,
or the land will turn to prostitution and be filled with wickedness."
(LEVITICUS 19:29)

Question: "What about boys and men? Are they involved in sex trafficking solely as perpetrators?"

Answer: No. Sadly, men and boys are also victims trapped in this form of modern-day slavery and are forced to sell their bodies for sex. While many victims' advocacy agencies focus on sexually exploited girls, awareness has risen in recent years about the numbers of boys and men who are also prostituted victims.[203]

Regardless of whether a victim is male or female, both are equally deserving and in need of rescue from the powerful enemy of exploitation.

He rescued me from my powerful enemy,
from my foes, who were too strong for me.
(2 SAMUEL 22:18)

SEXUAL ADDICTION

The Way Out of the Web

God's Heart on Sexual Addiction

God loves you and has a heart of grace and compassion for you.

"The Lord is gracious and compassionate, slow to anger and rich in love. The Lord is good to all; he has compassion on all he has made" (PSALM 145:8–9).

God wants you to regularly remind yourself of who He is.

"O Lord, you are so good, so ready to forgive, so full of unfailing love for all who ask for your help" (PSALM 86:5 NLT).

God wants you to see yourself through His eyes.

"You are precious in my eyes, and honored, and I love you" (ISAIAH 43:4 ESV).

God wants you to pursue holiness and learn to control your body.

"God's will is for you to be holy, so stay away from all sexual sin. Then each of you will control his own body and live in holiness and honor" (1 THESSALONIANS 4:3–4 NLT).

God wants you to run and flee from sexual sin.

"Run from sexual sin! No other sin so clearly affects the body as this one does. For sexual immorality is a sin against your own body" (1 CORINTHIANS 6:18 NLT).

God placed our sin and guilt on Christ so we could be forgiven.

"But he was pierced for our transgressions, he was crushed for our iniquities; the punishment that brought us peace was on him, and by his wounds we are healed. We all, like sheep, have gone astray, each of us has turned to our own way; and the Lord has laid on him the iniquity of us all" (ISAIAH 53:5–6).

God extends complete and total forgiveness to you.

"Finally, I confessed all my sins to you and stopped trying to hide my guilt. I said to myself, 'I will confess my rebellion to the Lord.' And you forgave me! All my guilt is gone" (PSALM 32:5 NLT).

God wants you in His presence—to cleanse you of the guilt and shame you feel.

"Let us go right into the presence of God with sincere hearts fully trusting him. For our guilty consciences have been sprinkled with Christ's blood to make us clean, and our bodies have been washed with pure water" (HEBREWS 10:22 NLT).

God wants you to replace the lies you've been led to believe with His truth.

"Guide me in your truth and teach me, for you are God my Savior, and my hope is in you all day long" (PSALM 25:5)

God wants you to find your identity in Him—as His beloved child.

"See what great love the Father has lavished on us, that we should be called children of God! And that is what we are!" (1 JOHN 3:1)

God wants you to fight sin—avoiding and getting rid of things that tempt you.

"So if your eye—even your good eye—causes you to lust, gouge it out and throw it away . . . And if your hand—even your stronger hand—causes you to sin, cut it off and throw it away" (MATTHEW 5:29–30 NLT).

God wants you to seek accountability.

"As iron sharpens iron, so one person sharpens another" (PROVERBS 27:17).

God can use counselors to help you find victory over sexual addiction.

"For by wise guidance you can wage your war, and in abundance of counselors there is victory" (PROVERBS 24:6 ESV).

God wants you to help others who struggle with sexual addiction.

"Brothers and sisters, if someone is caught in a sin, you who live by the Spirit should restore that person gently. But watch yourselves, or you also may be tempted. Carry each other's burdens, and in this way you will fulfill the law of Christ" (GALATIANS 6:1–2).

Do you not know that your bodies are temples
of the Holy Spirit, who is in you,
whom you have received from God?
You are not your own; you were bought at a price.
Therefore honor God with your bodies.
(1 CORINTHIANS 6:19–20)

The Shame of Sexual Addiction

S—Secretive: living a double life

H—Hollow: prioritizing sexual passion over a person

A—Abusive: exploiting others and debasing yourself

M—Mood-altering: using sexual passion for comfort or to avoid working through painful emotions

E—Essential: convincing yourself that sex is the most important thing in life

People are slaves to whatever has mastered them.
(2 Peter 2:19)

The Spiral of Sexual Addiction

Curiosity is a seemingly harmless temptation to view people as sexual objects.
"Each person is tempted when they are dragged away by their own evil desire and enticed" (James 1:14).

Addiction is a recurring stimulus in the brain.
"Do not be deceived: God cannot be mocked. A man reaps what he sows" (Galatians 6:7).

Compulsive masturbation is a response of sexual self-comfort to relieve the arousal.
"Jesus replied, 'Very truly I tell you, everyone who sins is a slave to sin'" (John 8:34).

Escalation is the need for more explicit or shocking sexuality.
"Having lost all sensitivity, they have given themselves over to sensuality so as to indulge in every kind of impurity, and they are full of greed" (Ephesians 4:19).

Desensitization is when shocking sexuality no longer produces the same stimulation.
"Are they ashamed of their detestable conduct? No, they have no shame at all; they do not even know how to blush" (Jeremiah 6:15).

Key Verse to Memorize

Flee from sexual immorality.
All other sins a person commits
are outside the body,
but whoever sins sexually,
sins against their own body.
(1 Corinthians 6:18)

Acting out is a compulsion to do (to enact) what has been seen and imagined.
"The acts of the flesh are obvious: sexual immorality, impurity and debauchery" (Galatians 5:19).

Despair is the feeling of disgust that comes in response to the inappropriate and addictive sexual behavior.
"I do not understand what I do. For what I want to do I do not do, but what I hate I do" (Romans 7:15).

The Cycle of Sexual Addiction

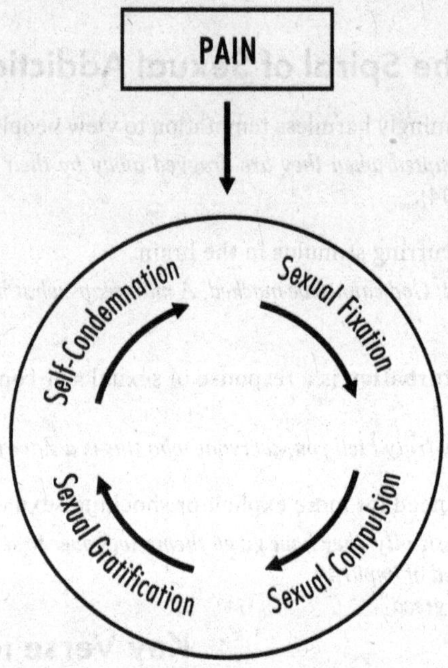

Unresolved pain fuels the cycle of sexual addiction. A struggler often turns to sex or pornography as a way to cope with emotional pain, past trauma, loneliness, or rejection. This leads to fixation on finding an outlet for sexual activity, followed by a compulsive drive to fulfill that desire. While gratification may bring momentary relief, it is short-lived, soon replaced by guilt, shame, and self-condemnation. These painful emotions reinforce the cycle, keeping the struggler trapped in addiction.

Breaking free requires finding healthy coping mechanisms, such as prayer, exercise, counseling, and accountability. Meditating on God's love and truth is key to freedom, remembering that in Christ, there is no condemnation.

There is now no condemnation for those who are in Christ Jesus.
(Romans 8:1)

Ways Out of the Web

Getting out of the web of sexual addiction involves addressing external (your environment) and internal factors (your heart). Sometimes strugglers address external factors and experience temporary victory, but without addressing the heart, the struggler will often stay trapped in the web.

External factors

- — Get an app on your phone and/or software on your computer that blocks access to pornographic sites. (Some include the option to send regular reports to an accountability partner.)
- — Delete any apps that often lead you into temptation, such as social media apps.
- — Set up or use your computer in a high-traffic or highly visible area of your home.
- — Identify the situations and times of day when you are prone to engage in addictive behaviors and take steps to be especially vigilant at those times.

"If your right eye causes you to stumble, gouge it out and throw it away"
(MATTHEW 5:29).

Internal factors

- — Identify the feelings that often precede or accompany the addictive behaviors (for example, sadness, shame, stress, loneliness, or frustration).
- — Identify any recurring thoughts that often precede or accompany the addictive behaviors (for example, "I'm a failure").
- — Identify any past pain or experiences that play a role in how the addictive behaviors began.
- — Talk with a trusted friend, pastor, or counselor about these thoughts, feelings, and experiences so that you can process them and develop new patterns of thinking and coping.

"Search me, God, and know my heart; test me and know my anxious thoughts. See if there is any offensive way in me, and lead me in the way everlasting"
(PSALM 139:23–24).

Purity

P—Participate in an accountability group dealing with sex addictions.

> *"Two are better than one, because they have a good return for their labor: If either of them falls down, one can help the other up. But pity anyone who falls and has no one to help them up"* (ECCLESIASTES 4:9–10).

U—Uphold boundary lines that must be off-limits.

> *"The prudent see danger and take refuge, but the simple keep going and pay the penalty"* (PROVERBS 27:12).

R—Rid yourself, your home, and your work area of all sexually addictive items.

"Wash and make yourselves clean. Take your evil deeds out of my sight; stop doing wrong. Learn to do right" (ISAIAH 1:16–17).

I—Incorporate the power of Christ daily when temptation overwhelms you.

"'My grace is sufficient for you, for my power is made perfect in weakness.' Therefore I will boast all the more gladly about my weaknesses, so that Christ's power may rest on me" (2 CORINTHIANS 12:9).

T—Take on positive habits of discipline, such as exercise, sports, regular sleep, and new hobbies.

"Whoever heeds discipline shows the way to life, but whoever ignores correction leads others astray" (PROVERBS 10:17).

Y—Yield your mind to meditating on and memorizing Scripture.

"Get rid of all moral filth and the evil that is so prevalent and humbly accept the word planted in you, which can save you" (JAMES 1:21).

God did not call us to be impure, but to live a holy life.
(1 THESSALONIANS 4:7)

How to Replace Lies with Truth

Lie: "I am dirty. God is disgusted with me."

Truth: God loves you. He washes you clean and makes you new by His Spirit.

"Once we, too, were foolish and disobedient. We were misled and became slaves to many lusts and pleasures . . . But—When God our Savior revealed his kindness and love, he saved us, not because of the righteous things we had done, but because of his mercy. He washed away our sins, giving us a new birth and new life through the Holy Spirit" (TITUS 3:3–5 NLT).

Lie: "God won't forgive me again."

Truth: God's grace is greater than our sin. He forgives all our sin.

"O Lord, you are so good, so ready to forgive, so full of unfailing love for all who ask for your help" (PSALM 86:5 NLT).

Lie: "I am worthless and unlovable."

Truth: You matter to God. You have God-given worth because He created you, and nothing can separate you from His love.

"You are precious to me. You are honored, and I love you" (ISAIAH 43:4 NLT).

Lie: "The temptation is too strong. I can't control it."

Truth: With God's help, you can overcome temptation. God is faithful to show you a way out.

"The temptations in your life are no different from what others experience. And God is faithful. He will not allow the temptation to be more than you can stand. When you are tempted, he will show you a way out so that you can endure" (1 CORINTHIANS 10:13 NLT).

Lie: "I can't change. There is no hope for me."

Truth: You can change. No matter how many times you've fallen or how deeply ensnared you feel—with God, there is always hope.

"There is surely a future hope for you, and your hope will not be cut off" (PROVERBS 23:18).

My Personalized Plan

I will . . .

Decide that I really do want to be set free.

"Prepare your minds for action and exercise self-control" (1 PETER 1:13 NLT).

Dispel the myth that I don't need help.

"Create in me a pure heart, O God, and renew a steadfast spirit within me" (PSALM 51:10).

Key Passage to Read

1 Thessalonians 4:1-8

Deal with any past abuse, seeking the Lord (and professional help if needed) for recovery.

"He heals the brokenhearted and binds up their wounds" (PSALM 147:3).

Discern the inner need(s) I have tried to satisfy through sexual passion.[204]

"You desired faithfulness even in the womb; you taught me wisdom in that secret place" (PSALM 51:6).

Determine to let Jesus meet my needs.

"My God will meet all your needs" (PHILIPPIANS 4:19).

Dedicate my life to the Lord Jesus.

"Whoever wants to be my disciple must deny themselves and take up their cross daily and follow me. For whoever wants to save their life will lose it, but whoever loses their life for me will save it" (LUKE 9:23–24).

Questions & Answers

Question: "At what point does normal sexual desire turn into lust?"

Answer: It is natural to be attracted to someone, but unnatural to *sexualize* a person. When your mind moves from normal attraction to consuming passion to do a sexually impure act, then you experience lust.

Do not let sin reign in your mortal body so that you obey its evil desires.
(ROMANS 6:12)

Question: "Pornography is harmless, so why should it ever be illegal?"

Answer: Pornography is far from harmless. Everyone who's been caught in the web of sexual addiction has obliterated that myth.

Pornography is addictive and often leads to abuse of others.

All of us would be wise to share the resolve of King David:

I will not look with approval
on anything that is vile.
(PSALM 101:3)

Question: "Since God created the human body as sexual, what's wrong with nudity and pornography?"

Answer: God ordained human sexuality for intimacy in marriage and for procreation. Pornography and indiscriminate nudity are designed simply to arouse sexual lust.

"Anyone who looks at a woman lustfully has already
committed adultery with her in his heart."
(MATTHEW 5:27–28)

SEXUAL ASSAULT & RAPE RECOVERY

Rescued, Redeemed, Restored

God's Heart on Sexual Harassment and Assault

God instructs us to love one another and treat one another with kindness and respect, just as we want to be treated.

"Finally, all of you, be like-minded, be sympathetic, love one another, be compassionate and humble" (1 PETER 3:8).

"So in everything, do to others what you would have them do to you, for this sums up the Law and the Prophets" (MATTHEW 7:12).

God commands us and anyone who would sexually harass another not to engage in any distasteful, objectionable, nasty, or unsavory talk, but to compliment and encourage one another.

"Do not let any unwholesome talk come out of your mouths, but only what is helpful for building others up according to their needs, that it may benefit those who listen" (EPHESIANS 4:29).

God's standard for sexual activity is that it be limited to husband and wife only, and that He will judge all who are sexually immoral according to His holy standard.

"Marriage should be honored by all, and the marriage bed kept pure, for God will judge the adulterer and all the sexually immoral" (HEBREWS 13:4).

God warns that impurity of speech or action is out of place for His holy people.

"Among you there must not be even a hint of sexual immorality, or of any kind of impurity, or of greed, because these are improper for God's holy people. Nor should there be obscenity, foolish talk or coarse joking, which are out of place, but rather thanksgiving" (EPHESIANS 5:3–4).

God examines our hearts to see if they are pure, for if our hearts are pure, then our thoughts, desires, words, and actions will be pure, putting an end to sexual harassment and assault.

"The things that come out of a person's mouth come from the heart, and these defile them. For out of the heart come evil thoughts—murder, adultery, sexual immorality, theft, false testimony, slander" (MATTHEW 15:18–19).

God keeps constant watch over His own and attends to the cry of those wounded by sexual harassment or assault, but He is against evildoers who perpetrate such harmful and wicked sexual acts.

"The eyes of the LORD are on the righteous, and his ears are attentive to their cry; but the face of the LORD is against those who do evil, to blot out their name from the earth" (PSALM 34:15–16).

God is our avenger and He exacts judgment on those who harm us through sinful actions.

"He is the God who pays back those who harm me" (PSALM 18:47 NLT).

God heals our wounded hearts, sets us free from mental and emotional bondage to our abusers, and releases us from the dark cloak of sin that often envelops us.

"The Spirit of the Sovereign LORD is on me [Jesus], *because . . . He has sent me to bind up the brokenhearted, to proclaim freedom for the captives and release from darkness for the prisoners"* (ISAIAH 61:1).

God watches over us to protect us, but He will silence, break, and confine to darkness the wicked who sin against Him by sinning against us in a sexual manner.

"He will guard the feet of his faithful servants, but the wicked will be silenced in the place of darkness . . . Those who oppose the LORD will be broken. The Most High will thunder from heaven; the LORD will judge the ends of the earth" (1 SAMUEL 2:9–10).

God feels compassion toward you and longs to help you and to shepherd you.

"When he saw the crowds, he had compassion on them, because they were harassed and helpless, like sheep without a shepherd" (MATTHEW 9:36).

What Sexual Assault Says vs. What God's Heart Says

Sexual Assault says: "You are all alone."

God's Heart says: "I am always with you and will never leave you or forsake you."

"Be strong and courageous. Do not be afraid or terrified because of them, for the LORD your God goes with you; he will never leave you nor forsake you" (DEUTERONOMY 31:6).

Sexual Assault says: "You are unimportant."

God's Heart says: "You are highly valued by Me and the lifeblood that flows throughout your body is precious to Me."

"He will take pity on the weak and the needy and save the needy from death. He will rescue them from oppression and violence, for precious is their blood in his sight" (PSALM 72:13–14).

Sexual Assault says: "You are beyond hope."

God's Heart says: "Your hope is Christ, who has taken up permanent residence within you, making it impossible for you to ever be without hope because you will never be without Him."

"There is surely a future hope for you, and your hope will not be cut off" (PROVERBS 23:18).

Sexual Assault says: "You are not worthy of love."

God's Heart says: "Even before you were born I loved you and sent My Son to die for you, and nothing you can do or not do will ever separate you from My love."

Key Verse to Memorize

"Do not fear, for I am with you;
do not be dismayed, for I am your God.
I will strengthen you and help you;
I will uphold you
with my righteous right hand."
(ISAIAH 41:10)

"I am convinced that neither death nor life, neither angels nor demons, neither the present nor the future, nor any powers, neither height nor depth, nor anything else in all creation, will be able to separate us from the love of God that is in Christ Jesus our Lord" (ROMANS 8:38–39).

Sexual Assault says: "You are not worthy of help."

God's Heart says: "I am your ever-present help, your constant source of strength. Call on Me and I will sustain and uphold you."

"Do not fear, for I am with you; do not be dismayed, for I am your God. I will strengthen you and help you; I will uphold you with my righteous right hand" (ISAIAH 41:10).

Sexual Assault says: "You are not worthy of compassion."

God's Heart says: "I am full of compassion for you and stand ready to cover you like a blanket with My comfort and shower you with tender mercies."

"The Father of compassion and the God of all comfort . . . comforts us in all our troubles, so that we can comfort those in any trouble with the comfort we ourselves receive from God" (2 CORINTHIANS 1:3–4).

Common Characteristics of Acquaintance Rapists

Appears emotionally immature

Acts aggressive or too forward

Views others as adversaries

Sees victims as conquests

Lacks empathy toward others

Lacks social consciousness

Boasts about physical prowess

Encroaches on your activities

Behaves jealously toward you

Acts possessive of you

Invades your personal space

Accuses you of being uptight

Asks intrusive questions about your life

Uses the "blame game" to make you feel guilty

Commands your attention when you are with others

Demands your compliance when you say *no*

Exhibits seething or short-tempered anger

Projects a dominant, forceful impression

Interjects "we" words to be included with you

Speaks negatively about women in general

Seeks to isolate you

Uses charm to lower your defenses

Ignores your stated boundaries

Tries to touch you inappropriately

There is no fear of God
before their eyes.
Even on their beds they plot evil;
they commit themselves to a sinful course
and do not reject what is wrong.
(Psalm 36:1, 4)

Common Characteristics of Rapists[205]

Poor self-image

Twisted view of sexuality

Difficulty establishing and maintaining intimate relationships

Low tolerance for frustration

Lack of sensitivity to the feelings of others

Pattern of seeking immediate gratification without regard for negative repercussions

Look of normalcy in some areas of life, such as having a wife and children

Key Passage to Read

Lamentations 3:17–26

Respectable, responsible, and rewarding job

Keen ability to detect vulnerable women by observing their walk, posture, attire, facial expressions, speech, and behavior

Preference for attacking women in the privacy of their own homes

"It is from within, out of a person's heart,
that evil thoughts come—sexual immorality . . .
adultery . . . deceit, lewdness."
(Mark 7:21–22)

My Personalized Plan

I will . . .

Face what happened to me.

— I will acknowledge that this experience is now part of my history—my life—which is an unfolding story written by God.

"All the days ordained for me were written in your book before one of them came to be" (Psalm 139:16).

Invite Jesus into my struggle.

— I will not face what happened and my reactions to it by myself—I will invite God into my pain.

"When you go through deep waters, I will be with you. When you go through rivers of difficulty, you will not drown. When you walk through the fire of oppression, you will not be burned up; the flames will not consume you" (ISAIAH 43:2 NLT).

Find my identity in Christ.

— I will consciously remind myself that Jesus has cleansed me and made me whole and nothing can change that reality.

"He [God] *saved us, not because of righteous things we had done, but because of his mercy. He saved us through the washing of rebirth and renewal by the Holy Spirit"* (TITUS 3:5).

Trust God to heal my memories with real truth.

— I will stop the endless loop of traumatic memories playing in my mind by replacing them with truths about God's goodness and grace.

"Give me a sign of your goodness, that my enemies may see it and be put to shame, for you, LORD, have helped me and comforted me" (PSALM 86:17).

Live in God's forgiveness.

— I will develop an attitude of forgiveness in my heart before God toward my attacker.

"Leave room for God's wrath, for it is written: 'It is mine to avenge; I will repay,' says the Lord" (ROMANS 12:19).

See myself through God's eyes.

— I will begin each day by recalling what God has revealed to me about how He sees me: I am His child; I am precious to Him; I am accepted and loved by Him.

"You are precious and honored in my sight, and . . . I love you" (ISAIAH 43:4).

Form supportive, positive relationships.

— I will reach out to safe people I know I can trust.

"A friend loves at all times, and a brother is born for a time of adversity" (PROVERBS 17:17).

Give myself time to experience restoration and renewal.

— I will not rush God's timing, but rather will respond and cooperate with Him as His Spirit guides me step-by-step through the healing process.

"He has made everything beautiful in its time. He has also set eternity in the human heart; yet no one can fathom what God has done from beginning to end" (ECCLESIASTES 3:11).

Move toward others with love, even in the midst of suffering.

- I will become more sensitive to and look for others around me who are hurting and will reach out to help them in whatever way I can.

"Praise be to the God and Father of our Lord Jesus Christ, the Father of compassion and the God of all comfort, who comforts us in all our troubles, so that we can comfort those in any trouble with the comfort we ourselves receive from God"
(2 CORINTHIANS 1:3–4).

Questions & Answers

Question: "My boss made a pass at me and is threatening to fire me if I don't 'play nice.' Is this a form of sexual harassment?"

Answer: Yes. The phrase "quid pro quo" is Latin for "this for that." When a person in a position of power over someone else promises a reward for sex or threatens a repercussion if sex is denied, these are quid pro quo types of sexual harassment.

Another type of sexual harassment is when sexual advances result in severe intimidation that affects the victim's ability to function effectively. This *hostile environment* is another type of sexual harassment that can be produced by a person in power over a peer.[206]

They will be paid back with harm for the harm they have done.
Their idea of pleasure is to carouse in broad daylight.
They are blots and blemishes, reveling in their pleasures.
(2 PETER 2:13)

Question: "Does God care about my suffering?"

Answer: God cares deeply about your suffering as demonstrated by the fact . . .

- He is close to you when you are brokenhearted.

"The LORD is close to the brokenhearted and
saves those who are crushed in spirit."
(PSALM 34:18)

- He keeps a record of your grief and holds your tears.

You keep track of all my sorrows.
You have collected all my tears in your bottle.
You have recorded each one in your book.
(PSALM 56:8 NLT)

SEXUAL INTEGRITY

Balancing Your Passion with Purity

God's Heart on Sexual Intimacy

The man and the woman will establish a separate family unit from their parents.

"That is why a man leaves his father and mother . . ." (GENESIS 2:24).

The married couple will cleave—bond—to each other as the priority relationship.

"And is united to his wife . . ." (GENESIS 2:24).

The "one flesh" sexual relationship will begin after the God-ordained marriage between husband and wife.

"And they become one flesh" (GENESIS 2:24).

The sexual and emotional intimacy in marriage will be open and vulnerable with moral purity between husband and wife.

"Adam and his wife were both naked, and they felt no shame" (GENESIS 2:25).

Marriage partners will not be burdened by the fear or shame of pregnancy out of wedlock.

"God blessed them and said to them, 'Be fruitful and increase in number'" (GENESIS 1:28).

The intimate relationship will represent the intimate oneness that true believers have with the Lord.

"As a bridegroom rejoices over his bride, so will your God rejoice over you" (ISAIAH 62:5).

"Haven't you read," he [Jesus] *replied,*
"that at the beginning the Creator 'made them male and female,'
and said, 'For this reason a man will leave his father and mother
and be united to his wife, and the two will become one flesh'?"
(MATTHEW 19:4–5)

What Is Sexual Integrity?

Sexual integrity is consistently living your life according to the highest moral sexual standards—consistently guarding your mind, will, and emotions from sexual impurity.

"Whoever walks in integrity walks securely, but whoever takes crooked paths will be found out" (PROVERBS 10:9).

Sexual integrity is to be the same in the dark as you are in the light—the same in private as you are in public—not double-minded with contradictory thoughts, words, and deeds. The person without integrity *"is double-minded and unstable in all they do"* (James 1:8).

What Is Sexual Purity?

Sexual purity is chastity or freedom from sexually immoral attitudes and actions.

"Set an example for the believers in speech, in conduct, in love, in faith and in purity" (1 TIMOTHY 4:12).

Sexual purity doesn't "just happen." Because of our bent to sin, we need to take an active role in purifying our hearts, which will in turn purify our attitudes and actions.

"Come near to God and he will come near to you. Wash your hands, you sinners, and purify your hearts, you double-minded" (JAMES 4:8).

Seven Underlying Reasons for "Giving In"

1. **Lack of self-worth**

   "'I know the plans I have for you,' declares the LORD, 'plans to prosper you and not to harm you, plans to give you hope and a future'" (JEREMIAH 29:11).

2. **Lack of self-control**

   "Like a city whose walls are broken through is a person who lacks self-control" (PROVERBS 25:28).

3. **Lack of self-respect**

   "Show proper respect to everyone, love the family of believers, fear God, honor the emperor" (1 PETER 2:17).

4. **Lack of emotional intimacy**

   "I have loved you with an everlasting love; I have drawn you with unfailing kindness" (JEREMIAH 31:3).

5. **Lack of communication**

   "It [the grace of God] *teaches us to say 'No' to ungodliness and worldly passions, and to live self-controlled, upright and godly lives in this present age"* (TITUS 2:12).

6. **Lack of boundaries**

   "The LORD *is close to the brokenhearted and saves those who are crushed in spirit"* (PSALM 34:18).

7. **Lack of discretion**

   "My son, do not let wisdom and understanding out of your sight, preserve sound judgment and discretion" (PROVERBS 3:21).

The LORD *will guide you always;*
he will satisfy your needs in a sun-scorched land
and will strengthen your frame.
You will be like a well-watered garden,
like a spring whose waters never fail.
(ISAIAH 58:11)

Three Subtle Seduction "Hooks" to Avoid

1. **Sexually driven advertising**

   "Their idea of pleasure is to carouse in broad daylight. They are . . . reveling in their pleasures while they feast with you. With eyes full of adultery, they never stop sinning" (2 PETER 2:13–14).

2. **Inappropriate/adult television programs and social media accounts**

   "They mouth empty, boastful words and, by appealing to the lustful desires of the flesh, they entice people who are just escaping from those who live in error. They promise them freedom, while they themselves are slaves of depravity—for 'people are slaves to whatever has mastered them'" (2 PETER 2:18–19).

3. **Explicit sites or apps on smartphones, computers, and the Internet**

   "Be alert and of sober mind. Your enemy the devil prowls around like a roaring lion looking for someone to devour. Resist him, standing firm in the faith, because you know that the family of believers throughout the world is undergoing the same kind of sufferings" (1 PETER 5:8–9).

Key Verses to Memorize

Do you not know that your bodies are
temples of the Holy Spirit, who is in you,
whom you have received from God?
You are not your own;
you were bought at a price.
Therefore honor God with your bodies.
(1 CORINTHIANS 6:19–20)

Reasons for Sexual Integrity

I want God's blessing on my life.

"I urge you, brothers and sisters, in view of God's mercy, to offer your bodies as a living sacrifice, holy and pleasing to God—this is your true and proper worship" (ROMANS 12:1).

I don't want to do anything that will hinder my prayer life with God.

"If I had cherished sin in my heart, the Lord would not have listened" (PSALM 66:18).

I don't want anyone else to take the place of God in my life.

"Jesus replied: 'Love the Lord your God with all your heart and with all your soul and with all your mind'" (MATTHEW 22:37).

I want to live a life of integrity, being the same in the dark as I am in the light—the same in public as I am in private.

"I know, my God, that you test the heart and are pleased with integrity" (1 CHRONICLES 29:17).

I want others to see the power of Christ in me.

"His divine power has given us everything we need for a godly life through our knowledge of him who called us by his own glory and goodness" (2 PETER 1:3).

I strive always to keep my conscience clear
before God and man.
(ACTS 24:16)

Invest in Integrity

I—Invite others to walk the road of sexual integrity with you.

"Two are better than one, because they have a good return for their labor: If either of them falls down, one can help the other up. But pity anyone who falls and has no one to help them up" (ECCLESIASTES 4:9–10).

N—Never put yourself or your loved one in a tempting situation.

"Do not offer any part of yourself to sin as an instrument of wickedness, but rather offer yourselves to God as those who have been brought from death to life; and offer every part of yourself to him as an instrument of righteousness" (ROMANS 6:13).

T—Trust God to meet your need for love.

"Let the morning bring me word of your unfailing love, for I have put my trust in you. Show me the way I should go, for to you I entrust my life" (PSALM 143:8).

E—Enjoy others instead of using others.

"Love must be sincere. Hate what is evil; cling to what is good. Be devoted to one another in love. Honor one another above yourselves" (ROMANS 12:9–10).

G—Give yourself to only sexually pure relationships.

"Now that you have purified yourselves by obeying the truth so that you have sincere love for each other, love one another deeply, from the heart" (1 PETER 1:22).

R—Refuse to justify any sexual impurity.

"Watch and pray so that you will not fall into temptation. The spirit is willing, but the flesh is weak" (MATTHEW 26:41).

I—Isolate yourself from people who tempt you.

"Do not be misled: 'Bad company corrupts good character'" (1 CORINTHIANS 15:33).

T—Transform your mind through the written Word of God.

"I have hidden your word in my heart that I might not sin against you" (PSALM 119:11).

Y—Yield to Christ, who lives in you, trusting Him to produce in you a life of purity.

"I have been crucified with Christ and I no longer live, but Christ lives in me. The life I now live in the body, I live by faith in the Son of God, who loved me and gave himself for me" (GALATIANS 2:20).

Myths About Sex

Myth: "If it feels good, it must be good."

Truth: Sin can feel good, but that doesn't mean sin is good.

"The one whose walk is blameless is kept safe, but the one whose ways are perverse will fall into the pit" (PROVERBS 28:18).

Myth: "I need sex in order to feel good about myself."

Truth: Real love is not self-seeking.

"It [Love] *does not dishonor others, it is not self-seeking"* (1 CORINTHIANS 13:5).

Myth: "A husband prefers his wife to be sexually experienced."

Truth: Premarital sex can breed jealousy and distrust in a marriage.

"Jealousy arouses a husband's fury, and he will show no mercy when he takes revenge" (PROVERBS 6:34).

Myth: "Multiple sex partners give me more experience."

Truth: Multiple experiences breed comparisons and dissatisfaction.

"Do not share in the sins of others. Keep yourself pure" (1 TIMOTHY 5:22).

Myth: "Sexual flirtation is harmless."

Truth: Sexual flirtation harms the conscience and leads to sexual arousal and physical involvement.

"Flee the evil desires of youth and pursue righteousness, faith, love and peace, along with those who call on the Lord out of a pure heart" (2 TIMOTHY 2:22).

Myth: "As long as I'm not married, I should be able to have sex with whomever I want."

Truth: The only instance where God blesses two people in a sexual relationship is within a husband-and-wife marital relationship.

"'For this reason a man will leave his father and mother and be united to his wife, and the two will become one flesh.' So they are no longer two, but one flesh" (MARK 10:7–8).

When You Choose to Wait

Emotionally—You have freedom from guilt, freedom from anxiety, freedom from grief, freedom from emotional scars.

"Do not be anxious about anything, but in every situation, by prayer and petition, with thanksgiving, present your requests to God. And the peace of God, which transcends all understanding, will guard your hearts and your minds in Christ Jesus" (PHILIPPIANS 4:6–7).

Physically—You have no premarital pregnancy, no unwanted child, no sexual disease, no abortion consequences.

"Flee from sexual immorality. All other sins a person commits are outside the body, but whoever sins sexually, sins against their own body" (1 CORINTHIANS 6:18).

Socially—You have positive relationships, positive self-image, positive values, positive reputation.

"Commit your way to the LORD; trust in him and he will do this: He will make your righteous reward shine like the dawn, your vindication like the noonday sun" (PSALM 37:5–6).

Spiritually—You have a pure conscience before God, a pure vision for God's will, a pure motive initiated by God, and a pure relationship with God.

"Blessed are the pure in heart, for they will see God" (MATTHEW 5:8).

My Personalized Plan[207]

I will . . .

Write out my vow to be sexually pure from this day on.

— Share my pledge with my parents, a special friend, or someone else I trust who knows the Lord.

"When you make a vow to God, do not delay to fulfill it. He has no pleasure in fools; fulfill your vow" (ECCLESIASTES 5:4).

Find friends who hold the same commitment.

— Abstaining from sex is easier alongside close friends who honor the same vow.

"I appeal to you . . . that you may be perfectly united in mind and thought" (1 CORINTHIANS 1:10).

Pray for the right accountability partner.

— Ask someone who cares about me that I deeply respect to hold me accountable sexually. Ideally, this person should be several years older, one who will ask candid questions and "speak the truth in love."

"Wounds from a friend can be trusted, but an enemy multiplies kisses" (PROVERBS 27:6).

Key Passage to Read

1 Thessalonians 4:3–8

Develop a proactive strategy for countering sexual triggers.

— I will not be alone in my date's home. I will use an Internet filter or a blocking service.

"Do not set foot on the path of the wicked or walk in the way of evildoers" (PROVERBS 4:14).

Make a list of goals I have for life.

— Develop short-term goals (six months to two years) and long-term goals (two to ten years), telling my family and friends so they can encourage me.

"We are God's handiwork, created in Christ Jesus to do good works, which God prepared in advance for us to do" (EPHESIANS 2:10).

Wear a chastity ring, bracelet, or necklace.

— A physical item can be a spiritual reminder of my commitment to sexual purity.

"Then I will ever sing in praise of your name and fulfill my vows day after day" (PSALM 61:8).

Write a love letter to my future mate.

— Tell my future marriage partner why I chose to save myself and share what purity means to me.

"Marriage should be honored by all, and the marriage bed kept pure, for God will judge the adulterer and all the sexually immoral" (HEBREWS 13:4).

Lend a hand in helping others.

— If I am busy, I am less likely to be preoccupied with sex. I can volunteer my time in service to others.

"Let your light shine before others, that they may see your good deeds and glorify your Father in heaven" (MATTHEW 5:16).

Rely on the spiritual beliefs or teachings of my church.

— Spiritual faith is a strong motivation to do what is right.

"Be on your guard; stand firm in the faith; be courageous; be strong" (1 CORINTHIANS 16:13).

Make a Promise List.

— "I promise I will practice sexual abstinence."

— "I promise I will date only those who are committed to sexual integrity."

— "I promise I will set sexual boundaries and stay within those boundaries."

— "I promise I will not be alone with a date in a bedroom, a parked car, or any other compromising place."

— "I promise I will guard my eyes, my mind, and my heart against sexual impurity."

— "I promise I will not take any drink or drug that would weaken my defenses."

— "I promise I will not look at pornography."

— "I promise I will not visit Internet sex sites."

Read this list at least once a week, renewing my vows to the Lord.

Since we have these promises, dear friends,
let us purify ourselves from everything that contaminates body and spirit,
perfecting holiness out of reverence for God.
(2 CORINTHIANS 7:1)

Questions & Answers

Question: "Is sexual temptation a sin?"

Answer: No. Temptation is not a sin, but to yield to temptation is a sin. We are all tempted in different areas. The issue is whether or not we give in to temptation. Only one person on earth experienced temptation in every area, yet was without sin—Jesus, our Savior.

We do not have a high priest who is unable
to empathize with our weaknesses,
but we have one who has been tempted in every way,
just as we are—yet he did not sin.
(HEBREWS 4:15)

Question: "Am I obligated to give sexual favors to someone who has spent money on me by buying me jewelry, taking me to dinner, going to the theater, or paying my rent?"

Answer: No. You are worth far more than any gift, favor, or dollar amount. You are made in the image of God, and it is far beneath your dignity to perform any type of sexual favor in return for any type of gift or "investment."

The body, however, is not meant for sexual immorality
but for the Lord, and the Lord for the body.
(1 CORINTHIANS 6:13)

Question: "I'm a teenage girl and have committed my life to the Lord. What can help me resist sexual temptation?"

Answer: Carry visual reminders of your highest ideals, values, and commitments. For example, many young people choose to wear a "purity ring" to symbolize their covenant to the Lord.

Godliness has value for all things, holding promise
for both the present life and the life to come.
(1 TIMOTHY 4:8)

SINGLE PARENTING

Success with God as Your Partner

God's Heart on Single Parenting

God views children as a gift to single parents.

"Children are a heritage from the LORD, offspring a reward from him" (PSALM 127:3).

God views single parents as worthy of their children's honor and obedience.

"Children, obey your parents in the Lord, for this is right. 'Honor your father and mother'—which is the first commandment with a promise—'so that it may go well with you and that you may enjoy long life on the earth'" (EPHESIANS 6:1-3).

God assigns to single parents the responsibility of imparting biblical truth to their children.

"Love the LORD your God with all your heart and with all your soul and with all your strength. These commandments that I give you today are to be on your hearts. Impress them on your children. Talk about them when you sit at home and when you walk along the road, when you lie down and when you get up" (DEUTERONOMY 6:5-7).

God instructs single parents to bring their children to Jesus.

"Let the little children come to me [Jesus], *and do not hinder them, for the kingdom of God belongs to such as these"* (LUKE 18:16).

God reveals Himself and His plan of salvation to children.

"Jesus said, 'I praise you, Father, Lord of heaven and earth, because you have hidden these things from the wise and learned, and revealed them to little children'" (MATTHEW 11:25).

God can use the faith and example of single parents to influence the child's spiritual development.

"I am reminded of your sincere faith, which first lived in your grandmother Lois and in your mother Eunice and, I am persuaded, now lives in you also" (2 TIMOTHY 1:5).

God wants you to lean on Him and trust Him as you navigate parenting.

"Trust in the LORD with all your heart and lean not on your own understanding; in all your ways submit to him, and he will make your paths straight" (PROVERBS 3:5-6).

God promises to be with you always for help and strength.

"God is our refuge and strength, an ever-present help in trouble" (PSALM 46:1).

God promises to help carry your burdens.

"Cast your cares on the Lord *and he will sustain you; he will never let the righteous be shaken"* (Psalm 55:22).

God wants you to receive and reflect the love of Jesus to your children.

"A new command I give you: Love one another. As I have loved you, so you must love one another" (John 13:34).

It was good for me to be afflicted
so that I might learn your decrees.
(Psalm 119:71)

Emotional Needs of Children

Security is the single most important need in a single-parent home. Children need to . . .

S—See that you are emotionally healthy and not insecure about the future.

"Blessed are those whose help is the God of Jacob, whose hope is in the Lord *their God"* (Psalm 146:5).

E—Experience a consistent, structured homelife brought about through wise parenting.

"By wisdom a house is built, and through understanding it is established" (Proverbs 24:3).

C—Continue to have the freedom to love both parents in the case of divorce or separation.

"Dear friends, since God so loved us, we also ought to love one another" (1 John 4:11).

U—Understand that they are not responsible for having only one parent at home.

"Understanding is a wellspring of life to him who has it" (Proverbs 16:22 nkjv).

R—Receive comfort so that someday they will be able to comfort others.

"Praise be to the God and Father of our Lord Jesus Christ, the Father of compassion and the God of all comfort, who comforts us in all our troubles, so that we can comfort those in any trouble with the comfort we ourselves receive from God" (2 Corinthians 1:3–4).

I—Identify their inner feelings and confront them.

"Search for peace, and work to maintain it. The eyes of the LORD watch over those who do right, and his ears are open to their prayers" (1 PETER 3:11-12 NLT).

T—Turn to the heavenly Father to find security in His family.

"See what great love the Father has lavished on us, that we should be called children of God!" (1 JOHN 3:1).

Y—Yield to the Lord their discontentment, realizing that there is no "perfect family."

"I have learned to be content whatever the circumstances" (PHILIPPIANS 4:11).

"Your dwelling place is secure,
your nest is set in a rock."
(NUMBERS 24:21)

Causes of Bitterness and Discontentment

Resentment toward ex-spouse or toward God

Reduction of income

Loss of friends and social life

Loss of identity

Loss of freedom because of bearing parenting responsibilities alone

Envy of friends who have spouses

Exhaustion from having to carry the load of parenting alone

Dos and Don'ts for Single Parents

Don't hang on to negative feelings.[208]
Do forgive the other parent.

"Bear with each other and forgive one another if any of you has a grievance against someone. Forgive as the Lord forgave you" (COLOSSIANS 3:13).

Don't try to be both father and mother.
Do be the wisest parent possible in your God-given role.

"A father to the fatherless, a defender of widows, is God in his holy dwelling" (PSALM 68:5).

Don't try to hide your emotions from your child.

Do be vulnerable. Let your child know who you really are as a person.[209]

"We have spoken freely to you . . . and opened wide our hearts to you" (2 Corinthians 6:11).

Don't criticize the other parent.[210]

Do mention positive attributes of the other parent and, if possible, give children the opportunity to build a relationship with the other parent.

"Set a guard over my mouth, Lord; keep watch over the door of my lips" (Psalm 141:3).

Key Verses to Memorize

For the Single Mother

You, God, see the trouble of the afflicted;
you consider their grief and take it in hand.
The victims commit themselves to you;
you are the helper of the fatherless.
(Psalm 10:14)

For the Single Father

Fathers, do not exasperate your children;
instead, bring them up in the training
and instruction of the Lord.
(Ephesians 6:4)

Don't live on borrowed money.

Do set a budget and involve the children in the planning.[211]

"Start children off on the way they should go, and even when they are old they will not turn from it. The rich rule over the poor, and the borrower is slave to the lender" (Proverbs 22:6–7).

Don't do everything for your children.

Do give them household chores with daily, weekly, and monthly schedules.[212]

"Diligent hands will rule, but laziness ends in forced labor" (Proverbs 12:24).

Don't accept disrespect from your children.

Do realize that when fear of rejection rules you, it can lead to passive parenting.

"Discipline your children, for in that there is hope; do not be a willing party to their death" (Proverbs 19:18).

Don't look to the world for advice and approval.

Do look to God and His Word for correction and instruction.

"Search me, God, and know my heart; test me and know my anxious thoughts. See if there is any offensive way in me, and lead me in the way everlasting" (Psalm 139:23–24).

Don't make your child feel guilty for continuing to love the other parent.

Do "be fair" not only to the other parent but to their parents as well (your child's grandparents).[213]

"Honor your father and your mother, so that you may live long in the land the L*ORD your God is giving you"* (EXODUS 20:12).

Don't shelter your child from the reality of their painful situation.

Do teach them about disappointment.[214]

"In this world you will have trouble. But take heart! I have overcome the world" (JOHN 16:33).

Goals for Personal Growth

A closer relationship with the Lord

A closer relationship with your children

A stronger sense of self-confidence

A stronger training ground to build character

A deeper joy in parenthood

A deeper joy in life

Consider it pure joy . . . whenever you face trials of many kinds,
because you know that the testing of your faith produces perseverance.
Let perseverance finish its work so that you may be mature
and complete, not lacking anything.
(JAMES 1:2–4)

Key Passages to Read

Psalm 145:8–9, 13–20

My Personalized Plan

I will . . .

Look to God for my strength and hope as I navigate single parenting.

"The L*ORD is my rock, my fortress and my deliverer; my God is my rock, in whom I take refuge, my shield and the horn of my salvation, my stronghold"* (PSALM 18:2).

Make a commitment to forgive my ex-spouse or others who have hurt or abandoned me.

"Get rid of all bitterness, rage and anger, brawling and slander, along with every form of malice. Be kind and compassionate to one another, forgiving each other, just as in Christ God forgave you" (EPHESIANS 4:31–32).

Find support with my church, family, and friends to provide the help I need.

"Remember your leaders, who spoke the word of God to you. Consider the outcome of their way of life and imitate their faith" (HEBREWS 13:7).

Rely on God's Word to help me provide a godly and peaceful home for my children.

"Everyone who hears these words of mine and puts them into practice is like a wise man who built his house on the rock" (MATTHEW 7:24).

Ask God to provide for me and my children financially.

"My God will meet all your needs according to the riches of his glory in Christ Jesus" (PHILIPPIANS 4:19).

Look to God's Word for correction and instruction as a single parent.

"Search me, God, and know my heart; test me and know my anxious thoughts. See if there is any offensive way in me, and lead me in the way everlasting" (PSALM 139:23–24).

Model humility and sacrificial, Christlike love to my children.

"Follow God's example, therefore, as dearly loved children and walk in the way of love, just as Christ loved us and gave himself up for us as a fragrant offering and sacrifice to God" (EPHESIANS 5:1–2).

Questions & Answers

Question: "My teenage son is rebellious and is getting into trouble. He says I am constantly nagging him. Should I give up trying to tell him what is right?"

Answer: No. Even if your son continues to make choices that are wrong, as a parent, you are responsible for communicating what is right.

The teaching of the wise is a fountain of life,
turning a person from the snares of death.
(PROVERBS 13:14)

Question: "I am a single parent with a ten-year-old daughter. She continues to argue and be disrespectful with me. What can I do to keep this from getting worse?"

Answer: Try to understand why she is acting this way. She might be hurt, frustrated, afraid, or going through a hard time. Be patient, praying for her heart and yours, that God will give you insight and wisdom. When necessary, set firm boundaries and communicate if those boundaries are broken. The choice is then hers to either respond to you respectfully or endure the repercussions. Persevere with her, encourage her regularly, and look to God's Word, trusted family, friends, and your church community for ongoing support and guidance.

Children are a heritage from the LORD,
offspring a reward from him.
(PSALM 127:3)

SINGLENESS

How to Be Single and Satisfied

God's Heart on Singleness

Singleness is a good state in which to be.

"To the unmarried and the widows I say: It is good for them to stay unmarried, as I do" (1 CORINTHIANS 7:8).

Singleness is a gift from God.

"I wish that all of you were as I am. But each of you has your own gift from God; one has this gift, another has that" (1 CORINTHIANS 7:7).

Singleness is the state in which to remain if separation occurs and reconciliation is impossible.

"A wife must not separate from her husband. But if she does, she must remain unmarried or else be reconciled to her husband. And a husband must not divorce his wife" (1 CORINTHIANS 7:10–11).

Singles can face crises and worldly difficulties with fewer complications and less complexity.

"Because of the present crisis, I think that it is good for a man to remain as he is" (1 CORINTHIANS 7:26).

Singles should not search for mates, but seek a deeper relationship with God.

"Are you pledged to a woman? Do not seek to be released. Are you free from such a commitment? Do not look for a wife" (1 CORINTHIANS 7:27).

Singles face fewer troubles in life.

"If you do marry, you have not sinned; and if a virgin marries, she has not sinned. But those who marry will face many troubles in this life, and I want to spare you this" (1 CORINTHIANS 7:28).

Singles have fewer concerns.

"I would like you to be free from concern. An unmarried man is concerned about the Lord's affairs—how he can please the Lord" (1 CORINTHIANS 7:32).

Singles can more single-mindedly focus on pleasing the Lord.

"I would like you to be free from concern. An unmarried man is concerned about the Lord's affairs—how he can please the Lord. But a married man is concerned about the affairs of this world—how he can please his wife—and his interests are divided. An unmarried woman or virgin is concerned about the Lord's affairs: Her aim is to be devoted to the Lord in both body and spirit. But a married woman is concerned about the affairs of this world—how she can please her husband" (1 CORINTHIANS 7:32–34).

Singles can have undivided devotion to the Lord.

"I am saying this for your own good, not to restrict you, but that you may live in a right way in undivided devotion to the Lord" (1 CORINTHIANS 7:35).

Singles have the right and the freedom to marry.

"If anyone is worried that he might not be acting honorably toward the virgin he is engaged to, and if his passions are too strong and he feels he ought to marry, he should do as he wants. He is not sinning. They should get married" (1 CORINTHIANS 7:36).

Singleness can be the happier state for a widow.

"In my judgment, she is happier if she stays as she is" (1 CORINTHIANS 7:40).

The LORD will fulfill his purpose for me;
your steadfast love, O LORD, endures forever.
(PSALM 138:8 ESV)

Myths About Singleness

Myth: "God's best is marriage. . . . Singleness is second best."

Truth: According to Scripture, singleness is referred to as the best state for having undivided devotion to the Lord.

"Are you free from such a commitment? Do not look for a wife. . . . I am saying this for your own good, not to restrict you, but that you may live in a right way in undivided devotion to the Lord" (1 CORINTHIANS 7:27, 35).

Myth: "Living in limbo is terrible. . . . Any decision is better than no decision."

Truth: God wants us to learn to be content in any state and to patiently wait on His timing.

"I have learned to be content whatever the circumstances" (PHILIPPIANS 4:11).

Myth: "All you need is another mate. . . . Then you will find fulfillment again."

Truth: Contentment and fulfillment are found in relationship with the Lord, who is always with you.

"Be content with what you have, because God has said, 'Never will I leave you; never will I forsake you'" (HEBREWS 13:5).

Myth: "After your mate dies, you are left incomplete and unfulfilled."

Truth: You may deeply grieve the loss of your spouse, but as a Christian, you are given complete fullness in Christ, whether married or single.

"You are complete in Him [Christ]*"* (Colossians 2:10 NKJV).

Myth: "Since God uses the family to build character, you will never become mature if you remain unmarried."

Truth: Your marital state does not determine the degree of your maturity. When you become a believer, God takes the responsibility to bring you to maturity.

"He who began a good work in you will carry it on to completion" (Philippians 1:6).

I wish that all men were as I am.
But each man has his own gift from God;
one has this gift, another has that.
(1 Corinthians 7:7)

Three Struggles Discontented Singles Share

The Struggle with Sexuality

- "How can I ignore my sexuality?"
- "How should I deal with my sexual desires?"
- "How am I to express my sexuality outside of marriage?"

"Offer your bodies as a living sacrifice, holy and pleasing to God—this is your true and proper worship" (Romans 12:1).

The Bondage of Bitterness

- "Why am I not receiving the best in life?"
- "Why is God punishing me?"
- "Why is life so unfair?"

"The Lord bestows favor and honor;
no good thing does he withhold from those whose walk is blameless" (Psalm 84:11).

Key Verse to Memorize

You are complete in Him.
(Colossians 2:10 NKJV)

The Fight with Fear

- "Will I be safe living alone?"
- "Will someone protect me from being hurt by others?"
- "Will I be all alone when I am old?"

"Do not fear, for I am with you; do not be dismayed, for I am your God. I will strengthen you and help you; I will uphold you with my righteous right hand" (Isaiah 41:10).

Choose to Be CONTENT

C—Confess the difficulty.

"Lord, I know that people's lives are not their own; it is not for them to direct their steps" (JEREMIAH 10:23).

O—Overcome the "greener grass" mentality.

"My God will meet all your needs according to the riches of his glory in Christ Jesus" (PHILIPPIANS 4:19).

N—Nourish a heart of gratitude.

"Rejoice always, pray continually, give thanks in all circumstances; for this is God's will for you in Christ Jesus" (1 THESSALONIANS 5:16–18).

T—Treasure your identity in Christ.

"The Lord will be at your side and will keep your foot from being snared" (PROVERBS 3:26).

E—Expect God to give you a ministry.

"Just as each of us has one body with many members, and these members do not all have the same function, so in Christ we, though many, form one body, and each member belongs to all the others. We have different gifts, according to the grace given to each of us. If your gift is prophesying, then prophesy in accordance with your faith; if it is serving, then serve; if it is teaching, then teach; if it is to encourage, then give encouragement; if it is giving, then give generously; if it is to lead, do it diligently; if it is to show mercy, do it cheerfully" (ROMANS 12:4–8).

N—Nurture a family of friends.

"A friend loves at all times" (PROVERBS 17:17).

T—Trust your future to God.

"Seek first his kingdom and his righteousness and all these things will be given to you as well" (MATTHEW 6:33).

What Does Healthy Singleness Mean?

Living by yourself with contentment

Learning not to need a mate to make your life meaningful or complete

Looking to God to satisfy the deepest needs and longings of your heart

Recognizing that being married is not better, merely different

Respecting *who* you are and *why* you are

Embracing your singleness as a gift from God and as His purpose for you

Pursuing God rather than a marriage partner

Feeling good about being free to make choices as God presents opportunities

Focusing on *becoming* the right kind of person rather than *looking for* the right person

Finding your fullness of joy in developing a more intimate relationship with God, family, and friends

My Personalized Plan

I will . . .

Turn to God when I am struggling with singleness.
"From the ends of the earth I call to you, I call as my heart grows faint; lead me to the rock that is higher than I" (PSALM 61:2).

Look to Christ for my identity, rather than marriage or a relationship.
"See what great love the Father has lavished on us, that we should be called children of God! And that is what we are!" (1 JOHN 3:1).

Ask God to help me embrace my singleness as a gift from Him.
"I wish that all of you were as I am. But each of you has your own gift from God; one has this gift, another has that" (1 CORINTHIANS 7:7).

Commit to pursuing the Lord above all else, whether I remain single or not.
"Seek the LORD and his strength; seek his presence continually!" (1 CHRONICLES 16:11 ESV).

Focus on becoming more like Christ.
"Grow in the grace and knowledge of our Lord and Savior Jesus Christ" (2 PETER 3:18).

Thank God for my friends and family and cherish these relationships.
"Give thanks in all circumstances; for this is God's will for you in Christ Jesus" (1 THESSALONIANS 5:18).

Look to God to satisfy my deepest needs and the longings of my heart.
"My God will meet all your needs according to the riches of his glory in Christ Jesus" (PHILIPPIANS 4:19).

Key Passage to Read

1 Corinthians chapter 7

Trust God with my future.

"Trust in the Lord with all your heart and lean not on your own understanding; in all your ways submit to him, and he will make your paths straight" (Proverbs 3:5–6).

Questions & Answers

Question: "How should I respond to people who keep telling me I need to be dating when I am content being single?"

Answer: People may want you to date and marry for any number of reasons. Generally, they mean well, so guard against feeling offended. Tell them you appreciate their interest, but you are really quite content to focus on being the person God created you to be. Explain that you have a full life and are sincerely content being single.

Godliness with contentment is great gain.
(1 Timothy 6:6)

Question: "What about God's statement in Genesis 2:18: *'It is not good for the man to be alone. I will make a helper suitable for him'*? Doesn't this mean that it is not good for men to remain single?"

Answer: When God created all living *things,* He created both male and female concurrently—at the same time so that they would multiply. However, when it came to human beings, He first created the man, Adam, and placed him *alone* in the garden of Eden. When God said that it was not good for the man to be alone, the statement was made when he was the only human being in existence. God changed the man's status from being alone by giving him Eve, another human being—a female helper through whom he could multiply and fill the earth with offspring.

God clearly does not intend every man to marry in order *not to be alone.* God intends for us to live in community.

Two are better than one,
because they have a good return for their labor.
(Ecclesiastes 4:9)

SPIRITUAL ABUSE

Religion at Its Worst

God's Heart on Spiritual Abuse

God wants you to use His Word as the standard for truth.

"Now the Berean Jews were of more noble character than those in Thessalonica, for they received the message with great eagerness and examined the Scriptures every day to see if what Paul said was true" (ACTS 17:11).

God wants you to hear His Word taught clearly, not in a distorted manner.

"We have renounced secret and shameful ways; we do not use deception, nor do we distort the word of God. On the contrary, by setting forth the truth plainly we commend ourselves to everyone's conscience in the sight of God" (2 CORINTHIANS 4:2).

God wants you to watch out for false teaching and false teachers.

"Watch out for false prophets. They come to you in sheep's clothing, but inwardly they are ferocious wolves" (MATTHEW 7:15).

God wants you to know that those who teach His Word will be judged more strictly.

"Not many of you should become teachers, my fellow believers, because you know that we who teach will be judged more strictly" (JAMES 3:1).

God wants you to stay away from those who cause divisions and lead others astray.

"Watch out for people who cause divisions and upset people's faith by teaching things contrary to what you have been taught. Stay away from them" (ROMANS 16:17 NLT).

God wants you to rely on His grace, not legalistic rules, to help you grow in your faith.

"Do not be carried away by all kinds of strange teachings. It is good for our hearts to be strengthened by grace, not by eating ceremonial foods, which is of no benefit to those who do so" (HEBREWS 13:9).

God offers healing from spiritual abuse.

"He heals the brokenhearted and binds up their wounds" (PSALM 147:3).

God wants you to be in a church that is devoted to faithfully teaching His Word.

"They devoted themselves to the apostles' teaching and to fellowship, to the breaking of bread and to prayer" (ACTS 2:42).

God wants His church to be led by spiritual leaders who humbly serve and lead by example.

"Care for the flock that God has entrusted to you. Watch over it willingly, not grudgingly—not for what you will get out of it, but because you are eager to serve God. Don't lord it over the people assigned to your care, but lead them by your own good example" (1 PETER 5:2–3 NLT).

God wants you to reach out to others who have experienced spiritually abusive treatment.

"The Father of compassion and the God of all comfort . . . comforts us in all our troubles, so that we can comfort those in any trouble with the comfort we ourselves receive from God" (2 CORINTHIANS 1:3–4).

"Come to me, all of you who are weary and carry heavy burdens, and I will give you rest."
(MATTHEW 11:28 NLT)

What Is Spiritual Abuse?

Spiritual abuse "occurs when someone in a position of spiritual authority misuses that authority . . . to control, coerce, or manipulate" others for what seems to be good and godly purposes, but are instead using it in their own self-interest.[215]

Spiritual abuse is the use of religious words or acts to manipulate someone for personal gain or to achieve a personal agenda, thereby harming that person's walk with God.

Spiritual abuse is often broadly defined as any misuse of Scripture whereby truth is twisted and which may or may not result in harming a person's relationship with God. The victim in this case may not be an individual, but truth itself.

Spiritual abuse is putting confidence in your position of authority and your perceived right to use those under your influence to accomplish your own personal agenda. However, God alone has the right, the wisdom, and the power to accomplish His plans and purposes for those He has created.

Symptoms of Spiritual Abuse[216]

Low self-worth	Limited transparency
Inordinate fear	Troubled relationships
Excessive guilt	High self-sufficiency
Unresolved anger	Misplaced priorities

Spiritual Abuse Self-Test[217]

Y / N Do you feel guilty if you miss church even one time?

Y / N Do you think God watches what you do, and if you don't do enough, He will punish or abandon you?

Y / N Do you feel excessive guilt for making even small mistakes?

Y / N Do you think that if you work harder or serve the Lord more, you can earn His forgiveness?

Y / N Does your family complain that you spend more time at church meetings than you do with them?

Y / N Do you donate to a ministry so God will bless you financially?

Y / N Do you see your minister as more important or more powerful than others in your life?

Y / N Do you look to your minister to offer fast fixes to lifelong struggles?

Y / N Do you struggle with making even small decisions without checking with your minister first?

Y / N Has following your faith led you into isolation, separating you from family and friends?

Y / N Do you quote Scripture in a conversation so often that people complain?

Y / N Have you been in an inappropriate relationship with someone in ministry?

Y / N Are your most significant relationships negatively impacted by your strong beliefs?

Y / N Has anyone ever suggested that a minister was manipulating you?

Key Verse to Memorize

It is for freedom that Christ has set us free. Stand firm, then, and do not let yourselves be burdened again by a yoke of slavery.
(Galatians 5:1)

How to Recover from Spiritual Abuse

R—Realize that you have been in a legalistic or abusive situation.

"Do not fear, for I am with you; do not be dismayed, for I am your God. I will strengthen you and help you; I will uphold you with my righteous right hand" (ISAIAH 41:10).

E—Exercise your freedom in Christ.

"If the Son sets you free, you will be free indeed" (JOHN 8:36).

C—Correct your concept of God.

"See what great love the Father has lavished on us, that we should be called children of God! And that is what we are!" (1 JOHN 3:1).

O—Open yourself up to healthy Christian relationships.

"Praise be to the God and Father of our Lord Jesus Christ, the Father of compassion and the God of all comfort, who comforts us in all our troubles, so that we can comfort those in any trouble with the comfort we ourselves receive from God" (2 CORINTHIANS 1:3–4).

V—Voice your cares and concerns to God.

"Trust in him at all times, you people; pour out your hearts to him, for God is our refuge" (PSALM 62:8).

E—Enlist the help of spiritually mature, grace-filled mentors.

"Walk with the wise and become wise, for a companion of fools suffers harm" (PROVERBS 13:20).

R—Rest in the finished work of Christ.

"God demonstrates his own love for us in this: While we were still sinners, Christ died for us" (ROMANS 5:8).

Y—Yield yourself to the Holy Spirit, who lives within you.

"Let us follow the Spirit's leading in every part of our lives" (GALATIANS 5:25 NLT).

"I am the good shepherd.
The good shepherd lays down his life for the sheep."
(JOHN 10:11)

Spiritually Healthy Churches[218]

Spiritual authority and power are applied to serving, equipping, and empowering the church—the body of Christ.

"Even the Son of Man did not come to be served, but to serve, and to give his life as a ransom for many" (Mark 10:45).

Believers in Jesus encourage others to imitate Christ, not themselves or leaders apart from Christ.

"Salvation is found in no one else, for there is no other name under heaven given to mankind by which we must be saved" (Acts 4:12).

The church's doctrinal beliefs and practices are biblically aligned, clearly communicated, and applied to leaders and members alike.

"When one rules over people in righteousness, when he rules in the fear of God, he is like the light of morning at sunrise on a cloudless morning, like the brightness after rain that brings grass from the earth" (2 Samuel 23:3–4).

Key Passage to Read

Galatians 3:1–14

The church belongs to God and exists to serve Him.

"Christ is also the head of the church, which is his body. He is the beginning, supreme over all who rise from the dead. So he is first in everything" (Colossians 1:18 NLT).

Devotion to Christ and building His kingdom is why the church exists—to encourage and equip the saints and to embrace and evangelize the lost.

"Love the Lord your God with all your heart and with all your soul and with all your mind and with all your strength" (Mark 12:30).

"No one can serve two masters. Either you will hate the one and love the other, or you will be devoted to the one and despise the other" (Luke 16:13).

Jesus said to them, "It is not the healthy
who need a doctor, but the sick.
I have not come to call the righteous, but sinners."
(Mark 2:17)

My Personalized Plan

I will . . .

Examine my own life.

"Examine yourselves to see whether you are in the faith; test yourselves. Do you not realize that Christ Jesus is in you—unless, of course, you fail the test?" (2 Corinthians 13:5).

Explore the actions of my pastor, my church, and other religious leaders in my life.

"Be shepherds of God's flock that is under your care, watching over them—not because you must, but because you are willing, as God wants you to be; not pursuing dishonest gain, but eager to serve; not lording it over those entrusted to you, but being examples to the flock" (1 PETER 5:2–3).

Educate myself with biblical truths about my freedom in Christ.

"Do your best to present yourself to God as one approved, a worker who does not need to be ashamed and who correctly handles the word of truth" (2 TIMOTHY 2:15).

Search me, God, and know my heart;
test me and know my anxious thoughts.
See if there is any offensive way in me,
and lead me in the way everlasting.
(PSALM 139:23–24)

Questions & Answers

Question: "What is at the heart of spiritual abuse?"

Answer: At the core of spiritual abuse is excessive control of others. Spiritual abuse is acting "spiritual" to benefit oneself by using self-centered efforts to control others.

Jesus said to them,
"The kings of the Gentiles lord it over them;
and those who exercise authority over them
call themselves Benefactors."
(LUKE 22:25)

Question: "Do I always have to submit to spiritual leaders, even when I know they are abusive? After all, the Bible says, *'Submit yourselves for the Lord's sake to every human authority'* (1 Peter 2:13)."

Answer: Spiritual abusers love to manipulate others by telling them that they must always submit to spiritual authority. This is wrong!

When the apostle Paul was facing trial at the hands of the Jewish religious leaders, he knew they wanted to execute him. Rather than submitting to religious leaders in Jerusalem who were not following God, Paul appealed to stand trial in Rome before the secular court of Caesar. However, before appealing to Caesar, Paul unknowingly insulted the high priest. When he was told whom he had insulted, Paul agreed that no one should speak evil about the ruler of the Jewish people.

At this the high priest Ananias ordered those standing near Paul to strike him on the mouth. Then Paul said to him, "God will strike you, you whitewashed wall! You sit there to judge me according to the law, yet you yourself violate the law by commanding that I be struck!" Those who were standing near Paul said, "How dare you insult God's high priest!" Paul replied, "Brothers, I did not realize that he was the high priest; for it is written: 'Do not speak evil about the ruler of your people.'" (Acts 23:2–5)

From this example we see that *respect should be shown* to those in spiritual authority, but we do not need to *obey* them if they don't line up with God's truth.

"We must obey God rather than any human authority."
(Acts 5:29 NLT)

SPIRITUAL WARFARE

Strategy for the Battle

God's Heart on Spiritual Warfare

God wants you to know He has already won the battle.

"He [Jesus] *disarmed the spiritual rulers and authorities. He shamed them publicly by his victory over them on the cross"* (COLOSSIANS 2:15 NLT).

God warns that the Enemy is real and wants to destroy you.

"Be alert and of sober mind. Your enemy the devil prowls around like a roaring lion looking for someone to devour" (1 PETER 5:8).

God wants you to remember who the true enemy is in this world.

"Our struggle is not against flesh and blood, but against the rulers, against the authorities, against the powers of this dark world and against the spiritual forces of evil in the heavenly realms" (EPHESIANS 6:12).

God wants you to look to Him for help when you are tempted.

"No temptation has overtaken you except what is common to mankind. And God is faithful; he will not let you be tempted beyond what you can bear. But when you are tempted, he will also provide a way out so that you can endure it" (1 CORINTHIANS 10:13).

God will help you withstand Satan's attacks.

"Submit yourselves, then, to God. Resist the devil, and he will flee from you" (JAMES 4:7).

God strengthens you with His Word to fight against the devil.

"Be strong in the Lord and in his mighty power. Put on the full armor of God, so that you can take your stand against the devil's schemes" (EPHESIANS 6:10–11).

God renews your mind, correcting lies from the Enemy and the world with His truth.

"Do not conform to the pattern of this world, but be transformed by the renewing of your mind. Then you will be able to test and approve what God's will is—his good, pleasing and perfect will" (ROMANS 12:2).

God frees you from accusation and condemnation of the Enemy.

"There is now no condemnation for those who are in Christ Jesus" (ROMANS 8:1).

God does not want you to live in fear but to know He is always with you.

"Do not fear, for I am with you; do not be dismayed, for I am your God. I will strengthen you and help you; I will uphold you with my righteous right hand" (ISAIAH 41:10).

God gives you other believers to help you in the battle.

"Surely you need guidance to wage war, and victory is won through many advisers" (PROVERBS 24:6).

As for you, you were dead in your transgressions
and sins, in which you used to live when you followed
the ways of this world and of the ruler of the
kingdom of the air [Satan], *the spirit who is now*
at work in those who are disobedient.
All of us also lived among them at one time,
gratifying the cravings of our flesh.
(EPHESIANS 2:1–3)

What Are the Three Enemies?

The World is that invisible system of ideas, activities, and purposes that Satan rules in opposition to God and His rule.[219]

"You adulterous people, don't you know that friendship with the world means enmity against God? Therefore, anyone who chooses to be a friend of the world becomes an enemy of God" (JAMES 4:4).

The Flesh—The "power of sin" (Romans chapter 7) is at work through *the flesh* of a person, whether saved or unsaved, and is demonstrated by going one's own way instead of God's way.

"I know that in me (that is, in my flesh) nothing good dwells; for to will is present with me, but how to perform what is good I do not find" (ROMANS 7:18 NKJV).

The Devil (Satan) is the supreme adversary of God and is leader of the spiritual forces of evil.

"He [the King, the Son of Man] *will say to those on his left, 'Depart from me, you who are cursed, into the eternal fire prepared for the devil and his angels'"* (MATTHEW 25:41).

The Battle Begins in the Mind

A thought (a lie) enters the mind from worldly, fleshly, or satanic influences.

A choice is made by the will to accept or reject the thought.

A habit is formed when continual choices are made to act on the thought.

A stronghold is developed when a habit becomes a deeply rooted, controlling behavior.[220]

"In your anger do not sin": Do not let the sun
go down while you are still angry,
and do not give the devil a foothold.
(EPHESIANS 4:26–27)

Overcome the World

F—Focus on Jesus as *God the Son.*

"In the beginning was the Word, and the Word was with God, and the Word was God. He was with God in the beginning. Through him all things were made; without him nothing was made that has been made. . . . The Word became flesh and made his dwelling among us. We have seen his glory, the glory of the one and only Son, who came from the Father, full of grace and truth" (JOHN 1:1–3, 14).

A—Acknowledge that Jesus has overcome the world.

"I have told you these things, so that in me you may have peace. In this world you will have trouble. But take heart! I have overcome the world" (JOHN 16:33).

Key Verse to Memorize

You, dear children, are from God
and have overcome them,
because the one who is in you is greater
than the one who is in the world.
(1 JOHN 4:4)

I—Identify with Jesus and know that His victory is your victory.

"You, dear children, are from God and have overcome them, because the one who is in you is greater than the one who is in the world" (1 JOHN 4:4).

T—Trust in the absolute truth of God's Word.

"All Scripture is God-breathed and is useful for teaching, rebuking, correcting and training in righteousness" (2 TIMOTHY 3:16).

H—Hold up God's Word as your measuring rod against the world's standards.

"I have hidden your word in my heart that I might not sin against you" (PSALM 119:11).

Defeat the Flesh

Acknowledge the war between the Holy Spirit and your fleshly habits.

"The flesh desires what is contrary to the Spirit, and the Spirit what is contrary to the flesh. They are in conflict with each other, so that you are not to do whatever you want" (Galatians 5:17).

Admit you were born with a sin nature, a natural bent to sin.

"Surely I was sinful at birth, sinful from the time my mother conceived me" (Psalm 51:5).

Accept Jesus Christ into your life to save you from the penalty of your sins, if you haven't already received His free gift of salvation.

"Small is the gate and narrow the road that leads to life, and only a few find it" (Matthew 7:14).

Agree that Christ's death on the cross for you brought death to the sin nature in you.

"We know that our old self was crucified with him so that the body ruled by sin might be done away with, that we should no longer be slaves to sin—because anyone who has died has been set free from sin" (Romans 6:6–7).

Appropriate the resurrection power of Christ within you to break the power of sin over you.

"Just as Christ was raised from the dead through the glory of the Father, we too may live a new life" (Romans 6:4).

Appreciate that you have been given a new nature.

"He has given us his very great and precious promises, so that through them you may participate in the divine nature, having escaped the corruption in the world caused by evil desires" (2 Peter 1:4).

Affirm that you are a new creation in Christ.

"If anyone is in Christ, the new creation has come: The old is gone. the new is here!" (2 Corinthians 5:17).

Ask Christ, who lives within you, to give you victory over self-centered habits.

"I can do all things through Christ who strengthens me" (Philippians 4:13 nkjv).

God's Strategy for Warfare[221]

Depend on God's power for victory.

— **Pray** often for God's protection.

— **Pray** for God to help you overcome your fear.

— **Pray** for God to give you His wisdom.

"Finally, be strong in the Lord and in his mighty power" (EPHESIANS 6:10).

Know your enemy.

— **The unsaved** are not your enemies.

— **Political and religious organizations** are not your enemies.

— **Satan, sin, and demonic spirits** are your real enemies.

"Put on the full armor of God, so that you can take your stand against the devil's schemes. For our struggle is not against flesh and blood, but against the rulers, against the authorities, against the powers of this dark world and against the spiritual forces of evil in the heavenly realms" (EPHESIANS 6:11–12).

Wear the battle gear.[222]

— **Have on** the ***belt of truth*** to combat Satan's lies.

— **Put on** the ***breastplate of righteousness*** to overcome temptation.

— **Wear** the ***shoes of peace***, knowing God is on your side.

— **Carry** the ***shield of faith*** to withstand doubt and unbelief.

— **Put on** the ***helmet of salvation*** to protect your mind.

— **Use** the ***sword of the Spirit*** accurately.

"Put on the full armor of God, so that when the day of evil comes, you may be able to stand your ground, and after you have done everything, to stand. Stand firm then, with the belt of truth buckled around your waist, with the breastplate of righteousness in place, and with your feet fitted with the readiness that comes from the gospel of peace. In addition to all this, take up the shield of faith, with which you can extinguish all the flaming arrows of the evil one. Take the helmet of salvation and the sword of the Spirit, which is the word of God" (EPHESIANS 6:13–17).

Pray always.[223]

"Pray in the Spirit on all occasions with all kinds of prayers and requests. With this in mind, be alert and always keep on praying for all the Lord's people" (EPHESIANS 6:18).

Stand Against Satan

Satan is not ***omnipotent***.

"The one who is in you is greater than the one who is in the world" (1 JOHN 4:4).

Satan is not ***omnipresent***.

"The LORD said to Satan, 'Where have you come from?' Satan answered the LORD, 'From roaming through the earth, going back and forth on it'" (JOB 1:7).

Satan is not ***omniscient***.

"Your heart became proud on account of your beauty, and you corrupted your wisdom because of your splendor" (Ezekiel 28:17).

Satan has been confined to boundaries.

"The Lord said to Satan, 'Very well, then, everything he [Job] *has is in your power, but on the man himself do not lay a finger'"* (Job 1:12).

Satan can't overcome resistance.

"Submit yourselves, then, to God. Resist the devil, and he will flee from you" (James 4:7).

Satan hates the blood of Christ.[224]

"They [believers] *triumphed over him by the blood of the Lamb"* (Revelation 12:11).

Satan is defeated by positive testimonies.

"They [believers] *triumphed over him . . . by the word of their testimony"* (Revelation 12:11).

Put on the full armor of God, so that when the day of evil comes,
you may be able to stand your ground,
and after you have done everything, to stand. Stand firm.
(Ephesians 6:13–14)

My Personalized Plan

I will . . .

Ask God to protect me.

"The Lord is faithful, and he will strengthen you and protect you from the evil one" (2 Thessalonians 3:3).

Look to God when I feel afraid or overwhelmed.

"From the ends of the earth I call to you, I call as my heart grows faint; lead me to the rock that is higher than I" (Psalm 61:2).

Remember that Jesus was tempted and He understands my struggle with my flesh.

"We do not have a high priest who is unable to empathize with our weaknesses, but we have one who has been tempted in every way, just as we are—yet he did not sin" (Hebrews 4:15).

Ask God for wisdom when I am confused.

"The LORD *gives wisdom; from his mouth come knowledge and understanding"* (PROVERBS 2:6).

Remember that Satan is my true enemy, not unbelievers or those who do not agree with my values and views.

"We are not fighting against flesh-and-blood enemies, but against evil rulers and authorities of the unseen world, against mighty powers in this dark world, and against evil spirits in the heavenly places" (EPHESIANS 6:12 NLT).

Key Passage to Read

Ephesians 6:10–18

Go to God's Word to equip me for battle.

"Put on the full armor of God, so that when the day of evil comes, you may be able to stand your ground, and after you have done everything, to stand" (EPHESIANS 6:13).

Correct the lies of the Enemy and the world with the truth of God's Word.

"The weapons we fight with are not the weapons of the world. On the contrary, they have divine power to demolish strongholds. We demolish arguments and every pretension that sets itself up against the knowledge of God, and we take captive every thought to make it obedient to Christ" (2 CORINTHIANS 10:4–5).

Not fight alone but enlist help from others.

"Two people are better off than one, for they can help each other succeed. If one person falls, the other can reach out and help. But someone who falls alone is in real trouble" (ECCLESIASTES 4:9–10 NLT).

Questions & Answers

Question: "When will this spiritual battle be over?"

Answer: For now, the kingdom of God and this present age coexist. A time will come when God eradicates all evil and judges Satan and his army—throwing them into the lake of fire. (Read Revelation 20:7-21:8.)

"'He will wipe every tear from their eyes.
There will be no more death' or mourning or crying
or pain, for the old order of things has passed away."
(REVELATION 21:4)

Question: "I'm constantly defeated in my thought life. How can I gain victory?"

Answer: Realize first that Satan is called "the father of lies," and he delights in defeating you (John 8:44). Read through the book of Philippians. Then take an inventory of every defeating thought and what you should be thinking instead. Then, as thoughts come, if they do not line up with Philippians 4:6–8, change your thinking!

Whatever is true, whatever is noble, whatever is right, whatever is pure, whatever is lovely, whatever is admirable—if anything is excellent or praiseworthy—think about such things.
(PHILIPPIANS 4:8)

Question: "If I sense that my loved ones are under spiritual attack, how do I pray for them? Will my prayers have any real effect?"

Answer: Yes, your prayers can have impact. Specifically pray that their faith will not fail. Jesus gave us this example when He prayed for His close friend Simon Peter.

"Simon, Simon, Satan has asked to sift all of you as wheat. But I have prayed for you, Simon, that your faith may not fail."
(LUKE 22:31–32)

STEALING

Catch the Thief Hiding in Your Heart

God's Heart on Stealing[225]

If you steal, you break one of God's commandments.

"You shall not steal" (EXODUS 20:15).

Stealing is contrary to God's nature and the order He created. If you are a Christian, you are not to be a thief because Christ, who lives in you, is not a thief.

"Just as he who called you is holy, so be holy in all you do; for it is written: 'Be holy, because I am holy'" (1 PETER 1:15–16).

If you steal, you must make restitution beyond the initial value.

"If the stolen animal is found alive in their possession—whether ox or donkey or sheep—they must pay back double" (EXODUS 22:4).

If you cannot make restitution, you should work for the one you have wronged until the debt is paid.

"If it happens after sunrise, the defender is guilty of bloodshed. Anyone who steals must certainly make restitution, but if they have nothing, they must be sold to pay for their theft" (EXODUS 22:3).

If something you borrow is damaged, lost, or stolen, you should pay for it.

"If anyone borrows an animal from their neighbor and it is injured or dies while the owner is not present, they must make restitution" (EXODUS 22:14).

If you find an item and do not try to locate its owner, you are stealing.

"If you come across your enemy's ox or donkey wandering off, be sure to return it" (EXODUS 23:4).

If you steal, it breaks God's heart because it breaks the law of love.

"The commandments, 'You shall not commit adultery,' 'You shall not murder,' 'You shall not steal,' 'You shall not covet,' and whatever other command there may be, are summed up in this one command: 'Love your neighbor as yourself.' Love does no harm to a neighbor. Therefore love is the fulfillment of the law" (ROMANS 13:9–10).

What Is Stealing?

Stealing means to take without right or permission that which belongs to another.[226]

Stealing can also mean to keep others from receiving what is rightfully theirs.[227]

"One person gives freely, yet gains even more; another withholds unduly, but comes to poverty" (PROVERBS 11:24).

Stealing (theft, larceny) is the most common crime in the U.S.[228]

Stealing is an umbrella word for various forms of theft.[229]

Stealing is forbidden by God in the Ten Commandments.

"You shall not steal" (DEUTERONOMY 5:19).

Types of Stealing[230]

T—Taking anything that is not yours, no matter how insignificant

"Whoever can be trusted with very little can also be trusted with much, and whoever is dishonest with very little will also be dishonest with much" (LUKE 16:10).

H—Hoarding belongings and supplies

"If anyone has material possessions and sees a brother or sister in need but has no pity on them, how can the love of God be in that person?" (1 JOHN 3:17).

I—Imposing on another's generosity

"The wicked borrow and do not repay, but the righteous give generously" (PSALM 37:21).

E—Evading prompt payment of debts

"Do not say to your neighbor, 'Come back tomorrow and I'll give it to you'—when you already have it with you" (PROVERBS 3:28).

V—Violating a personal "honor system"

"It is necessary to submit to the authorities, not only because of possible punishment but also as a matter of conscience" (ROMANS 13:5).

E—Extortion of others in order to "save a dollar"

"One who oppresses the poor to increase his wealth and one who gives gifts to the rich—both come to poverty" (PROVERBS 22:16).

S—Serving the god of materialism

"No one can serve two masters. Either he will hate the one and love the other, or he will be devoted to the one and despise the other. You cannot serve both God and money" (MATTHEW 6:24).

All a person's ways seem pure to them,
but motives are weighed by the LORD.
(PROVERBS 16:2)

To Catch a "Little Thief"

10 Guidelines for Parents[231]

1. **Pray** for discernment and wisdom when confronting a child.
2. **Be sure** your information and facts are correct.
3. **Meet** with the child in privacy.
4. **Begin by assuring** the child of your love for them.
5. **Offer** an opportunity for a confession by the child.
6. **If the child doesn't confess,** confront with love and concern.

   Encourage the child to tell the reason for taking something that did not belong to him or her.

   Appeal to the child's conscience.

   "How would you feel if someone stole from you?"

   "How do you think God feels about stealing?"
7. **Have the child return the item** and give something extra to the rightful owner as restitution.
8. **Give an example** of an apology. The child can say,

   "It was wrong of me to take this (name of item) that belongs to you. I want to return it and ask for your forgiveness."
9. **Ask the child**, "What will you do the next time you are tempted to steal?"
10. **Set boundaries** and consequences for possible dishonesty in the future.

Key Verse to Memorize

"Whoever can be trusted with very little
can also be trusted with much,
and whoever is dishonest with very little
will also be dishonest with much."
(LUKE 16:10)

Start children off on the way they should go,
and even when they are old they will not turn from it.
(PROVERBS 22:6)

Alibis and Answers

Alibi: "This will never be noticed or missed."

Answer: Even if I fool people, I can't fool God.

"The eyes of the LORD are everywhere, keeping watch on the wicked and the good" (PROVERBS 15:3).

Alibi: "I really don't want to be involved in stealing, but I don't want to lose my friend's approval."

Answer: I am to live for God's approval, not for the approval of people.

"Am I now trying to win the approval of human beings, or of God? Or am I trying to please people? If I were still trying to please people, I would not be a servant of Christ" (GALATIANS 1:10).

Alibi: "This is not really dishonest because they owe it to me."

Answer: I owe it to others to always do what is right and honorable.

"Give to everyone what you owe them: If you owe taxes, pay taxes; if revenue, then revenue; if respect, then respect; if honor, then honor" (ROMANS 13:7).

Alibi: "Once I get to the top, I will change my behavior."

Answer: I need to change my thinking (values); then my behavior will change.

"Do not conform to the pattern of this world, but be transformed by the renewing of your mind. Then you will be able to test and approve what God's will is—his good, pleasing and perfect will" (ROMANS 12:2).

Key Passage to Read

Titus 2:6–12

Alibi: "If I can get 'extra' money, I'll be able to give more to God."

Answer: God doesn't want stolen money—He wants a contrite heart.

"With what shall I come before the LORD and bow down before the exalted God? Shall I come before him with burnt offerings, with calves a year old? Will the LORD be pleased with thousands of rams, with ten thousand rivers of olive oil? Shall I offer my firstborn for my transgression, the fruit of my body for the sin of my soul? He has shown you, O mortal, what is good. And what does the LORD require of you? To act justly and to love mercy and to walk humbly with your God" (MICAH 6:6–8).

Alibi: "This will get me more cash to give to others."

Answer: God cares more about my character than my charity.

"A person may think their own ways are right, but the LORD weighs the heart. To do what is right and just is more acceptable to the LORD than sacrifice" (PROVERBS 21:2–3).

My Personalized Plan

I will . . .

Seek to understand God's standards on stealing.

"Love does no harm to a neighbor. Therefore love is the fulfillment of the law" (ROMANS 13:10).

Admit that my heart is deceitful, and ask God to reveal the ways I steal.

"Search me, God, and know my heart; test me and know my anxious thoughts. See if there is any offensive way in me, and lead me in the way everlasting" (PSALM 139:23–24).

Make a commitment to be totally honest, no matter the consequences.[232]

"You shall not steal; you shall not deal falsely; you shall not lie to one another" (LEVITICUS 19:11 ESV).

Remember that everything I do is seen by the eyes of a loving God, who holds me accountable.

"Your ways are in full view of the LORD, and he examines all your paths" (PROVERBS 5:21).

Think and pray before acting to make sure I am not rationalizing my behavior and choices.

"All a person's ways seem pure to them, but motives are weighed by the LORD" (PROVERBS 16:2).

Be sensitive and accountable to the Spirit of Christ alive in me.

"Since we live by the Spirit, let us keep in step with the Spirit" (GALATIANS 5:25).

Make restitution to those from whom I have stolen.

"Zacchaeus stood up and said to the Lord, 'Look, Lord! Here and now I give half of my possessions to the poor, and if I have cheated anybody out of anything, I will pay back four times the amount'" (LUKE 19:8).

No longer steal but work hard and live generously.

"Anyone who has been stealing must steal no longer, but must work, doing something useful with their own hands, that they may have something to share with those in need" (EPHESIANS 4:28).

Not attempt to gain money or profit through dishonest ways, but will seek to live righteously.

"Treasures gained by wickedness do not profit, but righteousness delivers from death" (PROVERBS 10:2 ESV).

Accept the forgiveness of God and continue to grow in Christlikeness.

"Grow in the grace and knowledge of our Lord and Savior Jesus Christ" (2 PETER 3:18).

"Whoever can be trusted with very little can
also be trusted with much, and whoever
is dishonest with very little will also
be dishonest with much."
(LUKE 16:10)

Questions & Answers

Question: "When is it wrong for me to copy other material?"

Answer: According to *New Oxford Dictionary of English*, a copyright is the exclusive legal right of the originator to control the use or sale of a work.[233] Unless the copyright owner gives permission or the work goes out of copyright, it is illegal to copy the work.

A fortune made by a lying tongue
is a fleeting vapor and a deadly snare.
(PROVERBS 21:6)

Question: "Is it plagiarism if I paraphrase someone rather than quote them directly?"

Answer: If you use what someone else has written and present it as your own, whether it is an exact quotation or a paraphrase, it is considered plagiarism. This is an infringement of copyright and is stealing.

You are permitted to quote other sources for review, criticism, or to illustrate or support your own points, but care must be taken to quote accurately and to give credit for sources.[234]

The way of the guilty is devious,
but the conduct of the innocent is upright.
(PROVERBS 21:8)

STRESS

How to Cope at the End of Your Rope

God's Heart on Stress

God is with you in times of stress.

"Do not fear, for I am with you; do not be dismayed, for I am your God. I will strengthen you and help you; I will uphold you with my righteous right hand" (ISAIAH 41:10).

God sees and knows your stress.

"You, God, see the trouble of the afflicted; you consider their grief and take it in hand" (PSALM 10:14).

God wants to give you peace when your heart is troubled, stressed, and afraid.

"Peace I leave with you; my peace I give you. I do not give to you as the world gives. Do not let your hearts be troubled and do not be afraid" (JOHN 14:27).

God wants to carry your burden and give you rest.

"Come to me, all you who are weary and burdened, and I will give you rest" (MATTHEW 11:28).

God wants to guide you when you're too stressed to make decisions.

"I will instruct you and teach you in the way you should go; I will counsel you with my loving eye on you" (PSALM 32:8).

God wants to strengthen you when you're weak and weary.

"He gives strength to the weary and increases the power of the weak" (ISAIAH 40:29).

God wants to deliver you from your stress.

"They cried out to the LORD in their trouble, and he delivered them from their distress" (PSALM 107:6).

God wants to comfort you in times of stress.

"I, yes I, am the one who comforts you" (ISAIAH 51:12 NLT).

God wants to use your stress to increase your dependence on Him.

"We were under great pressure, far beyond our ability to endure, so that we despaired of life itself. . . . But this happened that we might not rely on ourselves but on God, who raises the dead" (2 CORINTHIANS 1:8–9).

God wants you to talk to Him about your stress and set you free.

"In my distress I prayed to the LORD, and the LORD answered me and set me free" (PSALM 118:5 NLT).

God wants you to trust Him to be a refuge for you in times of stress.

"Trust in him at all times, you people; pour out your hearts to him, for God is our refuge" (PSALM 62:8).

God wants you to worship Him and acknowledge His constant presence even in times of stress.

"I will build an altar to God, who answered me in the day of my distress and who has been with me wherever I have gone" (GENESIS 35:3).

Those who hope in the LORD
will renew their strength.
They will soar on wings like eagles;
they will run and not grow weary,
they will walk and not be faint.
(ISAIAH 40:31)

Checklist for Burnout

Emotional Symptoms:

- ☐ I am plagued with guilt over not being as responsible or committed as I should be.
- ☐ I feel apathetic, anxious, and depressed.
- ☐ I have a great deal of self-doubt.
- ☐ I have a sense of hopelessness.
- ☐ I have decreased self-esteem.
- ☐ I have difficulty concentrating.
- ☐ I have increased irritability.
- ☐ I have less time and energy for relationships.

Physical Symptoms:

- ☐ I am susceptible to colds and viruses.
- ☐ I feel tired and lifeless most of the time.
- ☐ I grind my teeth at night and have trouble sleeping.
- ☐ I have a rapid pulse or high blood pressure.
- ☐ I have frequent, severe headaches.
- ☐ I have indigestion, diarrhea, or constipation often.

- ☐ I have lost or gained a lot of weight.
- ☐ I have tightness in my neck and shoulders or lower-back pain.

Spiritual Symptoms:

- ☐ I am apathetic toward Scripture.
- ☐ I am losing confidence in God to help me.
- ☐ I am too stressed to attend church.
- ☐ I fail to seek the counsel and support of others.
- ☐ I feel I am on my own.
- ☐ I feel God has given up on me.
- ☐ I feel like giving up on myself.
- ☐ I rarely pray or have quiet time anymore.

Four Stages of Stress

Stage 1—No Light
Insufficient Stress: No motivation to move responsibly

Stage 2—Green Light
Positive Stress: Motivation to move responsibly

Stage 3—Yellow Light
Negative Stress: Motivational warning signs to slow down movement

Stage 4—Red Light
Burnout: Movement suddenly stops and repair is necessary

Those who disregard discipline despise themselves,
but the one who heeds correction gains understanding.
(Proverbs 15:32)

The Root Cause of Stress

Wrong Belief: "My life is out of control. I feel helpless to cope with the stress in my life."

Right Belief: "God has allowed this stress in my life to bless me and to reveal my weaknesses. I am grateful for the pressures that have pressed me closer to Him and caused me to allow Christ to be my strength."

"My grace is sufficient for you,
for my power is made perfect in weakness."
Therefore I will boast all the more gladly
about my weaknesses, so that Christ's power
may rest on me. That is why, for Christ's sake,
I delight in weaknesses, in insults, in hardships,
in persecutions, in difficulties.
For when I am weak, then I am strong.
(2 CORINTHIANS 12:9–10)

Five Lies of Stress

Lie #1: "I will lose God's love if I fail."

Truth: God's love is always with you regardless of what you do.

"I am convinced that neither death nor life, neither angels nor demons, neither the present nor the future, nor any powers, neither height nor depth, nor anything else in all creation, will be able to separate us from the love of God that is in Christ Jesus our Lord" (ROMANS 8:38–39).

Lie #2: "When I'm not pleasing God, I feel His condemnation."

Truth: God's heart for you is not condemnation. He desires freedom for you and condemns only the sin that has you in bondage.

"There is now no condemnation for those who are in Christ Jesus, because through Christ Jesus the law of the Spirit who gives life has set you free from the law of sin and death" (ROMANS 8:1–2).

Lie #3: "I am not serving God if I'm not seeing tangible results."

Truth: You are to serve God in the way He chooses, but you are not responsible for God's timing or His harvest.

"Neither the one who plants nor the one who waters is anything, but only God, who makes things grow" (1 CORINTHIANS 3:7).

Lie #4: "I must appear to have it together and not allow my mistakes to show."

Truth: A spirit of humility is more impressive than a spirit of pride.

"Those who exalt themselves will be humbled, and those who humble themselves will be exalted" (MATTHEW 23:12).

Lie #5: "Keeping God's laws is the heart of the Christian message."

Truth: Reflecting God's grace is the heart of the Christian message.

"I consider my life worth nothing to me; my only aim is to finish the race and complete the task the Lord Jesus has given me—the task of testifying to the good news of God's grace" (ACTS 20:24).

Relieve Stress Overload

Stop and look at the real reason you are experiencing stress.

"Am I now trying to win the approval of human beings, or of God? Or am I trying to please people? If I were still trying to please people, I would not be a servant of Christ" (GALATIANS 1:10).

Stop, confess, and turn away from any known sin in your life.

"Whoever conceals their sins does not prosper, but the one who confesses and renounces them finds mercy" (PROVERBS 28:13).

Yield to God's sovereign control over your circumstances.

"In the LORD's hand the king's heart is a stream of water that he channels toward all who please him" (PROVERBS 21:1).

Yield to God your perceived rights and your expectations.

"Trust in the LORD with all your heart and lean not on your own understanding" (PROVERBS 3:5).

Resume speed—living in the presence of God.

"Blessed are those who have learned to acclaim you, who walk in the light of your presence, LORD" (PSALM 89:15).

Key Verses to Memorize

"Come to me, all you who are weary and burdened, and I will give you rest. Take my yoke upon you and learn from me, for I am gentle and humble in heart, and you will find rest for your souls. For my yoke is easy and my burden is light."
(MATTHEW 11:28-30)

My Personalized Plan

As I seek to manage the stress in my life, **I will . . .**

Seek to be healthy.

— I will eat healthy, get adequate sleep each night, avoid harmful substances, and exercise regularly (as I am able).

— I will get regular medical checkups and talk with my doctor about my stress if needed.

"Do you not know that your bodies are temples of the Holy Spirit, who is in you, whom you have received from God? You are not your own; you were bought at a price. Therefore honor God with your bodies" (1 CORINTHIANS 6:19-20).

Learn relaxation techniques.

— I will learn breathing techniques and other exercises to calm myself down when I am stressed.

— I will take a time-out as needed to give myself a few minutes to calm down in stressful situations.

"I have calmed and quieted myself, I am like a weaned child with its mother; like a weaned child I am content" (PSALM 131:2).

Express my emotions.

— I will talk with a trusted friend or family member, wise counselor, and especially with God about my stress and emotions.

— I will journal my thoughts and feelings regularly, especially when I am stressed.

"In my distress I prayed to the LORD, and the LORD answered me and set me free" (PSALM 118:5 NLT).

Draw near to God.

— I will pray and read God's Word daily, meditating on His truths and talking with Him honestly.

— I will attend church regularly to worship, receive encouragement from God's Word, and be with other believers.

"All the believers devoted themselves to the apostles' teaching, and to fellowship, and to sharing in meals (including the Lord's Supper), and to prayer" (ACTS 2:42 NLT).

Keep things in perspective.

— I will keep an eternal perspective and remember that my stress is temporary.

— I will remember God has promised me a future full of hope.

"Therefore we do not lose heart. Though outwardly we are wasting away, yet inwardly we are being renewed day by day. For our light and momentary troubles are achieving for us an eternal glory that far outweighs them all. So we fix our eyes not on what is seen, but on what is unseen, since what is seen is temporary, but what is unseen is eternal" (2 CORINTHIANS 4:16–18).

Replace negative thoughts.

— I will identify negative thought patterns that lead me to feel more stress.

— I will replace negative thoughts with the truth of God's Word.

"Whatever is true, whatever is noble, whatever is right, whatever is pure, whatever is lovely, whatever is admirable—if anything is excellent or praiseworthy—think about such things" (PHILIPPIANS 4:8).

Identify triggers.

- I will identify which situations, feelings, people, environments, and circumstances typically lead me to feel stressed.
- I will find healthy ways to prepare for and cope with those situations.

"Give careful thought to your ways" (HAGGAI 1:5).

Build boundaries.

- I will identify where I can create boundaries in my life to limit stressful interactions and prevent overextending myself.
- I will communicate my need for boundaries, time, and space as needed with the people in my life.

"Above all else, guard your heart, for everything you do flows from it" (PROVERBS 4:23).

Take time for myself.

- I will do at least one thing each day that brings me joy and gives me peace.
- I will take time to rest daily, weekly (Sabbath), and yearly (taking vacation time)—and not feel guilty about it.

"Yes, my soul, find rest in God; my hope comes from him" (PSALM 62:5).

Be in community.

- I will make time to be with friends and family to talk, share a meal together, or go out together.
- I will look into joining a local church, Bible study, book club, gym, exercise class, or other community group.

Key Passage to Read

1 Kings chapter 19

"Two people are better off than one, for they can help each other succeed. If one person falls, the other can reach out and help" (ECCLESIASTES 4:9–10 NLT).

Be thankful.

- I will write down a few things I am thankful for each day.
- I will give thanks to God for His many blessings and gracious gifts in my life.

"Give thanks in all circumstances; for this is God's will for you in Christ Jesus" (1 THESSALONIANS 5:18).

Rest in my identity in Christ.

- I will remember my identity is not in my job, performance, work, ministry, or accomplishments.

— I will rest in God's grace and find my identity in Christ as a beloved child of God.

"See what great love the Father has lavished on us, that we should be called children of God! And that is what we are!" (1 JOHN 3:1).

Give careful thought to the paths for your feet
and be steadfast in all your ways.
(PROVERBS 4:26)

Questions & Answers

Question: "In Gethsemane, how did Jesus mentally process the situation He was facing?"

Answer: Although Jesus knew He was about to be arrested and would face death, He acknowledged His Father's sovereignty and put His trust in God's ultimate control over the situation.

"Abba, Father," he said, "everything is possible for you."
(MARK 14:36)

Question: "How did Jesus outwardly express His emotions?"

Answer: Jesus responded to His pending crucifixion by releasing His anxiety to His Father in prayer. He admitted His desire to avoid the torturous death facing Him by asking His Father to remove the cross from His life. Yet, His heart remained submissive to His Father's will.

"Father, if you are willing, take this cup from me;
yet not my will, but yours be done."
(LUKE 22:42)

Question: "Did Jesus have a physical reaction to the trauma He experienced?"

Answer: Suffering physical torment as a result of His agony, Jesus perspired profusely. The Bible says, *"And being in anguish, he prayed more earnestly, and his sweat was like drops of blood falling to the ground"* (Luke 22:44).

Every crisis carries this challenging choice: You can choose to persevere and be changed, or you can choose to seek a way of escape.

This is how we know what love is: Jesus Christ laid down his life for us.
And we ought to lay down our lives for our brothers and sisters.
(1 JOHN 3:16)

SUCCESS THROUGH FAILURE

From Stumbling Stones to Stepping Stones

God's Heart on Failure

If you fail to live with your faith placed in Christ, you allow Satan to damage your life.

"Simon, Simon, Satan has asked to sift all of you as wheat. But I have prayed for you, Simon, that your faith may not fail. And when you have turned back, strengthen your brothers" (LUKE 22:31–32).

If you fail to let God initiate your plans, you will see plans fail.

"If their purpose or activity is of human origin, it will fail" (ACTS 5:38).

If you fail to do what you know is right, you are sinning against the Lord Himself.

"If anyone, then, knows the good they ought to do and doesn't do it, it is sin for them" (JAMES 4:17).

If you fail to forgive through the grace of God, a root of bitterness will grow.

"See to it that no one falls short of the grace of God and that no bitter root grows up to cause trouble and defile many" (HEBREWS 12:15).

If you fail to enter the "rest" of Christ, you will not have the peace of Christ.

"Since the promise of entering his rest still stands, let us be careful that none of you be found to have fallen short of it" (HEBREWS 4:1).

God's Heart on Success

If you put your trust in the Lord, you will be led by the Lord.

"Trust in the LORD with all your heart and lean not on your own understanding; in all your ways submit to him, and he will make your paths straight" (PROVERBS 3:5–6).

If you rely on God's Word, you will conquer sin in your life.

"I have hidden your word in my heart that I might not sin against you" (PSALM 119:11).

If you live in dependence on Christ, you will receive strength from Christ.

"I can do all this through him who gives me strength" (PHILIPPIANS 4:13).

If your "life source" is Christ, you will bear much fruit.

"Remain in me, as I also remain in you. No branch can bear fruit by itself; it must remain in the vine. Neither can you bear fruit unless you remain in me" (JOHN 15:4).

If you rely on Christ's power for your life, you will live a godly life.

"His divine power has given us everything we need for a godly life through our knowledge of him who called us by his own glory and goodness. Through these he has given us his very great and precious promises, so that through them you may participate in the divine nature, having escaped the corruption in the world caused by evil desires" (2 PETER 1:3–4).

Key Verse to Memorize

The one who calls you is faithful,
and he will do it.
(1 THESSALONIANS 5:24)

If you bear burdens of others in the name of Christ, you will fulfill the law of Christ.

"Carry each other's burdens, and in this way you will fulfill the law of Christ" (GALATIANS 6:2).

If you live a humble life, you will receive God's grace.

"He gives more grace. Therefore it says, 'God opposes the proud, but gives grace to the humble'" (JAMES 4:6 ESV).

Humble yourselves, therefore, under God's mighty hand,
that he may lift you up in due time.
Cast all your anxiety on him because he cares for you.
(1 PETER 5:6–7)

What Fear of Failure Produces

Paralysis—failing to take action or make decisions for *fear of being wrong*

Purposelessness—moving from one job to another with no real sense of commitment or direction for *fear of making a wrong decision*

Perfectionism—doing only those things that can be done flawlessly, those that carry little or no risk of failure, for *fear of criticism*

Pride—refusing to engage in certain activities for *fear of being less than the best and feeling inferior to someone else*

Paranoia—distrusting the motives of those who ask you to do things for *fear of being exposed as being less than adequate*

Procrastination—putting off an assignment or performing a task for *fear of doing it poorly*

There is no fear in love. But perfect love drives out fear,
because fear has to do with punishment.
The one who fears is not made perfect in love.
(1 JOHN 4:18)

The Primary Cause of Failure

P—Preoccupied with the opinions of others

"They loved human praise more than praise from God" (JOHN 12:43).

R—Refusing wise counsel

"Plans fail for lack of counsel, but with many advisers they succeed" (PROVERBS 15:22).

I—Ignoring the power of prayer

"You desire but do not have, so you kill. You covet but you cannot get what you want, so you quarrel and fight. You do not have because you do not ask God" (JAMES 4:2).

D—Depending on self-effort

"Are you so foolish? After beginning by means of the Spirit, are you now trying to finish by means of the flesh?" (GALATIANS 3:3).

E—Expecting praise and personal recognition

"All those who exalt themselves will be humbled, and those who humble themselves will be exalted" (LUKE 14:11).

Pride goes before destruction,
a haughty spirit before a fall.
(PROVERBS 16:18)

Faulty Thinking Checklist

Check any of the following thoughts that apply to you, and consider the more positive message in parentheses.

- ☐ Do you think you must avoid the hurt that results from having failed? (Hurt cannot be avoided in life. It gives opportunity for mental, emotional, and spiritual growth.)
- ☐ Do you think it would be terrible if you made a wrong decision? (Every wrong decision can teach you something of value and can be a stepping stone to making right decisions.)
- ☐ Do you think you must never make a mistake? (Mistakes are common to everyone.)

- ☐ Do you think God will reject you or be angry with you if you fail? (God knows you will fail and is pleased with your fortitude and persistent acceptance of challenges.)
- ☐ Do you think failure is an indication that you are stupid or weak? (Failure is universal, experienced by both the literate and the illiterate, the strong and the weak.)
- ☐ Do you think others will think less of you if you fail at something? (Others value you for your character traits and Christlike attitudes and actions rather than whether or not you fail at something.)
- ☐ Do you think it reflects badly on Christ when you fail? (Your failures provide a platform to show others that your security is in Christ, not in your successes.)
- ☐ Do you think failure is shameful and sinful? (Failing does not make you a failure. Failure is sinful only when it is a result of disobedience.)

"My thoughts are not your thoughts,
neither are your ways my ways,"
declares the LORD.
"As the heavens are higher than the earth,
so are my ways higher than your ways
and my thoughts than your thoughts."
(ISAIAH 55:8–9)

Change Your Focus

"Whatever is true, whatever is noble, whatever is right, whatever is pure, whatever is lovely, whatever is admirable—if anything is excellent or praiseworthy—think about such things."
(PHILIPPIANS 4:8)

True: Although I've experienced pain in my past, I will ignore Satan's lying accusations and focus on Your truth.

Noble: Since bitterness is really dishonoring to You, I release all of my bitterness out of respect for You.

Right: Although I am treated unjustly by others, I'm choosing to act in a way that is right in Your eyes toward others.

Pure: Although my heart hasn't always been pure, I will commit to a life that is pure.

Lovely: Even though others have shown disrespect, I will extend Jesus' loving respect.

Admirable: Even though I don't feel that others admire me, I want them to admire Christ.

Excellent: When my plans fail and I lose purpose, I will learn to excel with Your plans and purpose.

Praiseworthy: When I feel defeated with no sense of worth, I know that Jesus is praiseworthy and my worth is in Him.

My Personalized Plan

I will . . .

Look to God for my worth when I experience failure.
"Don't be afraid; you are worth more than many sparrows" (MATTHEW 10:31).

Look back on my past failures so I can learn from them.
"It was good for me to be afflicted so that I might learn your decrees" (PSALM 119:71).

Repent from ongoing sin in my life.
"Godly sorrow brings repentance that leads to salvation and leaves no regret, but worldly sorrow brings death" (2 CORINTHIANS 7:10).

Accept God's forgiveness for my sins and failures.
"You, Lord, are forgiving and good, abounding in love to all who call to you" (PSALM 86:5).

Key Passage to Read

1 Peter 5:6–10

Seek forgiveness from those whom I have hurt through my failures.
"Confess your sins to each other and pray for each other so that you may be healed. The prayer of a righteous person is powerful and effective" (JAMES 5:16).

Refuse to give up when I face trials and trouble.
"I do not consider myself yet to have taken hold of it. But one thing I do: Forgetting what is behind and straining toward what is ahead, I press on toward the goal to win the prize for which God has called me heavenward in Christ Jesus" (PHILIPPIANS 3:13–14).

Listen to and consider the wise counsel of others.
"Plans fail for lack of counsel, but with many advisers they succeed" (PROVERBS 15:22).

Commit my goals and plans to the Lord.
"Commit your actions to the LORD, and your plans will succeed" (PROVERBS 16:3 NLT).

Reach out to my friends and family for encouragement when I have trouble accomplishing something.

"May the God who gives endurance and encouragement give you the same attitude of mind toward each other that Christ Jesus had" (ROMANS 15:5).

Help others when they fail.

"Two people are better off than one, for they can help each other succeed. If one person falls, the other can reach out and help. But someone who falls alone is in real trouble" (ECCLESIASTES 4:9–10 NLT).

We know that in all things God works
for the good of those who love him,
who have been called according to his purpose.
(ROMANS 8:28)

Questions & Answers

Question: "I've had so many failures. Why should I even bother to keep trying?"

Answer: Scripture reveals many reasons to continue striving in hope. Romans 12:12 says, *"Be joyful in hope, patient in affliction, faithful in prayer."* Many people recognized for tremendous successes first experienced multiple failures. For example, Thomas Edison experienced thousands of failures before successfully inventing an effective and affordable light bulb. He is famously quoted as saying, "I have not failed. I've just found 10,000 ways that won't work."[235]

The Bible is also filled with people who suffered failures before finding success: Moses, David, Jonah, Peter, and Paul. But in each case, God continued to work in and through them—even through their sin and failures—to accomplish His purposes. No one has failed so much that they are outside the reach of God's grace. He can redeem anyone and any situation. The Bible says, *"Put your hope in the LORD, for with the Lord is unfailing love and with him is full redemption"* (Psalm 130:7).

Scripture also says that we have hope because God's love and compassion never fail. In fact, they are new every morning. *"This I call to mind and therefore I have hope: Because of the Lord's great love we are not consumed, for his compassions never fail. They are new every morning; great is your faithfulness"* (Lamentations 3:21–23). Because of this truth, there is grace for you each day to start fresh, learn from the past, and move forward with hope.

So don't give up. No matter how many times you've failed, the Lord can still work in and through you to accomplish His purposes.

Let us not become weary in doing good,
for at the proper time we will reap
a harvest if we do not give up.
(GALATIANS 6:9)

SUICIDE PREVENTION

Hope When Life Seems Hopeless

God's Heart on Suicide Prevention

God wants you to know it's never too late to find hope.

"Anyone who is among the living has hope" (Ecclesiastes 9:4).

God wants you to know there is hope for you.

"There is surely a future hope for you, and your hope will not be cut off" (Proverbs 23:18).

God wants you to know He is with you and can help you get through difficult times.

"So do not fear, for I am with you; do not be dismayed, for I am your God. I will strengthen you and help you; I will uphold you with my righteous right hand" (Isaiah 41:10).

God wants you to know you are loved and valued.

"You are precious to me. You are honored, and I love you" (Isaiah 43:4 NLT).

God wants you to know you have purpose.

"The Lord will fulfill his purpose for me; your steadfast love, O Lord, endures forever. Do not forsake the work of your hands" (Psalm 138:8 ESV).

God wants you to know your pain and suffering are not meaningless.

"We were crushed and overwhelmed beyond our ability to endure, and we thought we would never live through it. In fact, we expected to die. But as a result, we stopped relying on ourselves and learned to rely only on God, who raises the dead" (2 Corinthians 1:8–9 NLT).

God wants you to talk to someone and find help if you're having suicidal thoughts.

"In an abundance of counselors there is safety" (Proverbs 11:14 ESV).

God wants you to come to Him for refuge and help.

"The Lord is a shelter . . . a refuge in times of trouble" (Psalm 9:9 NLT).

God wants you to know He will not reject you when you come to Him.

"Whoever comes to me [Jesus] *I will never drive away"* (John 6:37).

God wants you to know He can heal your broken heart and the painful wounds of your past.

"He heals the brokenhearted and binds up their wounds" (Psalm 147:3).

God wants you to receive His free gift of salvation.

"God so loved the world that he gave his one and only Son, that whoever believes in him shall not perish but have eternal life" (John 3:16).

God wants you to have hope and rest in safety and security.

"You will be secure, because there is hope; you will look about you and take your rest in safety" (Job 11:18).

The Lord is gracious and righteous;
our God is full of compassion. . . .
when I was brought low, he saved me.
(Psalm 116:5–6)

Warning Signs of Suicide[236]

Being preoccupied with death, dying, or violence

Buying a gun, stockpiling pills, looking for a way to kill oneself

Displaying extreme mood swings

Feeling empty, hopeless, or like there is no reason to live

Feeling extremely sad, anxious, agitated, or full of rage

Feeling trapped or in unbearable physical or emotional pain

Increasing the use of alcohol or drugs

Making a plan to kill oneself (searching online, etc.)

Taking risks or engaging in reckless behavior

Saying goodbye to loved ones, putting affairs in order, giving away belongings

Showing rage or talking about seeking revenge

Sleeping too little or too much

Talking about wanting to die or wanting to kill oneself

Talking about being a burden to others

Talking about feelings of great guilt or shame

Withdrawing from family or friends or feeling isolated

Rescue me . . . do not let me sink;
Deliver me . . . from the deep waters.
(Psalm 69:14)

If you or someone you know is displaying any of these warning signs, seek help immediately. Call the **Suicide & Crisis Lifeline** at **988**. Or text the **Suicide & Crisis Lifeline** at **988** or text the word **HOME** to the **Crisis Text Line** at **741741**.

Suicide Assessment Questions[237]

Y / N **In the past month**, have you wished you were dead or wished you could go to sleep and not wake up?

Y / N **In the past month**, have you actually had thoughts about killing yourself?

Y / N **In the past month**, have you thought about how you might do this?

Y / N **In the past month**, have you had any intention of acting on these thoughts of killing yourself (as opposed to having the thoughts but definitely not acting on them)?

Y / N **In the past month**, have you started to work out or worked out the details of how to kill yourself? Do you intend to carry out this plan?

Y / N **In the past three months**, have you done anything, started to do anything, or prepared to do anything to end your life? (Examples: collected pills, obtained a gun, gave away valuables, wrote a will or suicide note, held a gun but changed your mind, cut yourself, tried to hang yourself, etc.)

If you answered *yes* to any of these questions, you should seek a behavioral health referral and contact the crisis numbers listed on the next page.

Key Verse to Memorize

There is surely a future hope for you
and your hope will not be cut off.
(Proverbs 23:18)

If you answered *yes* to questions 4, 5, or 6—you are at high risk of suicide and should seek immediate help:

— Call **911**.

— Call or text **988 (Suicide & Crisis Lifeline)**.

— Go to an **emergency room**.

Build a Support System

Make a list of names and phone numbers of people you can call for help (family, friends, pastor, doctor, etc.). **Note: If you are in crisis and need immediate assistance, call 988 or 911.**

My Contract of Hope

The following is a solemn binding contract. This contract cannot be declared null and void without the written agreement of both parties.

I promise that if I should consider harming myself, I will talk with ________ before I do anything destructive.

I sign my name as a pledge of my integrity.

Signature ______________________________ Date __________

Signature ______________________________ Date __________

Anyone who is among the living has hope.
(ECCLESIASTES 9:4)

NOTE: For more information on how to use this written Contract, see *Keys for Living* on Suicide Prevention.

My Personalized Plan

When I'm in despair and struggling with suicidal thoughts, **I will . . .**

Talk to someone.

I will reach out to someone I trust and honestly tell them what I'm thinking about doing.

"In an abundance of counselors there is safety" (PROVERBS 11:14 ESV).

Seek to be safe.

I will remove any harmful or lethal objects from my possession/home.

"But as for me, it is good to be near God. I have made the Sovereign LORD my refuge" (PSALM 73:28).

Hold on to hope.

I will try to put things in perspective and read God's Word to find true, lasting hope.

"We have this hope as an anchor for the soul, firm and secure" (HEBREWS 6:19).

Address physical issues.

I will talk with a doctor and consider any recommended treatments to help me.

"I discipline my body and keep it under control" (1 CORINTHIANS 9:27 ESV).

Take care of my emotional needs.

I will avoid unhealthy coping mechanisms and consider new, healthy ways of managing my emotions.

"In my distress I called to the LORD; I cried to my God for help" (PSALM 18:6).

Replace negative thoughts.

I will replace negative thoughts about myself by meditating on the truth of God's Word.

"Whatever is true, whatever is noble, whatever is right, whatever is pure, whatever is lovely, whatever is admirable—if anything is excellent or praiseworthy—think about such things" (PHILIPPIANS 4:8).

Key Passage to Read

Lamentations 3:19–26

Acknowledge that pain is temporary.

I will remember that God promises to one day put an end to all pain and suffering.

"He will wipe every tear from their eyes, and there will be no more death or sorrow or crying or pain. All these things are gone forever" (REVELATION 21:4 NLT).

Be in community.

I will seek the support of others and consider joining a community support group, a local church, or other helpful groups.

"Two people are better off than one, for they can help each other succeed. If one person falls, the other can reach out and help" (ECCLESIASTES 4:9–10 NLT).

Look to God for help.

I will regularly pray and search God's Word to find help, hope, strength, peace, and guidance.

"The LORD is my rock, my fortress, and my savior; my God is my rock, in whom I find protection. He is my shield, the power that saves me, and my place of safety" (PSALM 18:2 NLT).

Stay connected.

I will remember that even when I'm not in a crisis or having suicidal thoughts, it's important to stay connected with others.

"Let us not neglect our meeting together, as some people do, but encourage one another" (HEBREWS 10:25 NLT).

Questions & Answers

Question: "I've heard that incidents of suicide are lower among those who are religious. Is this true?"

Answer: Religious faith provides a number of protective factors against suicide, such as:

— A spiritually based support system
— A way of making sense of trials and suffering
— A greater sense of purpose in life
— A positive hope for the future
— A conviction that suicide is wrong
— A belief that one's life has inherent value
— A source of unconditional love (God)

Great is your love toward me;
you have delivered me from the depths.
(PSALM 86:13)

Question: "I promised I would keep my friend's thoughts about suicide a secret. If I tell, am I breaking the right to privacy?"

Answer: Never keep any possibility of suicide a secret. You are not betraying your friend. In fact, you may be the only one in a position to help save the life of your friend.

Say, "I didn't realize that what I was promising could actually hurt you. I care about you too much to keep that promise."

Encourage your friend to seek professional help.

Talk to an adult whom you trust *immediately.*

You may risk losing your friendship by breaking your promise, but keeping your promise and then losing your friend would be a far greater tragedy.

A prudent person foresees danger and takes precautions.
The simpleton goes blindly on and suffers the consequences.
(PROVERBS 27:12 NLT)

TEENAGERS

Helping Teens Through Turbulent Times

God's Heart on Teenagers

God wants you to love and accept your teenager unconditionally, as He loves and accepts you.

"A new command I give you: Love one another. As I have loved you, so you must love one another" (John 13:34).

God wants you to turn to His Word for guidance in your parenting.

"As for you, continue in what you have learned and have become convinced of, because you know those from whom you learned it, and how from infancy you have known the Holy Scriptures, which are able to make you wise for salvation through faith in Christ Jesus" (2 Timothy 3:14–15).

God wants you to remember not to judge or condemn based on age.

"Don't let anyone look down on you because you are young, but set an example for the believers in speech, in conduct, in love, in faith and in purity" (1 Timothy 4:12).

God wants you to set healthy boundaries for your teen and communicate them clearly.

"The boundary lines have fallen for me in pleasant places; surely I have a delightful inheritance" (Psalm 16:6).

God wants your teenager to have wise, godly friendships.

"Walk with the wise and become wise, for a companion of fools suffers harm" (Proverbs 13:20).

God wants you to remember that godly discipline produces peace.

"Discipline your children, and they will give you peace; they will bring you the delights you desire" (Proverbs 29:17).

God wants you to lead by example, pointing your teenager to Christ.

"Be shepherds of God's flock that is under your care, watching over them—not because you must, but because you are willing, as God wants you to be; not pursuing dishonest gain, but eager to serve; not lording it over those entrusted to you, but being examples to the flock" (1 Peter 5:2–3).

God wants you to train teenagers by giving them opportunities to grow.

"Train up a child in the way he should go: and when he is old, he will not depart from it" (Proverbs 22:6 KJV).

God wants you to praise and encourage your teenagers' good choices and behaviors.

"Encourage one another and build each other up, just as in fact you are doing" (1 THESSALONIANS 5:11).

God wants you to turn to Him in prayer for help guiding your teenager.

"If any of you lacks wisdom, you should ask God, who gives generously to all without finding fault, and it will be given to you" (JAMES 1:5).

Adolescence and Puberty

Adolescence is the transitional period of growth between childhood and adulthood characterized by dramatic emotional, social, and physical changes.[238]

Puberty is the age at which a person is first capable of sexual reproduction, characterized by dramatic physical changes.[239]

The onset of puberty occurs in girls between the ages of ten and seventeen (usually around age twelve) and in boys between the ages of twelve and nineteen (usually around fourteen).[240]

Picture of Passive Parenting

God holds parents responsible to guide and direct, to comfort and correct—even if their children object. Prayerfully consider the following questions and check off any items that resonate with you. Then allow the Holy Spirit to probe your heart for an honest appraisal of where you stand in God's courtroom of parental accountability.

- ☐ Do you avoid confronting the negative behavior of your teenager?
- ☐ Do you fail to discuss uncomfortable situations with your teen?
- ☐ Do you give in easily and readily accept excuses from your teenager?
- ☐ Do you cover up or make excuses for your teenager's behavior?
- ☐ Do you continually give your teenager additional chances without establishing consequences?
- ☐ Do you shield your teenager from outside repercussions caused by negative behavior?
- ☐ Do you fail to be consistent with rules, curfews, and limits for your teenager?
- ☐ Do you withhold love in the hopes of changing your teenager?
- ☐ Do you use comparisons and sarcasm to intimidate your teenager?
- ☐ Do you withhold discipline because of a fear of losing the love of your teenager?

Rescue those being led away to death;
hold back those staggering toward slaughter.
If you say, "But we knew nothing about this,"
does not he who weighs the heart perceive it?
Does not he who guards your life know it?
Will he not repay everyone according to what they have done?
(Proverbs 24:11–12)

"Thank Yous" of Appreciation from Teens

Live in such a way that one day you may hear—

"**Thank you** for giving me a Christian heritage."[241]

"**Thank you** for giving me honest answers to tough questions."

"**Thank you** for respecting my need for independence and for giving me some space."

"**Thank you** for giving me the freedom to fail."[242]

"**Thank you** for not rehearsing my wrongs."

"**Thank you** for forgiving my hurtful remarks."

"**Thank you** for being my parent and not my buddy."

"**Thank you** for being friendly to my friends."

"**Thank you** for providing more love than money."[243]

"**Thank you** for teaching me honesty and integrity."

"**Thank you** for displaying freedom from prejudice."

"**Thank you** for confronting wrong attitudes and actions."

"**Thank you** for saying *no* when it would have been easier to say *yes*."

"**Thank you** for being a godly parent whom I really respect."[244]

"**Thank you** for setting a Christlike example for me to follow."

Key Verses to Memorize

These commandments that I give you today
are to be on your hearts.
Impress them on your children.
Talk about them when you sit at home and
when you walk along the road,
when you lie down and when you get up.
(Deuteronomy 6:6–7)

How can a young person stay on the path of purity?
By living according to your word.
(PSALM 119:9)

Motivational Pointers for Parents

E—Examine your motive for wanting your teenager to change.

"Search me, God, and know my heart; test me and know my anxious thoughts. See if there is any offensive way in me, and lead me in the way everlasting" (PSALM 139:23–24).

N—Nurture the needs of your teenager.

"Do not let any unwholesome talk come out of your mouths, but only what is helpful for building others up according to their needs, that it may benefit those who listen" (EPHESIANS 4:29).

C—Create an environment where it is okay to fail.

"Accept one another, then, just as Christ accepted you, in order to bring praise to God" (ROMANS 15:7).

O—Orchestrate small steps to achievable goals.

"The hearts of the wise make their mouths prudent, and their lips promote instruction" (PROVERBS 16:23).

U—Use the Sandwich Method (praise, correction, encouragement) to confront failure.

"A person finds joy in giving an apt reply—and how good is a timely word!" (PROVERBS 15:23).

R—Recognize and compliment positive efforts and attitudes.

"Hope deferred makes the heart sick, but a longing fulfilled is a tree of life" (PROVERBS 13:12).

A—Admit your own feelings.

"[There is] *a time to weep and a time to laugh, a time to mourn and a time to dance"* (ECCLESIASTES 3:4).

G—Go to the Lord in prayer.

"Because he turned his ear to me, I will call on him as long as I live" (PSALM 116:2).

E—Ensure your own spiritual stability.

"I seek you with all my heart; do not let me stray from your commands" (PSALM 119:10).

My Personalized Plan

I will . . .

Strive to keep my relationship with God strong and regularly point my teenager to the Lord.

"Love the LORD your God with all your heart and with all your soul and with all your strength. These commandments that I give you today are to be on your hearts. Impress them on your children. Talk about them when you sit at home and when you walk along the road, when you lie down and when you get up" (DEUTERONOMY 6:5–7).

Communicate positively with my teenager.

"Do not let any unwholesome talk come out of your mouths, but only what is helpful for building others up according to their needs, that it may benefit those who listen" (EPHESIANS 4:29).

Examine my motives when I want my teen to change their actions or behaviors.

"Search me, God, and know my heart; test me and know my anxious thoughts. See if there is any offensive way in me, and lead me in the way everlasting" (PSALM 139:23–24).

Strive to create an environment where it is okay for my teenager to fail.

"Accept one another, then, just as Christ accepted you, in order to bring praise to God" (ROMANS 15:7).

Help my teenager establish achievable goals.

"Plans fail for lack of counsel, but with many advisers they succeed" (PROVERBS 15:22).

Confront failure lovingly, with praise, correction, and encouragement.

"A person finds joy in giving an apt reply—and how good is a timely word!" (PROVERBS 15:23).

Key Passages to Read

Book of Proverbs

Strive to recognize and compliment my teenager's positive efforts and attitudes.

"Kind words are like honey—sweet to the soul and healthy for the body" (PROVERBS 16:24 NLT).

Go to the Lord and my support system with my feelings when I am discouraged about my teenager.

"The LORD is my strength and my shield; my heart trusts in him, and he helps me" (PSALM 28:7).

Lift my teenager up regularly in prayer to the Lord.

"Pray in the Spirit on all occasions with all kinds of prayers and requests" (EPHESIANS 6:18).

Focus on my own walk with the Lord so I can be a Christlike example to my teenager.

"I seek you with all my heart; do not let me stray from your commands" (PSALM 119:10).

How can a young person stay on the path of purity?
By living according to your word.
(PSALM 119:9)

Questions & Answers

Question: "As a parent, I feel unloving when I discipline my teenager—even if he is guilty?"

Answer: The God-given role of a parent is to establish boundaries with rewards and repercussions. To "convict" a teenager for their wrong attitudes and actions is not unloving. Enforcing boundaries blesses them by enabling them to experience the consequences of knowing right from wrong.

It will go well with those who convict the guilty,
and rich blessing will come on them.
(PROVERBS 24:25)

Question: "Aren't teenagers too old for parental discipline?"

Answer: No. Accountability is necessary for everyone of any age.

My son, do not forget my teaching,
but keep my commands in your heart,
for they will prolong your life many years
and bring you peace and prosperity.
(PROVERBS 3:1–2)

TEMPTATION

Promise of Pleasure—Lured by a Lie

God's Heart on Temptation

God does not tempt people—temptation comes from internal desires and external influences.

"When tempted, no one should say, 'God is tempting me.' For God cannot be tempted by evil, nor does he tempt anyone; but each person is tempted when they are dragged away by their own evil desire and enticed. Then, after desire has conceived, it gives birth to sin; and sin, when it is full-grown, gives birth to death" (James 1:13–15).

God gives you the Holy Spirit to fight against temptation.

"Walk by the Spirit, and you will not gratify the desires of the flesh" (Galatians 5:16).

God always provides a way out of temptation.

"No temptation has overtaken you except what is common to mankind. And God is faithful; he will not let you be tempted beyond what you can bear. But when you are tempted, he will also provide a way out so that you can endure it" (1 Corinthians 10:13).

God can help you during temptation, as Jesus understands what it's like to be tempted.

"Because he himself suffered when he was tempted, he is able to help those who are being tempted" (Hebrews 2:18).

God instructs you to pray and stay alert so you do not fall into temptation.

"Watch and pray so that you will not fall into temptation. The spirit is willing, but the flesh is weak" (Matthew 26:41).

God does not want you to associate with people who will lead you into sin.

"Walk with the wise and become wise, for a companion of fools suffers harm" (Proverbs 13:20).

God wants you to fight temptation and take it seriously.

"If your right eye causes you to stumble, gouge it out and throw it away. It is better for you to lose one part of your body than for your whole body to be thrown into hell" (Matthew 5:29).

God gives you His Word to fight temptation.

"Man shall not live on bread alone, but on every word that comes from the mouth of God" (MATTHEW 4:4).

God calls you to submit to Him and resist the influence of the Enemy.

"Submit yourselves, then, to God. Resist the devil, and he will flee from you" (JAMES 4:7).

God instructs you to be vigilant in your fight against temptation and the Enemy.

"Be alert and of sober mind. Your enemy the devil prowls around like a roaring lion looking for someone to devour" (1 PETER 5:8).

God gives you other believers who can hold you accountable and help fight temptation.

"Two people are better off than one, for they can help each other succeed. If one person falls, the other can reach out and help. But someone who falls alone is in real trouble" (ECCLESIASTES 4:9–10 NLT).

God wants to renew your mind so you can stand strong when you are tempted.

"Do not conform to the pattern of this world, but be transformed by the renewing of your mind. Then you will be able to test and approve what God's will is—his good, pleasing and perfect will" (ROMANS 12:2).

Above all else, guard your heart,
for everything you do flows from it.
(PROVERBS 4:23)

Luring Lies of Temptation

Luring Lie #1: "Temptation is sinful."[245]

Truth: Temptation is not sin. Jesus was tempted in every way, yet He did not sin.

"We do not have a high priest who is unable to empathize with our weaknesses, but we have one who has been tempted in every way, just as we are—yet he did not sin" (HEBREWS 4:15).

Luring Lie #2: "God is tempting me!"[246]

Truth: Temptation is not from God, but it is *allowed* by God.

"When tempted, no one should say, 'God is tempting me.' For God cannot be tempted by evil, nor does he tempt anyone" (JAMES 1:13).

Luring Lie #3: "The devil made me do it!"[247]

Truth: Temptation is Satan's attempt to lure you into sin, but he can be resisted.

"Submit yourselves, then, to God. Resist the devil, and he will flee from you" (JAMES 4:7).

Luring Lie #4: "Somebody else made me do it."[248]

Truth: No one can make you kill, steal, lie, cheat, or commit any immoral act. You have a choice as to whether you give in to temptation or not.

"If sinful men entice you, do not give in to them" (PROVERBS 1:10).

Luring Lie #5: "A thought can't be sinful."[249]

Truth: An initial impure thought is not sinful, though it is a temptation. However, continuing with an unholy thought can make you captive to sin.

"Repent of this wickedness and pray to the Lord in the hope that he may forgive you for having such a thought in your heart. For I see that you are full of bitterness and captive to sin" (ACTS 8:22-23).

Key Verse to Memorize

No temptation has overtaken you except what is common to mankind. And God is faithful; he will not let you be tempted beyond what you can bear. But when you are tempted, he will also provide a way out so that you can endure it.
(1 CORINTHIANS 10:13)

Luring Lie #6: "God is angry at me when I'm tempted."[250]

Truth: God does not disapprove of you because you are tempted. He can use the temptation as a tool to develop your character.

"Consider it pure joy . . . whenever you face trials of many kinds, because you know that the testing of your faith produces perseverance. Let perseverance finish its work so that you may be mature and complete, not lacking anything" (JAMES 1:2-4).

Luring Lie #7: "What's the use? I've already blown it!"[251]

Truth: Failure is overcome by a change of focus: putting the past behind you and focusing on God's goal for you—Christlikeness. In Philippians 3:13-14, Paul shared how he appropriated this truth in his own life.

"I do not consider myself yet to have taken hold of it. But one thing I do: Forgetting what is behind and straining toward what is ahead, I press on toward the goal to win the prize for which God has called me heavenward in Christ Jesus" (PHILIPPIANS 3:13-14).

Because he himself [Jesus] *suffered*
when he was tempted, he is able
to help those who are being tempted.
(HEBREWS 2:18)

Turn from Temptation

Scriptures to read when tempted to . . .

Blame God

"When tempted, no one should say, 'God is tempting me.' For God cannot be tempted by evil, nor does he tempt anyone" (JAMES 1:13).

Complain

"Do everything without grumbling or arguing, so that you may become blameless and pure, 'children of God without fault in a warped and crooked generation.' Then you will shine among them like stars in the sky" (PHILIPPIANS 2:14–15).

Doubt God

"What is impossible with man is possible with God" (LUKE 18:27).

Give Up

"Since we are surrounded by such a great cloud of witnesses, let us throw off everything that hinders and the sin that so easily entangles. And let us run with perseverance the race marked out for us" (HEBREWS 12:1).

Lie

"Truthful lips endure forever, but a lying tongue lasts only a moment" (PROVERBS 12:19).

Lust

"You have heard that it was said, 'You shall not commit adultery.' But I tell you that anyone who looks at a woman lustfully has already committed adultery with her in his heart" (MATTHEW 5:27–28).

Quarrel

"Keep reminding God's people of these things. Warn them before God against quarreling about words; it is of no value, and only ruins those who listen" (2 TIMOTHY 2:14).

Scriptures to read when tempted to be . . .

Angry

"Take note of this: Everyone should be quick to listen, slow to speak and slow to become angry, because human anger does not produce the righteousness that God desires" (JAMES 1:19–20).

Discouraged

"We are hard pressed on every side, but not crushed; perplexed, but not in despair; persecuted, but not abandoned; struck down, but not destroyed" (2 CORINTHIANS 4:8–9).

Disobedient

"In fact, this is love for God: to keep his commands. And his commands are not burdensome" (1 JOHN 5:3).

Self-sufficient

"I am the vine; you are the branches. If you remain in me and I in you, you will bear much fruit; apart from me you can do nothing" (JOHN 15:5).

Key Passage to Read

Romans chapter 6

Unforgiving

"Bear with each other and forgive one another if any of you has a grievance against someone. Forgive as the Lord forgave you" (COLOSSIANS 3:13).

Vengeful

"Do not repay anyone evil for evil. Be careful to do what is right in the eyes of everyone. If it is possible, as far as it depends on you, live at peace with everyone. Do not take revenge, my dear friends, but leave room for God's wrath, for it is written: 'It is mine to avenge; I will repay,' says the Lord. On the contrary: 'If your enemy is hungry, feed him; if he is thirsty, give him something to drink. In doing this, you will heap burning coals on his head.' Do not be overcome by evil, but overcome evil with good" (ROMANS 12:17–21).

I have hidden your word in my heart
that I might not sin against you.
(PSALM 119:11)

Resisting Temptation

R—**Recognize** the source.

"Our struggle is not against flesh and blood, but against the rulers, against the authorities, against the powers of this dark world and against the spiritual forces of evil in the heavenly realms" (EPHESIANS 6:12).

E—**Expect** to win the war.[252]

"In all these things we are more than conquerors through him who loved us" (ROMANS 8:37).

S—**Search** your heart.

"Humble yourselves, therefore, under God's mighty hand, that he may lift you up in due time" (1 PETER 5:6).

I—**Imagine** the consequences.

"Because of your wrath there is no health in my body; there is no soundness in my bones because of my sin" (PSALM 38:3).

S—**Sense** God's presence.[253]

"Nothing in all creation is hidden from God's sight. Everything is uncovered and laid bare before the eyes of him to whom we must give account" (HEBREWS 4:13).

T—**Transform** your thoughts with truth.

"The weapons we fight with are not the weapons of the world. On the contrary, they have divine power to demolish strongholds. We demolish arguments and every pretension that sets itself up against the knowledge of God, and we take captive every thought to make it obedient to Christ" (2 CORINTHIANS 10:4–5).

In your struggle against sin, you have not yet resisted to the point of shedding your blood.
(HEBREWS 12:4)

The Freedom Formula for Self-Control

A New Purpose + A New Priority + A New Plan = A Transformed Life

Choose to reflect the character of Christ.

"Those God foreknew he also predestined to be conformed to the image of his Son" (ROMANS 8:29).

Choose to exchange your old habit for a new habit.

"Do not conform to the pattern of this world, but be transformed by the renewing of your mind" (Romans 12:2).

Choose to rely on Christ's strength, not your own strength.

"I can do all things through Christ who strengthens me" (Philippians 4:13 NKJV).

Choose to appropriate God's gift of self-control.

"With minds that are alert and fully sober, set your hope on the grace to be brought to you when Jesus Christ is revealed at his coming" (1 Peter 1:13).

We know that our old self was crucified with him
so that the body ruled by sin might be done away with,
that we should no longer be slaves to sin—
because anyone who has died has been
set free from sin.
(Romans 6:6–7)

My Personalized Plan

I will . . .

Turn to God when I am tempted.

"The Lord your God is with you, the Mighty Warrior who saves. He will take great delight in you; in his love he will no longer rebuke you, but will rejoice over you with singing" (Zephaniah 3:17).

Look to God to meet my legitimate needs rather than give in to temptation to meet my needs.

"No temptation has overtaken you except what is common to mankind. And God is faithful; he will not let you be tempted beyond what you can bear. But when you are tempted, he will also provide a way out so that you can endure it" (1 Corinthians 10:13).

Fill my mind with God's Word to help me resist temptation.

"I have stored up your word in my heart, that I might not sin against you" (Psalm 119:11 ESV).

Not allow my mind to dwell on tempting thoughts.

"Whatever is true, whatever is noble, whatever is right, whatever is pure, whatever is lovely, whatever is admirable—if anything is excellent or praiseworthy—think about such things" (Philippians 4:8).

Identify the triggers, environments, and people that lead me to temptation and set appropriate boundaries.

"Above all else, guard your heart, for everything you do flows from it" (PROVERBS 4:23).

Call on others to help me when I am tempted.

"By wise guidance you can wage your war, and in abundance of counselors there is victory" (PROVERBS 24:6 ESV).

Questions & Answers

Question: "What is the difference between a test, a trial, and a temptation? Aren't they really the same thing?"

Answer: No. Some aspects of tests, trials, and temptations may seem similar. In truth they are different, yet can overlap in some interesting ways.

- **Test**: God can and does use difficult situations in our lives to test us. Will we remain faithful and obedient to His call and commands when difficulties arise? In this case, withstanding temptation can in itself become a test!
- **Trial**: Suffering, enduring, and persevering through a lengthy hardship can seem more like trial and tribulation than a test or a temptation. Trials do have a beginning and an end, and they ultimately strengthen us in our weaknesses.
- **Temptation**: The Enemy of our souls uses every means of warfare at his disposal to steal, kill, and destroy. And when he can enlist our aid in our own destruction, he's all the more satisfied in the results.

Whenever we face tests, trials, and temptation we can wonder, *Why this? Why now? Why me?* We just need to remember what Scripture says . . .

I know, my God, that you
test the heart and are
pleased with integrity.
(1 CHRONICLES 29:17)

TERMINAL ILLNESS

How Can I Ever Let Go?

God's Heart on Terminal Illness

God wants you to come to Him with your fears about death.

"I sought the LORD, and he answered me; he delivered me from all my fears" (PSALM 34:4).

God draws near to you when you are hurting.

"The LORD is close to the brokenhearted and saves those who are crushed in spirit" (PSALM 34:18).

God is faithful to keep all of His promises.

"The LORD is trustworthy in all he promises and faithful in all he does" (PSALM 145:13).

God gives rest when you are weary and burdened.

"Come to me, all you who are weary and burdened, and I will give you rest" (MATTHEW 11:28).

God wants you to find peace in knowing that you will spend eternity with Him in heaven.

"Do not let your hearts be troubled. You believe in God; believe also in me. My Father's house has many rooms; if that were not so, would I have told you that I am going there to prepare a place for you?" (JOHN 14:1–2).

God anchors you with the hope of His Word and the hope of heaven.

"We have this hope as an anchor for the soul, firm and secure" (HEBREWS 6:19).

God loves you and has not forsaken you, even when He chooses not to heal.

"It is the LORD who goes before you. He will be with you; he will not leave you or forsake you. Do not fear or be dismayed" (DEUTERONOMY 31:8 ESV).

God wants you to allow your family and loved ones to help and comfort you as you approach death.

"But God, who comforts the downcast, comforted us by the coming of Titus" (2 CORINTHIANS 7:6).

God will comfort your loved ones after your death.

"Praise be to the God and Father of our Lord Jesus Christ, the Father of compassion and the God of all comfort, who comforts us in all our troubles, so that we can comfort those in any trouble with the comfort ourselves receive from God" (2 CORINTHIANS 1:3–4).

God will relieve your pain and restore your body in heaven.

"'He will wipe every tear from their eyes. There will be no more death' or mourning or crying or pain, for the old order of things has passed away. He who was seated on the throne said, 'I am making everything new!'" (REVELATION 21:4–5).

You guide me with your counsel,
and afterward you will take me into glory. . . .
My flesh and my heart may fail,
but God is the strength of my heart
and my portion forever.
(PSALM 73:24, 26)

Facing Death

Death is designed.

Embracing the God-given gift of life means accepting death as part of life. The moment you are born, you take the first step toward death. One of the characteristics of spiritual maturity is recognizing death as a natural part of life.

"There is a time for everything, and a season for every activity under the heavens: a time to be born and a time to die, a time to plant and a time to uproot" (ECCLESIASTES 3:1–2).

Key Verse to Memorize

Even though I walk through the valley
of the shadow of death,
I will fear no evil,
for you are with me;
your rod and your staff,
they comfort me.
(PSALM 23:4 ESV)

Death is a doorway.

Death can be a doorway to a more abundant (eternal) life, or it can be the gateway to eternal misery. Death is not an end to life but a beginning. We are born with a heart's desire to live forever, and only through faith in Christ can we reach out and embrace God's promise of eternal life.

"Enter through the narrow gate. For wide is the gate and broad is the road that leads to destruction, and many enter through it. But small is the gate and narrow the road that leads to life, and only a few find it" (MATTHEW 7:13–14).

Death is divine.

The reality for all Christians is that you have already died! God's desire for you as His child is death to self and submission to the divine life of Christ living within you, expressing His life through you.

"I have been crucified with Christ and I no longer live, but Christ lives in me. The life I now live in the body, I live by faith in the Son of God, who loved me and gave himself for me" (GALATIANS 2:20).

The living know that they will die.
(ECCLESIASTES 9:5)

Hospice Care

H—Home team effort—nursing, physician calls, family counseling, homemaking services, volunteer help, and spiritual support

O—Overall approach—physical, emotional, and spiritual care for the terminally ill and their families

S—Specialized services—physical therapy, medical equipment and supplies, nutritional counseling, meal planning, and other similar services

P—Pain control—efforts focused on preventing pain rather than giving relief on demand

I—Involvement with family

C—Cost-effectiveness

E—Emphasis on quality of life

We ought therefore to show hospitality to such people
so that we may work together for the truth.
(3 JOHN V. 8)

Preparing for Reality

R—Record your will.

"A will is in force only when somebody has died; it never takes effect while the one who made it is living" (HEBREWS 9:17).

E—Express your desires.

"By faith Joseph, when his end was near . . . gave instructions concerning the burial of his bones" (HEBREWS 11:22).

A—Arrange your affairs.

"David gave his son Solomon the plans for the portico of the temple. . . . 'All this,' David said, 'I have in writing as a result of the LORD's hand on me, and he enabled me to understand all the details of the plan'" (1 CHRONICLES 28:11, 19).

L—Leave a legacy of love.

"I thank God, whom I serve, as my ancestors did, with a clear conscience, as night and day I constantly remember you in my prayers. Recalling your tears, I long to see you, so that I may be filled with joy" (2 TIMOTHY 1:3–4).

I—Identify your fears.

"God is our refuge and strength, an ever-present help in trouble. Therefore we will not fear, though the earth give way and the mountains fall into the heart of the sea" (PSALM 46:1–2).

T—Trust your God.

"Trust in the LORD with all your heart and lean not on your own understanding; in all your ways submit to him, and he will make your paths straight" (PROVERBS 3:5–6).

Y—Yield your heart.

"As it is written: 'Eye has not seen, nor ear heard, nor have entered into the heart of man the things which God has prepared for those who love Him'" (1 CORINTHIANS 2:9 NKJV).

Leading the Way to the Lord

Start with prayer for God's blessing.

"The mouths of the righteous utter wisdom, and their tongues speaks what is just" (PSALM 37:30).

Seek to be alone with the person who is dying.

"When [Jesus] *was alone with his own disciples, he explained everything"* (MARK 4:34).

Speak directly about judgment and eternal life.

"People are destined to die once, and after that to face judgment" (HEBREWS 9:27).

Share the problem of sin in simple terms.

"All have sinned and fall short of the glory of God" (ROMANS 3:23).

State the consequences of sin.

"The wages of sin is death, but the gift of God is eternal life in Christ Jesus our Lord" (ROMANS 6:23).

Submit God's solution to sin.

"God demonstrates his own love for us in this: While we were still sinners, Christ died for us" (ROMANS 5:8).

Set forth the purpose of Jesus.

"God so loved the world that he gave his one and only Son, that whoever believes in him shall not perish but have eternal life" (JOHN 3:16).

Key Passage to Read

2 Corinthians 4:16–5:5

Single out Jesus Christ as the only way to be saved.

"Jesus answered, 'I am the way and the truth and the life. No one comes to the Father except through me'" (JOHN 14:6).

Suggest a prayer of salvation.

"Believe in the Lord Jesus, and you will be saved—you and your household" (ACTS 16:31).

Prayer of Salvation

"God, I want a real relationship with You.
I admit that many times I've chosen to go my own way
instead of Your way.
Please forgive me for my sins.
Jesus, thank You for dying on the cross
to pay the penalty for my sins.
Come into my life to be my Lord and my Savior.
Change me from the inside out and make me the person
You created me to be.
In Your holy name I pray. Amen."

My Personalized Plan

I will . . .

Turn to the Lord with any fears I am experiencing about death.

"God is our refuge and strength, an ever-present help in trouble. Therefore we will not fear, though the earth give way and the mountains fall into the heart of the sea" (PSALM 46:1–2).

Ask the Lord to help me leave a legacy of love.

"I thank God, whom I serve, as my ancestors did, with a clear conscience, as night and day I constantly remember you in my prayers. Recalling your tears, I long to see you, so that I may be filled with joy" (2 TIMOTHY 1:3–4).

Prepare a will and arrange my affairs.

"About that time Hezekiah became deathly ill, and the prophet Isaiah son of Amoz went to visit him. He gave the king this message: 'This is what the LORD says: Set your affairs in order, for you are going to die. You will not recover from this illness'" (2 KINGS 20:1 NLT).

Express my desires for end-of-life care to my family and loved ones.

"By faith Joseph, when his end was near . . . gave instructions concerning the burial of his bones" (HEBREWS 11:22).

Trust God as I face the end of my life and my future in eternity with Him.

"However, as it is written: 'What no eye has seen, what no ear has heard, and what no human mind has conceived'—the things God has prepared for those who love him" (1 CORINTHIANS 2:9).

Use my remaining time to share the hope I have and tell others about the Lord's salvation.

"We are therefore Christ's ambassadors, as though God were making his appeal through us. We implore you on Christ's behalf: Be reconciled to God" (2 CORINTHIANS 5:20).

Questions & Answers

Question: "Is it morally right for Christians to take pain medicine, or is that putting faith in prescriptions and not in God?"

Answer: God created everything in the earth and called it "good"—including plants with pain-relieving properties. With the medical knowledge available today, patients should not have to suffer great physical pain.

Fruit trees of all kinds will grow. . . . Their fruit will serve for food and their leaves for healing.
(EZEKIEL 47:12)

Question: "Is it always best to reveal the truth to a person who has been diagnosed as having a terminal illness?"

Answer: Yes. Most terminally ill patients instinctively know when they are not getting well. Dishonesty and deception rob them of dignity and the motivation to get their relationships and affairs in order before they die.

"Do not lie. Do not deceive one another."
(Leviticus 19:11)

Question: "What can I say to a friend who is grieving because of a terminal illness?"

Answer: Being there and listening are more important than talking. Be slow to use Scripture and, when you do, choose only those verses that are uplifting.

The words of the reckless pierce like swords,
but the tongue of the wise brings healing.
(Proverbs 12:18)

TIME MANAGEMENT

Wisdom to Maximize Your Minutes

God's Heart on Time Management

God is not bound by time like we are—He is eternal.

"Before the mountains were born or you brought forth the whole world, from everlasting to everlasting you are God. You turn people back to dust, saying, 'Return to dust, you mortals.' A thousand years in your sight are like a day that has just gone by, or like a watch in the night" (PSALM 90:2–4).

God does not change with the passage of time.

"Jesus Christ is the same yesterday and today and forever" (HEBREWS 13:8).

God created the world in such a way that time can be marked and measured.

"And God said, 'Let there be lights in the expanse of the heavens to separate the day from the night. And let them be for signs and for seasons, and for days and years'" (GENESIS 1:14 ESV).

God is in control of all time and history.

"From one man he made all the nations, that they should inhabit the whole earth; and he marked out their appointed times in history and the boundaries of their lands" (ACTS 17:26).

God wants you to know that your time is in His hands.

"I trust in you, LORD; I say, 'You are my God.' My times are in your hands" (PSALM 31:14–15).

God wants you to recognize that your time is limited and fleeting.

"LORD, remind me how brief my time on earth will be. Remind me that my days are numbered—how fleeting my life is. You have made my life no longer than the width of my hand. My entire lifetime is just a moment to you; at best, each of us is but a breath" (PSALM 39:4–5 NLT).

God wants you to use your time wisely—to do His will.

"Look carefully then how you walk, not as unwise but as wise, making the best use of the time, because the days are evil. Therefore do not be foolish, but understand what the will of the Lord is" (EPHESIANS 5:15–17 ESV).

God wants you to plan and manage your time, but allow Him to change your plans.

"You can make many plans, but the LORD's purpose will prevail" (PROVERBS 19:21 NLT).

God wants you to remember what He's done for you in the past.

"I will remember the deeds of the LORD" (PSALM 77:11).

God wants you to live in the present and not worry about the future.

"Do not worry about tomorrow, for tomorrow will worry about itself. Each day has enough trouble of its own" (MATTHEW 6:34).

God wants you—and everyone—to experience His salvation today.

"Now is the time of God's favor, now is the day of salvation" (2 CORINTHIANS 6:2).

God wants you to use your time for His glory as you look forward to spending eternity with Him.

"We are instructed to turn from godless living and sinful pleasures. We should live in this evil world with wisdom, righteousness, and devotion to God, while we look forward with hope to that wonderful day when the glory of our great God and Savior, Jesus Christ, will be revealed" (TITUS 2:12–13 NLT).

Teach us to number our days,
that we may gain a heart of wisdom.
(PSALM 90:12)

Hindrances to Effective Time Management

Argument: "If I don't do it, it won't get done!"

Answer: Decline or delegate tasks to alleviate feeling overwhelmed. Schedule all delegated tasks, providing those who help with specific due dates.

Argument: "Everyone is depending on me!"

Answer: Your perception may be distorted. Remember, someone could be manipulating you or you could be lying to yourself. Set appropriate boundaries.

Argument: "There's no way I can do everything that's on my schedule today. My social media interrupts me all day long!"

Answer: Take control of these interruptions by scheduling a specific amount of time each day to respond to these media outlets.

Argument: "Everyone knows that if they want the job done right, they should ask me to do it."

Answer: Recognize when others are taking advantage of you. Acknowledge that there are other talented people who are equally qualified to do the job.

Key Verse to Memorize

Be wise in the way you act . . . make the most of every opportunity.
(Colossians 4:5)

Argument: "There's no way I can check off everything on my to-do list!"

Answer: Prioritize three or four things you want to accomplish each day while including some unscheduled open time.

"Show me, Lord, my life's end
and the number of my days;
let me know how fleeting my life is."
(Psalm 39:4)

10 Timely Tips

1. **Identify the tasks** you dread most and do them first.
2. **Break enormous, overwhelming tasks into bite-sized pieces** to make doing them more manageable. Don't put them off.
3. **Group similar tasks back-to-back:** Return calls, answer letters, pay bills, file papers, and do shopping tasks together. Group errands geographically to avoid making extra side trips later.
4. **Pad your calendar** with an extra ten minutes if you are chronically late. Write what time you need to leave (including ten minutes pad time) on your calendar. Set an alarm or alert reminder.
5. **Wear an earpiece or headset** attached to your phone so that you can take care of phone calls while exercising, running errands, or doing other things.
6. **Filter mail.** Manage your email inbox using mail filters, smart mailboxes, and folders. Set up email rules to stop spam, automatically reroute incoming items to specific folders, and flag important senders.
7. **Use a "Do Not Disturb" sign** to minimize interruptions.
8. **Create a "not-to-do" list** by asking: "What would happen if someone else did this job or if it didn't get done?" If the answer is "nothing," cross it off your list.

9. **The more you own,** the more time you spend caring for "things." When you add something new, take away something old.

10. **Resist doing that "one last thing"** when you're ready to walk out the door.

The plans of the diligent lead to profit
as surely as haste leads to poverty.
(PROVERBS 21:5)

Trustworthy Time-Users

Be very careful, then, how you live—not as unwise but as wise,
making the most of every opportunity, because the days are evil.
Therefore do not be foolish, but understand what the Lord's will is.
(EPHESIANS 5:15–17)

Trustworthy time-users—are careful how they live (v. 15).

Trustworthy time-users—are not unwise, but wise (v. 15).

Trustworthy time-users—make the most of every opportunity (v. 16).

Trustworthy time-users—recognize that the days are evil (v. 16).

Trustworthy time-users—have learned not to be foolish (v. 17).

Trustworthy time-users—understand what the Lord's will is (v. 17).

Now it is required that those who have been
given a trust must prove faithful.
(1 CORINTHIANS 4:2)

My Personalized Plan

Nehemiah's rebuilding of the wall of Jerusalem illustrates eight time-management basics. These basics can teach me about the successful completion of any purpose or project God has for me. I will:

1. **Identify my life purposes**: Why has God put me on earth (for example, son/daughter, wife/husband, mother/father, employer/employee)?
   "The king asked, 'Well, how can I help you?' With a prayer to the God of heaven, I replied, 'If it please the king, and if you are pleased with me, your servant, send me to Judah to rebuild the city where my ancestors are buried'" (NEHEMIAH 2:4–5 NLT).

2. **Identify my goals leading to my purpose**: What do I want to accomplish today?

   "I also said to the king, 'If it please the king, let me have letters addressed to the governors of the province west of the Euphrates River, instructing them to let me travel safely through their territories on my way to Judah. And please give me a letter addressed to Asaph, the manager of the king's forest, instructing him to give me timber. I will need it to make beams for the gates of the Temple fortress, for the city walls, and for a house for myself.' And the king granted these requests, because the gracious hand of God was on me" (NEHEMIAH 2:7–8 NLT).

3. **Identify activities**: What will I have to do to make it happen?

   "The king, with the queen sitting beside him, asked, 'How long will you be gone? When will you return?' After I told him how long I would be gone, the king agreed to my request" (NEHEMIAH 2:6 NLT).

4. **Identify priorities**: What should I do first?

   "After dark I went out through the Valley Gate, past the Jackal's Well, and over to the Dung Gate to inspect the broken walls and burned gates. Then I went to the Fountain Gate and to the King's Pool, but my donkey couldn't get through the rubble. So, though it was still dark, I went up the Kidron Valley instead, inspecting the wall before I turned back and entered again at the Valley Gate" (NEHEMIAH 2:13–15 NLT).

5. **Identify how long it will take to do each item**: Do I have the time?

   "At last the wall was completed to half its height around the entire city, for the people had worked with enthusiasm" (NEHEMIAH 4:6 NLT).

6. **Identify the vital items**: What must be done now?

   "We worked early and late, from sunrise to sunset. And half the men were always on guard. I also told everyone living outside the walls to stay in Jerusalem. That way they and their servants could help with guard duty at night and work during the day" (NEHEMIAH 4:21–22 NLT).

7. **Identify flex time (pad time) to allow for the unexpected**: Have I allotted extra time?

   "When Sanballat and Tobiah and the Arabs, the Ammonites, and Ashdodites heard that the work was going ahead and that the gaps in the wall of Jerusalem were being repaired, they were furious. They all made plans to come and fight against Jerusalem and throw us into confusion. But we prayed to our God and guarded the city day and night to protect ourselves" (NEHEMIAH 4:7–9 NLT).

Key Passage to Read

Ecclesiastes chapter 3

8. **Identify involvement with others, as necessary**: Who could or should be included?

   "On October 2 the wall was finished—just fifty-two days after we had begun. When our enemies and the surrounding nations heard about it, they were frightened and humiliated. They realized this work had been done with the help of our God" (NEHEMIAH 6:15–16 NLT).

Whatever you do, work at it with all your heart,
as working for the Lord, not for human masters.
(COLOSSIANS 3:23)

Questions & Answers

Question: "I find that I increasingly spend too much time on social media and feel like I should avoid it altogether. What practical tips would you suggest to help me better manage my usage?"

Answer: The pull of social media can exacerbate the challenge of time management. But many of these symptoms can be better managed through a more deliberate emphasis on regulating time. Consider the following:

— Prioritize important activities and responsibilities *before* spending time on social media.

— Use the Screen Time (or similar) feature on your phone to monitor your usage and activity. These can be set up to send you regular alerts and notifications about your phone usage.

— Look into apps that you can download to monitor and limit time on your phone; some apps can even block social media usage after a set time.

— Quickly skim and reply to emails according to the need of a response.

— Use a timer to alert you when it's time to log off your social media sites and move on to another task.

— Determine to spend ten to fifteen minutes less per day on social media.

— Delete social media apps on your phone. If you want to visit those sites, use a computer—but only for a scheduled, limited time.

— Set boundaries with your phone or tablet. Use them only at scheduled times during the day.

— If hyper-concentrated focus is a problem, avoid social media before bedtime or prior to must-do tasks, such as paying bills or getting ready for work.

Surely God is my help;
the Lord is the one who sustains me.
(PSALM 54:4)

TRIALS

God's Refining Fire

God's Heart on Trials

God uses trials to show you the sufficiency of His power and grace.

"My grace is all you need. My power works best in weakness" (2 CORINTHIANS 12:9 NLT).

God uses trials to increase your trust in Him.

"Let those who suffer according to God's will entrust their souls to a faithful Creator while doing good" (1 PETER 4:19 ESV).

God uses trials to break pride and produce a heart of humility.

"So to keep me from becoming proud, I was given a thorn in my flesh" (2 CORINTHIANS 12:7 NLT).

God uses trials to reveal your sinfulness so that He might break the power of sin in your life.

"Surely it was for my benefit that I suffered such anguish. In your love you kept me from the pit of destruction; you have put all my sins behind your back" (ISAIAH 38:17).

God uses trials to lead you to a point of personal examination so that He might set you on a correction course.

"Search me, God, and know my heart; test me and know my anxious thoughts. See if there is any offensive way in me, and lead me in the way everlasting" (PSALM 139:23–24).

God uses trials to cause you to pour out your heart to Him.

"I cry aloud to the LORD; I lift up my voice to the LORD for mercy. I pour out before him my complaint; before him I tell my trouble. When my spirit grows faint within me, it is you who watch over my way" (PSALM 142:1–3).

God uses trials to show you that He hears you and encourages you.

"You, LORD, hear the desire of the afflicted; you encourage them, and you listen to their cry" (PSALM 10:17).

God uses trials to help you learn His ways.

"It was good for me to be afflicted so that I might learn your decrees" (PSALM 119:71).

God uses trials to keep you from going astray and to teach you obedience.

"Before I was afflicted I went astray, but now I obey your word" (PSALM 119:67).

God uses trials to produce maturity in you.

"Consider it pure joy, my brothers and sisters, whenever you face trials of many kinds, because you know that the testing of your faith produces perseverance. Let perseverance finish its work so that you may be mature and complete, not lacking anything" (JAMES 1:2–3).

God uses trials to develop compassion in you.

"The Father of compassion and the God of all comfort . . . comforts us in all our troubles, so that we can comfort those in any trouble with the comfort we ourselves receive from God" (2 CORINTHIANS 1:3–4).

God uses trials to bring glory to Himself.

"The sisters sent word to Jesus, 'Lord, the one you love is sick.' When he heard this, Jesus said, 'This sickness will not end in death. No, it is for God's glory so that God's Son may be glorified through it'" (JOHN 11:3–4).

"I have given them the glory that you gave me,
that they may be one as we are one—
I in them and you in me—so that they
may be brought to complete unity.
Then the world will know that you sent me
and have loved them even as you have loved me."
(JOHN 17:22–23)

Typical Types of Trials

T—Temporary Troubles

Loss of possessions

"One day . . . a messenger came to Job and said, 'The oxen were plowing and the donkeys were grazing nearby, and the Sabeans attacked and made off with them. . . .' While he was still speaking, another messenger came and said, 'The fire of God fell from the heavens and burned up the sheep and the servants . . .' While he was still speaking, another messenger came and said, 'The Chaldeans formed three raiding parties and swept down on your camels and made off with them'" (JOB 1:13–17).

Loss of security

"Surely, God, you have worn me out; you have devastated my entire household. You have shriveled me up—and it has become a witness; my gauntness rises up and testifies against me" (JOB 16:7–8).

R—Relational Ruptures

Loss of reputation

"I have become a laughingstock to my friends . . . a mere laughingstock, though righteous and blameless!" (Job 12:4).

Loss of acceptance and trust

"Oh, for the days when I was in my prime, when God's intimate friendship blessed my house, when the Almighty was still with me and my children were around me" (Job 29:4–5).

I—Inexplicable Injustices

Loss of understanding

"Does God pervert justice? Does the Almighty pervert what is right?" (Job 8:3).

Loss of insight

"Even if I washed myself with soap and my hands with cleansing powder, you would plunge me into a slime pit so that even my clothes would detest me" (Job 9:30–31).

A—All-Consuming Affliction

Loss of health

"So Satan went out from the presence of the Lord *and afflicted Job with painful sores from the soles of his feet to the crown of his head. Then Job took a piece of broken pottery and scraped himself with it as he sat among the ashes"* (Job 2:7–8).

Loss of stability

"Terrors overwhelm me; my dignity is driven away as by the wind, my safety vanishes like a cloud. And now my life ebbs away; days of suffering grip me" (Job 30:15–16).

L—Lingering Lament

Loss of loved ones

"Your sons and daughters were feasting and drinking wine at the oldest brother's house, when suddenly a mighty wind swept in from the desert and struck the four corners of the house. It collapsed on them and they are dead" (Job 1:18–19).

Loss of long-term dreams and opportunities

"I loathe my very life; therefore I will give free rein to my complaint and speak out in the bitterness of my soul" (Job 10:1).

S—Spiritual Suffering

Loss of peace

"When I think my bed will comfort me and my couch will ease my complaint, even then you frighten me with dreams and terrify me with visions, so that I prefer strangling and death, rather than this body of mine. I despise my life; I would not live forever. Let me alone; my days have no meaning" (Job 7:13–16).

Loss of purpose

"Why is light given to those in misery, and life to the bitter of soul, to those who long for death that does not come, who search for it more than for hidden treasure?" (JOB 3:20–21).

Called to Be in the Crucible

You are called to be committed.

"It is commendable if someone bears up under the pain of unjust suffering because they are conscious of God. But how is it to your credit if you receive a beating for doing wrong and endure it? But if you suffer for doing good and you endure it, this is commendable before God. To this you were called, because Christ suffered for you, leaving you an example, that you should follow in his steps. 'He committed no sin, and no deceit was found in his mouth.' When they hurled their insults at him, he did not retaliate; when he suffered, he made no threats. Instead, he entrusted himself to him who judges justly" (1 PETER 2:19–23).

You are called to be corrected.

"Endure hardship as discipline; God is treating you as his children. For what children are not disciplined by their father?" (HEBREWS 12:7).

You are called to be compassionate.

"Praise be to the God and Father of our Lord Jesus Christ, the Father of compassion and the God of all comfort, who comforts us in all our troubles, so that we can comfort those in any trouble with the comfort we ourselves receive from God. For just as we share abundantly in the sufferings of Christ, so also our comfort abounds through Christ" (2 CORINTHIANS 1:3–5).

You are called to be courageous.

"Everyone who wants to live a godly life in Christ Jesus will be persecuted" (2 TIMOTHY 3:12).

You are called to be a conqueror.

"No, in all things we are more than conquerors through him who loved us" (ROMANS 8:37).

You are called to be Christlike.

"Those God foreknew he also predestined to be conformed to the image of his Son" (ROMANS 8:29).

What Sets Us Up for the Crucible?

Stumbling

"Some of the wise will stumble, so that they may be refined, purified and made spotless until the time of the end, for it will still come at the appointed time" (DANIEL 11:35).

Wickedness

"Many will be purified, made spotless and refined, but the wicked will continue to be wicked. None of the wicked will understand, but those who are wise will understand" (DANIEL 12:10).

Untested ways

"I have made you a tester of metals and my people the ore, that you may observe and test their ways" (JEREMIAH 6:27).

Rebellion

"They are all hardened rebels, going about to slander" (JEREMIAH 6:28).

Key Verse to Memorize

"When you walk through the fire,
you will not be burned;
the flames will not set you ablaze."
(ISAIAH 43:2)

Corruption

"They are bronze and iron; they all act corruptly" (JEREMIAH 6:28).

Hardness

"The bellows blow fiercely to burn away the lead with fire" (JEREMIAH 6:29).

Unrepentance

"The refining goes on in vain; the wicked are not purged out" (JEREMIAH 6:29).

"They are called rejected silver,
because the LORD has rejected them."
(JEREMIAH 6:30)

The Root Cause of Discontentment in the Crucible

Wrong Belief: "Life is not fair! I don't deserve this much heartache and disappointment."

Right Belief: "There are no accidents in life. Since God is sovereign over every situation in my life, I will see my disappointment as God's appointment to build Christlike character in me. I know that at the end of this temporary trial, I will emerge as purified gold."

"But he knows the way that I take;
when he has tested me, I will come forth as gold.
My feet have closely followed his steps;
I have kept to his way without turning aside.
I have not departed from the commands of his lips;
I have treasured the words of his mouth more than my daily bread."
(JOB 23:10–12)

10 Steps to Accepting God's Sovereignty

1. **Seek** God in prayer for discernment in your circumstances.
   "Is anyone among you in trouble? Let them pray" (JAMES 5:13).

2. **Open** your heart to God with complete honesty about your feelings.
   "Cast your cares on the LORD and he will sustain you; he will never let the righteous be shaken" (PSALM 55:22).

3. **Remember** God's love for you.
   "Though he brings grief, he will show compassion, so great is his unfailing love" (LAMENTATIONS 3:32).

4. **Expect** God to change your life through the truth He reveals to you.
   "It was good for me to be afflicted so that I might learn your decrees" (PSALM 119:71).

5. **Realize** that God is all-powerful and sovereign over your circumstances.
   Pilate said, "Don't you realize I have power either to free you or to crucify you?" (JOHN 19:10).
   Jesus answered, "You would have no power over me if it were not given to you from above" (v. 11).

6. **Trust** God to work through all things to prove your faith and to bring Him praise, glory, and honor.
   "The God of all grace, who called you to his eternal glory in Christ, after you have suffered a little while, will himself restore you and make you strong, firm and steadfast" (1 PETER 5:10).

7. **Invest** time in studying God's Word and in prayer.
   "I meditate on your precepts and consider your ways. I delight in your decrees; I will not neglect your word" (PSALM 119:15–16).

8. **Gain** an eternal perspective of God's purposes for your present pain.
   "'Neither this man nor his parents sinned,' said Jesus, 'but this happened so that the works of God might be displayed in him'" (JOHN 9:3).

9. **Turn** to Christ, who provides you with His power for victory.

   "He gives strength to the weary and increases the power of the weak" (ISAIAH 40:29).

10. **Yield** to God's sovereignty. You may never understand or have any answers for your suffering.

    "Trust in the LORD with all your heart and lean not on your own understanding; in all your ways submit to him, and he will make your paths straight" (PROVERBS 3:5–6).

My Personalized Plan

Thankfulness—I will thank God for all that He is doing in my life.

"Give thanks in all circumstances; for this is God's will for you in Christ Jesus" (1 THESSALONIANS 5:18).

Joy—I will rejoice in the Lord, knowing that the outcome of every trial is in His hands.

"We rejoice in our sufferings, knowing that suffering produces endurance" (ROMANS 5:3 ESV).

Confession—I will ask God to search my heart, and I will confess any hidden sin.

"Whoever conceals their sins does not prosper, but the one who confesses and renounces them finds mercy" (PROVERBS 28:13).

Humility—I will remember that God gives grace to the humble.

"He gives us more grace. That is why Scripture says: 'God opposes the proud but shows favor to the humble'" (JAMES 4:6).

Obedience—I will listen to and obey God's Word.

"This is love: that we walk in obedience to his commands. As you have heard from the beginning, his command is that you walk in love" (2 JOHN V. 6).

Wisdom—I will saturate my mind with Scripture.

"I meditate on your precepts and consider your ways. I delight in your decrees; I will not neglect your word" (PSALM 119:15–16).

Prayer—I will not worry, but pray about everything.

"Do not be anxious about anything, but in every situation, by prayer and petition, with thanksgiving, present your requests to God. And the peace of God, which transcends all understanding, will guard your hearts and your minds in Christ Jesus" (PHILIPPIANS 4:6–7).

Trust—I will entrust myself to God, who judges justly.

"When they hurled their insults at him, he did not retaliate; when he suffered, he made no threats. Instead, he entrusted himself to him who judges justly" (1 PETER 2:23).

Dependence—I will act in the power of Christ.

"I can do all things through Christ who strengthens me" (PHILIPPIANS 4:13 NKJV).

Endurance—I will look to the Lord for deliverance.

"No temptation has overtaken you except what is common to mankind. And God is faithful; he will not let you be tempted beyond what you can bear. But when you are tempted, he will also provide a way out so that you can endure it" (1 CORINTHIANS 10:13).

Key Passage to Read

James 1:2–18

Praise—I will focus on God's greatness, not on my circumstances.

"I will praise you every day; yes, I will praise you forever. Great is the LORD! He is most worthy of praise! No one can measure his greatness" (PSALM 145:2–3 NLT).

Ministry—I will look for ways to reach out and help others.

"Don't be afraid of suffering for the Lord. Work at telling others the Good News, and fully carry out the ministry God has given you" (2 TIMOTHY 4:5 NLT).

We know that in all things God works
for the good of those who love him, who
have been called according to his purpose.
(ROMANS 8:28)

Questions & Answers

Question: "Aren't trials and suffering the result of sin?"

Answer: Sometimes yes, sometimes no. In some situations, suffering can be the direct result of a person's destructive choices. In other cases, God allows the innocent to suffer in order to display His power and divine purposes.

His disciples asked him, "Rabbi, who sinned,
this man or his parents, that he was born blind?"
"Neither this man nor his parents sinned,"
said Jesus, "but this happened so that
the works of God might be displayed in him."
(JOHN 9:2–3)

Question: "Does God care about my suffering?"

Answer: Know that your heavenly Father loves you deeply and cares greatly about your suffering as demonstrated by the fact that:

He is close to you when you are brokenhearted.

The LORD is close to the brokenhearted
and saves those who are crushed in spirit.
(PSALM 34:18)

He stays with you in the midst of trouble—to sustain you, help you, and deliver you.

Surely God is my help;
the Lord is the one who sustains me. . . .
You have delivered me from all my troubles.
(PSALM 54:4, 7)

He keeps a record of your grief and He collects your tears.

You keep track of all my sorrows.
You have collected all my tears in your bottle.
You have recorded each one in your book.
(PSALM 56:8 NLT)

He promises to one day wipe away your tears—and there will be no more suffering.

"He will wipe every tear from their eyes,
and there will be no more death or sorrow or crying or pain.
All these things are gone forever."
(REVELATION 21:4 NLT)

Remember, God's ways are always just. He never does wrong.

He is the Rock, his works are perfect,
and all his ways are just.
A faithful God who does no wrong,
upright and just is he.
(DEUTERONOMY 32:4)

THE UNBELIEVING MATE

Bridging the Spiritual Divide

God's Heart on Marriage and Unbelieving Mates

God's Heart on Marriage

God presents marriage as good and worthy of His favor.

"He who finds a wife finds what is good and receives favor from the L*ORD"* (PROVERBS 18:22).

God sees the person you married as your partner for life.

"They are no longer two, but one flesh. Therefore what God has joined together, let no one separate" (MATTHEW 19:6).

God portrays marriage as a picture of the sacrificial love of Christ (being willing to lay down your personal rights for your mate).

"Husbands, love your wives, just as Christ loved the church and gave himself up for her" (EPHESIANS 5:25).

God set apart the marriage relationship as the means by which He would bring children into the world and populate the earth He had created.

"God blessed them and said, 'Be fruitful and multiply. Fill the earth and govern it'" (GENESIS 1:28 NLT).

God's Heart for the Unbelieving Mate

God desires all people—including your unbelieving mate—to be saved.

"[God] *wants all people to be saved and to come to a knowledge of the truth"* (1 TIMOTHY 2:4).

God provided only one way to be saved—through faith in the Lord Jesus Christ alone.

"Salvation is found in no one else, for there is no other name under heaven given to mankind by which we must be saved" (ACTS 4:12).

God wants you and your unbelieving mate to be assured of your salvation.

"Very truly I tell you, whoever hears my word and believes him who sent me has eternal life and will not be judged but has crossed over from death to life" (JOHN 5:24).

God wants you to tell others—including your unbelieving mate—about His salvation.

"We are therefore Christ's ambassadors, as though God were making his appeal through us. We implore you on Christ's behalf: Be reconciled to God" (2 CORINTHIANS 5:20).

Though one may be overpowered, two can defend themselves.
A cord of three strands is not quickly broken.
(ECCLESIASTES 4:12)

Checklist of Common Issues[254]

Place a ✓ if your answer is *yes*, or an × if your answer is *no*.

- ☐ I love both God and my spouse, but sometimes that love seems to be diametrically opposed to each other.
- ☐ I feel torn between my unbelieving spouse and God.
- ☐ I find that I'm less and less interested in the recreational activities my spouse and I used to enjoy together.
- ☐ I struggle with a judgmental attitude and am often mentally critical of my unbelieving mate's actions and words.
- ☐ I've been unable to persuade my spouse to attend church.
- ☐ I don't attend church as regularly as I used to.
- ☐ I feel that my marriage lacks meaning and depth, and thus, I feel isolated and alone.
- ☐ I am tempted to look outside my marriage for the oneness I so strongly desire.
- ☐ I was previously happy in my marriage, but am experiencing more stress because we have very different priorities in life now.
- ☐ I doubt my ability to persevere long enough in my marriage for my unbelieving mate to become a Christian.
- ☐ I want our kids to go to church with me, but my spouse doesn't want them to attend church.
- ☐ I am fearful that my teenage children will be overly influenced by my spouse's focus on worldly things.
- ☐ I can see that disagreements in our home about faith and church are having an adverse effect on our children.
- ☐ I am daily faced with the reality that my spouse may never accept Jesus Christ as Lord and Savior.

Contributing Issues

Marrying because of parental or peer pressure or fear of missing out

Marrying due to premarital sexual activity

Marrying for fear of being alone

Marrying for financial security

Marrying according to cultural dictates

Marrying an unbeliever in direct disobedience to the Lord's instruction

"But my people would not listen to me;
Israel would not submit to me.
So I gave them over to their stubborn hearts
to follow their own devices."
(PSALM 81:11–12)

Reasons Some Resist Belief in Christ

Follows another faith

"'You are my witnesses,' declares the LORD, *'and my servant whom I have chosen, so that you may know and believe me and understand that I am he. Before me no god was formed, nor will there be one after me'"*
(ISAIAH 43:10).

Experienced little or no spiritual influence as a child

"Those along the path are the ones who hear, and then the devil comes and takes away the word from their hearts, so that they may not believe and be saved" (LUKE 8:12).

Believes in a "higher power" but rejects Jesus

"Do not let your hearts be troubled. You believe in God; believe also in me" (JOHN 14:1).

Key Verses to Memorize

Live wisely among those
who are not believers,
and make the most of every opportunity.
Let your conversation be gracious
and attractive so that you will have
the right response for everyone.
(COLOSSIANS 4:5–6 NLT)

Views the Bible as corrupted over time or a fairy tale

"The word of God is alive and powerful. It is sharper than the sharpest two-edged sword, cutting between soul and spirit, between joint and marrow. It exposes our innermost thoughts and desires" (HEBREWS 4:12 NLT).

Considers Christianity to be a "crutch" for weak people

"But he said to me, 'My grace is sufficient for you, for my power is made perfect in weakness.' Therefore I will boast all the more gladly about my weaknesses, so that Christ's power may rest on me" (2 CORINTHIANS 12:9).

Key Passage to Read

1 Corinthians 7:12–16

Suffered spiritual abuse or had a negative experience with Christians

"He knows those who are false, and he takes note of all their sins" (JOB 11:11 NLT).

Thinks scientific evidence precludes belief in God as unnecessary or foolish

"'My thoughts are nothing like your thoughts,' says the LORD. 'And my ways are far beyond anything you could imagine. For just as the heavens are higher than the earth, so my ways are higher than your ways and my thoughts higher than your thoughts'" (ISAIAH 55:8–9 NLT).

Judges faith in Jesus by the failings seen in His followers, and wants no part of Christianity

"Everyone has sinned; we all fall short of God's glorious standard. Yet God, in his grace, freely makes us right in his sight. . . . People are made right with God when they believe that Jesus sacrificed his life, shedding his blood. . . . God did this to demonstrate his righteousness, for he himself is fair and just, and he makes sinners right in his sight when they believe in Jesus" (ROMANS 3:23–26 NLT).

My Personalized Plan

To be a winsome witness, **I will be . . .**

Pardoning—quick to forgive

Patient—willingly waiting without complaining

Peaceable—not argumentative or hostile

Peaceful—exuding an inner tranquility

Perceptive—demonstrating keen insight and understanding of others

Persevering—unwavering in commitment

Polite—respectful in speech and behavior

Positive—choosing to look for the good while still being realistic and hope-filled

Prayerful—believing God is sovereign over life and personal in relationship

Precise—setting and keeping boundaries

Prepared—not easily knocked off-center

Protective—always keeping others' best interest at heart

Professional—willing to share their faith and testimony when asked

The Biblical Love Test

Answer these questions honestly and ask the Lord to reveal any areas where you need to grow.

— **Am I** slow to lose patience with my spouse?
— **Am I** thoughtful and considerate of my mate's feelings and needs?
— **Am I** content with my life and my marriage?
— **Am I** anxious to impress my spouse or others?
— **Am I** cherishing inflated ideas of my own importance?
— **Am I** practicing good manners toward my mate?
— **Am I** pursuing selfish advantage within my marriage?
— **Am I** touchy and easily irritated or angered by my spouse?
— **Am I** harboring ill will toward my mate?
— **Am I** gloating when my spouse is wrong or fails at something?
— **Am I** eager to share the joy of my mate?
— **Am I** conscientious about speaking truthfully to my spouse?
— **Am I** quick to protect and defend the reputation of my spouse?
— **Am I** unwavering in my trust that God is working in the life of my mate?
— **Am I** always hopeful of receiving God's best for my marriage?
— **Am I** committed to persevere in my love for my spouse?

Love is patient, love is kind. It does not envy,
it does not boast, it is not proud.
It does not dishonor others, it is not self-seeking,
it is not easily angered, it keeps no record of wrongs.
Love does not delight in evil but rejoices with the truth.
It always protects, always trusts, always hopes, always perseveres.
Love never fails.
(1 CORINTHIANS 13:4–8)

Questions & Answers

Question: "Being married to an unbeliever is too hard. I am so unhappy. I know God will forgive me if I get a divorce. Doesn't God want me to be happy? Wouldn't it be better for me to be in a Christian marriage where I could serve Him more?"

Answer: God has allowed your situation for a reason. Determine to see your life as a testimony of God's love. Your happiness does not depend on your husband's salvation but on your relationship with the Lord. Understand that your "happiness" is not God's goal. His goal is your transformation into the likeness of Jesus. Your service to God is not a matter of emotion but of will. God *allows* divorce in cases of marital infidelity or abandonment by an unbeliever, but He does not endorse divorce.

Shall we go on sinning so that grace
may increase? By no means!
(ROMANS 6:1–2)

Question: "What can I do if my mate insists on teaching our children beliefs that are contrary to God's Word?"

Answer: Teach your children the truth as presented in God's Word. Seek to balance your spouse's beliefs with your own. Do not malign your mate, but ask God to protect your children's hearts and minds against false doctrine. Specifically pray for and trust your children to God's care, knowing He loves them infinitely more than you do. Also, remember God can bring clarity to their thought processes in ways you cannot imagine.

"Even more blessed are all who hear the
word of God and put it into practice."
(LUKE 11:28 NLT)

VERBAL & EMOTIONAL ABUSE

Victory Over the Power of Abuse

God's Heart on Verbal and Emotional Abuse

God cares about your pain.

"You have seen my troubles, and you care about the anguish of my soul" (PSALM 31:7 NLT).

God understands the pain of abuse.

"He [Jesus] *was despised and rejected by mankind, a man of suffering, and familiar with pain"* (ISAIAH 53:3).

God offers healing from the pain of abuse.

"He heals the brokenhearted and binds up their wounds" (PSALM 147:3).

God affirms your worth as His special creation.

"You are precious and honored in my sight, and . . . I love you" (ISAIAH 43:4).

God wants to be your refuge and help you process your emotions with Him.

"Trust in him at all times, you people; pour out your hearts to him, for God is our refuge" (PSALM 62:8).

God longs for you to understand the power of words.

"The tongue has the power of life and death, and those who love it will eat its fruit" (PROVERBS 18:21).

God desires your speech to be encouraging, not abusive.

"Don't use foul or abusive language. Let everything you say be good and helpful, so that your words will be an encouragement to those who hear them" (EPHESIANS 4:29 NLT).

God calls for abusive people to change.

"Give up your violence and oppression and do what is just and right" (EZEKIEL 45:9).

God will judge and call everyone to account for the words they speak.

"I tell you, on the day of judgment people will give account for every careless word they speak" (MATTHEW 12:36 ESV).

God wants you to establish boundaries in your life and in your relationships.

"Guard your heart above all else, for it determines the course of your life" (PROVERBS 4:23 NLT).

God provides you with opportunities to help others who have experienced abusive treatment.

"The Father of compassion and the God of all comfort . . . comforts us in all our troubles, so that we can comfort those in any trouble with the comfort we ourselves receive from God" (2 CORINTHIANS 1:3–4).

God will one day end all abuse and pain.

"He will wipe every tear from their eyes, and there will be no more death or sorrow or crying or pain. All these things are gone forever" (REVELATION 21:4 NLT).

Power belongs to you, God,
and with you, Lord, is unfailing love.
(PSALM 62:11–12)

The Cost of Being Constantly Abused

Loss of clear conscience: increased guilt or shame

Loss of faith: increased fear

Loss of freedom: increased vigilance

Loss of friendship: increased isolation

Loss of happiness: increased emotional flatness

Loss of hope: increased despair

Loss of inner peace: increased "peace at any price" behavior

Loss of optimism: increased pessimism

Loss of pride: increased self-hatred

Loss of safety: increased sense of danger

Loss of security: increased desire to escape

Loss of self-assurance: increased insecurity

Loss of self-confidence: increased self-consciousness

Loss of self-perception: increased self-criticism

My Personalized Plan

I will . . .

Look to the Lord.

- — I will read God's Word and pray regularly.
- — I will get involved in a local church to grow in my relationship with God.

"Look to the LORD and his strength; seek his face always" (1 CHRONICLES 16:11).

Process my emotions.

- — I will be honest about the pain and emotions I've felt as a result of the abuse I experienced.
- — I will talk with God and trustworthy people to process my thoughts and emotions, as well as journal my experience.

"In my distress I called to the LORD; I cried to my God for help" (PSALM 18:6).

Find support.

- — I will seek the help of a counselor, if needed, to help me heal, grow, and develop healthy relationships.
- — I will develop a support system with my family, friends, and local church, as well as look into online and community resources for further support.

"Two people are better off than one, for they can help each other succeed. If one person falls, the other can reach out and help" (ECCLESIASTES 4:9–10 NLT).

Key Passage to Read

Matthew 12:34–37

Replace lies with truth.

- — I will identify the lies I believe about myself, about others, about life, and about God.
- — I will look to God's Word to replace those lies with truth.

"You will know the truth, and the truth will set you free" (JOHN 8:32).

Set boundaries.

- — I will set healthy boundaries to protect myself and others from further abuse.
- — I will enforce repercussions and maintain those boundaries when they are crossed.

"The peace of God, which transcends all understanding, will guard your hearts and your minds in Christ Jesus" (PHILIPPIANS 4:7).

Help others.

— I will trust God to use me, even the pain of my past, to help others who have been impacted by abuse.

— I will look for opportunities to share my story, listen to others, and point people to the Lord.

"'Though the mountains be shaken and the hills be removed, yet my unfailing love for you will not be shaken nor my covenant of peace be removed,' says the LORD, who has compassion on you" (ISAIAH 54:10).

Questions & Answers

Question: "What hope is there for someone who's been broken by abuse?"

Answer: God offers great hope for the one who's been broken by abuse. That hope is found in Him (see Proverbs 23:18). That means that no matter what has happened in the past, no matter how much pain you feel in the present, no matter how much fear you have about the future . . . *there is hope*. Seek God in His Word and pray for His comfort and healing.

The LORD is close to the brokenhearted
and saves those who are crushed in spirit.
(PSALM 34:18)

Question: "How can I overcome the pain I suffered in the past? Why do I keep repeating the same unhealthy relational patterns and how can I change them?"

Answer: God often allows the difficulties we experience in life to wake us up to our need to understand our personal attitudes and actions. Then, with that understanding we can take responsibility for them. You will be drawn to the same relational dynamics over and over until you overcome the past by allowing God to heal and restore you. Reclaiming your life through discipline will produce a harvest of peace and righteousness in you.

God disciplines us for our good,
in order that we may share in his holiness.
No discipline seems pleasant at the time, but painful.
Later on, however, it produces a harvest of righteousness
and peace for those who have been trained by it.
(HEBREWS 12:10–11)

VIOLENCE

Understand It—and Stop It

God's Heart on Violence

God hates violence.

"The LORD examines the righteous, but the wicked, those who love violence, he hates with a passion" (PSALM 11:5).

God judges those who are violent.

"God said to Noah, 'I am going to put an end to all people, for the earth is filled with violence'" (GENESIS 6:13).

God is angry with violent behavior.

"Must they also fill the land with violence and continually arouse my anger?" (EZEKIEL 8:17).

God prohibits violent people from positions of church leadership.

"Since an overseer manages God's household, he must be blameless—not overbearing, not quick-tempered, not given to drunkenness, not violent, not pursuing dishonest gain" (TITUS 1:7).

God commands those who are violent to change.

"Give up your violence and oppression and do what is just and right" (EZEKIEL 45:9).

"Never will I leave you; never will I forsake you."
So we say with confidence,
"The Lord is my helper; I will not be afraid.
What can mere mortals do to me?"
(HEBREWS 13:5–6)

God's Heart for the Victim

God hears the cry of the battered and abused.

"You, LORD, hear the desire of the afflicted; you encourage them, and you listen to their cry" (PSALM 10:17).

God holds victims of violence by the hand and reassures them of His provision for them.

"I am the LORD your God who takes hold of your right hand and says to you, Do not fear; I will help you" (ISAIAH 41:13).

God will rescue victims of abuse and violence.

"He will rescue them from oppression and violence, for precious is their blood in his sight" (PSALM 72:14).

God confirms the victim's value and worth.

"Are not five sparrows sold for two pennies? Yet not one of them is forgotten by God. Indeed, the very hairs of your head are all numbered. Don't be afraid; you are worth more than many sparrows" (LUKE 12:6–7).

God brings good out of violent, evil deeds and brings violent people to disaster.

"The LORD works out everything to its proper end—even the wicked for a day of disaster" (PROVERBS 16:4).

Rescue me, LORD, from evildoers;
protect me from the violent,
who devise evil plans in their hearts
and stir up war every day.
(PSALM 140:1–2)

Common Characteristics of a Violent or Abusive Person[255]

Aggressive behavior (pushing, shoving, restraining the victim)

Blaming others; not taking responsibility for one's own actions

Breaking or destroying the victim's property or belongings

Constant insults or demeaning comments

Controlling behavior (dictating how the victim spends their time or money)

Escalating the relationship quickly (proposing too fast, moving in together early)

Extreme jealousy or possessiveness

Forcing or pressuring the victim to engage in sexual acts or drug/alcohol use

Hypersensitivity or unpredictable behavior

Isolating the victim (preventing the victim from spending time with family and friends)

Limiting or preventing the victim's ability to make their own decisions

Threatening behavior (verbal threats, intimidation, using a weapon)

Your ways are in full view of the LORD,
and he examines all your paths.
The evil deeds of the wicked ensnare them;
the cords of their sins hold them fast.
For lack of discipline they will die,
led astray by their own great folly.
(PROVERBS 5:21–23)

Building Healthy Boundaries

Begin a new way of thinking about myself, God, and violence.

"Do not conform to the pattern of this world, but be transformed by the renewing of your mind. Then you will be able to test and approve what God's will is—his good, pleasing and perfect will" (ROMANS 12:2).

Overcome my fear of the unknown by trusting God with the future.

"When I am afraid, I put my trust in you. . . . I sought the LORD, and he answered me; he delivered me from all my fears" (PSALM 56:3; 34:4).

Obey the biblical mandate to hold violent people accountable.

"Call the evildoer to account for his wickedness that would not otherwise be found out" (PSALM 10:15).

Inform supportive friends, relatives, and authorities when I experience violence.

"Carry each other's burdens, and in this way you will fulfill the law of Christ" (GALATIANS 6:2).

Key Verse to Memorize

I eagerly expect and hope that
I will in no way be ashamed,
but will have sufficient courage
so that now as always
Christ will be exalted in my body,
whether by life or by death.
(PHILIPPIANS 1:20)

Develop God's perspective on biblical love, submission, and authority.

"Submit to one another out of reverence for Christ" (EPHESIANS 5:21).

Admit my own hurt and anger while practicing forgiveness.

"See to it that no one falls short of the grace of God and that no bitter root grows up to cause trouble and defile many" (HEBREWS 12:15).

Recognize any codependent patterns I may have developed and change the way I respond.

"Am I now trying to win the approval of human beings, or of God? Or am I trying to please people? If I were still trying to please people, I would not be a servant of Christ" (GALATIANS 1:10).

Identify healthy boundaries for myself and commit to maintaining them.

"A hot-tempered person must pay the penalty; rescue them, and you will have to do it again" (PROVERBS 19:19).

Ensure my personal safety immediately.

"In peace I will lie down and sleep, for you alone, LORD, make me dwell in safety" (PSALM 4:8).

My Personalized Plan

I will . . .

Ask God to help me overcome my fear of violence by trusting Him with the future.

"When I am afraid, I put my trust in you" (PSALM 56:3).

Obey the biblical mandate to hold violent people accountable.

"Call the evildoer to account for his wickedness that would not otherwise be found out" (PSALM 10:15).

Enlist the aid of authorities when I experience violence.

"The authorities are God's servants, sent for your good" (ROMANS 13:4 NLT).

Process my emotions with the Lord and trustworthy people, whether anger, hurt, fear, or confusion.

"Trust in him at all times, you people; pour out your hearts to him, for God is our refuge" (PSALM 62:8).

Seek help for my safety and recovery, whether physical, mental, or emotional.

"In an abundance of counselors there is safety" (PROVERBS 11:14 ESV).

Ask God to help me recognize any unhealthy relationship patterns I may have developed and change the way I respond.

"I the LORD search the heart and examine the mind, to reward each person according to their conduct, according to what their deeds deserve" (JEREMIAH 17:10).

Develop healthy boundaries for myself and commit to maintaining them.

"A hot-tempered person must pay the penalty; rescue them, and you will have to do it again" (PROVERBS 19:19).

Ensure my personal safety and the safety of my children above all else.

"A prudent person foresees danger and takes precautions" (PROVERBS 27:12 NLT).

Key Passage to Read

Psalm 37

Trust the Lord to heal and comfort me.

"He heals the brokenhearted and binds up their wounds" (PSALM 147:3).

Pray for those who hurt me—that the Lord would help them change their ways.

"Bless those who curse you. Pray for those who hurt you" (LUKE 6:28 NLT).

Show me the wonders of your great love,
you who save by your right hand
those who take refuge in you from their foes.
(PSALM 17:7)

Questions & Answers

Question: "I am angry with God. If He is just, why does He allow abuse?"

Answer: Your anger over the injustice of abuse is justified, but you are living with misplaced blame. Realize, God created everyone with free choice. He gives all people the freedom to do right or wrong, even when those choices go against His will. So God is not to blame when people choose to do wrong. They are to blame. They are the guilty ones—not God. But rest assured, God is a just God who hates violence.

God is just: He will pay back trouble to those who trouble you.
(2 THESSALONIANS 1:6)

Question: "What is dating violence, and how prevalent is it among adolescents?"

Answer: Dating violence is the intentional use of physical, sexual, verbal, or emotional violence by a person to harm, threaten, intimidate, or control another person in a dating relationship.[256] Because it is perpetrated by someone known and trusted by the victim, it is a betrayal that leaves mental, emotional, and psychological wounds that require great care and extended time to heal. Sadly, some are impacted for a lifetime. Estimates vary, but data from the CDC indicates "about 1 in 12 teens experience physical dating violence and about the same number face sexual dating violence."[257]

Keep me as the apple of your eye;
hide me in the shadow of your wings
from the wicked who are out to destroy me;
from my mortal enemies who surround me.
(Psalm 17:8–9)

WIDOWHOOD

Wisdom in a Wilderness

God's Heart on Widowhood

God is a protector and defender of widows.

"A father to the fatherless, a defender of widows, is God in his holy dwelling" (PSALM 68:5).

God sustains and cares for widows.

"He cares for the orphans and widows, but he frustrates the plans of the wicked" (PSALM 146:9 NLT).

God does not want widows to be taken advantage of, exploited, or mistreated.

"You must not exploit a widow or an orphan. If you exploit them in any way and they cry out to me, then I will certainly hear their cry" (EXODUS 22:22–23 NLT).

God calls His people to look after and care for widows.

"Religion that God our Father accepts as pure and faultless is this: to look after orphans and widows in their distress and to keep oneself from being polluted by the world" (JAMES 1:27).

God wants the children and grandchildren of widows to care for them.

"Take care of any widow who has no one else to care for her. But if she has children or grandchildren, their first responsibility is to show godliness at home and repay their parents by taking care of them. This is something that pleases God" (1 TIMOTHY 5:3–4 NLT).

God sees your pain and grief.

"I will be glad and rejoice in your unfailing love, for you have seen my troubles, and you care about the anguish of my soul" (PSALM 31:7 NLT).

God wants you to cry out to Him with your hurt and anger.

"Out of the depths I cry to you, LORD" (PSALM 130:1).

God will meet your needs.

"My God will meet all your needs according to the riches of his glory in Christ Jesus" (PHILIPPIANS 4:19).

God wants your hope to be in Him.

"Now a true widow, a woman who is truly alone in this world, has placed her hope in God. She prays night and day, asking God for his help" (1 TIMOTHY 5:5 NLT).

God promises to wipe away all your tears.

"He will wipe every tear from their eyes, and there will be no more death or sorrow or crying or pain. All these things are gone forever" (REVELATION 21:4 NLT).

God comforts you and can you use to comfort others.

"The Father of compassion and the God of all comfort . . . comforts us in all our troubles, so that we can comfort those in any trouble with the comfort we ourselves receive from God" (2 CORINTHIANS 1:3–4).

God wants you to trust Him with your future.

"Those who know your name trust in you, for you, LORD, have never forsaken those who seek you." (PSALM 9:10).

A father to the fatherless, a defender of widows,
is God in his holy dwelling.
(PSALM 68:5)

Characteristics of the Widowed

M—Marooned: feeling abandoned and deserted by mate

O—Overwhelmed: feeling unable to handle life alone

U—Useless: feeling without purpose in life

R—Resentful: feeling angry at God for allowing mate to die

N—Numbness: feeling unable to accept daily reality

I—Isolated: feeling loss at not being a part of other couples' activities

N—Neglected: feeling lonely and misunderstood by others

G—Guilty: feeling remorse over past attitudes and actions

The cords of death entangled me,
the anguish of the grave came over me;
I was overcome by distress and sorrow.
(PSALM 116:3)

Surface Causes of Pain

— **Loss** of companionship
— **Lonely** marriage bed
— **Lifestyle** changes

— **Low** self-worth
— **Lack** of healthy self-sufficiency
— **Locked** into the past
— **Left** to raise children alone
— **Limited** financial resources
— **Living** life through children
— **Looking** for another marriage partner

See to it that no one falls short of
the grace of God and that no bitter root grows up
to cause trouble and defile many.
(HEBREWS 12:15)

Special Ministries for the Widowed

Prayer: Fasting and praying on behalf of others

"There was also a prophet, Anna, the daughter of Penuel, of the tribe of Asher. She was very old; she had lived with her husband seven years after her marriage, and then was a widow until she was eighty-four. She never left the temple but worshiped night and day, fasting and praying" (LUKE 2:36–37).

Counsel: Counseling with godly wisdom

"Naomi said to Ruth her daughter-in-law, 'It will be good for you, my daughter, to go with the women who work for him, because in someone else's field you might be harmed'" (RUTH 2:22).

Teaching: Training others in sound doctrine and how to live a godly life

"You, however, must teach what is appropriate to sound doctrine. Teach the older men to be temperate, worthy of respect, self-controlled, and sound in faith, in love and in endurance. Likewise, teach the older women to be reverent in the way they live, not to be slanderers or addicted to much wine, but to teach what is good. Then they can urge the younger women to love their husbands and children, to be self-controlled and pure, to be busy at home, to be kind, and to be subject to their husbands, so that no one will malign the word of God" (TITUS 2:1–5).

Key Verses to Memorize

For the Widow

A father to the fatherless,
a defender of widows,
is God in his holy dwelling.
(PSALM 68:5)

For the Widower

It is God who arms me with strength
and keeps my way secure.
(PSALM 18:32)

Service: Working to meet the needs of others

"So Ruth gleaned in the field until evening. Then she threshed the barley she had gathered, and it amounted to about an ephah. She carried it back to town, and her mother-in-law saw how much she had gathered. Ruth also brought out and gave her what she had left over after she had eaten enough" (RUTH 2:17–18).

Hospitality: Extending a generous and warm welcome to guests

"Go at once to Zarephath in the region of Sidon and stay there. I have directed a widow there to supply you with food" (1 KINGS 17:9).

Giving: Recognizing and providing for the financial needs of Christians

"As Jesus looked up, he saw the rich putting their gifts into the temple treasury. He also saw a poor widow put in two very small copper coins. 'Truly I tell you,' he said, 'this poor widow has put in more than all the others. All these people gave their gifts out of their wealth; but she out of her poverty put in all she had to live on'" (LUKE 21:1–4).

Dos and Don'ts of Healthy Grieving

Don't let self-pity dominate your thoughts.

Do learn to find contentment in Christ.

"I have learned to be content whatever the circumstances" (PHILIPPIANS 4:11).

Don't become consumed with regret.

Do learn from and accept the past.

"Look straight ahead, and fix your eyes on what lies before you" (PROVERBS 4:25 NLT).

Don't ignore memories and feelings—both positive and negative.

Do allow yourself to feel your emotions and to reflect on your memories.

"I thank my God every time I remember you" (PHILIPPIANS 1:3).

Don't isolate yourself.

Do seek the support of others and look to the Lord to meet your needs.

"Two people are better off than one, for they can help each other succeed. If one person falls, the other can reach out and help" (ECCLESIASTES 4:9–10 NLT).

Don't compare your circumstances to the circumstances of others.

Do focus on what God wants you to do in your situation.

"Teach me to do your will, for you are my God; may your good Spirit lead me on level ground" (PSALM 143:10).

Don't busy yourself with distractions in an effort to avoid your grief.

Do set aside time to process your grief through prayer, journaling, conversations, etc.

"In my distress I prayed to the LORD, *and the* LORD *answered me and set me free"* (PSALM 118:5 NLT).

Don't make major decisions while grieving.

Do establish priorities and seek wise counsel.

"The wisdom of the prudent is to give thought to their ways" (PROVERBS 14:8).

Key Passage to Read

The book of Ruth

Don't define yourself by your grief.

Do find your identity in Christ as a beloved child of God.

"See what great love the Father has lavished on us, that we should be called children of God! And that is what we are!" (1 JOHN 3:1).

"My grace is sufficient for you,
for my power is made perfect in weakness."
(2 CORINTHIANS 12:9)

My Personalized Plan

Recognize my grief.

— Be honest about my pain.
— Share my pain with another.
— Allow my inner feelings to show outwardly.

"'Where have you laid him?' he asked. 'Come and see, Lord,' they replied. Jesus wept. Then the Jews said, 'See how he loved him!'" (JOHN 11:34–36).

Realize my insufficiency.

— Acknowledge my grief and pain to God in prayer.
— Admit I am powerless to carry the grief alone.
— Know I will realize "His sufficiency" through my insufficiency.

"But he said to me, 'My grace is sufficient for you, for my power is made perfect in weakness.' Therefore I will boast all the more gladly about my weaknesses, so that Christ's power may rest on me. That is why, for Christ's sake, I delight in weaknesses, in insults, in hardships, in persecutions, in difficulties. For when I am weak, then I am strong" (2 CORINTHIANS 12:9–10).

Relinquish control.

— Recognize God's sovereign control over my life.

— Give my personal dreams and desires to God.

— Become more aware of the presence of the Holy Spirit and yield to His control.

"Trust in the LORD with all your heart and lean not on your own understanding; in all your ways submit to him, and he will make your paths straight" (PROVERBS 3:5–6).

Respond to God's grace.

— Recognize that God loves me and has not deserted me.

— Spend time in God's Word. Personalize and memorize key scriptures (Psalm 32:8, 34:18, 68:5, 147:3; Isaiah 43:2; Jeremiah 29:11; Romans 8:18).

— Allow God to meet my emotional needs.

"Let us then approach God's throne of grace with confidence, so that we may receive mercy and find grace to help us in our time of need" (HEBREWS 4:16).

Rebuild my life.

— Recognize that God has a new purpose for my life.

— Be active in church and fellowship with other Christians.

— Become involved in the lives of others.

"The God of all grace, who called you to his eternal glory in Christ, after you have suffered a little while, will himself restore you and make you strong, firm and steadfast" (1 PETER 5:10).

Questions & Answers

Question: "Since my husband's death, I've not been open to dating another man. I feel guilty when I have any joy in the presence of another man. Are these feelings right?"

Answer: If you have feelings for another man, don't live with false guilt. When a mate in a loving, caring marriage dies, the surviving mate is more likely to be open to exploring the possibility of remarriage, for they have experienced the beauty that such a partnership can bring. However, your sense of guilt may be a normal result of not having fully grieved your loss. Conversely, one who has had a difficult marriage may be less open to remarriage.

By law a married woman is bound to her husband
as long as he is alive, but if her husband dies,
she is released from the law that
binds her to him. . . . But if her husband dies,
she is released from that law and is not
an adulteress if she marries another man.
(ROMANS 7:2–3)

Question: "I am a widower with children who adored their mother. Now a caring woman has entered my life and is interested in a more personal relationship with all of us. I don't want her presence to lessen the children's love of their mother. What is best for the children?"

Answer: Genuine love is not like steam that evaporates into thin air. Ask the Lord to reveal His will for you regarding this woman. Meanwhile, know that the loving memories of the children's mother are tucked safely within each child's heart.

Love never fails.
(1 CORINTHIANS 13:8)

WORRY

The Joy Stealer

God's Heart on Worry

God wants you to remember that He is good and gracious and cares about you with compassion.

"The LORD is gracious and compassionate, slow to anger and rich in love. The LORD is good to all; he has compassion on all he has made" (PSALM 145:8–9).

God wants you to remember He promises to meet your needs.

"The LORD will guide you always; he will satisfy your needs in a sun-scorched land and will strengthen your frame" (ISAIAH 58:11).

God wants you not to live in a state of worry.

"Do not worry about tomorrow, for tomorrow will worry about itself. Each day has enough trouble of its own" (MATTHEW 6:34).

God wants you to trust Him when you're worried—to have faith and not fear.

"When I am afraid, I put my trust in you" (PSALM 56:3).

God wants to be close to you when worries break your heart.

"The LORD is close to the brokenhearted; he rescues those whose spirits are crushed" (PSALM 34:18 NLT).

God wants you to look to Him when you're filled with worry.

"When anxiety was great within me, your consolation brought me joy" (PSALM 94:19).

God wants you to look to His Word when you're tempted to worry.

"As pressure and stress bear down on me, I find joy in your commands" (PSALM 119:143 NLT).

God wants you to give Him all your worries because He cares for you.

"Give all your worries and cares to God, for he cares about you" (1 PETER 5:7 NLT).

God wants you to encourage others when they are worried.

"Encourage one another and build each other up" (1 THESSALONIANS 5:11).

God wants you to talk with Him about everything that's worrying you, and thank Him for how He will use the trials in your life.

"Don't worry about anything; instead, pray about everything. Tell God what you need, and thank him for all he has done. Then you will experience God's peace, which exceeds anything we can understand. His peace will guard your hearts and minds as you live in Christ Jesus" (PHILIPPIANS 4:6–7 NLT).

I prayed to the LORD, and he answered me.
He freed me from all my fears.
Those who look to him for help will be radiant with joy.
(PSALM 34:4–5 NLT)

Symptoms of Worry[258]

If you habitually worry, you might justify your negative mindset with these thoughts . . .

— "I worry so nothing bad will happen."
— "I feel better when I worry."
— "I worry because I care!"
— "Worrying gives me something to do."
— "Everyone worries. It's not a big deal."
— "It's the way God made me."
— "I can't stop worrying."
— "I worry when I'm around negative people."
— "I don't want to worry, but I can't help it."
— "Worrying isn't the worst thing to do."
— "Worrying doesn't hurt anyone."
— "I worry that I'm the only one who worries."

Destructive Worry vs. Constructive Concern[259]

Worry	Concern
Promotes inaction	Prompts action
Disrupts a plan	Puts a plan together
Feels out of control	Takes control where possible
Ignores or blocks reality	Demonstrates the ability to see reality
Distracts from the problem	Focuses on the problem
Shows self-absorbed, selfish tendencies	Feels empathy or compassion
Is destructive, unhealthy, misplaced	Is constructive, healthy, focused
Remains immature; stunts growth	Produces maturity and growth

Why Do We Worry?

D—Distorted thinking

> *"Which of you, if your son asks for bread, will give him a stone? Or if he asks for a fish, will give him a snake? If you, then, though you are evil, know how to give good gifts to your children, how much more will your Father in heaven give good gifts to those who ask him!"* (MATTHEW 7:9–11).

I—Illusion of control

> *"Now listen, you who say, 'Today or tomorrow we will go to this or that city, spend a year there, carry on business and make money.' Why, you do not even know what will happen tomorrow. What is your life? You are a mist that appears for a little while and then vanishes. Instead, you ought to say, 'If it is the Lord's will, we will live and do this or that'"* (JAMES 4:13–15).

S—Super responsibility

> *"With minds that are alert and fully sober, set your hope on the grace to be brought to you when Jesus Christ is revealed"* (1 PETER 1:13).

T—Transferred guilt

> *"When I kept silent, my bones wasted away through my groaning all day long. For day and night your hand was heavy on me; my strength was sapped as in the heat of summer. Then I acknowledged my sin to you and did not cover up my iniquity. I said, 'I will confess my transgressions to the LORD'—and you forgave the guilt of my sin"* (PSALM 32:3–5).

R—Runaway emotions

"I sought the Lord, *and he answered me; he delivered me from all my fears"* (Psalm 34:4).

U—Unhealthy need

"Am I now trying to win the approval of human beings, or of God? Or am I trying to please people? If I were still trying to please people, I would not be a servant of Christ" (Galatians 1:10).

S—Spiritual starvation

"Taste and see that the Lord *is good; blessed is the one who takes refuge in him. . . . The lions may grow weak and hungry, but those who seek the* Lord *lack no good thing"* (Psalm 34:8, 10).

T—Trampled self-image

"How precious to me are your thoughts, God! How vast is the sum of them! Were I to count them, they would outnumber the grains of sand—when I awake, I am still with you" (Psalm 139:17–18).

Those who know your name trust in you,
for you, Lord, *have never forsaken those who seek you.*
(Psalm 9:10)

Rationalizations of Worriers

1. **Rationalization**: "I feel sure that what I'm worried about will happen."

   The Truth: "Most of what I worry about rarely or never happens."

   God's Truth: *"Trust in the* Lord *with all your heart; do not depend on your own understanding. Seek his will in all you do, and he will show you which path to take"* (Proverbs 3:5–6 NLT).

2. **Rationalization**: "It makes sense to worry because terrible things happen to me all the time."

   The Truth: "Looking back, I can see that terrible things have rarely happened to me."

   God's Truth: *"Surely God is my salvation; I will trust and not be afraid. The* Lord, *the* Lord *himself, is my strength and my defense; he has become my salvation"* (Isaiah 12:2).

3. **Rationalization**: "Worry helps to prepare me for what might happen."

   The Truth: "The future is in God's hands, so there's no reason for me to worry about this."

God's Truth: *"Commit everything you do to the* Lord. *Trust him, and he will help you"* (Psalm 37:5 NLT).

4. **Rationalization**: "If I worry about this, then maybe I can keep it from happening."

   The Truth: "I do not control the future—God does, and I can trust His plan for my life."

   God's Truth: *"'I know the plans I have for you,' declares the* Lord, *'plans to prosper you and not to harm you, plans to give you hope and a future'"* (Jeremiah 29:11).

5. **Rationalization**: "Worrying is better than doing nothing about it."

   The Truth: "Spending inordinate amounts of time worrying accomplishes nothing."

   God's Truth: *"Trust in him at all times, you people; pour out your hearts to him, for God is our refuge"* (Psalm 62:8).

Key Verses to Memorize

Don't worry about anything;
instead, pray about everything.
Tell God what you need,
and thank him for all he has done.
Then you will experience God's peace,
which exceeds anything we can understand.
His peace will guard your hearts and minds
as you live in Christ Jesus.
(Philippians 4:6–7 NLT)

Considerations for Overcoming Worry

Get sufficient sleep.

Exercise regularly.

Eat a balanced diet of healthy foods.

Avoid caffeine, alcohol, and drugs.

Make time for fun and recreation

Plan outdoor activities on sunny days.

Keep your home organized and tidy.

Live in the present, not in the past or the future.

Play music that enhances your sense of calm, peace, and joy.

Pace your daily activities and don't take on more than you can reasonably accomplish.

Take charge of your time by scheduling daily activities and responsibilities.

Spend time with positive, hopeful people.

Plan ahead how you will deal with potentially stressful situations.

Talk about your feelings with safe people.

My Personalized Plan

If I want my worries to vanish, then I must learn new ways of thinking and develop methods for changing my former thinking patterns. Although my thoughts and memories may not be erased, the rehearsed words can be replaced as I focus on the wisdom of Philippians 4:6–9:

Do not be anxious about anything, but in every situation,
by prayer and petition, with thanksgiving,
present your requests to God.
And the peace of God, which transcends all understanding,
will guard your hearts and your minds in Christ Jesus.
Finally, brothers and sisters, whatever is true,
whatever is noble, whatever is right, whatever is pure,
whatever is lovely, whatever is admirable—
if anything is excellent or praiseworthy—think about such things.
Whatever you have learned or received or heard from me,
or seen in me—put it into practice.
And the God of peace will be with you.

I will choose not to worry or be anxious about anything (v. 6).

Key Passage to Read

Luke 12:22–34

I will bring every situation that concerns me to God rather than worrying about it (v. 6).

I will tell God what I need, and thank Him for all He's done for me (v. 6).

I will focus on having a heart of praise and thankfulness (v. 6).

I will let His peace guard all of my thoughts and feelings—my entire mind and heart (v. 7).

I will direct my thoughts, intentionally fixing them on what is true, honorable, right, pure, lovely, admirable, excellent, and praiseworthy (v. 8).

I will act in a way that reflects God's life—His words, His teachings, His actions, His character, His example in thought, word, and deed (v. 9).

I will continually remember that the God of peace will be with me . . . *always* (v. 9).

Questions & Answers

Question: "What is the difference between fear and worry?"

Answer: Fear is an *emotional* reaction to a perceived, *present* danger. Worry is *mental distress* over a possible, undesired happening in the *future.*

Fear *focuses on present events*; it is energizing when it propels a person to action in a way that removes or lessens real danger.

Worry is distracting and can lead to distress, despair, and even depression and anxiety. In addition, worry is unproductive because it projects problems and unknown future events.

Call on me in the day of trouble;
I will deliver you, and you will honor me.
(Psalm 50:15)

Question: "In what ways does worry steal joy?"

Answer: Trying to maintain control in situations and circumstances over which you have no control is exhausting. If your thoughts, your energy, your days, your nights, and your heart are filled with worry, where is there room for joy in your life? If you're always worried about what's yet to come, how can you experience joy in the here and now?

Jesus doesn't want you to live your life consumed by worrying about what might or might not happen. He promises to take care of you and meet all of your needs. When you empty your life of the woes of worry, you have ample space for the joy of the Lord—joy found in His presence, His promises, and His peace.

When doubts filled my mind,
your comfort gave me renewed hope and cheer
(Psalm 94:19 NLT)

NOTES

Introduction

1. James T. Fisher and Lowell S. Hawley, *A Few Buttons Missing: The Case Book of a Psychiatrist* (J.B. Lippincott, 1951), 273.
2. For more on the three inner needs (or longings), see Lawrence J. Crabb Jr., *Understanding People: Why We Long for Relationship* (Zondervan, 2013), 17–18, 124–27; Robert S. McGee, *The Search for Significance: Seeing Your True Worth Through God's Eyes*, rev. ed. (Thomas Nelson Publishers, 2003), 6–11, 21–24.

The Abortion Dilemma

3. Nancy Michels, *Helping Women Recover from Abortion* (Bethany House, 1988), 11–28.

Abuse Recovery

4. Candace Walters, *Invisible Wounds: What Every Woman Should Know About Sexual Assault* (Multnomah Books, 1988), 62.
5. Ellen Bass and Laura Davis, *The Courage to Heal: A Guide for Women Survivors of Child Sexual Abuse* (Harper & Row, 1988), 49.
6. Rich Buhler, *Pain and Pretending* (Thomas Nelson, 1991), 65.
7. Mark Gregston, *The Phenomenon of Cutting* (Heartlight Publishing, 2016), 7–14; American Psychiatric Association, *DSM-V: Diagnostic and Statistical Manual of Mental Disorders*, 5th ed. (American Psychiatric Association, 2013), 803–5.

Adoption

8. Kay Marshall Strom and Douglas R. Donnelly, *The Complete Adoption Handbook*, rev. and updated ed. (Zondervan, 1992), 138–39.
9. Strom and Donnelly, *The Complete Adoption Handbook*, 139.

Adultery

10. Kay Marshall Strom, *Helping Women in Crisis: A Handbook for People Helpers* (Zondervan, 1986), 90–91.

Aging Well

11. Jim Conway and Sally Conway, *Maximize Your Mid-Life* (Tyndale House Publishers, 1987), 18–26.

Alcohol & Drug Abuse

12. American Psychiatric Association, "What Is a Substance Use Disorder?" reviewed by Hector Colon-Rivera and Alena Balasanova, December 2020, https://www.psychiatry.org/patients-families/addiction/what-is-addiction.
13. Gregory L. Jantz and Ann McMurray, *Healing the Scars of Addiction: Reclaiming Your Life and Moving into a Healthy Future* (Revell, 2018), 91–101.

Alzheimer's & Dementia

14. Alzheimer's Association, "10 Early Signs and Symptoms of Alzheimer's," accessed August 10, 2023, www.alz.org/alzheimers-dementia/10_signs.
15. Alzheimer's Association, "Stages of Alzheimer's," accessed August 10, 2023, www.alz.org/alzheimers-dementia/stages.
16. Patricia B. Smith, Mary Mitchell Kenan, and Mark Edwin Kunik, *Alzheimer's for Dummies* (Wiley Publishing, Inc., 2004), 17–24.

17. Eric Suni and Dr. Nilong Vyas, "How Lack of Sleep Impacts Cognitive Performance and Focus," article updated July 18, 2023, www.sleepfoundation.org/sleep-deprivation/lack-of-sleep-and-cognitive-impairment.
18. Daniel Amen, *Making a Good Brain Great* (Three Rivers Press, 2005), 91; National Institute on Aging, "Maintaining a Healthy Weight," accessed August 28, 2023, www.nia.nih.gov/health/maintaining-healthy-weight#eat.
19. National Institute on Aging, "Maintaining a Healthy Weight."
20. Amen, *Making a Good Brain Great*, 93.
21. Amen, 172.
22. National Institute on Aging, "Reducing Your Risk of Dementia," accessed August 15, 2023, https://order.nia.nih.gov/publication/reducing-your-risk-of-dementia.

Anger

23. David R. Mace, *Love & Anger in Marriage* (Zondervan, 1982), 47.
24. For more on the three inner needs (or longings), see Lawrence J. Crabb Jr., *Understanding People: Why We Long for Relationship* (Zondervan, 2013), 17–18, 124–27; Robert S. McGee, *The Search for Significance: Seeing Your True Worth through God's Eyes*, rev. ed. (Thomas Nelson, 2003), 6–11, 21–24.
25. Gary Jackson Oliver and H. Norman Wright, *When Anger Hits Home: Taking Care of Your Anger Without Taking It Out on Your Family* (Moody Press, 1992), 97.
26. Mace, *Love & Anger in Marriage*, 46.
27. Crabb, *Understanding People*, 17–18, 124–27; McGee, *The Search for Significance*, 6–11, 21–24.
28. Mace, *Love & Anger in Marriage*, 47–50.
29. Crabb, *Understanding People*, 17–18, 124–27; McGee, *The Search for Significance*, 6–11, 21–24.
30. Crabb, 17–18, 124–27; McGee, 6–11, 21–24.

Anxiety

31. William Backus, *The Good News about Worry: Applying Biblical Truth to Problems of Anxiety and Fear* (Bethany House Publishers, 1991), 66–67.
32. Anxiety and Depression Association of America, "Myths and Misconceptions About Anxiety," accessed October 22, 2019, https://adaa.org/understanding-anxiety/myth-conceptions.

Atheism & Agnosticism

33. Norman Geisler, *Baker Encyclopedia of Christian Apologetics* (Baker Books, 1999), 292.
34. Geisler, *Baker Encyclopedia of Christian Apologetics*, 275–76.
35. Geisler, *Baker Encyclopedia of Christian Apologetics*, 113–14.
36. Geisler, "Freud, Sigmund," in *Baker Encyclopedia of Christian Apologetics*.
37. Geisler, "Hume, David," in *Baker Encyclopedia of Christian Apologetics*.

The Bible: Is It Reliable?

38. *Merriam-Webster Collegiate Dictionary*, s.v. "Bible," accessed March 9, 2024, http://www.merriam-webster.com/dictionary/Bible.
39. James Strong, *Strong's Greek Lexicon*, Online Bible Millennium Edition v. 1.13 (Timnathserah Inc., July 6, 2002).
40. Paige Patterson, *The Issue Is Truth*, Shophar Papers, vol. 1 (Criswell Center of Biblical Studies, 1979), 13.
41. Patterson, *The Issue Is Truth*, 14.
42. James Montgomery Boice, *Standing on the Rock: Biblical Authority in a Secular Age* (Baker, 1994), 136–143.

The Blended Family

43. Michelle Cresse, *Jigsaw Families: Solving the Puzzle of Remarriage* (Aglow, 1989), 20.
44. Cresse, *Jigsaw Families*, 22–23.
45. Tom Frydenger and Adrienne Frydenger, *The Blended Family* (Chosen, 1984), 32.
46. Angela Elwell Hunt, *Loving Someone Else's Child* (Tyndale House, 1992), 55.
47. Tom Frydenger and Adrienne Frydenger, *Resolving Conflict in the Blended Family* (Chosen, 1991), 34.
48. Frydenger and Frydenger, *The Blended Family*, 59.
49. Hunt, *Loving Someone Else's Child*, 223.
50. Hunt, 28.
51. Frydenger and Frydenger, *The Blended Family*, 151–53.
52. Frydenger and Frydenger, *The Blended Family*, 92.
53. Charles Cerling, *Remarriage: Opportunity to Grow* (Power, 1988), 88–89.
54. Don Houck and LaDean Houck, *Remarried with Children: A Blended Couple's Journey to Harmony* (Here's Life, 1991), 179.
55. Hunt, *Loving Someone Else's Child*, 147–48.
56. Frydenger and Frydenger, *The Blended Family*, 176–78.
57. Cerling, *Remarriage: Opportunity to Grow*, 87.
58. Frydenger and Frydenger, *The Blended Family*, 103.
59. Cerling, *Remarriage: Opportunity to Grow*, 91–92.
60. Frydenger and Frydenger, *The Blended Family*, 129–33.

Boundaries

61. Henry Cloud and John Townsend, *Boundaries with Kids: When to Say Yes, When to Say No to Help Your Children Gain Control of Their Lives* (Zondervan, 1998), 43–44.

Bullying

62. Rachel Simmons, "The Nine Most Common Myths About Bullying," *Newsweek*, updated October 15, 2010, accessed February 24, 2025, https://www.newsweek.com/nine-most-common-myths-about-bullying-74185.
63. U.S. Department of Health and Human Services, "Facts About Bullying," *StopBullying.gov*, accessed March 31, 2025, https://www.stopbullying.gov/resources/facts.
64. U.S. Department of Health and Human Services, "Effects of Bullying," *StopBullying.gov*, accessed March 31, 2025, https://www.stopbullying.gov/bullying/effects.
65. *Collins English Dictionary*, "Bullycide" (HarperCollins), accessed April 2, 2025, https://www.collinsdictionary.com/dictionary/english/bullycide.
66. *Medical News Today*, "Bullying and Suicide: The Relationship and More," February 15, 2024, accessed April 2, 2025, https://www.medicalnewstoday.com/articles/bullying-and-suicide.

Caregiving

67. Alzheimer's Association, *How to Manage Stress: 10 Ways to Be a Healthier Caregiver*, adapted from a handout distributed through local chapters of the Greater Dallas Area Alzheimer's Association.

Child Evangelism

68. James Strong, *Strong's Greek Lexicon*, Online Bible Millennium Edition v. 1.13 (Timnathserah Inc., July 6, 2002); W. E. Vine, *Vine's Complete Expository Dictionary of Biblical Words*, electronic ed. (Thomas Nelson, 1996).
69. Strong, *Strong's Greek Lexicon*.

Childhood Sexual Abuse

70. Maxine Hancock and Karen Burton Mains, *Child Sexual Abuse: Hope for Healing*, rev. ed. (Harold Shaw Publishers, 1997), 122–26.
71. Grant Martin, *Please Don't Hurt Me* (Victor Books, 1987), 51–59.
72. Martin, *Please Don't Hurt Me*, 52–60.

Codependency

73. Melody Beattie, *Codependent No More: How to Stop Controlling Others and Start Caring for Yourself* (Harper, 1987), 37–49.
74. Roseann Lloyd and Merle A. Fossum, *True Selves: 12 Step Recovery from Codependency* (HarperCollins, 1991), 120.
75. Dr. Robert Hemfelt, Dr. Frank Minirth, and Dr. Paul Meier, *Love Is a Choice* (Thomas Nelson, 1989), 180–84.
76. Pia Mellody, Andrea Wells Miller, and J. Keith Miller, *Facing Love Addiction: Giving Yourself the Power to Change the Way You Love* (HarperOne, 2003), 78–79.
77. Mellody, Miller, and Miller, *Facing Love Addiction*, 166–69, 196–98.
78. Mellody, Miller, and Miller, 90–92.
79. Mellody, Miller, and Miller, 86–92.
80. Mellody, Miller, and Miller, 102–108.
81. Mellody, Miller, and Miller, 108–113.

Conflict Resolution

82. G. Brian Jones and Linda Phillips-Jones, *A Fight to the Better End* (Victor Books, 1989), 16–17.
83. Jones and Phillips-Jones, *A Fight to the Better End*, 17.
84. For types of conflict see Jones and Phillips-Jones, *A Fight to the Better End*, 16.
85. Josh McDowell, *Resolving Conflict* (Thomas Nelson, 2000), 11.

Confrontation

86. Josh McDowell, *Resolving Conflict* (Focus on the Family, 1989), 8–10.
87. Deborah Smith Pegues, *Confronting Without Offending: Biblical Strategies for Effective Personal and Business Confrontation* (Vincom, 1995), 3.

Considering Marriage

88. H. Norman Wright, *So You're Getting Married* (Regal, 1985), 7.
89. Wright, *So You're Getting Married*, 248.

Crisis & Trauma

90. American Psychological Association, "Trauma," in *APA Dictionary of Psychology*, accessed April 1, 2025, https://dictionary.apa.org/trauma.
91. *Oxford English Dictionary*, s.v. "crisis, n.," Oxford University Press, accessed April 1, 2025, https://www.oed.com/view/Entry/44539.
92. Merriam-Webster.com Dictionary, s.v. "crisis," accessed April 4, 2025, https://www.merriam-webster.com/dictionary/crisis.
93. *Merriam-Webster Dictionary*, s.v. "trauma," accessed April 1, 2025, https://www.merriam-webster.com/dictionary/trauma.
94. Hope for the Heart, *Foundations of Care: Group Study Facilitator Manual* (Plano, TX: Hope for the Heart, n.d.), Session 7, 166–168.
95. Hope for the Heart, *Foundations of Care*, Session 10, 262–263.

96. "Complex Trauma: What is it and how does it affect people?" Complex Trauma Resources, accessed April 4, 2025, https://www.complextrauma.org/complex-trauma/complex-trauma-what-is-it-and-how-does-it-affect-people/.
97. Tim Fletcher, "60 Characteristics of Complex Trauma," *Tim Fletcher* Co., March 9, 2024, https://www.timfletcher.ca/blog/60-characteristics-of-complex-trauma.

Critical Spirit

98. William D. Backus, *Telling Each Other the Truth* (Bethany House, 1985), 106–108.

Cults

99. Watchman Fellowship, "Patterns in the Cults," accessed February 10, 2025, used by permission, https://www.watchman.org/ProfilePatterns.pdf.
100. Rick Branch and Carmen Branch, *Friendshipping* (Utah Missions, 1986).

Dating

101. Don Raunikar, *Choosing God's Best: Wisdom for Lifelong Romance* (Multnomah Publishers, 1998), 20–29.

Decision-Making

102. Bobb Biehl, "Wisdom Checklist" (Bobb Biehl, 2015).
103. Damon Zahariades, *How to Make Better Decisions: 14 Smart Tactics for Curbing Your Biases, Managing Your Emotions, & Making Fearless Decisions in Every Area of Your Life!* (ArtofProductivity.com, 2024), 15–43.
104. Zahariades, How to Make Better Decisions, 189–91.

Depression

105. American Psychiatric Association (APA), *Diagnostic and Statistical Manual of Mental Disorders*, 5th edition, text revision (American Psychiatric Association, 2013), 160–161; National Institute of Mental Health, *Depression*, NIH Publication No. 24-MH-8079, U.S. Department of Health and Human Services, National Institutes of Health, 2024, accessed April 1, 2025, https://www.nimh.nih.gov/health/publications/depression.
106. June Hunt, Hope for the Heart Bible Studies, *Overcoming Depression: Walking from Darkness into the Dawn* (Rose Publishing/Aspire Press, 2017), 51–52.
107. For PET scan images, see Frank B. Minirth, *In Pursuit of Happiness* (Fleming H. Revell, 2004), 189–90

Divorce

108. David A. Thompson, *Counseling and Divorce*, Resources for Christian Counseling, ed. Gary R. Collins (Word, 1989), 44–45; Ronald M. Supanic and Dennis L. Baker, *When All Else Fails* (Fleming H. Revell, 1986), 103–115.

Domestic Abuse

109. "Survivor Resources," Texas Council on Family Violence, accessed April 1, 2025, https://tcfv.org/find-help/survivor-resources/; National Domestic Violence Hotline, "Safety Planning While Living with an Abusive Partner," *The Hotline*, accessed April 1, 2025, https://www.thehotline.org/resources/safety-planning-while-living-with-an-abusive-partner/.

The Dysfunctional Family

110. Nancy LeSourd, *No Longer the Hero: The Personal Pilgrimage of an Adult Child* (Thomas Nelson, 1991), 175–77.
111. David Mains, *Healing the Dysfunctional Church Family* (Victor Books, 1992), 145–46.

112. LeSourd, *No Longer the Hero*, 198-204.
113. Jim Conway, *Adult Children of Legal and Emotional Divorce: Healing Your Long-Term Hurt* (InterVarsity Press, 1990), 127-240.
114. LeSourd, *No Longer the Hero*, 173-74.

Envy & Jealousy

115. Alice Fryling, *Reshaping a Jealous Heart: How to Turn Dissatisfaction into Contentment* (InterVarsity Press, 1994), 15-17.

Forgiveness

116. John Nieder and Thomas M. Thompson, *Forgive & Love Again: Healing Wounded Relationships* (Harvest House Publishers, 1991), 173-85; Robert Jeffress, *When Forgiveness Doesn't Make Sense* (WaterBrook, 2000), 107-123.
117. Nieder and Thompson, *Forgive & Love Again*, 47-51.
118. Lewis B. Smedes, *Forgive and Forget: Healing the Hurts We Don't Deserve* (Harper & Row, 1984), 21-26.
119. Smedes, *Forgive and Forget*, 27-30.

Friendship

120. Shelley E. Taylor et al., "Biobehavioral Responses to Stress in Females: Tend-and-Befriend, Not Fight-or-Flight," *Psychological Review* 107, no. 3 (2000): 411-29, https://doi.org/10.1037/0033-295X.107.3.411.
121. Taylor et al., "Biobehavioral Responses to Stress in Females."

God: Who Is He?

122. Nathan Stone, *Names of God in the Old Testament* (Moody Publishers, 1944), 7-17.
123. Stone, *Names of God in the Old Testament*, 30-42.
124. Paul Enns, *The Moody Handbook of Theology* (Moody Publishers, 1989), 185-86.

The Holy Spirit

125. Charles Caldwell Ryrie, *The Holy Spirit* (Moody Publishers, 1965), 17-20; David Hocking, *The Dynamic Difference* (Harvest House Publishers, 1988), 14-18.
126. Charles R. Swindoll and Bryce Klabunde, *He Gave Gifts: Bible Study Guide*, rev. ed. (Insight for Living, 1998), 82-89.

Homosexuality & SSA

127. Joe Dallas, *Desires in Conflict* (Harvest House Publishers, 1991), 127-28.
128. Dallas, *Desires in Conflict*, 91.
129. Robert A. J. Gagnon, *The Bible and Homosexual Practice: Texts and Hermeneutics* (Abingdon Press, 2001), 395-431.

Hope

130. *American Heritage Electronic Dictionary* (Houghton Mifflin, 1992), s.v. "hope."
131. W. E. Vine, *Vine's Complete Expository Dictionary of Biblical Words*, electronic ed. (Thomas Nelson, 1996), s.v. "hope."

Identity & Self-Image

132. See *New Oxford Dictionary of English*, electronic ed. (Oxford University Press, 1998), s.v. "identity crisis."

Infertility

133. Jill Baughan, *A Hope Deferred: A Couple's Guide to Coping with Infertility* (Multnomah, 1989), 15; John Van Regenmorter, Sylvia Van Regenmorter, and Joe S. McIlhaney Jr., *Dear God, Why Can't We Have a Baby? A Guide for the Infertile Couple* (Baker, 1986), 9.
134. John Van Regenmorter and Sylvia Van Regenmorter, "Infertility: Everyone's Problem," *Stepping Stones*, February-March 1987, 1; Laura Zarecor, "Secondary Infertility Hurts, Too," *Stepping Stones*, August-September 1988, 2.
135. Baughan, *A Hope Deferred*, 14-15.
136. Baughan, 18.
137. Baughan, 112-28; Van Regenmorter, Van Regenmorter, and McIlhaney, *Dear God*, 75-83.
138. Baughan, *A Hope Deferred*, 138-40.
139. Baughan, 30-52; Van Regenmorter, Van Regenmorter, and McIlhaney, *Dear God*, 35-56.
140. Everett L. Worthington Jr., *Counseling for Unplanned Pregnancy and Infertility*, vol. 10, Resources for Christian Counseling, ed. Gary R. Collins (Word, 1987), 229.
141. Van Regenmorter, Van Regenmorter, and McIlhaney, *Dear God*, 139-48; Worthington, Counseling for Unplanned Pregnancy, 229.
142. Van Regenmorter, Van Regenmorter, and McIlhaney, *Dear God*, 149-55; Worthington, Counseling for Unplanned Pregnancy, 223-29.
143. Van Regenmorter, Van Regenmorter, and McIlhaney, *Dear God*, 139-48; Worthington, *Counseling for Unplanned Pregnancy*, 229.

Intimacy

144. Terry Hershey, *Intimacy: The Longing of Every Human Heart* (Harvest House Publishers, 1984), 166, 189-90.
145. Hershey, *Intimacy*, 32-36.
146. Hershey, *Intimacy*, 24; Janet G. Woititz, *Struggle for Intimacy* (Health Communications, 1985), 73.
147. For more on the three inner needs (or longings), see Lawrence J. Crabb Jr., *Understanding People: Why We Long for Relationship* (Zondervan, 2013), 17-18, 124-27; Robert S. McGee, *The Search for Significance: Seeing Your True Worth through God's Eyes*, rev. ed. (Thomas Nelson, 2003), 6-11, 21-24.

Loneliness

148. J. Oswald Sanders, *Facing Loneliness: The Starting Point of a New Journey* (Discovery House, 1990), 23-24.
149. Sanders, *Facing Loneliness*, 24.
150. Sanders, 23-25.
151. Tom Varney, *Loneliness* (NavPress, 1992), 16.

Lying vs. Truthfulness

152. Jerry E. White, *Honesty, Morality & Conscience* (NavPress, 1978), 172.
153. Devlin Donaldson and Steve Wamberg, *Pinocchio Nation: Embracing Truth in a Culture of Lies* (Pinion, 2001), 26.

Manipulation

154. Tim Kimmel, *Powerful Personalities* (Focus on the Family, 1993), 36-39.
155. Kimmel, *Powerful Personalities*, 37-38; Jan Silvious, *Please Don't Say You Need Me: Biblical Answers for Codependency* (Pyranee Books, 1989), 56.
156. Kimmel, *Powerful Personalities*, 48, 143-44; Barbara Sullivan, *The Control Grip: a Woman's Guide to Freedom from the Need to Manage People and Circumstances* (Bethany House, 1991), 67-69.

157. Kimmel, *Powerful Personalities*, 46–48, 97.
158. Kimmel, 61–62, 64–66.
159. Kimmel, 64–66; Sullivan, *The Control Grip*, 64–68.
160. Kimmel, *Powerful Personalities*, 53–54.
161. Kimmel, 46–48.
162. Sullivan, *Control Grip*, 67–68; Kimmel, *Powerful Personalities*, 61–62; Paul F. Schmidt, *Coping with Difficult People*, Christian Care Books, ed. Wayne E. Oates, vol. 6 (Westminster Press, 1980), 100–101.
163. James J. Messina, "Eliminating Manipulation: Tools for Handling Control Issues," A Tools-for-Coping Series Book (Kendall Hunt Publishing, 1992), accessed December 16, 2019, http://www.coping.us/toolsforhandlingcontrol/eliminatemanipulation.html.
164. Silvious, *Please Don't Say You Need Me*, 31; Kimmel, *Powerful Personalities*, 202–203.
165. Henry Cloud and John Townsend, *Boundaries: When to Say Yes, When to Say No, To Take Control of Your Life* (Zondervan, 1992), 199–201.

Midlife Crisis

166. Jim Conway and Sally Conway, *Maximize Your Mid-Life*, Pocket Guides (Tyndale House, 1987), 18–26.
167. Conway and Conway, *Maximize Your Mid-Life*, 18–26.

New Age Spirituality

168. Mary Baker Eddy, *Science and Health with Key to the Scriptures* (Christian Science Publishing, 1906), 472–73; Foundation for Inner Peace, *A Course in Miracles*, 2nd ed. (Viking, 1996), 1:402, 405; 2:403.
169. Napoleon Hill, *Think and Grow Rich* (Fawcett Books, 1937), 32; see also Ernest Holmes, *The Science of Mind* (Dodd, Mead and Company, 1938), 32.

The Occult

170. Frank York, "Rescuing the Devil's Teenager," *Focus on the Family Citizen*, October 1989, 7–8.

Overeating

171. Bill Perkins, *Fatal Attractions: Overcoming Our Secret Addictions* (Harvest House, 1991), 48–49.
172. Lawrence J. Crabb Jr., *Understanding People: Deep Longings for Relationship*, Ministry Resources Library (Zondervan, 1987), 15–16; Robert S. McGee, *The Search for Significance*, 2nd ed. (Rapha, 1990), 27–30.

Parenting

173. Horst Robert Balz and Gerhard Schneider, *Exegetical Dictionary of the New Testament*, vol. 3 (Eerdmans, 1993), 53.
174. Robert Laird Harris, Gleason Leonard Archer, and Bruce K. Waltke, *Theological Wordbook of the Old Testament*, electronic ed. (Moody Press, 1999), no. 115.

Pregnancy . . . Unplanned

175. The Helpline, "My Three Choices," accessed March 31, 2025, https://thehelpline.org/unplanned-pregnancy/general-information/my-three-choices/; Sylvia Boothe, *No Easy Choices: The Dilemma of Crisis Pregnancy* (New Hope, 1990), 23–56; Carolyn Owens and Linda Roggow, *Pregnant and Single*, rev. ed. (Pyranee, 1990), 31–43; Henrietta VanDerMolen, *Pregnant & Alone: How You Can Help an Unwed Friend*, Heart and Hand (Harold Shaw, 1989), 35–88.
176. VanDerMolen, *Pregnant & Alone*, 2–3; Frederica Mathewes-Green, *Real Choices: Offering Practical, Life-Affirming Alternatives to Abortion* (Multnomah, 1994), 131–34.

Prejudice

177. Derald Wing Sue, *Counseling the Culturally Diverse: Theory and Practice*, 5th ed. (John Wiley & Sons, Inc., 2008), 114–15.

Pride & Humility

178. W. Phillip Keller, *Predators in Our Pulpits* (Harvest House Publishers, 1988), 47–54.
179. Material in this section is adapted from Charles W. Colson, *Born Again* (Chosen Books, 1976), 114–15.

Purpose in Life

180. Patrick Morley, *The Man in the Mirror: Solving the 24 Problems Men Face* (Zondervan, 2000), 91.

Reconciliation

181. James Pittman, *What Do You Do with a Broken Relationship?* (Radio Bible Class, 2002), 6–7, 12–13.
182. Don Baker, *Restoring Broken Relationships* (Harvest House, 1989), 88–89.
183. Pittman, *What Do You Do with a Broken Relationship?* 8, 18–20.
184. Pittman, 11.
185. Ken Sande, *The Peacemaker: A Biblical Guide to Resolving Personal Conflict* (Baker, 1991), 197–204; Pittman, *What Do You Do with a Broken Relationship?* 22–26.
186. Myron Rush, *Hope for Hurting Relationships* (Victor Books, 1989), 123.
187. Pittman, *What Do You Do with a Broken Relationship?* 23.
188. Pittman, 23–24.
189. Pittman, 22.

Rejection & Abandonment

190. *Merriam-Webster Online Dictionary*, s.v. "reject," https://www.merriam-webster.com/dictionary/reject.
191. *Merriam-Webster*, s.v. "reject."
192. *Merriam-Webster*, s.v. "reject."
193. *Merriam-Webster*, s.v. "accept," https://www.merriam-webster.com/dictionary/accept.
194. Robert S. McGee, *The Search for Significance: Book and Workbook*, revised (Rapha, 1987), 219–20.
195. Marshall Bryant Hodge, *Your Fear of Love: Your Guide to the Enjoyment of Love, Sex, Family, and Friendship* (Doubleday, 1967), 26.
196. Charles Solomon, *The Ins and Out of Rejection* (Heritage House, 1976), 42–47.

Satan, Demons, and Satanism

197. Mark I. Bubeck, *The Adversary* (Moody Publishers, 1975), 58.
198. Bob Passantino and Gretchen Passantino, *Satanism*, Zondervan Guide to Cults & Religious Movements, ed. Alan W. Gomes (Zondervan, 1995), 72.
199. Neil T. Anderson and Steve Russo, *The Seduction of our Children* (Harvest House Publishers, 1991), 96–97; Mark I. Bubeck, *The Satanic Revival* (San Bernadino, CA: Here's Life, 1991), 26–27.
200. Anderson and Russo, *The Seduction of our Children*, 98; Jerry Mungadze, *Satanic Cults: What You Really Need to Know* (Mirror Productions, 1990), audiocassettes.

Sex and Human Trafficking

201. Congress.gov., "H.R.3244 - 106th Congress (1999-2000): Victims of Trafficking and Violence Protection Act of 2000," October 28, 2000, https://www.congress.gov/bill/106th-congress/house-bill/3244.

202. Katie Dupere, "6 Crucial Facts About Human Trafficking - And How You Can Help," *Mashable*, July 30, 2015, https://mashable.com/2015/07/30/human-trafficking-facts/#ODsVoTa59PqS.

203. Mags Gullo, "Male Sex Trafficking: The Invisible Victims," *Ranch Hands Rescue*, accessed March 31, 2025, https://ranchhandsrescue.org/male-sex-trafficking-the-invisile-victims/.

Sexual Addiction

204. Lawrence J. Crabb Jr., *Understanding People: Why We Long for Relationship* (Zondervan, 2013), 17–18, 124–27; Robert S. McGee, *The Search for Significance: Seeing Your True Worth through God's Eyes*, rev. ed. (Thomas Nelson, 2003), 6–11, 21–24.

Sexual Assault & Rape Recovery

205. Candace Walters, *Invisible Wounds: What Every Woman Should Know About Sexual Assault* (Multnomah Press, 1988), 30–31.

206. U.S. Equal Employment Opportunity Commission, "Sexual Harassment," accessed April 2, 2025, https://www.eeoc.gov/sexual-harassment.

Sexual Integrity

207. Marilyn Morris, *ABC's of the Birds and Bees for Parents of Toddlers to Teens*, 2nd ed. (Charles River, 2000), 297–300. Used by permission.

Single Parenting

208. Robert G. Barnes Jr., *Single Parenting: A Wilderness Journey* (Tyndale House, 1988), 25–28.

209. Joseph Warren Kniskern, *When the Vow Breaks: A Survival and Recovery Guide for Christians Facing Divorce* (Broadman & Holman, 1993), 239.

210. Dandi Daley Knorr, *Just One of Me: Confessions of a Less-Than-Perfect Single Parent* (Harold Shaw, 1989), 164.

211. Barnes, *Single Parenting*, 155–66.

212. Barnes, 145–54.

213. Kniskern, *When the Vow Breaks*, 239.

214. Kniskern, 239.

Spiritual Abuse

215. David Johnson and Jeff VanVonderen, *The Subtle Power of Spiritual Abuse: Recognizing and Escaping Spiritual Manipulation and False Spiritual Authority Within the Church* (Bethany House Publishers, 1991), 20.

216. David A. Seamands, *Healing Grace: Let God Heal You from the Performance Trap* (Victor Books, 1988), 12–19.

217. Stephen Arterburn and Jack Felton, *Toxic Faith: Experiencing Healing from Painful Spiritual Abuse* (WaterBrook Press, 2001), 263–64.

218. Jeff VanVonderen, *When God's People Let You Down* (Bethany House Publishers, 1995), 193–200.

Spiritual Warfare

219. See Mark I. Bubeck, *The Adversary: The Christian Versus Demon Activity* (Moody Publishers, 1975), 22; Thomas Ice and Robert Dean Jr., *A Holy Rebellion* (Harvest House Publishers, 1990), 46–47.

220. Danny Daniels, "The Building Up and Tearing Down of Strongholds," in *Spiritual Warfare*, ed. Ras Robinson (Fulness House, 1979), 20; Jim Logan, *Reclaiming Surrendered Ground* (Moody Publishers, 1995), 34–38; Ed Murphy, *The Handbook for Spiritual Warfare* (Thomas Nelson, 1992), 134.
221. Mark I. Bubeck, *Overcoming the Adversary* (Moody Publishers, 1984), 73–120.
222. David Jeremiah, *Spiritual Warfare*, Turning Point (Walk Thru the Bible Ministries, 1995); J. Oswald Sanders, *Satan Is No Myth* (Moody Publishers, 1975), 93–99.
223. Bubeck, *Overcoming the Adversary*, 121–29; Sanders, *Satan Is No Myth*, 99–100.
224. See Sanders, *Satan Is No Myth*, 121.

Stealing

225. Russell Kelfer, *The Issue of Integrity* (Discipleship Tape Ministries, 2002); www.dtm.org.
226. *Merriam-Webster Online Dictionary*, s.v. "stealing," https://www.merriam-webster.com/dictionary/stealing.
227. *Merriam-Webster*; Kelfer, *The Issue of Integrity*.
228. Pew Research Center. "What the Data Says About Crime in the U.S.," *Pew Research Center*, April 24, 2024, https://www.pewresearch.org/short-reads/2024/04/24/what-the-data-says-about-crime-in-the-us/.
229. "Stealing," *Merriam-Webster Collegiate Dictionary*; *New Oxford Dictionary of English*, electronic ed. (Oxford University Press, 1998).
230. Kelfer, *The Issue of Integrity*.
231. Jerry E. White, *Honesty, Morality & Conscience* (NavPress, 1978), 118–23.
232. White, *Honesty, Morality & Conscience*, 79–80.
233. "Copyright," *New Oxford Dictionary of English*, electronic ed., (Oxford University Press, 1998).
234. *The Chicago Manual of Style*, 15th ed. (University of Chicago Press, 2003), 106–144.
235. Thomas Edison National Historical Park, "Famous Quotes," accessed March 31, 2025, https://www.thomasedison.org/edison-quotes.

Suicide Prevention

236. "Warning Signs of Suicide," National Institute of Mental Health, U.S. Department of Health and Human Services, https://www.nimh.nih.gov/health/publications/warning-signs-of-suicide; "Suicide," *MedlinePlus*, U.S. National Library of Medicine, accessed March 31, 2025, https://medlineplus.gov/suicide.html#cat_79.
237. The Columbia Lighthouse Project, "The Columbia Protocol for Families, Friends, and Neighbors," accessed November 19, 2020, https://cssrs.columbia.edu/the-columbia-scale-c-ssrs/cssrs-for-families-friends-and-neighbors/.

Teenagers

238. David G. Myers, *Psychology*, 2nd ed. (Worth, 1989), 89.
239. Myers, *Psychology*, 90.
240. Bruce Narramore and Vern C. Lewis, *Parenting Teens* (Tyndale House, 1990), 33, 49.
241. Paul Warren and Bruce Grant, *Kids in Crisis* (Minirth-Meier Clinic, n.d.), audiocassette.
242. John White, *Parents in Pain: Overcoming the Hurt & Frustration of Problem Children* (InterVarsity Press, 1979), 164.
243. Ross Campbell, *How to Really Love Your Teenager*, rev. ed. (Victor Books, 1993), 29–35.
244. Warren and Grant, *Kids in Crisis*.

Temptation

245. Erwin W. Lutzer, *How to Say No to a Stubborn Habit: Even When You Feel Like Saying Yes* (Victor Books, 1986), 50–51; Charles F. Stanley, *Temptation* (Oliver-Nelson, 1988), 160–63.

246. Don Baker, *Lord, I've Got a Problem* (Harvest House Publishers, 1988), 92–93; Stanley, *Temptation*, 41–42.
247. Stanley, 40–41.
248. Stanley, 33–45.
249. William Backus and Marie Chapian, *Why Do I Do What I Don't Want to Do?* (Bethany House, 1984), 117.
250. Stanley, *Temptation*, 168–69.
251. Stanley, 176–77.
252. Institute in Basic Youth Conflicts, "Ten Steps to Conquer Impure Thoughts," in *Training Faithful Men* (1976), 1.
253. Institute in Basic Youth Conflicts, "Ten Steps to Conquer Impure Thoughts," 5.

The Unbelieving Mate

254. Michael Fanstone, *Unbelieving Husbands and the Wives Who Love Them* (Ann Arbor, MI: Servant Publications, 1994), 29–39.

Violence

255. National Domestic Violence Hotline, "Domestic Abuse Warning Signs," *The Hotline*, accessed March 31, 2025, https://www.thehotline.org/identify-abuse/domestic-abuse-warning-signs/; "Early Signs of an Abusive Man," *Medical News Today*, accessed March 31, 2025, https://www.medicalnewstoday.com/articles/early-signs-of-an-abusive-man#signs.
256. "FAMILY CODE CHAPTER 71. DEFINITIONS," Section 71.0021, Family Code, Texas Constitution and Statues, statutes.capitol.texas.gov/Docs/FA/htm/FA.71.htm.
257. Zara Abrams, "Up to 19% of Teens Experience Dating Violence. Psychologists Want to Break the Cycle," *Monitor on Psychology*, October 1, 2023, https://www.apa.org/monitor/2023/10/disrupting-teen-dating-violence.

Worry

258. Archibald D. Hart, *The Anxiety Cure: You Can Find Emotional Tranquility and Wholeness* (Thomas Nelson, 1999), 6–7; Deborah F. Bruce, "How Worrying Affects the Body," November 22, 2024, https://www.webmd.com/balance/guide/how-worrying-affects-your-body#1.
259. Linda Mintle, *Letting Go of Worry: God's Plan for Finding Peace and Contentment* (Harvest House Publishers, 2011), 20–22.

A Legacy of Hope

Special thanks to June Hunt for her unwavering commitment to God's Word, her compassionate heart for hurting people, decades of faithful ministry, and countless hours spent developing, editing, and teaching the 100+ topic *Keys for Living Library.*

June Hunt, MA, is an author, broadcaster, counselor, singer, speaker, and the founder of Hope for the Heart. She began the ministry in 1986 to provide God's truth for today's problems. June developed the 100+ topic *Keys for Living Library* to provide biblical hope and practical help on real-life issues.

Since 1995, June has shared compassionate biblical guidance with thousands of callers on her award-winning radio broadcast, *Hope in the Night*, a live, call-in counseling program, which she continues to host each weeknight.

A visionary with a heart to bring people together, June also founded The Hope Center in 2009, which serves as the permanent home for more than 60 nonprofit Christian ministries, allowing collaboration for greater kingdom impact.

June is a true model of integrity, compassion, and a servant's heart. The Lord has turned June's simple desire to help people find answers to life's toughest challenges into a worldwide ministry of hope, impacting more than 60 countries on 6 continents in over 35 languages. Those who have had the privilege of serving the Lord alongside June, benefitting from her wise care and counsel, or simply enjoying the warmth of her voice and guitar, can attest to the impact June has made for the kingdom.

www.hopefortheheart.org